Chris Webb & Artur Hojan

The Chelmno Death Camp

History, Biographies, Remembrance

Chris Webb & Artur Hojan

THE CHELMNO DEATH CAMP

History, Biographies, Remembrance

Bibliografische Information der Deutschen Nationalbibliothek
Die Deutsche Nationalbibliothek verzeichnet diese Publikation in der Deutschen Nationalbibliografie; detaillierte bibliografische Daten sind im Internet über http://dnb.d-nb.de abrufbar.

Bibliographic information published by the Deutsche Nationalbibliothek
Die Deutsche Nationalbibliothek lists this publication in the Deutsche Nationalbibliografie; detailed bibliographic data are available in the Internet at http://dnb.d-nb.de.

Cover design: Tom Nixon

∞
Gedruckt auf alterungsbeständigem, säurefreien Papier
Printed on acid-free paper

ISBN-13: 978-3-8382-1206-7
© *ibidem*-Verlag, Stuttgart 2019
Alle Rechte vorbehalten

Das Werk einschließlich aller seiner Teile ist urheberrechtlich geschützt. Jede Verwertung außerhalb der engen Grenzen des Urheberrechtsgesetzes ist ohne Zustimmung des Verlages unzulässig und strafbar. Dies gilt insbesondere für Vervielfältigungen, Übersetzungen, Mikroverfilmungen und elektronische Speicherformen sowie die Einspeicherung und Verarbeitung in elektronischen Systemen.

All rights reserved. No part of this publication may be reproduced, stored in or introduced into a retrieval system, or transmitted, in any form, or by any means (electronical, mechanical, photocopying, recording or otherwise) without the prior written permission of the publisher. Any person who does any unauthorized act in relation to this publication may be liable to criminal prosecution and civil claims for damages.

Printed in the EU

Table of Contents

Foreword 15

Author's Introduction 19

With Grateful Thanks 23

Abbreviations 25

Part I
The Hell Called Chełmno 27

Chapter I
November 1941
Chełmno Death Camp Established 29

Chapter II
December 1941
Mass Murder Begins 41

Chapter III
January 1942
The Slaughter Intensifies—Eichmann's Visit—
Prisoner Escapes 45

Chapter IV
February–March 1942
Mass Murder Continues—Hans Bothmann Arrives 73

Chapter V
April–May 1942
Deportations from the Litzmannstadt Ghetto 81

Chapter VI
June–August 1942
Exhumation and Cremation 91

Chapter VII
September 1942
The Gehsperre Deportation from
the Litzmannstadt Ghetto—Höss Visit 99

Chapter VIII
October 1942–April 1943
End of the First Phase 107

Chapter IX
The Second Phase February 1944–July 1944
The Waldlager Re-Established 115

Chapter X
August 1944–January 1945
The Liquidation of the Camp 137

Part II
Survivors, Victims, Perpetrators
and the Aftermath 145

Chapter XI
Jewish Survivors and Victims Roll of Remembrance 147

Chapter XII
The Perpetrators
Sonderkommando Kulmhof Garrison 362

Chapter XIII
The Polish *Arbeitskommando* 396

Chapter XIV
Testimonies and Trials 400

Chapter XV
Epilogue 416

Appendix I
Letter from Rabbi Szulman—Grabow 425

Appendix II
List of Transports to Chełmno 427

Appendix III
Inspection Protocol— Ostrowski Factory Koło 429

Appendix IV
The Extermination Center 431

Appendix V
My Tribute to Artur Hojan 437

Illustrations 441

Documents, Drawings, Maps 463

Table of Equivalent Ranks 484

Glossary of Nazi Terms 486

Selected Bibliography 492

Sources and Acknowledgements 494

Index of Names 497

Dedicated to Artur Hojan and all of the victims of the Chełmno Death Camp

For Zuzia, Freya and Lilli

"He who comes here, does not walk away alive."
Inscription on the basement wall, in the Mansion at Chełmno

In addition *Hauptsturmführer* Lange said to us that the orders to exterminate the Jews had been issued by Hitler and Himmler.
Kurt Möbius – *SS Sonderkommando* Kulmhof

The gassed people were thrown out of the vehicle and piled like rubbish. They were grabbed either by their legs or hair. Above the grave, there were two men throwing the bodies into it. Inside the hole there were another two men putting the corpses in layers, faces down, in a way that one person's legs met another person's head.
Szlamek Bajler
Szlamek escaped from Chełmno on January 19, 1942. He wrote a report on Chełmno. He perished in the Bełżec death camp after being deported from Zamość in April 1942.

Foreword

Chełmno is still relatively unknown, even amongst esteemed historians of the Holocaust. The importance of Chełmno in the development of the Holocaust is also not well understood and is certainly under researched.

Chełmno was the first death camp on *Reich* territory, and played a hugely important role in the plans of *Gauleiter* Arthur Greiser to develop the *Warthegau* into the model district (*Gau*), cleansed of Jews and other "undesirables." Greiser's relationship with Himmler, the *Reichsführer-SS*, allowed him to take a much more pivotal role in the development and organization of the Holocaust in the *Warthegau*, including the death camp Chełmno, than any other Nazi District leader. Greiser was a frequent visitor to Chełmno and it was Greiser's civil administration that organized the delivery of Jews to Chełmno.

Jewish Ghettoization began first in the *Warthegau* in 1940, and Łódź was the first large scale Jewish ghetto in Nazi occupied Europe. It was Greiser who sought approval from Adolf Hitler to kill the first 100,000 Jews of the *Warthegau* in 1941. There are direct links between the killing of mental patients between 1939 and 1941 in the *Warthegau* by Herbert Lange, and the development of Chełmno the death camp, with Lange as its first Commandant. It was Lange who devised the methodology and the organization of the camp and it was he who recruited the personnel. Chełmno was an integral part of the development of the racial policies that Greiser adopted for the *Warthegau* region.

Chełmno was the first Nazi death camp when it began operations in early December 1941. In Chełmno the gas vans were the first mass use of poison gas to kill Jews. Chełmno was the only death camp to use gas vans as its primary method of killing. Because of its proximity to Berlin, Chełmno became a testing ground for techniques for disposing the bodies of the dead victims. It was Colonel Paul Blobel under the auspices of *Sonderkommando 1005*, who developed the techniques in Chełmno, later used in the Aktion Reinhardt camps of

Bełżec, Sobibór and Treblinka, Auschwitz-Birkenau and all over occupied Eastern Europe, to dig up and burn the bodies of untold numbers of victims of the Nazi regime.

These firsts and interconnections make Chełmno and the killing of the Jews in the *Warthegau* almost unique in the annals of the Holocaust, but are also insightful in how the Holocaust itself developed. The number of histories published about the Chełmno death camp number less than ten. Chris's book is therefore timely. As always Chris brings his own style to the difficulty of how to write about the Nazi death camps, while respecting the memory of the victims. His book covers the development of the camp and racial program, its operations, the key events, the accounts of the brave Jews who escaped from this hell, the detailed Roll of Remembrance, the perpetrators and the post-War trials, right up to the modern-day.

This book is also important for me, as Chris has graciously coauthored with my late colleague Artur Hojan. I worked with Artur for eight years in researching Nazi War Crimes in the *Warthegau* and beyond. Artur's knowledge, especially of the killing of mental patients in Nazi occupied Western Poland was exceptional. This led to Artur and I setting up the *Tiergartenstrasse 4* Association in 2005 to research Nazi War Crimes. The Association is now established in Berlin, as *Tiergarten4 Association e.v* with a library and research center. Chris has quite rightly dedicated the book to our friend and colleague Artur and his memory.

I wish Chris the best of luck with this book on Chełmno that is a worthy successor to his books on the *Aktion Reinhardt* camps and Auschwitz Concentration Camp.

Cameron Munro
Tiergarten4 Association e.V.

A crucial extension to our body of knowledge on the Holocaust, *The Chełmno Death Camp: History, Biographies, Remembrance* is an authoritative and well-researched account of the construction, historical context and liquidation of Hitler's first death camp.

Drawing on detailed accounts from Jewish prisoners, perpetrator biographies and war crimes trials, Chris Webb and the late Artur Hojan paint a characteristically rich picture of the atrocities that happened at Chełmno, as well as providing an impactful list of remembrance.

Going forward, this book is a great resource for modern historians and students of the Holocaust who wish to understand more about how Chełmno sparked wider developments in the systematic murder of over six million Jews from 1941 to 1945.
Lest we forget!

Dr. William Allchorn is Associate Director of the Center for the Analysis of the Radical Right (CARR) and a Postdoctoral Researcher at the University of Leeds.

Author's Introduction

Artur and Chris – Łódź 2005

This book chronologically tells the story of the Chełmno death camp that the Nazis created in late 1941, in central Poland. Chełmno was the first death camp to murder the Jews using gas, though not in static gas chambers, but using gas-vans. I am deeply indebted to the work of Kryzysztof Gorczyca and Zdzisław Lorek, whose unpublished *Chełmno Day By Day* account has been invaluable. Also Patrick Montague's book *Chełmno and the Holocaust* published in 2012, has also been heavily quoted. There is simply too little published work and research in respect of the Chełmno death camp and this book hopes to cover previously uncharted territory, with new accounts and new information. Also an invaluable source has been the book *Chełmno Witnesses Speak* published by the District Museum in Konin, Poland.

In September 2005, Artur Hojan planned and guided Cameron Munro and myself on a visit to the former death camp in Chełmno, and numerous places connected with the T4 Euthanasia *"Aktions,"* in what was called the *Warthegau*, during the War. We also visited major cities like Poznań and Łódź and smaller places like Dąbie, Grabow and Koło, all closely bound up with the history of the Chełmno death camp. During this trip I had the good fortune to meet Zdzisław Lorek in person, a real expert on Chełmno.

Four years later another research trip to Chełmno was undertaken: Artur again produced the trip schedule. Our group of intrepid Holocaust researchers consisted of Arthur Hojan, Cameron Munro, Professor Matthew Feldman, Chris Webb and our Polish driver Krystof.

We were based in Kutno, and toured a number of places near Chełmno, such as Krośniewice, Sompolno, not previously visited, plus Dąbie, Zawadka, Łódź and Warsaw. I have included in this book some of the photographs taken on these two trips to provide the reader with a better understanding of how these places look now, and the horrors that once took place in this region of Poland.

Chełmno death camp has been generally neglected compared to other camps such as Auschwitz and Treblinka, but that should not be so, and this work demonstrates the vital role it played, and the need to be fully documented in this terrible tragedy that was the Holocaust.

This account begins with the establishment of the camp, and the commencement of mass murder by the use of gas vans in December 1941. It contains the detailed accounts of escapees Szlamek Bajler, who survived Chełmno only to lose his life in another of Hitler's slaughterhouses Bełżec in April 1942, and Michał Podchlebnik, who survived the hell that was Chełmno, and lived to see the Nazis defeated.

All sides in this modern tragedy are represented, the other Jewish survivors, such as Shimon Srebnik and M. Zurawski and Jewish victims, the German police and *SS*, the Polish workers who assisted the Nazis, the Polish and German residents of Chełmno and other places in the *Warthegau*.

A Roll of Remembrance of the Jews deported from Germany to Chełmno, has been created using the Bundesarchiv online resource the *Gedenkbuch* as well as names gleaned from the few survivors' accounts. The power of this website cannot be underestimated, 520 pages with over 5,000 names. To reproduce this would swamp the book, and a compromise has had to be found. Instead every surname has been included, which in no way diminishes those who have not been included, but does provide the reader nevertheless with a sense of the scale of the destruction.

The members of the *Sonderkommando Kulmhof* have been meticulously researched by the late Artur Hojan and by Cameron Munro, from *Tiergartenstrasse4 Association* in Berlin. It is thanks to Artur in particular that so many biographies have been compiled, of the men responsible for these ghastly crimes against humanity. Their initial findings have been updated and improved, with additional information and more biographies included.

The events of the post-war are captured, including testimonies and trials as well as personal accounts of our trips to Chełmno, and the surrounding villages all connected with the death camp's history, including some modern-day photographs, along with some rare documents to embellish the account.

With Grateful Thanks

This book owes everything to my late friend Artur Hojan. I first met Artur in Kraków in the summer of 2004, when the ARC Website group undertook their second field trip to Poland, visiting a host of sites connected with the Holocaust. Artur was from Kościan, in Poland and at that time he was learning English. During the trip he acted as one of our guides, and we became firm friends.

The following year in September 2005, I visited Chełmno for the first time, with Cameron Munro and Artur, who had established their own Holocaust research site. During that trip we met Zdzisław Lorek, who provided me with maps, documentation and research material about Chełmno some of which has been used in this book.

Artur sadly lost his life in December 2013, in the midst of writing a book on Chełmno, some of which he shared with me, and this has been incorporated in this work. Thus it is only fair that he has been given a co-writing credit. For Artur's family this is an important legacy, in recognition of his many years of dedicated research, and something tangible for generations to come. I am grateful to his wife Ada, for allowing me to include some of the work he started, but sadly did not finish.

Firstly I must thank Tom Nixon for his cover design and support, which is much appreciated. I am also grateful for the proof reading and copy-editing work of Tania Mühlberger, who really brings so much to the table. I must in this respect thank Professor Matthew Feldman, for introducing Tania to me, and his support for this book. Professor Feldman visited Chełmno with me in 2009, and has supported this work in so many ways. I cannot thank him enough.

I also want to thank the late Sir Martin Gilbert, who kindly gave me copies of his maps and drawings to use in my ventures. He was always a great inspiration to me, and always kind and generous with his knowledge and support. I have again used his fine maps to enrich my work.

I must place on record my thanks to Cameron Munro, Robert Parzer and Reinald Purmann from the *Tiergartenstrasse4*

Association in Berlin. As always, they have provided material, support, advice and expertise, which was invaluable. Cameron in particular is an expert in his own right on Euthanasia in the *Warthegau* and Chełmno in particular. This work owes a great deal to him, and I am proud to call him my friend. He kindly wrote the foreword to this book, and he is an inspiration in the field of Holocaust research. I first met Cameron in 2004, on the Second Field Trip to Poland undertaken by the ARC Group that I co-founded in 2001. This group initially focused on the *Aktion Reinhardt* mass murder program, but subsequently covered other aspects of the Holocaust. The photograph of Artur and me in Łódź was taken by Cameron, during our 2005 trip, and this particular trip was one of the most memorable I have taken part in.

In terms of institutions I am grateful for the assistance given by the staff of the Wiener Library, including its former head of photo archives Marek Jaros, who kindly gave me a number of photographs of Chełmno from their archives, which appear in this book. I must thank Elise Bath who has taken over from Marek for her kind permission to use the photographs.

The Wiener Library also provided a number of documents, and records from the International Military Tribunal held after the end of the Second World War, and I am very grateful for the help and guidance of Howard Falkensohn, who specializes in this particular field. The Wiener Library also provided other material that has been much appreciated, and they deserve much credit and support. They truly are a national treasure.

I am also grateful to Alla Kucherenko from Yad Vashem who has helped me to locate a number of rare and important documents regarding Chełmno and these have been reproduced in this book and it is much improved by their inclusion.

The Bundesarchiv in Berlin has also helped me with my research and I must thank Lutz Moeser for his patience and efforts in looking through numerous files of personnel who served at Chełmno, as well as their support with photographs and documents.

Abbreviations

AK	Armia Krajowa – Polish Home Army
ARC	Aktion Reinhard Camps website
BBC	British Broadcasting Corporation
GFH	Ghetto Fighters House, Israel
H.E.A.R.T.	Holocaust Education and Archive Research Team
HHS	Holocaust Historical Society, UK
KL	Konzentrationslager (Concentration Camp)
NA	National Archives, Kew, London
NSKK	National Sozialistische Kraftfahr Korps (National Socialist Motor Corps)
POW	Prisoner of War
PPS	Polish Socialist Party
RSHA	Reich Security Main Office
SD	Sicherheitsdienst (Security Service)
SIPO	Sicherheitspolizei (Security Police)
SS	Schutzstaffel (Protection Squad)
TAP	Secret Polish Army
TOW	Military Organization Union (Polish)
USHMM	United States Holocaust Memorial Museum
WL	Wiener Library, London
WVHA	Administration and Economic Main Office of the SS
YVA	Yad Vashem Archives

Part I
The Hell Called Chełmno

Chapter I
November 1941
Chełmno Death Camp Established

Chełmno, or as it was known during the Nazi occupation, *Kulmhof,* is located 50 kilometers north of Łódź, and 13 kilometers from Koło, otherwise known as *Warthbrücken* during this period. This area of Poland was recognized at that time as the *Warthegau.* The *Warthegau* was incorporated into the *Reich,* this included Wielkopolska (Greater Poland Voivodeship: with its Capital Poznań), Kujawy (Opole Voivodeship) and the Łódź region.

Arthur Greiser, the *Gauleiter* of *Reichsgau Wartheland (Warthegau)* and Wilhelm Koppe, the Higher *SS* and Police Leader, whose headquarters were based in *Posen,* today Poznań, sought solutions to overcome the overcrowding of ghettos within their sphere of influence. They called upon the services of *SS-Hauptsturmführer* Herbert Lange, who had been in command of a special unit *(Sonderkommando)* charged with murdering the disabled and mentally-ill in Soldau, in East Prussia and other locations within the *Warthegau,* such as Kościan and Osieczna. These executions were undertaken by shooting and by the use of gas vans *(Sonderwagen),* and were carried out under the auspices of the euthanasia program in the *Reich* that was known as the *T4,* program. *T4* was the abbreviation derived from the address of its headquarters in Berlin, *Tiergarten 4,* which was run by *SS-Oberführer* Viktor Brack, Chief of the Head Office II of Adolf Hitler's private Chancellery.

Herbert Lange was born in Menzlin, Pomerania on September 29, 1909. He studied law, but failed to obtain a degree and became a police officer. After serving in *Einsatzgruppe VI* under Erich Naumann, prior to the invasion of Poland in September 1939, Lange went to *Posen,* where he became Commandant of Fort VII for a brief period, between October 10–16, 1939. Here he selected the staff he required and admitted the first prisoners.[1]

Herbert Lange was then appointed head of the *Sonderkommando Lange*, and this *Kommando* conducted a series of gassing *Aktionen* asylums at Owińska, Dziekanka, Gniezno, Gostynin, Kochanówska near Łódź, Kościan, Warta and other places, from October 1939 to mid-1940. It is estimated that during these *Aktionen* and gassings at the stationary gas chamber at Fort VII, in *Posen*, that at least 10,000 patients were murdered by these means.[2]

One of the witnesses to these gassings at Fort VII in *Posen* was Henryk Maliczak, who was arrested in November 1939 and incarcerated in a *Gestapo* prison in Kościan. He was later transferred to Fort VII, where he was imprisoned in the cell designated *SK (Sonderkommando)*. He recalled the gassing of patients from the hospital in Owińska:

> We were initially employed in transporting and burying the corpses of the mentally ill. The first victims came from the psychiatric hospital in Owińska. They were transported by truck to Fort VII and gassed in a bunker, the door and window had been hermetically sealed. I saw how members of the camp staff and others, dressed in *SS* uniforms, observed the gassing through a window in the door of the bunker. A special group of approximately ten *SS* men, not Fort VII personnel, transported the mentally ill from the hospital in Owińska and gassed them. This group was commanded by an *SS* man named Lange.
> The gassing occurred in this way two or three times over a period of several days.... The victims were calm; I suppose they had been tranquillized with injections. Our role in this activity consisted of carrying the corpses of the victims to trucks that transported them to forests near the town of Oborniki Śląskie. Here we threw the corpses into previously dug pits. We learned from members of Lange's *Kommando*, that the victims came from Owińska and were mentally ill. They tried to put us at ease, saying that such people had to be eliminated.[3]
> Returning to the use of mobile gas-vans, they were constructed with a hermetically closed cargo hold, where the victims were incarcerated, and

---

[1] Artur Hojan – Chełmno *SS Personnel* unpublished paper.
[2] Ibid., p. 1.
[3] P. Montague, *Chełmno and the Holocaust*, I. B. Tauris and Co. Ltd, London 2012, p. 20.

from the outside they looked like refrigerator vans. To camouflage their true purpose there was a sign that read, *Kaiser's Kaffee-Geschäft* and a cup of steaming coffee was also depicted. The gas—carbon monoxide (CO) was pumped into the interior from steel bottles installed in the driver's cabin.[4]

A detailed description of the *Kaiser's Kaffee-Geschäft* gas-vans was provided by Wacław Berlowski who was employed at the Kochanówska hospital in Łódź from 1933 to 1941 as a metalworker / locksmith and who repaired the *Sonderwagen*:

> They were regular trucks with canvas coverings. Only one of them was a completely closed, metal vehicle, the interior of which was hermetically panelled with wood. This van had no windows. I repaired the van together with Antoni Bula.
> The inscription "Café Kaiser"[5] was written on the side of the van. During the repair work we noticed that the pipe led out from the motor. This pipe was flexible; it led out from the middle of the motor, from underneath and was connected to the body of the rear compartment. We also noticed that there was a grated opening in the floor of the vehicle. The pipe running from the motor led to this opening. This pipe was attached to an adaptor.
> Antoni Bula can provide additional details as he is a professional driver. When we saw this pipe, Bula said that it was for gassing people. This vehicle was never washed by personnel from the hospital, but occasionally Jews were brought from the city to do it. The vehicle was gone from the hospital for three to four hours at a time after transporting a group of patients.[6]

After the Euthanasia *T4-Aktionen* in the *Warthegau*, Lange's *Kommando* was sent to Soldau in East Prussia, and to the Konin region. This was at the request of Wilhelm Rediess, the Higher SS and Police Leader for East Prussia. He wanted Lange and his *Sonderkommando* to liquidate asylum inmates in the Zichenau region under his jurisdiction. According to the agreement reached with the *RSHA*, between May 21 and June 8, 1940, *Sonderkommando* Lange "evacuated"

---

[4] Krystof Gorczyca, Zdzisław Lorek, *Day After Day in the extermination camp Kulmhof am Ner* – unpublished draft, pp. 8–9.
[5] Should read "Kaiser's Kaffee Geschäft ".
[6] P. Montague, *Chełmno and the Holocaust*, I. B. Tauris and Co. Ltd, London 2012, p. 26.

1,558 "burdensome persons" brought to the so-called *Durchgangslager Soldau*. These people were killed in the camp by shooting and the use of *Kaiser's Kaffee Geschäft* gas-vans using gas cylinders. After these arduous *Aktionen* in Soldau, the members of *Sonderkommando* Lange involved in these murderous activities were granted a holiday in the Netherlands, which cost more than *RM*. 3,000. Lange was then transferred to the post of head of the Economics Crimes Department of the Criminal Police in *Posen*.[7]

Following the Nazi invasion of the Soviet Union on June 22, 1941, some two months later on August 16, 1941, Erich von dem Bach-Zelewski, Higher *SS* and Police Leader *Mitte* requested that *Sonderkommando* Lange come to his headquarters in Baranowicze, to give a demonstration of his killing process. This information was contained in a captured German Police decode intercepted by the British Intelligence Service at Bletchley Park. This was followed by another decoded message, by von dem Bach on August 18, 1941.[8]

Another decoded message intercepted by the British Intelligence Service on October 3, 1941, stated that a Senior Physician Freyberg, of the Army High Command requested that *Sonderkommando* Lange should be sent to Novgorod in Russia, to clear out three asylums, so they could be used by the *Wehrmacht*. A Junkers JU52 aircraft was to be provided for Lange and his assistants, as well as their equipment. Heinrich Himmler agreed the request. Whilst very little is known, it is unlikely that Himmler's orders were ignored. The Junkers JU52 most probably carried carbon monoxide bottles and piping, in order to convert the rooms in the asylums into provisional gas chambers.[9]

According to the testimony of Herbert Lange's driver and adjutant Walter Burmeister, the search for a suitable site to carry out the extermination of the Jews in the *Warthegau* commenced in the autumn of 1941. Lange and Dr. Walther Becht, the *Landrat* and

---

[7] Artur Hojan – *Chełmno SS Personnel* unpublished paper, p. 2.
[8] National Archives Kew HW16/32.
[9] Ibid., HW16/32.

Kreisleiter of the Nazi Party in *Warthbrücken*, visited Chełmno and decided that Chełmno was the ideal location for a death camp.

A few days later Herbert Lange and Walter Burmeister returned to Chełmno and local schoolteacher Erhard Michelsohn, one of the Germans who had been resettled into the village of Chełmno recalled:

> One day in the winter of 1941/42 several cars drove to the town hall opposite the school and several men in field-grey uniforms got out. I could observe this from the school. They went into the town hall and conferred there with *Amtskommissar* Schulz. Afterwards Schulz told me that a *Sonderkommando* would establish a Transit-Camp in Chełmno. The SS men told him that Jews would pass through here on their way to Russia.[10]

Herbert Lange told his driver Walter Burmeister:

> To make it plain from the start, absolute secrecy is crucial. I have orders to form a special commando in Chełmno. Other staff from *Posen* and from the State Police in *Litzmannstadt*,[11] are going to join us. We have a tough but important job to do.[12]

Chełmno was chosen because of its central location within the *Warthegau*, and its important transport links with *Warthbrücken* (Koło), a key station on the *Posen–Warschau* railroad line. There was a narrow gauge railway line from *Warthbrücken* (Koło), to Dąbie, that passed through Chełmno, but in the first phase of the death camp's activity, the bridge over the Rigilowka stream was destroyed in the 1939 invasion. Thus the Jewish deportees were transported on the narrow gauge track to Powiercie and from there the journey to Chełmno was completed by trucks. After the bridge was repaired in the autumn of 1942, the transports went directly to Chełmno.

The Jews were also deported from the Łódź ghetto and from locations in the vicinity of Chełmno by road. From Łódź they travelled in trucks from via Łęczyca–Grabow–Koło or a shorter route Łódź–

---

[10] P. Montague, *Chełmno and the Holocaust*, I.B. Tauris and Co. Ltd, London 2012, p.51.
[11] Litzmannstadt was the German name for Łódź.
[12] L. Rees, *Auschwitz. The Nazis and the Final Solution*, BBC Books, London 2005, p. 86.

Poddębice–Uniejów–Dąbie–Koło, which was a journey of approximately 70 kilometers.

The final destination was the 19th Century Manor House of Baron von Bistram, which was transformed into a place of extermination by the Nazis during November 1941. It was partly destroyed during the First World War and was under State supervision from 1918. It was located at the edge of the village, about 150 meters from the road, on the high bank of the valley of the River Ner, which is a tributary of the River Warta. The Manor House was also known as the Mansion, the Palace, the *Schloss* (Castle), or simply the *Haus* (House).

The Manor House area of almost 3 hectares, together with farm buildings, the park and the garden was separated from the village with a high fence some two and a half-three meters high made of boards. From the side by the river there was a fence made of netting, which had been put up before the Second World War. There were two entrance gates: the first one was located near the church, and it was constructed as a sluice: when guards opened one gate, the second gate was closed. The so-called Manor House was a substantial building, three storeys high. At the front façade there were two symmetrically placed entrances leading to, through wide galleries with stairs, the high ground floor. The garden façade had one entrance leading to a large patio. On the north-north western gable wall there was an entrance to the cellars from the inside of the building led by narrow stairs located near the southern entrance. Also there was a building in the grounds that was the Granary.

Approximately 150 meters south-east of the Manor House there was a neo-Gothic church separated from the estate by a road. During the first phase of the camp's activities the church was used as a garage for vans, according to the villagers who lived in Chełmno and then as a transit and a sorting place of the possessions taken from the victims.[13]

Chełmno was unlike the other death camps established in Poland, such as Bełżec, Lublin, Sobibór and Treblinka, in the first phase

---

[13] Krystof Gorczyca, Zdzisław Lorek, *Day After Day in the extermination camp Kulmhof am Ner* – unpublished draft, p. 23.

of its existence. After the people had been gassed in the gas-vans, the victims were driven in the gas-vans to the so-called *Waldlager* in the Rzuchów forest. In the forest the mass graves were located within the camp's area, where the victims were buried. In the other extermination camps the mass graves were located near the stationary gas chamber facilities.

Mass graves and later furnaces were located in two forest clearings, of approximately 5 hectares. The clearings were some 5 kilometers north-west of the Manor House, on the road to *Warthbrücken* (Koło), the forest belonged to the Ladorudz forest administration region, walk 77, under the supervision of the Forest Administration in Koło.[14]

The method of mass extermination at Chełmno was the use of gas-vans, which were used by Lange in Chełmno, a new more humane method of killing, was suggested. In November 1941, a new type of gas-van was introduced. As before, these were hermetically closed vans, but this time those inside the rear of the vehicle were killed by means of exhaust fumes, which were introduced from the exhaust pipe to the compartment containing the victims, using a flexible metal-strengthened spiral pipe connected to it. This outlet was additionally secured by a perforated sheet.

The *RSHA—Reich* Security Main Office II D 3a was responsible for the construction of the gas-vans, also known in German as *Sonderwagen*, recruitment of drivers and the provision of spare parts for the *Sonderwagen*. Two types of vehicles were used, a smaller version with a 3.5 tonnes payload which accommodated 50 persons, these were Diamond, Opel Blitz and Renault vehicles and a larger version with a payload of 70–80 persons, Sauer and Magrius vehicles with petrol engines. These gas vans had an air tight car-body and looked like furniture vans. Exhaust fumes were fed into the car-body by means of a removable tube. A barred lamp illuminated the interior.[15]

---

[14] Ibid., p. 23.
[15] www.deathcamps.org/gasvans. ARC - online resource.

The *RSHA* ordered both series from the plant *Gaubschat Fahrzeugwerke GmbH* in Berlin– Neukölln on the pretext of meeting the requirements of secure transportation of bodies of those who died due to typhoid epidemic. They were made of precisely pressed boards upholstered with sheet from inside and were equipped with hermetical doors. On the floor there was a wooden grille, as in bath, preventing the blockade of the exhaust fumes from the inside. In the driver's cabin there was a window, through which it was checked whether the exhaust fumes were working. The whole thing was painted dark grey.[16]

Having covered the camp and the chosen method of extermination, it is the turn of the perpetrators and their helpers, who commenced Phase One of the camps murderous activities. We have already mentioned the Commandant Herbert Lange and his deputy Herbert Otto, who both arrived in Chełmno on November 15, 1941. Immediately they were joined by between 10–15 *SS*-Officers. They were further strengthened by a unit of policemen *(Schutzpolizei)* and military policemen, who were accommodated in several buildings in Chełmno village.

The military policemen and *Schutzpolizei* were deployed from Litzmannstadt (Łódź) mainly from the 1st and 2nd companies of the 21st Station Battalion of Police Reserves. They were deployed by the Chief of the Police in Łódź, *SS-Brigadeführer* Karl-Wilhelm Albert. Another group came from *Posen* whilst others came directly from an *Aktion* in Konin. One of those who came from *Posen* was *Hauptscharführer* Karl Heinl and he gave the following account:

> I was to report to *Polizeimeister* Lenz at the *Posen Gestapo (Stapo)* office, in order to be incorporated into a guard squad together with other police officials. *Revierleutnant* Graf personally passed this order on to me. I do not know who from the *Kommando* of the *Schutzpolizei* passed on this order. I was not told either, for what purpose or in what place this *Kommando* was to be employed.
> As ordered I went to the *Gestapo* office in *Posen* on the following day. The aforementioned *Polizeimeister* Lenz, whom I did not know, met me

---

[16] Krystof Gorczyca, Zdzisław Lorek, *Day After Day in the extermination camp Kulmhof am Ner* – unpublished draft, p. 23.

at the entrance. Altogether, five or six police officials met there, who like Lenz came from the police districts in *Posen*. As far as I remember there were:
Polizei-Oberwachtmeister Hannes Runge
Polizei-Wachtmeister Max Sommer
Polizei-Hauptwachtmeister Simon Haider
Polizei-Oberwachtmeister Erich Kretschmer
I cannot now recall the other persons. We asked Lenz for what purpose we were being employed, but he told us he did not know. He told us to go to the canteen and wait for him. Then he went to the *Stapo* office. In the afternoon, at about three o'clock, Lenz appeared and ordered us to depart. In front of the *Stapo* office we got into a truck, which was driven by a member of the *Stapo*, *Oberscharführer* Erwin Bürstinger. He drove us via Koło to the village of Chełmno. After we arrived there, Lenz assigned us quarters in a house in the village, where we spent the night in a big room.[17]

The SS men were originally housed in the building of the local volunteer fire department, the so-called *Deutsches Haus*, but later when the police detachment was quartered in the *Deutsches Haus*, they moved into private homes in Chełmno village. Barracks to house the additional policemen drafted in, were erected next to the *Deutsches Haus*.

Lange and his driver Burmeister stayed in the local *gmia* (community) building. *Sonderkommando* Lange also requisitioned houses to serve as a kitchen and canteen. They also took over the presbytery, which stood opposite the church. The local Priest, Father Karol Morozewicz was arrested by the Germans and he later perished in the Dachau Concentration Camp on May 3, 1942.

The guard deployment at Chełmno was divided into three sub-units and these were known as detachments.

These were:

Transportkommando – Transportation Detachment
Hauskommando – Manor House Detachment
Waldkommando – Forest Detachment

---

[17] P. Montague, *Chełmno and the Holocaust*, I.B. Tauris and Co. Ltd, London 2012, pp. 51–52.

The first of the detachments was mainly responsible for the escort of the deported during the transportation to the death camp. To transport the victims and prisoner-workers they used a truck covered with tarpaulin and a bus. Later there were three trucks. The commanding officer had a car.

The Manor House detachment kept guard duty around the buildings in the village, guarded and hurried the victims who were already on the Manor House grounds, and supervised the group of prisoners-workers.

The forest detachment guarded parts of the camp located in the Rzuchówski forest, and performed other functions as well in relation to the supervision of burying and burning the bodies and covering up the traces of their crimes.

The *SS-Sonderkommando* members who were part of the original death camp personnel were as follows:

Hauptsturmführer – Herbert Lange
Obersturmführer – Herbert Otto
Rottenführer – Walter Burmeister
Hauptscharführer – Friedrich Neumann
Hauptscharführer – Erwin Bürstinger
Hauptscharführer – Alfred Behm
Hauptscharführer – Johannes Runge
Hauptscharführer – Karl Heinl[18]
Unterscharführer – Erich Kretschmer
Polizeimeister – Wilhelm Lenz
Polizeiwachtmeister – Max Sommer
Polizei-Hauptwachtmeister – Simon Haider[19]

The German camp personnel were assisted by a group of Polish prisoners, who became co-workers in this place of horror. There were eight men who had previously been incarcerated in Fort VII in *Posen*, and some of these men had been involved in the *T4 Aktionen* and

---

[18] Some reports claim that Karl Heinl arrived in Chełmno at the end of January 1942, but the above report would seem to place him there at the start of operations.

[19] P. Montague, *Chełmno and the Holocaust*, I.B. Tauris and Co. Ltd, London 2012, p. 53.

the extermination of Jews in the Konin district. These men arrived at Chełmno on November 15, 1941 and were:

Lech Jaskolski
Marian Libelt
Henryk Maliczak
Henryk Mania
Franciszek Piekarski
Stanisław Polubinski
Kajetan Skrzypczynski
Stanisław Szymanski[20]

With the personnel in place, the first tasks were to make the Manor House secure and move out the residents who were living there. *Amtskommissar* Schulz acted as the liaison man between the local population and the *Sonderkommando*. The Manor House residents were made to clean it thoroughly under the supervision of the village administrator Jakob Semmler, and then evacuated their homes.

Members of the *Sonderkommando* carried out minor repairs, basement windows were boarded over and later bricked in, and a local carpenter was ordered to make a number of benches and to modify the existing ones in the church for use in the Manor House.

The grounds of the Manor House were made secure and a wooden fence approximately three meters high was constructed on three sides. A large gate was built on the front side where the driveway met the main road. The rear of the Manor House, facing the River Ner, was sectioned off with a wire fence. A second wooden fence was built in front of the Manor House enclosing the courtyard. This fence had two gates located in the northwest and southeast sides.

Inside the Manor House, near the main entrance on the left side of the building, was a door that led downstairs to the basement and a small landing. A long corridor just over one meter wide and illuminated with gas lamps, led to the right. On the left hand side of the corridor were as many as seven rooms. On the right side were four rooms, about the same size as those on the other side of the corridor,

---

[20] Ibid., pp. 227–229.

as well as one other much smaller room. The corridor ended at a door that led outside on the right side of the building. A wooden ramp enclosed on two sides was built there.[21]

At the end of November 1941, a number of policemen were added to the *Sonderkommando Kulmhof*. On November 24, 1941, *Oberleutnant* Harold Lang arrived to take up duty in Chełmno, although his stay was brief. The following day on November 25, 1941, *Oberwachtmeister* Franz Schalling arrived from Łódź, with another group of policemen. Two days later Theodor Malzmüller also arrived at the camp, with a group of policemen from Police Battalion XXI, also previously based in Łódź.[22]

Franz Schalling described in an interview with Claude Lanzmann for the film "Shoah" his arrival at Chełmno:

> We were on permanent guard duty, protecting military objectives: mills, the roads, when Hitler went to East Prussia. It was dreary, and we were told, "We need men who want to break out from this routine." So we volunteered: we were issued winter uniforms, overcoats, fur hats, fur-lined boots, and two or three days later we were told, "We're off!" We were put aboard two or three trucks... I don't know... they had benches, and we rode and rode. Finally we arrived; the place was crawling with SS men and Police. Our first question was, "What goes on here?" They said, "You'll find out!"
> We were told to report to the *Deutsches Haus*, German Headquarters, the only stone building in the village. We were taken into it. An SS man immediately told us, "This is a top secret mission!"
> "A top secret mission: Sign this." We each had to sign. There was a form ready for each of us, a pledge of secrecy. We never even got to read it through. No, just sign, promising to shut up about whatever we'd see. Not say a word. After we'd signed we were told: "Final Solution of the Jewish question." We didn't understand what that meant. It all looked normal.[23]

---

[21] P. Montague, *Chełmno and the Holocaust*, I.B. Tauris and Co. Ltd, London 2012, pp. 54–55.

[22] Krystof Gorczyca, Zdzisław Lorek, *Day After Day in the extermination camp Kulmhof am Ner* – unpublished draft, p. 52.

[23] C. Lanzmann, *Shoah*, Pantheon Books, New York, 1985, pp. 73–74.

Chapter II
December 1941
Mass Murder Begins

On December 1, 1941, members of the *Sonderkommando Lange* carried out the final liquidation of the Kalisz ghetto and the remaining 100 inhabitants were murdered by gassing in the gas-vans in the Jedlenki forest near Głuchów.[24]

The Polish *Arbeitskommando* dug the first mass graves in the Rzuchówski forest on December 4, 1941, and the following day members of the *Sonderkommando Lange* went to the Koło ghetto in a car and truck. They selected 30 Jewish workers who were forced into the truck. This was the first Jewish work-commando in the history of Chełmno, but their survival was short-lived.

December 8, 1941 marked the start of the mass murder of Jews in the Chełmno death camp, indeed in Poland itself, with the first transport of Jews from nearby *Warthbrücken* (Koło).

Franz Schalling recalled the arrival of transports:

> In the winter of 1941/42, then we were assigned to our stations. Our guard post was at the side of the road, a sentry box in front of the castle. We could see. We were at the gatehouse. When the Jews arrived, the way they looked—half-frozen, starved, dirty, and already half-dead: Old people, children. Think of it! The long trip here, standing in a truck, packed in. Who knows if they knew what was in store. They didn't trust anyone, that's for sure. After months in the ghetto, you can imagine!
> I heard an *SS* man shout at them: "You're going to be deloused and have a bath. You're going to work here." The Jews consented. They said, "Yes, that's what we want to do. They were hustled into two or three big rooms on the first floor. They had to undress, give up everything, rings, gold, everything......
> Then stark naked they had to run down more steps to an underground corridor that led back up to the ramp, where the gas-van awaited them..... they were beaten. Blows fell everywhere, and the Jews

---

[24] Krystof Gorczyca, Zdzisław Lorek, *Day After Day in the extermination camp Kulmhof am Ner* – unpublished draft, p. 26.

understood. They screamed; it was frightful! Frightful! I know because we went down to the cellar when they were all in the van. We opened the cells of the work detail, the Jewish workers who collected stuff thrown into the yard out of a first floor window.

Franz Schalling was asked to describe the gas vans and the method of mass murder:

> Just big trucks, like moving vans, with two rear doors; It went like this a Pole yelled "Gas," then the driver got under the van to hook up the pipe that fed the gas into the van, from the motor.[25]

One of those who witnessed the deportations of the Jews from this town was Michał Podchlebnik. He and his wife had been resettled to the nearby village of Bugaj, but he worked for a German in Koło, under a work permit and he recalled:

> At three o'clock, everyone was entered on an A or B list – those able or unable to work. Then they were taken and locked in the synagogue and the Jewish school. The next day they were taken by transport to Chełmno. Everyone was told where they were going. It was said that Chełmno is an assembly point for further transports to the east. Sick people and pregnant women were treated with excessive politeness; they were taken during the last day of the ghetto's liquidation.
> The drivers were given special instructions, so that all could hear, to drive cautiously because they would be carrying sick people. Those leaving were ordered to take indispensable items and clothing. The trucks were loaded with between 40 and 60 people. During this time the names of the people leaving were read out loud and they were marked off from the registration list with red ink.
> I personally helped with the loading of the trucks. When the last transport was loaded, I asked if I could go to Chełmno to visit my family. They told me I couldn't, because it was impossible to return from there.[26]

On December 7, 1941, approximately 700 people arrived at the Manor House, where they were incarcerated for the night. The following day they were loaded into the *Kaiser's Kaffee Sonderwagen*,

---

[25] C. Lanzmann, *Shoah*, Pantheon Books, New York, 1985, pp. 75–76.
[26] P. Montague, *Chełmno and the Holocaust*, I.B. Tauris and Co. Ltd, London 2012, p. 64.

taken to the Rzuchówski forest, gassed and buried. This process for the Jews of Koło was repeated until December 11, 1941.[27]

Three days later on December 14, 1941, approximately 500 Jews from the nearby village of Czachulec, were murdered in Chełmno and on the same day 975 Jews from the nearby village of Dąbie, six kilometers south of Chełmno, were locked in the Catholic Church before being taken to Chełmno to share the same fate.

On December 15/16, 1941, two groups of gypsies from the *Litzmannstadt* ghetto numbering approximately 8,300 were transported in trucks from gypsy camps direct to Chełmno, where they were murdered.[28]

SS-Unterscharführer Kurt Möbius arrived from Łódź on December 19, 1941, and was put in charge of organizational work in the Manor House. The day after his arrival he was taken to the Forest Camp and he gave an account of what he saw, after the war:

> There was a large clearing in the forest surrounded by one or two cordons of guard posts. There was a large grave in the clearing that had been dug by four or five Polish workers. The grave had the following dimensions; five to six meters deep, eight meters wide and twenty meters long. About one-eighth of it was filled with bodies.[29]

Rottwachtmeister Jakob Wildermuth, a policeman who worked in the *Waldlager*, also recalled the mass graves:

> In the first clearing, there were two mass graves about 30 meters long, ten meters wide and three meters deep. In the second clearing, there was a mass grave about 30 meters long, ten meters wide and three meters deep. In the third clearing, there was a mass grave about 12 meters long, ten meters wide, and three meters deep. When I started my duty in Chełmno, the mass grave in the third clearing had already been filled with corpses. The mass grave in the second clearing was half-filled with

---

[27] Krystof Gorczyca, Zdzisław Lorek, *Day After Day in the extermination camp Kulmhof am Ner* – unpublished draft, p. 54.
[28] Krystof Gorczyca, Zdzisław Lorek, *Day After Day in the extermination camp Kulmhof am Ner* – unpublished draft, p. 55.
[29] P. Montague, *Chełmno and the Holocaust*, I.B. Tauris and Co. Ltd, London 2012, pp. 91–92.

corpses. The other mass graves had only been prepared and were filled with corpses later.[30]

Sometime, just prior to the deportation of the Jews from Koło to Chełmno in December 1941, Heinrich May the local Forester recalled an event in the forest near Chełmno:

> A few weeks later my youngest son returned home from school for vacation. I took him around through Koło and Chełmno. Near the district 77—the road ran through the northern strip of the district—there was a large, closed van stuck in a ditch. It was attached to another vehicle trying to get it out of the ditch back on to the road, which also became blocked.
> My son got out of the car and went up to the men in police uniforms near the van. I heard them address my son harshly, so I also got out and walked in their direction. The vehicle in the ditch was about four meters long and two meters high and the rear end was closed with an iron bar and padlocked. A peculiar, unpleasant smell was coming from the van and the men. When I asked if the road would be passable soon, they answered rudely that they would move out of the way a bit. Then they told me to leave quickly. A few days later my son was in Koło. After he returned home, he told me that Jews from Koło had been herded together by gendarmes and driven away in trucks.[31]

Transports of gypsies from the *Litzmannstadt* ghetto resumed on December 29, 1941, for two days, with approximately 4,000 deported in trucks to Chełmno where they were murdered.[32]

---

[30] Ibid., p. 92.
[31] *Chełmno Witnesses Speak*, Konin – Łódź 2004, pp. 154–155.
[32] Krystof Gorczyca, Zdzisław Lorek, *Day After Day in the extermination camp Kulmhof am Ner* – unpublished draft, pp. 56–57.

Chapter III
January 1942
The Slaughter Intensifies—Eichmann's Visit—Prisoner Escapes

With the start of the new year of 1942, a number of important changes of personnel took place at Chełmno. Fritz Ismer who was appointed to look after the valuables came from Łódź. His assistant Karl Göde also arrived in early January. Two gas van drivers *Oberscharführer* Basler and Franz Walter also arrived in either late December 1941, or early January 1942.

Stanisław Polubinski, one of the Polish *Arbeitskommando* in Chełmno was taken to the hospital in *Warthbrücken* (Koło), showing symptoms of typhus. He recovered from this, but was murdered by the Germans in Fort VII, in *Posen*, during 1943.

On January 2, 1942, 30 gravediggers from the Kłodawa ghetto were sent to Chełmno, and two days later another 16 gravediggers went to Chełmno from the Kłodawa ghetto.[33]

Between January 5, 1942 and January 12, 1942, approximately 5,000 Gypsies were transported directly from *Litzmannstadt* to Chełmno in trucks. They belonged to the Lalleri tribe and came from Burgenland, Austria, on November 5, 1941. They were incarcerated in a "Gypsy Camp," which had been established on the border of the ghetto at Brzezinska Street. They arrived at the Radogoszcz railway station and were escorted to the camp by SS guards. Among the deportees were a Jewish doctor, Dr. Fickelburg and an unknown Jewish nurse.[34] The Gypsy Camp was guarded by gendarmes from the 132nd

---

[33] Krystof Gorczyca, Zdzisław Lorek, *Day After Day in the extermination camp Kulmhof am Ner* – unpublished draft, p. 57.
[34] Martin Gilbert, *The Holocaust – The Jewish Tragedy*, William Collins, London 1987, p. 251.

Schutzpolizei battalion under the command of Eugen Jansen, who contracted typhus and died on December 23, 1941.[35]

Hauptscharführer Fritz Ismer on his arrival at Chełmno, with two other policemen, recalled the liquidation of the Gypsies in Chełmno:

> When we reported to Lange, he instructed us to go with him by car to the forest, which was about five kilometres away, in order to witness the commando in action. Lange had told us before that everything that happened there was top secret and that we had to keep absolutely silent about everything.
> When we arrived at the forest, one of the policemen who guarded it reported to us. The Forest Camp was a short distance off the country road and a dirt road led to it. Lange told us to come closer. We could see a clearing in the forest and a grey van that was parked there with the rear doors open. The van was full of bodies, which were taken out by a Jewish labour squad and thrown into a mass grave. The dead people looked like Gypsies. There were men, women and children there. The bodies were clothed.
> When I saw this I began to feel sick and had to vomit. When I rallied a little, Lange told me, "You'll get used to it." We stayed there for only about ten minutes. I think two more vans came during this time. They were also full of Gypsies. When we came back Lange told us that he wanted to show us the mansion. In the area of the mansion we saw people go directly from the trucks into the gas vans. Those people were Gypsies too.[36]

On January 5, 1942,[37] Szlamek Bajler who lived in the town of Izbica Kujawska was ordered to assemble for work, and the following day on Tuesday January 13, he reported to the police station. He managed to escape from Chełmno on Monday January 19, 1942. He made his way to the Warsaw ghetto, where he made contact with Emanuel Ringelblum and wrote an account of his experiences at Chełmno for Ringelblum's *Oneg Shabbat* group. These experiences included witnessing the mass murder of Gypsies from Łódź, and Jews deported to Chełmno from the local area, including his own home-town.

---

[35] L. Dobroszycki, *The Chronicle of the Łódź Ghetto 1941–1944*, Yale University Press, New Haven and London 1984, p. 82 and 101.

[36] P. Montague, *Chełmno and the Holocaust*, I.B. Tauris and Co. Ltd, London 2012, p. 66.

[37] Incorrectly stated as January 12, 1942 in Szlamek's testimony.

Szlamek Bajler was also known by the names Wiener and Grojnowski, possibly false names, for self-preservation.

Szlamek Bajler survived Chełmno, but he was deported from Zamość, in south-eastern Poland, with other members of his family on April 11, 1942, to the nearby Bełżec death camp, where he perished.[38] His detailed and very moving account of life and death in Chełmno covered thirteen days and certain entries have been extracted to provide the reader with the main points he experienced:

Tuesday, January 6, 1942

We arrived at 12:30 noon. At both doors stood *Gestapo* men and gendarmes doing guard duty. When we came in the second courtyard we were pushed out of the lorry. From here onwards we were in the hands of black uniformed *SS* men, all of them high ranking *Reich* Germans.

We were ordered to hand over all our money and valuables. After this fifteen men were selected. I among them and taken down to the cellar rooms of the *Schloss*. We fifteen were confined in one room, the remaining fourteen in another. It was still bright daylight outside, but down in the cellar it was pitch dark.

Some Ethnic German on the domestic staff provided us with straw. Later a lantern was also brought. At around eight in the evening we received unsweetened black coffee and nothing else. We were all in a depressed mood. One could only think of the worst, some were close to tears. We kissed each other and took leave. It was unimaginly cold and we lay down close together. In this manner we spent the whole night without shutting our eyes. We only talked about the deportation of Jews, particularly from Kolo and Dabie. The way it looked, we had no prospect of ever getting out again. [39]

---

[38] C. Webb, *The Bełżec Death Camp, History, Biographies, Remembrance*, ibidem-Verlag, Stuttgart, 2016, pp. 114–115.
[39] Martin Gilbert, *The Holocaust – The Jewish Tragedy*, William Collins, London 1987, pp. 252 -253.

Wednesday, January 7, 1942

At seven in the morning, the gendarme on duty knocked and ordered us to get up. We hadn't slept anyway, because of the cold. It took half an hour till they brought us black coffee and bread from our provisions. We drew some meagre consolation from this and told each other there was a God in heaven; we would after all be going to work.

At about 8:30 in the morning, we were led into the courtyard. Six of us had to go into the second cellar room to bring out two corpses. The dead were from Klodawa, and had hanged themselves. They were conscript grave-diggers. Their corpses were thrown on a lorry. We met the other fourteen enforced grave-diggers from Izbica. As soon as we came out of the cellar, we were surrounded by twelve gendarmes and *Gestapo* men with machine guns.

We got on the lorry together with the twenty-nine enforced grave-diggers and the two corpses: our escort were six gendarmes with machine guns. Behind us came another vehicle with ten gendarmes and two civilians. We drove in the direction of Kolo for about seven kilometers till turning left into the forest: after half a kilometer we halted at a clear path. We were ordered to get down and line up in double file.

An *SS* man ordered us to fall in with our shovels, dressed despite the frost, only in shoes, underwear, trousers, and shirts. Our coats, hats, gloves, had to remain in a pile on the ground. The two civilians took all the shovels and pick-axes down from the lorry. Eight of us who weren't handed any tools had to take down the two corpses.

Already on our way to the forest we saw about fourteen men, enforced grave-diggers from Klodawa, who had arrived before us and were at work in their shirtsleeves. The picture was as follows: twenty-one men in two's, behind them eight men with two corpses, ringed by armed Germans. The people from Klodawa were also guarded by twelve gendarmes. All in all we were guarded by thirty gendarmes.

As we approached the ditches the men from Klodawa asked us in whispers, 'Where are you from?' We answered, 'From Izbica.' They asked us how many of us there were and we replied, 'Twenty-nine.' This exchange took place while we worked.

The eight men without tools carried the two corpses to the ditch and threw them in. We didn't have to wait long before the next lorry arrived with fresh victims. It was specially constructed. It looked like a normal large lorry, in grey paint with two hermetically closed rear doors. The inner walls were of steel metal. There weren't any seats. The floor was covered by a wooden grating, as in public baths, with straw mats on top. Between the driver's cab and the rear part were two peepholes. With a torch one could observe through these peepholes if the victims were already dead.

Under the wooden grating were two tubes about fifteen centimeters thick which came out of the cab. The tubes had small openings from which gas poured out. The gas generator was in the cab, where the same driver sat all the time. He wore a uniform of the SS death's head units and was about forty years old. There were two such vans.

When the lorries approached, we had to stand at a distance of five meters from the ditch. The leader of the guard detail was a high-ranking SS man, an absolute sadist and murderer. He ordered that eight men were to open the doors of the lorry. The smell of gas that met us was overpowering. The victims were gypsies from Łódź. Strewn about the van were all their belongings: accordions, violins, bedding, watches, and other valuables.

After the doors had been open for five minutes, orders were screamed at us, 'Here! You Jews! Get in there and turn everything out!' The Jews scurried into the van and dragged the corpses away. The work didn't progress quickly enough. The SS leader fetched his whip and screamed, 'The devil. I'll give you a hand straight away!' He hit out in all directions on people's heads, ears and so on, till they collapsed. Three of the eight who couldn't get up again were shot on the spot.

When the others saw this they clambered back on their feet and continued the work with their last reserves of energy. The corpses were thrown one on top of another, like rubbish on a heap. We got hold of them by the feet and the hair. At the edge of the ditch stood two men who threw in the bodies. In the ditch stood an additional two men, who packed them in head to feet, facing downwards.

The orders were issued by an *SS* man who must have occupied a special rank. If any space was left, a child was pushed in. Everything was done very brutally. From up above the *SS* man indicated to us with a pine twig how to stack the bodies. He ordered where the head and feet, where the children and the belongings were to be placed. All this was accompanied by malicious screams, blows and curses. Every batch comprised 180–200 corpses. For every three vanloads twenty men were used to cover up the corpses. At first this had to be done twice, later up to three times, because nine vans arrived—that is nine times sixty corpses.

At exactly twelve o'clock the *SS* leader with the whip ordered, 'Put your shovels down!' We had to line up in double file to be counted again. Then we had to climb out of the ditch. We were surrounded by guards all the time. We even had to excrete on the spot. We went to the spot where our belongings were. We had to sit on them close together. The guards continued to surround us. We were given cold bitter coffee and a frozen piece of bread. That was our lunch. That's how we sat for half an hour. Afterwards we had to line up, were counted and led back to work.

What did the dead look like? They weren't burnt or black: their faces were unchanged. Nearly all the dead were soiled with excrement. At about five o'clock we stopped work. The eight men who had worked with the corpses had to lie on top of them face downwards. An *SS* man with a machine gun shot at their heads. The man with the whip screamed, 'The devil, get dressed quickly!' We dressed quickly and took the shovels with us. We were counted and escorted to the lorry by gendarmes and *SS* men. We had to put the shovels away. Then we were counted again and pushed into the lorry.

The journey to the *Schloss* took about fifteen minutes. We travelled together with the men from Klodawa and talked very quiety together. I said to my colleagues, 'My mother wanted to lead me to a white wedding canopy, she wont even have the experience of leading me to a black one.' We cried softly and spoke in whispers, so the gendarmes sitting at the back shouldn't hear us.

On the first day, the following happened: it was ten in the morning. A certain Giter from Bydgoszcz, a fat individual, resident in Izbica during the war, belonged to the group of 'eight' and was unable to keep up with the speed of the work. The SS man with the whip ordered him to undress. He flogged him and others till they lost consciousness. His body looked black as spleen. He had to lie down alone in the ditch, where he was shot.

It turned out there were many more rooms in the *Schloss*. We numbered twenty in our room, with fifteen more in the adjacent one. There weren't any other enforced grave-diggers. As soon as we came into the cold dark cellar, we threw ourselves down on the straw and cried about everything that had befallen us. The fathers wept from pain at never seeing their little ones again. A fifteen-year-old boy by the name of Moniek Halter embraced and kissed me. Weeping, he said to me, 'Ah Schlomo, even if I die a victim, my mother and sister should at least stay alive.' Meir Pitrowski, forty-years-old from Izbica, my neighbor on the straw, kissed me and said, 'Who knows if I will ever see them again, and what is going to happen to them?'

Gershon Prashker, a fifty-five-year-old from Izbica, said, 'We have a great God up in heaven and must pray to him. He wont desert us—that's why we must all now together say the 'prayer of confession and penitence before death.' Amid great pain and tears we recited the prayer. It was a very depressing sight. The sergeant-major knocked at the door, shouting, 'Quiet, you Jews, or I shoot.' We continued the prayer softly with choking voices.

At 7:30 in the evening they brought us a pot of thin kohlrabi soup. We couldn't swallow anything for crying and pain. It was very cold and we had no covers at all. One of us exclaimed, 'Who knows who among us will be missing tomorrow.' We pressed close together and lapsed into exhausted fitful sleep haunted by terrible dreams. We slept for about four hours. Then we ran about the room freezing cold and debated the fate that was in store for us.[40]

---

[40] Ibid. pp. 253–258.

Monday, January 12, 1942

At 5 a.m. six people got up and recited Psalms amid crying and wailing. Some of the others made fun of us because of our piety. They said there was no God. This consolation struck them as youthful foolishness. We replied that our life was in the hands of God. If all this was his will then we accepted it with love, all the more so as the days of the Messiah were approaching. After the morning prayer and Kaddish, in which even Eisenstab took part, we recited the prayer of penitence.

At 7 a.m. they brought us coffee and bread. Some of the men from Izbica drank up all the coffee. The others got very annoyed and said we were already facing death and had to behave with dignity. It was decided to share out a little coffee to everyone in future. At 8:30 we were already at work. At 9:30 the first gas van appeared.

Among the 'eight' were Aharon Rosenthal, Schlomo Babiacki, and Schmuel Bibedgal, all of them aged between fifty and sixty. On this day we were absolutely slave-driven. They wouldn't even wait till the gas smell had evaporated. You can imagine the screams of the tortured people. Immediately after the first van, the second one arrived. By twelve o'clock noon, the third had already come.

When we went to lunch the 'eight' remained behind to dispatch the last transport. Meanwhile a black limousine arrived and four officers got out. They heard a report from 'Big Whip' after which they shook his hand most appreciatively. 'Big Whip' then once again beat the 'eight' violently to his joy and satisfaction. When the SS men left, the 'eight' received their meagre lunch. That afternoon the work lasted till six. Nine transports, each of sixty Jews from Klodawa, were buried: fivehundred people from Klodawa in all.

My friend Getzel Chrzastowski screamed terribly for a moment when he recognized his fourteen-year-old son, who had just been thrown into the ditch. We had to stop him, too, from begging the German to shoot him. We argued it was necessary to survive this suffering, so we might revenge ourselves later and pay the Germans back. After work the five oldest men in the detail that handled the corpses were shot and we had to cover the grave as quickly as possible.

Because of the late hour—it was already very dark—the Germans feared there may be an uprising. We were hurriedly split into groups and chased into the lorries. Seven gendarmes travelled with us. In the evening at seven we returned to our place of refuge.

The sons of Rosenthal and Bibedgal, whose fathers had been killed that day, cried bitterly. We tried to console them and said it didn't matter whom fate struck down first: we would all die anyway. On this occasion these two also took part in the prayer of the mourners. After supper which as always consisted of kohlrabi soup, black coffee, and dry bread—all shared out justly, as agreed—Mosche Lesek said the prayer of penitence. He wanted to take his life, so he would not have to watch the sufferings of his nearest. He gave away all his belongings: bread, syrup, and clothes.

In the meantime, we heard a noise in the corridor. The other group in the adjacent room told us through the wall the Germans had captured an escaped Jew from Klodawa. Next morning they told us the following details: the captured escaper, Mahmens Goldman[41], had told them in detail how the Jews were driven into the gas vans.

When they arrived at the *Schloss*, they were first treated most politely. An elderly German, around sixty, with a long pipe in his mouth, helped the mothers to lift the children down from the lorry. He carried babies, so that the mothers could alight more easily and helped dotards to reach the *Schloss*.

The unfortunate ones were deeply moved by this gentle and mild manner. They were led into a warm room which was heated by two stoves. The floor was covered with wooden gratings as in a bath house. The elderly German and the SS officer spoke to them in this room. They assured them they would be taken to the Łódź Ghetto. There they were expected to work and be productive. The women would look after the household, the children would go to school, and so on. In order to get there, however, they had to undergo delousing. For that purpose they needed to undress down to their underwear.

---

[41] Goldman was executed in the forest on Tuesday 13, January 1942.

Their clothes would be passed through hot steam. Valuables and documents should be tied up in a bundle and handed over for safe keeping.

Whoever had kept banknotes, or had sewn them into their clothes, should take them out without fail, otherwise they would get damaged in the steam oven. Moreover, they would all have to take a bath. The elderly German politely requested those present to take a bath and opened a door from which 15–20 steps led down. It was terribly cold there. Asked about the cold, the German said gently they should walk a bit further, it would get warmer. They walked along a lengthy corridor to some steps leading to a ramp. The gas van had driven up to the ramp.

The polite behavior ended abruptly and they were all driven into the van with malicious screams. The Jews realized immediately they were facing death. They screamed, crying the prayer, 'Hear O Israel.' At the exit of the warm room was a small chamber in which Goldman hid. After he had spent 24 hours there in the icy cold and was already quite stiff, he decided to look for his clothes and to save himself. He was caught and pushed in among the grave-diggers. There his comrades tried to cheer him up, gave him food and trousers and a jacket.

We then discussed his story excitedly. Everybody said if they had been in Goldman's place they would have done better for themselves. At about three in the morning Mosche Lesek woke us all. He kissed and took leave of everybody. He had prepared a rope to hang himself. He already had the noose round his neck, when his strength left him. He simply couldn't take his own life.[42]

Wednesday, January 14, 1942

They brought us bitter coffee and bread. Immediately after breakfast Krzewacki from Klodawa, who had long contemplated suicide, put a noose around his neck. He begged Chrzatowski to remove the small packet from under his feet and shove it into his mouth, so that his

---

[42] Ibid. pp. 268–271.

breathing would stop sooner. Chrzatowski fulfilled his request and Krzewacki died an easy death. He committed suicide because he couldn't bear to watch the murderous deeds any longer. We cut him down and placed him against the wall.

Immediately after this Gershon Swietoplawski from Izbica also wanted to commit suicide. He had been Krzewacki's colleague in digging. He said he had dug with Krzewacki and wanted to lie in the ditch with him. Because of the late hour nobody wanted to help him. The guard could turn up at any moment. He quickly took a rope and tied a noose round his neck. He stood with his feet on the ground and bent forward to throttle himself more quickly. While he tortured himself in this way, there was a knock at the door.

Young Moniek Halter quickly cut the rope. Swietoplawski fell to the ground choking. When the guard had gone, on the one hand we didn't want to save him, but on the other hand, we couldn't bear to watch his torments. We begged Getzel Chrzatowski to put an end to them. Chrzatowski tied a noose tightly around Swietoplawski's neck, pinned his body down with his feet, and tugged hard at the rope, till he had throttled Swietoplawski. We left both corpses lying uncovered in the cellar. They remained there for a few days.

At eight in the morning, we were already at the ditches. Around ten o'clock there appeared the first van with Jewish victims from Izbica. By noon we had already dispatched five overloaded transports. Out of one of these transports the corpse of a German civilian had been pulled out. The person concerned was one of the cooks. He had presumably strayed into the van in the following manner: he had probably noticed one of the Jews purloining some object and had run after him to reclaim it. At that very moment the doors had clanged shut. His shouting and knocking had been ignored; in this way he was gassed together with the others. Immediately after he had been lifted out of the van, a special car with an ambulance man aboard arrived from the *Schloss*. The corpse was taken back there.

Some of us thought he had been deliberately poisoned, so that no witness of this killing should remain alive.[43]

During the lunch break two carloads of *SS* men arrived, who viewed our slaughterhouse with pleasure. In the afternoon a further five transports were buried. From one of the vans a woman with a suckling at her breast was thrown out. The baby had perished while sucking its mother's milk.

In the light of headlamps we carried on working till seven in the evening. On this day one of the vans drove in error right up to the ditch. We heard the muted cries for help and knocking at the door of the tortured victims. At the end of the day six members of the 'eight' were shot. Back in the cellar we all burst into tears. After supper we said the evening prayer and the prayer of the mourning.[44]

Thursday, January 15, 1942

We again drove to work very early. On this occasion we rode in a bus. At a certain moment Moniek Halter called across to me, the windows of the vehicle could easily be opened with a hook. The thought of escape had lodged in my brain all the time. With all my being I wanted to reach the Jews who were still alive, to tell them about the atrocities taking place in Chełmno.

At 8 a.m. we were already at the place of work. At ten o'clock the first victims arrived—again from Izbica. Till noon we dispatched four overloaded transports. One van waited in line after the next. I must describe again how barbarously the corpses were examined. Imagine the following picture: one German[45] drags one corpse from the pile to one side, while another drags a corpse elsewhere. They searched the women's necks for golden chains. If they found any, they immediately tore them off. Rings were pulled off fingers. They

---

[43] This was not a German, but a Polish member of the *Arbeitskommando*, Marian Libelt.
[44] Martin Gilbert, *The Holocaust – The Jewish Tragedy*, William Collins, London 1987, pp. 272–273.
[45] These were not Germans, but Polish members of the *Arbeitskommando*.

pulled out gold teeth with pliers. Then the corpses were stood up, legs apart, so that a hand could be inserted into the posterior. In the case of women, an examination was also carried out in front. Although this examination took place every day while we worked, our blood and brains boiled.

At midday I received the sad news that my brother and parents had just been buried. At one o'clock we were already back at work. I tried to get closer to the corpses to take a last look at my nearest and dearest. Once I had a clod of frozen earth tossed at me, thrown by the benign German with the pipe. The second time 'Big Whip' shot at me. I don't know if the shot missed me deliberately or by accident. One thing is certain: I remained alive. I suppressed my anguish and concentrated on working fast, so as to forget my dreadful situation for five minutes. I remained lonely as a piece of stone. Out of my entire family, which comprised sixty people, I am the only one who survived.

Towards evening, as we helped to cover the corpses, I put my shovel down. Michael Podchlebnik followed my example and we said the prayer of the mourners together. Before leaving the ditch five of the 'eight' were shot. At seven in the evening we were taken back home. All those who hailed from Izbica were in absolute despair. We had realized that we should never see our relatives again. I was quite beside myself and indifferent to everything.

After the evening prayer, all those from Izbica said the prayer of mourning together. In the next room, we had learnt, were eighteen grave-diggers from Łódź. We heard through the wall that Rumkowski—the elder of the Jewish Council at Łódź—had ordered the deportation of 750 families from Łódź. We spent a night filled with nightmares and images of horror. The strongest among us tried again to open the bricked-in window.[46]

---

[46] Martin Gilbert, *The Holocaust – The Jewish Tragedy*, William Collins, London 1987, pp. 273–274.

Monday, January 19, 1942

We again boarded the bus in the morning. I let all the others get on in front of me and was the last one aboard. The gendarme sat in front. On this day no SS men rode behind us. To my right was a window, which could be opened easily. During the ride I opened the window. When fresh cold air streamed in I caught fright and quickly shut the window again. My comrades, among them Moniek Halter, in particular, encouraged me, however.

After I made a decision I softly asked my comrades to stand up so the draught of cold air shouldn't reach the gendarmes. I quickly pulled the window pane out of its frame, pushed my legs out and turned around. I held onto the door with my hand and pressed my feet against the hinges. I told my colleagues they should put the window pane back immediately after I had jumped. I then jumped at once.

When I hit the ground I rolled for a bit and scraped the skin off my hands. The only thing that mattered to me was not to break a leg. I would hardly have minded breaking an arm. The main thing was that I could walk in order to get to the next Jewish settlement. I turned round to see if they had noticed anything on the bus, but it continued its journey.

I lost no time, but ran as fast as I could across fields and woods. After an hour I stood before the farm of a Polish peasant. I went inside and greeted him in the Polish manner: 'Blessed be Jesus Christ.' While I warmed myself I asked cautiously about the distance to Chełmno. It was only 3 kilometers. I also received a piece of bread which I put in my pocket. As I was about to go the peasant asked me if I was a Jew—which I absolutely denied. I asked him why he suspected me, and he told me they were gassing Jews and Gypsies at Chełmno. I took my leave with the Polish greeting and went away.

An hour later I came to another Polish farm, where they gave me sweet white coffee and a piece of bread. The people there told me: they are gassing Jews and Gypsies at Chełmno, and when they have finished with them, it will be our turn. I laughed about that. They explained to me what route I should take. I carried on walking till I reached a German village. The German houses could be easily recognized because they were richly ornamented and had radio antennae on their roofs.

I decided to walk on bravely through the whole village. Only at the end of the village did I find a house that belonged to a Pole. It transpired that I was 10 kilometers away from Grabow, which had a Jewish community. I introduced myself as a Polish miner on the way to Grabow, in search of work. The householder sent me to the neighbouring town, where I was to ask for a certain Grabowski. Grabowski had a horse and cart and would surely take me to Grabow.

This time I could make detours but had to walk along the open road part of the way. When I suddenly saw military vehicles my heart nearly stopped. I already had visions of being captured. At the last moment I took a peasant woman's arm and turned off into a footpath with her. I asked her if she had any furs to sell? The vehicle drove past and I was saved. I appealed to God and my deceased parents they should help me to save the Jewish people.

At Grabowski's I introduced myself as a certain Witjowski, who was looking for work in Grabow. It turned out that he, Grabowski, had gone to the market at Dabie. His neighbor to whom I was sent had likewise gone to the market at Dabie. I wandered a bit further and pondered my ill-luck. Now and then I asked passers-by for directions. All the time I was on the alert for gendarmes because I didn't have any documents on me.

I finally reached a village seven kilometers away from Grabow. There I arranged with a Polish farmer that he would drive me to Grabow for 15 marks. I put on his fur coat and cap.

On Monday at two o'clock we arrived at Grabow. The Jews took me for an Ethnic German, because I didn't wear a star. I asked for the rabbi. I looked rough; in Chełmno we had no opportunity to wash and shave.

I asked where the rabbi lived. 'Who are you?' he asked. 'Rabbi, I am a Jew from the nether world!' He looked at me as if I were mad. I told him: 'Rabbi, don't think I am crazed and have lost my reason. I am a Jew from the nether world. They are killing the whole nation

Israel. I myself have buried a whole town of Jews, my parents, brothers, and the entire family. I have remained lonely as a piece of stone.'

I cried during the conversation. The rabbi asked: 'Where are they being killed?' I said: 'Rabbi, in Chełmno. They are gassed in the forest, and buried in mass graves.' His domestic—the rabbi was a widower—brought me a bowl of water for my swollen eyes. I washed my hands. The injury on my right hand began to hurt. When my story made the rounds, many Jews came, to whom I told all the details. They all wept. We ate bread and butter; I was given tea to drink and said the blessing.[47]

The Rabbi Jakub Szulman wrote postcards and letters informing others about what he had been told by Wiener and Podchlebnik and the contents are shown at Appendix I.

During his trial in Jerusalem, Adolf Eichmann, the Chief of the Jewish and Evacuation Affairs of the *Reich* Security Main Office *(RSHA)* in Berlin, had his interview with Israeli Police Captain Avner Less replayed to the court on April 19, 1961. In the interview Eichmann's visit to *Chełmno / Kulmhof* was covered. During the interview Eichmann mistakenly identified the visit as going to *Kulm*, but he really meant *Kulmhof*:

> I went there, I reported to the *Stapoleit* at *Litzmannstadt,* I enquired there and they gave me an account: this was a special unit which the *Reichsführer* had detailed and it was under the command of...now I do not know whether the *SS* and Police Leader of the *Warthegau* or the Higher *SS* and Police Leader of the *Warthegau*. This is as much as I remember, but I was given an exact description where *Kulm* was situated, where it was. Perhaps they also sent an official with me to find my way, certainly because I had to approach an authority which...which, let us say: this mediation, that it came from the Head Office of *Reich* Security on a mission on behalf of *Gruppenführer* Müller, that I should watch this in order to report to *Gruppenführer* Müller, this is no longer known to me today. I only know this: that I saw what could be described as follows: A room—if I remember correctly—possibly five times the size of this one, perhaps only four times as large. There were Jews inside, they were

---

[47] Martin Gilbert, *The Holocaust – The Jewish Tragedy*, William Collins, London 1987, pp. 277–279.

required to undress, and after that a completely closed truck arrived and the doors in front were opened and it came up to some kind of platform; and the naked Jews were obliged to go inside. Afterwards the truck was closed and began to move.

L. How many people were in the truck?
E. I cannot tell you this exactly. I could not even watch what was going on exactly, all the time I did not look at it; I was far too upset. I told this to Müller, also, at the time I reported.
He did not derive much benefit from my report. Afterwards I rode after the truck, certainly with one of the men who knew the way—and there I saw the most horrible thing that I had ever seen in my life:
It drove up to a long ditch, the doors were opened, and the bodies were thrown out, as if they were still alive—their limbs were so supple. They were thrown into the ditch—I could still see how a civilian was removing teeth with pliers, and then I moved away from there. I entered the car and went away, and I did not speak at all. From then on I sat next to the driver for hours without exchanging a word with him. By then I was "fixed," then I was "finished." I only know further that a doctor in a white coat said to me that I should look through the peephole in the partition to see how they were inside the vehicle. I refused to do this. I couldn't...I couldn't say another word. I had to get away.
I came to Berlin, I reported to *Gruppenführer* Müller, I described those things to him exactly as I am doing now—more I couldn't say to him: More precisely I said to him.: "Terrible," I said, "the Inferno...I cannot...this is...that I cannot..." I said to him.[48]

Adolf Eichmann himself gave the date of his visit to Chełmno as January 13, 1942, although Szlamek Bajler's detailed accounts state that SS officers visited the *Waldlager* on Monday 12, January 1942, and on Wednesday 14, January 1942. Possibly one of the visiting parties was the visit of Eichmann.[49]

Another key eyewitness to the mass killings that took place in Chełmno during January 1942, was Michał Podchlebnik, who provided testimony to Judge Władysław Bednarz on June 9, 1945 in Koło:

> Before the war and at the beginning of the German occupation, I had resided permanently in Koło. In late December 1941, formations of the

---

[48] www.Nizkor.org Eichmann Trial Transcripts – online resource.
[49] Krystof Gorczyca, Zdzisław Lorek, *Day After Day in the extermination camp Kulmhof am Ner* – unpublished draft, p. 62.

NSKK (National Socialist Motor Corps) surrounded the town of Koło—their members wore black military field-caps and green uniforms. Jews were driven out of their flats and led to the house of the Jewish Committee at 6 Rzeznicza Street. Entire families were deported and each person could take a pack of weight not exceeding 10 kilograms.
They were placed in a Jewish temple and in the aforementioned building housing the Jewish Committee, which was attached to the synagogue. When cars arrived, entire Jewish families left the building carrying their baggage. In front of the building, by the entrance, there was an SS officer sitting at a table. He had a list of all Jewish residents of Koło and ticked off their names of all those that were getting into the vehicles. The baggage was loaded into a trailer. The guards and members of the Jewish Committee said that the Jews would be transported "to work at a railroad." About 40 people were loaded in each car. Two trucks transported Jews from Koło. The drivers were German. About 1,000 people were driven away each day.
Among the members of the escort team for the vehicles, was a *Volksdeutscher* Siuda from the village of Kościelec, who at that time worked for the military police. He said to the Jews, "Don't be afraid. They are going to take you to the Barlogi train station and from there to the East." He was known among local Jews and they believed his words. Each truck made 10–12 rides a day, which made us believe that the Jews were driven off not far from Koło.
I did not go only because, at that time, I was a resident of the village of Bugaj in Koło County, and my name was not on the list of Koło residents. I led my father, mother, sister with her five children, and my brother with his wife and three children to the truck. I helped load packs into the trailer. I even volunteered to go with my parents, but I was not allowed to. I witnessed a situation when a person known as Goldberg, a sawmill owner from Koło, applied to the German authorities to be appointed the manager of the East Camp for Jews from Koło, after his son had been driven away. The application was accepted and he was promised to be appointed the manager.
In the meantime, some little boy accidentally came to the Jewish Committee house and said that the Jews were not transported to the train station in the village of Barlogi, but to Chełmno, which he had seen himself. The Germans explained that in Chełmno they only select the strongest workers to work in the West. The ill were driven off on the last day. The drivers were told to drive slowly and carefully. The operation in Koło lasted four–five days.
In early January 1942—I cannot remember the exact date, but I remember it was a Friday—on the order of the Jewish Committee, I worked on

the demolition of a barn in Bugaj. From there 14 local Jews and I were taken to the gendarmerie station. Allegedly we were arrested because my cousin Mordka Podchelbnik had escaped. Gendarme Szplit, a *Volksdeutscher* from the village of Babiak, who once had had some conflict with a Jew named Dankowski, also from Babiak, said the following about the Jew, "He won't live long now." Dankowski was arrested in the morning. On Saturday at about 4 p.m. a truck brought 15 Jews from the village of Izbica. At the same time a smaller car brought an SS officer, whom I knew from the mentioned Koło operation (he ticked off the names of Jews getting into the truck). We and the Jews from Izbica were loaded into a truck and taken to Chełmno.

Let me point out that all the Jews in the vehicle were well built, strong and capable of doing even the toughest work. The car rolled into the palace grounds in Chełmno. The whole terrain was surrounded by a recently erected two and a half to three metre high fence made of wooden boards. The fence had no gaps so that nobody could see what was going on inside. The gates were opened and the truck drove into the grounds and stopped in front of the palace. After a while another gate was opened and the car was let into the inner palace grounds. When the vehicle was entering the inner grounds, I raised the tarpaulin and noticed a pile of used clothes. We got out of the truck, SS men formed a double line leading as far as the palace basement. We were counted and locked in the basement. In order to hurry us to move fast between the two rows of SS men, they repeatedly hit us with gun butts shouting, "Faster, Faster!"

Throughout all Sunday nothing happened. We were just sitting in the basement doing nothing. For physiological needs there was a bucket, which was carried out and emptied by one of my inmates under a strong escort. The inmate noticed that there were guards all over the place.

Many signatures appeared on the basement wall, among others, the signature of Mr. Kaliski from the town of Dąbie. There was also a significant line in Yiddish, "He who comes here, does not walk away alive." We had no illusions about our fate.

On Monday morning, 30 Jews were taken to work, in the woods. Ten others, including me stayed in the basement. There was a window in the basement, but it had been nailed up with wooden boards. At about 8 a.m. a truck stopped in front of the palace. I heard a German's voice, he was talking to those who had just arrived. He said, "You will go to the East. There are large areas where you can work. All you have to do now is to put on some clean clothes you will be given and take a shower." Then the newcomers started clapping their hands. Sometime later we heard a shuffle of bare feet in the basement corridor near our cell. We heard the German's shouting, "Faster, Faster!" I realized they were leading the Jews to the inner grounds. Suddenly, I heard a truck door slam, followed by an outburst of screaming and banging on the truck's walls. Then I heard the engine start and after six-seven minutes, when the screams fainted and died, the truck left the palace grounds.

Next we were ordered to go to a large room upstairs. On the floor we could see men's clothes and women's coats and shoes scattered about. We were told to carry all the clothes and shoes to some other room quickly. In the new room there were already a lot of other clothes and shoes. We put the shoes in a separate pile. Having finished the task, we were herded back to the basement cell. Another truck arrived and the whole procedure was repeated. This lasted all day long. I noticed that more trucks arrived at the grounds, then left. I came to the conclusion that trucks leaving Chełmno must have had a larger carrying capacity. I would like to point out that in the room where the Jews undressed there were two stoves, both giving off a significant amount of heat.

When our inmates returned from the woods in the evening, they said that they had all been burying Jews from Kłodawa, in a common grave in the woods. They removed the corpses from large black vans, in which, according to their accounts, Jews had been poisoned with exhaust fumes. The corpses were in underwear, in the van there were some towels and pieces of soap. This convinced me that Jews, having undressed, were given towels and soap and led to the basement, where allegedly they were supposed to take a shower. Three or four of those working in the wood that day, did not return, as they had been working badly and had been shot on the spot.

The following day, I volunteered to work in the woods. While I was leaving, I saw a large van, with its back end up against the palace. The door was open. A footbridge made it easier to get into the vehicle. What drew my attention was a wooden grate on the van floor, just like those in a bath-house. About 30 workers including me were loaded into two vehicles—a truck and a bus—and driven to woods near Chełmno. We were escorted by about thirty SS men.

In the woods there was a trench serving as a mass grave for the murdered Jews. We were ordered to dig the trench further. In order to do so, we were given shovels and pickaxes. At about 8 a.m. the first car from Chełmno arrived. When the van's door was opened, dark smoke with a white tint belched out from the inside. We were not allowed to approach the van at that moment and could not look in the direction of the open door. I noticed that the Germans, having opened the door, ran away from the vehicle. I cannot tell whether the gas coming out from the inside was an exhaust gas or some other gasses. We usually had to wait for so long that I did not smell the gas. Gas masks were not used. After three, four minutes had passed; three Jews went into the van. These were Neumüller from Koło, Chaim from Babiak, and one more whose name I cannot remember. They threw out the corpses from the vehicle onto the ground.

The corpses were haphazardly piled one on another as high as half way up the side of the van. Some of those murdered died holding their loved ones in their arms. The corpses generally did not look bad. I did not notice anyone with their tongue sticking out of their mouths or with any un-natural bruises. The bodies were still warm. I could not smell any gas. Some were still alive. In such cases SS men killed them by shooting them in the back of the head. After the van had been emptied of bodies, it returned to Chełmno.

Two Jews passed the corpses to two "Ukrainians,"[50] whose names I do not know. They spoke Polish and wore civilian clothes. There was one more "Ukrainian" but he was accidentally trapped in the van and gassed along with other Jews. They tried to rescue him by artificial respiration but the attempt was unsuccessful. I was there and saw it myself.[51]

The "Ukrainians" pulled out gold teeth from the corpses' mouths, tore off little sacks with money from their necks, pulled off wedding rings, watches and so on. The corpses were searched over very precisely. The "Ukrainians" were looking for gold and valuables, even in women's reproductive organs and anuses. They did not use rubber gloves. The valuables found were placed in a special suitcase. It was not the SS men who searched through the corpses. They just attentively watched the "Ukrainians" doing it. After the bodies had been searched, they were placed in trenches in layers. They were placed very tightly in layers facing down, in such a way, that someone's head touched someone else's feet. They had not been stripped of their underwear. The trench was six metres deep, six to seven metres wide—at the top. Four to five corpses were placed on the first layer on the bottom, on the last, upper layer there were as many as 30 bodies. Then the bodies were buried under a 1metre thick layer of earth. I noticed a few times that after a night the earth had been dug up in some places, exposing the corpses, buried on the previous day. I heard that this happened when the terrain was not guarded during the night. When I worked there, the length of the trench-grave

---

[50] These were not Ukrainians, but Polish members of the *Arbeitskommando*, this may have been claimed to avoid the fact that Poles collaborated in the mass murder of Jews.

[51] This was Marian Libelt; see Biographies of the Polish *Arbeitskommando*.

was over ten metres. About 1,000 people were buried a day, which filled three to four metres of trench.

The van, in which the victims were gassed, could take 80–90 persons at a time. During my stay in Chełmno, two cars were used simultaneously. In addition, there was another van, the largest of the three, but it was out of order and remained in Chełmno in the yard. I saw it had had one wheel taken off. Twelve to thirteen vans a day arrived in the woods. On this basis I figured that about 1,000 people were gassed every day. Jews who carried the corpses from the van had to remove the wooden floor grate from the vehicle and clean the car thoroughly. The valuables were also placed in the suitcase. The towels and pieces of soap were collected separately and driven back on a daily basis.

The third van which came to Chełmoński Square on that day, Tuesday—brought the bodies of my wife and two children—a 7-year old boy and a 4-year old girl. They were thrown out of the vehicle. I laid myself down near my wife's body and wanted to be shot. An SS man approached me and said, "This burly man can still work very well." He whipped me three times and forced me to continue working.

At midday they gave us food. We had to get out of the trench without shovels and form a circle. The SS men formed an outer circle around us. We were given black coffee and food brought in packs by Jews. Generally, we were fed well. That evening Krzewacki from Kłodawa hung himself in the basement. Another Jew, whose name I cannot remember either, did the same. I was going to hang myself too, but was finally persuaded not to do that.

I worked 10 days in Chełmno. The process of exterminating the Jews was repeated every day. The woods were not fenced in at that time. There were no furnaces for burning corpses either. I witnessed the extermination of Jews from Bugaj and then Izbica. On Friday they brought Gypsies from Łódź. On Saturday the first transport from the Łódź ghetto arrived. At the time of arrival, our labour group underwent selection. The weakest 20 Jews were killed and replaced with Jews from Łódź. All night we talked with our new companions. They were locked in a separate cell. They asked us whether the camp was good and whether they would receive much bread. When I told them the truth, they answered, "We volunteered to work in Koło." Since the very beginning I had been trying to persuade my inmates to escape, but they were so depressed, they could not make up their minds.

During my stay in Chełmno, I saw Zimmermann, arrive at the Chełmno woods. He was accompanied by two Germans I did not know. He examined the corpses, talked to SS-Officers and laughed. Soon he went back to Koło. I did not see any locals contacting SS men. The Chełmno woods were guarded by about eighty SS men. On the basis of my observations, the total number of SS men serving in Chełmno was about 120–130. When on duty they were generally sober. Their duties remained the same, and so I was well familiar with the faces of those who escorted us. The SS men wore gendarme uniforms and SS badges on their collars. It appeared that they were housed in the village, but I do not know that exactly. We worked until dusk. During work we were often beaten. If somebody did not work efficiently, he had to lie down on a pile of corpses and was shot in the back of the head with a pistol. The gendarmes did not talk to one another in our presence. When they talked to us, these were just brief exchanges. Sometimes they threw a package of cigarettes into the trench, so that we could smoke. The drivers were all German. Actually I do not know—they wore civilian clothes. But for sure they were not Koło residents. Where the SS men doing their service in Chełmno came from, I do not know. I cannot remember any names. The executions every day looked the same. The SS men were extremely cruel towards Jewish workers and punished them even for a minor offence. They killed for any reason.

On the way to work, I noticed that one of the windows on the bus could be lowered. I told my companion Wiener from Izbica (whose first name I cannot remember). I suggested an escape attempt. The following day on the way to work we intended to jump through the window and run away to the woods. However, we were separated and I had to get into the truck, while Wiener got into the bus. I decided to escape on my own. When the truck was in the woods, I asked the escorting SS man for a cigarette. When he gave me what I wanted, I stepped back and my companions surrounded him asking for cigarettes for themselves. With a sudden movement I cut the tarpaulin, on the driver's side, with a knife I had on me and jumped out of the car.

They started shooting at me, but all bullets missed the target. Luckily the bus did not follow the truck, so I was only shot at from the truck. The fact that the bus did not follow, made me think that Wiener must have escaped and consequently the bus had to be stopped. While I was running away through the woods, some man on a bicycle tried to stop me... shooting at me with a pistol. I managed to escape. I went into some barn and hid in the hay. The following morning I heard some peasants near the barn talking about Germans looking for some escaped Jews.

After two days, during which I did not eat anything, I snuck out of the barn and headed in the direction of Grabow town. On my way I stopped at some peasant's cottage—I do not know his name. He gave me some food and a hat, shaved me and showed the way. In Grabow I met Wiener from Izbica. Then I went to the town of Rzeszów and lost all contact with the region of Chełmno. Wiener probably died in the Zamość region in south-eastern Poland,[52] I think in 1944.[53]

With two escapes on the same day, January 19, 1942, of Bajler and Podchlebnik, the Germans understandably took precautions to avoid a repeat. All the Jewish workers were shackled in leg irons, which made escaping virtually impossible. The second change was the method of transportation between the mansion and the Rzuchówski forest. Instead of using the bus and truck the Jewish workers were taken to and brought back from the forest in a gas van.[54]

SS-Unterscharführer Alois Häfele arrived in Chełmno from *Posen* on January 28, 1942. He was placed in charge of organizing the work of the Jewish *Arbeitskommando* in the Palace. He recalled his arrival at *Kulmhof*:

> The entire detachment was taken in several trucks to a place called *Kulmhof*. We arrived there in the evening and were received by *Hauptsturmführer* Lange, who showed us our quarters. It was a large room in a building that must have been the administration building.
> The next morning the whole squad had to gather in front of the quarters. Lange and his deputy *Unterscharführer* Plate arrived. Lange gave a speech, explaining that *Kulmhof* was the place where Jews from the *Warthegau* were gassed and that our task was to guard and blockade the forest camp, the mansion and the village, so that no unauthorized people could see what was going on. We would have nothing to do with the extermination of the Jews themselves. Finally, Plate said that anyone remiss in fulfilling his duties, or who refused to obey orders, would be immediately sent to a concentration camp. Next we were given our assignments.[55]

From January 17, 1942, the first transport of Jews from the *Litzmannstadt* ghetto arrived in Chełmno. This deportation *"Aktion"*

---

[52] Wiener / Bajler died in the Bełżec death camp in April 1942, having been deported from Zamość.
[53] *Chełmno Witnesses Speak*, Konin – Łódź 2004, pp. 119–124.
[54] P. Montague, *Chełmno and the Holocaust*, I.B. Tauris and Co. Ltd, London 2012, p. 114.
[55] P. Montague, *Chełmno and the Holocaust*, I.B. Tauris and Co. Ltd, London 2012, p. 58.

briefly covered in the statements by Szlamek Bajler and Michał Podchlebnik, needs to be covered in more depth. This deportation "*Aktion*" was halted on January 30, 1942, but it resumed in February 1942. This murderous "*Aktion*" saw 10,003 Jews deported to Chełmno in this first phase. A key figure of the German administration intimately interwoven in the history of the *Litzmannstadt* ghetto and the Chełmno death camp was Hans Biebow.

Hans Biebow was born on December 18, 1902, in Bremen, Germany. After graduating from secondary school he found employment in the district branch of the Stuttgart Insurance Company. This was short-lived and he sought employment in the cereal and foodstuff bank in Bremen. He later owned his own coffee business, which was very successful, employing around 250 staff. When the *Litzmannstadt* ghetto was established in the spring of 1940, Biebow was put in charge of its food and economic office, that in October 1940 was re-designated the ghetto administration (*Ghettoverwaltung*).

Hans Biebow played a major role and managed the ghetto in a ruthless manner, obsessed with productivity, starved the population and played a full part in the deportation of the Jews to their deaths first in Chełmno during the years 1942 to 1944, with the final liquidation taking place in August 1944, when the remainder of the ghetto was sent to Auschwitz Concentration Camp to be murdered there.[56]

The other major figure in the *Litzmannstadt* ghetto was Mordechai Chaim Rumkowski who was born on March 27, in the village of Illino, Byelorussia. He received only a minimal formal education. He was a partner in a large velvet factory in before the First World War, but this and other business ventures failed.

He channelled his great energy and boundless ambition into child welfare and he built up a well-known orphanage in Helenówek, near Łódź, and was its director until 1939. From 1931, he served on the board of the Łódź *kehillah*, the Jewish community council, leading its Zionist faction.

After the Germans occupied Łódź, the *kehillah* was replaced by a Council of Elders and Rumkowski was ordered by the Germans to

---

[56] A. Adelson and R. Lapides, *Łódź Ghetto*, Viking Penguin, New York, 1989, pp. 496–497.

become its chairman, the so-called "Eldest of the Jews." When the Łódź ghetto was established, he became its virtual ruler.[57]

Heinrich May a German forester whose area of responsibility included the Rzuchówski forest witnessed one of these deportations from Łódź, which travelled to Koło railway station via Kutno. At Koło the Jews were taken to the Jewish synagogue. May takes up his eyewitness statement:

> I saw a transport of those unhappy people marching through Koło. Men, women, children and old people. A horse-drawn vehicle drove behind the column, evidently to pick up those incapable of marching. In the vicinity of the post office I saw a woman who carried in her arms a small child, obviously only several months old; she tripped and fell down. The child was probably already half-frozen, because I did not hear any screams. A policeman grabbed the child by one leg and threw it on the vehicle like a piece of wood.
> Some of those whose knees shook with fright and cold and who could not keep up with the column were driven forward by rough pushes with rifle butts. I saw two pretty, well-dressed girls who held an emaciated woman between them. It was probably their mother. The two girls dragged the woman along with difficulty. When she could go no further and collapsed on the road, the two girls endeavoured to put her back on her feet. In so doing, they fell somewhat behind the others. One of the accompanying gendarmes immediately dashed toward the group and yelled, "You dirty bunch of Jews, you probably would like to ride." Silently people stood on the roads and looked at this sad line of people.[58]

Another eyewitness to the arrival in Koło of those Jews resettled from the *Litzmannstadt* ghetto was August Piella. He was one of the handfuls of guards who escorted the Jews from Koło railway station to the Jewish synagogue, which was used as a collection point. He recalled the scene at the synagogue:

> At the entrance to the synagogue, high-ranking officers counted the people entering the building and from this I knew that the transports numbered over 1,000 people. In the synagogue, *Polizeimeister* Draheim collected money from the Jews for straw that was brought to the synagogue.

---

[57] A. Adelson and R. Lapides, *Łódź Ghetto*, Viking Penguin, New York, 1989, p. 504.
[58] P. Montague, *Chełmno and the Holocaust*, I.B. Tauris and Co. Ltd, London 2012, pp. 68–69.

The men who supplied the straw and the cart that brought the weakest people were paid with the money collected. Draheim and *Polizeimeister* Gerolis donated the rest of the money for "German Policeman's Day," so they told us.
The Jews were brought in the afternoon. They spent the night in the synagogue and in the morning trucks arrived from Chełmno and took away the people, who were packed very tightly together and without their baggage. The *Sonderkommando* from Chełmno took away the Jews from the synagogue because none of us were permitted to go there.[59]

Due to concerns raised by the public, these tragic processions were halted and trucks from the *Sonderkommando Kulmhof* collected the deportees and drove them in the direction of Chełmno, until March 1942, when the arrangements were modified again.

SS-Unterscharführer Kurt Möbius described how the Jews were dealt with, when they arrived at the mansion:

> After the Jews arrived at the mansion, they waited in the yard for some time. There they heard a speech, which was given by Plate or me. They were told that they would go to a large camp in Austria where they would have to work. But first they were told, they would have to take a bath, and their clothes would have to be deloused. Plate and I gave the speeches so that the Jews would remain unaware of their fate and do as they were told.
> Next, the Jewish people—men, women and children—were taken to the ground floor of the mansion. The Polish workers helped with this. They went through a straight corridor and entered two large rooms connected by a door. There the Jews undressed, under my supervision. They were not separated by sex. Before this, they had to turn over their valuables. The Polish workers collected these items in baskets.
> Next, as many people as could fit into a gas van at one time were taken from the rooms. On one side of the corridor, there was a door that led to the basement. There was a sign on it that read *"Zum Bade"* (To the Baths). The group that was led to the gas vans always consisted of 35 to 40 people. The stairs led down to a corridor that first went straight and then turned right. The people had to turn right and go to a platform where the gas van stood, with its doors open. There was a board wall on either side of the platform that ended at the doors of the van.
> Usually the Jewish people went to the gas vans quietly, believing what they had been told. The Polish workers accompanied them. They had

---

[59] Ibid., p. 69.

leather whips and beat those who were insubordinate, suspicious, or who wouldn't enter the vans.

Transports came every day except Sundays. During my stay in *Kulmhof*, it happened only two or three times that there were no transports at all on a weekday or that the transports were very small. When there were only a few Jews, they were kept in the basement and gassed on the following day. About five to ten transports came per day. I know this because I gave the speeches to the Jews every day and it happened five to eight sometimes even ten times a day. On average there was about 100 people in each transport. When there were so many of them that they could not fit in the two rooms, some of them had to wait in the yard.

The speech was given several times by *Sturmscharführer* Albert Plate. In May or June 1942, *Polizeimeister* Alois Häfele helped me with my work in the mansion. He also made speeches and carried out the same functions as I did. The number of the guards in the basement depended on the size of the transport. Sometimes there was only one or two, but for larger transports there were eight to ten policemen there.[60]

Stanisław Kaszynski, the former secretary of the Chełmno *gmina*, wrote a letter to the Swiss consulate in Łódź, which contained information about the establishment of a death camp at Chełmno. Herbert Lange, the Commandant, somehow found out about this and he arrested Stanisław Kaszynski in the *gmina* office on January 31, 1942, and took him to the mansion.

---

[60] P. Montague, *Chełmno and the Holocaust*, I.B. Tauris and Co. Ltd, London 2012, pp. 77–78.

Chapter IV
February–March 1942
Mass Murder Continues—
Hans Bothmann Arrives

On February 1, 1942, Sompolno, near Konin, was suddenly swarming with German Police. Shortly after midnight, in the early hours of February 2, 1942, the *Gestapo* and German Police broke into Jewish homes. They ordered the inhabitants to dress quickly and herded them into trucks, which took them to a large wooden garage next to the train station. Over 1000 people were pushed into this unheated building. A few Jews managed to slip through the dragnet and found shelter with Polish neighbours, but only a handful survived the war.

The people herded in the garage by the train station were sent to the Chełmno death camp, where they were murdered in gas vans. Those Jews who were kept behind to clear the vacated Jewish property and furniture were sent to the Łódź ghetto in June 1942.[61]

On February 3, 1942, Stanisław Kaszynski, who was incarcerated in the mansion, was being taken to Lange's office, when he broke free and ran down the gully between the church and the mansion. A guard escorting him shot three times and killed him. The body was taken back to the mansion by a couple of local villagers and was probably buried in the Rzuchówski forest.

Jan Oliskiewicz, who worked in the *Landratsamt* (County Administration Ofiice) in Koło, had been approached by Stanisław Kaszynski, to translate a letter into German, later recalled the events of this affair:

> On December 13, 1941, but I'm not sure of the date, Kaszynski came to me with a request to translate a letter into German. This letter was to be sent to the Swiss consulate in Łódź. It contained information about the liquidation by gas, of the Jews in the camp at Chełmno, as well as the

---

[61] www.holocausthistoricalsociety.org.uk/sompolnoghetto – (HHS Online resource).

murder of the Gypsies. The letter also touched upon a whole series of questions not connected with the camp at Chełmno.

On February 5, 1942, members of the *Sonderkommando* took me to Chełmno, where I was interrogated in the matter of the *Kaszynski* letter. The day before I was arrested, I found out that Kaszynski had been shot. I stubbornly maintained that I burned the translation of the letter, and that it had not been sent. I was badly beaten and put in a cell in the basement of the mansion.

In the neighbouring cells were Jews, women and men, whose voices I heard because the guards forced them to sing constantly. This singing continued for a couple of days. One morning before dawn, I heard the sound of clanging chains: a clanging as if something was being taken from the basement. A couple of times a Jew was brought to my cell, wearing only a shirt despite the frost. The Jew took the excrement bucket from the cell.

I heard voices outside in a mumbled language, not exactly Polish and not exactly German. In fragments of conversation among the guards, I heard about some bodies lying "*durcheinander*" (strewn in a mess) in the trucks. During the day, I heard shots, in series of four or five.

I had been arrested on February 5, 1942; I heard the shots on February 8 and 9, 1942. In the morning I heard a vehicle driving up to the mansion. Afterwards I heard the sound of a lot of bare feet running above me. After shouts of "*Genug, genug*" (Enough, enough), the footsteps stopped. I heard the sound of slamming doors, then for some five minutes, the sound of a motor. Then it drove off. I had the impression that as one vehicle left, another one arrived.[62]

Jan Oliskiewicz was eventually released after spending some sixteen days in the basement cells in the mansion. He was freed on the condition that he "forgot everything he had seen in the camp".[63]

Karolina Kaszynski, the wife of Stanisław Kaszynski, was arrested on February 21, 1942, for spreading information about Chełmno. She was incarcerated in the Women's Prison in 13 Gdanska Street in Łódź and in June 1942, she was moved to the *Gestapo* prison on Sterlinga

---

[62] P. Montague, *Chełmno and the Holocaust*, I.B. Tauris and Co. Ltd, London 2012, pp. 213–214.
[63] Ibid., p. 214.

Street. Her fate is unknown, but in all probability she was murdered by the Germans.[64]

The following day, February 22, 1942, saw the resumptions of the transports from the *Litzmannstadt* ghetto to Chełmno, and up to February 28, 1942, 7025 Jews arrived at Chełmno, to be murdered at the camp.

The underground newspaper *"Undzer Hofnung"* (Unsere Hoffnung) on March 1, 1942, published the information provided by Szlamek Bajler, on the exterminations that were taking place in Chełmno.[65]

On March 2, 1942, the methods of arrival were changed. After arriving at Koło railway station, the deportees were transferred by narrow-gauge railway open freight cars to Powiercie. At Powiercie, they were made to disembark and march to the Zawadka Mill, where they were quartered for the night, before being taken to Chełmno in trucks by road.[66]

Heinrich May was an eyewitness to an arrival of a Jewish transport at Powiercie:

> One day I went to the Powiercie estate manager on business. I walked through the estate park to the place where the narrow-gauge railway wagons were unloaded. From behind the hedge I observed what was happening there. A group of people formed a column along a dirt road. A few ill people were lying on the grass by the railway track. Others dressed their wounds, brought them something to drink and tried to ease their pain. When the column was already formed, two gendarmes appeared and drove the ill with blows from the butts of guns. One of the Jews, who was caring for the ill shouted indignantly, "Even cattle aren't treated in this way." I understood that sentence because it was in German. The gendarme raised his pistol in the direction of the Jew. I thought he just wanted to scare him, but then a shot rang out. The man fell. He tried to stand up, but fell again. He remained there, lying calmly with his head on the railway track. Light-red, frothy blood was streaming out of his mouth. The frightened ill got up and staggered to join the column.

---

[64] Krysztof Gorczyca, Zdzisław Lorek, *Day After Day in the extermination camp Kulmhof am Ner* – unpublished draft, p. 71.
[65] Ibid., p. 73.
[66] Ibid., p. 73.

One of them was too weak and fell again. One shot and he didn't get up again. The gendarmes took four Jews from the column. They had to load those who had been shot into the truck parked nearby. I heard one of the gendarmes say, "You filthy pigs."[67]

Oberwachtmeister Heinrich Beck arrived from Łódź on March 3, 1942, along with other policemen to reinforce the members of the *Sonderkommando Kulmhof*.[68] On March 2 and March 3, deportations took place from Krośniewice and Żychlin. The transport from Żychlin was taken to Krośniewice in carts, and then to Koło by train.[69]

Whilst Chełmno was in the midst of handling the deportations from Łódź, Herbert Lange was replaced as the Commandant of Chełmno by Wilhelm Schulte on a temporary basis and then by Hans Johann Bothmann, who arrived in Chełmno on March 9, 1942. Hans Bothmann was born in Lohe-Rickelshof on November 11, 1911. After the invasion of Poland he arrived in *Posen*, with other members of *Einsatzgruppe VI*. Prior to taking up his post in Chełmno, he was a member of the State Police in *Posen*, with the rank of *SS-Hauptsturmführer* and *Kriminalkommissar* (Superintendent) in the police.[70]

Bothmann's deputy was *SS-Hauptscharführer* and *Kriminalsekretär* Albert Plate, who was born on December 31, 1903, in Baut-Rustringen; he later committed suicide whilst fighting in Yugoslavia, on October 4, 1944.[71]

On March 13, 1942, *SS-Unterscharführer* Friedrich Maderholz arrived from Łódź, with other policemen for service in Chełmno. He was assigned to sentry duty at Zawadka Mill.[72]

---

[67] Chełmno Witnesses Speak, Konin – Łódź 2004, p. 157.
[68] Krystof Gorczyca, Zdzisław Lorek, *Day After Day in the extermination camp Kulmhof am Ner* – unpublished draft, p. 73.
[69] Ibid., p. 73.
[70] Artur Hojan – *Chełmno SS Personnel* unpublished paper, p. 3.
[71] Ibid., p. 13.
[72] Krystof Gorczyca, Zdzisław Lorek, *Day After Day in the extermination camp Kulmhof am Ner* – unpublished draft, p. 74.

A commission from Berlin and the head of the *Ghetto-Verwaltung* in *Litzmannstadt*, Hans Biebow visited Chełmno on March 14, 1942, in order to encourage the *Sonderkommando Kulmhof* to murder more Jews.[73]

Four days later on March 18, 1942, the transport from *Litzmannstadt* ghetto included in its numbers Salomon Hercberg, arrived in Chełmno. Hercberg the Jewish Order Service commandant of the Central Prison in *Litzmannstadt* had hidden in his three apartments, enormous quantities of gold, jewellery, valuables, food, clothing, alcohol and other things, which were discovered in raids conducted by the German Criminal Police. Hercberg, his wife and three sons were taken to Radogoszcz train station on March 17, 1942, and were put on a train to Chełmno. The downfall of Hercberg caused a sensation in the ghetto. The whole family perished in Chełmno.[74]

On March 24, 1942, Gustav Hüfing arrived in Chełmno to take over the duties as head of the police detachment.[75]

Two days later on March 26, 1942, the construction of a road leading to the palace, under the supervision of *SS-Unterscharführer* Alois Häfele commenced.[76] On the same day, 6,000 Jews were deported to Chełmno from the Jewish ghetto in Kutno. Anton Mehring arrived in Chełmno to perform sentry duty in the forest camp, on March 27, 1942.[77]

A number of other policemen such as Wilhelm Schulte and Gustav Fiedler also were transferred from Łódź to Chełmno, as recalled by Wilhelm Schulte, on the same day, March 27, 1942:

> We were taken by truck to the railway station in Łódź. Our commander was *Polizeihauptwachtmeister* Gustav Fiedler. We had to get into the first carriage of a train that stood on the platform ready to leave. There were Jews in the remaining six or seven carriages. As I recall, a railway

---

[73] Ibid., p. 75.
[74] L. Dobroszycki, *The Chronicle of the Łódz Ghetto 1941–1944*, Yale University Press, New Haven and London 1984, pp. 137–138.
[75] Krystof Gorczyca, Zdzisław Lorek, *Day After Day in the extermination camp Kulmhof am Ner* – unpublished draft, p. 77.
[76] Ibid., p. 77.
[77] Ibid., p. 77.

employee had locked the doors of those carriages. I cannot remember if there was a special police or *SS* squad to watch the Jews. As I recall, it was not our duty to watch the transport. The train then went to Koło. The Jews had to leave the train there and get into carriages of a narrow gauge train. It proceeded under the control of *SS* men and young policemen, whom I had seen before in *Polizeibattalion Litzmannstadt*. We got into a bus and were taken to Chełmno.

The next day, Hüfing assigned us to our guard service. About 15 people including me were in the group that was commanded by *Polizeihauptwachtmeister* Fiedler. We were to guard a mill that was located outside of Chełmno. It was called "the mill guard." In the afternoon of the same day we went by bus in the direction of Koło. Fiedler was in command. We got off the bus on a country road after about seven or eight kilometres, where the narrow gauge railroad crossed the Koło-Dąbie road. The bus went back to *Kulmhof*.

After a while a train with 250 to 300 Jews arrived. We took control of them and escorted them to the mill, which was about two kilometres away. Bothmann and Plate, who came by car, were present. The train was escorted by policemen who served in *Kulmhof*. After we had come to the mill, the Jews were put in a large room, where they slept. The policemen from the mill guard were accommodated in a house next to the mill. It also served as our guardroom.

Fiedler appointed three guard shifts, which changed every two hours. Our task was to watch the Jews, so that they did not escape. Policemen who were not on guard duty were required to be on call. The next morning trucks from *Kulmhof* came to the mill and the Jews were taken away. After the mill had been cleaned, the guard detachment was taken back to *Kulmhof* on the bus. Then we had time off.[78]

The Nazis were keen to camouflage the crimes they were committing at Chełmno, and Heinrich May outlined what took place:

> In the spring of 1942, I was called to the State Forestry Office in *Posen*. There I was told to report to *SS-Oberführer* Dr. Melhorn in the *Reich* Governor's Office. When I turned up there, *SS-Oberführer* Dr. Melhorn implied I must have known what was going on in Chełmno. Then he warned me to keep it strictly secret, if not I would surely not avoid the death penalty. He also told me that the commander of the special *SS*

---

[78] P. Montague, *Chełmno and the Holocaust*, I.B. Tauris and Co. Ltd, London 2012, p. 70.

unit, *Sturmbannführer*[79] Bothmann was authorised to contact me about the reforestation of the burial fields in district 77. He said it was vital that those graves be concealed. Then he added at worst we would have to report those graves as the ones of the murdered German civilians –*Volksdeutsche*.[80]

Heinrich May recalled other measures to conceal the crimes at the Rzuchówski forest:

> One day Forest Manager Kranold from the Forestry Office in *Posen* told me that 30,000 Poles were to be executed in the forests under his authority. Melhorn stated that district 77 would have to be enclosed with wooden poles. The concealment was absolutely urgent and had to be carried out immediately.[81]

One of the changes introduced by Hans Bothmann at the end of March 1942 was the use of machinery to excavate the mass graves and cover them over. Heinrich May the forester who was responsible for Rzuchówski forest, part of district 77, recalled:

> After a few days the commandant of the special unit, *SS-Sturmbannführer* Bothmann turned up at my house to talk over the concealment works..... I went with Bothmann to district 77 and I was terrified entering that place for the first time.
> In one of the clearings, enlarged by cutting down some of the trees, I saw a grave about two hundred metres long and five metres wide. The grave was covered with earth that was about two metres high. A bit further on I saw another grave fifty metres long. In the neighbouring clearing there was one more grave about one hundred and fifty metres long. About three quarters of the length of the grave was covered up. From my side it was still open. I did not have enough courage to go there and look into it.
> Soon after an enclosed truck appeared, which was moving backwards and then stopped right in front of the open part of the grave. The gendarme opened the van and I saw a pile of naked bodies. I was standing about eighty metres from the van. A group of half-naked forced labourers, supervised by one of the gendarmes, hurried to throw the corpses into the grave. Bothmann told me that the bodies had to be positioned

---

[79] Bothmann was not a *Sturmbannführer* in rank but a *SS-Hauptsturmführer*.
[80] *Chełmno Witnesses Speak*, Konin – Łódź 2004, pp. 157–158.
[81] Ibid., p. 158.

precisely; otherwise not enough of them would fit into the grave. Parallel to the grave, a motorized excavator with a conveyor belt was digging another grave. The conveyor belt was also used to cover up the graves.[82]

---

[82] *Chełmno Witnesses Speak*, Konin – Łódź 2004, p. 158.

Chapter V
April–May 1942
Deportations from
the Litzmannstadt Ghetto

Deportations continued at the beginning of the month from the *Litzmannstadt* ghetto, as well as smaller towns and villages in the *Warthegau,* such as Grabow, Gostynin, Łęczyca, Osięciny, Sanniki and others. The *Transportkommando* from Chełmno travelled to these locations and brought Jews to their death in Chełmno. Wilhelm Schulte described how this worked:

> The group was made up of six to eight men, mostly the same ones. But from time to time Fiedler appointed other people to help them. I was appointed to this group several times. Our task was to escort six to eight trucks, which were in *Kulmhof,* as the Jews were being brought from various neighbouring villages.
> Sometimes we had to go as far as 60 kilometres from Chełmno and take the Jews from there. *Polizeioberwachtmeister* Kretschmer was the commanding officer of this escort. As far as I know the transports were organized by *Scharführer* Richter, who drove it to the villages and took over command of the Jews from the SS men and policemen who were guarding them. I do not remember from what villages we took Jews. They were always ready for the transport.
> Kretschmer ordered me to get into a truck with the Jews, sit on the tailgate and watch them so that no one escaped. Policemen escorting the other trucks had the same task. During the drive, Kretschmer rode in the first truck, beside the driver. Richter drove in his car in front of us. The Jews were always transported to the mansion in *Kulmhof,* where they were taken over by Häfele or Möbius.
> Our trucks left the villages at 20-minute intervals, so they did not all get to *Kulmhof* at the same time. Many times I also escorted Jews from the ghetto in Łódź. *Gestapo* men in civilian clothes handed over these Jews to Richter.
> Members of the escort detachment wore coveralls during the transports. Policemen in the detachment had to have a leather whip during these trips; it was Bothmann's order. I also had such a leather whip. A Pole who worked in the mansion gave it to me; it had been made by a Jewish

craftsman. It was made out of a single piece of leather, something like a dog whip. Kretschmer also had a whip like this and he ordered us to beat the Jews if they didn't walk fast enough.
Many times I saw policemen beating Jews in accordance with this order. I used my whip several times in this situation, but I did not really beat them; I only touched those people who did not get onto the trucks fast enough, to make them go faster. But it surely cannot be considered a beating so that the Jews could feel pain.[83]

This phase of the *Litzmannstadt* ghetto deportations ended on April 3, 1942, which saw 34,074 Jews murdered in Chełmno between February and April 1942.

On April 10, 1942, *SS-Hauptscharführer* Wilhelm Heuckelbach arrived from Łódź. The following day, Szlamek Bajler was deported from the Zamość ghetto and murdered in the Bełżec death camp.[84]

Wilhelm Heuckelbach recalled that on his second day in the camp, April 12, 1942, he was on duty at the main gate at the mansion when two trucks arrived and he gave testimony after the war, of what took place:

> Then the people had to get out of the trucks and they were welcomed by a police officer. He gave a speech saying that they were in a transit camp, where they would be washed and deloused. Next they would be taken to a labour camp in the *Reich*. Before they were taken to the baths they had to go inside the mansion and remove their clothes. They had to deposit their valuables, which would be given back to them later.
> The Jews went inside the mansion. There were men, women and children. I followed them and guarded the position at the doors to the two rooms. After the Jews had undressed, they were led downstairs to the basement by a police officer, who counted them.
> Then, following orders, I went to the right side of the mansion, where there was a platform and a gas van. It was a truck with an enclosed compartment. The colour was grey. The doors were in the back of the van. The gas van stood at the platform with its doors open. I could see the Jews, who were brought through the basement, enter the vans.

---

[83] P. Montague, *Chełmno and the Holocaust*, I.B. Tauris and Co. Ltd, London 2012, pp. 71–72.

[84] Krystof Gorczyca, Zdzisław Lorek, *Day After Day in the extermination camp Kulmhof am Ner* – unpublished draft, p. 79.

After all the people had entered the gas van, the driver closed the doors and locked them. Then he turned on the engine. Shortly after that I could hear screaming and pounding against the walls of the van. After about ten minutes the screams died down and I knew the people were dead. The driver let the engine run for another few minutes and then he drove away.

Many times I also stood at the position in the basement when the Jews arrived at the mansion and after undressing were led to the gas vans. The Jews mostly walked to the vans quietly, because they knew from the speech that they were going to the baths. But sometimes during my service in the basement it happened that the Jews did not want to walk into the vans. In such cases I had to use my hands to push and hit the people, so that they would move on. Several times I beat Jews when they did not want to walk on. But it surely was not a real beating so that they felt pain. Each time I only threatened them with my whip and touched some of the Jews slightly to make them walk on. I felt sorry for the poor people and it was impossible for me to beat them harshly.[85]

Heinrich Himmler, *Reichsführer-SS* met with Adolf Hitler at his *Wolfschanze* headquarters near the town of Kętrzyn on April 16, 1942, and from there, Himmler flew to *Posen*, where he met *Gauleiter* Arthur Grieser and *HSSPF* Wilhelm Koppe. Himmler visited *Warthbrücken* (Koło) and the nearby village of Osiek Moczydła on April 17, 1942, meeting with Baltic Germans who had recently been resettled in the area.

Josef Islinger arrived in Chełmno from Łódź during April 1942, and he recalled what happened the day after his arrival:

> We were welcomed by two SS officers: *SS-Hauptsturmführer* Bothmann and *SS-Untersturmführer* Plate. Bothmann delivered a speech explaining to us that a secret affair of state was being carried out in *Kulmhof*. We were to keep silent about everything we saw and heard; otherwise we would face serious punishments. We were to become members of the *Polizeiwachtkommando* and serve as guards. He did not explain anything else, particularly what was going on in *Kulmhof*.
> Sergeant Otto Böge gave us our assignments. I became a member of a group under the command of *Polizeimeister* Haider. The task of this group was to guard a certain forest area near Chełmno. At first we didn't

---

[85] P. Montague, *Chełmno and the Holocaust*, I.B. Tauris and Co. Ltd, London 2012, p. 79.

know why we were guarding the forest. Haider assigned us to several positions around the forest. Our task was to ensure that no one entered the woods. Eventually, from hearsay, I found out what was happening. A Jewish labour detachment worked in the forest—it consisted of about 15 to 20 people.

At first, I mounted guard on the outer perimeter of the forest camp. Depending on where I mounted guard, I could sometimes see the gas vans drive into the forest camp. During my service there, I could see that everything I had heard from hearsay was true. I saw two large mass graves in the forest, about 20 to 30 metres long, six to eight metres wide, and four metres deep.

One of the mass graves was already filled with dead bodies and covered with earth. The other one was half-filled at that time. The gas vans came many times a day and stopped at the grave. The members of the Jewish labour detachment, whose legs were shackled, opened the back doors of the gas vans and took out the bodies that were inside.

Next, the bodies were stacked in layers inside the mass grave. The gas vans, full of bodies, came five to ten times a day. I estimate that there were always about 50 bodies in the smaller vans and 70 in the larger ones. The forest camp was supervised by *Polizeimeister* Lenz. *Polizeioberwachtmeister* Runge was second in command. Lenz and Runge always urged the Jews on who were unloading the gas vans. They reviled the Jews with terms like, "swine." Sometimes they also beat the Jews with sticks.

Almost every day, in the evening, several Jews from the labour squad were shot in the forest camp, before the group was transported back to Chełmno. Only those Jews who were unable or unwilling to work were shot. Usually there were five or six, but sometimes up to ten were shot. *Polizeimeister* Lenz carried out most of the executions. He ordered the Jews to lay face down on the edge of the mass grave. Then he took his gun and shot them in the back of the neck. The other Jews had to throw the bodies into the grave. I also recall that Plate carried out those executions from time to time. He often visited the forest camp and supervised our work.[86]

Deportations from Włocławek commenced on April 30, 1942, and lasted for two days, seeing some 3,500 Jews murdered in Chełmno. On the following day Arthur Greiser wrote a letter to *RFSS* Heinrich Himmler stating that "the special treatment of about 100,000 Jews in

---

[86] P. Montague, *Chełmno and the Holocaust*, I.B. Tauris and Co. Ltd, London 2012, pp. 92–93.

the territory of my district, approved by you in agreement with the Chief of the *Reich* Main Security Office, *SS-Obergruppenführer* Heydrich, can be completed within the next 2–3 months.... The number of persons infected with open Tuberculosis is estimated at 35,000 ... I could take responsibility for my suggestion to have cases of open TB exterminated among the Polish race here in the *Warthegau*.[87]

On May 3, 1942, *SS-Hauptscharführer* Gustav Laabs arrived in Chełmno after working for the *RSHA* in Berlin and subsequently transferred to the *SS und Polizeiführer's* office in *Posen*. Gustav Laabs immediately started driving the gas vans.[88] Another new gas van driver *SS-Oberscharführer* Oskar Hering arrived in Chełmno at the same time, from *Posen*.

Between May 4 and May 16, 1942, some 10,914 Jews were deported from the *Litzmannstadt* ghetto to Chełmno. Wilhelm Schulte testified after the war:

> I often stood at the main gate of the mansion and let in the transport of Jews. The Jews were received there by Häfele or by *Polizeimeister* Möbius. They always gave the speech to the Jews before they entered the mansion. Bothmann and Plate were always sometimes present and gave the speech. They told the Jews that they were in a transit camp where they would be washed and deloused. Afterwards they would be transported to a labour camp. First they should go inside the mansion, take off their clothes, and deposit their valuables, because they would be taken to baths by truck.
> When the Jews entered the mansion, I followed them and, in accordance with Häfele's instructions, I guarded the doors to the rooms where the Jews had to undress. Either Häfele or Möbius supervised the undressing. Several Poles who worked in the mansion collected valuables in baskets. I also saw Häfele collecting valuables from time to time, but not Möbius. After the Jews had undressed, a Pole took them downstairs to the basement, Häfele or Möbius followed them. The Pole, Häfele and Möbius had leather whips. I don't know if they used them to beat the Jews in the basement. When the Jews went downstairs to the basement, I went outside to the right side of the mansion where the gas vans were parked. I could see the Jews going over the platform naked into the gas van. The back doors were closed by the gas van drivers Laabs and Hering. They

---

[87] IMT Nuremberg, *Document NO-246*, Wiener Library London.
[88] Artur Hojan – *Chełmno SS Personnel* unpublished paper, p. 10.

then turned on the engines of their trucks, which began the process of gassing. I noticed it because the people, who were inside the vans knocked against the walls and screamed, frightened to death.

SS-Hauptscharführer Gustav Laabs recalled what happened, a few days after his arrival, when Hans Bothmann put him and Hering to work driving the gas vans, dealing with the transports of Jews from Łódź:

> Shortly afterwards, Bürstinger ordered me to back up the van that had been assigned to me to the ramp, which was on the side of the mansion by the park. The ramp was made of wood and sloped down into the basement corridor. The sides were comprised of a board wall about 2.5 metres tall. The front was enclosed by the van. Bürstinger opened the doors of the van after I had backed the van up to the ramp. He had unlocked the doors with a key that hung in the driver's cab. After the doors were opened, the ramp was completely enclosed so that one could not see into it, nor could one exit from it.
> I stayed in the cab because Bürstinger ordered me to do so. Bürstinger left the ramp through the basement corridor.
> After about half an hour, I heard loud calls from the basement hall and saw in the rear view mirror barefooted people run into the van. I did not see the people themselves, but through the gap between the right door and the van's body I saw bare feet. From this I concluded that the people were undressed. I knew they entered the van because it shook.
> When the van was full, the doors were closed and locked, apparently by Bürstinger, because he then hung the keys back up in the cab. Then Bürstinger ordered a Polish civilian to get under the van and do something there. Bothmann, who came out through the basement, ordered me to start the motor and let it run for 20 minutes. I started the motor and after about one minute I heard terrible moaning and screaming coming from inside the van.
> I was overcome with fear and jumped out of the cab—it was now clear to me that the exhaust gas led into the van in order to kill people. Bothmann yelled at me and ordered me to get back inside. I sat and waited. I couldn't do anything because I was afraid of Bothmann. Slowly the moans and cries faded away after several minutes.
> After about ten minutes a police official sat down beside me, and Bothmann ordered me to drive. But before this the Pole crept under the van and, as was now clear to me, disconnected the inflow of the exhaust gas into the van. The policeman who sat beside me told me where I was to drive. After about three kilometres we came to a clearing in a forest area that lay along the road to Koło.

When we arrived there, the policeman told me to stop at a mass grave, where under the supervision of a police official, a Jewish labour squad was working. There were several other policemen standing in a circle, apparently standing guard. The police official who supervised the labour squad told me to back the van up to the mass grave. The policeman who came with me unlocked the doors. Some members of the labour squad were then ordered to open the doors. When the doors were opened, eight to ten corpses fell out of the van. The labour squad then threw the rest out of the van.

After the van had been emptied, I drove it back to the mansion. On the way, I met Hering with his van. In the van I was driving, about 50 people were gassed. The same number was probably gassed in Hering's van. At the mansion some Jews who obviously belonged to the mansion labour squad had to clean the inside of the van, with water and disinfectants. To do this, they had to take out two wooden grates from the floor of the van. After the van had been cleaned and the grates put back in, Häfele ordered me to drive back to the ramp.[89]

The deportations from Łódź were described in *The Chronicle of the Łódź Ghetto*, the entry for Thursday, May 7, 1942, reads as follows:

A transport of former residents of Hamburg and Düsseldorf left the ghetto today. Possessions down to the smallest parcels continue to be taken away. They are only left their bread and at times, bits of some other food as well.

The transports are conveyed in the following manner. In the afternoon hours, the deportees make their way to the Central Prison or to the small buildings surrounded by barbed wire on Szklana Street. There they remain for the night, and the next day at noon they are assembled into groups and escorted under guard to the camp in Marysin, where they are lodged in the school building on Jonscher Street and in five small buildings on Okopowa Street.

They receive food at these assembly points—a ration of bread, *ersatz* coffee, and soup. Each person is supplied with a loaf of bread for the journey, free of charge. At four o'clock in the morning, special detachments of the Order Service, already expert at performing such onerous tasks, transport the deportees by tram to the Radogoszcz side-track station. Half-an-hour before the train departs—which occurs at 7 o'clock a.m on the dot—secret police *(Gestapo)* officials accompanied by regular German police, arrive by automobile. By then the deportees have been

---

[89] P. Montague, *Chełmno and the Holocaust*, I.B. Tauris and Co. Ltd, London 2012, pp. 80–81.

lined up by the Order Service, in groups of ten in front of the compartment doors, at a distance of two metres from the train.
Then they take their places under the eyes of the police. It is then that they are ordered to throw away the things they had brought with them. The largest pieces of luggage have already been taken away by the Order Service at the assembly points; those items and those taken away at the station, are later sent to the office on Rybna Street. Porters carry the sick and the very elderly onto the trains. There are medical stations in operation at the assembly points, and a medical team is on duty at the train station as well.
The story circulating through the ghetto concerning the beating of deportees is worth correcting. Such incidents, with minor exceptions are not taking place. The train is made up of third-class carriages, as in the previous resettlements. Each person leaving the ghetto is given a seat. The train returns the same day at 8 o'clock p.m.[90]

A transport of 260 Christian Jews, including Maria Regina Fuhrmann, a Carmelite nun who had been deported from Vienna to the *Litzmannstadt* ghetto, left for Chełmno on May 10, 1942, also on this transport was the well-known pianist Leopold Birkenfeld, who had been deported to the ghetto from Vienna.[91]

During the night on May 15, 1942, six Jewish prisoners escaped from Chełmno and despite a search by members of the *Sonderkommando* remained at large. The *Gestapo* in *Posen* issued a warrant for their arrest. The *Gestapo* in *Posen*, two days later, on May 18, 1942, issued another warrant stating that five Jews have been captured and one was still on the run.[92]

At the end of May 1942, as one of the Sauer gas van engines was started at the ramp with victims loaded inside, there was an explosion that caused a fire. One of the guards *Wachtmeister* Alexander Steinke suffered burns and had to be taken to hospital in *Warthbrücken*.[93]

---

[90] L. Dobroszycki, *The Chronicle of the Łódź Ghetto 1941–1944*, Yale University Press, New Haven and London 1984, pp. 164–165.
[91] Krystof Gorczyca, Zdzisław Lorek, *Day After Day in the extermination camp Kulmhof am Ner* – unpublished draft, p. 85.
[92] Ibid., p. 86 and p. 87.
[93] Ibid., p. 89.

Martha Michelsohn, the wife of the German schoolteacher in Chełmno recalled in the film "Shoah", by Claude Lanzmann:

> I was born in Laage, and I was sent to *Kulmhof*. They were looking for volunteer settlers, and I signed up. That's how I got there, first in *Warthbrücken* (Koło), then Chełmno (*Kulmhof*). This was the whole village. A very small village, straggling along the road. Just a few houses. There was the church, the castle, a store too, the administrative building and the school. The castle was next to the church, with a high board fence around both. My house was opposite the church—just opposite 150 feet.

Martha Michelson was asked if she saw the gas vans?

> Yes from the outside. They shuttled back and forth. I never looked inside; I didn't see Jews in them. I only saw things from outside—the Jews arrival, their disposition, how they were loaded aboard. Since World War I, the castle had been in ruins. Only part of it could still be used. That's where the Jews were taken.[94]

Martha Michelson described the arrival of the Jewish deportees:

> The Jews came in trucks and later there was a narrow-gauge railway that they arrived on. They were packed tightly in the trucks, or in the cars of the narrow-gauge railway. Lots of women and children; Men too, but most of them were old.
> The strongest were put in work details. They walked with chains on their legs. In the morning they fetched water, looked for food and so on. These weren't killed right away. That was done later. I don't know what became of them. They didn't survive anyway.

She was asked if people could speak to the Jewish work squad as they moved through the village.

> Yes there were guards. Anyway, people wanted nothing to do with all that. Do you see? Gets on your nerves, seeing that everyday. You can't force a whole village to watch such distress! When the Jews arrived, when they were pushed into the church or the castle .... And the screams! It was frightful! Depressing, day after day, the same spectacle. It was terrible. A sad sight. They screamed. They knew what was happening. At first they thought they were going to be deloused. But they soon

---

[94] C. Lanzmann, *Shoah*, Pantheon Books, New York, 1985, pp. 81–82.

understood. Their screams grew wilder and wilder. Horrifying screams. Screams of terror! Because they knew what was happening to them.[95]

---

[95] Ibid., pp. 92–94.

Chapter VI
June–August 1942
Exhumation and Cremation

As mentioned in the previous chapter the Nazis were determined to conceal the crimes they were committing in the Rzuchówski forest and Heinrich May recalled:

> I ordered a large quantity of juniper seeds in a seed store to reforest the clearings. Some pines and birches were planted as well..... Bothmann was accompanied by *Hauptwachtmeister* Plate, who made an impression of being very insidious. When I returned to that place with Bothmann in the summer of 1942, in the period when the wooden fences were being put up, I saw the graves; an unbearable, strong, sweetish odour wafted up above the whole place. I had to cover my nose and I left the place as soon as possible. Bothmann showed me large round heaps of earth on the long graves, above which, one could still see clouds of vapour. Bothmann told me about 250,000 people had been buried there and another 100,000 would be buried soon.[96]

On June 5, 1942, Willi Just wrote a letter to his superior *SS-Obersturmbannführer* Walter Rauff, the head of *Gruppe II D* of the *Reich Security Main Office*, who was responsible for vehicles including gas vans. The letter suggested technical modifications, the number of victims and the explosion of the *Sonderwagen*:

> Since December 1941, for example 97,000 have been processed using three vans without any faults developing in these vehicles. The well-known explosion in *Kulmhof* must be treated as a special case.[97]

SS-Standartenführer Paul Blobel was born on August 13, 1894, in Potsdam. After serving in the First World War, Paul Blobel worked as an architect in Düsseldorf. He joined the police in 1933, and a year later was recruited into the *Sicherheitsdienst (SD)*—the Security Service of the *SS*. In June 1941, prior to the German invasion of the Soviet

---

[96] *Chełmno Witnesses Speak*, Konin – Łódź 2004, p. 159.
[97] Holocaust Historical Society (HHS Archives).

Union, he was appointed to lead the *Sonderkommando* 4a of *Einsatzgruppe C*.

Paul Blobel organized the infamous Babi Yar massacre in Kiev, where over two days, on September 29 and 30, 1941, a total of 33,771 Jews were executed in the Babi Yar ravine, which was just beyond the Lukyanovka Jewish cemetery.[98]

In June 1942, Blobel was appointed to lead "*Aktion 1005*" which was established to remove all traces of the Nazi extermination policy in the East, and Blobel arrived in Chełmno on June 12, 1942, in order to determine the most effective method of body disposal to achieve the objectives the *Kommando* had been set. Transports were suspended, whilst the exhumation and cremation was carried out.[99]

Blobel set to work immediately exhuming the corpses from the mass graves and burning the corpses. This included the use of thermite bombs, and forester Heinrich May recalled:

> One day Bothmann appeared in the forestry's office and told me that he had orders from higher authority to burn all the corpses. He had already had the graves opened and attempted to burn the bodies with thermite bombs. Now he wished to try to carry out the order with firewood and he requested great amounts of it.
>
> During the burning with thermite bombs, a forest fire had been caused, whereby a portion of the woods surrounding the field of graves burned down. The charred woods could not be cut down since otherwise a view of the field of graves would have become possible to see from the road. I approached the *Landesforstamt* in regard to the ordered firewood and I was advised to deliver the wood.
>
> At first I ordered all young woods in question to be searched and delivered great quantities of branches and faggots. However, this was not sufficient, and I had to deliver cordwood. Finally, the consumption became so great that I changed over to making clearings in older woods.
>
> For many months, a terrible stench laid over the entire vicinity. When the wind was blowing from the west, the sickening odour could be noticed up to the forestry house in Balice forester's lodge, situated about 15 kilometres in a straight line from the graves.....

---

[98] G.Reitlinger, *The Final Solution*, Vallentine, Mitchell, London, 1968, p. 248.

[99] Krystof Gorczyca, Zdzisław Lorek, *Day After Day in the extermination camp Kulmhof am Ner* – unpublished draft, p. 92.

> During the construction of the fence I talked with the *Hauptwachtmeister* of the gendarmerie, if I remember correctly, his name was Lenz.... For instance, he told me during the first winter, it was quite hard because the earth was frozen and they did not have an excavator.....
> After many attempts, cremation of the bodies was performed in pits about three metres deep and four metres in diameter, reinforced with stones on the sides. The corpses were burnt in the fire inside the pits. The remaining long bones were pulled out and ground in a motor grinder placed in a wooden barrack. I do not know for what purpose this bone meal was used. There must have been lots of it.

Heinrich May described another visit to the *Waldlager*, in the Rzuchówski forest:

> During my last visit to the graveyard, when the juniper seeds were being sewn, Bothmann showed me the bone grinder. In the barracks there were a few full sacks. Bothmann said to one of the people employed there, "Itzig, bring me some meal from the sack." The old man untied one of the sacks and brought two handfuls of snow-white finely ground bone meal. Bothmann asked him, "Do you know what this is?" The man was silent. Bothmann explained, "These are your fellow countrymen, people of the same race as you." The man answered calmly and patiently, "What can one do?" His accent told me he was a German too......
> During the process of burning corpses in open pits, one of the workers who had to throw the bodies into the flames, jumped into the fire, perhaps in a fit of madness. One of the gendarmes standing by shouted, "Shoot, shoot!" Maybe he was one with a remaining spark of human feelings. But another gendarme shouted, "Don't shoot. We want to see how long he will remain alive." They looked at their watches and counted how long the man kept shouting until he turned silent.[100]

Another person who described the bone grinder was *SS-Hauptscharführer* Wilhelm Heukelbach who worked as a guard in the mansion and the Rzuchówski forest camp:

> I had heard there was a bone grinder in the forest camp where the bone fragments from the crematoria were ground. One night, when I was standing sentry in the forest camp, I had a closer look. It was situated not far from the crematoria and was covered with a roof. There was a large funnel on the top where the bone fragments must have been

---

[100] *Chełmno Witnesses Speak*, Konin – Łódź 2004, pp. 159–161.

poured in. There were several bags full of ground up bones near the mill. The bags were open so I could see what was inside.[101]

Blobel's remit was to eradicate all traces of the crimes being committed in Chełmno. This meant exhuming and cremating the victims in the mass graves and the use of a bone grinder was essential for this. On July 16, 1942, the deputy chief of the *Ghettoverwaltung* in *Litzmannstadt*, Friedrich Ribbe, wrote a letter to Chaim Rumkowski, the Chairman, Eldest of the Jews, asking "if there was a Bone Mill in the ghetto, as *Sonderkommando Kulmhof* is interested in such a mill."

The *Litzmannstadt* ghetto did not possess such a machine and a bone mill was obtained from the firm of Schriever and Company in Hannover. Walter Burmeister brought the bone mill and compressor to the Forest Camp. The mill weighed about five and a half tons and was transported on a five-ton truck and trailer. The bone mill was powered by a gas-driven generator and was supervised by Gustav Fiedler and Kurt Hoffman.[102]

The Jewish craftsmen working in the Chemno death camp communicated with the outside world by writing on scraps of paper. One of these notes written in Yiddish was found on the road near the Rzuchówski forest. As it mentions the burning of corpses, this means it must have been written after Blobel's arrival in Chełmno. The note read:

> These are the Jews who worked in the death camp *Kulmhof* between Koło and Dąbie:
> 1. Josef Herszkowicz from Kutno
> 2. Mojzesz Plocker from Kutno
> 3. Fajwel Plocker from Kutno
> 4. Szyja Szlamowicz from Grabow, near Łódź
> 5. Noech Wolf Judkiewicz from Łódź
> 6. Chaskel Zarak from Łęczyca
> 7. Motel Szymkie from Łęczyca
> 8. Chaskiel (son) Wachtel from Łęczyca
> 9. Beniek Jastrzebski from Łęczyca

---

[101] P. Montague, *Chełmno and the Holocaust*, I.B. Tauris and Co. Ltd, London 2012, pp. 117–118.
[102] Ibid., p. 117.

10. Aron Nussbaum from Sanok
11. Iser Strasburg from Lutomiersk
12. Gecel Stajer from Turek

These are the last Jews who worked for the *Gestapo* in Chełmno, which is located between Dąbie and Koło. These are the last days of our lives, so we are sending word about ourselves. Perhaps this note will find its way to relatives or friends of these people, so that they will know that all the Jews who were taken from Łódź were killed in a horrible manner. They were tortured and burned. Be healthy and, if you survive, avenge us.[103]

Although transports were suspended, one significant transport arrived in Chełmno on July 10, 1942, consisting of children from the village of Lidice. On June 10, 1942, the Nazis destroyed the Czech village of Lidice, as a reprisal measure for the killing of Reinhard Heydrich, the Deputy Protector, Bohemia-Moravia, and the chief architect of the "Final Solution of the Jewish Question". The men were shot on the spot, the women were sent to Concentration Camps and 88 children were sent to Łódź.

Dr. Walter Dongus of the Race and Settlement Office examined the children to see which children were suitable for "Germanization," out of the 88 only 7 were deemed suitable and the remaining 81 were sent to Chełmno for "special handling." One of the local residents of Chełmno witnessed the arrival of this transport. She asked one of the Jews who worked in the kitchen, Toporski, about it. He told her that they were from the Protectorate.[104]

Returning to the establishment of crematoria in the Forest Camp, Blobel constructed four crematoria measuring approximately eight meters by eight meters and these furnaces were in operation by mid-July 1942. Two larger crematoria were built, as these were more efficient than the field-furnaces. Rozalia Peham, the wife of one of the guards, Josef Peham, described the new crematoria:

---

[103] P. Montague, *Chełmno and the Holocaust*, I.B. Tauris and Co. Ltd, London 2012, pp. 83–84.
[104] Ibid., p. 127.

> Two crematoria were built. I don't know how they were installed because, of course, I was never there. I know only that the ovens had tall chimneys and were so constructed that they had a very strong draught. The bodies were arranged in layers in these ovens. Between each layer of bodies was a layer of wood. Gasoline was poured over the pile of bodies and wood when the corpses were to be burned in the fire.[105]

Transports to the Chełmno death camp resumed with the final liquidation of the open ghetto in Czachulec on July 20, 1942, and at the end of the month with the liquidation of 750 Jews from Lutomiersk, in Łask County.

During August 1942, a number of deportations from Bełchatów, Sieradz, Łask, Wieluń and other places arrived in Chełmno for "special handling." One of the largest deportations took place over three days, August 24–26, 1942, from Zduńska Wola and one eyewitness Rafal Lewkowicz recalled the liquidation of the ghetto:

> The liquidation of the ghetto began in the early morning hours of August 24. This did not cause a panic among the inhabitants because most already knew what was in store for them. Many had known since the winter of 1941, when according to the son of Dr. Lemberg, two Polish railroad men came overnight to see my father. They said they had confidential information for him. Later they said the Nazi's had evacuated several villages around Chełmno and that the trucks arrived there with Jews but left stuffed with clothing. They were convinced that the mass extermination of Jews was occurring there. My father decided to inform the local Jewish communities about this horrible discovery. He wrote anonymous letters with the information that the Jews were not going to work, as the Germans said, but to their death. We also sent word about this to Łódź. Aware of the fate that awaited them, many hid in basements and attics, while others went to the assembly point at Steszydzka Street, completely resigned or in despair. This behaviour had an influence on the particularly aggressive course of the ghetto's liquidation.
> A significantly strong contingent of *SS* police, including a special unit known as the *Rollkommando,* and the entire unit of the *Schutzpolizei* in Zduńska Wola, with its chief Hermann Funke, were mobilized for the operation. Also participating in the operation were *Gestapo* officials from Łódź, Gunther Fuchs and Albert Richter, as well as the head of the *Ghettoverwaltung* Hans Biebow, and section heads Erich Czarnulla,

---

[105] Ibid., p. 116.

Wilhelm Ribbe and Franz Seifert. Biebow and his associates were there to conduct the selection of the Jews, who were to strengthen the workshops of the Łódź ghetto and to secure the property of Zduńska Wola's Jews.

Following the initial segregation of the Jews at the assembly point on Steszydzka Street and murdering the sick, infirm and many elderly, the others were hustled through the streets to the Jewish cemetery, where a cordon of SS men were waiting. Another selection was conducted here, among screams and beatings by among others Biebow and the *Gestapo* officers. Everyone was divided into two groups. One group comprised young people, able to work, while the other included the elderly, children and the sick. Horrible scenes played out here when children were taken away from their mothers. Many chose death rather than separation from their loved ones.

While this selection was occurring at the cemetery, other *SS* and police detachments, with the help of Jewish police, searched the ghetto, murdering anyone who crossed their path. Those murdered in this way included elderly people and children, as well as the patients of the Jewish hospital on Ogrodowa Street. Dozens were killed on the first day of this operation. Dozens more were killed in the following two days. The corpses of those killed were taken to the cemetery and buried in prepared graves.

Those assembled at the cemetery languished there for two days without food or water. The cemetery was illuminated at night to prevent the two groups from intermingling. Those who tried to mingle were killed. The guards also shot into the crowd without reason, killing several dozen people.

On August 25 and 26, the larger of the two groups, comprising 8,594 people were loaded into trucks and transported to Chełmno. The smaller group of 1169 people was taken by train to the ghetto in Łódź.[106]

---

[106] P. Montague, *Chełmno and the Holocaust*, I.B. Tauris and Co. Ltd, London 2012, pp. 120–121.

Chapter VII
September 1942
The Gehsperre Deportation from the Litzmannstadt Ghetto—Höss Visit

In early September 1942, two Jews who had been deported from the Sieradz on August 22, 1942, were made to work in the Rzuchówski forest, as gravediggers escaped. The two men were Yitzhak Justmann and Chaim Widawski, and they sought refuge in Piotrków Trybunalski. They made their way to the home of Rabbi Moshe Lau, and his son Naphtali Lau-Lavie gave this account:

> Two young men in their twenties—Chaim Widawski and Yitzhak Justmann arrived in the ghetto seeking shelter. On the way to our home, they noticed that the *Volksdeutsche Gestapo* agent Emmering was following them. In order to lose him, they went in separate directions. Justmann went in the direction of the Great Synagogue and lost Emmering and found sanctuary in the Wajsberg home, where he was well hidden, while Widawski arrived at our home with the Jewish policeman Checinski on his tail, who tried to stop him. Hearing the commotion on the stairs, my father went out to see what was happening and with a firm voice ordered the policeman to leave the man alone, who, crying, thanked my father for saving him. Distraught and weeping, Widawski asked for water and the opportunity to tell his story.
> A calmer Widawski said that, together with Justmann, he escaped from a "commando" that buried victims of the death camp in Chełmno. No one in the ghetto had yet heard the name of that place.
> My father took Widawski into his office and closed the door. After about an hour he came out and told me to summon several of his friends, among whom were members of the pre-war community council: Mosze Nordman, Baruch Zylberszac, Hirsch-Leib Krakowski, Meir Abramsom, Fiszel Lubiner, Mordechai Michelson, Bunim Kaminski, Rabbi Mosze Temkin and Dr. Sztajn. Soon everyone was gathered in my father's study to hear Widawski recount his experience in Chełmno. My father wrote down his every word and asked many questions to check the veracity of his story.
> Widawski told about murdering people with exhaust fumes in special trucks, the exhaust pipes of which were directed into the hermetically

sealed rear compartment full of people. In the course of the half an hour trip from the mansion in Chełmno, where the people were imprisoned, to the clearing in the forest, where large rectangular pits were dug, everyone was murdered with the exhaust fumes from the vehicle's engine. Widawski and his friend were among the group whose task was throwing the corpses from the truck and carrying them to the pit. There, four other people threw the corpses into the hole where another group arranged the bodies so as many as possible could be packed together. Infants and babies were placed into any empty spaces. Lime was poured over each layer of bodies, on which the next layer of bodies was placed. After the final layer was placed in the grave, the Germans ordered the eight men in the hole to lay face down after which they were shot.

Among the tasks assigned to the group throwing the corpses out of the vans was cleaning them before they left for a new transport. "We worked like machines, unaware of what we were doing. The entire time I recited the *Kaddish* for the victims whom the van brought regularly every hour. Among the bodies that we pulled from the van I recognized relatives from Sieradz, and worst of all my fiancé to whom I had proposed two months previously," Widawski said, his voice breaking.

That tragic day while returning to the mansion in Chełmno, where they were isolated from those designated for death, Widawski and Justmann decided to escape from that hell at any price and whatever the consequences. That very night they managed to escape and after four days reached us in Piotrków.

Naively, I believed that nothing could horrify me after my own experiences at Auschwitz. But Widawski's story halted by sobs, dispelled that illusion. He talked compulsively, with Father writing everything in his notebook, pressing him for further details. The others listened, petrified. No one moved or spoke. At one point my father told me to take Widawski to the dining room, where my mother had prepared some food for him. When he was eating his first hot meal since who knows when, my father prepared a plan of escape for Widawski and his friend Justmann, who was hiding in the Wajsberg's apartment, not far from the synagogue.

Both were near the psychological breaking point, but as the *Gestapo* were aware of their presence, they had to escape from Piotrków as soon as possible. It was already curfew when I took Widawski to the nearby Goldring's home. There, the two fugitives were dressed in uniforms of

Polish railroad employees and given the necessary documents and money. Widawski held my hand convulsively not wanting to let go.[107]

Both Justmann and Widawski survived the Holocaust. Justmann settled in the United States of America, whilst Widawski set up his business and home in Antwerp, Belgium.

One of the most tragic events in the history of Chełmno was the infamous Nazi deportation *"Aktionen"* carried out in the *Litzmannstadt* ghetto, which became known as the *"Gehsperre"* deportations between September 3, 1942 and September 12, 1942. These *"Aktionen"* were aimed at the elderly and the children, aiming to turn the *Litzmannstadt* ghetto into a labor camp.

Dawid Sierakowiak, a Jewish resident of the ghetto kept a diary, which was discovered by a Polish gentile Waclaw Szkudlarek in an apartment in Łódź, after the city was liberated. Dawid Sierakowiak died in August 1943. The ghetto hospitals were the first to be targeted by the Germans and Dawid described what took place, in his diary:

Tuesday, September 1
In the morning, the areas around the hospitals were surrounded by guards. All the sick without exception were loaded on trucks and taken out of the ghetto. There was a terrible panic, because it's no secret, thanks to people who've recently come from the provinces, how the German's "take care" of such evacuees.
Hellish scenes occurred during the moving of the sick. People knew they were going to their death! They fought the Germans, and were thrown onto the trucks by force. In the meantime, a good many of the sick escaped from the hospitals which the Germans got to a little later. It's said that even the sick in the Marysin preventorium were shipped out. In our office nobody could think about work—I'm now in an office which distributes payments to the families of people working in Germany. It seems no work was done in other offices and factories either. People are fearing for their children and for the elderly who aren't working.

Wednesday, September 2
Having discovered that many of the sick escaped, the Germans are demanding they be brought back. On the basis of hospital records, the homes of the escapees' relatives have been searched and the sick

---

[107] P. Montague, *Chełmno and the Holocaust*, I.B. Tauris and Co. Ltd, London 2012, pp. 138–139.

captured. On this occasion, the Jewish police committed a crime unlike anything it seems to me, committed previously in the ghetto.

Thursday, September 3
It seems the Germans have asked that all children up to the age of 10 be delivered, most probably to be murdered. The situation resembles what happened in all the surrounding small towns prior to deportations and differs only in the precision and subtlety which prevails here. There everything was sudden and unexpected.[108]

On September 4, 1942, at 4 o'clock p.m, Rumkowski and Warszawski, the head of many factories, spoke at 13 Lutomierska Street, where they said sacrificing the children and elderly is necessary, according to the entry in Dawid Sierakowiak's diary.[109]

Extracts from the Speech by Chaim Rumkowski, the Eldest of the Jews, Litzmannstadt Ghetto

A grievous blow has struck the ghetto. They are asking us to give up the best we possess—the children and the elderly. I was unworthy of having a child of my own, so I gave the best years of my life to children. I've lived and breathed with children. I never imagined I would be forced to deliver this sacrifice to the altar with my own hands. In my old age I must stretch out my hands and beg: Brothers and sisters—hand them over to me! Fathers and mothers, give me your children!
The taking of the sick from the hospitals caught me completely by surprise. And I give you the best proof there is of this: I had my own nearest and dearest among them, and I could do nothing for them.... Yesterday afternoon, they gave me the order to send more than 20,000 Jews out of the ghetto, and if not—"We will do it!" So, the question became: "Should we take it upon ourselves, do it ourselves, or leave it for others to do?" Well, we—that is, I and my closest associates—thought first not about, "How many will perish?" but "How many is it possible to save?" And we reached the conclusion that, however hard it would be for us, we should take the implementation of this order into our own hands. I must

---

[108] A. Adelson and R. Lapides, *Łódź Ghetto*, Viking Penguin London and New York, 1989, pp. 319–320.
[109] Ibid., p. 332.

perform this difficult and bloody operation—I must cut off limbs in order to save the body itself—I must take children because, if not, others may be taken as well, God forbid.

I have no thought of consoling you today. Nor do I wish to calm you. I must lay bare your full anguish and pain. I come to you like a bandit, to take from you what you treasure most in your hearts! I have tried, using every possible means, to get the order revoked. I tried—when that proved to be impossible—to soften the order. Just yesterday I ordered a list of children aged nine—I wanted, at least, to save this one age group, the nine to ten year-olds. But I was not granted this concession. On only one point did I succeed in saving the ten-year olds, and up! Let this be a consolation in our profound grief.

I understand you, mothers; I see your tears, all right. I also feel what you feel in your hearts, you fathers who will have to go to work the morning after your children have been taken from you, when just yesterday you were playing with your dear little ones. All this I know and feel. Since four o'clock yesterday, when I first found out about this order, I have been utterly broken. I share your pain. I suffer because of your anguish, and I don't know how I'll survive this—where I'll find the strength to do so.

I must tell you a secret: they requested 24,000 victims, 3,000 a day for eight days. I succeeded in reducing the number to 20,000, but only on condition that these would be children below the age of ten. Children ten and over are safe. Since the children and aged together equal only some 13,000 souls, the gap will have to be filled with the sick.

One needs the heart of a bandit, to ask from you what I am asking. But put yourself in my place, think logically, and you'll reach the conclusion that I cannot proceed any other way. The part that can be saved is much larger than the part that must be given away.[110]

Another eyewitness to the deportations from Łódź was Paul Beder and he provided a post-war statement at the former Belsen Concentration Camp, in Germany, on January 2, 1946:

> I was taken to the Łódź ghetto in March 1940 because I am a Jew and had to live at Wolborska 25 until August 1944. I was then sent to Auschwitz for three weeks and from there, to the Dora Concentration Camp near Nordhausen. At the end of March 1945, I was transferred to Belsen where I was liberated by the British, on 15 April 1945.

---

[110] A. Adelson and R. Lapides, *Łódź Ghetto*, Viking Penguin London and New York, 1989, pp. 328–331.

On 31 December 1945, I was taken to the Belsen Detention Cells, where during an identification parade consisting of five men, I picked out the man referred to in my deposition as Seifert. He was in charge of the administration of the ghetto in Łódź.

I was employed by the Food Office at the ghetto and so often came into contact with Seifert. I know that he was largely responsible for the appalling conditions in the ghetto and especially for the inadequate rations and feeding arrangements which must have been the direct cause of the death of many thousands of the ghetto inmates.

Between 1942 and 1944, when the ghetto was finally dissolved many different transports of men, women and children were sent away for extermination. Since on such occasions I was always employed on loading the victims on to the Lorries, I saw Seifert take an active part in the selections. The people had to come downstairs and line up in front of Seifert who made some stand to one side. These people were then loaded on to the lorries and never seen or heard of again.

In September 1942, I was present when Seifert selected my four sisters, Mala Beder, Regina Beder, Ibka Beder, Sala Beder and my brother Schimson Beder, all Polish Jews, outside Wolborska 25, to be taken away with a transport that left Łódź for extermination. He also included an old friend of mine the Polish Jewess Friedman, who lived at Wolborska 25. They were made to mount the waiting trucks together with many others who had been selected by Seifert and that was the last I ever saw or heard of them.

During the round up for this extermination transport in September 1942, I was again employed on loading the people who had been selected on to the Lorries. I naturally tried to make them as comfortable as possible and so told them to sit as closely as feasible. Seifert supervised the loading and when he noticed what I was doing, came up to me and said, "Dont'make such a fuss with these creatures, just pile them on, one on top of the other and when the Lorry is filled, get up and jump on their bodies in order to make room for some more." When I would not do so, Seifert drew his pistol and threatened to shoot me for disobeying his order.

During the same round up in September 1942, I remember on one occasion our Lorries drew up outside the Hospital in the *Drewnowska Strasse*. Seifert was with us at the time and as we arrived there were a number of people in the streets nearby. No one was supposed to be out and when Seifert saw the people he drew his revolver and fired at them. I saw him hit a boy of about 16, who fell to the ground, screaming loudly. Seifert thereupon went up to him and I saw him fire three shots into the boy's head. The boy did not move again......

> During the round up in September 1942, near the hospital in the *Drewnowska Strasse*, a man and a woman, aged approximately 45 and 35 respectively, tried to escape from the transport that was just being made up. They were just trying to climb over a fence when Biebow arrived in his car. He saw them and drove his car up to them. I saw him take them to a nearby potato field and there he made them kneel down facing each other very closely, so that their faces touched. He then went behind the woman, drew his revolver and shot her through the back of her neck. The bullet must have penetrated her neck and then struck the man, because they both collapsed and did not move again.[111]

Over the course of the period September 1 to September 12, 1942, some 15,685 Jews were deported from the *Litzmannstadt* ghetto to the death camp at Chełmno. A final transport of 6,000 Jews was deported from Zelów to Chełmno, on September 14, 1942.[112]

The Commandant's Office in Auschwitz received written authorization on September 15, 1942, from Richard Glücks, the Head of Branch D of the *WVHA* for a trip by car to Łódź in the *Warthegau*, dated September 16, 1942. The purpose of the trip was to inspect an experimental facility of "field ovens" to be used in connection with *"Aktion Reinhardt."* The following day Commandant Rudolf Höss, *SS-Untersturmführer* Franz Hössler and *SS-Hauptsturmführer* Walter Dejaco visited the extermination facility at Chełmno on the River Ner, and witnessed the methods being tested by *SS-Standartenführer* Paul Blobel. Rudolf Höss in his memoirs recalled their visit to the camp:

> Hössler and I went to *Kulmhof* on a tour of inspection. Blobel had various makeshift ovens constructed, which were fired with wood and petrol refuse. He had also attempted to dispose of the bodies with explosives, but their destruction had been very incomplete. The ashes were distributed over the neighbouring countryside, after first being ground to a powder in a bone mill.
> On my visit to *Kulmhof*, I was also shown the extermination apparatus constructed out of Lorries, which had been designed to kill by using the exhaust gases from the engines. The officer in charge there, however,

---

[111] National Archives Kew, WO 311/1326/1.
[112] P. Montague, *Chełmno and the Holocaust*, I.B. Tauris and Co. Ltd, London 2012, p. 118.

described this method as being extremely unreliable, for the density of gas varied considerably and was often insufficient to be lethal. How many bodies lay in the mass graves at *Kulmhof*, or how many had already been cremated, I was unable to ascertain.[113]

Commandant Rudolf Höss returned to Auschwitz following this inspection and copied Blobel's method of burning the corpses in the open air, used at Chełmno. The camp authorities disposed of the corpses buried in Birkenau, under the supervision of *SS-Untersturmführer* Franz Hössler, without delay.

Following the visit of Rudolf Höss, two new ovens were constructed under the supervision of *SS-Hauptsturmführer* Johannes Runge. He obtained 60,000 bricks from the firm of Freudenreich in *Warthbrücken*. Runge's superiors were so pleased with his efforts in building the two ovens; Runge was awarded the War Services Cross, for his efforts, according to one of his colleagues.[114]

On September 19, 1942, one of the members of the Polish *Arbeitskommando*, Stanisław Szymanski was taken to Hans Bothmann's office and interrogated with regard to stealing jewellery from the Jewish victims. He was probably shot in the forest.[115]

---

[113] KL Auschwitz, *Seen By the SS*, Auschwitz Museum 1978, pp. 116–117.
[114] P. Montague, *Chełmno and the Holocaust*, I.B. Tauris and Co. Ltd, London 2012, p. 116.
[115] Ibid., p. 144.

Chapter VIII
October 1942–April 1943
End of the First Phase

From October onwards the transports of Jews to Chełmno ceased and the main focus of the camp was the exhumation and cremations in the Rzuchówski forest camp, and this continued for months. During October 1942, the *Sonderkommando* vacated the *gmina* building in Chełmno was handed back to the community, to be used as a school, but this was short-lived as the German school was closed down and relocated to Rzuchów.[116]

Erhard Michelsohn, the schoolteacher in the German school in Chełmno recalled that in October 1942, the school was closed down:

> The school was closed down due to a regulation of the District Administrator of Konin County, Becht. I received the decision on paper from my school inspector, who had his seat in Koło. Then I became a schoolteacher in *Schuchen*.
> When I used to teach in the old school in Chełmno, situated opposite the SS commandant's quarters, I noticed that Bothmann together with his fellows engaged themselves in orgies with German girls and women on a daily basis. As far as I know, the females were usually nurses from the hospital in Koło.
> Bothmann used to throw them out of the quarters building in the morning. They lay on the ground, drunk and naked. The school children watched this all. In response to the situation, I made a complaint to the inspector. As a result, the school was first moved to another location and then closed down. I remember that Bothmann came to me at that time and said that I would have to close the school down.[117]

On November 2, 1942, an invoice for a *Dieselmotor* purchased by the *SS-Sonderkommando Kulmhof*, was raised by the firm Motoren-Heyne in Leipzig. This document is shown below:

---

[116] Krystof Gorczyca, Zdzisław Lorek, *Day After Day in the extermination camp Kulmhof am Ner* – unpublished draft, p. 111.
[117] *Chełmno Witnesses Speak*, Konin – Łódź 2004, p. 201.

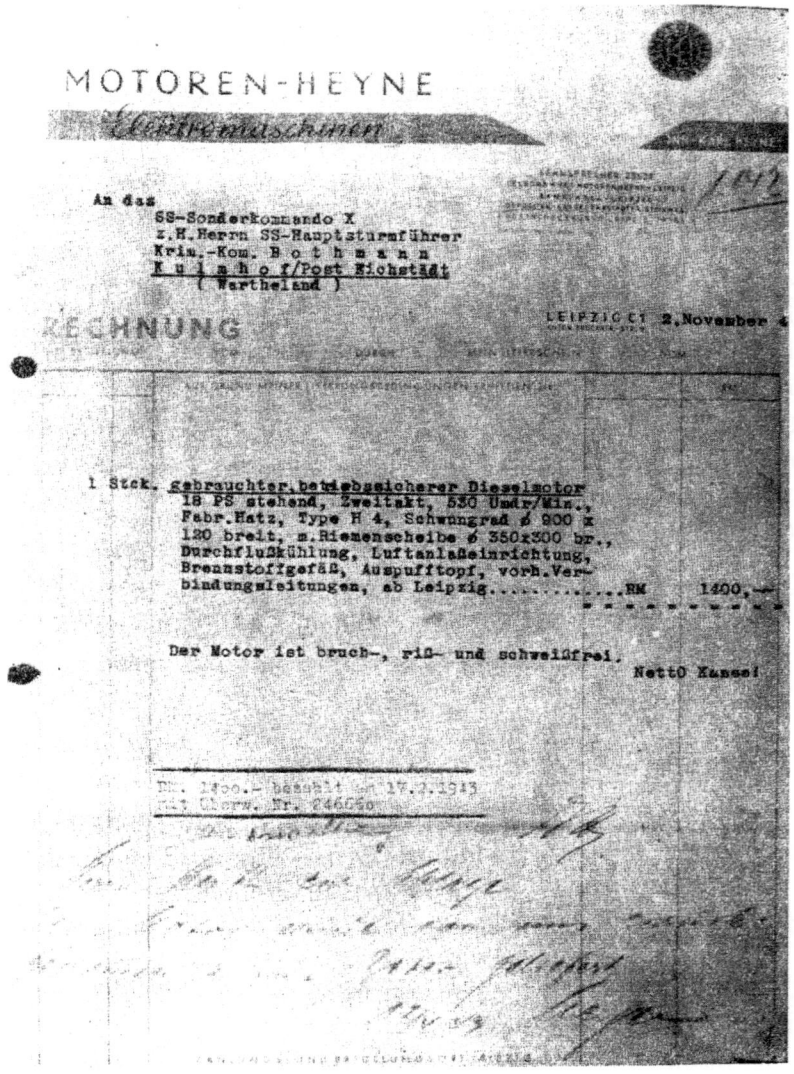

Doc. 1   Invoice for Diesel Motor—Motoren Heyne

A telegram sent by Abraham Stupp, Tel Aviv to Tartalower Miller at the Jewish World Congress in New York, United States of America on December 4, 1942, mentioned Chełmno, although incorrectly called it "Chelmna", among other places of horror, where the Jews were being exterminated. The telegram read as follows:

From part Poland annexed Germany deportations started January 1942. Jews sent village Chelmna. There murdered as follows; taken to barn and ordered "undress" then truck with specially built iron superstructure brought close barn door. People packed into—then truck hermetically closed driven neighbouring wood—there common graves dug; truck brought edge of pit and opened—dead bodies fell into pit arranged layers and poured upon lime and sand. Stop.[118]

In early 1943, a detailed report on the Chełmno death camp was published by the Jewish Frontier Association based in New York. The publication was titled, "The Massacre of a People" and this article has been reproduced in full and can be found in Appendix IV.[119]

Another invoice on February 3, 1943, was sent by *SS-Standartenführer* Blobel to the *Ghettoverwaltung* in *Litzmannstadt*, this time for *RM* 1,400, payable to the firm Motoren-Heyne in Leipzig. This document is shown below:

Doc. 2   Invoice to Paul Blobel re Diesel Motor from Motoren Heyne

---

[118] National Archives Kew, FO 371/ 30924.
[119] Wiener Library – OSP 2176.

Theodor Malzmüller, one of the policemen of the *Sonderkommando Kulmhof* recalled that:

> On March 5, 1943, *Gauleiter* Arthur Greiser arrived in Chełmno, along with fifteen high ranking SS officers, and the members of *Sonderkommando Kulmhof* were ordered to assemble in the courtyard of the mansion. Greiser thanked those assembled, "In the Name of the *Führer*," for the work they had done at Chełmno. He told them that the camp would shortly be dismantled. He also granted members of the camp with a reward of four weeks leave on one of his estates. Everyone assembled was invited to a "fellowship evening" in *Warthbrücken*.
> This "fellowship evening" party was held in the Riga restaurant in *Warthbrücken*, which was located at *Baltenstrasse 6*. Speeches followed dinner, given by Greiser and the Commandant Bothmann. Also in attendance was Dr. Otto Bradfisch, the head of the Łódź *Gestapo*. One of the *Sonderkommando* members Alois Häfele was personally promoted by Greiser to the rank of *Revierleutnant*. The party ended in the early morning hours.[120]

Gauleiter Greiser was so impressed with the *Sonderkommando Kulmhof's* personnel that he wrote to Heinrich Himmler, *Reichsführer-SS* on March 19, 1943:

> *Reichsführer*
> A few days ago I visited Lange's former *Sonderkommando*, which today is under the command of *SS-Hauptsturmführer, Kriminalkommissar* Bothmann and stationed in *Kulmhof, Kreis Warthbrücken,* until the end of the month.
> During my visit I was so struck by the conduct of the men of the *Sonderkommando* that I would not like to fail to bring it to your attention. The men have not only fulfilled the difficult task that has been set for them loyally, bravely, and in all respects appropriately, but also their soldierly conduct is exemplary.
> For example during a social evening to which I had invited them they gave me a contribution of 15,150 *RM* in cash which they had that day collected spontaneously. That means that each of these eighty-five men in the *Sonderkommando* had contributed about 180 *RM*. I have given instructions for the money to be put in the fund set up for the children of murdered ethnic Germans, unless you, *Reichsführer*, wish it to be put to another or better use.

---

[120] P. Montague, *Chełmno and the Holocaust*, I.B. Tauris and Co. Ltd, London 2012, p. 143.

The men further expressed the wish that all of them, if possible, be put under the command of their *Hauptsturmführer* Bothmann when they are transferred to their new assignment. I promised the men that I would communicate this wish to you, *Reichsführer*.

I should be grateful if you would give me permission to invite some of these men to be my guests on my country estate during their leave and to give them a generous allowance to make their leave more enjoyable.

Heil Hitler
(Signed) Greiser[121]

Theodor Malzmüller remembered that:

> A few days after Greiser's farewell party all members of the *SS-Sonderkommando* and the police guards received four weeks of special leave. Only a few members of the *SS-Sonderkommando* stayed behind in *Kulmhof.* One of these was *Polizei-Meister* Lenz. Then everybody had to report to *SS-Obergruppenführer* Kaltenbrunner, at State Security headquarters in Berlin on a particular day. He addressed us all and we were once again thanked on behalf of the *Führer* for our work in *Kulmhof.*
>
> We were then all detailed together to Yugoslavia to *SS*-Division Prinz Eugen, under the command of Bothmann. Here we were deployed against partisans in Yugoslavia and suffered very heavy losses. As far as I can recall, *SS-Untersturmführer* Plate committed suicide in Serbia, after being severely wounded. In the middle of 1944, some of those former members of the *SS-Sonderkommando* who were still alive were withdrawn from the *SS*-Division and sent back to *Kulmhof* to start up the extermination camp again.[122]

The Jewish craftsmen wrote another note to the outside world on April 2, 1943, which was found in the laundry in Pabiance, near Łódź, where warehouses for old clothes had been established. The note read:

April 2, 1943

> This card is written by people who have only several hours to live. Whoever reads this will find it difficult to believe whether it is the truth or not. But this is the tragic truth, for in this town are your brothers and

---

[121] Klee, Dressen, Riess, *Those Were The Days*, Hamish Hamilton, London 1991, pp. 222–223.
[122] Ibid., p. 219.

sisters who also died the same way. It is a place called Koło. This "human slaughterhouse" is located 12 kilometres from this town. We worked as craftsmen. Among others, there were tailors, leather workers, and shoemakers. There were seventeen craftsmen and so I give you the names of these people.
1. Pinkus Grün from Włocławek
2. Jonas Lew from Brzeziny
3. Ika Szama from Brzeziny
4. Zemad Szumiraj from Włocławek
5. Geszyp Majer from Kalisz
6. Symcha Wachtel from Łęczyca
7. Smlek Wachtel from Łęczyca
8. Beniek Jastrzebski from Łęczyca
9. Aron Nusbaum from Skępe
10. Iser Strasburg from Lutomiersk
11. Moniek Plocker from Kutno
12. Felek Plocker from Kutno
13. Josef Herszkowicz from Kutno
14. Chaskiel Zarak from Łęczyca
15. Wolf Judkiewicz from Łódź
16. Szyja Szlamowicz from Kalisz
17. Gecel from Turek
So these are the names, these are the people whom I list here. They are individuals from among the hundreds of thousands who died here.[123]

The Jewish work squads, including the craftsmen, mentioned above, who were incarcerated in the basement of the mansion were killed by being shot by Albert Plate. The final group of Jewish workers were buried by the Polish *Arbeitskommando*, according to Henryk Maliczak. When the camp was liquidated the surviving 6 members of this Polish group returned to Fort VII in *Posen*.

The fence around the mansion grounds was dismantled and removed and in the mansion itself all traces of the death camp were also removed. Gustav Laabs and Oskar Hering drove the *Sonderwagen* to the train station in *Warthbrücken*, where Burmeister and Bürstinger loaded them on a train.

---

[123] P. Montague, *Chełmno and the Holocaust*, I.B. Tauris and Co. Ltd, London 2012, p. 84.

At about noon on April 7, 1943, *SS-Standartenführer* Paul Blobel, who had returned to *Kulmhof* and with explosives, blew up the mansion, in order to eradicate all traces of the crimes that had been committed there. That same evening Fritz Herkner, the administrator of the Powiercie estate arrived at the mansion with a group of workers. They dismantled the structure and salvaged what they could from the smouldering ruins.

They removed ten wagons full of wood and then bricks, bowls, tools and chains. Everything was taken to the estate in Powiercie. Inside the granary, which was not destroyed, the upper floor was full of clothes and shoes, which also were taken to Powiercie for distribution to the local residents.

A small detachment of Police was assigned to guard the *Waldlager*, and on April 11, 1943, the remaining members of *Sonderkommando Kulmhof* left in trucks and returned to their former police locations.[124]

The first stage in the history of the Chełmno death camp had come to an end.

---

[124] Ibid., pp. 144–145.

Chapter IX
The Second Phase
February 1944–July 1944
The Waldlager Re-Established

Heinrich Himmler –*RFSS* visited Arthur Greiser in *Posen* on February 13 and 14, 1944, where he discussed that the *Litzmannstadt* ghetto would not be transformed into a concentration camp, and that the *Sonderkommando Kulmhof* under *SS-Hauptsturmführer* Bothmann would be re-established. Arthur Greiser wrote to *SS-Gruppenführer* Oswald Pohl, the head of the *SS-Wirtschafts- und Verwaltungshauptamt (WVHA)*, the following day[125]:

Posen, February 14, 1944
Top Secret

Dear Party Comrade Pohl,
On the occasion of the *Reichsführer's* visit to *Posen* yesterday and today, I had the opportunity to discuss and clear up two issues concerning your sphere of activity. The first issue is this:
The ghetto in *Litzmannstadt* is not to be transformed into a concentration camp, as was pointed out by *Oberführer* Beier and *Hauptsturmführer* Dr. Volk, who were sent to my *Gau* by your office. Their discussion took place in my office, in the *Reichsstatthalter* in *Posen*, on February 5. The decree issued by the *Reichsführer* on June 11, 1943, will therefore not be carried out. I have arranged the following with the *Reichsführer*:
(a) The ghetto's manpower will be reduced to a minimum and retain only as many Jews as are essential to the war economy.
(b) The ghetto therefore remains a *Gau* ghetto of the *Wartheland*.
(c) The reduction will be carried out by *Hauptsturmführer* Bothmann's special *Sonderkommando*, which has already had prior experience in the *Gau*. The *Reichsführer* will give orders to withdraw *Hauptsturmführer* Bothmann and his *Sonderkommando* from his mission in Croatia and again place him at the disposal of the *Wartheland*.

---

[125]   P. Montague, *Chełmno and the Holocaust*, I.B. Tauris and Co. Ltd, London 2012, p. 150.

(d) The utilization and administration of the contents of the ghetto remains in the hands of the *Wartheland*.
(e) After all Jews are removed from the ghetto and it is liquidated, the entire grounds of the ghetto are to go to the town of *Litzmannstadt*. The *Reichsführer* will then give appropriate instructions to the Main Trustee Office East (*Haupttreuhandstelle Ost*).
May I ask you to send me your suggestions in this matter as soon as possible.

With comradely greetings and *Heil Hitler*
Yours
Greiser

SS-Hauptsturmführer Bothmann assembled most of the members of the former *Sonderkommando Kulmhof* in Croatia. Bothmann told them that *Kulmhof* would once again be involved in the extermination of Jews. They travelled to *Posen*, via Berlin, and from there went by train to Koło, and the final leg of their journey was by truck to Chełmno.

It would appear that the *Sonderkommando* members arrived back in Chełmno sometime during March 1944. Stanisław Rubach, a journalist from the nearby town of Kościelec recorded that:

> March 19, 1944, after a year-long break, the news is circulating about the resumption of the camp in Chełmno. Basic preparations at the old granary on the estate are in full swing; it's being fenced. The people living in the houses nearby were removed. There are already more than 100 of the butchers in the village.[126]

Among the 100 plus butchers who formed part of the *SS-Sonderkommando Kulmhof*, the following personnel and the duties they performed were as follows:

---

[126] P. Montague, *Chełmno and the Holocaust*, I.B. Tauris and Co. Ltd, London 2012, p. 151.

Name	Rank	Role in Kulmhof
Hans Bothmann	*Hauptsturmführer*	Commandant
Walter Burmeister	*Unterscharführer*	Adjutant and Driver to Bothmann
Herbert Hiecke-Richter	*Hauptscharführer*	Valuables
Wilhelm Görlich	*Hauptscharführer*	Administration
Erwin Bürstinger	*Hauptscharführer*	Motor Pool
Gustav Laabs	*Hauptscharführer*	Gas Van Driver
Erwin Schmidt	*Hauptscharführer*	Canteen and Provisions
Johannes Runge	*Hauptscharführer*	Crematorium Supervisor
Erich Kretschmer	*Unterscharführer*	Crematorium Supervisor
Max Sommer	*Unterscharführer*	Assistant to Görlich
Alois Häfele	*Sturmscharführer*	Jewish Workers
Willi Lenz	*Polizeimeister*	Forest Camp Supervisor
Walter Piller	*Oberscharführer*	Deputy Commandant
Hermann Gielow	*Hauptscharführer*	Driver
Ernst Thiele	*Hauptscharführer*	Driver
Stefan Seidenglanz	*Scharführer*	Driver

Walter Piller, Hermann Gielow, Ernst Thiele and Ernst Burmeister all served in the so-called *Wetterkommando Legath*. Walter Piller testified after the war concerning his activities in this particular *"Kommando,"* which was commanded by *SS-Hauptsturmführer* Hans Legath, who was about thirty-five years of age and hailed from Munich:

> After the closure of the *Gestapo* offices in Inowrocław on November 1, 1943, due to the shortage of officers, I was transferred to the *Gestapo* post in Łódź. However, I did not begin my service until the middle of 1944,

because before that I was delegated to the *Wetterkommando* Legath, under the command of *Kriminal-Kommissar* and *SS-Hauptsturmführer* Hans Legath. He supervised Department IV H of the then-*Gestapo* station in Inowrocław. The department dealt with those party members in the Warta District who got rich through war speculation and corruption. All the members of the *Wetterkommando* Legath were ordered to assemble in Inowrocław, in the hall of the local *Gestapo* station, where *Kriminal-Kommissar* and *SS-Hauptsturmführer* Legath informed us of the nature of the work. All corpses of Polish citizens executed by firing squads and buried in the forests in the territory of the *Gestapo* headquarters in *Posen*, had to be dug up and cremated at the site. The ashes were ground on metal sheets into powder and some of it was used as a fertilizer in the VII Fort in Poznań; later the ashes were thrown into the flowing water so that all the traces of this work could be obliterated.

The opening of the graves and the pulling out of the corpses was done by Jews from the Łódź ghetto. This ghetto unit consisted of thirty people. Only strong individuals were selected to the unit twice (with ten new Jews each time), as some died on the job, while several others who could not, or did not want to perform the job were shot dead *by Kriminal-Sekretär* Michaelis or Schmerse, and in one case by me.

Execution orders were handed down by the unit commander..... these tasks were assigned to the expert, *Polizeimeister* Lenz. First he had to acquire the necessary equipment: shovels, pickaxes, metal sheets and together with the unit commandant, wood from the forest administration. After the equipment had been prepared, the work began. Apart from Lenz, all the officers were doing the job for the first time.

The individual graves where the executed Poles were buried were referred to as *Wetterstationen* (meteorological stations) and were all located within the jurisdiction of the *Gestapo* headquarters in Poznań, as well as the post in Inowrocław. As far as I can remember, the focus was on the following graves: Gniewkowo, near Inowrocław, the area around Strzelno, Gniezno, Oborniki, Szamotuły, Chodzież, Żnin, Międzychód, Leszno, Wągrowiec, Szubin, Kościan and a few others in the forests in the vicinity of Poznań.

The whole unit was lodged in hotels in the neighbouring towns or villages, in the meeting halls of inns, as well as in barracks and service buildings. The Jewish labor unit was housed in a temporary camp in Inowrocław and in Fort VII in Poznań. In other towns, they were transported to the prisons of the provincial courts. We organized food supplies outside the prisons and paid for them ourselves. During the day they got bread and coffee and additionally artificial honey, marmalade, and margarine. We had to supply our food ourselves. We received 15

Reich Marks and 10 cigarettes a day and three-quarters of a litre of vodka every ten days. We had to pay for the cigarettes, but the vodka and 15 *RM* came as a bonus in addition to our salaries. The *Wetterkommando* units from the *Gestapo* posts in Łódź and Ciechanów were provided for in the same way. The commandant of the *Wetterkommando* unit in Łódź was *SS-Hauptsturmführer* Fuchs. I do not know the other offices of these units and I cannot provide any information concerning them.

Walter Piller continued his testimony:

So now I will move onto the actual activities of the units. The graves at the execution site, over the three-and-a-half years, from 1939 to 1943, had collapsed. That meant they were visible to people. If there were any doubts, an iron rod was poked into the ground and it was determined that the graves were located in places where the earth gave way. The Jews dug up the graves—these were mass graves for 30–40 corpses and when the first layers of corpses were uncovered, they were pulled out with hooks (iron rods bent into a semi-circle at one end) until the grave was completely empty. Finally, the remaining bones and clothes were carefully picked out and the pit was filled in again with the same sand. They were covered with pieces of turf, so it was impossible to determine where the pit was located.

The *Schutzpolizei* unit under the command of *Polizeileutnant* Burmeister[127] was responsible for securing the site against intruders. Four helpers were assigned to the unit: Poles who were called "buddies," who had the right to inspect the graves from a close proximity. These Poles were with the *SS-Sonderkommando* Bothmann—earlier the *SS-Sonderkommando* Lange—as early as 1942 and they performed the same roles. I only know one by the last name. The first one was Keiteck. The next one was called Leo, another Heinrich (Henryk) and the fourth, Mania.[128] These so-called "buddies" helped dig up the pits and they knew the forests very well. Without these four Poles, graves rarely would have been found. Poles were also responsible for supervising the Jews and providing supplies. Their orders had to be obeyed.

Our task was to prevent any escape attempts. Furthermore, we were supposed to make sure, under order of the *Gestapo*, that the Jews were not beaten. The order given in connection with the whole campaign was handed down by the then *Reichsführer-SS* Himmler and had to be strictly obeyed. Such offences did not take place. Only *Polizeimeister*

---

[127] Ernst Burmeister was his full name.
[128] The four Polish members were Lech Jaskolski, Henryk Maliczak, Henry Mania and Kajtean Skrypczynski.

Lenz hit one Jew or another while they were burning the corpses; however, in such cases he was instantly reprimanded by commanding officer Legath. As soon as the corpses had been exhumed, they were thoroughly cremated under Lenz's supervision. If necessary, the area around the pit was cleared off and covered with iron sheets. As soon as the fire was lit, dead bodies were thrown into the pit and burned.

My responsibility in this unit was to secure ahead of time the sleeping quarters in the next town for the commander and the personnel, as well as for the Jewish brigade in prisons of the provincial courts that would be needed once the work came to an end in one place. There were difficulties involved in emptying out the accommodations I urgently needed for the *Wetterkommando* because in that period of time deportees from the Ukraine, Volhynia, and the Baltic States were being settled in the Warta District. In most cases I had to deal with the mayors and party officers. When everything was settled, I went back to the work site and reported the outcome to the commander. From then on, the sites were dealt with one after another until the objective was completed.

From November 1943 to mid-1944, on estimate 1200–1400 corpses were cremated in this way. I cannot cite the exact number, because the register was kept only by *Kriminal-Kommissar* Legath and I had no right to examine it. It is possible that Michaelis,[129] being his deputy, had more information. I remember exactly that there were 300 corpses buried in the forest near Oborniki. I heard these were patients from a hospital for the mentally ill near Poznań, who had been shot in the back of the head. The rest of the victims were Poles belonging to the Polish National Movement, who during the Polish rule treated *Volksdeutsche* badly......

In conclusion, what I can say about my activity in the unit is that I, like all other *Gestapo* officers, we had to be extremely vigilant in regards to escape attempts. We—Michaelis, Schmerse and I, were constantly reminded that time was of no importance when it came to security measures. Maintaining secrecy was of the most importance, the fast pace of work versus the precision of covering up all evidence. To prevent the Jews from escaping, their legs were shackled in chains the length of one pace. Every now and again the unit was inspected by the head of the *Gestapo* in Poznań, *Oberregierungsrat* and *Obersturmbannführer* Stosberg, as well as by Chief Inspector of the Warta District, *SS-Brigadeführer* Damzog from Poznań.

Both *Kriminal-Sekretär* Schmerse and I were not around to witness the liquidation of the *Wetterkommando* Legath, as we were both sent to the town of Rabka in the *Generalgouvernement*, in order to take a course for

---

[129] Erich Michaelis, *Kriminal-Sekretär* and *SS-Sturmscharführer*.

SS commanding officers. Neither of us completed the course. I returned to Inowrocław, to my family. I went to *Kriminal-Kommissar* Legath to receive my discharge, but he said that first I would have to help him liquidate the unit.

Thus Michaelis, Schmerse and I had to go to Poznań to return the equipment, cars and bedclothes supplied to us by the security police and the police. At the *Gestapo* headquarters in Poznań, I learned that we were to be assigned to the Bothmann *Sonderkommando*, Schmerse, as second-in-command, and I as a member. This may have occurred in the middle of 1944[130]. I cannot recollect the exact date. I was only aware of the fact that the Bothmann *Sonderkommando* was already in Chełmno and I was supposed to get ready to participate in the unknown activities of the unit.

After a one-week vacation, I went to Chełmno with *Kriminal-Sekretär* Schmerse, who held the position of second-in-command and a superior officer for only two days, because he fell ill and went to the hospital in Inowrocław, where he had to undergo stomach surgery. Since among all the unit officers, I held the highest rank after Schmerse, I was appointed by *SS-Hauptsturmführer* Bothmann as his deputy. This unit lasted until the first days of February 1945.[131]

Other members of the *Wetterkommando* Legath apart from Piller and Schmerse were also transferred to the *Sonderkommando* Bothmann in Chełmno. These included *SS-Hauptscharführer* Ernst Thiele, who was a driver, and *SS-Hauptscharführer* Hermann Gielow, Ernst Burmeister a *Polizeileutnant* and *Polizeimeister* Willi Lenz, who of course had already served at Chełmno, during the first phase.[132]

SS-Hauptscharführer Gustav Laabs recalled the *Sonderkommando's* return to Chełmno:

> In Chełmno we returned to our old quarters in the village houses. On the days that followed I had no work at all nor was I given any. As far as I remember, nothing had been built or started in the village, including

---

[130] Rudolf Kramp testified that he met Piller, Görlich and others in Chełmno during April 1944, so it would appear that Piller and others were in Chełmno earlier than mid-1944.
[131] *Chełmno Witnesses Speak*, Konin – Łódź 2004, pp. 172–176.
[132] Ibid., pp. 172–173.

the area of the former mansion. After a short time Hering[133] and I were ordered by Bothmann to go to the railroad station in Koło and pick up the two gas vans. Walter Burmeister drove us by car to the Koło train station where the two gas vans stood on a freight train. In my opinion, they were the same gas vans which we had driven during 1942 to 1943. We brought the vans to Chełmno and parked them on the grounds of the former mansion.[134]

As the *Waldlager* needed to be re-established, Rudolf Kramp, from the *Litzmannstadt* ghetto administrator was one of the people that delivered supplies and building material to the Chełmno death camp and he recalled after the war:

> In March 1944, I delivered furniture to Chełmno, which I unloaded in front of the staff building. Several days later, I delivered cement, which I unloaded next to the granary on the grounds of the former mansion. Burmeister, Richter and Runge took the cement from me. At this time, there were no Jewish workers in Chełmno. They carried the cement themselves. The area of the mansion was not fenced. There were no sentries.
> Several days later, I delivered more furniture. Altogether, at this time, I made about six trips. Besides me, Oswald Gossele also drove to Chełmno. I saw that barracks were being built and that the terrain was being fenced in. I delivered boards several times. The fence was being built by the SS men. At the end of April, Jewish workers were brought to Chełmno. Tusst and Schwind from the *Gestapo* brought them.
> About this same time I brought a load of iron rails and thick sheet iron. I believe this was at the end of April 1944. Policemen and SS men were brought in to supplement the *Sonderkommando*. At this time, other than Bothmann, I met Piller, Bothmann's deputy, Richter, Runge, Schmidt, Görlich, Lenz, Sommer, Laabs, Bürstinger and two others from Łódź.[135]

Members of the *Sonderkommando* enclosed the grounds of the former mansion with a barbed wire fence complete with warning signs that the fence was charged with electric current, but this was not the case. The Granary building was also enclosed by a barbed wire fence.

---

[133] Hering did not return in 1944 from fighting the partisans in Croatia.
[134] P. Montague, *Chełmno and the Holocaust*, I.B. Tauris and Co. Ltd, London 2012, p. 154.
[135] P. Montague, *Chełmno and the Holocaust*, I.B. Tauris and Co. Ltd, London 2012, p. 152.

The Granary was where the Jewish craftsmen were quartered. This contingent of specialized workers consisted of fifteen tailors and five shoemakers, who worked for the Germans.

Next to the Granary a large wooden barrack was erected, it had two rooms; the first room was lined with shelves and was a storeroom for items confiscated from the victims, whilst the other room was used as an office by Walter Burmeister. A shredding machine was brought from the *Litzmannstadt* ghetto, and this was positioned on the side of the barrack facing the Ner River, on a 3-by-5 meter platform. The shredding machine was used to shred low-quality clothing, which after shredding was packed and sent to the *Litzmannstadt* ghetto.[136]

Walter Piller testified about the Granary and the activities in the former mansion courtyard:

> Craftsmen were located in the upper cell in the form of 15 tailors and 5 shoemakers. The lower cell, which was almost twice as large, held 60–70 Jews who worked in the forest or in the courtyard of the former palace. Later a large tent was located in the yard that was about 80 metres long, 15 metres wide and 8 metres high. The confiscated clothes, which had been examined in the search for valuables were placed in that tent. Jewish stars were ripped off, and if a dark spot remained in their place, these garments along with all others in poor shape were shredded into pieces. The sorting of items and searching for valuables that might be sown in the clothes, was handled by the Jewish unit.
> The unit consisted of 40 or more Jews, aged 17–20. There were a few older men as well, but a significantly lower percent. The shredder came from the ghetto; it was propelled with a steam engine and operated by two Jews. The shredded material was transported to Łódź, while complete garments were allotted for use. But first it was thoroughly searched by the aforementioned unit, which was from time to time checked by *SS* members—Richter and Burmeister.
> The clothes destined for further use were prepared in the following way: the examined pieces were hung in one, and later three enclosed trucks—special vehicles used for gassing, and they remained there for 8–10 hours. To rid the things of vermin and germs, a chemical agent in powder form called "Diamethan" was used, which gave off a thick smoke that killed all vermin. Finally, the clothes were sorted and sent to the

---

[136] Ibid., p. 153.

Nationalsozialistische Volkswohlfahrt (National Socialist Welfare), in Koło, where they were handed out among displaced German persons, while the Poles employed in the construction of the Eastern Wall, who needed clothing, got the worst items.
Dishes were parcelled out in the same way. It needs to be pointed out that every single pair of shoes was torn into pieces in the tent to search for hidden valuables. It often happened that there were hollows in heels where gold necklaces had been hidden. The labour unit working in the palace courtyard was supplied as the need arose with new transports. Such a need arose if someone died or they did not want to work. In the latter case, of those who did not want to work, they were shot by Bothmann and in one case by Bürstinger. As far as I recall, this happened in five or six cases.[137]

Next to the tent, a deep hole was dug, and a fire was kept burning in it to serve as an incinerator for personal papers, documents, photographs that were collected from the victims. One of the first tasks the *Hauskommando* had to deal with was an unpleasant task. Coming from the ruined mansion was a foul stench. In the basement area the *Hauskommando* discovered a number of rotting corpses, which were loaded into a truck, which took the remains to the *Waldlager*, for disposal.[138]

In the *Waldlager*, two wooden barracks were constructed, some distance from the main road. These two barracks served as an undressing barrack and an antechamber to the gas vans. The barracks were approximately 10 meters wide by 20 meters long and stood side by side. They were located near the large field in which the new crematoria were to be erected. There were no windows on the sides facing the field. The barracks were entered through doors on the opposite side from the field. A wooden fence surrounded these two barracks.

The *Waldkommando* began building the two large crematoria, during May 1944, under the supervision of *SS-Hauptscharführer* Johannes Runge. The new ovens were located a couple of meters north of the location of the original ovens constructed in 1942. The foundations of the crematoria were approximately three-and-a-half meters below ground. The walls widened as they approached ground level, reaching dimensions of approximately 17 meters long by 17

---

[137] *Chełmno Witnesses Speak*, Konin – Łódź 2004, pp. 185–186.
[138] P. Montague, *Chełmno and the Holocaust*, I.B. Tauris and Co. Ltd, London 2012, p. 153 and 155.

meters wide. They were made of fireproofed bricks brought from a factory in *Warthbrücken*. The grating was made of railway rails, brought from the *Litzmannstadt* ghetto by Rudolf Kramp.

To ventilate the fire, each oven had air vents on either side. The vents provided a flow of air down into the ash pit. To clean out the oven, the workers had to pass through a chute, about 8 meters long, which led down to the ash pit. The chute was tall enough so that a stooping man could walk through it. The entire apparatus was underground and unlike the first ovens there were no chimneys. When the ovens were not operational they were covered with a roof of pine branches, so they were camouflaged from planes flying overhead.[139]

On May 8, 1944, the commandant of Chełmno, Hans Bothmann stays overnight in Łódź, as a guest of Hans Biebow. A meeting takes place with the *Gestapo* Chief of Łódź, Dr. Otto Bradfisch, with Bothmann and Biebow in attendance.[140]

Ernst Burmeister, *Revierleutnant*, who had served in the *Wetterkommando* Legath and in the police guarding the *Litzmannstadt* ghetto, headed the *Polizeiwachtkommando* in *Kulmhof* until August 1944, when he transferred to Warsaw, along with 40 other policemen, to quell the Warsaw Uprising. He recalled his arrival at the camp, which occurred on May 30, 1944:

> Bothmann assigned us some empty houses in the village as accommodation. Then I asked Bothmann what was going on in *Kulmhof* and what the task of my squad would be. He explained to me that an extermination camp for Jews had been set up near *Kulmhof* in the forest. He and a squad of SS men had just been building several barracks and a crematorium there. When this was completed, transports of Jews would come to *Kulmhof*. These Jews would first be accommodated in the church in the village and then transported to the forest camp and killed there. The corpses would be burnt in the crematorium. My task was merely to secure the entire forest camp from outside. He then ordered me to place sentries around the forest camp.

---

[139] P. Montague, *Chełmno and the Holocaust*, I.B. Tauris and Co. Ltd, London 2012, pp. 155–156.

[140] Krystof Gorczyca, Zdzisław Lorek, *Day After Day in the extermination camp Kulmhof am Ner* – unpublished draft, p. 130.

On the first day in *Kulmhof*, Bothmann drove me to the so-called forest camp. Two barracks and a crematorium were constructed in a clearing. The clearing was about 120 metres long and 80 metres wide. Bothmann told me to place a line of sentries around the camp and I did so. Later when the actual extermination of the Jews was being carried out, he told me that more sentries would have to be placed inside the forest camp. After about 14 days or three weeks, the forest camp was ready and the first transports of Jews arrived.[141]

On June 23, 1944, the first of ten transports left the *Litzmannstadt* ghetto bound for *Kulmhof*, this resettlement *"Aktion"* lasted until July 14, 1944, and some 7,186 Jews perished in the death camp. Ernst Burmeister, *Revierleutnant*, recalled the arrival of the first transport of Jews from *Litzmannstadt* to arrive at the railroad station in Koło, in this second phase of the camps existence:

> Train transports with Jews arrived at the railway station in *Warthbrücken* (Koło). There the Jews had to change to the narrow gauge track which went to *Kulmhof*. When the first transport arrived in *Warthbrücken*, Bothmann told me to accompany him and guard this transport of Jews from *Warthbrücken* to *Kulmhof*, with about 20 policemen from my squad. Bothmann himself drove me and the squad to *Warthbrücken*. As we arrived, a transport with about 500 to 600 Jews arrived. It was accompanied by a police squad under the command of a police officer. Bothmann took over this transport from the police officer, and afterwards, under the command of Bothmann, we took the Jewish people by the narrow gauge train to *Kulmhof*, where they were accommodated in the village church. Then I had to assign sentries to guard the church.[142]

Ernst Burmeister continued with his account into what happened next to the deportees from *Litzmannstadt:*

> The next morning members of the *Sonderkommando* took these Jews, men and women, in trucks to the forest camp. I went to the forest camp to see what happened to these people. The Jews had to get off the vehicles in front of the big barracks in the forest camp. They were gathered together in the yard in front of the barracks, which was surrounded by a fence the height of a man.
> Bothmann told them that they would go to work in Germany, but first they would have to be examined by a doctor and, in order to prevent an

---

[141]   Ibid., p. 157.
[142]   Ibid., p. 158.

epidemic, to take a bath. For this purpose they would have to undress in the barrack, take soap and a towel, and enter a van, which would drive them to the bath. And so it happened.

The Jews entered the barrack and afterward they came out naked. Then they had to enter a van, after having been led through a gangway enclosed by a wooden fence. The van was a so-called gas van, which had an enclosed body and was similar to a furniture van. After they had gotten inside this van, the doors in the back were closed by an SS man. After the doors were closed, the van drove immediately in the direction of the crematorium.[143]

Two of the Jewish workers from this period managed to survive the second phase of Chełmno death camp, they were Szymon Srebnik and Mordka (Mieczysław) Zurawski and they both testified after the war to Judge Władyslaw Bednarz in June and July 1945. These accounts provide the most detailed account of what took place in Chełmno during 1944. Szymon Srebnik was the first to be deported to Chełmno, so we will start with his account, which he gave on June 29, 1945, in Koło:

> Up to March 1944, I had been in the Łódź ghetto, from where I was then driven off to Chełmno. In Łódź I worked in the ghetto in the so-called "metal department." In March 1944, the Germans organized a round-up. They caught me while I was on a streetcar and led me to Balucki Square where there were some cars from Chełmno. We were loaded inside and driven off. Besides me, there were 50 other Jews on the truck. Among them there were Zydenfeld, Berek, Miodownik, Kalmuszewicz, Huskiel. I cannot recall any other names.
>
> The Germans took us to a granary on the grounds of the Chełmno palace. There were no other Jews. We found out that we were in the *Sonderkommando* camp. An hour later the prisoners were divided into two groups. The stronger and better workers were sent to the woods; they formed the so-called "*Waldkommando*." Weaker and younger ones, I was among them, were left to work in the so-called "*Hauskommando*." The *Waldkommando* chief was Lenz. Other Germans employed in the woods were Runge and Kretschmer. The *Hauskommando* chief was Häfele. The *Waldkommando* consisted of about 40 Jews; the remainder was assigned to the *Hauskommando*. We were all shackled. The shackles prevented us from walking in a normal way. We had to take very short

---

[143] P. Montague, *Chełmno and the Holocaust*, I.B. Tauris and Co. Ltd, London 2012, p. 161.

steps. The shackles on our ankles were also chained to our waists. We slept in the granary on a cement floor. It was very cold.

The members of the *Waldkommando* told us that they were burning two furnaces in the woods. They did not know what purpose they would serve, but they expected the furnaces might be used to make charcoal. The furnaces were very primitive. They stood on a cement foundation and were narrow at the bottom, gradually becoming wider at the top. They were approximately three metres (10 feet) tall. The width was about the same. The fire grate was made of narrow-gauge railroad railings. There was neither a chimney nor a special trench for better draught. Later I was in the woods a few times, so I could see the furnaces. Officers Runge and Kretschmer were responsible for the construction of the furnaces. The construction process lasted about two weeks. Jews building the furnaces were sometimes killed for entertainment. Lenz and the *Sonderkommando* Chief Commissar Bothmann showed extreme cruelty. At times, out of 30 workers sent to the woods, only 14 returned.

The groups of workers were constantly supplied with new men brought from Łódź. Although each of eight transports brought 30 workers, it was still not enough, because so many of them were killed. When the first transport arrived, there were only 18 Jewish workers in Chełmno. The rest had been killed. The corpses were buried in a pile of sand. After the furnaces became operational, the bodies were burned.

The workers were given 200 grams of bread a day, some coffee in the morning, and one-half litre of soup for dinner. Only after the first transport had arrived, did we get any blankets. We were constantly beaten during work. They hit us with their hands or spades. Obviously, blows from a spade resulted in death or mutilation, which actually equalled death, as those unable to work were finished off. The Germans killed in the following way: they called a Jew named Moniek Reich, who had to remove the shackles from those to be killed. Then they ordered them to lie on the ground and shot them in the back of the head.

The first transport came at the beginning of April from Łódź. In the morning Bothmann ordered the *Hauskommando* out of the granary. We were ordered to move baggage that had been unloaded near the narrow-gauge railroad track, in the place where it met the road. The prisoners were already locked in the church. We carried their belongings to the park, where two barracks had been built, one larger than the other. The confiscated clothes were sorted in the smaller building. Suitcases were put on one side and the sorted items on the other. The belongings were sorted by the *Hauskommando*. The most valuable items, new suits were kept in the smaller building. Valuables were given to Burmeister.

The transported prisoners were taken to the woods by trucks at six in the morning. But before that the *Waldkommando*, consisting of about 30 people, had already left for the woods. The Jews did not expect any danger on the way. Three trucks transported prisoners to the woods. They were not allowed to take any baggage. In the evening fellow prisoners from the *Waldkommando* told us what had happened in the woods. After the trucks arrived, the Jews were ordered to go to one of the barracks in the woods. The Germans told them to take off their clothes and put them in a separate pile, because they would put them back on after bathing. The underwear also had to be removed. Women could leave their panties on. Signs on the walls of the barracks read, "to the bath-house," and "to the Doctor." The Jews were driven out of the barracks and loaded into a van of a special type. If they refused to get in, the Germans used force.

There were three vans: a larger one and two smaller ones. The larger van could hold up to 170 people, while the smaller ones, 100–120. The van doors were locked with a bolt and a padlock. Then, the engine was started. The exhaust fumes entered the interior of the van and suffocated those inside. The exhaust pipe went from the engine along the chassis and into the van, through a hole in the car's floor, which was covered with a perforated sheet of metal. The hole was located more or less in the middle of the chassis. The van's floor was also covered with a wooden grate, just like the one in the bath-house. This was to prevent the prisoners from clogging the exhaust pipe. The vehicles were specially adapted vans. On one of them, under a new coat of paint, one could see a trade name. I cannot remember the name, but it started with the word "Otto." I do not know the make of the engine.

The chauffeurs were Bürstinger, Laabs, and Gielow. Shouting and banging on the door lasted about four minutes. The van was not moving at that time. After the shouting faded, the vehicle started moving in the direction of the crematoriums. When the van reached its destination, its door was unlocked to let the fumes out. Then two Jews went inside and threw out the bodies. The gas coming out had all the characteristics of the exhaust fumes (colour and smell). I cannot be mistaken here. The corpses, having been searched through, were placed in the furnace. Both crematoriums were built in the same clearing in the woods, several metres from each other. They were located at the entrance of the clearing and vehicles drove past them when they arrived at the place. However, the furnaces were covered with branches, so they would not be noticed.

The corpses were searched through by a Jew called Vidland[144] who took off rings and pulled out gold teeth. He was supervised by Piller. Each furnace was operated by 12 Jewish workers, who placed the corpses between layers of chipped wood. Before setting them on fire, gasoline was poured over the pile of bodies. The capacity of one furnace was more or less the same as of one van. Runge operated one crematorium and Kretschmer the other. Lenz was their superior. It took approximately one hour for the corpses to burn. Then a new pile of bodies was added. There were a few instances of unintended self-incineration: a Jew trying to set fire to a pile of bodies died in the flames himself. The bones were ground with the use of a hand-operated grinder on a cement surface near the woods. I did not see any grinding machine. The ground bones were carried out of the woods, more or less every second night, together with the ash. I cannot remember the name of the Gendarme supervising the Jewish workers grinding bones.

The Jews' clothes were stored in the other barracks in the woods. They had to be carried to the barracks rapidly before another truck arrived. Here the witness was shown a van found in the Ostrowski's factory in Koło. This is the van used in Chełmno for gassing. This is the vehicle I mentioned in my testimony, with the word "Otto" on its door......

Transports arrived in Chełmno every second day. Each transport carried from 700 to 1,000 people. I estimate that in 1944 alone, 15,000 Jews were brought to Chełmno. However, I did not count them—my assumption is based on what the Gendarmes had said before the transports had arrived... the transports arrived for two months. All of them with no exception first went to the ghetto, and only then were they directed to Chełmno. This is how Jews from abroad arrived. There were Jews from France, Czechoslovakia, the *Reich* (Berlin, Vienna, Hamburg) and even Jewish citizens of England. One Jewish Englishman named Alex worked in the *Waldkommando* for some time. I cannot remember the last names of any of the foreign Jews. I can only remember there was Dr. Proskauer, a Jew from Hamburg. As far as the Polish Jews are concerned, I can remember the following names: Icek Koltan, Mojsze Koltan, Henryk Oberfest and his brother, Henoch Erlich, Wolek Erhlich, Mordka Mordkiewicz and Abram Mordkiewicz, Szmul Paschwalski, Dr. Wajs (9 Zawiszy Street) with his family, Dr. Miller from Łódź and Mandelsohn (brought by Kramp).

The camp was liquidated and the barracks dismantled. Machines for shredding clothes and underwear were sent back. The furnaces were also dismantled. In the granary there were still 87 Jewish workers. Those were

---

[144] His name according to Zurawski was Frydland.

tailors and shoemakers. They lived upstairs. The number of workers decreased and finally there were 47 of them left—22 tailors and 25 courtyard workers.[145]

The second Jewish prisoner who escaped certain death, along with Szymon Srebnik, on the night of January 17, 1945, was Mordka Zurawski, and he testified before Judge Władysław Bednarz on July 31, 1945, in Koło, and his testimony was as follows:

> Before the war I lived in Włocławek. During the German occupation, after the Włocławek Ghetto had been liquidated, I was forced to work in Poznań and later (after a year) in the Łódź Ghetto. I worked there at the Radogoszcz (*Radegast*) station.
> In spring, transports of Jews started passing through Radogoszcz in some direction unknown to me. The transports carried between 700–1,000 people. I cannot remember whether there were any Jews from abroad. The railroad cars used were usually the same. I searched the cars through after the train had returned, and in one of them I read the following words; "We are traveling in a death train." I did not take the words seriously, so when I was assigned to the next transport, I did nothing to get myself out of it. I was convinced the transports were bound for places where people would work. The transports were escorted, as I found out later, by the *Sonderkommando Kulmhof*.
> On May 10, 1944, I went with the seventh transport. I remember there was nobody there bearing my last name. We walked to the Radogoszcz station. We could take as many belongings as we were able to carry. We reached Koło by train. There we were reloaded onto a narrow-gauge railway car that took us to Chełmno. The train stopped near the church. We were ordered off and divided into groups of four. Six Jews were selected for work—I was among them. The rest of the Jews were locked in the church.
> My companions and I were shackled; they put chains around our legs tightly and tied the chains to our waists so that we could only walk. I was assigned to the *Waldkommando* and I was ordered to quickly unload wood shipped from the Kościelec forest. The manager of the *Waldkommando* was *Wachtmeister* Lenz.[146] He shot one of the Jews because the latter was getting onto the truck too slowly. Besides, Lenz beat Jews no matter if they worked well or badly. Once he beat me so hard that that I

---

[145] *Chełmno Witnesses Speak*, Konin – Łódź 2004, pp. 125–128.
[146] *Polizeimeister* was the correct rank.

lost consciousness and later he poured cold water over me to bring me around. I slept in the granary.

Later I was ordered to stand in for a Jew named Finkelstein, who operated one of the crematoriums—Finkelstein himself was killed during an escape attempt. When another transport arrived, I was already operating the furnace and could see how the Jews were executed. From the early morning, groups of Jews were brought from the Chełmno church to the forest by trucks. When in the church *Wachtmeister* Häfele[147] told the Jews that they could expect a better fate. That was the reason they were so calm.

In the forest, they got off near the barracks and were told to undress and prepare for a bath. In the barracks there were boards saying: "To the bathroom." I had never worked at the barracks so I could not watch the process at close range. I saw it from a distance of about 200 metres. The Jews had to strip naked. Then they were led to a corridor protected by a wooden fence, at the end of which gas vans were ready to receive their victims. The Jews generally got into the vans peacefully. I would like to mention that while inside the barracks they were given a towel and a piece of soap to make them believe that they were going to take a bath. All the naked Jews were herded into the car and the door was locked.

When the engine started, the exhaust fumes entered the interior through a specially constructed pipe, suffocating all those inside. Four minutes later the groans died out, the van started moving towards the crematoriums. The corpses were dropped near one of them and the van returned to the barracks. Two vans were used: a bigger one that held 130 people, and a smaller one that held about 80–90. The interiors of the vehicles were covered with sheet metal and sealed. The vans were painted black. I do not know their make. The exhaust pipe entered the interior through the floor. It was covered with perforated sheet metal. On the floor there was a wooden grate, just like one might see in a bathroom. I do not know how they fixed the pipe, so that the fumes went inside the van, instead of out of it. We were not allowed to look at the construction of the vehicles.

I pulled the corpses out of the van and could only see the interior. After the door had been opened, we had to wait about eight minutes before we could go inside. I could not tell whether they added some chemical agents to the gasoline. I would like to point out that the victims closest to the pipe opening were burnt so terribly, that their skin was coming off their bodies. Having thrown the corpses out of the van, we washed and cleaned the grate on the floor.

---

[147] *Sturmscharführer* was the correct rank.

The towels and soap were thrown away. I would like to mention that everybody had his or her own towel and soap and no one got any from the camp warehouses. On the floor one could often find some gold or money. Before being burnt, the corpses were searched through. The body searches were carried out by Moniek, Reich and Frydland and supervised by Lenz and Hannes. They took off rings and pulled out gold teeth. Then the corpses were thrown into the furnaces.

In the forest, there were two identical crematoriums. The tops of the crematoria were at the ground level (they formed a pit). The furnace was four metres deep, six metres wide, and ten metres long. The sides of the furnace gradually narrowed towards the bottom and in the place where they reached the grate. The width was approximately one metre and the length one-and-a half metres. The grates were made of the rails from a narrow-gauge railroad track; it can still be found near the place where the crematoriums used to be located. The sides were made from chamotte brick and concrete. Under the grate, there was an ash pit linked with another pit to ensure the proper flow of air to the furnace. A layer of wood was set on fire, on which dead bodies were placed. The corpses had to be arranged in such a way that they did not touch one another. In the lowest layer there were 12 people. Their bodies were then covered with another layer of chipped wood and another layer of corpses. In this way the furnace could hold up to 100 bodies at a time.

As the corpses burned down, the free space created at the top was filled with another layer of bodies and wood. The corpses burnt quickly; they turned to ash in more or less 15 minutes. The ash was then removed from the ash pit with pokers of a special type. These were long iron poles with a 40-centimetre-long iron plate at the end. Removing the ash was a very difficult and hazardous job. No one could keep on with it longer than two-three days, after which the worker was unable to continue and was killed.

The bones and ashes were packed in sacks, made of blankets brought by the transported Jews. But first the bones had to be crushed with wooden stamps on a special cement foundation, so that it was impossible to recognize they were human bones. The sacks were usually driven out of the forest at night. Jews were not used to doing that..... I would like to point out that while the bones were being crushed, the workers had to stand on the ash, which was still very hot. In this way they burnt their feet very severely.

The work in the woods lasted from dawn to dusk. During that time, there was only one 10-minute break for bread and coffee. We worked in shackles all the time. The clearing was surrounded by gendarmes with sub-machine guns, standing 10 metres one from another. The workers were sometimes killed without any reason. There was no single day without killings.

In 1944, ten transports arrived in Chełmno, each of which brought 700–1,000 people. Transports carrying 700 victims were completed by smaller groups (brought by trucks). The total number of people who died in Chełmno in 1944 reached 10,000. Häfele spoke about this. I do not know what the Nazi plans concerning Chełmno, or, more precisely, the extermination camp, were. The Germans did not say anything about that. I did not hear that the Chełmno extermination camp was being prepared to receive Jews from Hungary or certain groups of Poles. At the time I was in Chełmno, transports with foreign Jews did not arrive.

However, there might have been such transports before my arrival. Only Jews were put to death in Chełmno. The acts of killing of Poles and Germans were only sporadic. During my whole stay in Chełmno, I saw corpses of non-Jews only once. One day, at five in the morning four corpses were brought to Chełmno. I do not know who they were. The only thing I can say is that they were not circumcised. Their bodies were buried in the ground, as there was no transport on that day. They were cremated the following day. The corpses must have been brought from Łódź. In a phone conversation I overheard that Łódź requested a truck, which was later sent there.

I have not heard about the case of the burning of two priests in the crematoriums. However, I did see with my own eyes two Jews dressed in Hasidic pre-death clothes, similar to cassocks worn by priests, being exhumed and burnt. I would like to remark that eight to ten people from each transport were forced to write letters to their families, notifying them, that they were staying in Leipzig, or Munich together with other Jews and that they were doing fine. The "letters" were written in the "bath-house." I would like to point out that those who wrote letters were not put to death in the vans. They were led near the crematoriums and shot in the head. In one case *Wachtmeister* Hannes pushed one of the Jewish workers into the flames. I cannot recall the Jew's name. This Hannes also axed one of the workers.

Sometimes those thrown out of the van were still alive. In spite of that, they were thrown into the furnaces. If the victims screamed too loudly, they were gunned down. I heard that a worker Finkelstein had to throw his own sister, who was still alive, into the furnace. I do not know any further details concerning this matter, as the incident had taken place before my arrival.

Sometimes during the day, Bothmann came to the forest and ordered us to line up. He selected a few workers who, in his opinion, had been working in the camp for too long. Moniek Reich removed the shackles from the feet of those selected. Then Bothmann ordered them to lie on the ground with their faces down and killed them himself. Sometimes only small transports came from the Łódź Ghetto, the people were gunned down near the crematoriums and then cremated.[148]

---

[148] *Chełmno Witnesses Speak*, Konin – Łódź 2004, pp. 130–133.

Chapter X
August 1944–January 1945
The Liquidation of the Camp

The ten transports from the *Litzmannstadt* ghetto during June and July 1944 signalled the end of mass extermination at the Chełmno death camp. The tide of war had changed against the Nazis, and by the end of July 1944, the Soviet advance had crossed the Vistula River, which was only 130 kilometers east *of Litzmannstadt.*

On July 24, 1944, *Oberwachtmeister* Bruno Simon, a guard in the forest camp, drowned in the River Ner.[149]

The *Litzmannstadt* ghetto was finally liquidated during the month of August 1944. Some 54,500 ghetto residents were murdered not at Chełmno, but at the Auschwitz-Birkenau Concentration Camps. Among those killed were Mordechai Chaim Rumkowski, the Eldest of the Jews, and members of his family, on August 29, 1944.

Having lost its *"raison d-etre,"* with the liquidation of the *Litzmannstadt* ghetto accomplished, the death camp authorities now had to dispose of the victims belongings and once again eradicate all traces of the crimes committed there. Firstly, the size of the *Polizeiwachtkommando* was reduced. Bothmann ordered Ernst Burmeister to select 40 members of the police detachment, who were to perform duties guarding the border between the *Warthegau* and the *Generalgouvernement.* Ernst Burmeister and his squad however, went to Warsaw on August 8, 1944, to quell the Warsaw Uprising. What remained in Chełmno was a guard detachment of approximately 40 policemen to guard about 100 prisoners.[150]

---

[149] Krystof Gorczyca, Zdzisław Lorek, *Day After Day in the extermination camp Kulmhof am Ner* – unpublished draft, p. 137.
[150] P. Montague, *Chełmno and the Holocaust*, I.B. Tauris and Co. Ltd, London 2012, p. 169.

On Saturday August 26, 1944, a Jewish prisoner from the *Waldkommando*, Finkelsztajn[151], was shot and killed by *Wachtmeister* Arthur Sliwke, whilst trying to escape.[152] He originally hailed from Pabiance. According to the testimony of Szymon Srebnik, Finkelsztajn was forced to throw his sister into the furnace. She regained consciousness and shouted, "You murderer, why are you throwing me into the furnace? I am still alive."[153]

During September / October 1944, the *Waldkommando* dismantled the two barracks in the Forest Camp, the building materials were shipped to *Warthbrücken*. The two crematoria were dismantled in stages, the first one during mid-September, supervised by *SS-Hauptscharführer* Johannes Runge, who had supervised their construction. Some of the bricks removed were taken to the estate in Powiercie, where they were used to make drainage channels in a greenhouse.[154]

Mieczysław Zurawski testified about the liquidation on July 31, 1945:

> September and October 1944, were the months of the camp liquidation. The crematoriums were destroyed and the debris was spread along the paths in the forest. It is possible that the remains of one of the crematoriums are still in the ground. The barracks were dismantled and the "death vans" were sent by rail to Berlin. The number of Chełmno workers was gradually being decreased. One day 60 workers were sent allegedly to another camp in Mühlental. In fact these Jews were put to death. Later we found their clothes in a warehouse at the place of annihilation. In Chełmno, the workers stayed in the granary. On the first floor there were tailors and shoemakers, and on the ground floor, there were the *Hauskommando* and the *Waldkommando*.[155]

The *Sonderwagen* was sent back to Berlin on October 3, 1944, on Bothmann's orders. The two gas vans were loaded by Laabs and

---

[151] Also recorded as Finkelstein by M. Zurawsk.
[152] Krystof Gorczyca, Zdzisław Lorek, *Day After Day in the extermination camp Kulmhof am Ner* – unpublished draft, p. 139.
[153] *Chełmno Witnesses Speak*, Konin – Łódź 2004, pp. 129.
[154] P. Montague, *Chełmno and the Holocaust*, I.B. Tauris and Co. Ltd, London 2012, pp. 169–170.
[155] *Chełmno Witnesses Speak*, Konin – Łódź 2004, p. 133.

Runge and they accompanied the *Sonderwagen* to Berlin. They drove the vans to a large motor pool in Oranienburg, and then returned back to Chełmno. The round trip took about a week to complete.[156]

On September 15, 1944, Hans Biebow, the head of the *Litzmannstadt* ghetto German administration ordered six tailors to board a truck. After a three hour journey the truck arrived in Chełmno. Among the tailors were Mordkiewicz and Oberferst, who were both highly regarded, and who worked exclusively for German and Jewish dignitaries in the ghetto. These two men and the four others were ordered to get out of the vehicle taking their sewing machines with them. The tailors were given worn out clothing to wear, and were placed in leg irons and taken to the granary building. There they were able to talk to the prisoners already imprisoned there.

Also on this transport of the tailors from the *Litzmannstadt* ghetto were the Mandels family. Dr. Sima Mandels, her husband and two children. Dr. Mandels was the director of the paediatric department at the *Litzmannstadt* ghetto hospital on Lagiewnicka Street. The family were sentenced to death by Hans Biebow. During a visit to the hospital one evening, a drunken Biebow encountered the Mandel's 16-year old daughter in a hallway. He grabbed her and forced her into an office. The girl rejected Biebow's sexual advances and screaming, attempted to fight him off. Whether she was raped or not, that is unclear, but Biebow drew his pistol and shot her in the face. She survived the attack, but Biebow ordered that the entire family be sent to Chełmno. When the truck arrived in Chełmno, the tailors exited the vehicle, the Mandels family were taken to the *Waldlager* and were all killed.[157]

On December 1, 1944, the group of craftsmen incarcerated in the granary wrote a last letter to the world and buried it in the grounds of the mansion:

Announcement to our future nation:

---

[156] P. Montague, *Chełmno and the Holocaust*, I.B. Tauris and Co. Ltd, London 2012, p. 170.
[157] Ibid., p. 171.

I describe to you the life of the Jewish nation from September 1, 1939 to December 1, 1944, and in what way they oppressed us. We were taken, young and old, to between the towns of Koło and Dąbie. We were taken to the forest; there we were gassed, shot, and burned. And so we ask so that our future brothers ... for our German murderers. Witnesses to our oppression are the Poles who live in this area. Once again we ask that this murder be made known throughout the whole world and to all the press. The last Jews who... here wrote this. We survived until December 1, 1944.
Illegible signature[158]

On January 17, 1945, 25 Jews from the *Hauskommando* and 22 craftsmen were held prisoner in the granary. Bruno Israel was on guard duty at the granary. *SS-Hauptsturmführer* Hans Bothmann arrived at the guardhouse around one o'clock in the morning. The entire *Sonderkommando* was assembled. Bothmann told them that the Red Army had occupied Łódź, and that the *Sonderkommando* was to be disbanded. He then said that the Jewish workers were to be shot immediately and burned in the forest, the following morning. Bothmann's Mercedes automobile and a truck drove to the granary and stopped, their headlights illuminated the building and the entire area was surrounded by a police detachment.[159]

Szymon Srebnik testified about the events of the night of January 17, 1945, to Judge Władysław Bednarz in Koło, on June 29, 1945:

> When the Soviet Army was advancing quickly, one night we were ordered to leave the granary in groups of five. I cannot remember the date. The area was lit with car headlights. I went outside in the first group of five. Lenz ordered us to lie down on the ground. He shot everybody in the back of the head. I lost consciousness and regained it when there was no one around. All the SS men were shooting inside the granary. I crawled to the car lighting the spot and broke both headlights. Under the cover of darkness I managed to run away. The wound was not deadly. The bullet went through the neck and mouth and pierced the nose and then went out.
> I hid in Wieczorek's barn, they did not find me. Later I learned that while killing the Jews, Lenz and Haase also died. I saw their bodies. When the

---

[158] Ibid., p. 172.
[159] P. Montague, *Chełmno and the Holocaust*, I.B. Tauris and Co. Ltd, London 2012, p. 172.

two went inside, the Jews hung one of them and shot the other one with his own weapon. Apart from me, one other person managed to save his life that night. It was Max Zurawski, who pushed his way past the gendarmes and escaped.[160]

Mordka Zurawski also testified before Judge Władysław Bednarz on July 31, 1945, in Koło, and his testimony was as follows:

On the night of January 17, Lenz entered the granary and called out five people. After a while we heard five shots. We knew it signified our deaths, and that they would call us out in groups of five to kill us all. I knocked on the ceiling with a wooden board in order to alarm the tailors and shoemakers on the first floor. I decided to save my life. I stood by the door hidden under a blanket with a knife in hand.

After the fourth group of five had been led out of the granary and the door was being locked, I charged the door with great force, probably making Lenz, who was locking it, fall over. I ran madly straight ahead stabbing my way through. I felt as if I were unconscious. As I later found out, in this act of madness one of the gendarmes lost his nose, and another his ear. They were shooting at me and one bullet reached the muscle of my right thigh. One of the gendarmes hit my leg with the butt of a gun, but I kept on running. I got through the fence injuring my right arm to the bone and kept on running towards the woods.

The Germans organized a chase. Lying in a ditch I heard the gendarme Ruwenach and some other gendarmes warning the residents in nearby houses about my escape. I managed to get through to the village of Umien, where I hid in a barn and stayed there throughout the night and the following day. While I was trying to escape, I saw that the granary was on fire. I also heard shots. Just to mention, while in the granary before the escape attempt, I had gotten rid of the shackles, which otherwise would have hampered my movements. I had hidden large tailor scissors that I used to cut the wire connecting the chain links.

I spent one more night in Mrs. Przyblska's barn, after revealing my presence to her. I gave her two rings in exchange for her kindness. Antoni Ludwicki, a resident of Chełmno, came to Mrs. Przyblska's and he recognized me. He blackmailed me into giving him a watch and a wedding ring, in exchange for silence. I was afraid of Ludwicki since he had denounced a Jew named Finkelstein, when the latter had escaped. He saw Finkelstein running away and sent some girl to alarm the gendarme Sliwke. Then he showed Sliwke the route Finkelstein had taken. The gendarme shot Finkelstein at the moment when the Jew's escape attempt

---

[160] *Chełmno Witnesses Speak*, Konin – Łódź 2004, pp. 128–129.

could have been successful. If it had not been for Ludwicki, Finkelstein would have saved his life. I heard about Ludwicki's deed from the gardener Miszczak's wife. I would like to mention that Ludwicki's sister, Hela Ludwicki had a child with *Wachtmeister* Häfele. At the time when Ludwicki was trying to blackmail me, the Russian army had already reached Chełmno.[161]

Walter Piller in his testimony regarding the end of operations at Chełmno on January 17, 1945, recalled:

> One night under the orders of Bothmann, the whole unit was woken up and had to assemble. At the assembly, we were told that the Red Army had taken over Łódź and so the unit had to be dissolved immediately. In prison[162] there were still 20 craftsmen, while below there were still 20–25 workers. I must point out that the tent, the shredding machine, the steam engine and the special vehicles had not been in the courtyard for a few weeks, maybe even a month. The unit should have been dissolved much earlier, however, Bothmann had not received any orders, so he started the liquidation process on his own initiative. His decision must have been influenced by the fact that the Red Army was continually advancing and Bothmann didn't want to encounter any problems during the liquidation.
>
> The remaining labour force, already mentioned, was to be executed in the morning, at dawn and cremated in the forest. The furnaces had already been destroyed. I mean, as far as I can remember, the first one was dismantled in the middle of September 1944, while the other one at the beginning of January 1945. The bricks were transported back to Koło, the foundation was removed to the last brick, in order to obliterate the traces. The furnaces were dismantled under the direction of Runge.
>
> So the prison remained in the palace courtyard in Chełmno with 40–45 Jewish workers. First the lower cell was opened to shoot those 20–25 Jews in front of the prison building. Every few minutes Lenz led five Jews outside at a time; then Bothmann, Lenz and I killed them with a shot to the back of the head. While the third group was coming out of the prison, one of the Jews escaped; he was a cook and all I know is that his first name is Maks.[163]
>
> Despite taking up chase by Bothmann, an SS-member, and four officers of the reserve forces, Maks managed to escape. In the guardhouse, I informed all of the gendarmerie posts via telephone about the search, but

---

[161] *Chełmno Witnesses Speak*, Konin – Łódź 2004, pp. 133–134.
[162] This was the Granary Building.
[163] The prisoner was Mordka Zurawski.

he was not caught. After Bothmann and the five people brought in had started the chase and he had ordered me to take care of the rest of the labour unit with a shot to the back of the head, Lenz brought out the remaining five from the lower cell, who were killed by Lenz and myself.

Walter Piller continued his testimony:

But there were still the 20 craftsmen left in the upper cell. Without my order, Lenz took a certain *Wachtmeister Schupo*[164] to the upper cell so that five Jews could be removed and shot in the same way, as with the lower cell. As soon as Lenz opened the cell door, four Jews threw themselves at him and pulled him into the cell. Then they took his pistol away and opened fire at two *Wachtmeisters* standing by the door. The door on the ground floor was locked only after Bothmann had returned from the unsuccessful search for the escapee and gave the order to do so.

After Bothmann, Häfele and I called out several times for them to release Lenz and leave the cell in groups of five, the answer was the firing of the pistol taken away from Lenz. Then one of the Jews called out that Lenz had hung himself. We could not check it out because the prisoners set fire to the prison and the flames were coming out of the roof. The fire spread twice as fast, because above the upper cell, wood was being dried to run the cars (*Holzgaswagen*).

However, the door on the ground floor was opened by Häfele because we assumed that the craftsmen would leave of their own will. But only two tailors went as far as the stairs and then fell to the floor, probably due to suffocation. Putting out or halting the fire would not have been humanly possible. Bothmann decided to let the prison burn down completely, despite the fact Lenz was still inside. Judging by the fire, Lenz was no longer alive, so the killed Jews lying in front of the prison were also carried into the burning building and abandoned to the flames.

In the morning, when the fire was slowly dying out and the glow could hardly be seen in the distance, Bothmann told me and Görlich to open a metal cabinet standing in one of the rooms and to burn all the secret documents kept there. The ash was to be spread in the open fields. We carried out the order, packed our belongings and the equipment in the quarters, and headed to Koło with all the other police officers in a closed transport. There the police unit was left with the local gendarmerie; the *Hauptmann* of the gendarmerie was named Stark.

Finally, the *SS-Sonderkommando* Bothmann headed for Poznań through Konin. In Konin we spent the night locked up in the local *Gestapo* station and we tried to phone and wire the head of the *Gestapo*

---

[164] This was Haase.

headquarters in Łódź, Dr. Bradfisch. However, all the wires had already been cut, but a detailed report of the camp liquidation procedure was typed up and wired to the Inspector of the Security Police and the *SD*, *SS-Brigadeführer* Damzog. In the reply that came a few hours later, also by wire, Bothmann received word that his unit should head to Poznań as quickly as possible and report to the *Gestapo* station in Poznań.

Bothmann was sent as a liaison officer of the Security Police to *SS-Reichsführer* Himmler in Wałcz. Of course he took his old friends Bürstinger and Burmeister as a chauffeur and escort. All the other members of the unit were assigned to various fighting units in order to participate in the battle against Russia.

After a few days spent in the waiting room of the headquarters of the new *Gestapo* commandant, Dr. Lange, after the evacuation of Grollman's Fort, I was assigned to an infantry division—*Hauptmann* Kohler's combat unit, and participated in several battles in Poznań until I was taken captive on February 23, 1945. On February 21, 1945, I was wounded in my right forearm by a heavy howitzer at a command post near the Poznań Citadel. All the other members of the *Sonderkommando* Bothmann were also assigned to German combat units. The last time I saw Runge and Gielow was after the battles in the Hugger Brewery. I do not know what happened to them later. I cannot say anything about the other members of the unit with the exception of Görlich and Schmidt, who I once saw at the Citadel in Poznań.[165]

---

[165] *Chełmno Witnesses Speak*, Konin – Łódź 2004, pp. 186–188.

Part II
Survivors, Victims, Perpetrators and the Aftermath

Chapter XI
Jewish Survivors and Victims
Roll of Remembrance

Survivors

BAJLER, Szlamek, He was deported to Chełmno death camp on January 13, 1942, from the town of Izbica Kujawska. He was selected for work in the "death brigade" who worked at emptying the gas vans and digging mass graves. He escaped from Chełmno on January 19, 1942, and made his way to Grabow. There he made contact with the local Rabbi, Jakub Szulman, and he told him about what was happening at Chełmno, and he urged the Rabbi to warn the world. Rabbi Jakub Szulman sent a postcard to his relatives in the Łódź ghetto, warning them of the mass murder in Chełmno.

From Grabow, Szlamek went to Piotrkow Trybunalski where he obtained a certificate from the Jewish Council bearing the name Jakub Grojnowski. He then made his way to Warsaw where he made contact with Emanuel Ringelblum and warned him of what the Nazis were doing in Chełmno.

Szlamek Bajler left Warsaw and went to live with his brother and sister-in-law, Fela Bajler, in Zamość. When the deportations from Zamość commenced as part of *Aktion Reinhardt*, Szlamek once again made contact with Ringelblum and his *Oneg Shabbat* group, sending them a letter informing them that "Bełżec is the same as *Kulmhof.*"

Szlamek was deported from the Zamość ghetto along with his brother, sister-in-law, and other members of the family on April 11, 1942, to the Bełżec death camp, where they all perished. Their fate was related to Emanuel Ringelblum, by Fela Bajler's son.

JUSTMANN, Yitzhak. There is nothing known about his formative years. He was deported to Chełmno from Sieradz at the end of August 1942. He was incarcerated in Chełmno, and employed in the *Waldkommando* as a gravedigger. He escaped from Chełmno along with Chaim Widawski and they both made their way to Piotrkow

Trybunalski. They left there in September 1942, dressed as Polish railway employees. Nothing is known about his time in hiding. According to the Widawski family, he was re-united with Chaim in Tel Aviv, Israel in 1955. Justmann, later, settled in Chicago, in the United States of America, where he passed away.

PODCHLEBNIK, Michał. He returned to Koło after the war and took part in Władysław Bednarz's investigation into the War crimes committed at Chełmno. He resumed his pre-War profession as a cattle trader in Koło. He settled in Zeilsheim, Germany, before settling in Israel in 1949, where he found employment in a confectionary plant and later as a partner in a laundry business. Michał, having lost his first wife and two children, a boy aged 7 and a girl aged 4, remarried a survivor from Auschwitz and they had two sons.

In 1961, he testified at the Adolf Eichmann trial in Jerusalem, Israel and also at the Chełmno trial that was held in Bonn, then West Germany, in 1963. Michał suffered for years with problems with his knee, and later on he developed a heart condition. Michał Podchlebnik died from heart disease in September 1985, after making a brief appearance in "Shoah," the acclaimed film by Claude Lanzmann.

ROJ, Abram. Born on January 8, 1916, in Przedecz, He was the son of Icek and Sura Roj. He grew up in Izbica Kujawska. Abram became a tailor's apprentice to help support his mother, four sisters and a brother—all of whom died in Chełmno.

Roj was called up for military service in August 1938, and in March 1939, he was assigned to the 69th Infantry Regiment, stationed in Gniezno. During the German invasion in September 1939, he was captured by the Germans and he was sent to Stalag XIA in Altengrabow. Roj was identified as a Jew by his fellow soldiers, and he was released from the Prisoner of War camp in March 1940. He returned to Izbica Kujawska, where he picked up his old trade as a tailor.

He was taken to Chełmno from his hometown during January 1942, where he was employed in the *Waldkommando* as a gravedigger. He escaped from Chełmno on Friday, January 16, 1942, at ten in the evening. He eventually returned to Izbica Kujawska, after being liberated by the Russians. He met another Holocaust survivor Taube Pakin, formerly Frolich, and the pair moved to Berlin, the American sector, where they married on October 26, 1945.

After co-owning a casino in the city, Abram and Taube emigrated to the United States of America, and they arrived after sailing from Germany, in New York, on July 11, 1951, and settled in Hartford, Connecticut, and he changed his name to Roy.

Abram returned to his boyhood profession and worked for a custom tailoring establishment and later he established his own tailoring and dry cleaning business, the couple had a baby girl that was born in 1955, and they were proud parents when she was accepted into Harvard University in 1973. Abram suffered from ill-health throughout the post-war years, and in 1967, he had a heart attack. He died on June 10, 1975.

SREBNIK, Szymon. He was treated for his wounds by the Red Army in Dąbie and later in Koło, and then he stayed at the Miszczak's home in Chełmno, whilst he recovered from his wounds. He subsequently returned to Łódź, his hometown, before deciding to leave Poland.

He met his future wife Hava, in a Jewish *kibbutz* in Milan, Italy, whilst en-route to Israel. The couple married in 1949, and settled in Nes Ziona, and had two daughters in the early 1950's. He found employment in the construction industry, and was employed as an electrician in the Defence industry.

Srebnik testified at the trial of Adolf Eichmann in Jerusalem, in 1961, and also at the Chełmno trial that was held in Bonn, then West Germany, in 1963. During the mid-1970's Srebnik returned to Chełmno, where he took part in the "Shoah" film by Claude Lanzmann. He retired in 1992, after a long professional career. The last living survivor of Chełmno he died from cancer on August 15, 2006. He was survived by his wife, two children, five grandchildren and three great-grand children.

WIDAWSKI, Chaim (Yerachmiel). Born during May 1913, in Sieradz, to Joshua and Chaya Widawski. His father worked in the spirts business. He was deported to Chełmno from Sieradz at the end of August 1942. He was incarcerated in Chełmno, and was employed in the *Waldkommando* as a gravedigger.

He escaped from Chełmno along with Yitzhak Justmann and they both made their way to Piotrkow Trybunalski. They left there in September 1942, dressed as Polish railway employees. He was liberated from his hiding place in Zilna, Slovakia, by the Red Army on April 30, 1945.

Two years later in 1947, he settled in Berlin and the following year married Malke Tauber, who hailed from Oświęcim, and she had survived being incarcerated in the Auschwitz Concentration Camp. The couple had three children and he ran a successful distillery business and later a nylon stocking factory. In 1953, both businesses were sold and the Widawski family moved to Antwerp, in Belgium, where a fourth child was born.

The family entered the industrial diamond business and became a pillar of the Antwerp Jewish community. At the end of the 1950's and the beginning of the 1960's, he worked to bring Jewish orphan children, saved from the Holocaust by Polish Christian families, to Belgium. Some were cared for in the Widawski home, before new homes were found for them in Canada, Israel and the United States of America.

While visiting Israel in the 1960's, Widawski met with Meir Grünfeld, the man who had sheltered him throughout most of the war. In 1972, again in Israel, he met with Naphtali Lau-Levi, who, along with his father, helped save his life in Piotrkow Trybunalski, just after escaping from Chełmno with Yitzhak Justmann. Chaim (Yerachmiel) Widawski died in April 1986, after suffering a heart attack.

ZURAWSKI, Mieczysław. He returned to Włocławek, where he had lived before the War. Zurawski provided testimony to the Polish government's investigation conducted by Judge Władysław Bednarz.

Zurawski was also a witness at the trials of former *Gauleiter* Arthur Greiser and Chełmno guard Hermann Gielow. He emigrated to Israel in the early 1950's. He provided his testimony at the trial of Adolf Eichmann in Jerusalem in 1961 and also at the Chełmno trial that was held in Bonn, then West Germany, in 1963. Mieczysław Zurawski passed away on March 5, 1989.

Victims

This chapter will cover the biographies of the Jews deported from the *Reich* to the Łódź ghetto then onto Chełmno death camp, where they were murdered. The source for this information is the

Bundesarchiv Memorial Website. Over 5,000 names have been recorded as having been deported from the *Reich*, and murdered at Chełmno. In view of this, an approach has been taken, that every surname has been included, thus providing the reader with a sense of the scale of destruction, whilst accepting that in a book of this nature, a full listing is impractical.

It does not mean that those excluded are any less important, but websites such as the *Bundesarchiv* can be easily consulted. Of course it goes without saying that we apologize in advance to anyone searching for relatives that are not included. Also compiling this kind of Roll of Remembrance always carries a risk of incorrect information and whilst every effort is made to ensure it is accurate, I must apologize in advance for any errors made. In some instances the entries have been cross-referenced with another online resource, the Yad Vashem Central Database of Shoah Victims, in order to find additional information or verify the entries.

What is very noticeable in compiling this list of victims who were deported from the *Reich* to Chełmno is that they all ended up at the death camp having first been deported to the ghetto in Łódź (*Litzmannstadt*). There were no direct transports to Chełmno from the *Reich*, unlike the other extermination centres in Poland, thus making the Chełmno death camp unique.

Victims from the *Reich*—Murdered at Chełmno
A-Z Alphabetical Listing
Extract of Memorial List by Individual Surname

AARON, Selma: Born on December 31, 1883, in Cologne. She was deported from Cologne on October 22, 1941, to the Łódź ghetto. She was deported from Łódź to Chełmno during May 1942, where she perished.

ABENDROTH, Margarete: Born on December 4, 1888, in Berlin. She was deported from Berlin on October 24, 1941, to the Łódź ghetto. She was deported from Łódź to Chełmno on May 11, 1942, where she perished on May 11, 1942.

ABRAHAM, Anna: Born on October 31, 1884, in Cologne. She was deported from Düsseldorf on October 27, 1941, to the Łódź ghetto. She was deported from Łódź to Chełmno on May 14, 1942, where she perished on May 15, 1942.

ABRAMCZYK, Flora: Born on December 13, 1872, in Berlin. She was deported from Berlin on October 18, 1941, to the Łódź ghetto. She was deported from Łódź to Chełmno on May 7, 1942. She perished in Chełmno on May 7, 1942.

ADAM, Hertha: Born on August 8, 1888, in Koronowo, Poland. She was deported from Berlin on October 18, 1941, to the Łódź ghetto. She was deported from Łódź to Chełmno on May 8, 1942. She perished in Chełmno on May 8, 1942.

ADELHEIM, Johanna: Born on May 20, 1890, in Hamburg. She was deported from Hamburg on October 25, 1941, to the Łódź ghetto. She was deported from Łódź to Chełmno on May 15, 1942, where she perished.

ADLER, Anschel: Born on December 29, 1885. He was expelled from Leipzig on October 28, 1938, to Poland. He was deported from Łódź to Chełmno on March 26, 1942, where he perished.

ALBERSHEIM, Wilhelmine: Born on September 22, 1875, in Witten. She was deported from Cologne on October 22, 1941, to the Łódź ghetto. She was deported from Łódź to Chełmno during May 1942, where she perished.

ALBERT, Clara: Born on September 27, 1887, in Kcynia, Poland. She was deported from Berlin on October 24, 1941, to the Łódź ghetto. She was deported from Łódź to Chełmno on May 4, 1942. She perished in Chełmno on May 4, 1942.

ALEMBIK, Chaja: Born on February 6, 1878, in Warsaw, Poland. She was imprisoned in the *Sammelstelle* on *Levetzowstrasse* in Berlin. She was deported from Berlin on November 1, 1941, to the Łódź ghetto. She was deported from Łódź to Chełmno on May 14, 1942. She perished in Chełmno on May 14, 1942.

ALEXANDER, Bertha: Born on November 3, 1893, in Lauenberg. She was deported from Hamburg on October 25, 1941, to the Łódź ghetto.

She was deported from Łódź to Chełmno on May 4, 1942, where she perished.

ALLMEIER, Adelheid: Born on July 2, 1871, in Schweich. She was deported from Cologne on October 30, 1941, to the Łódź ghetto. She was deported from Łódź to Chełmno during September 1942, where she perished.

ALPERT, Jakob: Born on February 22, 1879, in Plöwken. He was deported from Berlin on October 24, 1941, to the Łódź ghetto. He was deported from Łódź to Chełmno on May 15, 1942, where he perished.

ALSBERG, Martha: Born on February 19, 1895, in Witten. She was deported from Cologne on October 22, 1941 to the Łódź ghetto. She was deported to Chełmno where she perished.

ALTMANN, Adolf: Born on September 23, 1883, in Katowice, Poland. He was deported from Düsseldorf on October 27, 1941, to the Łódź ghetto. He was deported from Łódź to Chełmno on May 8, 1942. He perished in Chełmno on May 9, 1942.

ALTSCHUL, Karoline: Born on January 8, 1886, in Cologne. She was deported from Cologne on October 22, 1941, to the Łódź ghetto. She was deported from Łódź to Chełmno on May 12, 1942, where she perished.

AMSTER, Dora: Born on February 22, 1877, in Tarnów, Poland. She was deported from Berlin on November 1, 1941, to the Łódź ghetto. She was deported from Łódź to Chełmno on May 9, 1942, where she perished.

ANDERS, Lizzie: Born on January 15, 1893, in Hamburg. She was deported from Berlin on October 18, 1941, to the Łódź ghetto. She was deported from Łódź to Chełmno on May 8, 1942, where she perished.

ANDRES, Ferdinand: Born on July 27, 1886, in Krefeld. He was deported from Düsseldorf on October 27, 1941, to the Łódź ghetto. He was deported from Łódź to Chełmno on May 8, 1942. He perished in Chełmno on May 9, 1942.

ANSCHEL, Berta: Born on December 15, 1901, in Goleniów. She was deported from Berlin on November 1, 1941, to the Łódź ghetto. She was deported from Łódź to Chełmno. She perished in Chełmno on May 8, 1942.

ANSCHLAWSKI, Selma: Born on July 24, 1898, in Tilsit. She was deported from Hamburg on October 25, 1941, to the Łódź ghetto. She was deported from Łódź to Chełmno on May 12, 1942, where she perished.

ANTMANN, Sofie: Born on February 17, 1886, in Horodenka, Poland. She was deported from Cologne on October 22, 1941, to the Łódź ghetto. She was deported from Łódź to Chełmno on May 11, 1942, where she perished.

APFEL, Henny: Born on March 19, 1879, in Groseneder. She was deported from Düsseldorf on October 27, 1941, to the Łódź ghetto. She was deported from Łódź to Chełmno on May 8, 1942. She perished in Chełmno on May 9, 1942.

APFELBAUM, Ettel: Born on July 3, 1907, in Perechinsko, Ukraine. She was deported from Düsseldorf on October 27, 1941, to the Łódź ghetto. She was deported from Łódź to Chełmno on July 7, 1944. She perished in Chełmno on July 8, 1944.

APISDORF, Regina: Born on April 18, 1890, in Zubowmosty, Poland. She was deported from Berlin on October 27–29, 1941, to the Łódź ghetto. She was deported from Łódź to Chełmno on May 5, 1942, where she perished.

APT, Gertrud: Born on August 25, 1928, in Neheim. She was deported from Cologne on October 30, 1941, to the Łódź ghetto. She was deported from Łódź to Chełmno on June 28, 1944, where she perished.

ARCHENHOLD, Julius: Born on January 10, 1885, in Lichtenau. He was deported from Düsseldorf on October 27, 1941, to the Łódź ghetto. He was deported from Łódź to Chełmno during September 1942, where he perished.

ARENDS, Karl: Born on May 28, 1896, in Weener. He was deported from Düsseldorf on October 27, 1941, to the Łódź ghetto. He was deported from Łódź to Chełmno on June 26, 1944. He perished in Chełmno on June 27, 1944.

ARENDSTEIN, Gertrud: Born on June 4, 1886, in Berlin. She was deported from Berlin on October 27–29, 1941, to the Łódź ghetto. She was deported from Łódź to Chełmno, where she perished on May 7, 1942.

ARENDT, Klara: Born on November 27, 1880, in Königsberg. She was deported from Düsseldorf on October 27, 1941, to the Łódź ghetto. She was deported from Łódź to Chełmno on May 8, 1942. She perished in Chełmno on May 9, 1942.

ARENSBERG, Erich: Born on June 11, 1900, in Wattenschied. He was deported from Düsseldorf on October 27, 1941, to the Łódź ghetto. He was deported from Łódź to Chełmno on May 14, 1942. He perished in Chełmno on May 15, 1942.

ARMER, Rudolf: Born on October 11, 1903, in Berlin. He was deported from Berlin on October 27–29, 1941, to the Łódź ghetto. He was deported from Łódź to Chełmno on May 4, 1942. He perished in Chełmno on May 4, 1942.

ARNDT, Arthur: Born on December 31, 1885, in Wielen, Poland. He was deported from Berlin on October 18, 1941, to the Łódź ghetto. He was deported from Łódź to Chełmno on May 8, 1942, where he perished.

ARNSTEIN, Doris: Born on March 7, 1897, in Cronheim. She was deported from Düsseldorf on October 27, 1941, to the Łódź ghetto. She was deported from Łódź to Chełmno on May 8, 1942. She perished in Chełmno on May 9, 1942.

ARON, Abraham: Born on October 10, 1924, in Cologne. He was deported from Cologne on October 30, 1941, to the Łódź ghetto. He was deported from Łódź to Chełmno during May 1942, where he perished.

ARONADE, Rosa: Born on April 28, 1889, in Nakło, Poland. She was deported from Berlin on October 27–29, 1941, to the Łódź ghetto. She was deported from Łódź to Chełmno on May 5, 1942, where she perished.

ARONSOHN, Elisabeth: Born on October 13, 1906, in Berlin. She was deported from Berlin on October 18, 1941, to the Łódź ghetto. She

was deported from Łódź to Chełmno on May 8, 1942, where she perished.

ARONSON, Edith: Born on August 9, 1935, in Berlin. She was deported from Berlin on November 1, 1941, to the Łódź ghetto. She was deported from Łódź to Chełmno on September 11, 1942. She perished in Chełmno on September 11, 1942.

ARRONGE, Emilie: Born on February 25, 1881, in Hochneukirch. She was deported from Cologne on October 22, 1941, to the Łódź ghetto. She was deported from Łódź to Chełmno on May 4, 1942. She perished in Chełmno on May 4, 1942.

ARTMANN, Eidel: Born on April 9, 1881, in Niebylow, Poland. She was expelled during October 1938, to Zbąszyń, Poland. She was deported from Düsseldorf on October 27, 1941, to the Łódź ghetto. She was deported from Łódź to Chełmno on May 12, 1942. She perished in Chełmno on May 13, 1942.

ASCH, Berta: Born on February 7, 1882, in Aachen. She was deported from Cologne on October 30, 1941, to the Łódź ghetto. She was deported from Łódź to Chełmno during June 1944, where she perished.

ASCHER, Franz: Born on May 4, 1881, in Schlochau. He was deported from Berlin on October 27–29, 1941, to the Łódź ghetto. He was deported from Łódź to Chełmno on May 5, 1942, where he perished.

ATLAS, Cirla: Born on November 15, 1886, in Bandrów, Poland. She was deported from Berlin on October 27–29, 1941, to the Łódź ghetto. She was deported from Łódź to Chełmno on September 21, 1942. She perished in Chełmno on September 21, 1942.

AUERBACH, Emma: Born on April 5, 1878, in Ichenhausen. She was deported from Cologne on October 30, 1941, to the Łódź ghetto. She was deported from Łódź to Chełmno during May 1942, where she perished.

AUMANN, Selma: Born on October 14, 1898, in Eisenbach. She was deported from Düsseldorf on October 27, 1941, to the Łódź ghetto. She was deported from Łódź to Chełmno on May 8, 1942, where she perished.

AUSADERER, Ruth: Born on July 21, 1905, in Berlin. She was deported from Berlin on October 27–29, 1941, to the Łódź ghetto. She was deported from Łódź to Chełmno on May 4, 1942, where she perished.

AUSSENBERG, Lina: Born on November 18, 1909, in Cologne. She was deported from Cologne on October 22, 1941, to the Łódź ghetto. She was deported from Łódź to Chełmno during May 1942, where she perished.

AWERBUCH, Frieda: Born on June 6, 1885, in Kraków, Poland. She was deported from Berlin on October 24, 1941, to the Łódź ghetto. She was deported from Łódź to Chełmno on July 10, 1944. She perished in Chełmno on July 10–12, 1944.

BAB, Arthur: Born on December 25, 1871, in Messeritz. He was deported from Berlin on October 18, 1941, to the Łódź ghetto. He was deported from Łódź to Chełmno on May 12, 1942, where he perished.

BACH, Albert: Born on September 12, 1895, in Waren. He was deported from Düsseldorf on October 27, 1941, to the Łódź ghetto. He was deported from Łódź to Chełmno during September 1942, where he perished.

BACHENHEIMER, Johanna: Born on November 26, 1888, in Rauschenberg. She was deported from Düsseldorf on October 27, 1941, to the Łódź ghetto. She was deported from Łódź to Chełmno on May 9, 1942. She perished in Chełmno on May 10, 1942.

BACHMANN, Wally: Born on February 11, 1907, in Berlin. She was deported from Berlin on October 18, 1941, to the Łódź ghetto. She was deported from Łódź to Chełmno on May 8, 1942. She perished in Chełmno on May 8, 1942.

BACHSCHÜTZ, Flora: Born on February 22, 1888, in Berlin. She was deported from Berlin on October 27–29, 1941, to the Łódź ghetto. She was deported from Łódź to Chełmno on May 5, 1942. She perished in Chełmno on May 5, 1942.

BACK, Berta: Born on April 29, 1885, in Hildesheim. She was deported from Düsseldorf on October 27, 1941, to the Łódź ghetto. She was deported from Łódź to Chełmno on July 12, 1944. She perished in Chełmno on July 13, 1944.

BÄCHER, Margarete: Born on March 20, 1899, in Malchow. She was deported from Berlin on October 18, 1941, to the Łódź ghetto. She was deported from Łódź to Chełmno on May 8, 1942, where she perished.

BAHR, Alfred: Born on October 10, 1929, in Cologne. He was deported from Cologne on October 30, 1941, to the Łódź ghetto. He was deported from Łódź to Chełmno during May 1942, where he perished.

BÄHR, Hedwig: Born on November 11, 1890, in Cologne. She was deported from Cologne on October 30, 1941, to the Łódź ghetto. She was deported from Łódź to Chełmno during May 1942, where she perished.

BÄR, Albert: Born on December 27, 1887, in Puderbach. He was deported from Cologne on October 30, 1941, to the Łódź ghetto. He was deported from Łódź to Chełmno during May 1942, where he perished.

BÄRWALD, Emma: Born on March 13, 1869, in Magdeburg. She was deported from Berlin on November 1, 1941, to the Łódź ghetto. She was deported from Łódź to Chełmno on May 8, 1942. She perished in Chełmno on May 8, 1942.

BÄUMEL, Wilhelm: Born on August 28, 1880, in Oslov. He lived in Leipzig, but emigrated to Czechoslovakia on May 5, 1936. He was deported from Prague to the Łódź ghetto on October 16, 1941. He was deported from Łódź to Chełmno on May 20, 1942, where he perished.

BAGAINSKI, Julius: Born on May 6, 1921, in Berlin. He was deported from Berlin on October 18, 1941, to the Łódź ghetto. He was deported from Łódź to Chełmno on May 7, 1942. He perished in Chełmno on May 7, 1942.

BALAI, Emma: Born on July 7, in Iskrzyczn, Poland. She was deported from Berlin on October 18, 1941, to the Łódź ghetto. She was deported from Łódź to Chełmno during April 1942, where she perished.

BALL, Hedwig: Born on January 16, 1896, in Przemysl, Poland. She was deported from Berlin on October 27-29, 1941, to the Łódź ghetto. She was deported from Łódź to Chełmno on May 4, 1942. She perished in Chełmno on May 4, 1942.

BALSAM, Zita: Born on January 6, 1904, in Swenigorodka, Kiev, Russia. She was deported from Berlin on October 18, 1941, to the Łódź ghetto. She was deported from Łódź to Chełmno on May 8, 1942. She perished in Chełmno on May 8, 1942.

BAMBERGER, Joseph: Born on March 21, 1874, in Bad Kreuznach. He was imprisoned in the *Sammelstelle* on *Levetzowstrasse*, Berlin. He was deported from Berlin on October 27–29, 1941, to the Łódź ghetto. He was deported from Łódź to Chełmno on May 14, 1942. He perished in Chełmno on May 14, 1942.

BANDMANN, Alma: Born on February 3, 1879, in Hamburg. She was deported from Hamburg on October 25, 1941, to the Łódź ghetto. She was deported from Łódź to Chełmno on May 10, 1942, where she perished.

BARAN, Margarete: Born on August 16, 1887, in Berlin. She was deported from Berlin on October 27, 1941, to the Łódź ghetto. She was deported from Łódź to Chełmno on May 5, 1942. She perished in Chełmno on May 5, 1942.

BARME, Bertha: Born on January 27, 1879, in Witten. She was deported from Cologne on October 30, 1941, to the Łódź ghetto. She was deported from Łódź to Chełmno during September 1942, where she perished.

BARNAS, Minna: Born on May 1, 1882, in Berlin. She was deported from Berlin on November 1, 1941, to the Łódź ghetto. She was deported from Łódź to Chełmno on May 9, 1942. She perished in Chełmno on May 9, 1942.

BARON, Henriette: Born on March 18, 1903, in Berlin. She was deported from Berlin on October 18, 1941, to the Łódź ghetto. She was deported from Łódź to Chełmno on May 8, 1942, where she perished.

BARTELS, Clara: Born on April 27, 1884, in Koronowo, Poland. She was deported from Berlin on November 1, 1941, to the Łódź ghetto. She was deported from Łódź to Chełmno on May 9, 1942. She perished in Chełmno on May 9, 1942.

BARUCH, Berta: Born on May 23, 1909, in Hausberge. She was deported from Cologne on October 30, 1941, to the Łódź ghetto. She

was deported from Łódź to Chełmno during May 1942, where she perished.

BASCH, Helene: Born on May 25, 1901, in Eggesin. She was deported from Berlin on October 27–29, 1941, to the Łódź ghetto. She was deported from Łódź to Chełmno on May 5, 1942. She perished in Chełmno on May 5, 1942.

BASCHWITZ, Cacilie: Born on August 11, 1867, in Bromberg, Poland. She was deported from Berlin on November 1, 1941, to the Łódź ghetto. She was deported from Łódź to Chełmno on May 13, 1942. She perished in Chełmno on May 13, 1942.

BASSFREUND, Adele: Born on March 5, 1869, in Strzelno, Poland. She was deported from Berlin on October 18, 1941, to the Łódź ghetto. She was deported from Łódź to Chełmno on May 4, 1942. She perished in Chełmno on May 4, 1942.

BAUER, Felix: Born on September 11, 1897, in Gladenbach. She was deported from Cologne on October 30, 1941, to the Łódź ghetto. She was deported from Łódź to Chełmno during May 1942, where she perished.

BAUM, Amalie: Born on March 7, 1891, in Welschbillig. She was deported from Cologne on October 30, 1941, to the Łódź ghetto. She was deported from Łódź to Chełmno where she perished.

BAUMANN, Gertrud: Born on December 30, 1876, in Berlin. She was deported from Berlin on October 24, 1941, to the Łódź ghetto. She was deported from Łódź to Chełmno on May 4, 1942. She perished in Chełmno on May 4, 1942.

BAUMBLATT, Anna: Born on December 15, 1892, in Berlin. She was deported from Berlin on October 18, 1941, to the Łódź ghetto. She was deported from Łódź to Chełmno on May 4, 1942. She perished in Chełmno on May 4, 1942.

BAUMER, Abraham: Born on January 29, 1899, in Pilica, Poland. He was deported from Berlin on October 24, 1941, to the Łódź ghetto. He was deported from Łódź to Chełmno on May 4, 1942. He perished in Chełmno on May 4, 1942.

BAUMGARTEN, Bertha: Born on March 22, 1886, in Berlin. She was deported from Berlin on October 24, 1941, to the Łódź ghetto. She was deported from Łódź to Chełmno on September 10, 1942. She perished in Chełmno on September 10, 1942.

BAUSER, Erna: Born on July 31, 1902, in Breslau, Poland. She was deported from Berlin on October 24, 1941, to the Łódź ghetto. She was deported from Łódź to Chełmno on May 4, 1942. She perished in Chełmno on May 4, 1942.

BECKER, Else: Born on April 1, 1888, in Łódź, Poland. She was imprisoned in the *Sammelstelle* on Levetzowstrasse, Berlin. She was deported from Berlin on November 1, 1941, to the Łódź ghetto. She was deported from Łódź to Chełmno on September 11, 1942. She perished in Chełmno on September 11, 1942.

BEER, Anna: Born on March 13, 1869, in Soehren. She was deported from Berlin on November 1, 1941, to the Łódź ghetto. She was deported from Łódź to Chełmno on September 8, 1942. She perished in Chełmno on September 8, 1942.

BEERMANN, Carola: Born on October 5, 1896, in Kassel. She was deported from Cologne on October 22, 1941, to the Łódź ghetto. She was deported from Łódź to Chełmno on May 10, 1942, where she perished.

BEHR, Abraham: Born on October 8, 1868, in Lobzenica, Poland. He was deported from Berlin on November 1, 1941, to the Łódź ghetto. He was deported from Łódź to Chełmno on May 9, 1942. He perished in Chełmno on May 9, 1942.

BEHRENS, Alina: Born on December 26, 1884, in Schweich. She was deported from Cologne on October 30, 1941, to the Łódź ghetto. She was deported from Łódź to Chełmno during May 1942, where she perished.

BEIN, Betty: Born on November 13, 1895, in Wronki, Poland. She was deported from Berlin on November 1, 1941, to the Łódź ghetto. She was deported from Łódź to Chełmno on May 9, 1942. She perished in Chełmno on May 9, 1942.

BEITH, Günther: Born on June 14, 1933, in Hamburg. He was deported from Hamburg on October 25, 1941, to the Łódź ghetto. He was deported from Łódź to Chełmno on May 10, 1942, where he perished.

BELAU, Emma: Born on April 10, 1901, in Poznań Poland. She was deported from Berlin on October 24, 1941, to the Łódź ghetto. She was deported from Łódź to Chełmno on May 4, 1942. She perished in Chełmno on May 4, 1942.

BELITZER, Regina: Born on August 5, 1875, in Berlin. She was deported from Berlin on October 27–29, 1941, to the Łódź ghetto. She was deported from Łódź to Chełmno on May 6, 1942, where she perished.

BENDA, Emmy: Born on August 24, 1887, in Berlin. She was deported from Berlin on October 18, 1941, to the Łódź ghetto. She was deported from Łódź to Chełmno on May 4, 1942. She perished in Chełmno on May 4, 1942.

BENDER, Emma: Born on June 5, 1891, in Polch. She was deported from Düsseldorf on October 27, 1941, to the Łódź ghetto. She was deported from Łódź to Chełmno on May 9, 1942. She perished in Chełmno on May 10, 1942.

BENDIK, Jenny: Born on September 13, 1875, in Soldau. She was deported from Düsseldorf on October 27, 1941, to the Łódź ghetto. She was deported from Łódź to Chełmno on May 13, 1942. She perished in Chełmno on May 14, 1942.

BENDIT, Bernhard: Born on January 20, 1866, in Lobzenica, Poland. He was deported from Berlin on October 24, 1941, to the Łódź ghetto. He was deported from Łódź to Chełmno on May 13, 1942. He perished in Chełmno on May 13, 1942.

BENGER, Hermann: Born on February 17, 1888, in Katowice, Poland. He was deported from Berlin on October 24, 1941, to the Łódź ghetto. He was deported from Łódź to Chełmno on May 4, 1942. He perished in Chełmno on May 4, 1942.

BENJAMIN, Adele: Born on April 29, 1885, in Gros-Steinheim. She was deported from Cologne on October 22, 1941, to the Łódź ghetto. She was deported from Łódź to Chełmno during May 1942, where she perished.

BENZIAN, Margarete: Born on January 12, 1874, in Berlin. She was deported from Berlin on November 1, 1941, to the Łódź ghetto. She was deported from Łódź to Chełmno on May 8, 1942. She perished in Chełmno on May 8, 1942.

BENZION, Herta: Born on July 3, 1904, in Berlin. She was deported from Berlin on October 24, 1941, to the Łódź ghetto. She was deported from Łódź to Chełmno on May 15, 1942. She perished in Chełmno on May 15, 1942.

BEREND, Franz: Born on August 19, 1881, in Hannover. He was deported from Hamburg, on October 25, 1941, to the Łódź ghetto. He was deported from Łódź to Chełmno on May 12, 1942, where he perished.

BERG, Alfred: Born on May 4, 1921, in Cologne. He was deported from Cologne on October 30, 1941, to the Łódź ghetto. He was deported from Łódź to Chełmno during May 1942, where he perished.

BERGEL, Marianne: Born on February 12, 1878, in Geldern. She was deported from Düsseldorf on October 27, 1941, to the Łódź ghetto. She was deported from Łódź to Chełmno during September 1942, where she perished.

BERGER, Alexander: Born on August 8, 1886, in Mayen. He was imprisoned in Dachau Concentration Camp in November 1938. He was deported from Düsseldorf on October 27, 1941, to the Łódź ghetto. He was deported from Łódź to Chełmno during September 1942, where he perished.

BERGMANN, Betti: Born on February 17, 1886, in Labiau. She was deported from Berlin on November 1, 1941, to the Łódź ghetto. She was deported from Łódź to Chełmno on May 9, 1942, where she perished.

BERKHEIM, Alfred: Born on December 9, 1884, in Berlin. He was deported from Berlin on November 1, 1941, to the Łódź ghetto. He was deported from Łódź to Chełmno on May 8, 1942, where he perished.

BERKOWICZ, David: Born on November 4, 1896, in Krzepice, Poland. He was expelled from Duisburg on October 28, 1938, to Zbąszyń, Poland. He was deported from Düsseldorf on October 27, 1941, to the

Łódź ghetto. He was deported from Łódź to Chełmno on July 14, 1944. He perished in Chełmno on July 15, 1944.

BERL, Gertrud: Born on August 17, 1885, in Lyck. She was imprisoned in the *Sammelstelle* on *Levetzowstrasse*, Berlin. She was deported from Berlin on October 18, 1941, to the Łódź ghetto. She was deported from Łódź to Chełmno on May 8, 1942. She perished in Chełmno on May 8, 1942.

BERLIN, Emmy: Born on November 4, 1885, in Cologne. She was deported from Cologne on October 22, 1941, to the Łódź ghetto. She was deported from Łódź to Chełmno on May 4, 1942, where she perished.

BERLOWITZ, Anna: Born on July 27, 1879, in Bublitz. She was deported from Berlin on October 24, 1941, to the Łódź ghetto. She was deported from Łódź to Chełmno on May 4, 1942. She perished in Chełmno on May 4, 1942.

BERMANN, Jenny: Born on April 15, 1883, in Zell. She was deported from Cologne on October 22, 1941, to the Łódź ghetto. She was deported from Łódź to Chełmno on May 6, 1942, where she perished.

BERNDT, Rosa: Born on October 12, 1879, in Graudenz, Poland. She was deported from Cologne on October 22, 1941, to the Łódź ghetto. She was deported from Łódź to Chełmno during May 1942, where she perished.

BERNHARD, Irene: Born on January 12, 1912, in Munstermaifeld. She was deported from Düsseldorf on October 27, 1941, to the Łódź ghetto. She was deported from Łódź to Chełmno on May 9, 1942. She perished in Chełmno on May 10, 1942.

BERNHARDT, Adelheid: Born on February 21, 1876, in Swinenmunde. She was deported from Berlin on November 1, 1941, to the Łódź ghetto. She was deported from Łódź to Chełmno on May 9, 1942. She perished in Chełmno on May 9, 1942.

BERNHAUT, Jakob: Born on November 12, 1888, in Kolomea. He was deported from Berlin on October 18, 1941, to the Łódź ghetto. He was deported from Łódź to Chełmno on June 26, 1944. He perished in Chełmno on June 26, 1944.

BERNSOHN, Hermann: Born on November 13, 1877, in Podbusz, Poland. He was imprisoned in the *Sammelstelle* on *Levetzowstrasse*, Berlin. He was deported from Berlin on October 24, 1941, to the Łódź ghetto. He was deported from Łódź to Chełmno on May 4, 1942. He perished in Chełmno on May 4, 1942.

BERNSTEIN, Antonie: Born on July 28, 1891, in Hamburg. He was deported from Hamburg on October 25, 1941, to the Łódź ghetto. He was deported from Łódź to Chełmno on May 4, 1942, where he perished.

BERNTHAL, Edith: Born on October 13, 1891, in Görlitz. She was deported from Hamburg on October 25, 1941, to the Łódź ghetto. She was deported from Łódź to Chełmno, where she perished.

BESEN, Josefine: Born on January 8, 1899, in Kuty, Poland. She was deported from Düsseldorf on October 27, 1941, to the Łódź ghetto. She was deported from Łódź to Chełmno during September 1942, where she perished.

BESTEHER, Hedwig: Born on February 26, 1894, in Berlin. She was deported from Berlin on October 18, 1941, to the Łódź ghetto. She was deported from Łódź to Chełmno on May 4, 1942, where she perished.

BESTHOF, Alma: Born on August 7, 1895, in Bleicherode. She was deported from Düsseldorf on October 27, 1941, to the Łódź ghetto. She was deported from Łódź to Chełmno on May 8, 1942. She perished in Chełmno on May 9, 1942.

BETTELHEISER, Hermann: Born on December 31, 1877, in Laasphe. He was deported from Cologne on October 22, 1941, to the Łódź ghetto. He was deported from Łódź to Chełmno during May 1942. He perished in Chełmno on May 6, 1942.

BETTENHAUSEN, Alice: Born on April 30, 1905, in Barmen-Elberfeld. She was deported from Düsseldorf on October 27, 1941, to the Łódź ghetto. She was deported from Łódź to Chełmno on June 26, 1944. She perished in Chełmno on June 27, 1944.

BETTMANN, Leo: Born on January 30, 1902, in Cologne. He was deported from Cologne on October 22, 1941, to the Łódź ghetto. He was deported from Łódź to Chełmno on May 6, 1942, where he perished.

BEUTLER, Marion: Born on August 15, 1905, in Berlin. She was deported from Berlin on October 27–29, 1941, to the Łódź ghetto. She was deported from Łódź to Chełmno on May 5, 1942. She perished in Chełmno on May 5, 1942.

BEZEN, Bilba: Born on December 5, 1939, in Hamburg. She was deported from Hamburg on October 25, 1941, to the Łódź ghetto. She perished in Chełmno on September 29, 1942.

BIBERFELD, Dorothea: Born on June 20, 1886, in Obornik, Poland. She was deported from Berlin on October 18, 1941, to the Łódź ghetto. She was deported from Łódź to Chełmno on May 7, 1942, where she perished.

BIBO, Elsa: Born on November 28, 1888, in Erfurt. She was deported from Berlin on October 18, 1941, to the Łódź ghetto. She was deported from Łódź to Chełmno on May 8, 1942. She perished in Chełmno on May 8, 1942.

BICK, Anna: Born on April 10, 1896, in Frille. She was deported from Berlin on November 1, 1941, to the Łódź ghetto. She was deported from Łódź to Chełmno on May 8, 1942. She perished in Chełmno on May 8, 1942.

BIER, Albertine: Born on February 11, 1921, in Cologne. She was deported from Cologne on October 30, 1941, to the Łódź ghetto. She was deported from Łódź to Chełmno during May 1942, where she perished.

BIERMANN, Margarete: Born on November 6, 1885, in Berlin. She was deported from Berlin on November 1, 1941, to the Łódź ghetto. She was deported from Łódź to Chełmno on May 9, 1942, where she perished.

BIESUNSKI, Adele: Born on July 8, 1905, in Daugavpils, Russia. She was deported from Düsseldorf on October 27, 1941, to the Łódź ghetto. She was deported from Łódź to Chełmno on May 6, 1942. She perished in Chełmno on May 7, 1942.

BILSKI, Charlotte: Born on December 12, 1903, in Wriezen. She was deported from Berlin on October 24, 1941, to the Łódź ghetto. She

was deported from Łódź to Chełmno on May 4, 1942, where she perished.

BING, Manfred: Born on December 17, 1890, in Frankfurt am Main. He was deported from Düsseldorf on October 27, 1941, to the Łódź ghetto. He was deported from Łódź to Chełmno during September 1942, where he perished.

BIRMANN, Josef: Born on November 5, 1889, in Przedbórz, Poland. He was expelled from Hamburg on October 28, 1938, to Zbąszyń, Poland. He was imprisoned in the Zbąszyń internment camp until the summer of 1939. He was deported from the Łódź ghetto to Chełmno where he perished.

BIRN, Samuel: Born on August 2, 1875, in Andrychów, Poland. He was deported from Berlin on October 18, 1941, to the Łódź ghetto. He was deported from Łódź to Chełmno on May 7, 1942. He perished in Chełmno on May 7, 1942.

BLACH, Betti: Born on September 21, 1885, in Rosenthal. She was deported from Cologne on October 22, 1941, to the Łódź ghetto. She was deported from Łódź to Chełmno during May 1942, where she perished.

BLANCKE, Otto: Born on September 20, 1876, in Hameln. He was deported from Cologne on October 22, 1941, to the Łódź ghetto. He was deported from Łódź to Chełmno on May 9, 1942, where he perished.

BLANKENSTEIN, Martha: Born on December 25, 1866, in Poznań, Poland. She was deported from Berlin on October 18, 1941, to the Łódź ghetto. She was deported from Łódź to Chełmno on May 8, 1942. She perished in Chełmno on May 8, 1942.

BLASS, Auguste: Born on October 12, 1877, in Kydran. She was deported from Berlin on October 18, 1941, to the Łódź ghetto. She was deported from Łódź to Chełmno on May 8, 1942. She perished in Chełmno on May 8, 1942.

BLATT, Isaak: Born on November 4, 1884, in Sieniawa, Poland. He was imprisoned from November 17, 1938, until December 21, 1938, in the Dachau Concentration Camp. He was deported from Düsseldorf on

October 27, 1941, to the Łódź ghetto. He was deported from Łódź to Chełmno on May 5, 1942. He perished in Chełmno on May 6, 1942.

BLATTBERG, Osias: Born on December 1, 1891, in Mielec, Poland. He was deported from Cologne on October 30, 1941, to the Łódź ghetto. He was deported from Łódź to Chełmno during May 1942, where he perished.

BLAUKOPF, Berko: Born on May 3, 1886, in Gogolina. She was deported from Berlin on October 18, 1941, to the Łódź ghetto. She was deported from Łódź to Chełmno on May 7, 1942. She perished in Chełmno on May 7, 1942.

BLAUSTEIN, Berthold: Born on June 17, 1900, in Berlin. He was deported from Cologne on October 30, 1941, to the Łódź ghetto. He was deported from Łódź to Chełmno during May 1942, where he perished.

BLEICH, Markus: Born on January 15, 1891, in Skalat, Poland. He was expelled from Hamburg on October 28, 1938, to Zbąszyń, Poland. He was imprisoned in Hamburg-Fuhlsbüttel during 1939–1940. He was deported from Hamburg on October 25, 1941, to the Łódź ghetto. He was deported from Łódź to Chełmno on April 25, 1942, where he perished.

BLIMBAUM, Sofie: Born on May 25, 1896, in Kolomea, Poland. She emigrated from Leipzig on July 1, 1939, to Poland. She was deported from the Łódź ghetto to Chełmno on March 15, 1942, where she perished.

BLITSTEIN, Gertrud: Born on April 9, 1868, in Berlin. She was deported from Berlin on October 27–29, 1941, to the Łódź ghetto. She was deported from Łódź to Chełmno on May12, 1942. She perished in Chełmno on May 12, 1942.

BLITZBLUM, Friedrich: Born on May 21, 1935, in Essen. He was deported from Düsseldorf on October 27, 1941, to the Łódź ghetto. He was deported from Łódź to Chełmno on May 11, 1942. He perished in Chełmno on May 12, 1942.

BLOCH, Helga: Born on April 1, 1929, in Berlin. She was deported from Berlin on October 27–29, 1941, to the Łódź ghetto. She was deported from Łódź to Chełmno on May 5, 1942, where she perished.

BLOCK, Ida: Born on July 19, 1882, in Westerkappeln. She was deported from Cologne on October 22, 1941, to the Łódź ghetto. She was deported from Łódź to Chełmno during May 1942, where she perished.

BLUHM, Hedwig: Born on December 13, 1887, in Osche. She was deported from Berlin on October 24, 1941, to the Łódź ghetto. She was deported from Łódź to Chełmno on May 4, 1942. She perished in Chełmno on May 4, 1942.

BLUM, David: Born on August 30, 1879, in Kestrich. He was imprisoned from November 15, 1938, until November 19, 1938, in the Dachau Concentration Camp. He was deported from Cologne on October 30, 1941, to the Łódź ghetto. He was deported from Łódź to Chełmno on June 23, 1944, where he perished.

BLUMENAU, Clara: Born on November 14, 1891, in Krefeld. She was deported from Düsseldorf on October 27, 1941, to the Łódź ghetto. She was deported from Łódź to Chełmno on May 6, 1942. She perished in Chełmno on May 7, 1942.

BLUMENFELD, Ilse: Born on December 8, 1934, in Berlin. She was deported from Berlin on October 24, 1941, to the Łódź ghetto. She was deported from Łódź to Chełmno on May 13, 1942, where she perished.

BLUMENKRON, Mathilde: Born on January 18, 1902, in Cologne. She was deported from Cologne on October 22, 1941, to the Łódź ghetto. She was deported from Łódź to Chełmno during May 1942, where she perished.

BLUMENRATH, Berta: Born on October 2, 1877, in Dortmund. She was deported from Düsseldorf on October 27, 1941, to the Łódź ghetto. She was deported from Łódź to Chełmno on May 7, 1942. She perished in Chełmno on May 8, 1942.

BLUMENTHAL, Albert: Born on April 3, 1878, in Pattensen. He was deported from Düsseldorf on October 27, 1941, to the Łódź ghetto. He was deported from Łódź to Chełmno during September 1942, where he perished.

BLUMGARDT, Erich: Born on March 27, 1908, in Cologne. He was deported from Cologne on October 22, 1941, to the Łódź ghetto. He was deported from Łódź to Chełmno on September 21, 1942, where he perished.

BOAS, Clara: Born on July 23, 1874, in Freystadt. She was deported from Berlin on November 1, 1941, to the Łódź ghetto. She was deported from Łódź to Chełmno on May 9, 1942. She perished on May 9, 1942.

BOCK, Renate: Born on November 28, 1899, in Berlin. She was deported from Berlin on November 1, 1941, to the Łódź ghetto. She was deported from Łódź to Chełmno on May 9, 1942. She perished in Chełmno on May 9, 1942.

BOHM, Elsa: Born on April 7, 1877, in Ixelles, Brussels, Belgium. She was imprisoned in the *Sammelstelle* on *Levetzowstrasse*, Berlin. She was deported from Berlin on October 24, 1941, to the Łódź ghetto. She was deported from Łódź to Chełmno on May 4, 1942. She perished in Chełmno on May 4, 1942.

BOHRMANN, Amanda: Born on May 19, 1882, in Hasloch. She was deported from Düsseldorf on October 27, 1941, to the Łódź ghetto. She was deported from Łódź to Chełmno on May 5, 1942. She perished in Chełmno on May 6, 1942.

BONDY, Johanna: Born on December 17, 1883, in Cologne. She was deported from Cologne on October 22, 1941, to the Łódź ghetto. She was deported from Łódź to Chełmno during May 1942, where she perished.

BONEM, Alice: Born on February 17, 1876, in Frankfurt am Main. She was deported from Cologne on October 30, 1941, to the Łódź ghetto. She was deported from Łódź to Chełmno during May 1942, where she perished.

BONHEIM, Margarete: Born on March 10, 1888, in Dessau. She was deported from Berlin on October 18, 1941, to the Łódź ghetto. She was deported from Łódź to Chełmno on May 8, 1942, where she perished.

BONIFACIUS, Lotte: Born on July 14, 1898, in Elbing. She was deported from Hamburg on October 25, 1941, to the Łódź ghetto. She was deported from Łódź to Chełmno on May 18, 1942, where she perished.

BORCHARDT, Hanna: Born on January 16, 1877, in Goral. She was deported from Berlin on October 18, 1941, to the Łódź ghetto. She was deported from Łódź to Chełmno on May 8, 1942, where she perished.

BORCHERT, Anna: Born on May 7, 1921, in Berlin. She was deported from Berlin on October 27–29, 1941, to the Łódź ghetto. She was deported from Łódź to Chełmno on May 5, 1942. She perished in Chełmno on May 5, 1942.

BORCK, Emil: Born on October 23, 1867, in Breslau, Poland. He was deported from Berlin on October 24, 1941, to the Łódź ghetto. He was deported from Łódź to Chełmno on September 11, 1942, where he perished.

BORKOWSKI, Samuel: Born on December 20, 1903, in Baku, Russia. He was deported from Düsseldorf on October 27, 1941, to the Łódź ghetto. He was deported from Łódź to Chełmno on May 13, 1942. He perished in Chełmno on May 14, 1942.

BORNHEIM, Margot: Born on December 11, 1929, in Kaiserswerth. She was deported from Düsseldorf on October 27, 1941, to the Łódź ghetto. She was deported from Łódź to Chełmno during September 1942, where she perished.

BORNSTEIN, Jakob: Born on September 16, 1894, in Kraków, Poland. He was deported from Berlin on October 18, 1941, to the Łódź ghetto. He was deported from Łódź to Chełmno on May 8, 1942. He perished in Chełmno on May 8, 1942.

BORODKIN, Rosa: Born on June 25, 1884, in Breslau, Poland. She was deported from Berlin on November 1, 1941, to the Łódź ghetto. She was deported from Łódź to Chełmno on May 8, 1942. She perished in Chełmno on May 8, 1942.

BOROSCHEK, Karl: Born on June 3, 1899, in Jarotschin, Poland. He was deported from Berlin on October 24, 1941, to the Łódź ghetto. He was deported from Łódź to Chełmno on September 13, 1942. He perished in Chełmno on September 13, 1942.

BOROWSKI, Mendel: Born on June 11, 1936. He was deported from the Łódź ghetto to Chełmno on July 12, 1944, where he perished.

BOTSHAIM, Hindla: Born on March 20, 1895, in Puławy, Poland. She was deported from Berlin on October 27–29, 1941, to the Łódź ghetto. She was deported from Łódź to Chełmno on September 10, 1942. She perished in Chełmno on September 10, 1942.

BOUSCHER, Eduard: Born on May 22, 1899, in Solingen. He was imprisoned in the Dachau Concentration Camp between November 17, 1938 and December 15, 1938. He was deported from Düsseldorf on October 27, 1941, to the Łódź ghetto. He was deported from Łódź to Chełmno on May 13, 1942. He perished in Chełmno on May 14, 1942.

BOYGEN, Sonja: Born on December 15, 1930, in Hamburg. She was expelled on October 28, 1938, to Zbąszyń, Poland. She was deported from Berlin on November 1, 1941, to the Łódź ghetto. She was deported from Łódź to Chełmno on April 28, 1942. She perished in Chełmno on April 28, 1942.

BRACH, Milli: Born on February 19, 1892, in Berlin. She was deported from Berlin on October 18, 1941, to the Łódź ghetto. She was deported from Łódź to Chełmno on May 8, 1942, where she perished.

BRACK, Ilse: Born on March 10, 1904, in Barmen-Elberfeld. She was deported from Düsseldorf on October 27, 1941, to the Łódź ghetto. She was deported from Łódź to Chełmno on May 12, 1942. She perished in Chełmno on May 13, 1942.

BRAGENHEIM, Erna: Born on January 28, 1888, in Berlin. She was deported from Hamburg on October 25, 1941, to the Łódź ghetto. She was deported from Łódź to Chełmno on May 10, 1942, where she perished.

BRAM, Erwin: Born on January 14, 1904, in Berlin. He was deported from Berlin on October 27–29, 1941, to the Łódź ghetto. He was deported from Łódź to Chełmno on May 4, 1942. He perished in Chełmno on May 4, 1942.

BRAMM, Hertha: Born on July 15, 1895, in Berlin. She was deported from Berlin on October 27–29, 1941, to the Łódź ghetto. She was

deported from Łódź to Chełmno on May 6, 1942. She perished in Chełmno on May 6, 1942.

BRANDT, Alfred: Born on February 16, 1899, in Gros-Strehlitz. He was deported from Berlin on October 24, 1941, to the Łódź ghetto. He was deported from Łódź to Chełmno on July 3, 1944, where he perished.

BRASCH, Arno: Born on February 11, 1909, in Eberswalde. He was deported from Berlin on November 1, 1941, to the Łódź ghetto. He was deported from Łódź to Chełmno on May 4, 1942. He perished in Chełmno on May 4, 1942.

BRAUER, Herta: Born on August 14, 1911, in Solingen. She was deported from Düsseldorf on October 27, 1941, to the Łódź ghetto. She was deported from Łódź to Chełmno on May 5, 1942. She perished in Chełmno on May 6, 1942.

BRAUN, Frieda: Born on April 3, 1889, in Poznań, Poland. She was deported from Berlin on November 1, 1941, to the Łódź ghetto. She was deported from Łódź to Chełmno on May 9, 1942. She perished in Chełmno on May 9, 1942.

BRAUNSCHWEIGER, Ella: Born on July 3, 1891, in Deutschdorf. She was deported from Hamburg on October 25, 1941, to the Łódź ghetto. She was deported from Łódź to Chełmno on September 11, 1942, where she perished.

BRAV, Adolf: Born on November 29, 1890, in Tarnów, Poland. He was imprisoned on November 17, 1938, in Dachau Concentration Camp. He was deported from Düsseldorf on October 27, 1941, to the Łódź ghetto. He was deported from Łódź to Chełmno on May 6, 1942. He perished in Chełmno on May 7, 1942.

BREITENSTEIN, Johanna: Born July 13, 1883, in Altenwalde. She was deported from Berlin on November 1, 1941, to the Łódź ghetto. She was deported from Łódź to Chełmno on May 8, 1942. She perished in Chełmno on May 8, 1942.

BREMER, Regina: Born on February 28, 1907, in Berlin. She was deported from Berlin on October 24, 1941, to the Łódź ghetto. She was deported from Łódź to Chełmno on May 4, 1942, where she perished.

BRESLAUER, Adele: Born on October 14, 1877, in Buschkau. She was deported from Berlin on October 18, 1941, to the Łódź ghetto. She was deported from Łódź to Chełmno on May 8, 1942. She perished in Chełmno on May 8, 1942.

BRESSLER, Moritz: Born on November 1, 1879, in Schildberg. He was deported from Berlin on October 18, 1941, to the Łódź ghetto. He was deported from Łódź to Chełmno on May 8, 1942, where he perished.

BREUMANN, Ella: Born on September 29, 1899, in Mallwischken. She was deported from Berlin on October 18, 1941, to the Łódź ghetto. She was deported from Łódź to Chełmno on May 8, 1942, where she perished.

BRIEGER, Klara: Born on April 15, 1892, in Mainz. She was deported from Cologne on October 30, 1941, to the Łódź ghetto. She was deported from Łódź to Chełmno during May 1942, where she perished.

BRILL, Neuma: Born on May 17, 1906, in Minsk, Russia. She was deported from Berlin on October 24, 1941, to the Łódź ghetto. She was deported from Łódź to Chełmno on May 4, 1942. She perished in Chełmno on May 4, 1942.

BRILLES, Hedwig: Born on March 9, 1879, in Neumark. She was deported from Berlin on October 27–29, 1941, to the Łódź ghetto. She was deported from Łódź to Chełmno on May 4, 1942. She perished in Chełmno on May 4, 1942.

BRINGER, Ida: Born on March 7, 1900, in Zolynia, Poland. She was deported from Cologne on October 22, 1941, to the Łódź ghetto. She was deported from Łódź to Chełmno during May 1942, where she perished.

BRINITZER, Erna: Born August 14, 1891, in Schrimm, Poland. She was imprisoned in the *Sammelstelle* on *Levetzowstrasse,* Berlin. She was deported from Berlin on October 18, 1941, to the Łódź ghetto. She was deported from Łódź to Chełmno on May 8, 1942. She perished in Chełmno on May 8, 1942.

BRINK, Joseph: Born on March 1, 1875, in Emden. He was deported from Berlin on October 24, 1941, to the Łódź ghetto. He was deported from Łódź to Chełmno on May 12, 1942. He perished in Chełmno on May 12, 1942.

BRINN, Julius: Born on October 9, 1871, in Schippenbell. He was deported from Berlin on November 1, 1941, to the Łódź ghetto. He was deported from Łódź to Chełmno on May 12, 1942, where he perished.

BRODEK, Frieda: Born on December 5, 1879, in Berlin. She was deported from Berlin on October 18, 1941, to the Łódź ghetto. She was deported from Łódź to Chełmno on May 8, 1942. She perished in Chełmno on May 8, 1942.

BRODER, Nelly: Born on August 17, 1898, in Vienna, Austria. She was deported from Berlin on October 24, 1941, to the Łódź ghetto. She was deported from Łódź to Chełmno on May 4, 1942. She perished in Chełmno on May 4, 1942.

BRODT, Charlotte: Born on May 21, 1920, in Düsseldorf. She was deported from Düsseldorf on October 27, 1941, to the Łódź ghetto. She was deported from Łódź to Chełmno on May 5, 1942. She perished in Chełmno on May 6, 1942.

BROMBERGER, Anni: Born on April 10, 1925, in Berlin. She was deported from Berlin on October 24, 1941, to the Łódź ghetto. She was deported from Łódź to Chełmno on May 4, 1942. She perished in Chełmno on May 4, 1942.

BRONSTEIN, David: Born on June 10, 1882, in Odessa, Russia. He was deported from Düsseldorf on October 27, 1941, to the Łódź ghetto. He was deported from Łódź to Chełmno on May 6, 1942. He perished in Chełmno on May 7, 1942.

BRUCH, Ludwig: Born on May 21, 1876, in Vettweiss. He was deported from Cologne on October 22, 1941, to the Łódź ghetto. He was deported from Łódź to Chełmno during May 1942, where he perished.

BRUCHFELD, Lotte: Born on February 10, 1908, in Cologne. She was deported from Cologne on October 22, 1941, to the Łódź ghetto. She was deported from Łódź to Chełmno on May 4, 1942, where she perished.

BRUCK, Julia: Born on June 16, 1870, in New York, United States of America. She was deported from Berlin on October 24, 1941, to the

Łódź ghetto. She was deported from Łódź to Chełmno on May 12, 1942. She perished in Chełmno on May 12, 1942.

BRUCKMANN, Max: Born on September 24, 1881, in Krefeld. He was deported from Cologne on October 22, 1941, to the Łódź ghetto. He was deported from Łódź to Chełmno during May 1942, where he perished.

BRÜCK, Gisela: Born on February 26, 1938, in Berlin. She was deported from Berlin on October 27–29, 1941, to the Łódź ghetto. She was deported from Łódź to Chełmno on May 4, 1942. She perished in Chełmno on May 4, 1942.

BRÜCKMANN, Henny: Born on April 4, 1910, in Hannover. She was deported from Hamburg on October 25, 1941, to the Łódź ghetto. She was deported from Łódź to Chełmno on September 10, 1942, where she perished.

BRÜGGERMANN, Else: Born on May 3, 1885, in Birnbaum. She was imprisoned in the *Sammelstelle* on *Levetzowstrasse*, Berlin. She was deported from Berlin on November 1, 1941, to the Łódź ghetto. She was deported from Łódź to Chełmno on May 4, 1942. She perished in Chełmno on May 4, 1942.

BRÜNELL, Hannelore: Born on December 14, 1930, in Goch. She was deported from Düsseldorf on October 27, 1941, to the Łódź ghetto. She was deported from Łódź to Chełmno on May 6, 1942. She perished in Chełmno on May 7, 1942.

BRUMEL, Gertrud: Born on May 16, 1915, in Wasungen. She was deported from Prague on October 31, 1941, to the Łódź ghetto. She was deported from Łódź to Chełmno on May 8, 1942, where she perished.

BUCHEIMER, Rosalie: Born on March 9, 1888, in Cologne. She was deported from Cologne on October 22, 1941, to the Łódź ghetto. She was deported from Łódź to Chełmno on May 4, 1942. She perished in Chełmno on May 8, 1942.

BUCHOLZ, Gertrud: Born on February 13, 1867, in Poznań, Poland. She was deported from Berlin on October 18, 1941, to the Łódź ghetto. She was deported from Łódź to Chełmno on September 12, 1942. She perished in Chełmno on September 12, 1942.

BUD, Elise: Born on May 29, 1883, in Berlin. She was deported from Berlin on October 27–29, 1941, to the Łódź ghetto. She was deported from Łódź to Chełmno on May 4, 1942, where she perished.

BÜCHENBACHER, Sophie: Born on February 6, 1877, in Fürth. She was deported from Cologne on October 22, 1941, to the Łódź ghetto. She was deported from Łódź to Chełmno during May 1942, where she perished.

BUKOFZER, Erich: Born on August 26, 1922, in Würzburg. He was deported from Berlin on October 27–29, 1941, to the Łódź ghetto. He was deported from Łódź to Chełmno on May 7, 1942. He perished in Chełmno on May 7, 1942.

BULLEMER, Johanna: Born on January 11, 1895, in Berlin. She was deported from Berlin on October 24, 1941, to the Łódź ghetto. She was deported from Łódź to Chełmno on May 4, 1942. She perished in Chełmno on May 4, 1942.

BUONAVENTURA, Fritz: Born on August 6, 1906, in Landeshut. He was deported from Berlin on October 18, 1941, to the Łódź ghetto. He was deported from Łódź to Chełmno on September 10, 1942. He perished in Chełmno on September 10, 1942.

BURCHARD, Sara: Born on September 1, 1876, in Margonin. She was deported from Berlin on November 1, 1941, to the Łódź ghetto. She was deported from Łódź to Chełmno on May 4, 1942. She perished in Chełmno on May 4, 1942.

BURCHARDI, Regina: Born May 10, 1879, in Egelsbach. She was deported from Cologne on October 22, 1941, to the Łódź ghetto. She was deported from Łódź to Chełmno on May 4, 1942. She perished in Chełmno on May 4, 1942.

BURG, Martin: Born on May 9, 1895, in Berlin. He was deported from Berlin on October 24, 1941, to the Łódź ghetto. He was deported from Łódź to Chełmno on May 4, 1942, where he perished.

BURGER, Johanna: Born on May 26, 1883, in Mitzkowo, Poland. She was deported from Berlin on October 24, 1941, to the Łódź ghetto. She was deported from Łódź to Chełmno on May 4, 1942. She perished in Chełmno on May 4, 1942.

BURGMANN, Betty: Born on October 11, 1874, in Bengel. She was deported from Düsseldorf on October 27, 1941, to the Łódź ghetto. She was deported from Łódź to Chełmno during September 1942, where she perished.

BURZINSKA, Cyria: Born on March 7, 1885, in Piotrków. She was deported from Düsseldorf on October 27, 1941, to the Łódź ghetto. She was deported from Łódź to Chełmno on May 6, 1942. She perished in Chełmno on May 7, 1942.

BUSCHHOFF, Hilde: Born on February 4, 1910, in Betzdorf. She was deported from Cologne on October 30, 1941, to the Łódź ghetto. She was deported from Łódź to Chełmno during September 1942, where she perished.

BUTOW, Anna: Born on May 4, 1881, in Könitz. She was deported from Berlin on November 1, 1941, to the Łódź ghetto. She was deported from Łódź to Chełmno on May 8, 1942. She perished in Chełmno on May 8, 1942.

BUTTNER, Lucie: Born on June 30, 1883, in Sandersleben. She was deported from Berlin on October 18, 1941, to the Łódź ghetto. She was deported from Łódź to Chełmno on May 8, 1942. She perished in Chełmno on May 8, 1942.

BUXBAUM, Emma: Born on October 26, 1881, in Nümbrecht. She was deported from Cologne on October 22, 1941, to the Łódź ghetto. She was deported from Łódź to Chełmno on May 6, 1942, where she perished.

BYTHINER, Kurt: Born on February 13, 1928, in Berlin. He was deported from Berlin on November 1, 1941, to the Łódź ghetto. He was deported from Łódź to Chełmno on May 6, 1942. He perished in Chełmno on May 6, 1942.

BYTINSKI, Ursula: Born on April 21, 1924, in Berlin. She was deported from Berlin on October 27–29, 1941, to the Łódź ghetto. She was deported from Łódź to Chełmno on May 4, 1942. She perished in Chełmno on May 4, 1942.

CAHEN, Ruth: Born on February 16, 1910, in Cologne. She was deported from Cologne on October 22, 1941, to the Łódź ghetto. She was deported from Łódź to Chełmno during June 1944, where she perished.

CAHN, Hedwig: Born on May 30, 1900, in Krefeld. She was deported from Düsseldorf on October 27, 1941, to the Łódź ghetto. She was deported from Łódź to Chełmno on May 6, 1942. She perished in Chełmno on May 7, 1942.

CALLMANN, Johanna: Born on September 7, 1911, in Cologne. She was deported from Cologne on October 30, 1941, to the Łódź ghetto. She was deported from Łódź to Chełmno during May 1942, where she perished.

CALM, Else: Born on February 27, 1878, in Berlin. She was deported from Berlin on October 18, 1941, to the Łódź ghetto. She was deported from Łódź to Chełmno on May 8, 1942. She perished in Chełmno on May 8, 1942.

CALMER, Richard: Born on March 24, 1874, in Cologne. He was deported from Cologne on October 22, 1941, to the Łódź ghetto. He was deported from Łódź to Chełmno during May 1942, where he perished.

CAMNITZER, Hertha: Born on November 23, 1899, in Berlin. She was deported from Berlin on November 1, 1941, to the Łódź ghetto. She was deported from Łódź to Chełmno on May 10, 1942. She perished in Chełmno on May 10, 1942.

CAPAUNER, Johanna: Born on October 8, 1876, in Lipine. She was deported from Berlin on November 1, 1941, to the Łódź ghetto. She was deported from Łódź to Chełmno on September 7, 1942, where she perished.

CAPPEL, Fanny: Born on April 8, 1887, in Cologne. She was deported from Düsseldorf on October 27, 1941, to the Łódź ghetto. She was deported from Łódź to Chełmno on May 6, 1942. She perished in Chełmno on May 7, 1942.

CARO, Gunda: Born on June 2, 1874, in Kozmin, Poland. She was deported from Berlin on October 18, 1941, to the Łódź ghetto. She was deported from Łódź to Chełmno on September 7, 1942, where she perished.

CARSCH, Adele: Born on December 18, 1896, in Mülheim. She was deported from Düsseldorf on October 27, 1941, to the Łódź ghetto. She was deported from Łódź to Chełmno on May 6, 1942. She perished in Chełmno on May 7, 1942.

CASPARI, Salomon: Born on November 28, 1877, in Rosenberg. He was deported from Berlin on November 1, 1941, to the Łódź ghetto. He was deported from Łódź to Chełmno on May 6, 1942. He perished in Chełmno on May 6, 1942.

CASPARIUS, Franziska: Born on October 4, 1876, in Viersen. She was deported from Düsseldorf on October 27, 1941, to the Łódź ghetto. She was deported from Łódź to Chełmno on May 6, 1942. She perished in Chełmno on May 7, 1942.

CASPARY, Hedwig: Born on January 30, 1880, in Wielen, Poland. She was imprisoned in the *Sammelstelle* on *Levetzowstrasse*, Berlin. She was deported from Berlin on November 1, 1941, to the Łódź ghetto. She was deported from Łódź to Chełmno on May 15, 1942. She perished in Chełmno on May 15, 1942.

CASPER, Marie: Born on May 20, 1883, in Stolp. She was deported from Berlin on October 18, 1941, to the Łódź ghetto. She was deported from Łódź to Chełmno on May 8, 1942. She perished in Chełmno on May 8, 1942.

CASSEL, Artur: Born on October 14, 1877, in Lauenburg. He was deported from Berlin on October 24, 1941, to the Łódź ghetto. He was deported from Łódź to Chełmno on September 10, 1942. He perished in Chełmno on September 10, 1942.

CASSIRER, Hilde: Born on May 15, 1902, in Kolberg. She was deported from Berlin on November 1, 1941, to the Łódź ghetto. She was deported from Łódź to Chełmno on May 9, 1942. She perished in Chełmno on May 9, 1942.

CENDROWICZ, Ruchla: Born on March 5, 1873, in Kalisch, Poland. She was deported from Berlin on October 27–29, 1941, to the Łódź ghetto.

She was deported from Łódź to Chełmno on May 13, 1942. She perished in Chełmno on May 13, 1942.

CHAIM, Johanna: Born on May 23, 1892, in Luckenwalde. She was deported from Cologne on October 22, 1941, to the Łódź ghetto. She was deported from Łódź to Chełmno during May 1942. She perished in Chełmno on May 10, 1942.

CHASKEL, Martin: Born on September 4, 1875, in Poznań, Poland. He was deported from Cologne on October 22, 1941, to the Łódź ghetto. He was deported from Łódź to Chełmno on May 5, 1942, where he perished.

CHMIELNIEKA, Ester: Born on March 14, 1888, in Kielce, Poland. She was deported from Berlin on October 27–29, 1941, to the Łódź ghetto. She was deported from Łódź to Chełmno on May 6, 1942. She perished in Chełmno on May 6, 1942.

CHOJNACKI, Lena: Born on June 5, 1913, in Falkenstein. She was expelled from Leipzig to Poland during the 1930's. She was deported from the Łódź ghetto to Chełmno on April 12, 1942, where she perished.

CHRAPLEWSKI, Bianka: Born on August 20, 1899, in Bartschin. She was deported from Berlin on October 27–29, 1941, to the Łódź ghetto. She was deported from Łódź to Chełmno on May 4, 1942. She perished in Chełmno on May 4, 1942.

CHRAPLOWSKY, Arnold: Born on November 15, 1886, in Belgard. He was imprisoned until December 20, 1938, in Sachsenhausen Concentration Camp. He was deported from Berlin on October 27–29, 1941, to the Łódź ghetto. He was deported from Łódź to Chełmno on May 4, 1942. He perished in Chełmno on May 4, 1942.

CIBULSKI, Edith: Born on September 1, 1934, in Berlin. She was deported from Berlin on October 27–29, 1941, to the Łódź ghetto. She was deported from Łódź to Chełmno on May 4, 1942. She perished in Chełmno on May 4, 1942.

CLAESSEN, Hans: Born on December 16, 1904, in Emmerich. He was imprisoned between November 17, 1938, and January 10, 1939, in Dachau Concentration Camp. He was deported from Cologne on

October 30, 1941, to the Łódź ghetto. He was deported from Łódź to Chełmno during June 1944, where he perished.

CLEFFMANN, Josefine: Born on March 29, 1880, in Wesel. She was deported from Cologne on October 22, 1941, to the Łódź ghetto. She was deported from Łódź to Chełmno during May 1942, where she perished.

COHEN, Anna: Born on July 6, 1885, in Schwerin. She was deported from Hamburg on October 25, 1941, to the Łódź ghetto. She was deported from Łódź to Chełmno on June 28, 1944. She perished in Chełmno on June 28, 1944.

COHN, Anneliese: Born on April 23, 1919, in Rheda. She was deported from Düsseldorf on October 27, 1941, to the Łódź ghetto. She was deported from Łódź to Chełmno on September 11, 1942. She perished in Chełmno on September 12, 1942.

COHNEN, Hugo: Born on September 21, 1877, in Jüchen. He was deported from Düsseldorf on October 27, 1941, to the Łódź ghetto. He was deported from Łódź to Chełmno on May 7, 1942. He perished in Chełmno on May 8, 1942.

CONRAD, Ella: Born on January 14, 1897, in Cologne. She was deported from Cologne on October 22, 1941, to the Łódź ghetto. She was deported from Łódź to Chełmno during July 1944. She perished in Chełmno on July 12, 1944.

CONRAK, Conrah: Born on August 29, 1882, in Neudamm. She was deported from Berlin on October 18, 1941, to the Łódź ghetto. She was deported from Łódź to Chełmno on May 8, 1942. She perished in Chełmno on May 8, 1942.

COPER, Calmann: Born on June 6, 1884, in Tuchel. He was deported from Berlin on October 27–29, 1941, to the Łódź ghetto. He was deported from Łódź to Chełmno on September 12, 1942. He perished in Chełmno on September 12–14, 1942.

COPPEL, Erna: Born on February 8, 1893, in Barmen-Elberfeld. She was deported from Düsseldorf on October 27, 1941, to the Łódź ghetto. She was deported from Łódź to Chełmno on June 26, 1944, where she perished.

CORNEL, Margit: Born on August 20, 1884, in Nagykáta, Hungary. She was deported from Berlin on October 18, 1941, to the Łódź ghetto. She was deported from Łódź to Chełmno on May 7, 1942. She perished in Chełmno on May 7, 1942.

COSSMANN, Ida: Born on July 18, 1895, in Zülpich. She was deported from Cologne on October 22, 1941, to the Łódź ghetto. She was deported from Łódź to Chełmno during May 1942, where she perished.

COURANT, Nuscha: Born on February 18, 1878, in Katowice, Poland. She was deported from Berlin on October 18, 1941, to the Łódź ghetto. She was deported from Łódź to Chełmno on May 13, 1942. She perished in Chełmno on May 13, 1942.

CREMER, Pauline: Born on June 11, 1880, in Hamburg. She was deported from Hamburg on October 25, 1941, to the Łódź ghetto. She was deported from Łódź to Chełmno on May 4, 1942, where she perished.

CRONER, Frieda: Born on December 13, 1875, in Wehrda. She was deported from Berlin on October 18, 1941, to the Łódź ghetto. She was deported from Łódź to Chełmno on May 8, 1942. She perished in Chełmno on May 8, 1942.

CUDKOWICZ, Rolf: Born on April 1, 1936, in Chemnitz. He was expelled from Chemnitz to Poland on October 28, 1938. He was deported from the Łódź ghetto to Chełmno on September 10, 1942, where he perished.

CUSSEL, Ernst: Born on July 26, 1887, in Hamm. He was deported from Düsseldorf on October 27, 1941, to the Łódź ghetto. He was deported from Łódź to Chełmno on May 7, 1942. He perished in Chełmno on May 8, 1942.

CUSTODIS, Elise: Born on May 11, 1901, in Cologne. She was deported from Cologne on October 22, 1941, to the Łódź ghetto. She was deported from Łódź to Chełmno during May 1942, where she perished.

CWERN, Jan: Born on December 31, 1917, in Essen. He was deported from Düsseldorf on October 27, 1941, to the Łódź ghetto. He was deported from Łódź to Chełmno on May 7, 1942. He perished in Chełmno on May 8, 1942.

CYTRYN, Henni: Born on January 12, 1890, in Sanok, Poland. She was deported from Berlin on October 27–29, 1941, to the Łódź ghetto. She was deported from Łódź to Chełmno on May 5, 1942. She perished in Chełmno on May 5, 1942.

CZAPSKI, Else: Born on March 9, 1889, in Bernstadt. She was deported from Berlin on October 18, 1941, to the Łódź ghetto. She was deported from Łódź to Chełmno on July 5, 1944. She perished in Chełmno on July 5, 1944.

DAGOWITSCH, Feige: Born on December 5, 1902, in Jarosław, Poland. She was deported from Berlin on November 1, 1941, to the Łódź ghetto. She was deported from Łódź to Chełmno on May 9, 1942. She perished in Chełmno on May 9, 1942.

DAHL, David: Born on March 18, 1885, in Dormagen. He was deported from Cologne on October 30, 1941, to the Łódź ghetto. He was deported from Łódź to Chełmno during September 1942, where he perished.

DAHLHEIMER, Flora: Born on August 11, 1897, in Schotten. She was deported from Frankfurt am Main on October 20, 1941, to the Łódź ghetto. She was deported from Łódź to Chełmno during September 1942, where she perished.

DAMMANN, Friederike, Born on December 23, 1888, in Frankfurt am Main. She was deported from Berlin on November 1, 1941, to the Łódź ghetto. She was deported from Łódź to Chełmno on May 9, 1942. She perished in Chełmno on May 9, 1942.

DANIEL, Else: Born on April 5, 1901, in Neuklunkwitz. She was deported from Berlin on November 1, 1941, to the Łódź ghetto. She was deported from Łódź to Chełmno on May 9, 1942. She perished in Chełmno on May 9, 1942.

DANIELSOHN, Frida: Born on August 30, 1899, in Berlin. She was deported from Berlin on October 27–29, 1941, to the Łódź ghetto. She was deported from Łódź to Chełmno on September 10, 1942. She perished in Chełmno on September 10, 1942.

DANNENBAUM, Charlotte: Born on November 13, 1891, in Hagenbach. She was deported from Düsseldorf on October 27, 1941, to the Łódź ghetto. She was deported from Łódź to Chełmno during September 1942, where she perished.

DANZIGER, Paula: Born on July 8, 1891, in Vienna, Austria. She was deported from Berlin on October 24, 1941, to the Łódź ghetto. She was deported from Łódź to Chełmno on May 5, 1942. She perished in Chełmno on May 5, 1942.

DAVID, Gertrud: Born on May 27, 1888, in Berlin. She was deported from Berlin on October 27–29, 1941, to the Łódź ghetto. She was deported from Łódź to Chełmno on May 5, 1942. She perished in Chełmno on May 5, 1942.

DAVIDMANN, Max: Born on January 25, 1905, in Berlin. He was deported from Berlin on November 1, 1941, to the Łódź ghetto. He was deported from Łódź to Chełmno on May 9, 1942. He perished in Chełmno on May 9, 1942.

DAVIDSOHN, Ella: Born on March 8, 1874, in Soldau. She was deported from Berlin on October 18, 1941, to the Łódź ghetto. She was deported from Łódź to Chełmno on May 8, 1942. She perished in Chełmno on May 8, 1942.

DAVIDSON, Martha: Born on September 19, 1879, in Schleusingen. She was deported from Düsseldorf on October 27, 1941, to the Łódź ghetto. She was deported from Łódź to Chełmno on May 7, 1942. She perished in Chełmno on May 8, 1942.

DAWIDOWICZ, Bronisława: Born on November 16, 1894, in Przedmość, Poland. She emigrated from Breslau to Poland. She was deported from the Łódź ghetto to Chełmno on September 10, 1942, where she perished.

DELIK, Else: Born on March 25, 1890, in Danzig. She was deported from Berlin on October 27–29, 1941, to the Łódź ghetto. She was deported from Łódź to Chełmno on May 4, 1942. She perished in Chełmno on May 4, 1942.

DEMBER, Julia: Born on October 18, 1883, in Mayen. She was deported from Cologne on October 22, 1941, to the Łódź ghetto. She was deported from Łódź to Chełmno during September 1942, where she perished.

DESSLER, Erna: Born on November 2, 1890, in Dortmund. She was deported from Cologne on October 30, 1941, to the Łódź ghetto. She was deported from Łódź to Chełmno during May 1942, where she perished.

DETTMANN, Anni: Born on May 6, 1907, in Hamburg. She was deported from Hamburg on October 25, 1941, to the Łódź ghetto. She was deported from Łódź to Chełmno on April 7, 1942, where she perished.

DEUTSCH, Fritz: Born on October 30, in Berlin. He was deported from Berlin on October 27–29, 1941, to the Łódź ghetto. He was deported from Łódź to Chełmno on May 5, 1942. He perished in Chełmno on May 5, 1942.

DIENSTFERTIG, Ella: Born on May 3, 1873, in Oels. She was deported from Berlin on November 1, 1941, to the Łódź ghetto. She was deported from Łódź to Chełmno on May 8, 1942. She perished in Chełmno on May 8, 1942.

DIETRICH, Marta: Born on November 19, 1893, in Trzemeszno, Poland. She was deported from Berlin on October 27–29, 1941, to the Łódź ghetto. She was deported from Łódź to Chełmno on May 4, 1942. She perished in Chełmno on May 4, 1942.

DIMENSTEIN, Eva: Born on March 22, 1914, in Berlin. She was deported from Berlin on October 24, 1941, to the Łódź ghetto. She was deported from Łódź to Chełmno on May 4, 1942, where she perished.

DINGFELDER, Kathe: Born on May 8, 1913, in Velbert. She was deported from Cologne on October 22, 1941, to the Łódź ghetto. She was deported from Łódź to Chełmno on May 12, 1942, where she perished.

DJUK, Maria: Born on July 2, 1882, in Istanbul, Turkey. She was deported from Düsseldorf on October 27, 1941, to the Łódź ghetto. She was deported from Łódź to Chełmno on May 9, 1942. She perished in Chełmno on May 10, 1942.

DOBRIN, Else: Born on March 10, 1914, in Lyck. She was imprisoned in the *Sammelstelle* on *Levetzowstrasse*, Berlin. She was deported from Berlin on November 1, 1941, to the Łódź ghetto. She was deported

from Łódź to Chełmno on May 9, 1942. She perished in Chełmno on May 9, 1942.

DOBRINER, Flora: Born on May 23, 1875, in Kiel. She was deported from Berlin on October 24, 1941, to the Łódź ghetto. She was deported from Łódź to Chełmno on May 4, 1942, where she perished.

DOBROWOLSKI, Else: Born on May 4, 1900, in Bonn. She was deported from Cologne on October 22, 1941, to the Łódź ghetto. She was deported from Łódź to Chełmno on May 4, 1942, where she perished.

DOKSCHITZKI, Miron: Born on May 28, 1894, in Minsk, Russia. He was deported from Berlin on October 27–29, 1941, to the Łódź ghetto. He was deported from Łódź to Chełmno on May 5, 1942. He perished in Chełmno on May 5, 1942.

DOMB, Max: Born on October 20, 1881, in Libau. He was deported from Cologne during 1941, to the Łódź ghetto. He perished in Chełmno during May 1942.

DOMBROWER, Edith: Born on August 10, 1921, in Berlin. She was imprisoned in the *Sammelstelle* on *Levetzowstrasse*, Berlin. She was deported from Berlin on October 18, 1941, to the Łódź ghetto. She was deported from Łódź to Chełmno on July 7, 1944. She perished in Chełmno on July 7, 1944.

DOMINSKY, Rebekka: Born on May 9, 1885, in Freystadt. She was deported from Berlin on October 27–29, 1941, to the Łódź ghetto. She was deported from Łódź to Chełmno on May 9, 1942. She perished in Chełmno on May 9, 1942.

DORN, Meta: Born on July 10, 1867, in Graudenz. She was imprisoned in the *Sammelstelle* on *Levetzowstrasse,* Berlin. She was deported from Berlin on October 18, 1941, to the Łódź ghetto. She was deported from Łódź to Chełmno on May 8, 1942. She perished in Chełmno on May 8, 1942.

DRATWA, Sara: Born on May 10, 1881, in Hamburg. She was deported from Hamburg on October 25, 1941, to the Łódź ghetto. She was deported from Łódź to Chełmno on May 10, 1942, where she perished.

DREIFUS, Hedwig: Born on February 15, 1883, in Telgte. She was deported from Cologne on October 30, 1941, to the Łódź ghetto. She was deported from Łódź to Chełmno during May 1942, where she perished.

DRESDNER, Herta: Born February 7, 1896, in Hamburg. She was deported from Hamburg on October 18, 1941, to the Łódź ghetto. She was deported from Łódź to Chełmno on May 10, 1942. She perished in Chełmno on May 10, 1942.

DRESSLER, Ruchla: Born on October 10, 1883, in Łódź, Poland. She was expelled from Chemnitz on October 28, 1938, to Poland. She was deported from Łódź to Chełmno where she perished.

DREYFUS, Albert: Born on October 3, 1873, in Altdorf. He was deported from Frankfurt am Main on October 20, 1941, to the Łódź ghetto. He was deported from Łódź to Chełmno during May 1942, where he perished.

DREYFUSS, Bernard: Born on March 1, 1880, in Albersweiler. He was deported from Düsseldorf on October 27, 1941, to the Łódź ghetto. He was deported from Łódź to Chełmno during September 1942, where he perished.

DROBINSKI, Liba: Born on November 18, 1871, in Odessa, Russia. She was deported from Berlin on November 1, 1941, to the Łódź ghetto. She was deported from Łódź to Chełmno on May 10, 1942. She perished in Chełmno on May 10, 1942.

DRUCKER, Ester: Born on January 2, 1896, in Dębica, Poland. She was deported from Berlin on November 1, 1941, to the Łódź ghetto. She was deported from Łódź to Chełmno on May 9, 1942, where she perished.

DRUTOWSKI, Elli: Born on December 13, 1877, in Vellahn. She was expelled from Hamburg on October 28, 1938, to Zbąszyń, Poland. She was imprisoned until the summer of 1939, in the Zbąszyń internment camp. She was deported from Hamburg on October 25, 1941, to the Łódź ghetto. She was deported from Łódź to Chełmno on May 10, 1942, where she perished.

DUBINSKA, Lea: Born on March 10, 1872, in Odessa, Russia. She was deported from Berlin on November 1, 1941, to the Łódź ghetto. She was deported from Łódź to Chełmno on May 9, 1942. She perished in Chełmno on May 9, 1942.

DUNJE, Hermann: Born on April 14, 1883, in Joniskis, Russia. He was deported from Berlin on October 24, 1941, to the Łódź ghetto. He was deported from Łódź to Chełmno on May 4, 1942. He perished in Chełmno on May 4, 1942.

DYMENTMANN, Chaim: Born on January 22, 1899, in Warsaw, Poland. He was deported from Berlin on November 1, 1941, to the Łódź ghetto. He was deported from Łódź to Chełmno on May 9, 1942. He perished in Chełmno on May 9, 1942.

ECKSTEIN, Elly: Born on October 2, 1883, in Unna. She was deported from Cologne on October 22, 1941, to the Łódź ghetto. She was deported from Łódź to Chełmno during May 1942, where she perished.

EDEL, Hermann: Born on November 9, 1891, in Lobsens, Poland. He was deported from Berlin on October 27–29, 1941, to the Łódź ghetto. He was deported from Łódź to Chełmno on May 4, 1942. He perished in Chełmno on May 4, 1942.

EDELSTEIN, Fanny: Born on March 22, 1883, in Laurahütte, (Huta Laura) Poland. She was deported from Berlin on October 27–29, 1941, to the Łódź ghetto. She was deported from Łódź to Chełmno on May 5, 1942. She perished in Chełmno on May 5, 1942.

EGER, Margarete: Born on March 13, 1878, in Berlin. She was deported from Berlin on October 24, 1941, to the Łódź ghetto. She was deported from Łódź to Chełmno on May 4, 1942. She perished in Chełmno on May 4, 1942.[166]

EGGENER, Alfred: Born on November 22, 1898, in Holten. He was deported from Cologne on October 30, 1941, to the Łódź ghetto. He was deported from Łódź to Chełmno during May 1942, where he perished.

---

[166] Margarete Eger is mentioned complete with family portrait in the book *Underground in Berlin*, by Marie Jalowicz Simon, published by Back Bay Books, 2016.

EHRENBAUM, Marta: Born on February 6, 1885, in Tessin. She was imprisoned in Fuhlsbüttel Concentration Camp during 1940. She was deported from Hamburg on October 25, 1941, to the Łódź ghetto. She was deported from Łódź to Chełmno on September 10, 1942, where she perished.

EHRENFELD, Ladislaus: Born on July 3, 1909, in Beregsurány, Hungary. He was deported from Berlin on October 27–29, 1941, to the Łódź ghetto. He was deported from Łódź to Chełmno on May 9, 1942. He perished in Chełmno on May 9, 1942.

EHRLICH, Edith: Born July 15, 1900, in Berlin. She was deported from Berlin on November 1, 1941, to the Łódź ghetto. She was deported from Łódź to Chełmno on May 9, 1942. She perished in Chełmno on May 9, 1942.

EHRMANN, Simson: Born on February 17, 1874, in Berlin. He was deported from Berlin on October 27–29, 1941, to the Łódź ghetto. He was deported from Łódź to Chełmno on May 13, 1942. He perished in Chełmno on May 13, 1942.

EICHEL, Frieda: Born on February 9, 1891, in Staudernheim. She was deported from Cologne on October 22, 1941, to the Łódź ghetto. She was deported from Łódź to Chełmno on May 4, 1942. She perished in Chełmno on May 4, 1942.

EICHELBAUM, Alice: Born on August 24, 1886, in Schloppe. She was deported from Berlin on October 18, 1941, to the Łódź ghetto. She was deported from Łódź to Chełmno on May 8, 1942. She perished in Chełmno on May 8, 1942.

EICHENGRÜN, Betty: Born on April 16, 1897, in Cologne. She was deported from Cologne on October 30, 1941, to the Łódź ghetto. She was deported from Łódź to Chełmno during May 1942, where she perished.

EICHENWALD, Herta: Born on April 9, 1905, in Schweich. She was deported from Düsseldorf on October 27, 1941, to the Łódź ghetto. She was deported from Łódź to Chełmno on May 7, 1942. She perished in Chełmno on May 8, 1942.

EICHOLD, Mathilde: Born on March 15, 1884, in Rockenhausen. She was deported from Berlin on October 24, 1941, to the Łódź ghetto. She was deported from Łódź to Chełmno on May 4, 1942. She perished in Chełmno on May 5, 1942.

EIGENFELD, Isaak: Born on April 2, 1884, in Perechinsko, Poland. He was deported from Düsseldorf on October 27, 1941, to the Łódź ghetto. He was deported from Łódź to Chełmno on May 14, 1942. He perished in Chełmno on May 15, 1942.

EIGER, Ruth: Born on September 27, 1911, in Kalleningken. She was deported from Berlin on October 18, 1941, to the Łódź ghetto. She was deported from Łódź to Chełmno on May 8, 1942. She perished in Chełmno on May 8, 1942.

EISENBERG, Alfred: Born on April 2, 1877, in Horn. He was deported from Cologne on October 30, 1941, to the Łódź ghetto. He was deported from Łódź to Chełmno during May 1942, where he perished.

EISENBLATT, Albert: Born on October 31, 1904, in Antwerp, Belgium. He was deported from Berlin on November 1, 1941, to the Łódź ghetto. He was deported from Łódź to Chełmno on May 9, 1942. He perished in Chełmno on May 9, 1942.

EISENFELD, Sara: Born on September 3, 1877, in Nisko, Poland. She was deported from Berlin on October 27–29, 1941, to the Łódź ghetto. She was deported from Łódź to Chełmno on May 11, 1942. She perished in Chełmno on May 11, 1942.

EISENSTADT, Gertrud: Born on August 3, 1882, in Markisch Friedland. She was deported from Berlin on November 1, 1941, to the Łódź ghetto. She was deported from Łódź to Chełmno on May 9, 1942. She perished in Chełmno on May 9, 1942.

EISERFEY, Ilse: Born on February 26, 1881, in Cologne. She was deported from Cologne during October 1941, to the Łódź ghetto. She was deported from Łódź to Chełmno on May 10, 1942. She perished in Chełmno on May 11, 1942.

EISIG, Frida: Born on August 29, 1880, in Berlin. She was deported from Berlin on October 27–29, 1941, to the Łódź ghetto. She was deported from Łódź to Chełmno on September 12, 1942. She perished in Chełmno on September 12, 1942.

EISNER, Sophie: Born on September 15, 1882, in Bütow. She was deported from Berlin on October 18, 1941, to the Łódź ghetto. She was deported from Łódź to Chełmno on May 8, 1942. She perished in Chełmno on May 8, 1942.

ELBERT, Lieselotte: Born on Jul 28, 1924, in Cologne. She was deported from Cologne on October 30, 1941, to the Łódź ghetto. She was deported from Łódź to Chełmno during June 1944, where she perished.

ELIAS, Auguste: Born on October 26, 1899, in Berlin. She was deported from Berlin on October 24, 1941, to the Łódź ghetto. She was deported from Łódź to Chełmno on May 4, 1942. She perished in Chełmno on May 4, 1942.

ELKAN, Ida: Born on January 30, 1878, in Hamm. She was deported from Cologne on October 30, 1941, to the Łódź ghetto. She was deported from Łódź to Chełmno during July 1944, where she perished.

ELSBACH, Ella: Born on October 16, 1897, in Walldorf. She was deported from Cologne on October 22, 1941, to the Łódź ghetto. She was deported from Łódź to Chełmno on May 4, 1942, where she perished.

EMANUEL, Bertha: Born on September 23, 1891, in Aldenhoven. She was deported from Cologne on October 22, 1941, to the Łódź ghetto. She was deported from Łódź to Chełmno during May 1942, where she perished.

ENGEL, Bella: Born on December 30, 1883, in Budapest, Hungary. She was deported from Berlin on October 27-29, 1941, to the Łódź ghetto. She was deported from Łódź to Chełmno on May 6, 1942. She perished in Chełmno on May 6, 1942.

ENGELARD, Betti: Born on July 17, 1927, in Berlin. She was deported from Berlin on October 24, 1941, to the Łódź ghetto. She was deported from Łódź to Chełmno on July 7, 1942. She perished in Chełmno on July 7, 1944.

EPHRAIM, Emillie: Born on March 8, 1886, in Osterath. She was deported from Düsseldorf on October 27, 1941, to the Łódź ghetto. She

was deported from Łódź to Chełmno on May 7, 1942. She perished in Chełmno on May 8, 1942.

EPPENHEIM, Hilda: Born on January 16, 1906, in Berlin. She was deported from Berlin on October 18, 1941, to the Łódź ghetto. She was deported from Łódź to Chełmno during September 1942, where she perished.

EPSTEIN, Helene: Born on June 26, 1895, in Żurawno, Poland. She was deported from Berlin on October 27–29, 1941, to the Łódź ghetto. She was deported from Łódź to Chełmno on May 5, 1942. She perished in Chełmno on May 5, 1942.

ERMANN, Rosa: Born on October 10, 1881, in Leiwen. She was deported from Luxembourg-Trier on October 16, 1941, to the Łódź ghetto. She was deported from Łódź to Chełmno on May 10, 1942, where she perished.

ERMOLNIKOFF, Frieda: Born on April 7, 1886, in Berlin. She was deported from Berlin on October 24, 1941, to the Łódź ghetto. She was deported from Łódź to Chełmno on May 4, 1942. She perished in Chełmno on May 4, 1942.

ERSZTER, Berty: Born on September 6, 1926, in Chemnitz. She was expelled from Chemnitz to Poland on October 28, 1938. She was deported from the Łódź ghetto to Chełmno on June 26, 1944, where she perished.

ESCHEN, Blanka: Born on September 4, 1880, in Samter, Poland. She was deported from Berlin on October 18, 1941, to the Łódź ghetto. She was deported from Łódź to Chełmno on May 8, 1942. She perished in Chełmno on May 8, 1942.

ESSER, Erna: Born on June 30, 1893, in Cologne. She was deported from Cologne on October 22, 1941, to the Łódź ghetto. She was deported from Łódź to Chełmno on May 10, 1942, where she perished.

ESSERHOLZ, Veronika: Born on June 1, 1895, in Cologne. She was deported from Cologne on October 22, 1941, to the Łódź ghetto. She was deported from Łódź to Chełmno during May 1942, where she perished.

ETTINGER, Abraham: Born on May 13, 1886, in Eppingen. He was deported from Berlin on October 18, 1941, to the Łódź ghetto. He was deported from Łódź to Chełmno on May 8, 1942. He perished in Chełmno on May 8, 1942.

EWERTH, Wilhelm: Born on June 25, 1897, in Berlin. He was deported from Berlin on October 27–29, 1941, to the Łódź ghetto. He was deported from Łódź to Chełmno on May 5, 1942. He perished in Chełmno on May 5, 1942.

FABIAN, Erna: Born on August 16, 1897, in Berlin. She was deported from Berlin on November 1, 1941, to the Łódź ghetto. She was deported from Łódź to Chełmno on May 5, 1942. She perished in Chełmno on May 5, 1942.

FABISCH, Hedwig: Born on June 7, 1889, in Graudenz. She was deported from Berlin on November 1, 1941, to the Łódź ghetto. She was deported from Łódź to Chełmno on May 8, 1942. She perished in Chełmno on May 8, 1942.

FÄRBER, Siegfried: Born on August 5, 1920, in Breslau. He was deported from Berlin on November 1, 1941, to the Łódź ghetto. He was deported from Łódź to Chełmno on May 14, 1942. He perished in Chełmno on May 14, 1942.

FAIBUSCH, Esther: Born on February 9, 1936, in Cologne. She was deported from Cologne on October 30, 1941, to the Łódź ghetto. She was deported from Łódź to Chełmno during May 1942, where she perished.

FALK, Auguste: Born on September 8, 1877, in Hamm. She was imprisoned in the *Sammelstelle* on *Levetzowstrasse*, Berlin. She was deported from Berlin on October 24, 1941, to the Łódź ghetto. She was deported from Łódź to Chełmno on May 4, 1942. She perished in Chełmno on May 4, 1942.

FALKENSTEIN, Betty: Born on March 6, 1892, in Lechenich. She was deported from Cologne on October 22, 1941, to the Łódź ghetto. She was deported from Łódź to Chełmno on May 11, 1942. She perished in Chełmno on May 11, 1942.

FALKSON, Helene: Born on March 17, 1873, in Kassel. She was deported from Berlin on October 27–29, 1941, to the Łódź ghetto. She was deported from Łódź to Chełmno on May 4, 1942. She perished in Chełmno on May 4, 1942.

FAMILIER, Gerda: Born on February 3, 1910, in Berlin. She was deported from Berlin on October 24, 1941, to the Łódź ghetto. She was deported from Łódź to Chełmno on May 4, 1942. She perished in Chełmno on May 4, 1942.

FEBER, Regina: Born on February 29, 1879, in Katowice. She was deported from Cologne on October 22, 1941, to the Łódź ghetto. She was deported from Łódź to Chełmno on May 4, 1942, where she perished.

FEDER, Fanny: Born on March 28, 1882, in Munich. She was deported from Berlin on October 18, 1941, to the Łódź ghetto. She was deported from Łódź to Chełmno on May 8, 1942. She perished in Chełmno on May 8, 1942.

FEDERMANN, Paula: Born on March 27, 1894, in Łódź, Poland. She was expelled from Leipzig on October 28, 1938, to Poland. She was deported from the Łódź ghetto to Chełmno on September 29, 1942, where she perished.

FEIBUSCH, Jenny: Born on October 24, 1880, in Fordon. She was deported from Berlin on October 18, 1941, to the Łódź ghetto. She was deported from Łódź to Chełmno on May 8, 1942. She perished in Chełmno on May 8, 1942.

FEIERTAG, Johanna: Born on July 16, 1886, in Berlin. She was deported from Berlin on October 18, 1941, to the Łódź ghetto. She was deported from Łódź to Chełmno on May 7, 1942. She perished in Chełmno on May 7, 1942.

FEIGE, Selma: Born on July 3, 1876, in Poznań, Poland. She was deported from Berlin on November 1, 1941, to the Łódź ghetto. She was deported from Łódź to Chełmno on May 9, 1942. She perished in Chełmno on May 9, 1942.

FEILER, Esther: Born on April 12, 1909, in Tarnów, Poland. She was deported from Berlin on October 24, 1941, to the Łódź ghetto. She was

deported from Łódź to Chełmno on May 4, 1942. She perished in Chełmno on May 4, 1942.

FELD, Klara: Born December 24, 1904, in Skołoszów, Poland. She was deported from Berlin on October 18, 1941, to the Łódź ghetto. She was deported from Łódź to Chełmno on May 8, 1942. She perished in Chełmno on May 8, 1942.

FELDHAHN, Alfred: Born June 8, 1880, in Mainstockheim. He was deported from Düsseldorf on October 27, 1941, to the Łódź ghetto. He was deported from Łódź to Chełmno on May 7, 1942. He perished in Chełmno on May 8, 1942.

FELDMANN, Elly: Born on July 9, 1888, in Düsseldorf. She was deported from Cologne on October 22, 1941, to the Łódź ghetto. She was deported from Łódź to Chełmno on September 10, 1942. She perished in Chełmno on September 14, 1942.

FELDMAR, Walli: Born on August 21, 1909, in Berlin. He was deported from Berlin on October 18, 1941, to the Łódź ghetto. He was deported from Łódź to Chełmno on May 9, 1942. He perished in Chełmno on May 9, 1942.

FELLS, Anne: Born on February 23, 1890, in Berent. She was deported from Hamburg on October 25, 1941, to the Łódź ghetto. She was deported from Łódź to Chełmno on May 15, 1942, where she perished.

FELSENTHAL, Bruno: Born on October 9, 1875, in Aachen. He was deported from Berlin on October 18, 1941, to the Łódź ghetto. He was deported from Łódź to Chełmno on May 13, 1942. He perished in Chełmno on May 13, 1942.

FENICHEL, Zerline: Born on July 14, 1896, in Berlin. She was deported from Berlin on October 18, 1941, to the Łódź ghetto. She was deported from Łódź to Chełmno on May 9, 1942. She perished in Chełmno on May 9, 1942.

FENSTER, Eva: Born on May 20, 1870, in Neustadt. She was deported from Berlin on November 1, 1941, to the Łódź ghetto. She was deported from Łódź to Chełmno on May 8, 1942. She perished in Chełmno on May 8, 1942.

FERBER, Berta: Born on August 3, 1882, in Mainz. She was deported from Cologne on October 22, 1941, to the Łódź ghetto. She was deported from Łódź to Chełmno during July 1944, where she perished.

FERNICH, Helene: Born on May 14, 1887, in Castrop-Rauxel. She was deported from Cologne on October 30, 1941, to the Łódź ghetto. She was deported from Łódź to Chełmno where she perished on September 13, 1942.

FERTIG, Sareli: Born on September 28, 1899, in Samocice, Poland. She was deported from Berlin on October 27–29, 1941, to the Łódź ghetto. She was deported from Łódź to Chełmno on June 30, 1944. She perished in Chełmno on June 30, 1944.

FEUER, Jenny: Born on July 31, 1886, in Berlin. She was deported from Berlin on October 27–29, 1941, to the Łódź ghetto. She was deported from Łódź to Chełmno on May 4, 1942. She perished in Chełmno on May 4, 1942.

FEUERSTEIN, Heinz: Born on October 3, 1904, in Poznań, Poland. He was deported from Berlin on November 1, 1941, to the Łódź ghetto. He was deported from Łódź to Chełmno on May 4, 1942. He perished in Chełmno on May 4, 1942.

FEYBUSCH, Julius: Born on May 7, 1891, in Stettin. He was deported from Berlin on October 18, 1941, to the Łódź ghetto. He was deported from Łódź to Chełmno on June 30, 1944. He perished in Chełmno on June 30, 1944.

FICHTELBERG, Sandor: Born on December 31, 1871, in Zmabar. He was deported from Berlin on November 1, 1941, to the Łódź ghetto. He was deported from Łódź to Chełmno during March 1942, where he perished.

FIDELMANN, Erna: Born on March 23, 1882, in Dresden. She was deported from Berlin on October 18, 1941, to the Łódź ghetto. She was deported from Łódź to Chełmno on May 8, 1942. She perished in Chełmno on May 8, 1942.

FINGER, Anna: Born on October 6, 1897, in Berlin. She was deported from Berlin on October 24, 1941, to the Łódź ghetto. She was

deported from Łódź to Chełmno on May 4, 1942. She perished in Chełmno on May 4, 1942.

FINK, Adele: Born on August 31, 1881, in Beek, Holland. She was deported from Cologne on October 30, 1941, to the Łódź ghetto. She was deported from Łódź to Chełmno where she perished during May 1942.

FINKEL, Jenny: Born on June 15, 1882, in Poznań, Poland. She was deported from Berlin on October 18, 1941, to the Łódź ghetto. She was deported from Łódź to Chełmno on May 9, 1942. She perished in Chełmno on May 9, 1942.

FINKELS, Tana: Born on April 19, 1940, in Berlin. She was deported from Berlin on October 18, 1941, to the Łódź ghetto. She was deported from Łódź to Chełmno during September 1942, where she perished.

FINKENSTEIN, Flora: Born on May 4, 1866, in Berlin. She was deported from Berlin on October 18, 1941, to the Łódź ghetto. She was deported from Łódź to Chełmno on September 7, 1942. She perished in Chełmno on September 7, 1942.

FISCHEL, Rita: Born on May 3, 1917, in Berlin. She was deported from Berlin on October 27-29, 1941, to the Łódź ghetto. She was deported from Łódź to Chełmno on May 8, 1942. She perished in Chełmno on May 8, 1942.

FISCHER, Heinz: Born on February 15, 1903, in Berlin. He was deported from Berlin on October 24, 1941, to the Łódź ghetto. He was deported from Łódź to Chełmno on May 4, 1942. He perished in Chełmno on May 4, 1942.

FISCHLERMAN, Hinda: Born on April 16, 1900, in Warsaw, Poland. She was deported from Berlin on November 1, 1941, to the Łódź ghetto. She was deported from Łódź to Chełmno on May 14, 1942. She perished in Chełmno on May 14, 1942.

FLANZREICH, Marion: Born on June 10, 1940, in Berlin. She was deported from Berlin on October 18, 1941, to the Łódź ghetto. She was deported from Łódź to Chełmno on May 8, 1942. She perished in Chełmno on May 8, 1942.

FLATAU, Frieda: Born on November 24, 1889, in Breslau. She was deported from Berlin on October 18, 1941, to the Łódź ghetto. She was deported from Łódź to Chełmno on May 8, 1942. She perished in Chełmno on May 8, 1942.

FLATAUER, Rudolf: Born on January 17, 1878, in Bischofswerder. He was deported from Berlin on October 18, 1941, to the Łódź ghetto. He was deported from Łódź to Chełmno on May 8, 1942. He perished in Chełmno on May 8, 1942.

FLATOW, Alice: Born on May 21, 1889, in Berlin. She was deported from Berlin on October 27–29, 1941, to the Łódź ghetto. She was deported from Łódź to Chełmno on May 9, 1942. She perished in Chełmno on May 9, 1942.

FLEISCHER, Ida: Born on August 7, 1889, in Demmelsdorf. She was deported from Berlin on November 1, 1941, to the Łódź ghetto. She was deported from Łódź to Chełmno on September 7, 1942. She perished in Chełmno on September 7, 1942.

FLEISCHMANN, Johanna: Born on July 19, 1877, in Jihlava. She was deported from Berlin on October 18, 1941, to the Łódź ghetto. She was deported from Łódź to Chełmno on May 8, 1942. She perished in Chełmno on May 8, 1942.

FLIESS, Hella: Born on February 28, 1923, in Berlin. She was deported from Berlin on October 27–29, 1941, to the Łódź ghetto. She was deported from Łódź to Chełmno on May 4, 1942. She perished in Chełmno on May 4, 1942.

FLONDER, Itta: Born on March 9, 1891, in Kłodawa, Poland. She lived in Danzig, and emigrated to Poland. She was deported from the Łódź ghetto during September 1942, where she perished.

FÖRSTER, Lilli: Born on July 3, 1909, in Berlin. She was deported from Berlin on October 27–29, 1941, to the Łódź ghetto. She was deported from Łódź to Chełmno on May 5, 1942. She perished in Chełmno on May 5, 1942.

FOGEL, Elias: Born on December 19, 1919, in Berlin. He was expelled from Berlin on October 28, 1938, to Zbąszyń, Poland. He was deported from Zduńska Wola to the Łódź ghetto. He was deported from Łódź to Chełmno on June 28, 1944, where he perished.

FONTHEIM, Harry: Born on May 24, 1881, in Diepholz. He was deported from Berlin on October 18, 1941, to the Łódź ghetto. He was deported from Łódź to Chełmno on May 8, 1942. He perished in Chełmno on May 8, 1942.

FRÄNKEL, Alma: Born on June 10, 1878, in Ostrich. She was deported from Düsseldorf on October 27, 1941, to the Łódź ghetto. She was deported from Łódź to Chełmno on May 6, 1942. She perished in Chełmno on May 7, 1942.

FRAJERMANN, Chaja: Born on January 13, 1870, in Janowitz, Poland. She was deported from Berlin on October 24, 1941, to the Łódź ghetto. She was deported from Łódź to Chełmno on May 13, 1942. She perished in Chełmno on May 13, 1942.

FRANK, Berta: Born on August 25, 1882, in Anhausen. She was deported from Düsseldorf on October 27, 1941, to the Łódź ghetto. She was deported from Łódź to Chełmno on May 6, 1942. She perished in Chełmno on May 7, 1942.

FRANKE, Taube: Born on May 18, 1878, in Gnesen, Poland. She was deported from Berlin on November 1, 1941, to the Łódź ghetto. She was deported from Łódź to Chełmno on May 8, 1942. She perished in Chełmno on May 8, 1942.

FRANKEN, Erna: Born on November 21, 1894, in Emmerich. She was deported from Düsseldorf on October 27, 1941, to the Łódź ghetto. She was deported from Łódź to Chełmno on May 7, 1942. She perished in Chełmno on May 8, 1942.

FRANKENSTEIN, Ella: Born on June 6, 1891, in Berlin. She was deported from Berlin on October 18, 1941, to the Łódź ghetto. She was deported from Łódź to Chełmno during September 1942, where she perished.

FRANKENTHAL, Edith: Born on August 10, 1908, in Berlin. She was deported from Berlin on October 24, 1941, to the Łódź ghetto. She was deported from Łódź to Chełmno on May 5, 1942. She perished in Chełmno on May 5, 1942.

FRANKFURT, Carl: Born on August 17, 1886, in Krefeld. He was imprisoned between November 17, 1938, and December 23, 1938, in Dachau Concentration Camp. He was deported from Düsseldorf on October 27, 1941, to the Łódź ghetto. He was deported from Łódź to Chełmno on May 7, 1942. He perished in Chełmno on May 8, 1942.

FRAYSTMANN, Chawa: Born on December 29, 1902, in Warsaw, Poland. She was deported from Berlin on November 1, 1941, to the Łódź ghetto. She was deported from Łódź to Chełmno on June 28, 1944. She perished in Chełmno on June 28, 1944.

FREIMARK, Therese: Born on October 6, 1893, in Cologne. She was deported from Cologne on October 22, 1941, to the Łódź ghetto. She was deported from Łódź to Chełmno on September 14, 1942. She perished in Chełmno on September 14, 1942.

FREIMUTH, Emil: Born on March 31, 1880, in Sedlice. He was imprisoned in Fuhlsbüttel Police prison during December 1939. He was deported from Hamburg on October 25, 1941, to the Łódź ghetto. He was deported from Łódź to Chełmno on September 2, 1942, where he perished.

FREIREICH, Hinda: Born on February 7, 1906, in Nowy Sącz, Poland. She was deported from Berlin on October 27–29, 1941, to the Łódź ghetto. She was deported from Łódź to Chemno on May 4, 1942. She perished in Chełmno on May 4, 1942.

FREITAG, Rosa: Born on May 7, 1891, in Nowy Tomyśl, Poland. She was deported from Düsseldorf on October 27, 1941, to the Łódź ghetto. She was deported from Łódź to Chełmno on May 7, 1942. She perished in Chełmno on May 8, 1942.

FRENKEL, Selma: Born on January 28, 1892, in Jüchen. She was deported from Cologne on October 22, 1941, to the Łódź ghetto. She was deported from Łódź to Chełmno on May 1, 1942, where she perished.

FRENSDORF, Erich: Born on April 24, 1924, in Hamburg. He was deported from Hamburg on October 25, 1941, to the Łódź ghetto. He was deported from Łódź to Chełmno on May 3, 1942, where he perished.

FREUDENBERG, Gertrud: Born on August 24, 1885, in Berlin. She was deported from Berlin on October 18, 1941, to the Łódź ghetto. She was deported from Łódź to Chełmno on July 7, 1944. She perished in Chełmno on July 7, 1944.

FREUND, Walter: Born on May 11, 1883, in Bielschowitz. He was deported from Berlin on November 1, 1941, to the Łódź ghetto. He was deported from Łódź to Chełmno on May 12, 1942. He perished in Chełmno on May 12, 1942.

FREUNDLICH, Johanna: Born on January 21, 1873, in Montau. She was deported from Berlin on October 18, 1941, to the Łódź ghetto. She was deported from Łódź to Chełmno on May 8, 1942. She perished in Chełmno on May 8, 1942.

FREY, Clara: Born on November 11, 1882, in Langendorf. She was deported from Berlin on October 18, 1941, to the Łódź ghetto. She was deported from Łódź to Chełmno on May 8, 1942. She perished in Chełmno on May 8, 1942.

FRIEDBERG, Kurt: Born on April 17, 1933, in Kirchberg. He was deported from Cologne on October 30, 1941, to the Łódź ghetto. He was deported from Łódź to Chełmno during May 1942, where he perished.

FRIEDBERGER, Gerd: Born on January 14, 1925, in Solingen. He was deported from Düsseldorf on October 27, 1941, to the Łódź ghetto. He was deported from Łódź to Chełmno on May 9, 1942. He perished in Chełmno on May 10, 1942.

FRIEDE, Elisabeth: Born on May 3, 1884, in Berlin. She was deported from Cologne on October 22, 1941, to the Łódź ghetto. She was deported from Łódź to Chełmno during May 1942. She perished in Chełmno on May 24, 1942.

FRIEDEBERG, Henriette: Born on December 14, 1867, in Birnbaum. She was deported from Berlin on October 24, 1941, to the Łódź ghetto. She was deported from Łódź to Chełmno during May 1942. She perished in Chełmno on May 12, 1942.

FRIEDEMANN, Erna: Born on February 18, 1903, in Stettin. She was deported from Berlin on October 27–29, 1941, to the Łódź ghetto. She was deported from Łódź to Chełmno on September 12, 1942. She perished in Chełmno on September 12, 1942.

FRIEDENSOHN, Meta: Born on December 5, 1885, in Berlin. She was deported from Berlin on October 18, 1941, to the Łódź ghetto. She was deported from Łódź to Chełmno on May 8, 1942. She perished in Chełmno on May 8, 1942.

FRIEDHEIM, Rosa: Born on December 29, 1885, in Essen. She was deported from Düsseldorf on October 27, 1941, to the Łódź ghetto. She was deported from Łódź to Chełmno on May 7, 1942. She perished in Chełmno on May 8, 1942.

FRIEDLANDER, Albertine: Born on July 7, 1874, in Rheydt. She was deported from Düsseldorf on October 27, 1941, to the Łódź ghetto. She was deported from Łódź to Chełmno on May 7, 1942. She perished in Chełmno on May 8, 1942.

FRIEDLICH, Laja: Born on September 5, 1874, in Podgórz. She was deported from Berlin on October 27–29, 1941, to the Łódź ghetto. She was deported from Łódź to Chełmno on May 4, 1942. She perished in Chełmno on May 4, 1942.

FRIEDMANN, Albert: Born on November 22, 1887, in Kobylin, Poland. He was deported from Berlin on October 27–29, 1941, to the Łódź ghetto. He was deported from Łódź to Chełmno on May 4, 1942. He perished in Chełmno on May 4, 1942.

FRÖHLICH, Anne: Born on May 3, 1923, in Koblenz. She was deported from Cologne on October 22, 1941, to the Łódź ghetto. She was deported from Łódź to Chełmno during May 1942. She perished in Chełmno on May 8, 1942.

FRÖLING, Flora: Born on September 29, 1898, in Barmen. She was deported from Cologne on October 22, 1941, to the Łódź ghetto. She was deported from Łódź to Chełmno on May 8, 1942, where she perished.

FROHNHAUSEN, Frieda: Born on October 10, 1885, in Bublitz. She was deported from Berlin on October 18, 1941, to the Łódź ghetto. She was deported from Łódź to Chełmno on May 8, 1942. She perished in Chełmno on May 8, 1942.

FROHWEIN, Ella: Born on August 22, 1885, in Strempt. She was deported from Düsseldorf on October 27, 1941, to the Łódź ghetto. She was deported from Łódź to Chełmno on May 7, 1942. She perished in Chełmno on May 8, 1942.

FROMM, Dorothea: Born on July 25, 1908, in Berlin. She was deported from Berlin on November 1, 1941, to the Łódź ghetto. She was deported from Łódź to Chełmno on June 9, 1942. She perished in Chełmno on June 9, 1942.

FROST, Georg: Born on May 6, 1904, in Wronki, Poland. He was deported from Berlin on October 27–29, 1941, to the Łódź ghetto. He was deported from Łódź to Chełmno on May 12, 1942. He perished in Chełmno on May 12, 1942.

FRÜCHTER, Berta: Born on December 11, 1879, in Borysław, Poland. She was deported from Berlin on November 1, 1941, to the Łódź ghetto. She was deported from Łódź to Chełmno on May 8, 1942. She perished in Chełmno on May 8, 1942.

FRUCHTZWEIG, Emillie: Born on September 30, 1885, in Dorsten. She was deported from Düsseldorf on October 27, 1941, to the Łódź ghetto. She was deported from Łódź to Chełmno on May 7, 1942. She perished in Chełmno on May 8, 1942.

FRUH, Else: Born on April 1, 1912, in Berlin. She was deported from Berlin on October 27–29, 1941, to the Łódź ghetto. She was deported from Łódź to Chełmno on May 5, 1942. She perished in Chełmno on May 5, 1942.

FRÜHLING, Else: Born on May 18, 1899, in Gniezno, Poland. She was deported from Berlin on October 27–29, 1941, to the Łódź ghetto. She was deported from Łódź to Chełmno on May 4, 1942. She perished in Chełmno on May 4, 1942.

FUCHS, Albert: Born on April 26, 1899, in Berlin. He was deported from Berlin on October 27–29, 1941, to the Łódź ghetto. He was deported from Łódź to Chełmno on May 4, 1942. He perished in Chełmno on May 4, 1942.

FÜRST, Julie: Born on November 25, 1907, in Kumehnen. She was deported from Berlin on October 18, 1941, to the Łódź ghetto. She was

deported from Łódź to Chełmno on May 8, 1942. She perished in Chełmno on May 8, 1942.

FÜRSTENBERG, Elfriede: Born on May 8, 1885, in Reichenbach. She was deported from Berlin on October 18, 1941, to the Łódź ghetto. She was deported from Łódź to Chełmno on May 8, 1942, where she perished.

FULTHEIM, Bianka: Born on May 14, 1880, in Gleicherwiesen. She was deported from Cologne on October 22, 1941, to the Łódź ghetto. She was deported from Łódź to Chełmno during May 1942, where she perished.

FURMANSKI, Elly: Born on June 17, 1894, in Hamburg. She was deported from Hamburg on October 25, 1941, to the Łódź ghetto. She was deported from Łódź to Chełmno on May 15, 1942, where she perished.

GABRIEL, Adolf: Born on September 25, 1872, in Wreschen, Poland. He was deported from Berlin on November 1, 1941, to the Łódź ghetto. He was deported from Łódź to Chełmno on May 9, 1942. He perished in Chełmno on May 9, 1942.

GÄRTNER, Helene: Born on May 11, 1882, in Rommerskirchen. She was deported from Cologne on October 22, 1941, to the Łódź ghetto. She was deported from Łódź to Chełmno during May 1942, where she perished.

GANDZIOR, Frieda: Born on November 15, 1885, in Sohrau. She was deported from Berlin on November 1, 1941, to the Łódź ghetto. She was deported from Łódź to Chełmno on May 9, 1942. She perished in Chełmno on May 9, 1942.

GANS, Berta: Born on July 12, 1915, in Cologne. She was deported from Cologne on October 22, 1941, to the Łódź ghetto. She was deported from Łódź to Chełmno during July 1944. She perished in Chełmno on July 10, 1944.

GAPPE, Paula: Born on September 3, 1884, in Koronowo, Poland. She was deported from Berlin on October 18, 1941, to the Łódź ghetto. She was deported from Łódź to Chełmno on May 8, 1942, where she perished.

GARAI, Moritz: Born on March 21, 1879, in Lonto, Hungary. He was deported from Prague on October 31, 1941, to the Łódź ghetto. He was deported from Łódź to Chełmno on May 8, 1942, where he perished.

GEDALJE, Amalie: Born on February 4, 1872, in Neubrück. She was deported from Berlin on November 1, 1941, to the Łódź ghetto. She was deported from Łódź to Chełmno on May 9, 1942. She perished in Chełmno on May 9, 1942.

GEISEL, Helene: Born on August 25, 1879, in Reichelsheim. She was deported from Cologne on October 22, 1941, to the Łódź ghetto. She was deported from Łódź to Chełmno during May 1942, where she perished.

GEISENHEIMER, Frieda: Born on June 2, 1889, in Cologne. She was deported from Cologne on October 30, 1941, to the Łódź ghetto. She was deported from Łódź to Chełmno during May 1942, where she perished.

GEISSLER, Charlotte: Born on May 28, 1913, in Berlin. She was deported from Berlin on October 24, 1941, to the Łódź ghetto. She was deported from Łódź to Chełmno on May 4, 1942. She perished in Chełmno on May 4, 1942.

GEIZMANN, Aron: Born on March 20, 1880, in Golowonesk, Russia. He was deported from Berlin on October 27–29, 1941, to the Łódź ghetto. He was deported from Łódź to Chełmno on May 10, 1942. He perished in Chełmno on May 10, 1942.

GELDERN, Elli: Born on May 25, 1916, in Bochum. She was deported from Düsseldorf on October 27, 1941, to the Łódź ghetto. She was deported from Łódź to Chełmno on May 13, 1942. She perished in Chełmno on May 14, 1942.

GELLER, Henry: Born on August 26, 1898, in Hamburg. He was deported from Hamburg on October 25, 1941, to the Łódź ghetto. He was deported from Łódź to Chełmno on May 10, 1942, where he perished.

GEMBICKI, Renate: Born on January 29, 1938, in Berlin. She was deported from Berlin on October 24, 1941, to the Łódź ghetto. She was

deported from Łódź to Chełmno on May 4, 1942. She perished in Chełmno on May 4, 1942.

GEMBITZ, Auguste: Born on October 13, 1876, in Gniezno, Poland. He was deported from Berlin on November 1, 1941, to the Łódź ghetto. He was deported from Łódź to Chełmno on May 8, 1942. He perished in Chełmno on May 8, 1942.

GENDLER, Werner: Born on March 18, 1927, in Berlin. He was deported from Berlin on October 27–29, 1941, to the Łódź ghetto. He was deported from Łódź to Chełmno on May 5, 1942. He perished in Chełmno on May 5, 1942.

GEPPERT, Rachela: Born on March 1, 1888, in Rawa Ruska. She was deported from Cologne on October 30, 1941, to the Łódź ghetto. She was deported from Łódź to Chełmno during May 1942, where she perished.

GERBER, Max: Born on April 21, 1877, in Obschilskin. He was deported from Berlin on October 24, 1941, to the Łódź ghetto. He was deported from Łódź to Chełmno on May 4, 1942. He perished in Chełmno on May 4, 1942.

GERECHTER, Anna: Born on January 6, 1887, in Kallies. She was deported from Berlin on November 1, 1941, to the Łódź ghetto. She was deported from Łódź to Chełmno on May 9, 1942. She perished in Chełmno on May 9, 1942.

GEROTHWOHL, Ignatz: Born on June 26, 1881, in Bingen. He was deported from Cologne on October 30, 1941, to the Łódź ghetto. He was deported from Łódź to Chełmno during September 1942, where he perished.

GERSMANN, Flora: Born on May 24, 1872, in Stęszew, Poland. She was deported from Berlin on October 18, 1941, to the Łódź ghetto. She was deported from Łódź to Chełmno on May 8, 1942, where she perished.

GERSON, Alfred: Born on February 23, 1886, in Leipzig. He was deported from Berlin on October 27–29, 1941, to the Łódź ghetto. He was deported from Łódź to Chełmno on May 5, 1942. He perished in Chełmno on May 5, 1942.

GERSTEL, Dorothea: Born on February 11, 1938, in Berlin. She was deported from Berlin on October 24, 1941, to the Łódź ghetto. She was deported from Łódź to Chełmno on June 26, 1944. She perished in Chełmno on June 26, 1944.

GERSZTENZANG, Szlama: Born on December 1, 1898, in Warsaw, Poland. He was deported from Hamburg on October 25, 1941, to the Łódź ghetto. He was deported from Łódź to Chełmno on September 12, 1942, where he perished.

GESSLER, Ernst: Born on July 20, 1889, in Hotzenplotz. He was deported from Prague on October 16, 1941, to the Łódź ghetto. He was deported from Łódź to Chełmno on May 8, 1942, where he perished.

GEWERZ, Egon: Born on March 7, 1934, in Berlin. He was deported from Berlin on October 24, 1941, to the Łódź ghetto. He was deported from Łódź to Chełmno on May 4, 1942. He perished in Chełmno on May 4, 1942.

GIDION, Jenny: Born on May 4, 1883, in Mülheim. She was deported from Düsseldorf on October 27, 1941, to the Łódź ghetto. She was deported from Łódź to Chełmno on May 7, 1942. She perished in Chełmno on May 8, 1942.

GIMPEL, Frieda: Born on April 5, 1890, in Lwow. She was deported from Berlin on October 18, 1941, to the Łódź ghetto. She was deported from Łódź to Chełmno on May 8, 1942. She perished in Chełmno on May 8, 1942.

GLADTKE, Elsa: Born on November 18, 1879, in Weinheim. She was deported from Düsseldorf on October 27, 1941, to the Łódź ghetto. She was deported from Łódź to Chełmno on May 7, 1942. She perished in Chełmno on May 8, 1942.

GLAJTMAN, Estera: Born on June 11, 1903, in Bedzin. She was deported from Berlin on November 1, 1941, to the Łódź ghetto. She was deported from Łódź to Chełmno on May 4, 1942, where she perished.

GLASENAPP, Kathe: Born on October 24, 1892, in Barmen-Elberfeld. She was deported from Düsseldorf on October 27, 1941, to the Łódź ghetto. She was deported from Łódź to Chełmno on May 12, 1942. She perished in Chełmno on May 13, 1942.

GLASER, Else: Born on December 24, 1899, in Hamburg. She was deported from Berlin on October 18, 1941, to the Łódź ghetto. She was deported from Łódź to Chełmno on May 8, 1942. She perished in Chełmno on May 8, 1942.

GLASS, Benno: Born on November 14, 1914, in Berlin. He was deported from Berlin on October 27–29, 1941, to the Łódź ghetto. He was deported from Łódź to Chełmno on May 5, 1942. He perished in Chełmno on May 5, 1942.

GLEITMANN, Laja: Born on June 23, 1890, in Niwka. She was deported from Berlin on October 27–29, 1941, to the Łódź ghetto. She was deported from Łódź to Chełmno on May 4, 1942. She perished in Chełmno on May 4, 1942.

GLICENSTEIN, Chaja: Born on November 20, 1892, in Łódź, Poland. She was expelled from Chemnitz on October 28, 1938, to Poland. She was deported from the Łódź ghetto to Chełmno on September 17, 1942, where she perished.

GLOGOWSKI, Max: Born on September 2, 1886, in Raszków, Poland. He was deported from Berlin on October 24, 1941, to the Łódź ghetto. He was deported from Łódź to Chełmno on May 4, 1942, where he perished.

GLÜCK, Olga: Born on February 13, 1886, in Leipzig. She was deported from Berlin on October 18, 1941, to the Łódź ghetto. She was deported from Łódź to Chełmno on May 8, 1942. She perished in Chełmno on May 8, 1942.

GLUSKIN, Abraham: Born on December 12, 1887, in Janówka. He was deported from Düsseldorf on October 27, 1941, to the Łódź ghetto. He was deported from Łódź to Chełmno on May 7, 1942. He perished in Chełmno on May 8, 1942.

GNIESŁAW, Laja: Born on March 30, 1911, in Praszka, Poland. She was expelled from Leipzig on October 28, 1938, to Poland. She was deported from the Łódź ghetto to Chełmno where she perished.

GÖRITZ, Rosa: Born on March 15, 1885, in Berlin. She was deported from Berlin on October 18, 1941, to the Łódź ghetto. She was deported

from Łódź to Chełmno on May 7, 1942. She perished in Chełmno on May 7, 1942.

GÖTZ, Margarete: Born on November 18, 1879, in Liegnitz. She was deported from Hamburg on October 25, 1941, to the Łódź ghetto. She was deported from Łódź to Chełmno on May 15, 1942, where she perished.

GÖTZER, Paula: Born on May 28, 1892, in Düsseldorf. She was deported from Cologne on October 22, 1941, to the Łódź ghetto. She was deported from Łódź to Chełmno during May 1942, where she perished.

GÖTZHOFF, Rosa: Born on December 17, 1891, in Kolbiel, Poland. She was deported from Cologne on October 22, 1941, to the Łódź ghetto. She was deported from Łódź to Chełmno on June 26, 1944, where she perished.

GOLDBARTH, Sara: Born on September 3, 1905, in Poznań, Poland. She was deported from Berlin on October 27–29, 1941, to the Łódź ghetto. She was deported from Łódź to Chełmno on May 5, 1942. She perished in Chełmno on May 5, 1942.

GOLDBERG, Ferdinand: Born on December 22, 1929, in Berlin. He was deported from Berlin on October 24, 1941, to the Łódź ghetto. He was deported from Łódź to Chełmno on May 15, 1942. He perished in Chełmno on May 15–17, 1942.

GOLDBERG-WELTMANN, Artur: Born on August 15, 1932, in Berlin. He was deported from Berlin on October 18, 1941, to the Łódź ghetto. He was deported from Łódź to Chełmno on May 8, 1942. He perished in Chełmno on May 8, 1942.

GOLDEMANN, Charlotte: Born on April 26, 1882, in Gołańcz, Poland. She was deported from Berlin on October 27–29, 1941, to the Łódź ghetto. She was deported from Łódź to Chełmno on May 4, 1942. She perished in Chełmno on May 4, 1942.

GOLDENRING, Charlotte: Born on January 11, 1880, in Warsaw, Poland. She was deported from Berlin on October 24, 1941, to the Łódź ghetto. She was deported from Łódź to Chełmno on May 4, 1942. She perished in Chełmno on May 4, 1942.

GOLDFINGER, Gertrud: Born on December 6, 1888, in Berlin. She was deported from Berlin on October 27–29, 1941, to the Łódź ghetto. She was deported from Łódź to Chełmno on May 4, 1942. She perished in Chełmno on May 4, 1942.

GOLDFREUND, Margarete: Born on July 1, 1887, in Berlin. She was deported from Berlin on November 1, 1941, to the Łódź ghetto. She was deported from Łódź to Chełmno on May 9, 1942. She perished in Chełmno on May 9, 1942.

GOLDMANN, Elisabeth: Born on March 12, 1871, in Wilhelmshöhe. She was deported from Berlin on November 1, 1941, to the Łódź ghetto. She was deported from Łódź to Chełmno on May 12, 1942. She perished in Chełmno on May 12, 1942.

GOLDSCHILD, Valeria: Born on July 16, 1874, in Labenz. She was deported from Berlin on October 27–29, 1941, to the Łódź ghetto. She was deported from Łódź to Chełmno on May 13, 1942, where she perished.

GOLDSCHMIDT, Bernhard: Born on March 12, 1901, in Hannover. He was deported from Berlin on October 18, 1941, to the Łódź ghetto. He was deported from Łódź to Chełmno on May 8, 1942. He perished in Chełmno on May 8, 1942.

GOLDSTAUB, Rosa: Born on February 6, 1873, in Leszno, Poland. She was deported from Berlin on October 24, 1941, to the Łódź ghetto. She was deported from Łódź to Chełmno on May 4, 1942. She perished in Chełmno on May 4, 1942.

GOLDSTEIN, Else: Born on June 30, 1890, in Krefeld. She was deported from Düsseldorf on October 27, 1941, to the Łódź ghetto. She was deported from Łódź to Chełmno on May 6, 1942. She perished in Chełmno on May 7, 1942.

GOLDSTROM, Ilse: Born on November 2, 1924, in Königsberg. She was deported from Berlin on October 18, 1941, to the Łódź ghetto. She was deported from Łódź to Chełmno on May 13, 1942. He perished in Chełmno on May 13, 1942.

GOLDSTÜCKER, Max: Born on December 6, 1878, in Breslau. He was deported from Berlin on October 18, 1941, to the Łódź ghetto. He was deported from Łódź to Chełmno on September 10, 1942. He perished in Chełmno on September 10, 1942.

GOLDWASSER, Maria: Born on October 10, 1895, in Berlin. She was deported from Berlin on October 27–29, 1941, to the Łódź ghetto. She was deported from Łódź to Chełmno on May 4, 1942. She perished in Chełmno on May 4, 1942.

GOLYSCHEFF, Jakob: Born on September 20, 1906, in Cherson, Russia. He was deported from Berlin on October 18, 1941, to the Łódź ghetto. He was deported from Łódź to Chełmno on May 8, 1942. He perished in Chełmno on May 8, 1942.

GOMPERTZ, Jenny: Born on August 2, 1889, in Kamp-Lintfort. She was deported from Düsseldorf on October 27, 1941, to the Łódź ghetto. She was deported from Łódź to Chełmno on May 6, 1942. She perished in Chełmno on May 7, 1942.

GONDORF, Erna: Born on August 4, 1887, in Obernau. She was deported from Cologne on October 22, 1941, to the Łódź ghetto. She was deported from Łódź to Chełmno during May 1942, where she perished.

GONSENHEIMER, Hanny: Born on November 28, 1903, in Kleve. She was deported from Düsseldorf on October 27, 1941, to the Łódź ghetto. She was deported from Łódź to Chełmno on May 6, 1942, where she perished.

GORDON, Alfred: Born on May 24, 1886, in Augsburg. He was deported from Hamburg on October 25, 1941, to the Łódź ghetto. He was deported from Łódź to Chełmno and he perished there during February 1942.

GOSSELS, Elise: Born on December 17, 1896, in Emden. She was deported from Berlin on October 24, 1941, to the Łódź ghetto. She was deported from Łódź to Chełmno on June 23, 1944. She perished in Chełmno on June 23, 1944.

GOTHEINER, Horst: Born on October 7, 1931. He emigrated to Poland from Bad Harzburg. He was deported from the Łódź ghetto to Chełmno on June 28, 1944, where he perished.

GOTTHELFT, Berta: Born on February 16, 1892, in Mannheim. She was deported from Berlin on October 27–29, 1941, to the Łódź ghetto. She was deported from Łódź to Chełmno on May 9, 1942. She perished in Chełmno on May 9, 1942.

GOTTLIEB, Selly: Born on January 12, 1886, in Hamburg. He was deported from Hamburg on October 25, 1941, to the Łódź ghetto. He was deported from Łódź to Chełmno on May 15, 1942, where he perished.

GOTTREICH, Lilian: Born on February 18, 1931, in Berlin. She was deported from Berlin on November 1, 1941, to the Łódź ghetto. She was deported from Łódź to Chełmno on May 9, 1942. She perished in Chełmno on May 9, 1942.

GOTTREICH-JACOBSOHN, Denny: Born on April 28, 1941, in Berlin. He was deported from Berlin on November 1, 1941, to the Łódź ghetto. He was deported from Łódź to Chełmno on May 9, 1942. He perished in Chełmno on May 9, 1942.

GOTTSCHALK, Frieda: Born on March 3, 1884, in Berlin. She was deported from Berlin on October 18, 1941, to the Łódź ghetto. She was deported from Łódź to Chełmno on May 8, 1942. She perished in Chełmno on May 8, 1942.

GOWA, Paula: Born on April 10, 1877, in Hamburg. She was deported from Hamburg on October 25, 1941, to the Łódź ghetto. She was deported from Łódź to Chełmno where she perished.

GRABISCHEWSKI, Schmul: Born on May 1, 1887, in Zgierz, Poland. He emigrated from Berlin to Poland. He was deported from the Łódź ghetto to Chełmno on September 8, 1942, where he perished.

GRABISZEWSKI, Sofie: Born on March 9, 1938, in Berlin. She emigrated from Berlin to Poland. She was deported from the Łódź ghetto to Chełmno on March 31, 1942, where she perished.

GRÄFNER, Rosa: Born on November 11, 1875, in Berlin. She was deported from Berlin on October 18, 1941, to the Łódź ghetto. She was deported from Łódź to Chełmno on May 8, 1942. She perished in Chełmno on May 8, 1942.

GRÄTZER, Ella: Born on July 13, 1885, in Prenzlau. She was deported from Berlin on October 18, 1941, to the Łódź ghetto. She was deported from Łódź to Chełmno on May 8, 1942. She perished in Chełmno on May 8, 1942.

GRAFF, Gertrud: Born on April 23, 1897, in Osche. She was deported from Berlin on October 27–29, 1941, to the Łódź ghetto. She was deported from Łódź to Chełmno on May 4, 1942. She perished in Chełmno on May 4, 1942.

GRAUMANN, Max: Born on July 1, 1899, in Cologne. He was deported from Cologne on October 22, 1941, to the Łódź ghetto. He was deported from Łódź to Chełmno during May 1942, where he perished.

GREBERMANN, Ellen: Born on March 20, 1934, in Berlin. She was deported from Berlin on November 1, 1941, to the Łódź ghetto. She was deported from Łódź to Chełmno on May 8, 1942. She perished in Chełmno on May 8, 1942.

GRELL, Kathe: Born on August 31, 1880, in Nikolaiken (Mikołajki). She was deported from Berlin on October 27–29, 1941, to the Łódź ghetto. She was deported from Łódź to Chełmno on May 4, 1942. She perished in Chełmno on May 4, 1942.

GRIES, Kurt: Born on June 30, 1896, in Berlin. He was deported from Berlin on October 27–29, 1941, to the Łódź ghetto. He was deported from Łódź to Chełmno on May 4, 1942. He perished in Chełmno on May 4, 1942.

GRIESS, Martha: Born on June 20, 1878, in Poznań, Poland. She was deported from Berlin on October 27–29, 1941, to the Łódź ghetto. She was deported from Łódź to Chełmno during September 1942, where she perished.

GRÖDEL, Albert: Born on June 2, 1885, in Frankfurt am Main. He was deported from Cologne on October 22, 1941, to the Łódź ghetto. He was deported from Łódź to Chełmno during July 1944, where he perished.

GRONOWSKI, Erika: Born on March 7, 1922, in Königsberg. She was deported from Berlin on November 1, 1941, to the Łódź ghetto. She was deported from Łódź to Chełmno on June 7, 1944. She perished in Chełmno on June 7, 1944.

GROS, Elsbeth: Born on May 26, 1908, in Berlin. She was deported from Berlin on October 27–29, 1941, to the Łódź ghetto. She was deported from Łódź to Chełmno on May 4, 1942. She perished in Chełmno on May 4, 1942.

GROSS, Manasche: Born on November 24, 1885, in Jarosław, Poland. He emigrated from Berlin to Poland. He was deported from the Łódź ghetto to Chełmno on October 1, 1942, where he perished.

GROSMANN, Manfred: Born on November 1, 1936, in Berlin. He was deported from Berlin on October 27–29, 1941, to the Łódź ghetto. He was deported from Łódź to Chełmno on September 12, 1942. He perished in Chełmno on September 12, 1942.

GROWALD, Edith: Born on December 29, 1904, in Berlin. She was deported from Berlin on October 18, 1941, to the Łódź ghetto. She was deported from Łódź to Chełmno on May 13, 1942. She perished in Chełmno on May 13, 1942.

GRÜN, Caroline: Born on January 6, 1880, in Kassel. She was deported from Berlin on October 27–29, 1941, to the Łódź ghetto. She was deported from Łódź to Chełmno on May 4, 1942. She perished in Chełmno on May 4, 1942.

GRÜNBERG, David: Born on October 25, 1918, in Barmen-Elberfeld. He was deported from Düsseldorf on October 27, 1941, to the Łódź ghetto. He was deported from Łódź to Chełmno on May 13, 1942. He perished in Chełmno on May 14, 1942.

GRÜNEBERG, Charlotte: Born on July 17, 1900, in Filehne, Poland. She was deported from Berlin on November 1, 1941, to the Łódź ghetto. She was deported from Łódź to Chełmno on May 9, 1942. She perished in Chełmno on May 9, 1942.

GRÜNEWALD, Margarete: Born on June 14, 1890, in Wongrowitz, Poland. She was deported from Düsseldorf on October 27, 1941, to the Łódź ghetto. She was deported from Łódź to Chełmno on May 6, 1942. She perished in Chełmno on May 7, 1942.

GRÜNFELD, Minna: Born on April 5, 1887, in Bleicherode. She was deported from Berlin on October 27–29, 1941, to the Łódź ghetto. She was deported from Łódź to Chełmno on May 10, 1942. She perished in Chełmno on May 10, 1942.

GRÜNSPAHN, Fritz: Born on July 7, 1892, in Berlin. He was deported from Berlin on October 27–29, 1941, to the Łódź ghetto. He was deported from Łódź to Chełmno on May 4, 1942. He perished in Chełmno on May 4, 1942.

GRÜNTHAL, Hugo: Born on April 20, 1876, in Breslau. He was deported from Berlin on October 18, 1941, to the Łódź ghetto. He was deported from Łódź to Chełmno on May 9, 1942. He perished in Chełmno on May 9, 1942.

GRÜNWALD, Kate: Born on February 13, 1911, in Gumbinnen. She was deported from Berlin on October 18, 1941, to the Łódź ghetto. She was deported from Łódź to Chełmno on May 8, 1942. She perished in Chełmno on May 8, 1942.

GRUMACH, Fritzi: Born on April 28, 1882, in Złotów (Flatow). She was deported from Berlin on October 27–29, 1941, to the Łódź ghetto. She was deported from Łódź to Chełmno on May 13, 1942. She perished in Chełmno on May 13, 1942.

GRÜNAU, Janette: Born on July 20, 1886, in Gosmansdorf. She was deported from Berlin on October 27–29, 1941, to the Łódź ghetto. She was deported from Łódź to Chełmno on May 4, 1942. She perished in Chełmno on May 4, 1942.

GRUNDMANN, Ella: Born on October 24, 1886, in Herford. She was deported from Cologne on October 22, 1941, to the Łódź ghetto. She was deported from Łódź to Chełmno during May 1942, where she perished.

GRÜNSFELD, Bertha: Born on July 7, 1877, in Culmsee. She was deported from Berlin on November 1, 1941, to the Łódź ghetto. She was deported from Łódź to Chełmno on May 8, 1942, where she perished.

GÜLZER, Bertha: Born on August 17, 1899, in Peczeniżyn, Poland. She was deported from Berlin on October 24, 1941, to the Łódź ghetto.

She was deported from Łódź to Chełmno during September 1942, where she perished.

GÜNTHER, Adolf: Born on October 17, 1878, in Kleve. He was deported from Cologne on October 30, 1941, to the Łódź ghetto. He was deported from Łódź to Chełmno during May 1942, where he perished.

GUGGENHEIM, Mathilde: Born on July 7, 1889, in Gailingen. She was deported from Berlin on October 24, 1941, to the Łódź ghetto. She was deported from Łódź to Chełmno on May 4, 1942. She perished in Chełmno on May 4, 1942.

GULKO, Hirsch: Born on August 12, 1877, in Odessa, Russia. He was deported from Berlin on October 27–29, 1941, to the Łódź ghetto. He was deported from Łódź to Chełmno on May 4, 1942. He perished in Chełmno on May 4, 1942.

GUMPERTZ, Margarete: Born on October 21, 1890, in Essen. She was deported from Düsseldorf on October 27, 1941, to the Łódź ghetto. She was deported from Łódź to Chełmno on May 5, 1942. She perished in Chełmno on May 6, 1942.

GUNZENHAUSER, Julie: Born on October 7, 1896, in Berleburg. She was deported from Cologne on October 30, 1941, to the Łódź ghetto. She was deported from Łódź to Chełmno during June 1944, where she perished.

GÜTERMANN, Selma: Born on February 6, 1877, in Schermeisel. She was deported from Berlin on October 27–29, 1941, to the Łódź ghetto. She was deported from Łódź to Chełmno on May 5, 1942. She perished in Chełmno on May 5, 1942.

GUTFELD, Berta: Born on January 19, 1891, in Graudenz. She was deported from Berlin on November 1, 1941, to the Łódź ghetto. She was deported from Łódź to Chełmno on May 9, 1942, where she perished.

GUTH, Julius: Born on April 17, 1897, in Charlottenburg. He was deported from Berlin on October 27–29, 1941, to the Łódź ghetto. He was deported from Łódź to Chełmno on May 12, 1942. He perished in Chełmno on May 12, 1942.

GUTKIND, Dora: Born on November 23, 1880, in Aachen. She was deported from Berlin on October 18, 1941, to the Łódź ghetto. She was

deported from Łódź to Chełmno on May 8, 1942. She perished in Chełmno on May 8, 1942.

GUTMANN, Anna: Born on May 7, 1905, in Kerschkow. She was deported from Berlin on October 27–29, 1941, to the Łódź ghetto. She was deported from Łódź to Chełmno on May 4, 1942. She perished in Chełmno on May 4, 1942.

GUTTMANN, Elly: Born on April 14, 1895, in Berlin. She was deported from Berlin on October 27–29, 1941, to the Łódź ghetto. She was deported from Łódź to Chełmno on May 6, 1942. She perished in Chełmno on May 6, 1942.

GUTWILEN, Abraham: Born on August 2, 1894, in Śmiłów. He was expelled from Gera on October 28, 1938, to Poland. He was deported from the Łódź ghetto to Chełmno on March 25, 1942, where he perished.

GUTWILLIG, Jenta: Born on November 20, 1883, in Lutowiska, Poland. She was deported from Berlin on October 27–29, 1941, to the Łódź ghetto. She was deported from Łódź to Chełmno on September 10, 1942. She perished in Chełmno on September 10, 1942.

HAAS, Lilli: Born on September 24, 1907, in Berlin. She was deported from Hamburg on October 25, 1941, to the Łódź ghetto. She was deported from Łódź to Chełmno on September 10, 1942, where she perished.

HABER, Albert: Born on September 21, 1887, in Mülheim. He was deported from Düsseldorf on October 27, 1941, to the Łódź ghetto. He was deported from Łódź to Chełmno during September 1942, where he perished.

HACHENBERG, Adele: Born on December 4, 1893, in Essen. She was deported from Düsseldorf on October 27, 1941, to the Łódź ghetto. She was deported from Łódź to Chełmno on May 6, 1942. She perished in Chełmno on May 7, 1942.

HACKELBERG, Hilde: Born on July 28, 1892, in Bonn. She was deported from Cologne on October 30, 1941, to the Łódź ghetto. She was deported from Łódź to Chełmno on May 7, 1942, where she perished.

HAGELBERG, Jenny: Born on February 3, 1886, in Berlin. She was deported from Cologne on October 30, 1941, to the Łódź ghetto. She was deported from Łódź to Chełmno during May 1942, where she perished.

HAHN, Heinz: Born on September 11, 1905, in Berlin. He was deported from Berlin on October 27–29, 1941, to the Łódź ghetto. He was deported from Łódź to Chełmno on May 4, 1942. He perished in Chełmno on May 4, 1942.

HAIMANN, Hannelore: Born on December 16, 1921, in The Hague, Holland. She was deported from Cologne on October 30, 1941, to the Łódź ghetto. She was deported from Łódź to Chełmno where she perished on July 5, 1944.

HAIN, Karoline: Born on November 18, 1882, in Ulmbach. She was deported from Cologne on October 22, 1941, to the Łódź ghetto. She was deported from Łódź to Chełmno during September 1942, where she perished.

HAKESBERG, Kurt: Born on July 21, 1914, in Erkeln. He was deported from Cologne on October 30, 1941, to the Łódź ghetto. He was deported from Łódź to Chełmno during May 1942, where he perished.

HALBER, Friederike: Born on December 26, 1875, in Bielefeld. She was deported from Düsseldorf on October 27, 1941, to the Łódź ghetto. She was deported from Łódź to Chełmno on May 6, 1942. She perished in Chełmno on May 7, 1942.

HALBERSBERG, Sara: Born on December 14, 1894, in Lublin, Poland. She was deported from Berlin on November 1, 1941, to the Łódź ghetto. She was deported from Łódź to Chełmno on May 5, 1942, where she perished.

HALLE, Margarethe: Born on September 23, 1877, in Poznań, Poland. She was deported from Berlin on October 18, 1941, to the Łódź ghetto. She was deported from Łódź to Chełmno on May 12, 1942. She perished in Chełmno on May 12, 1942.

HAMBURGER, Hulda: Born on July 5, 1871, in Katscher. She was deported from Berlin on October 18, 1941, to the Łódź ghetto. She was deported from Łódź to Chełmno on September 14, 1942. She perished in Chełmno on September 14, 1942.

HAMMEL, Fritz: Born on February 14, 1895, in Wollstein. He was deported from Berlin on November 1, 1941, to the Łódź ghetto. He was deported from Łódź to Chełmno on May 12, 1942. He perished in Chełmno on May 12, 1942.

HANNO, Else: Born on September 10, 1900, in Berlin. She was deported from Berlin on October 18, 1941, to the Łódź ghetto. She was deported from Łódź to Chełmno on May 8, 1942. She perished in Chełmno on May 8, 1942.

HARF, Moritz: Born on November 7, 1875, in Keyenberg. He was deported from Düsseldorf on October 27, 1941, to the Łódź ghetto. He was deported from Łódź to Chełmno on May 6, 1942. He perished in Chełmno on May 7, 1942.

HARLAM, Peter: Born on June 6, 1928, in Berlin. He was deported from Berlin on October 18, 1941, to the Łódź ghetto. He was deported from Łódź to Chełmno on May 13, 1942. He perished in Chełmno on May 13, 1942.

HARTH, Erna: Born on March 14, 1899, in Berlin. She was deported from Berlin on October 27–29, 1941, to the Łódź ghetto. She was deported from Łódź to Chełmno on May 15, 1942. She perished in Chełmno on May 15, 1942.

HARTOG, Adolf: Born on April 5, 1891, in Aurich. He was deported from Düsseldorf on October 27, 1941, to the Łódź ghetto. He was deported from Łódź to Chełmno on May 6, 1942. He perished in Chełmno on May 7, 1942.

HARTOGSOHN, Lea: Born on May 3, 1878, in Barnten. She was deported from Berlin on October 24, 1941, to the Łódź ghetto. She was deported from Łódź to Chełmno on May 12, 1942. She perished in Chełmno on May 12, 1942.

HASFELD, Eva: Born on December 10, 1913, in Warsaw, Poland. She was deported from Düsseldorf on October 27, 1941, to the Łódź ghetto. She was deported from Łódź to Chełmno on May 7, 1942. She perished in Chełmno on May 8, 1942.

HAUER, Helmut: Born on October 22, 1927, in Berlin. He was deported from Berlin on October 18, 1941, to the Łódź ghetto. He was deported from Łódź to Chełmno on May 7, 1942. He perished in Chełmno on May 7, 1942.

HAUPTMANN, Benno: Born on August 17, 1917, in Hamburg. He was deported from Hamburg on October 25, 1941, to the Łódź ghetto. He was deported from Łódź to Chełmno on May 10, 1942, where he perished.

HAUSER, Berta: Born on May 26, 1884, in Vienna, Austria. She was deported from Berlin on November 1, 1941, to the Łódź ghetto. She was deported from Łódź to Chełmno on May 8, 1942. She perished in Chełmno on May 8, 1942.

HAUSMANN, Eva: Born on January 31, 1916, in Düren. She was deported from Cologne on October 30, 1941, to the Łódź ghetto. She was deported from Łódź to Chełmno where she perished during May 1942.

HAYUM, Ilse: Born on April 17, 1933, in Saarburg. She was deported from Luxembourg–Trier on October 16, 1941, to the Łódź ghetto. She was deported from Łódź to Chełmno where she perished on June 28, 1944.

HECHT, Hermann: Born on June 1, 1884, in Kempen, Poland. He was deported from Cologne on October 30, 1941, to the Łódź ghetto. He was deported from Łódź to Chełmno during September 1942, where he perished.

HEFFNER, Ruth: Born on December 22, 1922, in Berlin. She was deported from Berlin on November 1, 1941, to the Łódź ghetto. She was deported from Łódź to Chełmno on May 5, 1942. She perished in Chełmno on May 5, 1942.

HEIDEMANN, Frieda: Born on October 13, 1882, in Frankfurt an der Oder. She was deported from Berlin on October 27–29, 1941, to the Łódź ghetto. She was deported from Łódź to Chełmno on May 4, 1942. She perished in Chełmno on May 4, 1942.

HEIDT, Martin: Born on December 17, 1902, in Cologne. He was deported from Cologne on October 22, 1941, to the Łódź ghetto. He was deported from Łódź to Chełmno on September 10, 1942, where he perished.

HEILBERG, Rosi: Born on February 1, 1917, in Meudt. She was deported from Cologne on October 22, 1941, to the Łódź ghetto. She was deported from Łódź to Chełmno during May 1942, where she perished.

HEILBORN, Herbert: Born on November 17, 1897, in Cologne. He was imprisoned between November 15, 1938, and November 28, 1938, in Dachau Concentration Camp. He was deported from Cologne during October 1941, to the Łódź ghetto. He was deported from Łódź to Chełmno on May 8, 1942, where he perished.

HEILBRONN, Helene: Born on October 3, 1884, in Glehn. She was deported from Düsseldorf on October 27, 1941, to the Łódź ghetto. She was deported from Łódź to Chełmno during September 1942, where she perished.

HEILBRUNN, Ruth: Born on February 4, 1919, in Cologne. She was deported from Cologne on October 22, 1941, to the Łódź ghetto. She was deported from Łódź to Chełmno on May 5, 1942, where she perished.

HEILNER, Irma: Born on May 6, 1894, in Kissingen. She was deported from Cologne on October 22, 1941, to the Łódź ghetto. She was deported from Łódź to Chełmno during May 1942, where she perished.

HEIM, Irene: Born on September 24, 1911, in Borek, Poland. She was imprisoned in the Schönefeld Jewish Forestry Labor Camp. She was deported from Berlin on October 27–29, 1941, to the Łódź ghetto. She was deported from Łódź to Chełmno on May 5, 1942, where she perished.

HEIMANN, Adelheid: Born on May 10, 1887, in Berlin. She was deported from Berlin on November 1, 1941, to the Łódź ghetto. She was deported from Łódź to Chełmno on May 9, 1942. She perished in Chełmno on May 9, 1942.

HEIMBACH, Anna: Born on January 22, 1897, in Rheydt. She was deported from Cologne on October 22, 1941, to the Łódź ghetto. She was deported from Łódź to Chełmno on July 14, 1944, where she perished.

HEIMBERG, Edgar: Born on September 14, 1888, in Padberg. He was imprisoned in Fuhlsbüttel Concentration Camp between November 10, 1938, and November 30, 1938. He was deported from Hamburg on October 25, 1941, to the Łódź ghetto. He was deported from Łódź to Chełmno on April 25, 1942, where he perished.

HEIN, Rosa: Born on April 17, 1873, in Riesenburg. She was deported from Berlin on October 24, 1941, to the Łódź ghetto. She was deported from Łódź to Chełmno on May 13, 1942. She perished in Chełmno on May 13, 1942.

HEINE, Fritz: Born on November 10, 1884, in Berlin. He was deported from Berlin on October 24, 1941, to the Łódź ghetto. He was deported from Łódź to Chełmno on July 3, 1944. He perished in Chełmno on July 3, 1944.

HEINEBERG, Else: Born on September 28, 1881, in Lemgo. She was deported from Cologne on October 22, 1941, to the Łódź ghetto. She was deported from Łódź to Chełmno during May 1942, where she perished.

HEINEMANN, Emma: Born on March 25, 1882, in Neus. She was deported from Cologne on October 22, 1941, to the Łódź ghetto. She was deported from Łódź to Chełmno on May 24, 1942. She perished in Chełmno on May 24, 1942.

HEINRICH, Leonhard: Born on February 23, 1905, in Berlin. He emigrated to Czechoslovakia. He was deported from Prague on October 21, 1941, to the Łódź ghetto. He was deported from Łódź to Chełmno on May 10, 1942, where he perished.

HEISER, Paula: Born on October 23, 1878, in Kamen. She was deported from Cologne on October 30, 1941, to the Łódź ghetto. She was deported from Łódź to Chełmno where she perished on September 12, 1942.

HELD, Marie: Born on January 10, 1872, in Hamburg. She was deported from Berlin on October 18, 1941, to the Łódź ghetto. She was deported from Łódź to Chełmno on May 13, 1942. She perished in Chełmno on May 13, 1942.

HELDBERG, Laura: Born on September 16, in Lwów. She was deported from Hamburg on October 25, 1941, to the Łódź ghetto. She perished in Chełmno.

HELLENSTEIN, Hedwig: Born on November 8, 1901, in Mannheim. She was deported from Berlin on November 1, 1941, to the Łódź ghetto. She was deported from Łódź to Chełmno on May 9, 1942. She perished in Chełmno on May 9, 1942.

HELLER, Charlotte: Born on June 4, 1909, in Berlin. She was deported from Berlin on October 18, 1941, to the Łódź ghetto. She was deported from Łódź to Chełmno on May 8, 1942, where she perished.

HELLMANN, Max: Born on February 13, 1875, in Kleinsteinach. He was deported from Hamburg on October 25, 1941, to the Łódź ghetto. He was deported from Łódź to Chełmno on May 10, 1942, where he perished.

HELLWITZ, Wilhelmine: Born on November 20, 1886, in Trier. She was deported from Cologne on October 30, 1941, to the Łódź ghetto. She was deported from Łódź to Chełmno during September 1942, where she perished.

HELMANN, Klara: Born on March 20, 1884, in Zolynia, Poland. She was deported from Berlin on October 24, 1941, to the Łódź ghetto. She was deported from Łódź to Chełmno on May 15, 1942. She perished in Chełmno on May 15, 1942.

HENLE, Gert: Born on December 8, 1924, in Bonn. He was deported from Cologne on October 22, 1941, to the Łódź ghetto. He was deported from Łódź to Chełmno during May 1942, where he perished.

HENLEIN, Anna: Born on April 13, 1880, in Langenschwalbach. She was deported from Düsseldorf on October 27, 1941, to the Łódź ghetto. She was deported from Łódź to Chełmno on May 6, 1942. She perished in Chełmno on May 7, 1942.

HENTSCHEL, Margarete: Born on September 2, 1883, in Kurnik, Poland. She was deported from Berlin on October 18, 1941, to the Łódź ghetto. She was deported from Łódź to Chełmno on May 8, 1942. She perished in Chełmno on May 8, 1942.

HEPNER, Kathe: Born on February 22, 1887, in Berlin. She was deported from Frankfurt am Main on October 20, 1941, to the Łódź ghetto. She was deported from Łódź to Chełmno on May 10, 1942, where she perished.

HERMANN, Erich: Born on October 15, 1890, in Berlin. He was deported from Berlin on November 1, 1941, to the Łódź ghetto. He was deported from Łódź to Chełmno on May 9, 1942. He perished in Chełmno on May 9, 1942.

HERRSCHER, Rosel: Born on June 15, 1890, in Neckar-Steinach. She was deported from Frankfurt am Main on October 20, 1941, to the Łódź ghetto. She was deported from Łódź to Chełmno on May 9, 1942, where she perished.

HERSCHANDER, Helene: Born on August 1, 1884, in Berlin. She was deported from Hamburg on October 25, 1941, to the Łódź ghetto. She was deported from Łódź to Chełmno on May 11, 1942, where she perished.

HERSCHBERG, Charlotte: Born on October 2, 1889, in Berlin. She was deported from Berlin on November 1, 1941, to the Łódź ghetto. She was deported from Łódź to Chełmno on May 9, 1942. She perished in Chełmno on May 9, 1942.

HERSTATT, Hubert: Born on December 3, 1879, in Siegburg. He was deported from Cologne on October 30, 1941, to the Łódź ghetto. He was deported from Łódź to Chełmno during May 1942, where he perished.

HERTZ, Maximillian: Born on July 5, 1892, in Krefeld. He was deported from Düsseldorf on October 27, 1941, to the Łódź ghetto. He was deported from Łódź to Chełmno on May 6, 1942. He perished in Chełmno on May 7, 1942.

HERZ, Adelheid: Born on November 7, 1872, in Heilbronn. She was deported from Berlin on October 27–29, 1941, to the Łódź ghetto. She was deported from Łódź to Chełmno on May 9, 1942. She perished in Chełmno on May 9, 1942.

HERZBERG, Else: Born on July 2, 1887, in Düsseldorf. She was deported from Düsseldorf on October 27, 1941, to the Łódź ghetto. She was

deported from Łódź to Chełmno on May 6, 1942. She perished in Chełmno on May 7, 1942.

HERZBERGER, Leon: Born on December 31, 1875, in Kleve. He was imprisoned in the Spatzenberg prison between November 10, 1938 and November 19, 1938. He was deported from Düsseldorf on October 27, 1941, to the Łódź ghetto. He was deported from Łódź to Chełmno on May 7, 1942. He perished in Chełmno on May 8, 1942.

HERZENBERG, Irene: Born on August 10, 1888, in Darmstadt. She was deported from Berlin on October 18, 1941, to the Łódź ghetto. She was deported from Łódź to Chełmno on May 8, 1942. She perished in Chełmno on May 8, 1942.

HERZFELD, Hannelore: Born on May 30, 1923, in Schivelbein. She was deported from Berlin on October 27-29, 1941, to the Łódź ghetto. She was deported from Łódź to Chełmno on May 4, 1942. She perished in Chełmno on May 4, 1942.

HERZOG, Paula: Born on July 20, 1920, in Berlin. She was deported from Berlin on October 27-29, 1941, to the Łódźg hetto. She was deported from Łódź to Chełmno on May 5, 1942, where she perished.

HESS, Benno: Born on August 14, 1902, in Magdeburg. He was deported from Berlin on October 24, 1941, to the Łódź ghetto. He was deported from Łódź to Chełmno on May 4, 1942. He perished in Chełmno on May 4, 1942.

HESSE, Max: Born on November 13, 1898, in Leer. He was deported from Cologne on October 30, 1941, to the Łódź ghetto. He was deported from Łódź to Chełmno during May 1942, where he perished.

HESSENBERGER, Martha: Born on January 30, 1885, in Poznań, Poland. She was deported from Berlin on November 1, 1941, to the Łódź ghetto. She was deported from Łódź to Chełmno on May 9, 1942. She perished in Chełmno on May 9, 1942.

HEUMANN, Selma: Born on May 31, 1881, in Duisberg. She was deported from Düsseldorf on October 27, 1941, to the Łódź ghetto. She was deported from Łódź to Chełmno on May 6, 1942. She perished in Chełmno on May 7, 1942.

HEYDEMANN, Hugo: Born on May 9, 1875, in Baudach. He was deported from Berlin on October 27–29, 1941, to the Łódź ghetto. He was deported from Łódź to Chełmno on May 4, 1942, where he perished.

HEYMANN, Berta: Born on June 21, 1879, in Lutschmin, Poland. She was deported from Berlin on October 24, 1941, to the Łódź ghetto. She was deported from Łódź to Chełmno on May 4, 1942. She perished in Chełmno on May 4, 1942.

HILLER, Frieda: Born on October 19, 1887, in Schonlanke, Poland. She was deported from Berlin on November 1, 1941, to the Łódź ghetto. She was deported from Łódź to Chełmno on May 8, 1942. She perished in Chełmno on May 8, 1942.

HIMMELRICK, Kathe: Born on November 23, 1911, in Werl. She was deported from Düsseldorf on October 27, 1941, to the Łódź ghetto. She was deported from Łódź to Chełmno on July 12, 1944. She perished in Chełmno on July 13, 1944.

HIMMELWEIT, Irma: Born on October 14, 1914, in Crimmitschau. She was deported from Berlin on October 27–29, 1941, to the Łódź ghetto. She was deported from Łódź to Chełmno on May 4, 1942. She perished in Chełmno on May 4, 1942.

HIMMLER, Siegmund: Born on August 1, 1894, in Mardzina. He was deported from Berlin on November 1, 1941, to the Łódź ghetto. He was deported from Łódź to Chełmno on May 4, 1942. He perished in Chełmno on May 4, 1942.

HINRICHS, Emma: Born on June 11, 1910, in Oels. She was deported from Berlin on October 27–29, 1941, to the Łódź ghetto. She was deported from Łódź to Chełmno on May 4, 1942, where she perished.

HINZ, Gertrud: Born on March 9, 1885, in Sangerhausen. She was deported from Berlin on November 1, 1941, to the Łódź ghetto. She was deported from Łódź to Chełmno on May 8, 1942. She perished in Chełmno on May 8, 1942.

HIRSCH, Adolf: Born on July 4, 1882, in Hamburg. He was deported from Düsseldorf on October 27, 1941, to the Łódź ghetto. He was deported from Łódź to Chełmno on September 8, 1942. He perished in Chełmno on September 9, 1942.

HIRSCHBERG, Gertrud: Born on September 28, 1893, in Berlin. She was deported from Berlin on November 1, 1941, to the Łódź ghetto. She was deported from Łódź to Chełmno on May 8, 1942. She perished in Chełmno on May 8, 1942.

HIRSCHEL, Rosa: Born on April 7, 1884, in Hamburg. She was deported from Berlin on October 18, 1941, to the Łódź ghetto. She was deported from Łódź to Chełmno on May 8, 1942. She perished in Chełmno on May 8, 1942.

HIRSCHFELD, Johanna: Born on May 23, 1871, in Grodzisk, Poland. She was deported from Berlin on November 1, 1941, to the Łódź ghetto. She was deported from Łódź to Chełmno on May 9, 1942. She perished in Chełmno on May 9, 1942.

HIRSCHFELDT, Fritz: Born on June 15, 1902, in Braunsberg. He was deported from Berlin on October 18, 1941, to the Łódź ghetto. He was deported from Łódź to Chełmno on May 8, 1942. He perished in Chełmno on May 8, 1942.

HIRSCHHAHN, Rosa: Born on February 5, 1874, in Essen. She was deported from Cologne on October 22, 1941, to the Łódź ghetto. He was deported from Łódź to Chełmno on May 12, 1942, where she perished.

HIRTZ, Eugen: Born on February 10, 1905, in Krefeld. He was deported from Düsseldorf on October 27, 1941, to the Łódź ghetto. He was deported from Łódź to Chełmno on May 13, 1942. He perished in Chełmno on May 14, 1942.

HOBERG, Karola: Born on August 13, 1882, in Breslau. She was deported from Düsseldorf on October 27, 1941, to the Łódź ghetto. She was deported from Łódź to Chełmno on May 11, 1942. She perished in Chełmno on May 12, 1942.

HOCH, Regina: Born on February 15, 1892, in Łódź, Poland. She was expelled from Essen on October 28, 1938, to Zbąszyń, Poland. She was deported from the Łódź ghetto to Chełmno on March 28, 1942, where she perished.

HOCHBERGER, Zilli: Born on August 6, 1924, in Leipzig. He was expelled from Leipzig on October 28, 1938, to Poland. He was deported from the Łódź ghetto to Chełmno on September 9, 1942, where he perished.

HOCHDORF, Arnold: Born on April 27, 1881, in Stettin. He was deported from Cologne on October 22, 1941, to the Łódź ghetto. He was deported from Łódź to Chełmno during May 1942, where he perished.

HÖFLICH, Henriette: Born on March 5, 1896, in Aachen. She was deported from Cologne on October 30, 1941, to the Łódź ghetto. She was deported from Łódź to Chełmno during May 1942, where she perished.

HOFFMANN, Elenore: Born on September 23, 1871, in Berlin. She was deported from Berlin on November 1, 1941, to the Łódź ghetto. She was deported from Łódź to Chełmno on May 8, 1942. She perished in Chełmno on May 8, 1942.

HOFFSTADT, Margot: Born on August 5, 1922, in Cologne. She was deported from Cologne on October 30, 1941, to the Łódź ghetto. She was deported from Łódź to Chełmno during June 1944, where she perished.

HOFMANN, Jenny: Born on February 5, 1874, in Essen. She was deported from Cologne to the Łódź ghetto. She was deported from Łódź to Chełmno during May 1942, where she perished.

HOHENSTEIN, Adelheid: Born on February 21, 1872, in Tuchel. She was deported from Berlin on October 18, 1941, to the Łódź ghetto. She was deported from Łódź to Chełmno on May 8, 1942. She perished in Chełmno on May 8, 1942.

HOLDSTEIN, Alfred: Born on May 24, 1911, in Graudenz. He was deported from Berlin on October 18, 1941, to the Łódź ghetto. He was deported from Łódź to Chełmno on July 6, 1944. He perished in Chełmno on July 6, 1944.

HOLLÄNDER, Adelheid: Born on July 27, 1921, in Berlin. She was deported from Berlin on October 27–29, 1941, to the Łódź ghetto. She

was deported from Łódź to Chełmno on May 4, 1942. She perished in Chełmno on May 4, 1942.

HOLSTEIN, Betty: Born on June 17, 1884, in Hamburg. She was deported from Hamburg on October 25, 1941, to the Łódź ghetto. She was deported from Łódź to Chełmno on May 10, 1942, where she perished.

HOLZ, Bernd: Born on March 9, 1922, in Berlin. He was deported from Berlin on October 27–29, 1941, to the Łódź ghetto. He was deported from Łódź to Chełmno on May 4, 1942. He perished in Chełmno on May 4, 1942.

HOLZKNECHT, Berta: Born on July 21, 1889, in Dirmerzheim. She was deported from Cologne on October 22, 1941, to the Łódź ghetto. She was deported from Łódź to Chełmno on May 4, 1942, where she perished.

HOLZMANN, Dora: Born on May 11, 1889, in Koronowo, Poland. She was deported from Berlin on October 27–29, 1941, to the Łódź ghetto. She was deported from Łódź to Chełmno on May 5, 1942. She perished in Chełmno on May 5, 1942.

HOPE, Rolf: Born on November 16, 1910, in Brühl. He was imprisoned between November 15, 1938, and December 1, 1938, in Dachau Concentration Camp. He was deported from Cologne on October 22, 1941, to the Łódź ghetto. He was deported from Łódź to Chełmno on May 4, 1942, where he perished.

HOPP, Clara: Born on July 27, 1875, in Strzelno, Poland. She was deported from Berlin on November 1, 1941, to the Łódź ghetto. She was deported from Łódź to Chełmno on May 9, 1942. She perished in Chełmno on May 9, 1942.

HOPSTEIN, Estera: Born on May 5, 1873, in Łódź, Poland. She was deported from Berlin on October 18, 1941, to the Łódź ghetto. She was deported from Łódź to Chełmno on September 10, 1942. She perished in Chełmno on September 10, 1942.

HORN, Albert: Born on April 16, 1880, in Cologne. He was deported from Cologne on October 22, 1941, to the Łódź ghetto. He was deported from Łódź to Chełmno on May 5, 1942, where he perished.

HORNIK, Regina: Born on March 11, 1881, in Kolberg. She was deported from Berlin on October 24, 1941, to the Łódź ghetto. She was deported from Łódź to Chełmno on May 14, 1942. She perished in Chełmno on May 14, 1942.

HORWIITZ, Susanne: Born on April 27, 1881, in Stettin. She was deported from Cologne during October 1941, to the Łódź ghetto. She was deported from Łódź to Chełmno during May 1942, where she perished.

HORWITZ, Elfriede: Born on January 27, 1891, in Breslau. She was deported from Berlin on October 18, 1941, to the Łódź ghetto. She was deported from Łódź to Chełmno on May 7, 1942. She perished in Chełmno on May 7, 1942.

HÜNEBERG, Margarete: Born on October 13, 1907, in Essen. She was deported from Düsseldorf on October 27, 1941, to the Łódź ghetto. She was deported from Łódź to Chełmno on May 6, 1942. She perished in Chełmno on May 7, 1942.

HÜTTNER, Cacilie: Born on February 8, 1888, in Hamburg. She was deported from Hamburg on October 25, 1941, to the Łódź ghetto. She was deported from Łódź to Chełmno on September 12, 1942, where she perished.

HUFFMANN, Erna: Born on September 4, 1900, in Vienna, Austria. She was deported from Berlin on October 27–29, 1941, to the Łódź ghetto. She was deported from Łódź to Chełmno on May 4, 1942. She perished in Chełmno on May 4, 1942.

HUMBERG, Erich: Born on June 11, 1918, in Vreden. He was deported from Cologne on October 22, 1941, to the Łódź ghetto. He was deported from Łódź to Chełmno where he perished on June 26, 1944.

ICEK, Abram: Born on December 2, 1905, in Wieruszów, Poland. He was expelled from Dresden on October 28–29, 1938, to Zbąszyń, Poland. He was deported from the Pabianice ghetto to the Łódź ghetto during May 1942. He was deported from Łódź to Chełmno on June 28, 1944. He perished in Chełmno on June 28, 1944.

ICKOVICZ, Fiszel: Born on December 15, 1903, in Skierniewice, Poland. He was deported from Berlin on October 27–29, 1941, to the Łódź

ghetto. He was deported from Łódź to Chełmno on May 4, 1942. He perished in Chełmno on May 4, 1942.

IGLA, Rivka: Born on August 30, 1929, in Emden. She was expelled from Emden on October 28, 1938, to Poland. She was deported from the Łódź ghetto to Chełmno on September 12, 1942, where she perished.

IGLICK, Edgar: Born on February 6, 1902, in Berlin. He was deported from Berlin on October 24, 1941, to the Łódź ghetto. He was deported from Łódź to Chełmno on May 5, 1942, where he perished.

IHRING, Gertrud: Born on April 24, 1906, in Berlin. She was deported from Berlin on November 1, 1941, to the Łódź ghetto. She was deported from Łódź to Chełmno on May 9, 1942. She perished in Chełmno on May 9, 1942.

ILLFELDER, Paula: Born on December 14, 1884, in Iserlohn. She was deported from Düsseldorf on October 27, 1941, to the Łódź ghetto. She was deported from Łódź to Chełmno on May 6, 1942. She perished in Chełmno on May 7, 1942.

IMHOF, Amalie: Born on March 5, 1896, in Mülheim. She was deported from Berlin on October 18, 1941, to the Łódź ghetto. She was deported from Łódź to Chełmno on May 9, 1942. She perished in Chełmno on May 9, 1942.

INOW, Beatrice: Born on June 25, 1897, in Bochum. She was deported from Düsseldorf on October 27, 1941, to the Łódź ghetto. She was deported from Łódź to Chełmno on May 6, 1942. She perished in Chełmno on May 7, 1942.

IRES, val, Spira: Born on January 15, 1940, in Cologne. He was deported from Cologne on October 22, 1941, to the Łódź ghetto. He was deported from Łódź to Chełmno during September 1942, where he perished.

ISAAC, Bella: Born on June 21, 1895, in Aurich. She was deported from Düsseldorf on October 27, 1941, to the Łódź ghetto. She was deported from Łódź to Chełmno on May 13, 1942. She perished in Chełmno on May 14, 1942.

ISAAK, Alfred: Born on December 6, 1879, in Fürstenfelde. He was deported from Berlin on October 18, 1941, to the Łódź ghetto. He was deported from Łódź to Chełmno on May 8, 1942. He perished in Chełmno on May 8, 1942.

ISAY, Adolf: Born on January 12, 1880, in Mehring. He was deported from Düsseldorf on October 27, 1941, to the Łódź ghetto. He was deported from Łódź to Chełmno during September 1942, where he perished.

ISENTHAL, Katharina: Born on February 8, 1890, in Schmiedeberg. She was deported from Berlin on October 18, 1941, to the Łódź ghetto. She was deported from Łódź to Chełmno on May 9, 1942. She perished in Chełmno on May 9, 1942.

ISRAEL, Hugo: Born on September 18, 1869, in Rieder. He was deported from Berlin on October 24, 1941, to the Łódź ghetto. He was deported from Łódź to Chełmno on May 4, 1942. He perished in Chełmno on May 4, 1942.

ISRAELSOHN, Zipora: Born on January 13, 1871, in Falkenburg. She was deported from Berlin on October 27–29, 1941, to the Łódź ghetto. She was deported from Łódź to Chełmno on May 13, 1942. She perished in Chełmno on May 13, 1942.

ITALIENER, Gesine: Born on March 19, 1874, in Oude Pekela, Holland. She was deported from Berlin on October 24, 1941, to the Łódź ghetto. She was deported from Łódź to Chełmno on May 12, 1942. She perished in Chełmno on May 12, 1942.

IWANTER, Moritz: Born on July 11, 1882, in Eisleben. He was deported from Berlin on November 1, 1941, to the Łódź ghetto. He was deported from Łódź to Chełmno on May 8, 1942, where he perished.

JABLONOWER, Josef: Born on March 11, 1895, in Warsaw, Poland. He was deported from Düsseldorf on October 27, 1941, to the Łódź ghetto. He was deported from Łódź to Chełmno on June 28, 1944. He perished in Chełmno on June 29, 1944.

JABLONSKY, Erna: Born on November 11, 1895, in Berlin. She was deported from Berlin on October 27–29, 1941, to the Łódź ghetto. She was deported from Łódź to Chełmno on May 5, 1942. She perished in Chełmno on May 5, 1942.

JACHMANN, Gertha: Born on June 8, 1901, in Bublitz. She was deported from Berlin on November 1, 1941, to the Łódź ghetto. She was deported from Łódź to Chełmno on May 9, 1942. She perished in Chełmno on May 9, 1942.

JACHT, Alice: Born on November 11, 1895, in Berlin. She was deported from Berlin on October 27–29, 1941, to the Łódź ghetto. She was deported from Łódź to Chełmno on May 5, 1942. She perished in Chełmno on May 5, 1942.

JACKS, Else: Born on October 16, 1884, in Treten. She was deported from Berlin on November 1, 1941, to the Łódź ghetto. She was deported from Łódź to Chełmno on May 13, 1942. She perished in Chełmno on May 13, 1942.

JACOB, Amanda: Born on May 21, 1896, in Hörstgen. She was deported from Düsseldorf on October 27, 1941, to the Łódź ghetto. She was deported from Łódź to Chełmno on May 7, 1942. She perished in Chełmno on May 8, 1942.

JACOBI, Rosa: Born on June 22, 1891, in Poznań, Poland. She was deported from Berlin on November 1, 1941, to the Łódź ghetto. She was deported from Łódź to Chełmno on May 10, 1942. She perished in Chełmno on May 10, 1942.

JACOBIUS, Ruth: Born on August 20, 1913, in Sobowitz. She was deported from Berlin on October 24, 1941, to the Łódź ghetto. She was deported from Łódź to Chełmno on May 4, 1942. She perished in Chełmno on May 4, 1942.

JACOBOWITZ, Martha: Born on April 5, 1883, in Podwitz. She was deported from Berlin on November 1, 1941, to the Łódź ghetto. She was deported from Łódź to Chełmno on May 9, 1942. She perished in Chełmno on May 9, 1942.

JACOBSOHN, Alfred: Born on November 22, 1887, in Heilsberg. He was deported from Berlin on November 1, 1941, to the Łódź ghetto. He was deported from Łódź to Chełmno on September 10, 1942. He perished in Chełmno on September 10, 1942.

JACOBUS, Rosa: Born on June 14, 1900, in Berlin. She was deported from Berlin on November 1, 1941, to the Łódź ghetto. She was

deported from Łódź to Chełmno on May 8, 1942. She perished in Chełmno on May 8, 1942.

JACOBY, Anita: Born on June 16, 1930, in Berlin. She was deported from Berlin on October 27–29, 1941, to the Łódź ghetto. She was deported from Łódź to Chełmno on May 4, 1942. She perished in Chełmno on May 4, 1942.

JACUBOWITZ, Gertrud: Born on February 22, 1881, in Neumarkt. She was deported from Berlin on October 18, 1941, to the Łódź ghetto. She was deported from Łódź to Chełmno on May 8, 1942. She perished in Chełmno on May 8, 1942.

JAFFE, Paul: Born on November 21, 1911, in Hamburg. He was deported from Hamburg on October 25, 1941, to the Łódź ghetto. He was deported from Łódź to Chełmno on May 10, 1942, where he perished.

JAHISCH, Perla: Born on March 3, 1917, in Berlin. She was deported from Berlin on October 24, 1941, to the Łódź ghetto. She was deported from Łódź to Chełmno on May 13, 1942, where she perished.

JAKOB, Betty: Born on March 23, 1919, in Berlin. She was deported from Berlin on October 27–29, 1941, to the Łódź ghetto. She was deported from Łódź to Chełmno on May 5, 1942. She perished in Chełmno on May 5, 1942.

JAKOBI, Margot: Born on July 1, 1917, in Duisburg. She was deported from Cologne on October 22, 1941, to the Łódź ghetto. She was deported from Łódź to Chełmno on June 28, 1944. She perished in Chełmno on June 28, 1944.

JAKOBS, Renate: Born on July 19, 1925, in Aachen. She emigrated to Belgium on December 20, 1938. She was deported from Cologne on October 30, 1941, to the Łódź ghetto. She was deported from Łódź to Chełmno on June 26, 1944, where she perished.

JAKOBSTHAL, Else: Born on October 1, 1887, in Grodzisk, Poland. She was deported from Berlin on November 1, 1941, to the Łódź ghetto. She was deported from Łódź to Chełmno on May 9, 1942. She perished in Chełmno on May 9, 1942.

JAKUBOWITZ, Anna: Born on May 10, 1882, in Włoszczowa, Poland. She was deported from Düsseldorf on October 27, 1941, to the Łódź

ghetto. She was deported from Łódź to Chełmno on May 6, 1942. She perished in Chełmno on May 7, 1942.

JALOWITZ, Karl: Born on August 13, 1896, in Flatow. He was deported from Berlin on November 1, 1941, to the Łódź ghetto. He was deported from Łódź to Chełmno on July 5, 1942. He perished in Chełmno on July 5, 1942.

JANOWSKI, Manja: Born on October 6, 1897, in Łódź, Poland. She was deported from Cologne on October 22, 1941, to the Łódź ghetto. She was deported from Łódź to Chełmno on May 6, 1942, where she perished.

JARECKI, Alphons: Born on July 3, 1878, in Poznań, Poland. He was deported from Berlin on October 27–29, 1941, to the Łódź ghetto. He was deported from Łódź to Chełmno on May 4, 1942. He perished in Chełmno on May 4, 1942.

JASKULSKI, Edith: Born on April 5, 1932, in Berlin. She was deported from Berlin on October 24, 1941, to the Łódź ghetto. She was deported from Łódź to Chełmno on May 4, 1942. She perished in Chełmno on May 4, 1942.

JASTROW, Amalie: Born on March 17, 1872, in Landsberg. She was deported from Berlin on October 18, 1941, to the Łódź ghetto. She was deported from Łódź to Chełmno on May 4, 1942. She perished in Chełmno on May 4, 1942.

JEAN, Johanna: Born on May 2, 1900, in Oestringen. She was deported from Hamburg on October 25, 1941, to the Łódź ghetto. She was deported from Łódź to Chełmno on May 10, 1942, where she perished.

JEIDELS, Frieda: Born on April 24, 1875, in Karthaus. She was deported from Berlin on October 24, 1941, to the Łódź ghetto. She was deported from Łódź to Chełmno on May 8, 1942, where she perished.

JEROCHIM, Jenny: Born on August 2, 1873, in Stolpmünde. She was deported from Berlin on October 18, 1941, to the Łódź ghetto. She was deported from Łódź to Chełmno on May 8, 1942. She perished in Chełmno on May 8, 1942.

JEROZOLIMSKI, Szlama: Born on December 23, 1900, in Wielun. He was deported from Cologne on October 30, 1941, to the Łódź ghetto.

He was deported from Łódź to Chełmno during July 1944, where he perished.

JOACHIMSTHAL, Edgar: Born on June 17, 1890, in Eberswalde. He was deported from Berlin on October 24, 1941, to the Łódź ghetto. He was deported from Łódź to Chełmno on May 5, 1942. He perished in Chełmno on May 5, 1942.

JOELSOHN, Jacob: Born on February 2, 1877, in Pammin. He was deported from Berlin on November 1, 1941, to the Łódź ghetto. He was deported from Łódź to Chełmno on May 9, 1942. He perished in Chełmno on May 9, 1942.

JOHN, Ernestine: Born on July 23, 1890, in Czernowitz. She was deported from Berlin on October 18, 1941, to the Łódź ghetto. She was deported from Łódź to Chełmno on May 8, 1942. She perished in Chełmno on May 8, 1942.

JONAS, Abraham: Born on August 12, 1900, in Berlin. He was deported from Berlin on October 24, 1941, to the Łódź ghetto. He was deported from Łódź to Chełmno on September 13, 1942. He perished in Chełmno on September 13, 1942.

JONASSOHN, Hans: Born on October 8, 1901, in Duisburg. He was deported from Cologne on October 30, 1941, to the Łódź ghetto. He was deported from Łódź to Chełmno during May 1942, where he perished.

JONASSON, Frida: Born on December 1, 1878, in Magdeburg. She was deported from Berlin on October 18, 1941, to the Łódź ghetto. She was deported from Łódź to Chełmno on May 9, 1942. She perished in Chełmno on May 9, 1942.

JONG, Gerda: Born on June 29, 1919, in Barmen-Elberfeld. She was deported from Düsseldorf on October 27, 1941, to the Łódź ghetto. She was deported from Łódź to Chełmno on May 5, 1942. She perished in Chełmno on May 6, 1942.

JONSCHER, Liebe: Born on January 11, 1879, in Tuchel. She was deported from Berlin on November 1, 1941, to the Łódź ghetto. She was deported from Łódź to Chełmno on May 9, 1942. She perished in Chełmno on May 9, 1942.

JORDAN, Johanna: Born on December 15, 1897, in Rogowo, Poland. She was deported from Berlin on October 24, 1941, to the Łódź ghetto. She was deported from Łódź to Chełmno on September 10, 1942. She perished in Chełmno on September 10, 1942.

JOSEL, Gertrud: Born on November 9, 1893, in Lobedau. She was deported from Düsseldorf on October 27, 1941, to the Łódź ghetto. She was deported from Łódź to Chełmno on May 7, 1942. She perished in Chełmno on May 8, 1942.

JOSEPH, Else: Born on December 21, 1885, in Dortmund. She was deported from Berlin on October 18, 1941, to the Łódź ghetto. She was deported from Łódź to Chełmno on May 8, 1942. She perished in Chełmno on May 8, 1942.

JOSEPHSOHN, Alfred: Born on September 16, 1878, in Elbing. He was deported from Berlin on October 18, 1941, to the Łódź ghetto. He was deported from Łódź to Chełmno on May 8, 1942. He perished in Chełmno on May 8, 1942.

JUDA, Else: Born on May 16, 1932, in Berlin. She was deported from Berlin on November 1, 1941, to the Łódź ghetto. She was deported from Łódź to Chełmno on September 7, 1942. She perished in Chełmno on September 7, 1942.

JÜLICH, Hermann: Born on January 14, 1886, in Bad Münstereifel. He was deported from Cologne on October 30, 1941, to the Łódź ghetto. He was deported from Łódź to Chełmno during May 1942, where he perished.

JÜTTNER, Dorothea: Born on March 13, 1907, in Berlin. She was deported from Berlin on November 1, 1941, to the Łódź ghetto. She was deported from Łódź to Chełmno on May 12, 1942. She perished in Chełmno on May 12, 1942.

JURKE, Ellen: Born on January 29, 1924, in Berlin. She was deported from Berlin on October 27–29, 1941, to the Łódź ghetto. She was deported from Łódź to Chełmno on May 5, 1942. She perished in Chełmno on May 5, 1942.

JUST, Alice: Born on January 26, 1916, in Berlin. She was deported from Berlin on November 1, 1941, to the Łódź ghetto. She was deported

from Łódź to Chełmno on May 8, 1942. She perished in Chełmno on May 8, 1942.

KACZYNSKI, Kurt: Born on April 25, 1899, in Berlin. He was deported from Berlin on October 24, 1941, to the Łódź ghetto. He was deported from Łódź to Chełmno on May 5, 1942. He perished in Chełmno on May 5, 1942.

KÄMPFER, Ellen: Born on January 11, 1894, in Hamburg. She was deported from Hamburg on October 25, 1941, to the Łódź ghetto. She was deported from Łódź to Chełmno on May 10, 1942, where she perished.

KAFFE, Meta: Born on October 29, 1902, in Berlin. She was deported from Berlin on November 1, 1941, to the Łódź ghetto. She was deported from Łódź to Chełmno on May 9, 1942. She perished in Chełmno on May 9, 1942.

KAHL, Grete: Born on March 31, 1906, in Berlin. She was deported from Berlin on October 18, 1941, to the Łódź ghetto. She was deported from Łódź to Chełmno on May 9, 1942. She perished in Chełmno on May 9, 1942.

KAHN, Alfred: Born on February 27, 1914, in Essen. He was deported from Düsseldorf on October 27, 1941, to the Łódź ghetto. He was deported from Łódź to Chełmno on May 13, 1942. He perished in Chełmno on May 14, 1942.

KAHNWEILER, Lilli: Born on July 1, 1887, in Bonn. She was deported from Cologne on October 22, 1941, to the Łódź ghetto. She was deported from Łódź to Chełmno on May 6, 1942, where she perished.

KAIN, Siegbert: Born on February 3, 1921, in Brotdorf. He was deported from Cologne during October 1941, to the Łódź ghetto. He was deported from Łódź to Chełmno during May 1942, where he perished.

KAINER, Henriette: Born on November 29, 1877, in Brody. She was deported from Berlin on October 18, 1941, to the Łódź ghetto. She was deported from Łódź to Chełmno on May 8, 1942. She perished in Chełmno on May 8, 1942.

KAISER, Emmy: Born on February 16, 1903, in Berlin. She was deported from Berlin on October 24, 1941, to the Łódź ghetto. She was deported from Łódź to Chełmno on June 26, 1944. She perished in Chełmno on June 26, 1944.

KALB, Erna: Born on December 19, 1930, in Berlin. She was deported from Berlin on October 24, 1941, to the Łódź ghetto. She was deported from Łódź to Chełmno on May 4, 1942. She perished in Chełmno on May 4, 1942.

KALENSCHER, Regina: Born on September 7, 1886, in Berlin. She was deported from Berlin on November 1, 1941, to the Łódź ghetto. She was deported from Łódź to Chełmno on May 8, 1942. She perished in Chełmno on May 8, 1942.

KALISCHER, Meta: Born on September 20, 1889, in Zbiczno. She was deported from Berlin on October 18, 1941, to the Łódź ghetto. She was deported from Łódź to Chełmno on September 23, 1942, where she perished.

KALLMANN, Marie: Born on September 10, 1877, in Heilbronn. She was deported from Berlin on October 18, 1941, to the Łódź ghetto. She was deported from Łódź to Chełmno on May 8, 1942. She perished in Chełmno on May 8, 1942.

KAMINSKI, Hannah: Born on February 12, 1882, in Allenstein. She was deported from Berlin on November 1, 1941, to the Łódź ghetto. She was deported from Łódź to Chełmno on May 9, 1942. She perished in Chełmno on May 9, 1942.

KAMINSKY, Gertrud: Born on July 12, 1881, in Berlin. She was deported from Berlin on October 18, 1941, to the Łódź ghetto. She was deported from Łódź to Chełmno on May 8, 1942, where she perished.

KAMP, Edith: Born on August 24, 1918, in Dortmund. She was deported from Cologne on October 22, 1941, to the Łódź ghetto. She was deported from Łódź to Chełmno on May 6, 1942, where she perished.

KANN, Klara: Born on December 20, 1885, in Adorf. She was deported from Düsseldorf on October 27, 1941, to the Łódź ghetto. She was deported from Łódź to Chełmno on May 11, 1942. She perished in Chełmno on May 12, 1942.

KANTER, Kurt: Born on June 17, 1933, in Cologne. He was deported from Cologne on October 30, 1941, to the Łódź ghetto. He was deported from Łódź to Chełmno during May 1942, where he perished.

KANTOROWICZ, Leo: Born on December 2, 1928, in Gera. He was deported from Berlin on October 24, 1941, to the Łódź ghetto. He was deported from Łódź to Chełmno during March 1942, where he perished.

KAPLAN, Georg: Born on January 8, 1881, in Berlin. He was deported from Berlin on October 24, 1941, to the Łódź ghetto. He was deported from Łódź to Chełmno on May 8, 1942. He perished in Chełmno on May 8, 1942.

KARFIOL, Klara: Born on December 13, 1892, in Eisleben. She was deported from Berlin on October 18, 1941, to the Łódź ghetto. She was deported from Łódź to Chełmno on May 4, 1942. She perished in Chełmno on May 8, 1942.

KARGAUER, Norbert: Born on September 29, 1926, in Hamburg. He was deported from Hamburg on October 25, 1941, to the Łódź ghetto. He was deported from Łódź to Chełmno on May 10, 1942, where he perished.

KARIEL, Veronika: Born on March 1, 1892, in Wesel. She was deported from Cologne on October 30, 1941, to the Łódź ghetto. She was deported from Łódź to Chełmno during September 1942, where she perished.

KARPE, Thomas: Born on August 30, 1941, in Berlin. He was deported from Düsseldorf on October 27, 1941, to the Łódź ghetto. He was deported from Łódź to Chełmno during September 1942, where he perished.

KASCHMANN, Isaac: Born on July 16, 1886, in Bischhausen. He was deported from Düsseldorf on October 27, 1941, to the Łódź ghetto. He was deported from Łódź to Chełmno on May 7, 1942. He perished in Chełmno on May 8, 1942.

KASSEL, Rosalie: Born on December 14, 1911, in Königshütte, Poland. She was imprisoned in the *Sammelstelle* on *Levetzowstrasse,* Berlin. She was deported from Berlin on October 18, 1941, to the Łódź ghetto.

She was deported from Łódź to Chełmno on May 7, 1942. She perished in Chełmno on May 7, 1942.

KASTELLAN, Adele: Born on February 8, 1890, in Guhrau. She was deported from Berlin on November 1, 1941, to the Łódź ghetto. She was deported from Łódź to Chełmno on May 13, 1942, where she perished.

KATZ, Max: Born on March 10, 1879, in Badorf. He was deported from Düsseldorf on October 27, 1941, to the Łódź ghetto. He was deported from Łódź to Chełmno on May 13, 1942. He perished in Chełmno on May 14, 1942.

KATZENBERG, Jenny: Born on September 23, 1887, in Liblar. She was deported from Cologne on October 22, 1941, to the Łódź ghetto. She was deported from Łódź to Chełmno on May 5, 1942, where she perished.

KATZENELLENBOGEN, Eva-Lucie: Born on November 16, 1929, in Gros Mandelkow. She was deported from Berlin on October 27–29, 1941, to the Łódź ghetto. She was deported from Łódź to Chełmno on May 9, 1942. She perished in Chełmno on May 9, 1942.

KATZENSTEIN, Anneliese: Born on May 24, 1910, in Cottbus. She was deported from Cologne on October 22, 1941, to the Łódź ghetto. She was deported from Łódź to Chełmno where she perished on September 16, 1942.

KAUFFMANN, Paula: Born on May 13, 1880, in Erwitte. She was deported from Düsseldorf on October 27, 1941, to the Łódź ghetto. She was deported from Łódź to Chełmno on May 7, 1942. She perished in Chełmno on May 8, 1942.

KEDZIOREK, Rosa: Born on February 23, 1874, in Neuwedell. She was deported from Berlin on October 24, 1941, to the Łódź ghetto. She was deported from Łódź to Chełmno on May 5, 1942. He perished in Chełmno on May 5, 1942.

KELLER, Arnold: Born on January 20, 1888, in Lwow. He was deported from Berlin on October 18, 1941, to the Łódź ghetto. He was deported from Łódź to Chełmno on May 8, 1942. He perished in Chełmno on May 8, 1942.

KELMAN, Betty: Born on August 22, 1903, in Berlin. She was deported from Berlin on October 24, 1941, to the Łódź ghetto. She was deported from Łódź to Chełmno on May 4, 1942. She perished in Chełmno on May 4, 1942.

KEMPINSKI, Meta: Born on October 19, 1906, in Dornum. She was expelled from Hamburg on 28–29 October 1938, to Zbąszyń, Poland. She was deported from the Łódź ghetto to Chełmno on July 10, 1944, where she perished.

KEMPLER, Edith: Born on July 20, 1913, in Berlin. She was deported from Berlin on October 27–29, 1941, to the Łódź ghetto. She was deported from Łódź to Chełmno on May 5, 1942. She perished in Chełmno on May 5, 1942.

KERBS, Frieda: Born on August 27, 1883, in Neumagen. She was deported from Cologne on October 22, 1941, to the Łódź ghetto. She was deported from Łódź to Chełmno on April 5, 1942, where she perished.

KERN, Alice: Born on July 2, 1904, in Berlin. She was deported from Berlin on October 27–29, 1941, to the Łódź ghetto. She was deported from Łódź to Chełmno on May 4, 1942. She perished in Chełmno on May 4, 1942.

KERP, Frieda: Born on January 18, 1895, in Polch. She was deported from Düsseldorf on October 27, 1941, to the Łódź ghetto. She was deported from Łódź to Chełmno on June 28, 1944. She perished in Chełmno on June 29, 1944.

KICK, Henriette: Born on January 30, 1881, in Cologne. She was deported from Cologne on October 30, 1941, to the Łódź ghetto. She was deported from Łódź to Chełmno during May 1942, where she perished.

KIEFER, Ida: Born on February 19, 1885, in Heddesheim. She was deported from Frankfurt am Main on October 20, 1941, to the Łódź ghetto. She was deported from Łódź to Chełmno on September 23, 1942, where she perished.

KIEWE, Frieda: Born on September 17, 1889, in Wriezen. She was deported from Berlin on October 27–29, 1941, to the Łódź ghetto. She

was deported from Łódź to Chełmno on May 5, 1942. She perished in Chełmno on May 5, 1942.

KIKSMANN, Jacob: Born on January 10, 1870, in Mysłowice, Poland. He was deported from Berlin on November 1, 1941, to the Łódź ghetto. He was deported from Łódź to Chełmno on May 14, 1942, where he perished.

KIMEL, Abraham: Born on September 1, 1875, in Lwow. He was deported from Berlin on October 27–29, 1941, to the Łódź ghetto. He was deported from Łódź to Chełmno on September 7, 1942. He perished in Chełmno on September 7, 1942.

KINSKY, Henriette: Born on June 1, 1883, in Cammin. She was deported from Düsseldorf on October 27, 1941, to the Łódź ghetto. She was deported from Łódź to Chełmno on May 6, 1942. She perished in Chełmno on May 7, 1942.

KIRIASEFER, Sigmund: Born on January 3, 1878, in Jekaterinoslaw, Russia. He was deported from Berlin on October 18, 1941, to the Łódź ghetto. He was deported from Łódź to Chełmno on May 9, 1942. He perished in Chełmno on May 9, 1942.

KIRSCHBAUM, Hedwig: Born on September 30, 1881, in Kahnstein. She was deported from Düsseldorf on October 27, 1941, to the Łódź ghetto. She was deported from Łódź to Chełmno on May 6, 1942. She perished in Chełmno on May 7, 1942.

KIRSCHBERG, Eva: Born on April 7, 1890, in Cologne. She was deported from Cologne on October 30, 1941, to the Łódź ghetto. She was deported from Łódź to Chełmno during May 1942, where she perished.

KIRSCHENBAUM, Jenny: Born on August 6, 1901, in Santomischel, Poland. She was deported from Berlin on November 1, 1941, to the Łódź ghetto. She was deported from Łódź to Chełmno on May 8, 1942. She perished in Chełmno on May 8, 1942.

KIRSCHNER, Paula: Born on September 7, 1879, in Heidlingsfeld. She was deported from Berlin on October 18, 1941, to the Łódź ghetto. She was deported from Łódź to Chełmno on May 8, 1942, where she perished.

KIRSTEIN, Henriette: Born on May 30, 1870, in Bärwalde. She was deported from Berlin on November 1, 1941, to the Łódź ghetto. She was deported from Łódź to Chełmno on May 9, 1942. She perished in Chełmno on May 9, 1942.

KISCH, Erna: Born on May 10, 1891, in Freiberg. She was deported from Hamburg on October 25, 1941, to the Łódź ghetto. She was deported from Łódź to Chełmno on May 10, 1942, where she perished.

KIWI, Hermann: Born on February 22, 1879, in Oborniki, Poland. He was deported from Berlin on October 18, 1941, to the Łódź ghetto. He was deported from Łódź to Chełmno on May 8, 1942. He perished in Chełmno on May 8, 1942.

KIWIT, Emmy: Born on June 5, 1879, in Frankenstein. She was deported from Berlin on October 27–29, 1941, to the Łódź ghetto. She was deported from Łódź to Chełmno on May 5, 1942, where she perished.

KLABER, Klementine: Born on September 24, 1883, in Kyllburg. She was deported from Cologne on October 30, 1941, to the Łódź ghetto. She was deported from Łódź to Chełmno during May 1942, where she perished.

KLANDT, Clara: Born on June 29, 1866, in Sandow. She was deported from Berlin on November 1, 1941, to the Łódź ghetto. She was deported from Łódź to Chełmno on May 8, 1942. She perished in Chełmno on May 8, 1942.

KLARER, Jacob: Born on April 26, 1884, in Brzeżany, Poland. He was deported from Berlin on October 24, 1941, to the Łódź ghetto. He was deported from Łódź to Chełmno on May 5, 1942. He perished in Chełmno on May 5, 1942.

KLARMANN, Regina: Born on September 29, 1890, in Sniatyn, Poland. She was deported from Berlin on October 27–29, 1941, to the Łódź ghetto. She was deported from Łódź to Chełmno on May 4, 1942. She perished in Chełmno on May 4, 1942.

KLEBE, Margot: Born on August 10, 1926, in Cologne. She was deported from Cologne on October 22, 1941, to the Łódź ghetto. She was deported from Łódź to Chełmno during May 1942, where she perished.

KLECZEWSKI, Werner: Born on January 29, 1930, in Berlin. He was deported from Berlin on October 24, 1941, to the Łódź ghetto. He was deported from Łódź to Chełmno on May 4, 1942. He perished in Chełmno on May 4, 1942.

KLEE, Kurt: Born on February 27, 1902, in Cologne. He was deported from Cologne on October 30, 1941, to the Łódź ghetto. He was deported from Łódź to Chełmno during May 1942, where he perished.

KLEFISCH, Sibylia: Born on December 21, 1903, in Cologne. She was deported from Cologne on October 22, 1941, to the Łódź ghetto. She was deported from Łódź to Chełmno during May 1942, where she perished.

KLEIMANN, Malka: Born on November 14, 1887, in Oświęcim, Poland. She was deported from Berlin on October 27–29, 1941, to the Łódź ghetto. She was deported from Łódź to Chełmno on September 12, 1942. She perished in Chełmno on September 12, 1942.

KLEIN, Herbert: Born on July 11, 1929, in Berlin. He was deported from Berlin on October 27–29, 1941, to the Łódź ghetto. He was deported from Łódź to Chełmno on May 4, 1942. He perished in Chełmno on May 4, 1942.

KLESTADT, Friedrich: Born on May 10, 1889, in Bamberg. He was deported from Cologne on October 30, 1941, to the Łódź ghetto. He was deported from Łódź to Chełmno during May 1942. He perished in Chełmno on December 7, 1942.

KLINGER, Johanna: Born on October 21, 1886, in Soest. She emigrated from Hannover on July 2, 1939, to Poland. She was deported from the Łódź ghetto to Chełmno where she perished.

KLOPSTOCK, Paula: Born on October 19, 1883, in Lemgo. She was deported from Cologne on October 22, 1941, to the Łódź ghetto. She was deported from Łódź to Chełmno on May 5, 1942, where she perished.

KLOSS, Grete: Born on October 16, 1878, in Preusisch Stargard. She was deported from Berlin on October 27–29, 1941, to the Łódź ghetto. She was deported from Łódź to Chełmno on May 6, 1942. She perished in Chełmno on May 6, 1942.

KLÜGER, Sara: Born on July 5, 1887, in Jarotschin, Poland. She was deported from Berlin on October 24, 1941, to the Łódź ghetto. She was deported from Łódź to Chełmno on September 10, 1942. She perished in Chełmno on September 10, 1942.

KLUGE, Rosalie: Born on June 20, 1898, in Berlin. She was deported from Berlin on November 1, 1941, to the Łódź ghetto. She was deported from Łódź to Chełmno on June 28, 1944. She perished in Chełmno on June 28, 1944.

KNAPP, Henri: Born on September 9, 1933, in Berlin. He was deported from Berlin on October 24, 1941, to the Łódź ghetto. He was deported from Łódź to Chełmno on July 3, 1944. He perished in Chełmno on July 3, 1944.

KNECHT, Regina: Born on April 3, 1922, in Duisburg. She was deported from Düsseldorf on October 27, 1941, to the Łódź ghetto. She was deported from Łódź to Chełmno on July 12, 1944. She perished in Chełmno on July 13, 1944.

KNIEBEL, Josef: Born on March 15, 1886, in Buk, Poland. He was deported from Cologne on October 30, 1941, to the Łódź ghetto. He was deported from Łódź to Chełmno during May 1942, where he perished.

KNOPF, Jenny: Born on July 20, 1881, in Netzebruch. She was deported from Berlin on October 27–29, 1941, to the Łódź ghetto. She was deported from Łódź to Chełmno on May 6, 1942. She perished in Chełmno on May 6, 1942.

KOBURGER, Melanie: Born on September 6, 1874, in Friedelsheim. She was deported from Düsseldorf on October 27, 1941, to the Łódź ghetto. She was deported from Łódź to Chełmno during September 1942, where she perished.

KOCH, Joachim: Born on July 4, 1918, in Berlin. He was deported from Berlin on October 24, 1941, to the Łódź ghetto. He was deported from Łódź to Chełmno on May 15, 1942. He perished in Chełmno on May 15, 1942.

KOCHMANN, Berthold: Born on January 6, 1878, in Schokken. He was deported from Düsseldorf on October 27, 1941, to the Łódź ghetto.

He was deported from Łódź to Chełmno on May 6, 1942. He perished in Chełmno on May 7, 1942.

KÖLN, Erich: Born on November 28, 1898, in Berlin. He was deported from Berlin on October 24, 1941, to the Łódź ghetto. He was deported from Łódź to Chełmno on May 5, 1942. He perished in Chełmno on May 5, 1942.

KÖNIG, Klara: Born on April 14, 1880, in Graudenz. She was deported from Berlin on October 18, 1941, to the Łódź ghetto. She was deported from Łódź to Chełmno on May 12, 1942. She perished in Chełmno on May 12, 1942.

KÖNIGHEIM, Paula: Born on September 5, 1888, in Wittlich. She was deported from Cologne on October 30, 1941, to the Łódź ghetto. She was deported from Łódź to Chełmno during June 1942, where she perished.

KÖNIGSBERGER, Alice: Born on February 14, 1889, in Berlin. She was deported from Berlin on October 18, 1941, to the Łódź ghetto. She was deported from Łódź to Chełmno on May 9, 1942. She perished in Chełmno on May 9, 1942.

KÖNIGSFELD, Dorothea: Born on August 9, 1896, in Berlin. She was deported from Berlin on November 1, 1941, to the Łódź ghetto. She was deported from Łódź to Chełmno on May 8, 1942, where she perished.

KÖSTEN, Ida: Born on September 19, 1883, in Rożniątów, Poland. She was deported from Düsseldorf on October 27, 1941, to the Łódź ghetto. She was deported from Łódź to Chełmno on May 6, 1942. She perished in Chełmno on May 7, 1942.

KOGON, Hersch: Born on December 1878, in Slatopol, Russia. He was deported from Frankfurt am Main on October 20, 1941, to the Łódź ghetto. He was deported from Łódź to Chełmno on May 11, 1942, where he perished.

KOHLAGEN, Therese: Born on April 22, 1887, in Haupersweiler. She was deported from Cologne on October 22, 1941, to the Łódź ghetto. She was deported from Łódź to Chełmno on May 11, 1942, where she perished.

KOHLS, Berta: Born on March 30, 1886, in Krojanke. She was deported from Berlin on October 27–29, 1941, to the Łódź ghetto. She was deported from Łódź to Chełmno on May 6, 1942. She perished in Chełmno on May 6, 1942.

KOHN, Alfred: Born on June 7, 1879, in Liebotitz. He was deported from Düsseldorf on October 27, 1941, to the Łódź ghetto. He was deported from Łódź to Chełmno on May 6, 1942. He perished in Chełmno on May 7, 1942.

KOLATZKI, Berta: Born on May 24, 1892, in Brussels, Belgium. She was deported from Cologne on October 30, 1941, to the Łódź ghetto. She was deported from Łódź to Chełmno during May 1942, where she perished.

KONEGEN, Frida: Born on March 27, 1879, in Stettin. She was deported from Berlin on November 1, 1941, to the Łódź ghetto. She was deported from Łódź to Chełmno on May 11, 1942. She perished in Chełmno on May 11, 1942.

KONGRECKI, Auguste: Born on March 6, 1887, in Niedenstein. She was deported from Düsseldorf on October 27, 1941, to the Łódź ghetto. She was deported from Łódź to Chełmno on May 6, 1942. She perished in Chełmno on May 7, 1942.

KONINSKY, Henriette: Born on June 19, 1883, in Burgdorf. She was deported from Cologne on October 30, 1941, to the Łódź ghetto. She was deported from Łódź to Chełmno during May 1942, where she perished.

KOPPEL, Pauline: Born on March 4, 1892, in Kraków, Poland. She was deported from Berlin on October 24, 1941, to the Łódź ghetto. She was deported from Łódź to Chełmno on May 15, 1942. She perished in Chełmno on May 15, 1942.

KORANT, Anna: Born on June 5, 1880, in Berlin. She was deported from Berlin on October 18, 1941, to the Łódź ghetto. She was deported from Łódź to Chełmno on May 8, 1942, where she perished.

KORNBLUM, Johanna: Born on February 10, 1884, in Beuthen, Poland. She was deported from Berlin on October 27–29, 1941, to the Łódź ghetto. She was deported from Łódź to Chełmno on May 4, 1942, where she perished.

KORNGOLD, Rifka: Born on January 29, 1901, in Oświęcim, Poland. She was deported from Berlin on October 24, 1941, to the Łódź ghetto. She was deported from Łódź to Chełmno on May 15, 1942. She perished in Chełmno on May 15, 1942.

KORTE, Lilly: Born on May 11, 1890, in Berlin. She was deported from Berlin on November 1, 1941, to the Łódź ghetto. She was deported from Łódź to Chełmno on May 9, 1942. She perished in Chełmno on May 9, 1942.

KOSLOWSKI, Henriette: Born on June 17, 1898, in Berlin. She was deported from Berlin on October 24, 1941, to the Łódź ghetto. She was deported from Łódź to Chełmno on May 4, 1942. She perished in Chełmno on May 4, 1942.

KOSSMANN, Johanna: Born on June 18, 1882, in Cologne. She was deported from Cologne on October 22, 1941, to the Łódź ghetto. She was deported from Łódź to Chełmno during May 1942, where she perished.

KOSTEZKI, Rachila: Born on June 15, 1892, in Liepaja, Latvia. She was deported from Hamburg on October 25, 1941, to the Łódź ghetto. She was deported from Łódź to Chełmno on May 10, 1942, where she perished.

KOTEK, Elias: Born on September 29, 1887, in Łódź, Poland. He emigrated from Wuppertal to Poland. He was deported from the Łódź ghetto to Chełmno on April 1, 1942, where he perished.

KOWALSKI, Hinda: Born on September 19, 1900, in Łódź, Poland. She was deported from Düsseldorf on October 27, 1941, to the Łódź ghetto. She was deported from Łódź to Chełmno on May 13, 1942. She perished in Chełmno on May 14, 1942.

KRÄMER, Selma: Born on May 15, 1878, in Czernowitz. She was deported from Berlin on November 1, 1941, to the Łódź ghetto. She was deported from Łódź to Chełmno on May 4, 1942. She perished in Chełmno on May 4, 1942.

KRAKAUER, Else: Born on January 1, 1897, in Odenkirchen. She was deported from Berlin on October 18, 1941, to the Łódź ghetto. She was deported from Łódź to Chełmno on May 4, 1942. She perished in Chełmno on May 4, 1942.

KRAMARSKI, Max: Born on September 20, 1923, in Berlin. He was deported from Berlin on October 18, 1941, to the Łódź ghetto. He was deported from Łódź to Chełmno on May 13, 1942. He perished in Chełmno on May 13, 1942.

KRAMARZINSKY, Frieda: Born on March 15, 1868, in Zrobka, Russia. She was deported from Berlin on November 1, 1941, to the Łódź ghetto. She was deported from Łódź to Chełmno on May 9, 1942. She perished in Chełmno on May 9, 1942.

KRAMER, Josef: Born on June 22, 1927, in Berlin. He was deported from Berlin on November 1, 1941, to the Łódź ghetto. He was deported from Łódź to Chełmno on May 9, 1942. He perished in Chełmno on May 9, 1942.

KRATZ, Jacob: Born on July 7, 1870, in Nideggen. He was deported from Berlin on October 18, 1941, to the Łódź ghetto. He was deported from Łódź to Chełmno on May 9, 1942. He perished in Chełmno on May 9, 1942.

KREBS, Johanna: Born on March 1, 1885, in Bingen. She was deported from Berlin on October 18, 1941, to the Łódź ghetto. She was deported from Łódź to Chełmno on May 8, 1942. She perished in Chełmno on May 8, 1942.

KREISBERG, Mincia: Born on May 15, 1892, in Drohobycz. She was deported from Berlin on October 24, 1941, to the Łódź ghetto. She was deported from Łódź to Chełmno on May 4, 1942. She perished in Chełmno on May 4, 1942.

KREKLER, Hedwig: Born on May 19, 1880, in Dortmund. She was deported from Cologne on October 22, 1941, to the Łódź ghetto. She was deported from Łódź to Chełmno on April 5, 1942, where she perished.

KRESSE, Henriette: Born on November 23, 1885, in Düsseldorf. She was deported from Berlin on October 24, 1941, to the Łódź ghetto.

She was deported from Łódź to Chełmno on May 15, 1942, where she perished.

KREIGER, Abraham: Born on November 1, 1885, in Gorlice, Poland. He was deported from Düsseldorf on October 27, 1941, to the Łódź ghetto. He was deported from Łódź to Chełmno on May 6, 1942. He perished in Chełmno on May 7, 1942.

KRISCH, Hermann: Born on March 16, 1885, in Inowrocław, Poland. He was deported from Berlin on October 27–29, 1941, to the Łódź ghetto. He was deported from Łódź to Chełmno on May 5, 1942. He perished in Chełmno on May 5, 1942.

KROHN, Gertrud: Born on September 13, 1879, in Gniezno, Poland. She was deported from Berlin on October 27–29, 1941, to the Łódź ghetto. She was deported from Łódź to Chełmno on May 4, 1942, where she perished.

KRON, Selma: Born on April 6, 1890, in Spangenberg. She was deported from Hamburg on October 25, 1941, to the Łódź ghetto. She was deported from Łódź to Chełmno on May 1, 1942, where she perished.

KRONENBERGER, Augusta: Born on April 7, 1887, in Simmern. She was deported from Luxembourg –Trier on October 16, 1941, to the Łódź ghetto. She was deported from Łódź to Chełmno on May 7, 1942, where she perished.

KRONHEIM, Ulrike: Born on October 25, 1885, in Gardelegen. She was deported from Berlin on November 1, 1941, to the Łódź ghetto. She was deported from Łódź to Chełmno on May 6, 1942. She perished in Chełmno on May 6, 1942.

KRÜGER, Hedwig: Born on September 4, 1893, in Czempin, Poland. She was deported from Berlin on October 24, 1941, to the Łódź ghetto. She was deported from Łódź to Chełmno on May 5, 1942. She perished in Chełmno on May 5, 1942.

KRYPKA, Clara: Born on October 3, 1875, in Fordon. She was deported from Cologne on October 22, 1941, to the Łódź ghetto. She was deported from Łódź to Chełmno on May 5, 1942, where she perished.

KUBA, Adolf: Born on December 30, 1883, in Srem, Poland. He was deported from Berlin on October 27–29, 1941, to the Łódź ghetto. He was deported from Łódź to Chełmno on September 10, 1942. He perished in Chełmno on September 10, 1942.

KUCZINNA, Henriette: Born on October 17, 1911, in Goldap. She was deported from Berlin on October 27–29, 1941, to the Łódź ghetto. She was deported from Łódź to Chełmno on May 4, 1942. She perished in Chełmno on May 4, 1942.

KÜHNS, Irma: Born on January 14, 1902, in Breslau. She was deported from Berlin on October 18, 1941, to the Łódź ghetto. She was deported from Łódź to Chełmno on May 8, 1942, where she perished.

KUFERT, Icek: Born on July 8, 1900, in Lask, Poland. He was expelled from Berlin on October 28–29, 1938, to Poland. He was deported from the Łódź ghetto to Chełmno on June 28, 1944, where he perished.

KUGELMANN, Robert: Born on June 6, 1880, in Fritzlar. He was deported from Düsseldorf on October 27, 1941, to the Łódź ghetto. He was deported from Łódź to Chełmno on May 6, 1942. He perished in Chełmno on May 7, 1942.

KULP, Anna: Born on May 9, 1883, in Kartuzy, Poland. She was deported from Berlin on October 18, 1941, to the Łódź ghetto. She was deported from Łódź to Chełmno on May 8, 1942. She perished in Chełmno on May 8, 1942.

KUNTZ, Frieda: Born on June 23, 1901, in Stuhm. She was deported from Berlin on October 27–29, 1941, to the Łódź ghetto. She was deported from Łódź to Chełmno on May 5, 1942. She perished in Chełmno on May 5, 1942.

KUNZ, Max: Born on April 3, 1865, in Tiefenbach. He was deported from Berlin on October 18, 1941, to the Łódź ghetto. He was deported from Łódź to Chełmno on May 11, 1942. He perished in Chełmno on May 11, 1942.

KUPERBERG, Helena: Born on January 2, 1923, in Essen. She was expelled from Essen on October 28, 1938, to Zbąszyń, Poland. She was imprisoned in Zbąszyń Internment Camp until the summer of 1939. She was deported from the Łódź ghetto to Chełmno on February 23, 1942. She perished in Chełmno on February 23, 1942.

KUPFERMANN, Josef: Born on April 16, 1879, in Kolomea. He was deported from Düsseldorf on October 27, 1941, to the Łódź ghetto. He was deported from Łódź to Chełmno on May 6, 1942. He perished in Chełmno on May 7, 1942.

KUPFERSCHMIED, Sara: Born on January 6, 1888, in Gros Hermenau. He was deported from Berlin on October 24, 1941, to the Łódź ghetto. He was deported from Łódź to Chełmno on May 4, 1942. He perished in Chełmno on May 4, 1942.

KUPPERMANN, Henriette: Born on August 16, 1890, in Wola Duchacka, Poland. She was deported from Hamburg on October 25, 1941, to the Łódź ghetto. She was deported from Łódź to Chełmno on June 28, 1944, where she perished.

KUROPATWA, Therese: Born on May 7, 1886, in Culmsee. She was deported from Berlin on October 18, 1941, to the Łódź ghetto. She was deported from Łódź to Chełmno on May 8, 1942. She perished in Chełmno on May 8, 1942.

KURZ, Ellen: Born on November 30, 1934, in Berlin. She was deported from Berlin on October 18, 1941, to the Łódź ghetto. She was deported from Łódź to Chełmno on May 9, 1942. She perished in Chełmno on May 9, 1942.

KURZBERG, Hulda: Born on March 21, 1880, in Poznań, Poland. She was deported from Berlin on October 18, 1941, to the Łódź ghetto. She was deported from Łódź to Chełmno on May 8, 1942, where she perished.

KURZONDKOWSKI, Meta: Born on April 26, 1903, in Stretzin. She was deported from Berlin on October 27–29, 1941, to the Łódź ghetto. She was deported from Łódź to Chełmno on July 12, 1944. She perished in Chełmno on July 12, 1944.

KURZWEG, Doris: Born on February 15, 1895, in Berlin. She was deported from Berlin on October 27–29, 1941, to the Łódź ghetto. She was deported from Łódź to Chełmno on May 5, 1942. She perished in Chełmno on May 5, 1942.

KUSSEL, Hugo: Born on November 4, 1877, in Barmen-Elberfeld. He was deported from Düsseldorf on October 27, 1941, to the Łódź

ghetto. He was deported from Łódź to Chełmno on May 6, 1942. He perished in Chełmno on May 7, 1942.

KUTNER, Sophie: Born on June 29, 1881, in Berlin. She was deported from Berlin on October 18, 1941, to the Łódź ghetto. She was deported from Łódź to Chełmno on May 9, 1942. She perished in Chełmno on May 9, 1942.

KUTTNER, Olga: Born on March 10, 1874, in Tuchel. She was deported from Berlin on October 24, 1941, to the Łódź ghetto. She was deported from Łódź to Chełmno on September 10, 1942. She perished in Chełmno on September 10, 1942.

KUZNICKI, Frajda: Born on May 3, 1917, in Zduńska Wola, Poland. She was expelled from Frankfurt am Main on October 28–29, 1938, to Zbąszyń, Poland. She was expelled from the Łódź ghetto to Chełmno where she perished.

KUZNITZKY, Martha: Born on March 20, 1885, in Katowice, Poland. She was deported from Berlin on November 1, 1941, to the Łódź ghetto. She was deported from Łódź to Chełmno on May 8, 1942, where she perished.

LACHMANN, Betty: Born on August 18, 1889, in Allenstein. She was deported from Berlin on November 1, 1941, to the Łódź ghetto. She was deported from Łódź to Chełmno on May 9, 1942. She perished in Chełmno on May 9, 1942.

LANDAU, Anna: Born on August 1, 1889, in Tłumacz, Poland. She was expelled from Düsseldorf on May 19, 1936, to Stanislau, Poland. She was deported from Düsseldorf on October 27, 1941, to the Łódź ghetto. She was deported from Łódź to Chełmno on May 6, 1942. She perished in Chełmno on May 7, 1942.

LANDECK, Clara: Born on December 28, 1883, in Gros Linichen. She was deported from Berlin on October 18, 1941, to the Łódź ghetto. She was deported from Łódź to Chełmno on May 8, 1942. She perished in Chełmno on May 8, 1942.

LANDECKER, Frieda: Born on September 14, 1870, in Greifenberg. She was deported from Berlin on October 27–29, 1941, to the Łódź ghetto.

She was deported from Łódź to Chełmno on May 12, 1942. She perished in Chełmno on May 12, 1942.

LANDESMANN, Ruth: Born on January 12, 1938, in Weidenau. She emigrated from Siegen on December 8, 1938, to Poland. She was deported from the Łódź ghetto to Chełmno on September 10, 1942. She perished in Chełmno on September 10, 1942.

LANDSBERG, Veronika: Born on February 5, 1873, in Berlin. She was deported from Berlin on October 18, 1941, to the Łódź ghetto. She was deported from Łódź to Chełmno on May 8, 1942. She perished in Chełmno on May 8, 1942.

LANG, Martha: Born on March 20, 1879, in Berlin. She was deported from Berlin on October 18, 1941, to the Łódź ghetto. She was deported from Łódź to Chełmno on May 8, 1942. She perished in Chełmno on May 8, 1942.

LANG-PUCHOF, Josefine: Born on May 21, 1896, in Vienna, Austria. She was deported from Berlin on October 24, 1941, to the Łódź ghetto. She was deported from Łódź to Chełmno on May 9, 1942. She perished in Chełmno on May 9, 1942.

LANGE, Julius: Born on October 29, 1875, in Hamburg. He was deported from Cologne on October 22, 1941, to the Łódź ghetto. He was deported from Łódź to Chełmno during May 1942, where he perished.

LANGSTADT, Else: Born on August 26, 1880, in Altena. She was deported from Düsseldorf on October 27, 1941, to the Łódź ghetto. She was deported from Łódź to Chełmno on May 6, 1942. She perished in Chełmno on May 7, 1942.

LANOCH, Hanna: Born on December 9, 1886, in Cieszyn. She was deported from Berlin on October 27–29, 1941, to the Łódź ghetto. She was deported from Łódź to Chełmno on May 10, 1942. She perished in Chełmno on May 10, 1942.

LAPIDAS, Erna: Born on May 20, 1884, in Waldeck. She was deported from Berlin on October 24, 1941, to the Łódź ghetto. She was deported from Łódź to Chełmno on September 10, 1942. She perished in Chełmno on September 10, 1942.

LASCH, Leonore: Born on May 31, 1880, in Oelde. She was deported from Cologne on October 22, 1941, to the Łódź ghetto. She was deported from Łódź to Chełmno on May 5, 1942, where she perished.

LASER, Lilli: Born on August 15, 1898, in Berlin. She was deported from Berlin on October 18, 1941, to the Łódź ghetto. She was deported from Łódź to Chełmno on May 8, 1942. She perished in Chełmno on May 8, 1942.

LASKA, Hermann: Born on October 4, 1927, in Danzig. He was expelled from Danzig on November 12, 1938, to Poland. He was deported from the Łódź ghetto to Chełmno on March 1, 1942, where he perished.

LASKI, Caesar: Born on November 2, 1871, in Hamburg. He was deported from Hamburg on October 25, 1941, to the Łódź ghetto. He was deported from Łódź to Chełmno on May 10, 1942, where he perished.

LASZLO, Angela: Born on June 6, 1877, in Kisorosz, Hungary. She was deported from Berlin on October 24, 1941, to the Łódź ghetto. She was deported from Łódź to Chełmno on May 4, 1942. She perished in Chełmno on May 4, 1942.

LAUFER, Netty: Born on July 7, 1878, in Lancut, Poland. She was deported from Düsseldorf on October 27, 1941, to the Łódź ghetto. She was deported from Łódź to Chełmno on May 4, 1942. She perished in Chełmno on May 4, 1942.

LAUTMANN, Sara: Born on December 29, 1912, in Berlin. She was deported from Berlin on October 24, 1941, to the Łódź ghetto. She was deported from Łódź to Chełmno on May 4, 1942. She perished in Chełmno on May 4, 1942.

LAZARUS, Leopold: Born on March 9, 1871, in Golkrath. He was deported from Düsseldorf on October 27, 1941, to the Łódź ghetto. He was deported from Łódź to Chełmno on May 6, 1942. He perished in Chełmno on May 7, 1942.

LEBER, Sabine: Born on July 6, 1884, in Tarnów, Poland. She was deported from Düsseldorf on October 27, 1941, to the Łódź ghetto. She was deported from Łódź to Chełmno on May 7, 1942. She perished in Chełmno on May 8, 1942.

LEBRAM, Max: Born on June 2, 1883, in Berlin. He was deported from Düsseldorf on October 27, 1941, to the Łódź ghetto. He was deported from Łódź to Chełmno on May 7, 1942. He perished in Chełmno on May 8, 1942.

LEDERMANN, Regina: Born on February 28, 1903, in Slopia, Russia. She was deported from Berlin on October 27–29, 1941, to the Łódź ghetto. She was deported from Łódź to Chełmno on May 6, 1942, where she perished.

LEFEBRE, Horst: Born on March 9, 1921, in Hamburg. He was deported from Hamburg on October 25, 1941, to the Łódź ghetto. He was deported from Łódź to Chełmno on May 10, 1942, where he perished.

LEFFMANN, Emil: Born on April 10, 1883, in Kleve. He was deported from Düsseldorf on October 27, 1941, to the Łódź ghetto. He was deported from Łódź to Chełmno during September 1942, where he perished.

LEHMANN, Anna: Born on June 20, 1884, in Jarotschin, Poland. She was deported from Cologne on October 22, 1941, to the Łódź ghetto. She was deported from Łódź to Chełmno on May 6, 1942, where she perished.

LEIBENHAUT, Golda: Born on December 16, 1905, in Skole. She was deported from Berlin on October 27–29, 1941, to the Łódź ghetto. She was deported from Łódź to Chełmno on May 4, 1942, where she perished.

LEIBHOLZ, Georg: Born on June 7, 1884, in Hammerstein. He was deported from Berlin on November 1, 1941, to the Łódź ghetto. He was deported from Łódź to Chełmno on May 13, 1942, where he perished.

LEIPZIGER, Meta: Born on November 23, 1884, in Gniezno, Poland. She was deported from Berlin on October 18, 1941, to the Łódź ghetto. She was deported from Łódź to Chełmno on May 8, 1942. She perished in Chełmno on May 8, 1942.

LEISER, Hermann: Born on March 11, 1881, in Łobżenica, Poland. He was deported from Berlin on October 24, 1941, to the Łódź ghetto. He was deported from Łódź to Chełmno on May 4, 1942. He perished in Chełmno on May 4, 1942.

LEISTNER, Adele: Born on March 18, 1881, in Dortmund. She was deported from Düsseldorf on October 27, 1941, to the Łódź ghetto. She was deported from Łódź to Chełmno on May 7, 1942. She perished in Chełmno on May 8, 1942.

LEJBUSIEWICZ, Chawa: Born on September 9, 1902, in Końskie, Poland. She was deported from Düsseldorf on October 27, 1941, to the Łódź ghetto. She was deported from Łódź to Chełmno where she perished.

LEMLE, Johanna: Born on June 15, 1881, in Unna. She was deported from Cologne on October 22, 1941, to the Łódź ghetto. She was deported from Łódź to Chełmno during May 1942, where she perished.

LENNEBERG, Hermine: Born on February 25, 1882, in Cologne. She was deported from Düsseldorf on October 27, 1941, to the Łódź ghetto. She was deported from Łódź to Chełmno on May 6, 1942. She perished in Chełmno on May 7, 1942.

LENNHOFF, Sarah: Born on March 11, 1893, in Plettenberg. She was deported from Hamburg on October 25, 1941, to the Łódź ghetto. She was deported from Łódź to Chełmno on May 7, 1942, where she perished.

LENZ, Amalie: Born on June 2, 1902, in Cologne. She was deported from Cologne on October 22, 1941, to the Łódź ghetto. She was deported from Łódź to Chełmno on May 10, 1942, where she perished.

LEOPOLD, Else: Born on March 8, 1891, in Hamburg. She was deported from Hamburg on October 25, 1941, to the Łódź ghetto. She was deported from Łódź to Chełmno on May 15, 1942, where she perished.

LERMER, Rose: Born on October 2, 1900, in Kraków, Poland. She was deported from Berlin on October 18, 1941, to the Łódź ghetto. She was deported from Łódź to Chełmno on May 8, 1942. She perished in Chełmno on May 8, 1942.

LESCHZINER, Wilhelm: Born on December 8, 1877, in Königshütte, Poland. He was deported from Berlin on November 1, 1941, to the Łódź ghetto. He was deported from Łódź to Chełmno on May 8, 1942. He perished in Chełmno on May 8, 1942.

LES, Emma: Born on December 4, 1874, in Konitz. She was deported from Berlin on November 1, 1941, to the Łódź ghetto. She was deported from Łódź to Chełmno on May 9, 1942. She perished in Chełmno on May 9, 1942.

LESSER, Leonie: Born on January 6, 1889, in Hamburg. She was deported from Berlin on October 18, 1941, to the Łódź ghetto. She was deported from Łódź to Chełmno on May 8, 1942. She perished in Chełmno on May 8, 1942.

LESSNER, Meta: Born on July 8, 1890, in Miłosław, Poland. She was deported from Berlin on October 18, 1941, to the Łódź ghetto. She was deported from Łódź to Chełmno on May 8, 1942. She perished in Chełmno on May 8, 1942.

LETOCHA, Liesbet: Born on May 12, 1886, in Bernstadt. She was deported from Berlin on October 18, 1941, to the Łódź ghetto. She was deported from Łódź to Chełmno on May 8, 1942, where she perished.

LEUFER, Henny: Born on February 16, 1893, in Cologne. She was deported from Cologne on October 22, 1941, to the Łódź ghetto. She was deported from Łódź to Chełmno, where she perished on July 12, 1944.

LEVANO, Paula: Born on April 8, 1887, in Kommern. She was deported from Cologne on October 22, 1941, to the Łódź ghetto. She was deported from Łódź to Chełmno on May 6, 1942, where she perished.

LEVEN, Hermann: Born on May 7, 1876, in Gastorf. He was deported from Cologne on October 22, 1941, to the Łódź ghetto. He was deported from Łódź to Chełmno on May 6, 1942, where he perished.

LEVENBACH, Margarethe: Born on June 20, 1890, in Cologne. She was deported from Cologne on October 22, 1941, to the Łódź ghetto. She was deported from Łódź to Chełmno where she perished during May 1942.

LEVI, Cilly: Born on October 22, 1888, in Bresin. She was deported from Cologne on October 30, 1941, to the Łódź ghetto. She was deported from Łódź to Chełmno where she perished on July 7, 1944.

LEVIN, Berthold: Born on July 24, 1877, in Berlin. He was deported from Berlin on November 1, 1941, to the Łódź ghetto. He was deported from Łódź to Chełmno on May 14, 1942. He perished in Chełmno on May 14, 1942.

LEVISOHN, Manfred: Born on February 27, 1937, in Hamburg. He was deported from Hamburg on October 25, 1941, to the Łódź ghetto. He was deported from Łódź to Chełmno on September 12, 1942, where he perished.

LEVISON, Fanny: Born on December 15, 1878, in Cologne. She was deported from Düsseldorf on October 27, 1941, to the Łódź ghetto. She was deported from Łódź to Chełmno on May 5, 1942. She perished in Chełmno on May 6, 1942.

LEVITON, Hedwig: Born on November 25, 1877, in Inowrocław. She was deported from Berlin on November 1, 1941, to the Łódź ghetto. She was deported from Łódź to Chełmno on May 9, 1942. She perished in Chełmno on May 9, 1942.

LEVY, Edgar: Born on January 2, 1898, in Ahrensburg. He was deported from Berlin on October 24, 1941, to the Łódź ghetto. He was deported from Łódź to Chełmno on May 15, 1942. He perished in Chełmno on May 15, 1942.

LEWANDOWSKI, Manfred: Born on April 23, 1909, in Berlin. He was deported from Berlin on November 1, 1941, to the Łódź ghetto. He was deported from Łódź to Chełmno on July 12, 1944. He perished in Chełmno on July 12, 1944.

LEWI, Hedwig: Born on May 6, 1890, in Vandsburg. She was deported from Berlin on October 24, 1941, to the Łódź ghetto. She was deported from Łódź to Chełmno on May 10, 1942. She perished in Chełmno on May 10, 1942.

LEWIEN, Julius: Born on January 11, 1894, in Königsdorf. He was deported from Berlin on November 1, 1941, to the Łódź ghetto. He was deported from Łódź to Chełmno on May 9, 1942. He perished in Chełmno on May 9, 1942.

LEWIN, Charlotte: Born on March 15, 1889, in Berlin. She was deported from Berlin on November 1, 1941, to the Łódź ghetto. She was deported from Łódź to Chełmno on May 8, 1942. She perished in Chełmno on May 8, 1942.

LEWINIOWSKA, Minka: Born on November 17, 1892, in Nowy Sącz, Poland. She was deported from Hamburg on October 25, 1941, to the Łódź ghetto. She was deported from Łódź to Chełmno on September 15, 1942, where she perished.

LEWINNECK, Margarete: Born on November 1886, in Wernigerode. She was deported from Berlin on October 18, 1941, to the Łódź ghetto. She was deported from Łódź to Chełmno on May 8, 1942. She perished in Chełmno on May 8, 1942.

LEWINSKI, Erna: Born on May 13, 1895, in Penkuhl. She was deported from Berlin on November 1, 1941, to the Łódź ghetto. She was deported from Łódź to Chełmno on July 14, 1944. She perished in Chełmno on July 14, 1944.

LEWINSOHN, Betty: Born on June 1, 1894, in Driesen. She was deported from Berlin on November 1, 1941, to the Łódź ghetto. She was deported from Łódź to Chełmno on May 4, 1942. She perished in Chełmno on May 4, 1942.

LEWITH, Karoline: Born on March 5, 1882, in Danzig. She was deported from Hamburg on October 18, 1941, to the Łódź ghetto. She was deported from Łódź to Chełmno on May 8, 1942. She perished in Chełmno on May 8, 1942.

LEWKOWICZ, Alfred: Born on March 3, 1898, in Wongrowitz, Poland. He was deported from Berlin on October 27–29, 1941, to the Łódź ghetto. He was deported from Łódź to Chełmno on May 15, 1942. He perished in Chełmno on May 15, 1942.

LEWY, Max: Born on May 14, 1902, in Berlin. He was deported from Berlin on October 18, 1941, to the Łódź ghetto. He was deported from Łódź to Chełmno on May 5, 1942. He perished in Chełmno on May 5, 1942.

LEYSER, Leopold: Born on July 28, 1914, in Berlin. He was deported from Berlin on November 1, 1941, to the Łódź ghetto. He was deported from Łódź to Chełmno on May 8, 1942, where he perished.

LIBOWSKI, Grete: Born on August 15, 1876, in Graudenz. She was deported from Berlin on October 24, 1941, to the Łódź ghetto. She was

deported from Łódź to Chełmno on May 4, 1942. She perished in Chełmno on May 4, 1942.

LIBRACH, Gitla: Born on October 12, 1891, in Łódź, Poland. She was expelled from Halle on October 28–29, 1938, to Poland. She was deported from the Łódź ghetto to Chełmno on September 18, 1942. She perished in Chełmno on September 21, 1942.

LICHTENSTEIN, Alice: Born on February 1, 1924, in Berlin. She was deported from Berlin on October 18, 1941, to the Łódź ghetto. She was deported from Łódź to Chełmno on May 8, 1942. She perished in Chełmno on May 8, 1942.

LICHTHEIM, Margarete: Born on January 15, 1881, in Stettin. She was deported from Hamburg on October 25, 1941, to the Łódź ghetto. She was deported from Łódź to Chełmno on May 15, 1942. She perished in Chełmno on May 15, 1942.

LICHTIGFELD, Sala: Born on December 28, 1894, in Rohatyn, (now a city in the Ukraine). She was deported from Düsseldorf on October 27, 1941, to the Łódź ghetto. She was deported from Łódź to Chełmno during September 1942, where she perished.

LICHTMANN, Oskar: Born on April 19, 1900, in Błażowa, Poland. He was deported from Berlin on October 27–29, 1941, to the Łódź ghetto. He was deported from Łódź to Chełmno on May 6, 1942, where he perished.

LIEBENTHAL, Edith: Born on November 7, 1910, in Pattensen. She was deported from Berlin on October 18, 1941, to the Łódź ghetto. She was deported from Łódź to Chełmno on June 28, 1944. She perished in Chełmno on June 28, 1944.

LIEBERMANN, Bianca: Born on December 13, 1884, in Berlin. She was deported from Berlin on November 1, 1941, to the Łódź ghetto. She was deported from Łódź to Chełmno on May 9, 1942. She perished in Chełmno on May 9, 1942.

LIEBLEIN, Jenni: Born on December 12, 1915, in Berlin. She was deported from Berlin on November 1, 1941, to the Łódź ghetto. She was deported from Łódź to Chełmno on May 9, 1942. She perished in Chełmno on May 9, 1942.

LIEBRECHT, Walter: Born on February 12, 1885, in Berlin. He was deported from Berlin on October 27–29, 1941, to the Łódź ghetto. He was deported from Łódź to Chełmno on May 4, 1942. He perished in Chełmno on May 4, 1942.

LIEVENDAG, Meta: Born on September 4, 1897, in Schüttorf. She was deported from Cologne on October 22, 1941, to the Łódź ghetto. She was deported from Łódź to Chełmno during July 1944, where she perished.

LIFFMANN, Moritz: Born on December 18, 1882, in Mönchengladbach. He was deported from Düsseldorf on October 27, 1941, to the Łódź ghetto. He was deported from Łódź to Chełmno during September 1942, where he perished.

LILLENFELD, Hilde: Born on July 13, 1912, in Recklinghausen. She was deported from Düsseldorf on October 27, 1941, to the Łódź ghetto. She was deported from Łódź to Chełmno during September 1942, where she perished.

LILLENHEIM, Chana: Born on October 10, 1891, in Warsaw, Poland. She was deported from Berlin on October 24, 1941, to the Łódź ghetto. She was deported from Łódź to Chełmno on May 13, 1942. She perished in Chełmno on May 13, 1942.

LILLENTHAL, Albert: Born on April 27, 1867, in Arnswalde. He was deported from Berlin on October 24, 1941, to the Łódź ghetto. He was deported from Łódź to Chełmno on May 14, 1942. He perished in Chełmno on May 14, 1942.

LINDEMANN, Armin: Born on July 24, 1905, in Berlin. He was deported from Berlin on October 24, 1941, to the Łódź ghetto. He was deported from Łódź to Chełmno on May 7, 1942. He perished in Chełmno on May 7, 1942.

LINDENSTRAUSS, Arthur: Born on July 8, 1890, in Hamm. He was deported from Berlin on October 27–29, 1941, to the Łódź ghetto. He was deported from Łódź to Chełmno on May 5, 1942. He perished in Chełmno on May 5, 1942.

LINDMANN, Anita: Born on March 18, 1890, in Hamburg. She was deported from Berlin on October 27–29, 1941, to the Łódź ghetto. She

was deported from Łódź to Chełmno on May 9, 1942. She perished in Chełmno on May 9, 1942.

LINK, Editha: Born on May 26, 1911, in Treten. She was deported from Berlin on November 1, 1941, to the Łódź ghetto. She was deported from Łódź to Chełmno on May 13, 1942. She perished in Chełmno on May 13, 1942.

LINKER, Jetty: Born on July 14, 1888, in Kimpolung. She was deported from Berlin on October 18, 1941, to the Łódź ghetto. She was deported from Łódź to Chełmno on May 8, 1942, where she perished.

LINZ, Karoline: Born on November 25, 1876, in Rüdesheim am Rhein. She was deported from Cologne on October 22, 1941, to the Łódź ghetto. She was deported from Łódź to Chełmno during May 1942, where she perished.

LION, Helene: Born on August 8, 1878, in Obernkirchen. She was deported from Düsseldorf on October 27, 1941, to the Łódź ghetto. She was deported from Łódź to Chełmno on May 6, 1942. She perished in Chełmno on May 7, 1942.

LIPMANN, Margot: Born on February 5, 1881, in Berlin. She was deported from Berlin on November 1, 1941, to the Łódź ghetto. She was deported from Łódź to Chełmno on May 9, 1942, where she perished.

LIPPMANN, Melanie: Born on December 17, 1885, in Güsten. She was deported from Berlin on October 24, 1941, to the Łódź ghetto. She was deported from Łódź to Chełmno on May 5, 1942. She perished in Chełmno on May 5, 1942.

LIPSCHITZ, Georg: Born on October 29, 1883, in Strehlen. He was deported from Hamburg on October 25, 1941, to the Łódź ghetto. He was deported from Łódź to Chełmno on May 5, 1942, where he perished.

LISEK, Pessa: Born on January 22, 1882, in Iranad. She was deported from Cologne on October 30, 1941, to the Łódź ghetto. She was deported from Łódź to Chełmno during May 1942, where she perished.

LISSACK, Ida: Born on March 8, 1876, in Poznań, Poland. She was deported from Berlin on October 18, 1941, to the Łódź ghetto. She was

deported from Łódź to Chełmno on May 8, 1942. She perished in Chełmno on May 8, 1942.

LISSAUER, Gerda: Born on October 2, 1920, in Hamburg. She was deported from Hamburg on October 25, 1941, to the Łódź ghetto. She was deported from Łódź to Chełmno on May 15, 1942, where she perished.

LISSNER, Rieke: Born on December 18, 1870, in Czarnków, Poland. She was deported from Berlin on October 27–29, 1941, to the Łódź ghetto. She was deported from Łódź to Chełmno on May 4, 1942. She perished in Chełmno on May 4, 1942.

LISZEWSKY, Anneliese: Born on June 1, 1919, in Dierdorf. She was deported from Cologne on October 30, 1941, to the Łódź ghetto. She was deported from Łódź to Chełmno on June 28, 1944, where she perished.

LITTHAUER, Ernst: Born on June 26, 1896, in Berlin. He was deported from Berlin on November 1, 1941, to the Łódź ghetto. He was deported from Łódź to Chełmno on May 4, 1942. He perished in Chełmno on May 4, 1942.

LITTMANN, Lydia: Born on April 26, 1887, in Alt Karbe. She was deported from Berlin on October 18, 1941, to the Łódź ghetto. She was deported from Łódź to Chełmno on May 8, 1942. She perished in Chełmno on May 8, 1942.

LITTWACK, Liesbeth: Born on September 14, 1890, in Mrocza, Poland. She was deported from Berlin on October 27–29, 1941, to the Łódź ghetto. She was deported from Łódź to Chełmno on May 7, 1942, where she perished.

LIWSCHITZ, Gregor: Born on May 14, 1891, in Rostow, Russia. He was deported from Hamburg on October 25, 1941, to the Łódź ghetto. He was deported from Łódź to Chełmno on May 12, 1942, where he perished.

LOEB, Emmy: Born on November 17, 1877, in Cologne. She was deported from Cologne on October 22, 1941, to the Łódź ghetto. She was deported from Łódź to Chełmno during May 1942. She perished in Chełmno on May 12, 1942.

LÖBENSTEIN, Ella: Born on February 28, 1897, in Issum. She was deported from Cologne on October 30, 1941, to the Łódź ghetto. She was deported from Łódź to Chełmno during June 1944, where she perished.

LÖFFLER, Else: Born on May 25, 1892, in Freudental. She was deported from Berlin on November 1, 1941, to the Łódź ghetto. She was deported from Łódź to Chełmno on May 8, 1942, where she perished.

LÖVINSKI, Frieda: Born on July 23, 1893, in Fraustadt. She was deported from Berlin on November 1, 1941, to the Łódź ghetto. She was deported from Łódź to Chełmno on May 9, 1942. She perished in Chełmno on May 9, 1942.

LÖWE, Angelika: Born on February 3, 1898 in Silesia. She was deported from Berlin on October 27–29, 1941, to the Łódź ghetto. She was deported from Łódź to Chełmno on May 4, 1942. She perished in Chełmno on May 4, 1942.

LÖWENBACH, Else: Born on May 24, 1914, in Düren. She was deported from Cologne on October 22, 1941, to the Łódź ghetto. She was deported from Łódź to Chełmno on May 8, 1942, where she perished.

LÖWENBERG, Arthur: Born on April 22, 1887, in Wartenburg. She was deported from Berlin on November 1, 1941, to the Łódź ghetto. She was deported from Łódź to Chełmno on May 8, 1942. She perished in Chełmno on May 8, 1942.

LÖWENHEIM, Johanna: Born on November 7, 1912, in Berlin. She was deported from Berlin on November 1, 1941, to the Łódź ghetto. She was deported from Łódź to Chełmno on May 4, 1942. She perished in Chełmno on May 4, 1942.

LÖWENKOPF, Chana: Born during 1870, lived in Dresden. She was expelled from Dresden on October 28, 1938, to Poland. She was deported from the Łódź ghetto to Chełmno during May 1942, where she perished.

LÖWENSBERG, Ernst: Born on January 13, 1891, in Krefeld. He was deported from Cologne on October 22, 1941, to the Łódź ghetto. He was deported from Łódź to Chełmno during 1942, where he perished.

LÖWENSTEIN, Anna: Born on October 2, 1880, in Minden. She was deported from Cologne on October 22, 1941, to the Łódź ghetto. She was deported from Łódź to Chełmno on May 10, 1942. She perished in Chełmno on May 10, 1942.

LÖWENTHAL, Arthur: Born on December 2, 1887, in Pelplin. He was deported from Berlin on October 18, 1941, to the Łódź ghetto. He was deported from Łódź to Chełmno on May 8, 1942. He perished in Chełmno on May 8, 1942.

LÖWI, Emmy: Born on November 30, 1876, in Regensburg. She was deported from Berlin on October 18, 1941, to the Łódź ghetto. She was deported from Łódź to Chełmno on May 8, 1942. She perished in Chełmno on May 8, 1942.

LÖWY, Betty: Born on August 19, 1878, in Bublitz. She was deported from Berlin on October 27–29, 1941, to the Łódź ghetto. She was deported from Łódź to Chełmno on May 4, 1942. She perished in Chełmno on May 4, 1942.

LOHN, Rael: Born on October 2, 1885, in Telgte. She was deported from Cologne on October 22, 1941, to the Łódź ghetto. She was deported from Łódź to Chełmno on September 10, 1942, where she perished.

LOMNITZ, Elfriede: Born on June 8, 1887, in Ruda Śląska, Poland. She was deported from Berlin on October 18, 1941, to the Łódź ghetto. She was deported from Łódź to Chełmno on September 5, 1942. She perished in Chełmno on September 5, 1942.

LORBER, Hannchen: Born on November 11, 1869, in Leszno, Poland. She was deported from Berlin on November 1, 1941, to the Łódź ghetto. She was deported from Łódź to Chełmno on May 9, 1942. She perished in Chełmno on May 9, 1942.

LORCH, Johanna: Born on December 2, 1916, in Harsewinkel. She was deported from Cologne on October 22, 1941, to the Łódź ghetto. She was deported from Łódź to Chełmno during May 1942. She perished in Chełmno on May 9, 1942.

LORENZ, Meyer: Born on February 19, 1870, in Christburg. He was deported from Berlin on October 27–29, 1941, to the Łódź ghetto. He

was deported from Łódź to Chełmno on May 13, 1942. He perished in Chełmno on May 13, 1942.

LORIG, Siegfried: Born on November 25, 1882, in Mayen. He was deported from Düsseldorf on October 27, 1941, to the Łódź ghetto. He was deported from Łódź to Chełmno on May 7, 1942. He perished in Chełmno on May 8, 1942.

LOSER, Manfred: Born on June 23, 1921, in Berlin. He was deported from Berlin on October 24, 1941, to the Łódź ghetto. He was deported from Łódź to Chełmno on May 5, 1942. He perished in Chełmno on May 5, 1942.

LOSZYNSKI, Gustav: Born on December 6, 1881, in Murowana Goślina, Poland. He was deported from Berlin on October 18, 1941, to the Łódź ghetto. He was deported from Łódź to Chełmno on May 8, 1942. He perished in Chełmno on May 8, 1942.

LOUIS, Irma: Born on March 20, 1901, in Strasburg. She was deported from Hamburg on October 25, 1941, to the Łódź ghetto. She was deported from Łódź to Chełmno during May 1942, where she perished.

LUBASCH, Frieda: Born on October 24, 1898, in Berlin. She was deported from Berlin on November 1, 1941, to the Łódź ghetto. She was deported from Łódź to Chełmno on May 8, 1942. She perished in Chełmno on May 8, 1942.

LUBASCHER, Kurt: Born on December 31, 1926, in Solingen. He was deported from Düsseldorf on October 27, 1941, to the Łódź ghetto. He was deported from Łódź to Chełmno on September 7, 1942, where he perished.

LUBELSKY, Ruth: Born on July 24, 1932, in Hamburg. She was deported from Hamburg on October 25, 1941, to the Łódź ghetto. She was deported from Łódź to Chełmno on May 15, 1942, where she perished.

LUBINSKI, Richard: Born on September 7, 1896, in Breslau. He was deported from Hamburg on October 25, 1941, to the Łódź ghetto. He was deported from Łódź to Chełmno on May 10, 1942, where he perished.

LUBRANZCYK, Erna: Born on October 9, 1889, in Berlin. She was deported from Hamburg on October 25, 1941, to the Łódź ghetto. She

was deported from Łódź to Chełmno on May 12, 1942, where she perished.

LUCA, Lucian: Born on June 3, 1889, in Bucharest, Rumania. He was imprisoned in Fuhlsbüttel Police prison between November 11–12, 1938. He was deported from Hamburg on October 25, 1941, to the Łódź ghetto. He was deported from Łódź to Chełmno during June 1944, where he perished.

LUCAS, Betty: Born on January 8, 1888, in Krefeld. She was deported from Cologne on October 30, 1941, to the Łódź ghetto. She was deported from Łódź to Chełmno during May 1942, where she perished.

LUCHTENSTEIN, Hedwig: Born on January 12, 1889, in Strzelno, Poland. She was deported from Berlin on October 18, 1941, to the Łódź ghetto. She was deported from Łódź to Chełmno on May 8, 1942, where she perished.

LUDNOWSKY, Wilhelmine: Born on March 15, 1876, in Bornheim. She was deported from Cologne on October 22, 1941, to the Łódź ghetto. She was deported from Łódź to Chełmno on May 5, 1942, where she perished.

LUDWIG, Paula: Born on October 23, 1880, in Berlin. She was deported from Berlin on November 1, 1941, to the Łódź ghetto. She was deported from Łódź to Chełmno on May 10, 1942. She perished in Chełmno on May 10, 1942.

LÜBECK, Edmund: Born on February 22, 1884, in Berlin. He was deported from Berlin on November 1, 1941, to the Łódź ghetto. He was deported from Łódź to Chełmno on May 9, 1942. He perished in Chełmno on May 9, 1942.

LYPOLD, Berthold: Born on April 25, 1885, in Alsenz. He was deported from Cologne on October 30, 1941, to the Łódź ghetto. He was deported from Łódź to Chełmno during May 1942, where he perished.

MAAS, Dina: Born on June 27, 1889, in Hattingen. She was deported from Cologne on October 22, 1941, to the Łódź ghetto. She was deported from Łódź to Chełmno during May 1942, where she perished.

MACHTYNGER, Roza: Born on May 3, 1884, in Pińczów, Poland. She was deported from Berlin to the Łódź ghetto. She was deported from Łódź to Chełmno on March 20, 1942, where she perished.

MÄNGEN, Klara: Born on January 10, 1878, in Schlifferstadt. She was deported from Berlin on October 18, 1941, to the Łódź ghetto. She was deported from Łódź to Chełmno on May 8, 1942. She perished in Chełmno on May 8, 1942.

MÄRKER, Carl: Born on March 13, 1873, in Güsten. He was deported from Berlin on October 18, 1941, to the Łódź ghetto. He was deported from Łódź to Chełmno on May 8, 1942. He perished in Chełmno on May 8, 1942.

MAGASINER, Bertha: Born on May 30, 1893, in Kiew, Russia. She was deported from Berlin on November 1, 1941, to the Łódź ghetto. She was deported from Łódź to Chełmno on May 8, 1942. She perished in Chełmno on May 8, 1942.

MAGIER, Abraham: Born on May 31, 1935, in Berlin. He was deported from Berlin on October 24, 1941, to the Łódź ghetto. He was deported from Łódź to Chełmno on May 15, 1942. He perished in Chełmno on May 15, 1942.

MAGNUS, Elisabeth: Born on January 19, 1888, in Berlin. She was deported from Berlin on October 18, 1941, to the Łódź ghetto. She was deported from Łódź to Chełmno on May 8, 1942. She perished in Chełmno on May 8, 1942.

MAHNKE, Sara: Born on April 1, 1883, in Welschbillig. She was deported from Cologne on October 22, 1941, to the Łódź ghetto. She was deported from Łódź to Chełmno on May 4, 1942. She perished in Chełmno on May 4, 1942.

MAIER, Frieda: Born on August 19, 1889, in Wolfenbüttel. She was deported from Cologne on October 22, 1941, to the Łódź ghetto. She was deported from Łódź to Chełmno during July 1944. She perished in Chełmno on July 5, 1944.

MAINZER, Walter: Born on October 19, 1912, in Düsseldorf. He was deported from Düsseldorf on October 27, 1941, to the Łódź ghetto. He

was deported from Łódź to Chełmno on May 14, 1942. He perished in Chełmno on May 15, 1942.

MAJOR, Marja: Born on December 14, 1916, in Klein Raschen. She was deported from Berlin on November 1, 1941, to the Łódź ghetto. She was deported from Łódź to Chełmno on May 9, 1942, where she perished.

MALBIN, Ruth: Born on February 10, 1920, in Angerburg. She was deported from Berlin on October 24, 1941, to the Łódź ghetto. She was deported from Łódź to Chełmno on May 5, 1942, where she perished.

MALINOWSKI, Clara: Born on November 20, 1877, in Kempen. She was deported from Berlin on October 24, 1941, to the Łódź ghetto. She was deported from Łódź to Chełmno on May 4, 1942. She perished in Chełmno on May 4, 1942.

MALKUS, Lydia: Born on May 12, 1877, in Grodzisk, Poland. She was deported from Berlin on October 24, 1941, to the Łódź ghetto. She was deported from Łódź to Chełmno on May 4, 1942. She perished in Chełmno on May 4, 1942.

MALSCH, Amalie: Born on September 17, 1889, in Düsseldorf. She was deported from Düsseldorf on October 27, 1941, to the Łódź ghetto. She was deported from Łódź to Chełmno on May 6, 1942. She perished in Chełmno on May 7, 1942.

MAMBER, Rosa: Born on July 8, 1879, in Mosciska, Poland. She was deported from Berlin on November 1, 1941, to the Łódź ghetto. She was deported from Łódź to Chełmno on May 9, 1942. She perished in Chełmno on May 9, 1942.

MAMELOK, Grete: Born on June 2, 1897, in Hamburg. She was deported from Hamburg on October 25, 1941, to the Łódź ghetto. She was deported from Łódź to Chełmno on May 10, 1942, where she perished.

MANASSE, Frieda: Born on January 10, 1876, in Freiberg. She was deported from Berlin on October 27–29, 1941, to the Łódź ghetto. She was deported from Łódź to Chełmno on May 4, 1942. She perished in Chełmno on May 4, 1942.

MANDEL, Hedwig: Born on April 9, 1892, in Berlin. She was deported from Berlin on October 24, 1941, to the Łódź ghetto. She was deported from Łódź to Chełmno on May 4, 1942. She perished in Chełmno on May 4, 1942.

MANDELBAUM, Wanda: Born on July 13, 1891, in Gelsenkirchen. She was deported from Düsseldorf on October 27, 1941, to the Łódź ghetto. She was deported from Łódź to Chełmno on September 8, 1942, where she perished.

MANDUS, Luise: Born on September 10, 1877, in Breslau. She was deported from Berlin on October 24, 1941, to the Łódź ghetto. She was deported from Łódź to Chełmno on May 4, 1942. She perished in Chełmno on May 4, 1942.

MANES, Margarete: Born on August 5, 1902, in Solingen. She was deported from Düsseldorf on October 27, 1941, to the Łódź ghetto. She was deported from Łódź to Chełmno on July 5, 1944, where she perished.

MANGOLD, Ella: Born on July 2, 1883, in Hersfeld. She was deported from Cologne on October 22, 1941, to the Łódź ghetto. She was deported from Łódź to Chełmno on May 5, 1942, where she perished.

MANN, Paula: Born on August 23, 1877, in Cannstatt. She was deported from Cologne on October 30, 1941, to the Łódź ghetto. She was deported from Łódź to Chełmno during May 1942, where she perished.

MANNES, Julius: Born on August 6, 1883, in Wreschen, Poland. He was deported from Berlin on November 1, 1941, to the Łódź ghetto. He was deported from Łódź to Chełmno on May 8, 1942. He perished in Chełmno on May 8, 1942.

MANNHEIMER, Albert: Born on November 14, 1885, in Worms. He was deported from Berlin on October 18, 1941, to the Łódź ghetto. He was deported from Łódź to Chełmno on May 4, 1942. He perished in Chełmno on May 4, 1942.

MANSBACH, Johanna: Born on July 11, 1881, in Linnich. She was deported from Cologne on October 22, 1941, to the Łódź ghetto. She was deported from Łódź to Chełmno on May 11, 1942. She perished in Chełmno on May 11, 1942.

MANTEL, Jacob: Born on October 23, 1882, in Bacău, Rumania. He was deported from Berlin on October 18, 1941, to the Łódź ghetto. He was deported from Łódź to Chełmno on May 8, 1942, where he perished.

MANTEUFFEL, Elfriede: Born on October 23, 1889, in Neustadt an der Haardt. She was deported from Berlin on October 18, 1941, to the Łódź ghetto. She was deported from Łódź to Chełmno on May 8, 1942, where she perished.

MARCHAND, Emma: Born on February 24, 1877, in Oberhausen. She was deported from Düsseldorf on October 27, 1941, to the Łódź ghetto. She was deported from Łódź to Chełmno on May 14, 1942. She perished in Chełmno on May 15, 1942.

MARCUS, Charlotte: Born on July 15, 1893, in Storozynetz. She was deported from Berlin on October 24, 1941, to the Łódź ghetto. She was deported from Łódź to Chełmno on May 14, 1942. She perished in Chełmno on May 14, 1942.

MARCUSE, Hedwig: Born on October 9, 1891, in Schönbeck. She was deported from Berlin on October 24, 1941, to the Łódź ghetto. She was deported from Łódź to Chełmno on May 15, 1942. She perished in Chełmno on May 15, 1942.

MARCZAK, Dorothea: Born on August 1, 1881, in Schulzendorf. She was deported from Berlin on October 24, 1941, to the Łódź ghetto. She was deported from Łódź to Chełmno on May 12, 1942. She perished in Chełmno on May 14, 1942.

MARGONINER, Georg: Born on April 12, 1906, in Berlin. He was deported from Berlin on October 27–29, 1941, to the Łódź ghetto. He was deported from Łódź to Chełmno on May 5, 1942. He perished in Chełmno on May 5, 1942.

MARGONINSKI, Martha: Born on May 31, 1883, in Berlin. She was deported from Berlin on October 18, 1941, to the Łódź ghetto. She was deported from Łódź to Chełmno on May 8, 1942, where she perished.

MARGULIUS, Abraham: Born on November 27, 1879, in Żnin, Poland. He was deported from Berlin on October 24, 1941, to the Łódź ghetto. He was deported from Łódź to Chełmno on May 4, 1942. He perished in Chełmno on May 4, 1942.

MARKERT, Clara: Born on October 1, 1878, in Faluszlatina, Hungary. She was deported from Berlin on October 27–29, 1941, to the Łódź ghetto. She was deported from Łódź to Chełmno on May 10, 1942. She perished in Chełmno on May 10, 1942.

MARKIEL, Rose: Born on September 28, 1888, in Hamburg. She was deported from Hamburg on October 25, 1941, to the Łódź ghetto. She was deported from Łódź to Chełmno on May 10, 1942, where she perished.

MARKIEWICZ, Julius: Born on May 15, 1893, in Ostrowo, Poland. He was deported from Düsseldorf on October 27, 1941, to the Łódź ghetto. He was deported from Łódź to Chełmno on May 7, 1942. He perished in Chełmno on May 8, 1942.

MARKOWITZ, Abraham: Born on May 1, 1902, in Poddębice. He was deported from Hamburg on October 25, 1941, to the Łódź ghetto. He was deported from Łódź to Chełmno on May 10, 1942, where he perished.

MARKOWSKI, Else: Born on November 26, 1909, in Berlin. She was deported from Berlin on November 1, 1941, to the Łódź ghetto. She was deported from Łódź to Chełmno on May 5, 1942. She perished in Chełmno on May 5, 1942.

MARKSCHIESS, Markschies: Born on March 9, 1902, in Berlin. She was deported from Berlin on October 27–29, 1941, to the Łódź ghetto. She was deported from Łódź to Chełmno on May 4, 1942. She perished in Chełmno on May 4, 1942.

MARKUS, David: Born on November 20, 1881, in Essen. He was deported from Düsseldorf on October 27, 1941, to the Łódź ghetto. He was deported from Łódź to Chełmno on May 6, 1942. He perished in Chełmno on May 7, 1942.

MARKUSE, Bertha: Born on November 9, 1874, in Chełmno, Poland. She was deported from Berlin on October 18, 1941, to the Łódź ghetto. She was deported from Łódź to Chełmno on May 8, 1942. She perished in Chełmno on May 8, 1942.

MARSCHNER, Karlheinz: Born on October 26, 1926, in Berlin. He was deported from Berlin on November 1, 1941, to the Łódź ghetto. He

was deported from Łódź to Chełmno on May 9, 1942. He perished in Chełmno on May 9, 1942.

MARWILSKI, Arthur: Born on July 9, 1877, in Labiau. He was deported from Berlin on October 24, 1941, to the Łódź ghetto. He was deported from Łódź to Chełmno on September 12, 1942. He perished in Chełmno on September 12, 1942.

MARX, Andreas: Born on October 21, 1892, in Otzenrath. He was deported from Düsseldorf on October 27, 1941, to the Łódź ghetto. He was deported from Łódź to Chełmno on July 7, 1944. He perished in Chełmno on July 8, 1944.

MASCHKOWSKI, Hugo: Born on February 2, 1883, in Sierakowitz. He was deported from Berlin on November 1, 1941, to the Łódź ghetto. He was deported from Łódź to Chełmno on September 11, 1942. He perished in Chełmno on September 11, 1942.

MASUM, Anna: Born on August 17, 1890, in Cologne. She was deported from Cologne on October 22, 1941, to the Łódź ghetto. She was deported from Łódź to Chełmno during May 1942, where she perished.

MATHES, Johanna: Born on February 6, 1884, in Koronowo, Poland. She was deported from Berlin on October 18, 1941, to the Łódź ghetto. She was deported from Łódź to Chełmno on May 7, 1942. She perished in Chełmno on May 7, 1942.

MATHEWS, Julius: Born on November 2, 1882, in Berlin. He was deported from Berlin on October 24, 1941, to the Łódź ghetto. He was deported from Łódź to Chełmno on May 4, 1942. He perished in Chełmno on May 4, 1942.

MATTISSOHN, Jeanette: Born on November 26, 1876, in Ebersbach. She was deported from Berlin on October 24, 1941, to the Łódź ghetto. She was deported from Łódź to Chełmno on May 4, 1942. She perished in Chełmno on May 4, 1942.

MATZDORFF, Felix: Born on October 13, 1873, in Frankenstein. He was deported from Berlin on October 24, 1941, to the Łódź ghetto. He was deported from Łódź to Chełmno on September 7, 1942, where he perished.

MAUTNER, Alice: Born on September 10, 1876, in Berlin. She was deported from Berlin on October 18, 1941, to the Łódź ghetto. She was deported from Łódź to Chełmno on May 8, 1942. She perished in Chełmno on May 8, 1942.

MAY, Lilli: Born on May 22, 1887, in Hannover. She was deported from Berlin on October 18, 1941, to the Łódź ghetto. She was deported from Łódź to Chełmno on May 10, 1942, where she perished.

MAYER, Alfred: Born on March 23, 1908, in Berlin. He was deported from Berlin on October 27–29, 1941, to the Łódź ghetto. He was deported from Łódź to Chełmno on May 10, 1942. He perished in Chełmno on May 10, 1942.

MEERFISCH, Sara: Born on December 24, 1889, in Janów, Poland. She was deported from Berlin on November 1, 1941, to the Łódź ghetto. She was deported from Łódź to Chełmno on May 9, 1942, where she perished.

MEERSAND, Frieda: Born on July 26, 1914, in Berlin. She was deported from Berlin on October 24, 1941, to the Łódź ghetto. She was deported from Łódź to Chełmno on May 4, 1942. She perished in Chełmno on May 4, 1942.

MEHLER, Alfred: Born on March 13, 1878, in Cologne. He was deported from Düsseldorf on October 27, 1941, to the Łódź ghetto. He was deported from Łódź to Chełmno on May 14, 1942. He perished in Chełmno on May 15, 1942.

MEIER, Eva: Born on February 15, 1879, in Hamburg. She was deported from Berlin on November 1, 1941, to the Łódź ghetto. She was deported from Łódź to Chełmno on May 9, 1942. She perished in Chełmno on May 9, 1942.

MEIGNERS, August: Born on July 10, 1890, in Aschchabad, Russia. He was deported from Berlin on October 18, 1941, to the Łódź ghetto. He was deported from Łódź to Chełmno on May 8, 1942. He perished in Chełmno on May 8, 1942.

MEILICH, Hugo: Born on May 27, 1897, in Graudenz. He was deported from Berlin on October 24, 1941, to the Łódź ghetto. He was deported from Łódź to Chełmno on May 4, 1942. He perished in Chełmno on May 4, 1942.

MEINHARDT, Jenny: Born on June 12, 1877, in Berlin. She was deported from Berlin on November 1, 1941, to the Łódź ghetto. She was deported from Łódź to Chełmno on May 4, 1942. She perished in Chełmno on May 4, 1942.

MEITLIS, Elsa: Born on August 26, 1888, in Berlin. She emigrated from Berlin to Poland. She was deported from the Łódź ghetto to Chełmno on September 10, 1942, where she perished.

MELLER, Debora: Born on January 4, 1893, in Włocławek, Poland. She was expelled from Berlin to the Zbąszyń Internment Camp in Poland. She was deported from the Łódź ghetto to Chełmno on June 26, 1944, where she perished.

MENAHINI, Michan: Born on June 15, 1883, in Edirne. He was deported from Berlin on October 18, 1941, to the Łódź ghetto. He was deported from Łódź to Chełmno on May 8, 1942. He perished in Chełmno on May 8, 1942.

MENDEL, Arno: Born on July 7, 1932, in Berlin. He was deported from Berlin on November 1, 1941, to the Łódź ghetto. He was deported from Łódź to Chełmno on September 12, 1942. He perished in Chełmno on September 12, 1942.

MENDELS, Alwine: Born on July 19, 1906, in Loga. She was deported from Düsseldorf on October 27, 1941, to the Łódź ghetto. She was deported from Łódź to Chełmno on May 14, 1942. She perished in Chełmno on May 15, 1942.

MENDELSOHN, Casper: Born on February 24, 1875, in Riesenburg. He was deported from Berlin on November 1, 1941, to the Łódź ghetto. He was deported from Łódź to Chełmno on May 9, 1942. He perished in Chełmno on May 9, 1942.

MENDHEIM, David: Born on October 20, 1874, in Kolmar, Poland. He was deported from Berlin on November 1, 1941, to the Łódź ghetto. He was deported from Łódź to Chełmno on May 9, 1942. He perished in Chełmno on May 9, 1942.

MENKIS, Ryfka: Born on September 3, 1888, in Smarżowa, Poland. She was deported from Berlin on October 27–29, 1941, to the Łódź ghetto. She was deported from Łódź to Chełmno on May 6, 1942. She perished in Chełmno on May 6, 1942.

MENTESCH, Josef: Born on March 6, 1893, in Istanbul, Turkey. He was deported from Berlin on October 24, 1941, to the Łódź ghetto. He was deported from Łódź to Chełmno on May 13, 1942, where he perished.

MENZ, Ilse: Born on June 18, 1919, in Hamm. She was deported from Cologne on October 22, 1941, to the Łódź ghetto. She was deported from Łódź to Chełmno on May 10, 1942, where she perished.

MERZBACH, Gertrud: Born on November 24, 1893, in Königsberg. She was deported from Berlin on October 18, 1941, to the Łódź ghetto. She was deported from Łódź to Chełmno on May 8, 1942. She perished in Chełmno on May 8, 1942.

MESCHOULAM, Albert: Born on April 6, 1934, in Berlin. He was deported from Berlin on October 24, 1941, to the Łódź ghetto. He was deported from Łódź to Chełmno on May 13, 1942. He perished in Chełmno on May 13, 1942.

MESSERSCHMIDT, Hertha: Born on September 30, 1887, in Berlin. She was deported from Berlin on November 1, 1941, to the Łódź ghetto. She was deported from Łódź to Chełmno on May 9, 1942. She perished in Chełmno on May 9, 1942.

MESSOW, Elfriede: Born on December 12, 1872, in Zabrze, Poland. She was deported from Berlin on October 27–29, 1941, to the Łódź ghetto. She was deported from Łódź to Chełmno on May 4, 1942, where she perished.

METZENBERG, Charlotte: Born on April 13, 1888, in Berlin. She was deported from Berlin on November 1, 1941, to the Łódź ghetto. She was deported from Łódź to Chełmno on May 8, 1942. She perished in Chełmno on May 8, 1942.

METZGER, Raicha: Born on April 10, 1881, in Joniskis, Russia. She was deported from Berlin on October 24, 1941, to the Łódź ghetto. She was deported from Łódź to Chełmno on May 4, 1942. She perished in Chełmno on May 4, 1942.

MEYER, Alice: Born on July 4, 1926, in Essen. She was deported from Düsseldorf on October 27, 1941, to the Łódź ghetto. She was deported from Łódź to Chełmno on May 7, 1942. She perished in Chełmno on May 8, 1942.

MEYERFELD, Emma: Born on January 3, 1880, in Berlin. She was deported from Berlin on October 18, 1941, to the Łódź ghetto. She was deported from Łódź to Chełmno on May 8, 1942. She perished in Chełmno on May 8, 1942.

MEYERHOF, Fritz: Born on August 16, 1903, in Berlin. He was deported from Berlin on October 24, 1941, to the Łódź ghetto. He was deported from Łódź to Chełmno on May 14, 1942, where he perished.

MEYERHOFF, Henriette: Born on May 5, 1879, in Tetz. She was deported from Düsseldorf on October 24, 1941, to the Łódź ghetto. She was deported from Łódź to Chełmno on May 7, 1942. She perished in Chełmno on May 8, 1942.

MEYERS, Emillie: Born on June 9, 1916, in Düsseldorf. She was deported from Düsseldorf on October 27, 1941, to the Łódź ghetto. She was deported from Łódź to Chełmno on May 7, 1942. She perished in Chełmno on May 8, 1942.

MEYEROWITZ, Bogdan: Born on August 29, 1878, in Tomascheiten. He was deported from Berlin on November 1, 1941, to the Łódź ghetto. He was deported from Łódź to Chełmno on May 8, 1942. He perished in Chełmno on May 8, 1942.

MICHAELIS, Gertrud: Born on February 8, 1887, in Berlin. She was deported from Berlin on November 1, 1941, to the Łódź ghetto. She was deported from Łódź to Chełmno on May 5, 1942. She perished in Chełmno on May 5, 1942.

MICHEL, Auguste: Born on November 1, 1878, in Ostrowo, Poland. She was deported from Berlin on November 1, 1941, to the Łódź ghetto. She was deported from Łódź to Chełmno on May 4, 1942. She perished in Chełmno on May 4, 1942.

MICHELS, Betty: Born on March 7, 1883, in Cammin. She was deported from Berlin on October 24, 1941, to the Łódź ghetto. She was

deported from Łódź to Chełmno on May 4, 1942. She perished in Chełmno on May 4, 1942.

MIELZYNSKI, Flora: Born on February 26, 1878, in Rogoźno, Poland. She was deported from Berlin on October 24, 1941, to the Łódź ghetto. She was deported from Łódź to Chełmno on May 5, 1942. She perished in Chełmno on May 5, 1942.

MILCHNER, Flora: Born on November 2, 1888, in Berlin. She was deported from Berlin on October 18, 1941, to the Łódź ghetto. She was deported from Łódź to Chełmno on May 8, 1942. She perished in Chełmno on May 8, 1942.

MILDENBERG, Julius: Born on September 2, 1879, in Lengerich. He was deported from Düsseldorf on October 27, 1941, to the Łódź ghetto. He was deported from Łódź to Chełmno on May 7, 1942. He perished in Chełmno on May 8, 1942.

MILGRAM, Ilda: Born on May 1, 1927, in Gleiwitz, Poland. She was deported from Berlin on October 18, 1941, to the Łódź ghetto. She was deported from Łódź to Chełmno on May 4, 1942. She perished in Chełmno on May 4, 1942.

MILOSŁAWSKI, Arnold: Born on November 21, 1923, in Berlin. He was deported from Berlin on October 27–29, 1941, to the Łódź ghetto. He was deported from Łódź to Chełmno on September 12, 1942. He perished in Chełmno on September 12, 1942.

MINDUS, Franziska: Born on July 8, 1886, in Lübeck. She was deported from Hamburg on October 25, 1941, to the Łódź ghetto. She was deported from Łódź to Chełmno on May 15, 1942, where she perished.

MINNER, Agnes: Born on February 17, 1876, in Grand Rapids, United States of America. She was deported from Berlin on October 18, 1941, to the Łódź ghetto. She was deported from Łódź to Chełmno during September 1942, where she perished.

MISCH, Berta: Born on December 26, 1905, in Markoldendorf. She was deported from Cologne on October 30, 1941, to the Łódź ghetto. She was deported from Łódź to Chełmno during September 1942, where she perished.

MISCHKOWSKY, Margarete: Born on December 18, 1927, in Halberstadt. She was deported from Berlin on November 1, 1941, to the Łódź ghetto. She was deported from Łódź to Chełmno on May 8, 1942. She perished in Chełmno on May 8, 1942.

MITSCHKER, Meta: Born on February 25, 1894, in Berlin. She was deported from Berlin on November 1, 1941, to the Łódź ghetto. She was deported from Łódź to Chełmno on May 9, 1942. She perished in Chełmno on May 9, 1942.

MITZ, Sylvia: Born on June 22, 1894, in Hamburg. She was deported from Hamburg on October 25, 1941, to the Łódź ghetto. She was deported from Łódź to Chełmno on May 10, 1942, where she perished.

MODE, Hertha: Born on March 27, 1892, in Bromberg, Poland. She was deported from Berlin on October 18, 1941, to the Łódź ghetto. She was deported from Łódź to Chełmno on July 7, 1944. She perished in Chełmno on July 7, 1944.

MÖHRING, Frieda: Born on November 13, 1890, in Berlin. She was deported from Berlin on October 18, 1941, to the Łódź ghetto. She was deported from Łódź to Chełmno on May 8, 1942. She perished in Chełmno on May 8, 1942.

MÖLLERICH, Selma: Born on August 1, 1895, in Carolinensiel. She was deported from Hamburg on October 25, 1941, to the Łódź ghetto. She was deported from Łódź to Chełmno, where she perished.

MÖNCH, Bertha: Born on September 26, 1896, in Berlin. She was deported from Berlin on October 18, 1941, to the Łódź ghetto. She was deported from Łódź to Chełmno on May 9, 1942. She perished in Chełmno on May 9, 1942.

MOHL, Johanna: Born on August 11, 1924, in Cologne. She was deported from Cologne on October 30, 1941, to the Łódź ghetto. She was deported from Łódź to Chełmno where she perished on July 10, 1944.

MONDERER, Margot: Born on August 2, 1919, in Cologne. She was deported from Düsseldorf on October 27, 1941, to the Łódź ghetto. She was deported from Łódź to Chełmno on May 7, 1942. She perished in Chełmno on May 8, 1942.

MONETTA, Sara: Born on July 7, 1895, in Demblin, Poland. She was deported from Cologne on October 22, 1941, to the Łódź ghetto. She was deported from Łódź to Chełmno during May 1942, where she perished.

MORAWICKI, Martha: Born on September 25, 1934, in Duisburg. She was deported from Düsseldorf on October 27, 1941, to the Łódź ghetto. She was deported from Łódź to Chełmno on May 7, 1942. She perished in Chełmno on May 8, 1942.

MORAWIECKI, Lea: Born on July 29, 1904, in Jaworzno, Poland. She was deported from Düsseldorf on October 27, 1941, to the Łódź ghetto. She was deported from Łódź to Chełmno on May 7, 1942. She perished in Chełmno on May 8, 1942.

MORITZ, Karola: Born on January 21, 1904, in Gelnhausen. She was deported from Frankfurt am Main on October 20, 1941, to the Łódź ghetto. She was deported from Łódź to Chełmno on May 9, 1942, where she perished.

MOSCHKOWITZ, Elfriede: Born on July 4, 1900, in Berlin. She was deported from Berlin on November 1, 1941, to the Łódź ghetto. She was deported from Łódź to Chełmno on May 5, 1942. She perished in Chełmno on May 5, 1942.

MOSER, Marie: Born on December 31, 1884, in Darmstadt. She was deported from Hamburg on October 25, 1941, to the Łódź ghetto. She was deported from Łódź to Chełmno on September 15, 1942, where she perished.

MOSES, Albert: Born on November 5, 1880, in Mülheim. He was deported from Düsseldorf on October 27, 1941, to the Łódź ghetto. He was deported from Łódź to Chełmno on June 26, 1944. He perished in Chełmno on June 27, 1944.

MOSZKOWITZ, Marjem: Born on December 2, 1899, in Buczyna, Russia. She was deported from Berlin on November 1, 1941, to the Łódź ghetto. She was deported from Łódź to Chełmno on May 9, 1942. She perished in Chełmno on May 9, 1942.

MOTTEK, Sylvia: Born on September 3, 1882, in Berlin. She was deported from Berlin on October 27–29, 1941, to the Łódź ghetto. She

was deported from Łódź to Chełmno on May 4, 1942. She perished in Chełmno on May 4, 1942.

MOTULSKI, Lilly: Born on November 19, 1906, in Neidenburg. She was deported from Berlin on October 27–29, 1941, to the Łódź ghetto. She was deported from Łódź to Chełmno on May 4, 1942. She perished in Chełmno on May 4, 1942.

MUCHA, Emma: Born on April 6, 1885, in Berlin. She was deported from Berlin on October 18, 1941, to the Łódź ghetto. She was deported from Łódź to Chełmno on May 8, 1942. She perished in Chełmno on May 8, 1942.

MÜLLER, Dorothea: Born on February 1, 1885, in Küstrin. She was deported from Berlin on October 18, 1941, to the Łódź ghetto. She was deported from Łódź to Chełmno on May 15, 1942. She perished in Chełmno on May 15, 1942.

MÜNZER, Fanny: Born on January 4, 1875, in Krzyskowice, Poland. She was deported from Berlin on October 24, 1941, to the Łódź ghetto. She was deported from Łódź to Chełmno on May 14, 1942. She perished in Chełmno on May 14, 1942.

MULARSKI, Siegfried: Born on September 11, 1930, in Lübeck. He was deported from Hamburg on October 25, 1941, to the Łódź ghetto. He was deported from Łódź to Chełmno on September 10, 1942, where he perished.

MUSZKAT, Milva: Born on November 1, 1880, in Schwedt. She was deported from Berlin on October 18, 1941, to the Łódź ghetto. She was deported from Łódź to Chełmno on May 8, 1942. She perished in Chełmno on May 8, 1942.

MYRANTS, Ruth: Born on March 2, 1901, in Katowice, Poland. She was deported from Berlin on October 18, 1941, to the Łódź ghetto. She was deported from Łódź to Chełmno during September 1942, where she perished.

NACHSCHÖN, Louise: Born on March 22, 1872, in Czersk. She was deported from Berlin on October 18, 1941, to the Łódź ghetto. She was deported from Łódź to Chełmno on May 8, 1942. She perished in Chełmno on May 8, 1942.

NACHTIGALL, Minna: Born on April 19, 1880, in Hildesheim. She was deported from Berlin on November 1, 1941, to the Łódź ghetto. She was deported from Łódź to Chełmno on May 9, 1942. She perished in Chełmno on May 9, 1942.

NADEL, Markus: Born on January 23, 1883, in Kuńkowce, Poland. He was deported from Berlin on October 27–29, 1941, to the Łódź ghetto. He was deported from Łódź to Chełmno on May 4, 1942. He perished in Chełmno on May 4, 1942.

NADLER, Fryda: Born on April 30, 1881, in Dolina, Poland. She was deported from Berlin on October 24, 1941, to the Łódź ghetto. She was deported from Łódź to Chełmno on May 4, 1942. She perished in Chełmno on May 4, 1942.

NAGEL, Maximillian: Born on May 25, 1883, in Barmen-Elberfeld. He was deported from Hamburg on October 25, 1941, to the Łódź ghetto. He was deported from Łódź to Chełmno on May 14, 1942, where he perished.

NAGER, Elsbeth: Born on February 26, 1883, in Poznań, Poland. She was deported from Berlin on October 24, 1941, to the Łódź ghetto. She was deported from Łódź to Chełmno on May 4, 1942. She perished in Chełmno on May 4, 1942.

NATANNSEN, Hugo: Born on November 2, 1897, in Koslin. He lived in Hamburg. He was deported from Prague on November 3, 1941, to the Łódź ghetto. He was deported from Łódź to Chełmno on July 7, 1944, where he perished.

NATHAN, Hedwig: Born on August 7, 1891, in Berlin. She was deported from Berlin on October 18, 1941, to the Łódź ghetto. She was deported from Łódź to Chełmno on May 7, 1942. She perished in Chełmno on May 7, 1942.

NEHAB, Sella: Born on October 2, 1886, in Jastrow. She was deported from Berlin on October 27–29, 1941, to the Łódź ghetto. She was deported from Łódź to Chełmno on May 9, 1942. She perished in Chełmno on May 9–11, 1942.

NELKEN, Schmul: Born on March 6, 1874, in Opatów, Poland. He was deported from Berlin on October 18, 1941, to the Łódź ghetto. He was deported from Łódź to Chełmno on May 8, 1942, where he perished.

NELLHAUS, Wilhelm: Born on December 24, 1873, in Gros Lessen. He was deported from Berlin on October 27–29, 1941, to the Łódź ghetto. He was deported from Łódź to Chełmno on May 13, 1942, where he perished.

NETTER, Flora: Born on October 2, 1885, in Cologne. She was deported from Cologne on October 22, 1941, to the Łódź ghetto. She was deported from Łódź to Chełmno on May 6, 1942, where she perished.

NEUBAUER, Joachim: Born on July 2, 1926, in Berlin. He was deported from Berlin on October 27–29, 1941, to the Łódź ghetto. He was deported from Łódź to Chełmno on May 4, 1942. He perished in Chełmno on May 4, 1942.

NEUBIESER, Flora: Born on September 23, 1879, in Berlin. She was deported from Berlin on October 24, 1941, to the Łódź ghetto. She was deported from Łódź to Chełmno on May 13, 1942. She perished in Chełmno on May 13, 1942.

NEUBURG, Julius: Born on December 7, 1884, in Vinsbeck. He was imprisoned between November 17, 1938, and December 9, 1938, in Dachau Concentration Camp. He was deported from Düsseldorf on October 27, 1941, to the Łódź ghetto. He was deported from Łódź to Chełmno on September 14, 1942. He perished in Chełmno on September 15, 1942.

NEUBURGER, Chloe: Born on June 7, 1885, in Rouxville, South Africa. She was deported from Hamburg on October 25, 1941, to the Łódź ghetto. She was deported from Łódź to Chełmno during May 1942, where she perished.

NEUDING, Henriette: Born on June 14, 1897, in Oels. She was deported from Hamburg on October 25, 1941, to the Łódź ghetto. She was deported from Łódź to Chełmno on May 10, 1942, where she perished.

NEUGARTEN, Johanna: Born on March 23, 1876, in Ibbenbüren. She was deported from Düsseldorf on October 27, 1941, to the Łódź

ghetto. She was deported from Łódź to Chełmno on May 6, 1942. She perished in Chełmno on May 7, 1942.

NEUHAUS, Ruth: Born on October 25, 1918, in Bebra. She was deported from Hamburg on October 25, 1941, to the Łódź ghetto. She was deported from Łódź to Chełmno on July 12, 1944, where she perished.

NEUHOF, Mathilde: Born on May 6, 1880, in Alzey. She was deported from Berlin on October 18, 1941, to the Łódź ghetto. She was deported from Łódź to Chełmno on May 8, 1942. She perished in Chełmno on May 8, 1942.

NEUMANN, Hans: Born on May 21, 1926, in Friedland. He was deported from Berlin on October 18, 1941, to the Łódź ghetto. He was deported from Łódź to Chełmno on May 8, 1942. He perished in Chełmno on May 8, 1942.

NEUMARK, Manfred: Born on November 26, 1935, in Berlin. He was deported from Berlin on November 1, 1941, to the Łódź ghetto. He was deported from Łódź to Chełmno on May 13, 1942. He perished in Chełmno on May 13, 1942.

NEUSTADT, Johanna: Born on January 1, 1867, in Jaroschewo, Poland. She was deported from Berlin on October 27–29, 1941, to the Łódź ghetto. She was deported from Łódź to Chełmno on May 5, 1942. She perished in Chełmno on May 5, 1942.

NEUSTADTER, Lina: Born on July 29, 1894, in Hamburg. She was deported from Hamburg on October 25, 1941, to the Łódź ghetto. She was deported from Łódź to Chełmno on May 10, 1942, where she perished.

NEUWAHL, Ines: Born on February 19, 1923, in Cologne. She was deported from Cologne on October 22, 1941, to the Łódź ghetto. She was deported from Łódź to Chełmno during May 1942, where she perished.

NICLAS, Julia: Born on June 13, 1898, in Mülheim. She was deported from Cologne on October 30, 1941, to the Łódź ghetto. She was deported from Łódź to Chełmno during May 1942, where she perished.

NIENDORF, Elfriede: Born on July 10, 1881, in Zawodzie, Poland. She was deported from Berlin on October 18, 1941, to the Łódź ghetto.

She was deported from Łódź to Chełmno on May 8, 1942. She perished in Chełmno on May 8, 1942.

NIESEN, Kate: Born on February 23, 1891, in Barmen-Elberfeld. She was deported from Cologne on October 22, 1941, to the Łódź ghetto. She was deported from Łódź to Chełmno during May 1942, where she perished.

NOMBURG, Charlotte: Born on August 17, 1898, in Riddagshausen. She was deported from Berlin on October 18, 1941, to the Łódź ghetto. She was deported from Łódź to Chełmno on May 10, 1942. She perished in Chełmno on May 10, 1942.

NOSSECK, Betty: Born on January 24, 1880, in Flatow. She was deported from Berlin on November 1, 1941, to the Łódź ghetto. She was deported from Łódź to Chełmno on May 9, 1942. She perished in Chełmno on May 9, 1942.

NOSSEK, Hildegard: Born on January 2, 1906, in Berlin. She was deported from Berlin on October 27–29, 1941, to the Łódź ghetto. She was deported from Łódź to Chełmno on September 10, 1942. She perished in Chełmno on September 10, 1942.

NÜSSBAUM, Charlotte: Born on June 27, 1904, in Solingen. She was deported from Düsseldorf on October 27, 1941, to the Łódź ghetto. She was deported from Łódź to Chełmno during May 1942, where she perished.

NÜSSBAUM, Julie: Born on September 3, 1875, in Hersfeld. She was deported from Cologne on October 30, 1941, to the Łódź ghetto. She was deported from Łódź to Chełmno during May 1942, where she perished.

NÜSSHOLZ, Moses: Born on January 30, 1894, in Warsaw, Poland. He was deported from Berlin on October 27–29, 1941, to the Łódź ghetto. He was deported from Łódź to Chełmno on March 25, 1942. He perished in Chełmno on March 25, 1942.

OBERLÄNDER, Friedel: Born on November 28, 1890, in Paderborn. He was deported from Düsseldorf on October 27, 1941, to the Łódź ghetto. He was deported from Łódź to Chełmno on June 28, 1944. He perished in Chełmno on June 29, 1944.

OBERSCHUTZKY, Hedwig: Born on November 29, 1886, in Immenrode. She was deported from Düsseldorf on October 27, 1941, to the Łódź ghetto. She was deported from Łódź to Chełmno on May 6, 1942. She perished in Chełmno on May 7, 1942.

OBST, Paula: Born on February 18, 1878, in Zempelburg. She was deported from Berlin on November 1, 1941, to the Łódź ghetto. She was deported from Łódź to Chełmno on May 9, 1942. She perished in Chełmno on May 9, 1942.

OBSTLER, Rosalie: Born on August 1, 1898, in Kraków, Poland. She was deported from Berlin on October 27–29, 1941, to the Łódź ghetto. She was deported from Łódź to Chełmno on May 4, 1942, where she perished.

ÖSTREICH, Henny: Born on March 27, 1909, in Berlin. She was deported from Berlin on October 24, 1941, to the Łódź ghetto. She was deported from Łódź to Chełmno on May 14, 1942. She perished in Chełmno on May 14, 1942.

ÖTTINGER, Arno: Born on August 11, 1923, in Berlin. He was deported from Berlin on October 27–29, 1941, to the Łódź ghetto. He was deported from Łódź to Chełmno on May 4, 1942. He perished in Chełmno on May 4, 1942.

OHNHAUS, Moses: Born on November 12, 1876, in Wangen. He was deported from Düsseldorf on October 27, 1941, to the Łódź ghetto. He was deported from Łódź to Chełmno on May 6, 1942. He perished in Chełmno on May 7, 1942.

OLING, Jenny: Born on February 25, 1895, in Berlin. She was deported from Berlin on October 27–29, 1941, to the Łódź ghetto. She was deported from Łódź to Chełmno on May 4, 1942. She perished in Chełmno on May 4, 1942.

OLIVEN, Else: Born on December 8, 1879, in Karwen. She was deported from Düsseldorf on October 27, 1941, to the Łódź ghetto. She was deported from Łódź to Chełmno on May 6, 1942. She perished in Chełmno on May 7, 1942.

OPFER, Paula: Born on February 2, 1891, in Breslau. She was deported from Berlin on October 18, 1941, to the Łódź ghetto. She was deported from Łódź to Chełmno on May 7, 1942, where she perished.

OPPEL, Alice: Born on September 4, 1929, in Berlin. She was deported from Berlin on October 27–29, 1941, to the Łódź ghetto. She was deported from Łódź to Chełmno on May 7, 1942. She perished in Chełmno on May 7, 1942.

OPPENHEIM, Clara: Born on July 13, 1876, in Berlin. She was deported from Berlin on October 18, 1941, to the Łódź ghetto. She was deported from Łódź to Chełmno on May 9, 1942. She perished in Chełmno on May 9, 1942.

OPPENHEIMER, Adolf: Born on January 25, 1876, in Esens. He was deported from Düsseldorf on October 27, 1941, to the Łódź ghetto. He was deported from Łódź to Chełmno on May 13, 1942. He perished in Chełmno on May 14, 1942.

ORBACH, Elly: Born on March 20, 1899, in Berlin. She was deported from Berlin on October 18, 1941, to the Łódź ghetto. She was deported from Łódź to Chełmno on May 7, 1942, where she perished.

ORCHUDESCH, Kate: Born on November 7, 1889, in Berlin. She was deported from Berlin on November 1, 1941, to the Łódź ghetto. She was deported from Łódź to Chełmno on September 10, 1942. She perished in Chełmno on September 10, 1942.

ORENSTEIN, Marion: Born on October 24, 1927, in Berlin. She was deported from Berlin on October 18, 1941, to the Łódź ghetto. She was deported from Łódź to Chełmno on May 8, 1942. She perished in Chełmno on May 8, 1942.

ORTHEILER, Rachel: Born on March 29, 1879, in Bieringen. She was deported from Hamburg on October 25, 1941, to the Łódź ghetto. She was deported from Łódź to Chełmno, where she perished.

OSCHER, Luise: Born on February 18, 1886, in Pitschen. She was deported from Berlin on October 18, 1941, to the Łódź ghetto. She was deported from Łódź to Chełmno on May 8, 1942, where she perished.

OSSER, Hans: Born on July 3, 1927, in Hamburg. He was deported from Cologne on October 22, 1941, to the Łódź ghetto. He was deported from Łódź to Chełmno during May 1942, where he perished.

OSTBERG, Hedwig: Born July 24, 1881, in Bochum. She was deported from Cologne on October 22, 1941, to the Łódź ghetto. She was deported from Łódź to Chełmno on May 5, 1942. She perished in Chełmno on May 12, 1942.

OSTER, Benny: Born on July 3, 1879, in Xanten. He was deported from Cologne on October 22, 1941, to the Łódź ghetto. He was deported from Łódź to Chełmno on May 5, 1942, where he perished.

OSTROMOGILSKI, Lessa: Born on January 6, 1900, in Odessa, Russia. She was deported from Berlin on October 24, 1941, to the Łódź ghetto. She was deported from Łódź to Chełmno on May 5, 1942, where she perished.

OSTROWSKI, Willy: Born on February 20, 1884, in Berlin. He was deported from Berlin on November 1, 1941, to the Łódź ghetto. He was deported from Łódź to Chełmno on May 10, 1942, where he perished.

OSTWALD, Johanna: Born on July 24, 1878, in Altena. She was deported from Cologne on October 30, 1941, to the Łódź ghetto. She was deported from Łódź to Chełmno and she perished during May 1942.

OSWALD, Georg: Born on March 4, 1909, in Cologne. He was deported from Cologne on October 30, 1941, to the Łódź ghetto. He was deported from Łódź to Chełmno during May 1942, where he perished.

PACKSCHER, Franziska: Born on January 23, 1891, in Berlin. She was deported from Berlin on October 24, 1941, to the Łódź ghetto. She was deported from Łódź to Chełmno on May 5, 1942. She perished in Chełmno on May 5, 1942.

PADERSTEIN, Daisy: Born on July 30, 1886, in Berlin. She was deported from Berlin on November 1, 1941, to the Łódź ghetto. She was deported from Łódź to Chełmno on May 9, 1942. She perished in Chełmno on May 9, 1942.

PAGENER, Sofie: Born on December 29, 1888, in Cologne. She was deported from Düsseldorf on October 27, 1941, to the Łódź ghetto. She

was deported from Łódź to Chełmno on May 6, 1942. She perished in Chełmno on May 7, 1942.

PANDER, Kaethe: Born on August 17, 1890, in Berlin. She was deported from Berlin on October 18, 1941, to the Łódź ghetto. She was deported from Łódź to Chełmno on May 7, 1942. She perished in Chełmno on May 7, 1942.

PANITSCH, Nathan: Born on December 29, 1875, in Rawitsch, Poland. He was deported from Cologne on October 22, 1941, to the Łódź ghetto. He was deported from Łódź to Chełmno on May 7, 1942, where he perished.

PANKE, Helene: Born on February 6, 1888, in Berlin. She was deported from Berlin on November 1, 1941, to the Łódź ghetto. She was deported from Łódź to Chełmno on May 9, 1942. She perished in Chełmno on May 9, 1942.

PAPPENHEIMER, Carl: Born on October 10, 1875, in Stuttgart. He was deported from Berlin on October 27–29, 1941, to the Łódź ghetto. He was deported from Łódź to Chełmno on May 13, 1942. He perished in Chełmno on May 13, 1942.

PARISER, Johanna: Born on April 27, 1878, in Gniezno, Poland. She was deported from Berlin on November 1, 1941, to the Łódź ghetto. She was deported from Łódź to Chełmno on September 10, 1942, where she perished.

PASKUSZ, Roschen: Born on July 29, 1867, in Ost Grosefen. She was deported from Berlin on October 27–29, 1941, to the Łódź ghetto. She was deported from Łódź to Chełmno on May 13, 1942. She perished in Chełmno on May 13, 1942.

PAUL, Kathe: Born on May 6, 1905, in Wilhelmshaven. She was deported from Berlin on October 18, 1941, to the Łódź ghetto. She was deported from Łódź to Chełmno on May 8, 1942. She perished in Chełmno on May 8, 1942.

PEGLAU, Rolf: Born on July 21, 1921, in Berlin. He was deported from Berlin on October 18, 1941, to the Łódź ghetto. He was deported from Łódź to Chełmno on May 6, 1942. He perished in Chełmno on May 6, 1942.

PEISER, Arthur: Born on January 25, 1885, in Berlin. He was deported from Berlin on October 24, 1941, to the Łódź ghetto. He was deported from Łódź to Chełmno on May 4, 1942. He perished in Chełmno on May 4, 1942.

PELS, Juda: Born on November 15, 1862, in Emden. He was deported from Berlin on October 24, 1941, to the Łódź ghetto. He was deported from Łódź to Chełmno on May 7, 1942. He perished in Chełmno on May 7, 1942.

PELZER, Margot: Born on December 1, 1902, in Berlin. She was deported from Cologne on October 22, 1941, to the Łódź ghetto. She was deported from Łódź to Chełmno during July 1944, where she perished.

PELZIGER, Justine: Born on August 12, 1875, in Plock. She was deported from Berlin on October 24, 1941, to the Łódź ghetto. She was deported from Łódź to Chełmno on May 14, 1942. She perished in Chełmno on May 14, 1942.

PERETZ, Alice: Born on October 5, 1898, in Warsaw, Poland. She was deported from Berlin on October 24, 1941, to the Łódź ghetto. She was deported from Łódź to Chełmno on July 3, 1944. She perished in Chełmno on July 3, 1944.

PERGAMENT, Erich: Born on December 12, 1888, in Berlin. He was deported from Berlin on October 18, 1941, to the Łódź ghetto. He was deported from Łódź to Chełmno on May 8, 1942. He perished in Chełmno on May 8, 1942.

PERGAMENTER, Berta: Born on June 4, 1872, in Köthen. She was deported from Berlin on October 18, 1941, to the Łódź ghetto. She was deported from Łódź to Chełmno on May 8, 1942. She perished in Chełmno on May 8, 1942.

PERITZ, Hilda: Born on November 24, 1914, in Berlin. She was deported from Berlin on November 1, 1941, to the Łódź ghetto. She was deported from Łódź to Chełmno on May 9, 1942. She perished in Chełmno on May 9, 1942.

PERL, Liebe: Born on May 24, 1891, in Stettin. She was deported from Berlin on October 18, 1941, to the Łódź ghetto. She was deported from

Łódź to Chełmno on May 8, 1942. She perished in Chełmno on May 8, 1942.

PERLINSKI, Hugo: Born on October 1, 1890, in Gostin. He was deported from Hamburg on October 25, 1941, to the Łódź ghetto. He was deported from Łódź to Chełmno on March 30, 1942, where he perished.

PERLMUTTER, Chana: Born on August 1, 1886, in Halicz, Poland. She was deported from Berlin on October 24, 1941, to the Łódź ghetto. She was deported from Łódź to Chełmno on May 13, 1942. She perished in Chełmno on May 13, 1942.

PERLSTEIN, Alice: Born on July 27, 1877, in Berlin. She was deported from Cologne on October 30, 1941, to the Łódź ghetto. She was deported from Łódź to Chełmno during May 1942, where she perished.

PFEIL, Moritz: Born on December 7, 1867, in Trockenberg. He was deported from Berlin on October 18, 1941, to the Łódź ghetto. He was deported from Łódź to Chełmno on May 8, 1942. He perished in Chełmno on May 8, 1942.

PHIEBIG, Hans: Born on January 10, 1908, in Berlin. He was deported from Berlin on October 18, 1941, to the Łódź ghetto. He was deported from Łódź to Chełmno on May 13, 1942. He perished in Chełmno on May 13, 1942.

PHILIP, Sophie: Born on August 7, 1885, in Hamburg. She was deported from Hamburg on October 25, 1941, to the Łódź ghetto. She was deported from Łódź to Chełmno on May 15, 1942, where she perished.

PHILIPP, Paula: Born on September 9, 1877, in Reppen. She was deported from Berlin on October 27–29, 1941, to the Łódź ghetto. She was deported from Łódź to Chełmno on May 12, 1942. She perished in Chełmno on May 12, 1942.

PHILIPPI, Marie: Born on July 2, 1880, in Berlin. She was deported from Berlin on October 18, 1941, to the Łódź ghetto. She was deported from Łódź to Chełmno on May 8, 1942. She perished in Chełmno on May 8, 1942.

PHILIPPS, Emilie: Born on July 20, 1890, in Duisburg. She was deported from Düsseldorf on October 27, 1941, to the Łódź ghetto. She was deported from Łódź to Chełmno on May 6, 1942. She perished in Chełmno on May 7, 1942.

PHILIPPSBORN, Frieda: Born on June 22, 1883, in Ratibor. She was deported from Berlin on October 24, 1941, to the Łódź ghetto. She was deported from Łódź to Chełmno on May 14, 1942. She perished in Chełmno on May 14, 1942.

PHILIPPSTEIN, Jenni: Born on March 18, 1874, in Emden. She was deported from Berlin on October 24, 1941, to the Łódź ghetto. She was deported from Łódź to Chełmno on May 12, 1942. She perished in Chełmno on May 12, 1942.

PHILIPSOHN, Hans: Born on December 1, 1896, in Tolkemit. He was deported from Berlin on October 18, 1941, to the Łódź ghetto. He was deported from Łódź to Chełmno on May 8, 1942. He perished in Chełmno on May 8, 1942.

PHILIPSTHAL, Gertrud: Born on August 5, 1891, in Berlin. She was deported from Berlin on October 18, 1941, to the Łódź ghetto. She was deported from Łódź to Chełmno on May 8, 1942. She perished in Chełmno on May 8, 1942.

PIANKA, Minna: Born on October 10, 1893, in Warsaw, Poland. She was deported from Düsseldorf on October 27, 1941, to the Łódź ghetto. She was deported from Łódź to Chełmno during 1942, where she perished.

PICH, Betty: Born on October 13, 1900, in Bütow. She was deported from Berlin on October 18, 1941, to the Łódź ghetto. She was deported from Łódź to Chełmno on May 8, 1942. She perished in Chełmno on May 8, 1942.

PICK, Else: Born on October 10, 1891, in Swinemünde. She was deported from Berlin on November 1, 1941, to the Łódź ghetto. She was deported from Łódź to Chełmno on May 9, 1942. She perished in Chełmno on May 9, 1942.

PILCER, Martin: Born on February 22, 1927, in Berlin. He was deported from Berlin on October 27–29, 1941, to the Łódź ghetto. He was deported from Łódź to Chełmno on June 30, 1944. He perished in Chełmno on June 30, 1944.

PINCUS, Anna: Born on October 17, 1878, in Berlin. She was deported from Berlin on October 24, 1941, to the Łódź ghetto. She was deported from Łódź to Chełmno on May 13, 1942. She perished in Chełmno on May 13, 1942.

PINKOWITZ, Jenny: Born on August 24, 1877, in Ostrowo, Poland. She was deported from Berlin on October 18, 1941, to the Łódź ghetto. She was deported from Łódź to Chełmno on May 13, 1942. She perished in Chełmno on May 13, 1942.

PINKUS, Jakob: Born on November 24, 1880, in Mrotschen, (Mrocza) Poland. He emigrated from Danzig, to Poland. He was deported from the Łódź ghetto to Chełmno on September 10, 1942, where he perished.

PINOFF, Harry: Born on May 30, 1884, in Riga. He was deported from Berlin on November 1, 1941, to the Łódź ghetto. He was deported from Łódź to Chełmno on May 8, 1942. He perished in Chełmno on May 8, 1942.

PINTHUS, Frieda: Born on April 11, 1889, in Berlin. He was deported from Berlin on October 18, 1941, to the Łódź ghetto. He was deported from Łódź to Chełmno on May 8, 1942, where he perished.

PINTUS, Albert: Born on December 29, 1888, in Chmielno. He was deported from Berlin on October 27–29, 1941, to the Łódź ghetto. He was deported from Łódź to Chełmno on May 5, 1942. He perished in Chełmno on May 5, 1942.

PIORKOWSKY, Alice: Born on June 11, 1890, in Koblenz. She was deported from Cologne on October 22, 1941, to the Łódź ghetto. She was deported from Łódź to Chełmno on May 8, 1942, where she perished.

PIPPERSBERG, Gerd: Born on October 30, 1931, in Hamburg. He was deported from Hamburg on October 25, 1941, to the Łódź ghetto. He was deported from Łódź to Chełmno on May 15, 1942, where he perished.

PLAAT, Recha: Born on September 4, 1889, in Wesel. She was deported from Düsseldorf on October 27, 1941, to the Łódź ghetto. She was deported from Łódź to Chełmno on May 6, 1942. She perished in Chełmno on May 7, 1942.

PLASS, Franziska: Born on May 10, 1911, in Berlin. She was deported from Berlin on October 27–29, 1941, to the Łódź ghetto. She was deported from Łódź to Chełmno on May 13, 1942. She perished in Chełmno on May 13, 1942.

PLATAU, Hedwig: Born on May 31, 1884, in Neustadt. She was deported from Berlin on October 27–29, 1941, to the Łódź ghetto. She was deported from Łódź to Chełmno on May 4, 1942. She perished in Chełmno on May 4, 1942.

PLATZ, Ruth: Born on August 29, 1920, in Cologne. She was deported from Cologne on October 30, 1941, to the Łódź ghetto. She was deported from Łódź to Chełmno during May 1942, where she perished.

PLAUT, Anna: Born on October 4, 1880, in Nordhausen. She was deported from Berlin on October 18, 1941, to the Łódź ghetto. She was deported from Łódź to Chełmno on May 8, 1942, where she perished.

PLESSNER, Bertha: Born on June 9, 1907, in Hamburg. She was deported from Hamburg on October 25, 1941, to the Łódź ghetto. She was deported from Łódź to Chełmno on May 5, 1942, where she perished.

PLESNER, Ruth: Born on February 5, 1925, in Hamburg. She was deported from Hamburg on October 25, 1941, to the Łódź ghetto. She was deported from Łódź to Chełmno on May 5, 1942, where she perished.

PLONSKER, Erna: Born on April 30, 1908, in Bollendorf. She was deported from Luxembourg-Trier on October 16, 1941, to the Łódź ghetto. She perished in Chełmno during April 1942.

POCH, Dora: Born on July 1, 1879, in Leszno, Poland. She was deported from Cologne on October 22, 1941, to the Łódź ghetto. She was deported from Łódź to Chełmno during May 1942, where she perished.

PODBIELSKI, Eva: Born on September 18, 1920, in Königsberg. She was deported from Berlin on October 24, 1941, to the Łódź ghetto. She

was deported from Łódź to Chełmno on May 5, 1942, where she perished.

PÖDERL, Selma: Born on October 3, 1893, in Euskirchen. She was deported from Cologne on October 22, 1941, to the Łódź ghetto. She was deported from Łódź to Chełmno during May 1942, where she perished.

POHLMANN, Jontof: Born on October 21, 1869, in Christburg. He was deported from Berlin on October 27–29, 1941, to the Łódź ghetto. He was deported from Łódź to Chełmno on May 5, 1942. He perished in Chełmno on May 5, 1942.

POLAK, Ernst: Born on September 4, 1876, in Weener. He was deported from Cologne on October 30, 1941, to the Łódź ghetto. He was deported from Łódź to Chełmno during May 1942, where he perished.

POLITZER, Max: Born on September 6, 1888, in Lassee. He was imprisoned between November 15, 1938, and January 3, 1939, in Dachau Concentration Camp. He was deported from Vienna, Austria on November 2, 1941, to the Łódź ghetto. He perished in Chełmno on September 11, 1942.

POLKE, Wally: Born on May 3, 1879, in Glatz. He was deported from Berlin on October 18, 1941, to the Łódź ghetto. He was deported from Łódź to Chełmno on May 8, 1942, where he perished.

POLLACK, Camilla: Born on May 6, 1914, in Cologne. She was deported from Cologne on October 22, 1941, to the Łódź ghetto. She was deported from Łódź to Chełmno during May 1942, where she perished.

POLLACZEK, Rosa: Born on August 21, 1921, in Berlin. She was deported from Berlin on October 24, 1941, to the Łódź ghetto. She was deported from Łódź to Chełmno during May 1942, where she perished.

POLLEY, Elsa: Born on October 28, 1887, in Gumbinnen. She was deported from Berlin on November 1, 1941, to the Łódź ghetto. She was deported from Łódź to Chełmno on May 14, 1942. She perished in Chełmno on May 14, 1942.

POPPER, Rudolf: Born on June 2, 1895, in Mainz. He was deported from Berlin on November 1, 1941, to the Łódź ghetto. He was deported from Łódź to Chełmno on May 6, 1942, where he perished.

PORN, Anna: Born on December 8, 1909, in Buczacz, Poland. She was deported from Berlin on November 1, 1941, to the Łódź ghetto. She was deported from Łódź to Chełmno on May 9, 1942. She perished in Chełmno on May 9, 1942.

POSNER, Elise: Born on May 12, 1865, in Poznań, Poland. She was deported from Berlin on October 18, 1941, to the Łódź ghetto. She was deported from Łódź to Chełmno on May 8, 1942. She perished in Chełmno on May 8, 1942.

PRAGER, Leo: Born on June 21, 1872, in Berlin. He was deported from Berlin on November 1, 1941, to the Łódź ghetto. He was deported from Łódź to Chełmno on May 9, 1942. He perished in Chełmno on May 9, 1942.

PRELLER, Hedwig: Born on May 8, 1882, in Düsseldorf. She was deported from Düsseldorf on October 27, 1941, to the Łódź ghetto. She was deported from Łódź to Chełmno on May 10, 1942. She perished in Chełmno on May 11, 1942.

PREUSS, Max: Born on September 16, 1868, in Tilsit. He was deported from Berlin on October 18, 1941, to the Łódź ghetto. He was deported from Łódź to Chełmno on May 12, 1942. He perished in Chełmno on May 12, 1942.

PRINZ, Selma: Born on January 24, 1876, in Berlin. She was deported from Cologne on October 22, 1941, to the Łódź ghetto. She was deported from Łódź to Chełmno on May 5, 1942, where she perished.

PROSKAUER, Gerda: Born on June 17, 1922, in Berlin. She was deported from Berlin on October 18, 1941, to the Łódź ghetto. She was deported from Łódź to Chełmno on July 10, 1944. She perished in Chełmno on July 10, 1944.

PULKA, Gerda: Born on February 19, 1921, in Berlin. She was deported from Hamburg on October 25, 1941, to the Łódź ghetto. She was deported from Łódź to Chełmno on April 12, 1942, where she perished.

PUNITZER, Herbert: Born on August 19, 1891, in Cottbus. He was deported from Berlin on October 27–29, 1941, to the Łódź ghetto. He was deported from Łódź to Chełmno on May 4, 1942. He perished in Chełmno on May 4, 1942.

PUTZIGER, Arthur: Born on December 5, 1882, in Arnswalde. He was deported from Berlin on November 1, 1941, to the Łódź ghetto. He was deported from Łódź to Chełmno on May 9, 1942. He perished in Chełmno on May 9, 1942.

RABBINOWITZ, Martha: Born on September 15, 1878, in Sandersleben. She was deported from Berlin on October 18, 1941, to the Łódź ghetto. She was deported from Łódź to Chełmno on May 11, 1942. She perished in Chełmno on May 11, 1942.

RADOMSKY, Else: Born on June 30, 1905, in Berlin. She was deported from Berlin on October 24, 1941, to the Łódź ghetto. She was deported from Łódź to Chełmno on May 15 1942. She perished in Chełmno on May 15, 1942.

RADWANTZER, Erna: Born on March 19, 1903, in Berlin. She was deported from Berlin on November 1, 1941, to the Łódź ghetto. She was deported from Łódź to Chełmno on May 13, 1942. She perished in Chełmno on May 13, 1942.

RAK, Levi: Born on October 28, 1885, in Warsaw, Poland. He was deported from Düsseldorf on October 27, 1941, to the Łódź ghetto. He was deported from Łódź to Chełmno on May 6, 1942. He perished in Chełmno on May 7, 1942.

RAND, Anna: Born on November 1, 1894, in Tarnów, Poland. She emigrated from Bielefeld on May 8, 1940, to Austria. She was deported from Vienna, Austria on November 2, 1941, to the Łódź ghetto. She was deported from Łódź to Chełmno on May 7, 1942, where she perished.

RANDERATH, Adele: Born on October 6, 1876, in Flammersfeld. She was deported from Cologne on October 22, 1941, to the Łódź ghetto. She was deported from Łódź to Chełmno during May 1942, where she perished.

RAPHAELSON, Frieda: Born on September 14, 1899, in Mönchengladbach. She was deported from Berlin on October 18, 1941, to the Łódź ghetto. She was deported from Łódź to Chełmno on May 8, 1942. She perished in Chełmno on May 8, 1942.

RAPPAPORT, Malwine: Born on November 19, 1890, in Odessa, Russia. She was deported from Berlin on October 18, 1941, to the Łódź ghetto. She was deported from Łódź to Chełmno on May 8, 1942. She perished in Chełmno on May 8, 1942.

RAPS, Roschen: Born on April 13, 1926, in Kassel. She was deported from Berlin on October 27–29, 1941, to the Łódź ghetto. She was deported from Łódź to Chełmno on May 4, 1942. She perished in Chełmno on May 4, 1942.

RASBA, Chaye: Born on June 10, 1883, in Vilnius. She was deported from Berlin on November 1, 1941, to the Łódź ghetto. She was deported from Łódź to Chełmno on May 9, 1942. She perished in Chełmno on May 9, 1942.

RATHAUS, Chaskel: Born on September 5, 1872, in Tarnopol, Poland. He was deported from Berlin on October 24, 1941, to the Łódź ghetto. He was deported from Łódź to Chełmno on September 7, 1942. He perished in Chełmno on September 7, 1942.

RATKOWSKI, Gertrud: Born on April 27, 1882, in Frankfurt an der Oder. She was deported from Berlin on October 18, 1941, to the Łódź ghetto. She was deported from Łódź to Chełmno on May 8, 1942, where she perished.

RATZ, Szosza: Born on April 30, 1880, in Białystok, Poland. She was deported from Berlin on November 1, 1941, to the Łódź ghetto. She was deported from Łódź to Chełmno on May 9, 1942. She perished in Chełmno on May 9, 1942.

RAU, Cacillie: Born on June 8, 1874, in Rügenwalde. She was deported from Berlin on November 1, 1941, to the Łódź ghetto. She was deported from Łódź to Chełmno on May 8, 1942. She perished in Chełmno on May 8, 1942.

RAUCH, Estera: Born on March 2, 1900, in Lutowiska, Poland. She was deported from Berlin on October 27–29, 1941, to the Łódź ghetto. She was deported from Łódź to Chełmno on September 10, 1942. She perished in Chełmno on September 10, 1942.

RAWACK, Klara: Born on April 20, 1883, in Leszno, Poland. She was deported from Berlin on October 18, 1941, to the Łódź ghetto. She was deported from Łódź to Chełmno on May 15, 1942. She perished in Chełmno on May 15, 1942.

REBENSAFT, Feige: Born on May 1, 1880, in Brody, Poland. She was deported from Berlin on October 24, 1941, to the Łódź ghetto. She was deported from Łódź to Chełmno on September 10, 1942. She perished in Chełmno on September 10, 1942.

RECHTSCHAFFEN, Minna: Born on November 11, 1894, in Hamburg. She was expelled from Hamburg on October 28, 1938, to Zbąszyń, Poland. She was deported from Hamburg on October 25, 1941, to the Łódź ghetto. She was deported from Łódź to Chełmno on May 7, 1942, where she perished.

REDER, Rosalie: Born on October 13, 1887, in Großbüllesheim. She was deported from Cologne on October 30, 1941, to the Łódź ghetto. She was deported from Łódź to Chełmno during May 1942, where she perished.

REDNER, Berta: Born on August 13, 1902, in Lübeck. She was deported from Hamburg on October 25, 1941, to the Łódź ghetto. She was deported from Łódź to Chełmno on July 12, 1944, where she perished.

REGENSBURGER, Amalie: Born on August 28, 1878, in Dierdorf. She was deported from Cologne on October 30, 1941, to the Łódź ghetto. She was deported from Łódź to Chełmno on September 12, 1942, where she perished.

REHFELD, Lisbeth: Born on August 20, 1898, in Berlin. She was deported from Berlin on October 27–29, 1941, to the Łódź ghetto. She was deported from Łódź to Chełmno on May 4, 1942. She perished in Chełmno on May 4, 1942.

REICH, Julius: Born on February 6, 1870, in Berlin. He was deported from Berlin on October 18, 1941, to the Łódź ghetto. He was deported from Łódź to Chełmno on May 8, 1942. He perished in Chełmno on May 8, 1942.

REICHENBERG, Gerta: Born on July 17, 1910, in Solingen. She was deported from Düsseldorf on October 27, 1941, to the Łódź ghetto. She was deported from Łódź to Chełmno on May 6, 1942. She perished in Chełmno on May 7, 1942.

REICHENSTEIN, Laura: Born on October 17, 1885, in Perechinsko, Poland. She was deported from Düsseldorf on October 27, 1941, to the Łódź ghetto. She was deported from Łódź to Chełmno on May 6, 1942. She perished in Chełmno on May 7, 1942.

REICHHARDT, Lotte: Born on March 11, 1921, in Michelstadt. She was deported from Cologne on October 22, 1941, to the Łódź ghetto. She was deported from Łódź to Chełmno on May 9, 1942, where she perished.

REICHMANN, Martha: Born on February 16, 1883, in Birnbaum, Poland. She was deported from Berlin on November 1, 1941, to the Łódź ghetto. She was deported from Łódź to Chełmno on May 9, 1942. She perished in Chełmno on May 9, 1942.

REIDER, Sonja: Born on January 1, 1882, in Jelgava, Russia. She was deported from Hamburg on October 25, 1941, to the Łódź ghetto. She was deported from Łódź to Chełmno on May 10, 1942, where she perished.

REIF, Maria: Born on February 7, 1915, in Duisburg. She was deported from Cologne on October 30, 1941, to the Łódź ghetto. She was deported from Łódź to Chełmno where she perished during July 1944.

REILINGER, Flora: Born on August 4, 1878, in Kindenheim. She was deported from Berlin on October 18, 1941, to the Łódź ghetto. She was deported from Łódź to Chełmno on May 8, 1942, where she perished.

REINEMANN, Irma: Born on November 22, 1890, in Kitzingen. She was deported from Düsseldorf on October 27, 1941, to the Łódź ghetto. She was deported from Łódź to Chełmno on May 6, 1942. She perished in Chełmno on May 6, 1942.

REINHARD, Johanna: Born on May 21, 1900, in Jügesheim. She was deported from Cologne on October 22, 1941, to the Łódź ghetto. She

was deported from Łódź to Chełmno on May 6, 1942, where she perished.

REINS, Selma: Born on June 10, 1896, in Berlin. She was deported from Berlin on October 18, 1941, to the Łódź ghetto. She was deported from Łódź to Chełmno on May 10, 1942. She perished in Chełmno on May 14, 1942.

REISMANN, Bruno: Born on October 31, 1903, in Berlin. He was deported from Berlin on October 18, 1941, to the Łódź ghetto. He was deported from Łódź to Chełmno on May 8, 1942. He perished in Chełmno on May 8, 1942.

REISSMANN, Arthur: Born on November 27, 1879, in Leszno, Poland. He was deported from Berlin on October 18, 1941, to the Łódź ghetto. He was deported from Łódź to Chełmno on May 4, 1942. He perished in Chełmno on May 4, 1942.

REISSNER, Alice: Born on May 25, 1874, in Frankfurt am Main. She was deported from Berlin on October 24, 1941, to the Łódź ghetto. She was deported from Łódź to Chełmno on September 7, 1942. She perished in Chełmno on September 7, 1942.

REIWALD, Anna: Born on March 27, 1872, in Białośliwie, Poland. She was deported from Berlin on October 18, 1941, to the Łódź ghetto. She was deported from Łódź to Chełmno on May 8, 1942, where she perished.

REVERSZ, Hedwig: Born on March 2, 1881, in Trutnov. She was deported from Cologne on October 30, 1941, to the Łódź ghetto. She was deported from Łódź to Chełmno where she perished on September 12, 1942.

REWALD, Oskar: Born on January 18, 1877, in Stettin. He was deported from Berlin on October 24, 1941, to the Łódź ghetto. He was deported from Łódź to Chełmno on September 12, 1942. He perished in Chełmno on September 12, 1942.

REYERSBACH, Margarete: Born on April 16, 1889, in Hamburg. She was deported from Hamburg on October 25, 1941, to the Łódź ghetto. She was deported from Łódź to Chełmno on May 15, 1942, where she perished.

RIEHS, Helene: Born on August 22, 1882, in Cologne. She was deported from Cologne on October 22, 1941, to the Łódź ghetto. She was deported from Łódź to Chełmno on May 10, 1942, where she perished.

RIESENFELD, Ella: Born on June 3, 1887, in Striegau. She was deported from Berlin on October 27–29, 1941, to the Łódź ghetto. She was deported from Łódź to Chełmno on May 4, 1942. She perished in Chełmno on May 4, 1942.

RIESS, Edith: Born on October 2, 1905, in Altona. She was deported from Berlin on October 27–29, 1941, to the Łódź ghetto. She was deported from Łódź to Chełmno on May 4, 1942. She perished in Chełmno on May 4, 1942.

RING, Jenny: Born on November 2, 1887, in Berlin. She was deported from Berlin on October 24, 1941, to the Łódź ghetto. She was deported from Łódź to Chełmno on May 4, 1942, where she perished.

RINGER, Dora: Born on January 25, 1901, in Vilnius. She was deported from Berlin on October 27–29, 1941, to the Łódź ghetto. She was deported from Łódź to Chełmno on May 4, 1942. She perished in Chełmno on May 4, 1942.

RISCH, Paula: Born on July 25, 1876, in Poznań, Poland. She was deported from Berlin on October 18, 1941, to the Łódź ghetto. She was deported from Łódź to Chełmno on May 7, 1942, where she perished.

ROBERT, Flora: Born on March 22, 1872, in Lessen. She was deported from Düsseldorf on October 27, 1941, to the Łódź ghetto. She was deported from Łódź to Chełmno on May 7, 1942, where she perished.

ROCHOCZ, Zerline: Born August 3, 1874, in Luckau. She was deported from Berlin on October 27–29, 1941, to the Łódź ghetto. She was deported from Łódź to Chełmno on May 12, 1942. She perished in Chełmno on May 12, 1942.

ROCKMANN, Margarete: Born on April 8, 1911, in Berlin. She was deported from Berlin on October 27–29, 1941, to the Łódź ghetto. She was deported from Łódź to Chełmno on June 26, 1944. She perished in Chełmno on June 26, 1944.

RÖDELHEIMER, Julius: Born on August 26, 1887, in Fulda. He was deported from Cologne during October 1941, to the Łódź ghetto. He was deported from Łódź to Chełmno during May 1942, where he perished.

RÖHMANN, Edith: Born on August 29, 1909, in Berlin. She was imprisoned in the *Sammelstelle* on *Levetzowstrasse* in Berlin. She was deported from Berlin on October 24, 1941, to the Łódź ghetto. She was deported from Łódź to Chełmno on May 4, 1942. She perished in Chełmno on May 4, 1942.

ROER, Josef: Born on December 30, 1883, in Untermaubach. He was deported from Cologne on October 22, 1941, to the Łódź ghetto. He was deported from Łódź to Chełmno on September 28, 1942, where he perished.

RÖTTGEN, Emilie: Born on January 28, 1893, in Barmen-Elberfeld. She was deported from Düsseldorf on October 27, 1941, to the Łódź ghetto. She was deported from Łódź to Chełmno during 1942, where she perished.

ROGOFF, Gregor: Born on November 8, 1900, in Minsk, Russia. He was deported from Berlin on October 24, 1941, to the Łódź ghetto. He was deported from Łódź to Chełmno on May 4, 1942. He perished in Chełmno on May 4, 1942.

ROLLE, Pauline: Born on May 10, 1876, in Schlochau. She was deported from Berlin on November 1, 1941, to the Łódź ghetto. She was deported from Łódź to Chełmno on May 8, 1942. She perished in Chełmno on May 8, 1942.

ROMM, Recha: Born on December 17, 1875, in Friedrichsberg. She was deported from Berlin on November 1, 1941, to the Łódź ghetto. She was deported from Łódź to Chełmno on May 5, 1942. She perished in Chełmno on May 5, 1942.

ROSE, Max: Born on June 19, 1882, in Dorstfeld. He was deported from Berlin on October 18, 1941, to the Łódź ghetto. He was deported from Łódź to Chełmno on May 8, 1942. He perished in Chełmno on May 8, 1942.

ROSEMANN, Anna: Born on December 30, 1899, in Dorna Watra. She was deported from Berlin on October 24, 1941, to the Łódź ghetto.

She was deported from Łódź to Chełmno on May 4, 1942. She perished in Chełmno on May 4, 1942.

ROSEN, Rudolf: Born on August 12, 1895, in Stargard. He was deported from Hamburg on October 25, 1941, to the Łódź ghetto. He was deported from Łódź to Chełmno on May 10, 1942, where he perished.

ROSENBAUM, Arnold: Born on August 18, 1932, in Berlin. He was deported from Berlin on November 1, 1941, to the Łódź ghetto. He was deported from Łódź to Chełmno on May 9, 1942. He perished in Chełmno on May 9, 1942.

ROSENBERG, Albert: Born on July 28, 1880, in Osnabrück. He was deported from Hamburg on October 25, 1941, to the Łódź ghetto. He was deported from Łódź to Chełmno on May 15, 1942, where he perished.

ROSENBLATT, Erna: Born on December 22, 1897, in Lautenburg. She was deported from Berlin on October 24, 1941, to the Łódź ghetto. She was deported from Łódź to Chełmno on September 12, 1942. She perished in Chełmno on September 12, 1942.

ROSENBLUTH, Debora: Born on August 16, 1895, in Oleszyce, Poland. She was deported from Berlin on November 1, 1941, to the Łódź ghetto. She was deported from Łódź to Chełmno on May 9, 1942. She perished in Chełmno on May 9, 1942.

ROSENDAHL, Wilhelm: Born on January 2, 1881, in Gangelt. He was deported from Cologne on October 22, 1941, to the Łódź ghetto. He was deported from Łódź to Chełmno during May 1942, where he perished.

ROSENDORFF, Heinz: Born on August 24, 1922, in Schlochau. He was deported from Berlin on October 24, 1941, to the Łódź ghetto. He was deported from Łódź to Chełmno on May 15, 1942. He perished in Chełmno on May 15, 1942.

ROSENFELD, Ida: Born on March 16, 1874, in Babenhausen. She was deported from Berlin on October 27–29, 1941, to the Łódź ghetto. She was deported from Łódź to Chełmno on May 13, 1942. She perished in Chełmno on May 13, 1942.

ROSENKRANZ, Louise: Born on November 1, 1884, in Śmigiel, Poland. She was deported from Berlin on November 1, 1941, to the Łódź ghetto. She was deported from Łódź to Chełmno on May 9, 1942. She perished in Chełmno on May 9, 1942.

ROSENOW, Gertrude: Born on February 17, 1891, in Lautenburg. She was deported from Berlin on October 24, 1941, to the Łódź ghetto. She was deported from Łódź to Chełmno on May 4, 1942. She perished in Chełmno on May 4, 1942.

ROSENRAUCH, Manfred: Born on March 8, 1927, in Berlin. He was deported from Berlin on October 27–29, 1941, to the Łódź ghetto. He was deported from Łódź to Chełmno on May 4, 1942. He perished in Chełmno on May 4, 1942.

ROSENSTEIN, Erna: Born on January 21, 1904, in Loslau, Oberschlesien, Poland. She was deported from Cologne on October 22, 1941, to the Łódź ghetto. She was deported from Łódź to Chełmno during May 1942. She perished in Chełmno on May 14, 1942.

ROSENSTERN, Richard: Born on November 21, 1886, in Hannover. He was imprisoned in Fuhlsbüttel Police prison from May 29, 1941. He was deported from Hamburg on October 25, 1941, to the Łódź ghetto. He was deported from Łódź to Chełmno during May 1942, where he perished.

ROSENSTIEL, Adele: Born on January 22, 1884, in Hagen. She was deported from Düsseldorf on October 27, 1941, to the Łódź ghetto. She was deported from Łódź to Chełmno during September 1942, where she perished.

ROSENSTOCK, Henriette: Born on November 19, 1883, in Frankfurt am Main. She was deported from Cologne on October 22, 1941, to the Łódź ghetto. She was deported from Łódź to Chełmno during May 1942, where she perished.

ROSENTHAL, Alice: Born on October 31, 1896, in Berlin. She was deported from Berlin on October 27–29, 1941, to the Łódź ghetto. She was deported from Łódź to Chełmno on May 13, 1942. She perished in Chełmno on May 13, 1942.

ROSENTRETER, Fanny: Born on April 4, 1898, in Passau. She was deported from Hamburg on October 25, 1941, to the Łódź ghetto. She was deported from Łódź to Chełmno on May 10, 1942, where she perished.

ROSMARIN, Benjamin: Born on August 8, 1901, in Bedzin, Poland. He was deported from Düsseldorf on October 27, 1941, to the Łódź ghetto. He was deported from Łódź to Chełmno during September 1942, where he perished.

ROSNER, Else: Born on June 21, 1877, in Cammin. She was deported from Berlin on October 18, 1941, to the Łódź ghetto. She was deported from Łódź to Chełmno on May 10, 1942, where she perished.

ROTENBERG, Fanny: Born on June 24, 1896, in Leipzig. She was expelled from Leipzig to Poland on October 28, 1938. She was deported from the Łódź ghetto to Chełmno on July 14, 1944, where she perished.

ROTH, Ernestine: Born on December 11, 1870, in Schrimm, Poland. She was deported from Berlin on October 24, 1941, to the Łódź ghetto. She was deported from Łódź to Chełmno on May 4, 1942. She perished in Chełmno on May 4, 1942.

ROTHENBERG, Hanna: Born on August 6, 1891, in Berlin. She was deported from Berlin on October 24, 1941, to the Łódź ghetto. She was deported from Łódź to Chełmno on May 4, 1942. She perished in Chełmno on May 4, 1942.

ROTHER, Adolf: Born on February 24, 1875, in Częstochowa, Poland. He was deported from Berlin on October 27–29, 1941, to the Łódź ghetto. He was deported from Łódź to Chełmno on May 4, 1942, where he perished.

ROTHFELS, Roni: Born on May 3, 1898, in Bebra. She was deported from Cologne on October 22, 1941, to the Łódź ghetto. She was deported from Łódź to Chełmno where she perished on June 30, 1942.

ROTHHOLZ, Auguste: Born on March 20, 1898, in Wartenburg. She was deported from Berlin on November 1, 1941, to the Łódź ghetto. She was deported from Łódź to Chełmno on May 9, 1942, where she perished.

ROTHSCHILD, Johanna: Born on January 17, 1880, in Berlin. She was deported from Berlin on October 18, 1941, to the Łódź ghetto. She was deported from Łódź to Chełmno on May 8, 1942. She perished in Chełmno on May 8, 1942.

ROTHSTEIN, Selma: Born on July 5, 1890, in Angerburg. She was deported from Berlin on October 18, 1941, to the Łódź ghetto. She was deported from Łódź to Chełmno on May 8, 1942. She perished in Chełmno on May 8, 1942.

ROTTENSTEIN, Rosalie: Born on April 8, 1884, in Mezőkaszony, Hungary. She was deported from Berlin on October 27–29, 1941, to the Łódź ghetto. She was deported from Łódź to Chełmno during September 1942, where she perished.

RUBEN, Albert: Born on July 4, 1875, in Bruttig-Fankel. He was deported from Cologne on October 22, 1941, to the Łódź ghetto. He was deported from Łódź to Chełmno on May 6, 1942, where he perished.

RUBENS, Anna: Born on January 6, 1893, in Dortmund. She was deported from Cologne on October 22, 1941, to the Łódź ghetto. She was deported from Łódź to Chełmno during September 1942. She perished in Chełmno on September 17, 1942.

RUBENSOHN, Hertha: Born on August 21, 1900, in Barmen. She was deported from Cologne on October 22, 1941, to the Łódź ghetto. She was deported from Łódź to Chełmno on May 7, 1942, where she perished.

RUBENSTEIN, Jakob: Born on December 14, 1906, in Berlin. He was deported from Berlin on November 1, 1941, to the Łódź ghetto. He was deported from Łódź to Chełmno on May 8, 1942. He perished in Chełmno on May 8, 1942.

RUBIN, Efraim: Born on August 9, 1924, in Chemnitz. He was expelled from Chemnitz on October 28, 1938, to Poland. He was deported from the Łódź ghetto to Chełmno on March 15, 1942, where he perished.

RUBINFELD, Ida: Born on November 24, 1880, in Dubiecko, Poland. She was deported from Berlin on October 24, 1941, to the Łódź

ghetto. She was deported from Łódź to Chełmno on May 4, 1942. She perished in Chełmno on May 4, 1942.

RUBINSTEIN, Paula: Born on November 10, 1876, in Regensburg. She was deported from Cologne on October 22, 1941, to the Łódź ghetto. She was deported from Łódź to Chełmno during May 1942, where she perished.

RUBLACH, Luba: Born on October 28, 1899, in Nagartow, Russia. She was expelled from Hamburg on 28–29, October 1938, to Zbąszyń, Poland. She was deported from the Łódź ghetto to Chełmno on March 25, 1942, where she perished.

RUDEITZKI, Frida: Born on May 22, 1881, in Berlin. She was deported from Berlin on October 24, 1941, to the Łódź ghetto. She was deported from Łódź to Chełmno on May 15, 1942. She perished in Chełmno on May 15, 1942.

RUDERMANN, Cacilie: Born on December 30, 1917, in Berlin. She was deported from Berlin on November 1, 1941, to the Łódź ghetto. She was deported from Łódź to Chełmno on May 9, 1942. She perished in Chełmno on May 9, 1942.

RÜBSTECK, Amalia: Born on July 30, 1909, in Schiefbahn. She was deported from Cologne on October 22, 1941, to the Łódź ghetto. She was deported from Łódź to Chełmno during May 1942. She perished in Chełmno on May 12, 1942.

RÜCKERSBERG, Berta: Born on March 8, 1884, in Montabaur. She was deported from Hamburg on October 25, 1941, to the Łódź ghetto. She was deported from Łódź to Chełmno on May 10, 1942, where she perished.

RÜDENBERG, Else: Born on September 10, 1882, in Barmen-Elberfeld. She was deported from Düsseldorf on October 27, 1941, to the Łódź ghetto. She was deported from Łódź to Chełmno on May 7, 1942. She perished in Chełmno on May 8, 1942.

RUHR, Albert: Born on June 27, 1928, in Düsseldorf. He was deported from Düsseldorf on October 27, 1941, to the Łódź ghetto. He was deported from Łódź to Chełmno on May 7, 1942. He perished in Chełmno on May 8, 1942.

RUMPER, Leja: Born on April 10, 1872, in Tarnów, Poland. She was deported from Berlin on November 1, 1941, to the Łódź ghetto. She was deported from Łódź to Chełmno on May 9, 1942. She perished in Chełmno on May 9, 1942.

RUSS, Frieda: Born on January 3, 1876, in Brandenburg-Havel. She was deported from Berlin on October 18, 1941, to the Łódź ghetto. She was deported from Łódź to Chełmno on May 8, 1942. She perished in Chełmno on May 8, 1942.

RUSSECK, Passel: Born on September 18, 1933, in Plauen. She emigrated from Leipzig to Poland. She was deported from the Łódź ghetto to Chełmno on April 30, 1942, where she perished.

RYNARZEWSKI, Dora: Born on March 15, 1897, in Berlin. She was deported from Berlin on October 24, 1941, to the Łódź ghetto. She was deported from Łódź to Chełmno on May 4, 1942. She perished in Chełmno on May 4, 1942.

SAALFELD, Gertrud: Born on May 21, 1885, in Tasdorf. She was deported from Berlin on October 27–29, 1941, to the Łódź ghetto. She was deported from Łódź to Chełmno on May 4, 1942. She perished in Chełmno on May 4, 1942.

SABAN, Ida: Born on April 4, 1895, in Łódź, Poland. She was expelled from Plauen to Poland. She was deported from the Łódź ghetto to Chełmno on March 3, 1942, where she perished.

SABATZKY, Willy: Born on March 29, 1889, in Koslin. He was deported from Berlin on October 24, 1941, to the Łódź ghetto. He was deported from Łódź to Chełmno on May 4, 1942. He perished in Chełmno on May 4, 1942.

SABEL, Amanda: Born on March 22, 1876, in Siegburg. She was deported from Cologne on October 22, 1941, to the Łódź ghetto. She was deported from Łódź to Chełmno during May 1942, where she perished.

SABOR, Eva: Born on December 28, 1937, in Berlin. She was deported from Berlin on October 24, 1941, to the Łódź ghetto. She was deported from Łódź to Chełmno on September 12, 1942, where she perished.

SACHS, Ilse: Born on July 28, 1920, in Berlin. She was deported from Berlin on October 18, 1941, to the Łódź ghetto. She was deported from Łódź to Chełmno on May 7, 1942. She perished in Chełmno on May 7, 1942.

SACK, Josefine: Born on February 5, 1873, in Eydtkuhnen. She was deported from Berlin on October 24, 1941, to the Łódź ghetto. She was deported from Łódź to Chełmno on May 4, 1942. She perished in Chełmno on May 4, 1942.

SALAZIN, Frieda: Born on April 16, 1896, in Hornburg. She was deported from Berlin on November 1, 1941, to the Łódź ghetto. She was deported from Łódź to Chełmno on May 9, 1942, where she perished.

SALINGER, Eva: Born on August 21, 1899, in Laskownica, Poland. She was deported from Berlin on October 27–29, 1941, to the Łódź ghetto. She was deported from Łódź to Chełmno on May 4, 1942, where she perished.

SALM, Berta: Born on August 12, 1885, in Grevenstein. She was deported from Düsseldorf on October 27, 1941, to the Łódź ghetto. She was deported from Łódź to Chełmno on May 7, 1942. She perished in Chełmno on May 8, 1942.

SALMON, Mathilde: Born on July 22, 1867, in Otterberg. She was deported from Berlin on October 18, 1941, to the Łódź ghetto. She was deported from Łódź to Chełmno on May 8, 1942. She perished in Chełmno on May 8, 1942.

SALOMON, Alfred: Born on January 27, 1877, in Cologne. He was deported from Cologne on October 30, 1941, to the Łódź ghetto. He was deported from Łódź to Chełmno where he perished on May 15, 1942.

SALOMONIS, Johanna: Born on February 5, 1883, in Gromaden, Poland. She was deported from Berlin on November 1, 1941, to the Łódź ghetto. She was deported from Łódź to Chełmno on May 8, 1942. She perished in Chełmno on May 8, 1942.

SALZMANN, Arthur: Born on March 14, 1880, in Stettin. He was deported from Düsseldorf on October 27, 1941, to the Łódź ghetto. He was deported from Łódź to Chełmno on May 7, 1942. He perished in Chełmno on May 8, 1942.

SAMASKEWITZ, Marga: Born on April 15, 1935, in Pirmasens. She was deported from Berlin on October 18, 1941, to the Łódź ghetto. She was deported from Łódź to Chełmno on June 30, 1944. She perished in Chełmno on June 30, 1944.

SAMOSCH, Rosa: Born on August 25, 1880, in Berlin. She was deported from Berlin on October 24, 1941, to the Łódź ghetto. She was deported from Łódź to Chełmno on May 4, 1942. She perished in Chełmno on May 4, 1942.

SAMTER, Gertrud: Born on October 14, 1877, in Berlin. She was deported from Berlin on October 24, 1941, to the Łódź ghetto. She was deported from Łódź to Chełmno on May 15, 1942. She perished in Chełmno on May 15, 1942.

SAMUEL, Hertha: Born on May 21, 1900, in Gross Gottswalde. She was deported from Berlin on October 27–29, 1941, to the Łódź ghetto. She was deported from Łódź to Chełmno on May 4, 1942. She perished in Chełmno on May 4, 1942.

SANDERS, Johanna: Born on November 14, 1902, in Busendorf. She emigrated to Holland. She was deported from Cologne on October 30, 1941, to the Łódź ghetto. She was deported from Łódź to Chełmno where she perished on June 28, 1944.

SANDHEIM, Else: Born on April 29, 1878, in Zerbst. She was deported from Berlin on October 18, 1941, to the Łódź ghetto. She was deported from Łódź to Chełmno on May 4, 1942, where she perished.

SANDMANN, Rosa: Born on October 6, 1889, in Schubin, Poland. She was deported from Berlin on November 1, 1941, to the Łódź ghetto. She was deported from Łódź to Chełmno on May 11, 1942. She perished in Chełmno on May 11, 1942.

SARNER, Gertrud: Born on January 25, 1889, in Berlin. She was deported from Berlin on October 18, 1941, to the Łódź ghetto. She was deported from Łódź to Chełmno on May 8, 1942. She perished in Chełmno on May 8, 1942.

SASS, Fanny: Born on June 20, 1880, in Jarosław, Poland. She was deported from Berlin on November 1, 1941, to the Łódź ghetto. She was deported from Łódź to Chełmno on September 7, 1942. She perished in Chełmno on September 7, 1942.

SAUL, Georg: Born on July 23, 1886, in Starogard. He was deported from Berlin on October 27–29, 1941, to the Łódź ghetto. He was deported from Łódź to Chełmno on May 10, 1942, where he perished.

SAX, Betty: Born on July 17, 1887, in Berlin. She was deported from Berlin on October 27–29, 1941, to the Łódź ghetto. She was deported from Łódź to Chełmno on May 4, 1942. She perished in Chełmno on May 4, 1942.

SCHACHMANN, Jette: Born on October 27, 1875, in Lessen. She was deported from Berlin on November 1, 1941, to the Łódź ghetto. She was deported from Łódź to Chełmno on May 10, 1942. She perished in Chełmno on May 10, 1942.

SCHÄFER, Rosalie: Born on January 13, 1900, in Waldungen, Poland. She was deported from Berlin on October 27–29, 1941, to the Łódź ghetto. She was deported from Łódź to Chełmno on June 28, 1944. She perished in Chełmno on June 28, 1944.

SCHALLENBERG, Hildegard: Born on July 15, 1901, in Cologne. She was deported from Cologne on October 22, 1941, to the Łódź ghetto. She was deported from Łódź to Chełmno on May 5, 1942, where she perished.

SCHALSCHA, Else: Born on August 16, 1876, in Gross Gandern. She was deported from Berlin on October 18, 1941, to the Łódź ghetto. She was deported from Łódź to Chełmno on May 8, 1942. She perished in Chełmno on May 8, 1942.

SCHANZER, Betty: Born on September 26, 1929, in Siegen. She was deported from Berlin on October 27–29, 1941, to the Łódź ghetto. She was deported from Łódź to Chełmno on May 4, 1942. She perished in Chełmno on May 4, 1942.

SCHAPIRA, Lucie: Born on November 1, 1881, in Stettin. She was deported from Berlin on October 24, 1941, to the Łódź ghetto. She was deported from Łódź to Chełmno on May 4, 1942, where she perished.

SCHAPIRO, Louise: Born on March 31, 1879, in Gunzenhausen. She was deported from Berlin on October 27–29, 1941, to the Łódź ghetto.

She was deported from Łódź to Chełmno on May 4, 1942. She perished in Chełmno on May 4, 1942.

SCHARLINSKI, Charlotte: Born on October 20, 1913, in Christburg. She was deported from Berlin on October 27–29, 1941, to the Łódź ghetto. She was deported from Łódź to Chełmno on May 4, 1942. She perished in Chełmno on May 4, 1942.

SCHATTSCHNEIDER, Else: Born on April 19, 1884, in Berlin. She was deported from Hamburg on October 25, 1941, to the Łódź ghetto. She was deported from Łódź to Chełmno on May 15, 1942, where she perished.

SCHAUER, Helene: Born on March 21, 1879, in Mainz. She was deported from Berlin on November 1, 1941, to the Łódź ghetto. She was deported from Łódź to Chełmno on May 9, 1942. She perished in Chełmno on May 9, 1942.

SCHAUL, Marta: Born on November 11, 1894, in Stargard. She was deported from Berlin on October 27–29, 1941, to the Łódź ghetto. She was deported from Łódź to Chełmno on May 6, 1942. She perished in Chełmno on May 6, 1942.

SCHEFF, Gabriele: Born on September 17, 1895, in Wüstegiersdorf. She was deported from Berlin on October 18, 1941, to the Łódź ghetto. She was deported from Łódź to Chełmno on May 8, 1942. She perished in Chełmno on May 8, 1942.

SCHEFFLER, Rosa: Born on February 16, 1886, in Berlin. She was imprisoned in the *Sammelstelle* on *Levetzowstrasse* in Berlin. She was deported from Berlin on October 18, 1941, to the Łódź ghetto. She was deported from Łódź to Chełmno on May 7, 1942, where she perished.

SCHEIBERG, Klara: Born on April 10, 1878, in Mülheim. She was deported from Cologne on October 22, 1941, to the Łódź ghetto. She was deported from Łódź to Chełmno during September 1942, where she perished.

SCHEIDEMANN, Ella: Born on March 13, 1902, in Tilsit. She was deported from Berlin on November 1, 1941, to the Łódź ghetto. She was

deported from Łódź to Chełmno on May 8, 1942. She perished in Chełmno on May 8, 1942.

SCHEIER, Leopold: Born on June 26, 1874, in Hamburg. He was deported from Hamburg on October 25, 1941, to the Łódź ghetto. He was deported from Łódź to Chełmno on May 12, 1942. He perished in Chełmno on May 12, 1942.

SCHEIN, Fanny: Born on May 30, 1883, in Bârlad, Rumania. She was deported from Berlin on October 24, 1941, to the Łódź ghetto. She was deported from Łódź to Chełmno on May 4, 1942. She perished in Chełmno on May 4, 1942.

SCHEINER, Hedwig: Born on March 31, 1891, in Weyerbusch. She was deported from Cologne on October 22, 1941, to the Łódź ghetto. She was deported from Łódź to Chełmno during May 1942, where she perished.

SCHEINWECHSLER, Ernestine: Born on September 15, 1880, in Buschkau, Poland. She was deported from Berlin on November 1, 1941, to the Łódź ghetto. She was deported from Łódź to Chełmno on May 9, 1942. She perished in Chełmno on May 9, 1942.

SCHEMEL, Bruno: Born on February 22, 1873, in Sorau. He was deported from Berlin on November 1, 1941, to the Łódź ghetto. He was deported from Łódź to Chełmno on May 13, 1942. He perished in Chełmno on May 13, 1942.

SCHENDEL, Jenny: Born on October 19, 1881, in Berlin. She was deported from Berlin on November 1, 1941, to the Łódź ghetto. She was deported from Łódź to Chełmno on May 10, 1942, where she perished.

SCHERBEL, Arthur: Born on May 25, 1872, in Glogau, Poland. He was deported from Berlin on October 27–29, 1941, to the Łódź ghetto. He was deported from Łódź to Chełmno on May 13, 1942, where he perished.

SCHERMANN, Elise: Born on April 24, 1873, in Uman, Russia. She was deported from Berlin on October 18, 1941, to the Łódź ghetto. She was deported from Łódź to Chełmno on May 14, 1942. She perished in Chełmno on May 14, 1942.

SCHERZ, Aron: Born on September 27, 1880, in Pruchnik, Poland. He was deported from Berlin on October 27–29, 1941, to the Łódź ghetto. He was deported from Łódź to Chełmno on May 6, 1942. He perished in Chełmno on May 6, 1942.

SCHEUER, Rosa: Born on April 30, 1881, in Berlin. She was deported from Berlin on October 24, 1941, to the Łódź ghetto. She was deported from Łódź to Chełmno on May 10, 1942. She perished in Chełmno on May 10, 1942.

SCHEYE, Ruth: Born on May 6, 1935, in Cologne. She was deported from Cologne on October 30, 1941, to the Łódź ghetto. She was deported from Łódź to Chełmno where she perished during May 1942.

SCHEYER, Alice: Born on October 12, 1884, in Stuttgart. She was deported from Cologne on October 22, 1941, to the Łódź ghetto. She was deported from Łódź to Chełmno on May 5, 1942, where she perished.

SCHIEFER, Mathilde: Born on September 14, 1882, in Haaren. She was deported from Cologne on October 22, 1941, to the Łódź ghetto. She was deported from Łódź to Chełmno during May 1942, where she perished.

SCHIFFER, Else: Born on October 18, 1882, in Berlin. She was deported from Berlin on October 18, 1941, to the Łódź ghetto. She was deported from Łódź to Chełmno on May 9, 1942. She perished in Chełmno on May 9, 1942.

SCHILD, Marta: Born on September 3, 1896, in Kupferdreh. She was deported from Cologne on October 30, 1941, to the Łódź ghetto. She was deported from Łódź to Chełmno during September 1942, where she perished.

SCHILTZER, Rosa: Born on April 14, 1891, in Berlin. She was deported from Berlin on November 1, 1941, to the Łódź ghetto. She was deported from Łódź to Chełmno on May 8, 1942, where she perished.

SCHILZER, Grete: Born on September 15, 1895, in Berlin. She was deported from Berlin on November 1, 1941, to the Łódź ghetto. She was deported from Łódź to Chełmno on May 9, 1942. She perished in Chełmno on May 9, 1942.

SCHIMMELMANN, Frieda: Born on November 19, 1879, in Berlin. She was deported from Berlin on October 18, 1941, to the Łódź ghetto. She was deported from Łódź to Chełmno on May 8, 1942. She perished in Chełmno on May 8, 1942.

SCHINDEL, Karla: Born on January 24, 1925, in Chemnitz. She emigrated from Chemnitz to Poland. She was deported from the Łódź ghetto to Chełmno on July 14, 1944, where she perished.

SCHINDLER, Gitta: Born on September 28, 1932, in Berlin. She was deported from Berlin on October 18, 1941, to the Łódź ghetto. She was deported from Łódź to Chełmno on May 4, 1942. She perished in Chełmno on May 4, 1942.

SCHLEIMER, Meta: Born on July 2, 1879, in Neukrug. She was deported from Berlin on October 24, 1941, to the Łódź ghetto. She was deported from Łódź to Chełmno on May 4, 1942. She perished in Chełmno on May 4, 1942.

SCHLESINGER, Fritz: Born on October 8, 1886, in Berlin. He was deported from Berlin on October 24, 1941, to the Łódź ghetto. He was deported from Łódź to Chełmno on May 4, 1942. He perished in Chełmno on May 4, 1942.

SCHLEWINSKY, Johanna: Born on May 28, 1885, in Cottbus. She was deported from Berlin on November 1, 1941, to the Łódź ghetto. She was deported from Łódź to Chełmno on May 9, 1942. She perished in Chełmno on May 9, 1942.

SCHLIZ, Amalie: Born on February 3, 1877, in Danzig. She was deported from Berlin on October 18, 1941, to the Łódź ghetto. She was deported from Łódź to Chełmno on May 9, 1942. She perished in Chełmno on May 9, 1942.

SCHLOSS, Chana: Born on April 25, 1940, in Trier. She was deported from Luxembourg-Trier on October 16, 1941, to the Łódź ghetto. She was deported from Łódź to Chełmno on September 14, 1942. She perished in Chełmno on September 14, 1942.

SCHLOSS, Valeska: Born on January 18, 1881, in Berlin. She was deported from Berlin on November 1, 1941, to the Łódź ghetto. She was

deported from Łódź to Chełmno on May 9, 1942. She perished in Chełmno on May 9, 1942.

SCHMELZER, Louise: Born on January 10, 1889, in Vienna, Austria. She was deported from Berlin on October 24, 1941, to the Łódź ghetto. She was deported from Łódź to Chełmno on June 28, 1944. She perished in Chełmno on June 28, 1944.

SCHMIDT, Betty: Born on May 28, 1902, in Berlin. She was deported from Berlin on October 24, 1941, to the Łódź ghetto. She was deported from Łódź to Chełmno on May 15, 1942. She perished in Chełmno on May 15, 1942.

SCHMIEDMAYER, Gerda: Born on June 23, 1928, in Berlin. She was deported from Berlin on October 24, 1941, to the Łódź ghetto. She was deported from Łódź to Chełmno on May 4, 1942. She perished in Chełmno on May 4, 1942.

SCHMITZ, Selma: Born on February 26, 1896, in Zabrze, Poland. She was deported from Cologne on October 30, 1941, to the Łódź ghetto. She was deported from Łódź to Chełmno where she perished on September 10, 1942.

SCHMOLL, Agnes: Born on February 26, 1889, in Briesen. She was deported from Berlin on October 27–29, 1941, to the Łódź ghetto. She was deported from Łódź to Chełmno on May 4, 1942. She perished in Chełmno on May 4, 1942.

SCHMUL, Rosi: Born on March 10, 1921, in Berlin. She was deported from Berlin on November 1, 1941, to the Łódź ghetto. She was deported from Łódź to Chełmno on May 5, 1942. She perished in Chełmno on May 5, 1942.

SCHMULOWITZ, Gideon: Born on May 13, 1939, in Berlin. He was deported from Berlin on October 18, 1941, to the Łódź ghetto. He was deported from Łódź to Chełmno on May 9, 1942. He perished in Chełmno on May 9, 1942.

SCHNAPP, Feleg: Born on December 29, 1872, in Leszno, Poland. He was deported from Berlin on October 18, 1941, to the Łódź ghetto. He was deported from Łódź to Chełmno on May 9, 1942. He perished in Chełmno on May 9, 1942.

SCHNEIDER, Hulda: Born on May 23, 1895, in Rogoźno, Poland. She was deported from Berlin on October 27–29, 1941, to the Łódź ghetto. She was deported from Łódź to Chełmno on May 4, 1942. She perished in Chełmno on May 4, 1942.

SCHNITZER, Sara: Born on February 11, 1890, in Tarnopol, Poland. She was expelled from Leipzig on October 28, 1938, to Poland. She was deported from the Łódź ghetto to Chełmno on September 19, 1942, where she perished.

SCHNOCK, Heinz: Born on July 13, 1931, in Mönchengladbach. He was deported from Düsseldorf on October 27, 1941, to the Łódź ghetto. He was deported from Łódź to Chełmno during September 1942, where he perished.

SCHNOG, Seligmann: Born on February 22, 1887, in Cologne. He was deported from Cologne on October 22, 1941, to the Łódź ghetto. He was deported from Łódź to Chełmno during May 1942, where he perished.

SCHNOOK, Henny: Born on November 20, 1929, in Waldenrath. She was deported from Düsseldorf on October 27, 1941, to the Łódź ghetto. She was deported from Łódź to Chełmno during September 1942, where she perished.

SCHÖMANN, Frieda: Born on March 1, 1908, in Kröv. She was deported from Cologne on October 22, 1941, to the Łódź ghetto. She was deported from Łódź to Chełmno on May 10, 1942, where she perished.

SCHÖN, Isfried: Born on November 14, 1884, in Naumburg. He was deported from Berlin on November 1, 1941, to the Łódź ghetto. He was deported from Łódź to Chełmno on May 15, 1942. He perished in Chełmno on May 15, 1942.

SCHÖNBACH, Henriette: Born on August 17, 1888, in Schermbeck. She was deported from Cologne on October 22, 1941, to the Łódź ghetto. She was deported from Łódź to Chełmno at the beginning of May 1942, where she perished on May 5, 1942.

SCHÖNFELD, Hildegard: Born on March 27, 1923, in Cologne. She was deported from Cologne on October 22, 1941, to the Łódź ghetto. She

was deported from Łódź to Chełmno during May 1942, where she perished.

SCHÖNFELDT, Amalie: Born on January 18, 1878, in Berlin. She was deported from Berlin on November 1, 1941, to the Łódź ghetto. She was deported from Łódź to Chełmno on May 8, 1942. She perished in Chełmno on May 8, 1942.

SCHÖNHORN, Gertrude: Born on June 3, 1892, in Berlin. She was deported from Berlin on October 24, 1941, to the Łódź ghetto. She was deported from Łódź to Chełmno on May 4, 1942. She perished in Chełmno on May 4, 1942.

SCHÖNTHAL, Recha: Born on November 30, 1921, in Norden. She was deported from Berlin on October 24, 1941, to the Łódź ghetto. She was deported from Łódź to Chełmno on May 4, 1942. She perished in Chełmno on May 4, 1942.

SCHÖNWALD, Abraham: Born on October 21, 1877, in Przeworsk, Poland. He was deported from Hamburg on October 25, 1941, to the Łódź ghetto. He was deported from Łódź to Chełmno on May 15, 1942, where he perished.

SCHOPS, Clara: Born on June 14, 1876, in Gniewkowo, Poland. She was deported from Berlin on November 1, 1941, to the Łódź ghetto. She was deported from Łódź to Chełmno on May 9, 1942, where she perished.

SCHOR, Dora: Born on January 18, 1920, in Berlin. She was deported from Berlin on November 1, 1941, to the Łódź ghetto. She was deported from Łódź to Chełmno on May 8, 1942. She perished in Chełmno on May 8, 1942.

SCHORSCH, Röschen: Born on December 24, 1887, in Münden. She was deported from Cologne on October 22, 1941, to the Łódź ghetto. She was deported from Łódź to Chełmno during May 1942, where she perished.

SCHOTT, Hanna: Born on April 25, 1931, in Düsseldorf. She was deported from Düsseldorf on October 27, 1941, to the Łódź ghetto. She was deported from Łódź to Chełmno on September 12, 1942, where she perished.

SCHRAMM, Benjamin: Born on January 6, 1886, in Koronowo, Poland. He was deported from Berlin on October 27–29, 1941, to the Łódź ghetto. He was deported from Łódź to Chełmno on May 4, 1942. He perished in Chełmno on May 4, 1942.

SCHRANK, Helene: Born on March 25, 1887, in Monheim am Rhein. She was deported from Cologne on October 22, 1941, to the Łódź ghetto. She was deported from Łódź to Chełmno during May 1942, where she perished.

SCHREIBER, Karl: Born on September 1, 1881, in Vienna, Austria. He was deported from Berlin on October 18, 1941, to the Łódź ghetto. He was deported from Łódź to Chełmno during September 1942, where he perished.

SCHRÖDER, Helene: Born on April 25, 1879, in Hamburg. She was deported from Berlin on November 1, 1941, to the Łódź ghetto. She was deported from Łódź to Chełmno on May 13, 1942. She perished in Chełmno on May 13, 1942.

SCHRUBSKI, Byanka: Born on March 3, 1878, in Mogilno, Poland. She was deported from Berlin on November 1, 1941, to the Łódź ghetto. She was deported from Łódź to Chełmno on September 13, 1942. She perished in Chełmno on September 13, 1942.

SCHUBACH, Max: Born on September 27, 1883, in Mülheim. He was deported from Cologne on October 22, 1941, to the Łódź ghetto. He was deported from Łódź to Chełmno on May 5, 1942, where he perished.

SCHÜFTAN, Else: Born on August 31, 1889, in Brieg. She was deported from Berlin on November 1, 1941, to the Łódź ghetto. She was deported from Łódź to Chełmno on May 13, 1942. She perished in Chełmno on May 13, 1942

SCHÜLER, Jacques: Born on September 23, 1875, in Poznań, Poland. He was deported from Berlin on October 24, 1941, to the Łódź ghetto. He was deported from Łódź to Chełmno on May 13, 1942. He perished in Chełmno on May 13, 1942.

SCHÜLLER, Pauline: Born on September 18, 1900, in Cologne. She was deported from Cologne on October 22, 1941, to the Łódź ghetto. She

was deported from Łódź to Chełmno during May 1942, where she perished.

SCHULDE, Gertrude: Born on January 11, 1893, in Vienna, Austria. She was deported from Berlin on November 1, 1941, to the Łódź ghetto. She was deported from Łódź to Chełmno on September 10, 1942. She perished in Chełmno on September 10, 1942.

SCHULZ, Sara: Born on December 13, 1901, in Bjelzy, Russia. She was deported from Berlin on October 27–29, 1941, to the Łódź ghetto. She was deported from Łódź to Chełmno on May 5, 1942. She perished in Chełmno on May 5, 1942.

SCHULZE, Martha: Born on June 26, 1905, in Berlin. She was deported from Berlin on October 27–29, 1941, to the Łódź ghetto. She was deported from Łódź to Chełmno on May 5, 1942. She perished in Chełmno on May 5, 1942.

SCHUSTER, Olga: Born on January 24, 1885, in Hamburg. She was deported from Hamburg on October 25, 1941, to the Łódź ghetto. She was deported from Łódź to Chełmno on May 4, 1942, where she perished.

SCHWAB, Ruth: Born on January 25, 1925, in Cologne. She was deported from Cologne on October 22, 1941, to the Łódź ghetto. She was deported from Łódź to Chełmno during May 1942, where she perished.

SCHWABE, Herbert: Born on January 20, 1905, in Hildesheim. He was deported from Berlin on October 24, 1941, to the Łódź ghetto. He was deported from Łódź to Chełmno on May 4, 1942. He perished in Chełmno on May 4, 1942.

SCHWALB, Golda: Born on March 5, 1882, in Jarosław, Poland. She was deported from Berlin on October 24, 1941, to the Łódź ghetto. She was deported from Łódź to Chełmno on May 10, 1942. She perished in Chełmno on May 10, 1942.

SCHWARZ, Albert: Born on January 24, 1877, in Poznań, Poland. He was deported from Berlin on November 1, 1941, to the Łódź ghetto. He was deported from Łódź to Chełmno on May 9, 1942. He perished in Chełmno on May 9, 1942.

SCHWARZMANN, Rachel: Born on May 25, 1878, in Jarosław, Poland. She was deported from Berlin on October 27–29, 1941, to the Łódź ghetto. She was deported from Łódź to Chełmno on May 4, 1942. She perished in Chełmno on May 4, 1942.

SCHWEIZER, Josefine: Born on June 30, 1883, in Düsseldorf. She was deported from Düsseldorf on October 27, 1941, to the Łódź ghetto. She was deported from Łódź to Chełmno during May 1942, where she perished.

SCHWENK, Erich: Born on May 31, 1884, in Grottkau. He was deported from Berlin on October 27–29, 1941, to the Łódź ghetto. He was deported from Łódź to Chełmno on May 5, 1942. He perished in Chełmno on May 5, 1942.

SCHWERIN, Else: Born on June 17, 1896, in Berlin. She was deported from Berlin on October 18, 1941, to the Łódź ghetto. She was deported from Łódź to Chełmno on June 28, 1944. She perished in Chełmno on June 28, 1944.

SECKELS, Selma: Born on October 17, 1895, in Aurich. She was deported from Cologne on October 22, 1941, to the Łódź ghetto. She was deported from Łódź to Chełmno on May 6, 1942, where she perished.

SECKL, Friedrich: Born on July 13, 1891, in Vienna, Austria. He was deported from Frankfurt am Main on October 20, 1941, to the Łódź ghetto. He was deported from Łódź to Chełmno on May 4, 1942, where he perished.

SEEFELD, Bernd: Born on January 23, 1937, in Berlin. He was deported from Berlin on November 1, 1941, to the Łódź ghetto. He was deported from Łódź to Chełmno on May 9, 1942. He perished in Chełmno on May 9, 1942.

SEELIG, Rosa: Born on January 9, 1886, in Kempen, Poland. She was deported from Cologne on October 22, 1941, to the Łódź ghetto. She was deported from Łódź to Chełmno during May 1942, where she perished.

SEGINER, Isaak: Born on December 2, 1888, in Sanok, Poland. He was deported from Düsseldorf on October 27, 1941, to the Łódź ghetto.

He was deported from Łódź to Chełmno during May 1942, where he perished.

SEIDE, Elfriede: Born on November 22, 1877, in Gleiwitz, Poland. She was deported from Berlin on November 1, 1941, to the Łódź ghetto. She was deported from Łódź to Chełmno on May 4, 1942, where she perished.

SEIDEMANN, Moritz: Born on March 21, 1875, in Krefeld. He was deported from Berlin on October 18, 1941, to the Łódź ghetto. He was deported from Łódź to Chełmno on May 7, 1942. He perished in Chełmno on May 7, 1942.

SEIFERHELD, Milian: Born on January 30, 1881, in Langenselbold. She was deported from Cologne on October 22, 1941, to the Łódź ghetto. She was deported from Łódź to Chełmno during September 1942, where she perished.

SELBIGER, Rosa: Born on February 17, 1897, in Berlin. She was deported from Berlin on November 1, 1941, to the Łódź ghetto. She was deported from Łódź to Chełmno on May 9, 1942. She perished in Chełmno on May 9, 1942.

SELIG, Rita: Born on May 17, 1933, in Berlin. She was deported from Berlin on October 24, 1941, to the Łódź ghetto. She was deported from Łódź to Chełmno on September 12, 1942. She perished in Chełmno on September 12, 1942.

SELIGMANN, Amalie: Born on January 28, 1884, in Bonn. She was deported from Düsseldorf on October 27, 1941, to the Łódź ghetto. She was deported from Łódź to Chełmno on May 7, 1942. She perished in Chełmno on May 8, 1942.

SENFT, Amalie: Born on August 3, 1884, in Danzig. She was deported from Berlin on October 24, 1941, to the Łódź ghetto. She was deported from Łódź to Chełmno on May 4, 1942, where she perished.

SERETH, Gisela: Born on October 11, 1895, in Hamburg. She was deported from Cologne on October 22, 1941, to the Łódź ghetto. She was deported from Łódź to Chełmno during May 1942, where she perished.

SERVOS, Julius: Born on July 19, 1904, in Hamborn. He was deported from Düsseldorf on October 27, 1941, to the Łódź ghetto. He was deported from Łódź to Chełmno on June 26, 1944. He perished in Chełmno on June 27, 1944.

SICHEL, Werner: Born on July 1, 1931, in Cologne. He was deported from Cologne on October 22, 1941, to the Łódź ghetto. He was deported from Łódź to Chełmno on May 15, 1942, where he perished.

SIEMONTOWSKI, Ilse: Born on April 5, 1907, in Berlin. She was deported from Berlin on October 18, 1941, to the Łódź ghetto. She was deported from Łódź to Chełmno on May 9, 1942. She perished in Chełmno on May 9, 1942.

SILBERBACH, Adolf: Born on January 21, 1879, in Bad Salzuflen. He was deported from Cologne on October 22, 1941, to the Łódź ghetto. He was deported from Łódź to Chełmno during May 1942, where he perished.

SILBERBERG, Emma: Born on November 30, 1882, in Lippstadt. She was deported from Cologne on October 22, 1941, to the Łódź ghetto. She was deported from Łódź to Chełmno during early May 1942, where she perished on May 10, 1942.

SILBERBLATT, Rosel: Born on January 16, 1887, in Libau, Poland. He was deported from Cologne on October 30, 1941, to the Łódź ghetto. He was deported from Łódź to Chełmno during May 1942, where he perished.

SILBERMANN, Bertha: Born on June 28, 1890, in Aurich. She was deported from Berlin on October 24, 1941, to the Łódź ghetto. She was deported from Łódź to Chełmno on May 14, 1942. She perished in Chełmno on May 14, 1942.

SILBERSTEIN, Rosa: Born on June 1, 1882, in Leipzig. She was deported from Berlin on October 18, 1941, to the Łódź ghetto. She was deported from Łódź to Chełmno on May 14, 1942. She perished in Chełmno on May 14, 1942.

SILBIGER, Moritz: Born on May 19, 1882, in Wieliczka, Poland. He was imprisoned in Sachsenhausen Concentration Camp from November 11, 1938, to December 6, 1938. He was deported from Berlin on

October 27-29, 1941, to the Łódź ghetto. He was deported from Łódź to Chełmno on May 4, 1942, where he perished.

SIMENAUER, Lucie: Born on June 18, 1876, in Nikolai (Berlin). She was deported from Berlin on November 1, 1941, to the Łódź ghetto. She was deported from Łódź to Chełmno on May 9, 1942. She perished in Chełmno on May 9, 1942.

SIMKE, Elfriede: Born on November 21, 1879, in Luckau. She was deported from Berlin on October 27–29, 1941, to the Łódź ghetto. She was deported from Łódź to Chełmno on May 11, 1942, where she perished.

SIMON, Alice: Born on December 6, 1896, in Cologne. She was deported from Düsseldorf on October 27, 1941, to the Łódź ghetto. She was deported from Łódź to Chełmno on May 15, 1942. She perished in Chełmno on May 16, 1942.

SIMON-WOLFSKEHL, Erna: Born on December 12, 1901, in Geisenheim. She was deported from Frankfurt am Main on October 20, 1941, to the Łódź ghetto. She was deported from Łódź to Chełmno on June 28, 1944, where she perished.

SIMONS, Berta: Born on January 1, 1895, in Mittelsinn. She was deported from Cologne on October 22, 1941, to the Łódź ghetto. She was deported from Łódź to Chełmno, where she perished on June 26, 1944.

SIMONSTEIN, Martha: Born on January 31, 1884, in Swarzędz, Poland. She was deported from Berlin on October 18, 1941, to the Łódź ghetto. She was deported from Łódź to Chełmno on May 8, 1942. She perished in Chełmno on May 8, 1942.

SIMSON, Selma: Born on December 25, 1886, in Rosenberg. She was deported from Berlin on November 1, 1941, to the Łódź ghetto. She was deported from Łódź to Chełmno on May 7, 1942, where she perished.

SINGER, Elsa: Born on June 24, 1881, in Berlin. She was deported from Berlin on November 1, 1941, to the Łódź ghetto. She was deported from Łódź to Chełmno on May 9, 1942. She perished in Chełmno on May 9, 1942.

SIPPEL, Mathilde: Born on February 1, 1879, in Iserlohn. She was deported from Düsseldorf on October 27, 1941, to the Łódź ghetto. She was deported from Łódź to Chełmno on May 6, 1942. She perished in Chełmno on May 7, 1942.

SISTIG, Erna: Born on August 2, 1899, in Bonn. She was deported from Cologne on October 30, 1941, to the Łódź ghetto. She was deported from Łódź to Chełmno where she perished during May 1942.

SITZMANN, Karl: Born on December 23, 1886, in Unterriedenberg. He was deported from Berlin on October 27-29, 1941, to the Łódź ghetto. He was deported from Łódź to Chełmno on May 5, 1942, where he perished.

SKLARZ, Clara: Born on June 25, 1890, in Warsaw, Poland. She was deported from Berlin on October 27–29, 1941, to the Łódź ghetto. She was deported from Łódź to Chełmno on July 3, 1944. She perished in Chełmno on July 3, 1944.

SLATOPOLSKI, Horst: Born on April 1, 1926, in Berlin. He was deported from Berlin on October 24, 1941, to the Łódź ghetto. He was deported from Łódź to Chełmno on May 4, 1942. He perished in Chełmno on May 4, 1942.

SINSKI, Jakob: Born on October 23, 1896, in Zduńska Wola, Poland. He was expelled from Cologne on October 28, 1938, to Zbąszyń, Poland, where he was incarcerated in Zbąszyń Internment Camp until the Summer of 1939. He was deported from the Łódź ghetto to Chełmno on February 28, 1942, where he perished.

SLOTOWSKI, Paul: Born on March 8, 1879, in Neu Jucha. He was deported from Berlin on October 24, 1941, to the Łódź ghetto. He was deported from Łódź to Chełmno on May 4, 1942. He perished in Chełmno on May 4, 1942.

SMOLARSKI, Faivel: Born on June 9, 1895, in Łódź, Poland. He emigrated from Berlin to Poland. He was deported from Łódź to Chełmno, where he perished.

SOBERSKY, Herbert: Born on October 5, 1886, in Zeitz. He was imprisoned in Dachau Concentration Camp from November 15, 1938, to December 29, 1938. He was deported from Cologne on October 30,

1941, to the Łódź ghetto. He was deported from Łódź to Chełmno during May 1942, where he perished.

SOBOTKI, Johanna: Born on July 23, 1882, in Barmen-Elberfeld. She was deported from Düsseldorf on October 27, 1941, to the Łódź ghetto. She was deported from Łódź to Chełmno on September 10, 1942, where she perished.

SOLLINGER, Hanna: Born on November 23, 1892, in Lüdenhausen. She was deported from Düsseldorf on October 27, 1941, to the Łódź ghetto. She was deported from Łódź to Chełmno on May 6, 1942. She perished in Chełmno on May 7, 1942.

SOLMS, Else: Born on August 28, 1891, in Lauban. She was deported from Berlin on October 27–29, 1941, to the Łódź ghetto. She was deported from Łódź to Chełmno on May 4, 1942. She perished in Chełmno on May 4, 1942.

SOMMER, Hedwig: Born on October 15, 1879, in Lüxheim. She was deported from Düsseldorf on October 27, 1941, to the Łódź ghetto. She was deported from Łódź to Chełmno on May 6, 1942. She perished in Chełmno on May 7, 1942.

SOMMERBURG, Julie: Born on November 26, 1893, in Vienna, Austria. She was deported from Berlin on November 1, 1941, to the Łódź ghetto. She was deported from Łódź to Chełmno on May 4, 1942. She perished in Chełmno on May 4, 1942.

SOMMERFELD, Johanna: Born on May 15, 1896, in Cottbus. She was deported from Berlin on October 27–29, 1941, to the Łódź ghetto. She was deported from Łódź to Chełmno on May 4, 1942. She perished in Chełmno on May 4, 1942.

SOMMERFELDT, Margot: Born on July 28, 1908, in Berlin. She was deported from Berlin on October 18, 1941, to the Łódź ghetto. She was deported from Łódź to Chełmno on September 11, 1942. She perished in Chełmno on September 11, 1942.

SOMMERHAUSER, August: Born on September 11, 1910, in Nürnberg. He was deported from Berlin on October 27 -29, 1941, to the Łódź ghetto. He was deported from Łódź to Chełmno on September 7, 1942. He perished in Chełmno on September 7, 1942.

SONN, Levi: Born on September 20, 1879, in Neukirchen. He was deported from Cologne on October 22, 1941, to the Łódź ghetto. He was deported from Łódź to Chełmno during May 1942, where he perished.

SONNENBERG, Emma: Born on May 3, 1879, in Betzdorf. She was deported from Cologne on October 30, 1941, to the Łódź ghetto. She was deported from Łódź to Chełmno where she perished during May 1942.

SONNENBLICK, Blima: Born on May 24, 1883, in Tyrawa Wołoska, Poland. She was deported from Berlin on October 24, 1941, to the Łódź ghetto. She was deported from Łódź to Chełmno on September 2, 1942. She perished in Chełmno on September 2, 1942.

SONNENFELD, Arthur: Born on May 1, 1881, in Breslau. He was deported from Berlin on November 1, 1941, to the Łódź ghetto. He was deported from Łódź to Chełmno on May 8, 1942. He perished in Chełmno on May 8, 1942.

SONNENMARK, Elise: Born on April 1881, in Lednice. She was deported from Berlin on October 27–29, 1941, to the Łódź ghetto. She was deported from Łódź to Chełmno on May 6, 1942. She perished in Chełmno on May 6, 1942.

SORIN, Rosa: Born on July 23, 1879, in Odessa, Russia. She was deported from Düsseldorf on October 27, 1941, to the Łódź ghetto. She was deported from Łódź to Chełmno on May 6, 1942. She perished in Chełmno on May 7, 1942.

SORSKY, Marie: Born on February 7, 1905, in Berlin. She was deported from Berlin on November 1, 1941, to the Łódź ghetto. She was deported from Łódź to Chełmno on May 5, 1942. She perished in Chełmno on May 5, 1942.

SOSTHEIM, Alfred: Born on October 22, 1931, in Flamersheim. He was deported from Cologne on October 22, 1941, to the Łódź ghetto. He was deported from Łódź to Chełmno where he perished on May 10, 1942.

SPANDAU, Valeska: Born on July 30, 1883, in Neudamm. She was deported from Berlin on November 1, 1941, to the Łódź ghetto. She was

deported from Łódź to Chełmno on May 8, 1942. She perished in Chełmno on May 8, 1942.

SPANIER, Bella: Born on February 25, 1884, in Bremen. She was deported from Hamburg on October 25, 1941, to the Łódź ghetto. She was deported from Łódź to Chełmno on May 10, 1941, where she perished.

SPEIER-HOLSTEIN, Samuel: Born on September 17, 1895, in Cologne. He was deported from Cologne on October 22, 1941, to the Łódź ghetto. He was deported from Łódź to Chełmno during May 1942, where he perished.

SPERLING, Karolina: Born on March 28, 1877, in Ochtendung. She was deported from Berlin on October 27–29, 1941, to the Łódź ghetto. She was deported from Łódź to Chełmno on May 4, 1942. She perished in Chełmno on May 4, 1942.

SPET, Emma: Born on December 7, 1897, in Kąkolewicz, Poland. She was deported from Berlin on October 27–29, 1941, to the Łódź ghetto. She was deported from Łódź to Chełmno on June 26, 1944. She perished in Chełmno on June 26, 1944.

SPEYER, Else: Born on June 17, 1881, in Bochum. She was deported from Düsseldorf on October 27, 1941, to the Łódź ghetto. She was deported from Łódź to Chełmno on May 9, 1942. She perished in Chełmno on May 10, 1942.

SPICKER, Heinz: Born on May 31, 1911, in Berlin. He was deported from Berlin on November 1, 1941, to the Łódź ghetto. He was deported from Łódź to Chełmno on May 10, 1942. He perished in Chełmno on May 10, 1942.

SPIEGEL, Johanna: Born on January 23, 1921, in Oberaula. She was deported from Düsseldorf on October 27, 1941, to the Łódź ghetto. She was deported from Łódź to Chełmno on July 12, 1944. She perished in Chełmno on July 13, 1944.

SPIEGLER, Leopold: Born on March 23, 1881, in Rohonc, Hungary. He was deported from Berlin on October 24, 1941, to the Łódź ghetto. He was deported from Łódź to Chełmno on September 7, 1942. He perished in Chełmno on September 7, 1942.

SPIELDOCH, Paula: Born on January 29, 1892, in Berlin. She was deported from Berlin on October 24, 1941, to the Łódź ghetto. She was deported from Łódź to Chełmno on May 4, 1942. She perished in Chełmno on May 4, 1942.

SPIELMANN, Joachim: Born on January 15, 1938, in Berlin. He was deported from Berlin on October 27 -29, 1941, to the Łódź ghetto. He was deported from Łódź to Chełmno on May 4, 1942. He perished in Chełmno on May 4, 1942.

SPIRA, Arthur: Born on October 28, 1875, in Kraków, Poland. He was deported from Berlin on October 18, 1941, to the Łódź ghetto. He was deported from Łódź to Chełmno on May 8, 1942. He perished in Chełmno on May 8, 1942.

SPIRO, Erna: Born on August 6, 1891, in Werden. She was deported from Cologne on October 30, 1941, to the Łódź ghetto. She perished in Chełmno during May 1942.

SPITZ, Gisela: Born on June 29, 1878, in Tarnów, Poland. She was deported from Berlin on October 27–29, 1941, to the Łódź ghetto. She was deported from Łódź to Chełmno on September 12, 1942. She perished in Chełmno on September 12, 1942.

SPITZER, Berta: Born on January 31, 1881, in Düsseldorf. She was deported from Berlin on November 1, 1941, to the Łódź ghetto. She was deported from Łódź to Chełmno on May 8, 1942. She perished in Chełmno on May 8, 1942.

SPORN, Adelheid: Born on February 4, 1891, in Otzenrath. She was deported from Düsseldorf on October 27, 1941, to the Łódź ghetto. She was deported from Łódź to Chełmno during July 1944, where she perished.

SPRINGER, Gisela: Born on November 9, 1872, in Vienna, Austria. She was deported from Berlin on October 18, 1941, to the Łódź ghetto. She was deported from Łódź to Chełmno on May 8, 1942. She perished in Chełmno on May 8, 1942.

SQUAR, Elvira: Born on November 3, 1865, in Berlin. She was deported from Berlin on November 1, 1941, to the Łódź ghetto. She was

deported from Łódź to Chełmno on May 4, 1942. She perished in Chełmno on May 4, 1942.

STADTHAGEN, Lucie: Born on August 19, 1886, in Ober Kahlbude. She was deported from Berlin on October 24, 1941, to the Łódź ghetto. She was deported from Łódź to Chełmno on May 15, 1942. She perished in Chełmno on May 15, 1942.

STAHL, Leon: Born on October 26, 1885, in Bucharest, Rumania. He was deported from Berlin on October 24, 1941, to the Łódź ghetto. He was deported from Łódź to Chełmno on May 9, 1942, where he perished.

STECKEL, Margarete: Born on January 10, 1904, in Berlin. She was deported from Berlin on November 1, 1941, to the Łódź ghetto. She was deported from Łódź to Chełmno on May 7, 1942. She perished in Chełmno on May 7, 1942.

STEIER, Jakob: Born on December 29, 1885, in Zgierz, Poland. He was expelled from Berlin on October 28, 1938, to Zbąszyń, Poland. He was deported to the Łódź ghetto and from there he was deported to Chełmno on July 3, 1944, where he perished.

STEIN, Dora: Born on May 4, 1891, in Rheinbach. She was deported from Düsseldorf on October 27, 1941, to the Łódź ghetto. She was deported from Łódź to Chełmno on July 12, 1944. She perished in Chełmno on July 13, 1944.

STEINBERG, Frieda: Born on February 22, 1937, in Berlin. She was deported from Berlin on November 1, 1941, to the Łódź ghetto. She was deported from Łódź to Chełmno on May 9, 1942. She perished in Chełmno on May 9, 1942.

STEINBERGER, Selma: Born on June 8, 1884, in Alsfeld. She was deported from Cologne on October 22, 1941, to the Łódź ghetto. She was deported from Łódź to Chełmno where she perished during May 1942.

STEINER, Sophie: Born on July 10, 1889, in Horodenka, Poland. She was deported from Berlin on October 27–29, 1941, to the Łódź ghetto. She was deported from Łódź to a forced labor camp in Poznań on

November 11, 1941. She was deported to Chełmno on May 4, 1942. She perished in Chełmno on May 4, 1942.

STEINFELD, Bernhard: Born on August 24, 1894, in Versmold. He was deported from Cologne on October 22, 1941, to the Łódź ghetto. He was deported from Łódź to Chełmno during Septenber 1942. He perished in Chełmno on September 9, 1942.

STEINHAGEN, Max: Born on January 3, 1876, in Schloppe. He was deported from Berlin on October 24, 1941, to the Łódź ghetto. He was deported from Łódź to Chełmno on May 4, 1942. He perished in Chełmno on May 4, 1942.

STEINHART, Moritz: Born on September 11, 1877, in Ryczywół, Poland. He was deported from Berlin on October 27 -29, 1941, to the Łódź ghetto. He was deported from Łódź to Chełmno on May 13, 1942, where he perished.

STEINWEG, Sophia: Born on July 11, 1915, in Aachen. She was deported from Cologne on October 30, 1941, to the Łódź ghetto. She was deported from Łódź to Chełmno on May 4, 1942, where she perished.

STENISCHEWSKI, Benno: Born on May 15, 1900, in Strasburg. He was deported from Berlin on October 24, 1941, to the Łódź ghetto. He was deported from Łódź to Chełmno on May 4, 1942. He perished in Chełmno on May 4, 1942.

STEPHAN, Henriette: Born on April 5, 1895, in Berlin. She was deported from Berlin on October 24, 1941, to the Łódź ghetto. She was deported from Łódź to Chełmno on May 4, 1942. She perished in Chełmno on May 4, 1942.

STERN, Adolf: Born on July 15, 1880, in Büderich. He was deported from Düsseldorf on October 27, 1941, to the Łódź ghetto. He was deported from Łódź to Chełmno on May 6, 1942. He perished in Chełmno on May 7, 1942.

STERNBERG, Ellen: Born on April 8, 1925, in Bonn. She was deported from Cologne on October 30, 1941, to the Łódź ghetto. She was deported from Łódź to Chełmno during July 1944, where she perished.

STERNEFELD, Karl: Born on June 9, 1888, in Goch. He was imprisoned in Dachau Concentration Camp from November 17, 1938, to January

10, 1939. He was deported from Düsseldorf on October 27, 1941, to the Łódź ghetto. He was deported from Łódź to Chełmno on May 6, 1942. He perished in Chełmno on May 7, 1942.

STERNFELD, Max: Born on August 30, 1912, in Berlin. He was deported from Berlin on November 1, 1941, to the Łódź ghetto. He was deported from Łódź to Chełmno on May 8, 1942. He perished in Chełmno on May 8, 1942.

STERNHEIM, Selma: Born on August 12, 1888, in Dortmund. She was deported from Cologne on October 22, 1941, to the Łódź ghetto. She was deported from Łódź to Chełmno where she perished on May 6, 1942.

STERNLICHT, Regina: Born on April 4, 1896, in Cajar, Hungary. She was deported from Berlin on October 24, 1941, to the Łódź ghetto. She was deported from Łódź to Chełmno on May 4, 1942. She perished in Chełmno on May 4, 1942.

STERNSCHUSS, Rosa: Born on July 7, 1896, in Hamburg. She was deported from Cologne on October 30, 1941, to the Łódź ghetto. She was deported from Łódź to Chełmno during May 1942, where she perished.

STICH, Hedwig: Born on September 4, 1881, in Schubin, Poland. She was deported from Berlin on October 27–29, 1941, to the Łódź ghetto. She was deported from Łódź to Chełmno on May 4, 1942. She perished in Chełmno on May 4, 1942.

STIEBEL, Jakob: Born on April 12, 1887, in Kitzingen. He was deported from Düsseldorf on October 27, 1941, to the Łódź ghetto. He was deported from Łódź to Chełmno during September 1942, where he perished.

STIEFEL, Hannelore: Born on October 13, 1920, in Düsseldorf. She was deported from Düsseldorf on October 27, 1941, to the Łódź ghetto. She was deported from Łódź to Chełmno during July 1944, where she perished.

STITZKY, Elsa: Born on February 12, 1882, in Roździeń, Poland. She was deported from Berlin on October 27–29, 1941, to the Łódź ghetto. She

was deported from Łódź to Chełmno on May 5, 1942, where she perished.

STOCK, Eva: Born on March 9, 1935, in Cologne. She was deported from Cologne on October 30, 1941, to the Łódź ghetto. She was deported from Łódź to Chełmno during early May 1942, where she perished on May 10, 1942.

STOCKMANN, Rosa: Born on August 7, 1898, in Tarnogród, Poland. She was deported from Berlin on October 24, 1941, to the Łódź ghetto. She was deported from Łódź to Chełmno on June 28, 1944. She perished in Chełmno on June 28, 1944.

STOPPELMANN, Minna: Born on January 17, 1887, in Aurich. She was deported from Berlin on October 18, 1941, to the Łódź ghetto. She was deported from Łódź to Chełmno on May 4, 1942. She perished in Chełmno on May 4, 1942.

STRAUSS, Agnes: Born on August 18, 1892, in Duisburg. She was deported from Düsseldorf on October 27, 1941, to the Łódź ghetto. She was deported from Łódź to Chełmno on May 6, 1942. She perished in Chełmno on May 7, 1942.

STREISAND, Margarete: Born on August 5, 1882, in Grodzisk, Poland. She was deported from Berlin on October 27–29, 1941, to the Łódź ghetto. She was deported from Łódź to Chełmno on May 6, 1942. She perished in Chełmno on May 6, 1942.

STRUMPFNER, Alma: Born on March 10, 1879, in Mikołów, Poland. She was deported from Berlin on November 1, 1941, to the Łódź ghetto. She was deported from Łódź to Chełmno on May 9, 1942, where she perished.

STRUZIK, Elli: Born on November 7, 1915, in Berlin. She was deported from Berlin on November 1, 1941, to the Łódź ghetto. She was deported from Łódź to Chełmno on May 13, 1942. She perished in Chełmno on May 13, 1942.

STUDINSKI, Hedwig: Born on September 23, 1901, in Hötensleben. She was deported from Berlin on November 1, 1941, to the Łódź ghetto. She was deported from Łódź to Chełmno on May 15, 1942. She perished in Chełmno on May 15, 1942.

STURMLAUFER, Estera: Born on April 3, 1908, in Gizalki, Russia. She was deported from Berlin on October 24, 1941, to the Łódź ghetto. She was deported from Łódź to Chełmno on May 4, 1942. She perished in Chełmno on May 4, 1942.

STUTZINSKI, Jenny: Born on September 27, 1883, in Friedrichshof. She was deported from Berlin on October 24, 1941, to the Łódź ghetto. She was deported from Łódź to Chełmno on May 4, 1942. She perished in Chełmno on May 4, 1942.

SULTAN, Hedwig: Born on April 19, 1886, in Strasburg. She was deported from Berlin on October 18, 1941, to the Łódź ghetto. She was deported from Łódź to Chełmno on May 8, 1942. She perished in Chełmno on May 8, 1942.

SURTH, Jakob: Born on July 5, 1877, in Brühl. He was deported from Cologne on October 22, 1941, to the Łódź ghetto. He was deported from Łódź to Chełmno during May 1942, where he perished.

SUSSKIND, Hedwig: Born on October 12, 1878, in Krotoszyn, Poland. She was deported from Berlin on October 18, 1941, to the Łódź ghetto. She was deported from Łódź to Chełmno on May 13, 1942. She perished in Chełmno on May 13, 1942.

SUSSMANN, Carla: Born on July 12, 1935, in Berlin. She was deported from Berlin on November 1, 1941, to the Łódź ghetto. She was deported from Łódź to Chełmno on May 9, 1942. She perished in Chełmno on May 9, 1942.

SWARSENSKY, Margarete: Born on May 20, 1889, in Berlin. She was deported from Berlin on November 1, 1941, to the Łódź ghetto. She was deported from Łódź to Chełmno on May 10, 1942. She perished in Chełmno on May 10, 1942.

SWIATLOWSKI, Fedora: Born on September 14, 1930, in Essen. She was expelled from Essen on October 28, 1938, to Zbąszyń, Poland. She was deported from the Łódź ghetto to Chełmno on June 30, 1944, where she perished.

SZAJNFELD, Martha: Born on May 8, 1922, in Hamburg. She was expelled from Hamburg on October 28, 1938, to Zbąszyń, Poland. She was deported from the Łódź ghetto to Chełmno on June 28, 1944, where she perished.

SZAMATULSKI, David: Born on January 21, 1899, in Pinne, Poland. He was deported from Berlin on November 1, 1941, to the Łódź ghetto. He was deported from Łódź to Chełmno on May 9, 1942. He perished in Chełmno on May 9, 1942.

SZIGELZKY, Werner: Born on November 28, 1920, in Barmen-Elberfeld. He was deported from Düsseldorf on October 27, 1941, to the Łódź ghetto. He was deported from Łódź to Chełmno during 1942, where he perished.

SZMULEWICZ, Luser: Born on December 21, 1900, in Piotrków, Poland. He lived in Essen. He was imprisoned in Dachau Concentration Camp from November 17, 1938, to January 31, 1939. He was deported from Düsseldorf on October 27, 1941, to the Łódź ghetto. He was deported from Łódź to Chełmno on May 3, 1942. He perished in Chełmno on May 4, 1942.

SZYCMAN, Adolf: Born on June 23, 1926, in Berlin. He emigrated from Berlin to Poland. He was deported from the Łódź ghetto to Chełmno on July 7, 1944, where he perished.

SZYDLOWSKI, Martin: Born on May 6, 1939, in Duisburg. He was deported from Düsseldorf on October 27, 1941, to the Łódź ghetto. He was deported from Łódź to Chełmno on May 15, 1942. He perished in Chełmno on May 16, 1942.

SZYKMAN, Rosa: Born on June 14, 1898, in Radautz. She emigrated from Hamburg to Poland. She was deported from the Łódź ghetto to Chełmno on June 23, 1944, where she perished.

SZYNDELMACHER, Gitla: Born on December 13, 1905, in Żarki, Poland. She was deported from Berlin on November 1, 1941, to the Łódź ghetto. She was deported from Łódź to Chełmno on May 9, 1942. She perished in Chełmno on May 9, 1942.

TALAN, Rika: Born on July 29, 1896, in Daugavpils. She was deported from Hamburg on October 25, 1941, to the Łódź ghetto. She was deported from Łódź to Chełmno on May 10, 1942, where she perished.

TANN, Meta: Born on February 8, 1882, in Stettin. She was deported from Berlin on November 1, 1941, to the Łódź ghetto. She was deported from Łódź to Chełmno on May 4, 1942. She perished in Chełmno on May 4, 1942.

TANNENWALD, Leonore: Born on October 17, 1870, in Stettin. She was deported from Berlin on October 18, 1941, to the Łódź ghetto. She was deported from Łódź to Chełmno on May 8, 1942. She perished in Chełmno on May 8, 1942.

TASSELKRAUT, Dorothea: Born on December 29, 1879, in Rogoźno, Poland. She was deported from Berlin on October 27–29, 1941, to the Łódź ghetto. She was deported from Łódź to Chełmno on May 4, 1942. She perished in Chełmno on May 4, 1942.

TAUBENSCHLAG, Gerhard: Born on May 29, 1913, in Berlin. He was deported from Berlin on October 27–29, 1941, to the Łódź ghetto. He was deported from Łódź to Chełmno on May 4, 1942. He perished in Chełmno on May 4, 1942.

TAUSK, Bertha: Born on June 13, 1872, in Murowana Goślina, Poland. She was deported from Berlin on October 24, 1941, to the Łódź ghetto. She was deported from Łódź to Chełmno on May 4, 1942. She perished in Chełmno on May 4, 1942.

TEICH-BIRKEN, Isaak: Born on July 3, 1886, in Sieniawa, Poland. He was deported from Berlin on October 18, 1941, to the Łódź ghetto. He was deported from Łódź to Chełmno on May 8, 1942. He perished in Chełmno on May 8, 1942.

TEICHER, Helene: Born on April 24, 1877, in Brochnia. She was deported from Berlin on November 1, 1941, to the Łódź ghetto. She was deported from Łódź to Chełmno on May 9, 1942, where she perished.

TEITELBAUM, Helene: Born on September 27, 1929, in Berlin. She was deported from Berlin on October 24, 1941, to the Łódź ghetto. She was deported from Łódź to Chełmno on May 6, 1942. She perished in Chełmno on May 6, 1942.

TELLER, Sara: Born on August 11, 1877, in Vandsburg. She was deported from Berlin on October 24, 1941, to the Łódź ghetto. She was

deported from Łódź to Chełmno on May 5, 1942. She perished in Chełmno on May 5, 1942.

TETTELES, Cilli: Born on September 7, 1869, in Brody, Poland. She was deported from Berlin on October 18, 1941, to the Łódź ghetto. She was deported from Łódź to Chełmno on May 8, 1942, where she perished.

TEUTSCH, Paula: Born on April 27, 1880, in Neustadt. She was deported from Berlin on November 1, 1941, to the Łódź ghetto. She was deported from Łódź to Chełmno on May 13, 1942. She perished in Chełmno on May 13, 1942.

THALMANN, Arthur: Born on September 28, 1878, in Bochum. He was deported from Düsseldorf on October 27, 1941, to the Łódź ghetto. He was deported from Łódź to Chełmno on May 6, 1942. He perished in Chełmno on May 7, 1942.

THIELE, Johanna: Born on November 21, 1889, in Neurode. She was deported from Berlin on November 1, 1941, to the Łódź ghetto. She was deported from Łódź to Chełmno on May 9, 1942, where she perished.

THON, Feigel: Born on December 25, 1876, in Wiepitz. She was deported from Hamburg on October 25, 1941, to the Łódź ghetto. She was deported from Łódź to Chełmno on May 10, 1942, where she perished.

TICHAUER, Cacilie: Born on September 8, 1874, in Peiskretscham. She was deported from Berlin on October 18, 1941, to the Łódź ghetto. She was deported from Łódź to Chełmno on September 12, 1942. She perished in Chełmno on September 12, 1942.

TOBIAS, Thekla: Born on December 21, 1882, in Oberwambach. She was deported from Cologne on October 22, 1941, to the Łódź ghetto. She was deported from Łódź to Chełmno during May 1942, where she perished.

TODTMANN, Fritze: Born on June 4, 1883, in Żnin, Poland. He was deported from Berlin on November 1, 1941, to the Łódź ghetto. He was deported from Łódź to Chełmno on May 13, 1942. He perished in Chełmno on May 13, 1942.

TÖRLITZ, Franziska: Born on January 13, 1874, in Strelitz. She was deported from Berlin on November 1, 1941, to the Łódź ghetto. She was deported from Łódź to Chełmno on May 9, 1942, where she perished.

TOLLER, Louis: Born on January 11, 1877, in Tuchel. He was deported from Berlin on October 24, 1941, to the Łódź ghetto. He was deported from Łódź to Chełmno on September 10, 1942. He perished in Chełmno on September 10, 1942.

TRACHTENBRODT, Kate: Born on August 21, 1879, in Preußisch Eylau. She was imprisoned in the *Sammelstelle Levetzowstrasse*, Berlin. She was deported from Berlin on October 24, 1941, to the Łódź ghetto. She was deported from Łódź to Chełmno on May 14, 1942. She perished in Chełmno on May 14, 1942.

TRÄGER, Jakob: Born on August 2, 1886, in Rzeszów, Poland. He was deported from Düsseldorf on October 27, 1941, to the Łódź ghetto. He was deported from Łódź to Chełmno on May 6, 1942. He perished in Chełmno on May 7, 1942.

TRAUB, Elsa: Born on October 20, 1883, in Harburg. She was deported from Cologne on October 30, 1941, to the Łódź ghetto. She was deported from Łódź to Chełmno during May 1942, where she perished.

TREITELFELD, Hermann: Born on July 26, 1893, in Flatow. He was deported from Berlin on November 1, 1941, to the Łódź ghetto. He was deported from Łódź to Chełmno on May 8, 1942. He perished in Chełmno on May 8, 1942.

TREUHERZ, Dora: Born on March 2, 1905, in Krojanke. She was deported from Berlin on October 18, 1941, to the Łódź ghetto. She was deported from Łódź to Chełmno on May 8, 1942. She perished in Chełmno on May 8, 1942.

TROMPETER, Feigel: Born on January 15, 1884, in Oświęcim, Poland. She was deported from Berlin on November 1, 1941, to the Łódź ghetto. She was deported from Łódź to Chełmno on May 13, 1942. She perished in Chełmno on May 13, 1942.

TROPLOWITZ, Rosa: Born on August 11, 1884, in Cologne. She was deported from Cologne on October 30, 1941, to the Łódź ghetto. She

was deported from Łódź to Chełmno during May 1942, where she perished.

TUCHOLSKI, Dorothea: Born on September 3, 1895, in Roden. She was imprisoned in Ravensbrück Concentration Camp. She was deported from Berlin on November 1, 1941, to the Łódź ghetto. She was deported from Łódź to Chełmno on May 9, 1942. She perished in Chełmno on May 9, 1942.

TUERK, Hulda: Born on February 2, 1876, in Schwetz. She was deported from Berlin on November 1, 1941, to the Łódź ghetto. She was deported from Łódź to Chełmno on May 9, 1942. She perished in Chełmno on May 9, 1942.

TUGENDHAT, Marta: Born on April 23, 1873, in Berlin. She was deported from Berlin on October 18, 1941, to the Łódź ghetto. She was deported from Łódź to Chełmno on May 12, 1942. She perished in Chełmno on May 12, 1942.

TWOROGER, Markus: Born on October 18, 1888, in Kobyla Góra, Poland. He was deported from Berlin on November 1, 1941, to the Łódź ghetto. He was deported from Łódź to Chełmno on May 12, 1942. He perished in Chełmno on May 12, 1942.

UCKO, Else: Born on December 27, 1874, in Berlin. She was deported from Berlin on October 18, 1941, to the Łódź ghetto. She was deported from Łódź to Chełmno on May 8, 1942, where she perished.

UFFENHEIMER, Ludwig: Born on March 17, 1889, in Bingen. He was deported from Cologne on October 30, 1941, to the Łódź ghetto. He was deported from Łódź to Chełmno during May 1942, where he perished.

ULLMANN, Julia: Born on February 13, 1888, in Mönchengladbach. She was deported from Düsseldorf on October 27, 1941, to the Łódź ghetto. She was deported from Łódź to Chełmno on May 6, 1942. She perished in Chełmno on May 7, 1942.

ULRICH, Henriette: Born on June 10, 1885, in Brühl. She was deported from Berlin on October 18, 1941, to the Łódź ghetto. She was deported from Łódź to Chełmno on May 8, 1942, where she perished.

UNGER, Emma: Born on May 13, 1910, in Liegnitz. She was imprisoned in the *Sammelstelle Levetzowstrasse*, Berlin. She was deported from Berlin on November 1, 1941, to the Łódź ghetto. She was deported from Łódź to Chełmno on May 4, 1942. She perished in Chełmno on May 4, 1942.

URAM, Fanny: Born on September 9, 1894, in Morochów, Poland. She was deported from Berlin on October 24, 1941, to the Łódź ghetto. She was deported from Łódź to Chełmno on May 4, 1942. She perished in Chełmno on May 4, 1942.

UTITZ, Jeanette: Born on December 24, 1881, in Oldersum. She was deported from Berlin on October 18, 1941, to the Łódź ghetto. She was deported from Łódź to Chełmno on May 8, 1942. She perished in Chełmno on May 8, 1942.

VALK, Sara: Born on February 12, 1885, in Emden. She was deported from Berlin on October 23, 1941, to the Łódź ghetto. She was deported from Łódź to Chełmno on May 13, 1942. She perished in Chełmno on May 13, 1942.

VASEN, Adelheid: Born on December 26, 1873, in Neus. She was deported from Düsseldorf on October 27, 1941, to the Łódź ghetto. She was deported from Łódź to Chełmno on May 6, 1942. She perished in Chełmno on May 7, 1942.

VEIT, Paula: Born on October 27, 1895, in Hausen. She was deported from Cologne on October 30, 1941, to the Łódź ghetto. She was deported from Łódź to Chełmno during May 1942, where she perished.

VERSTANDIG, Gerhard: Born on October 15, 1933, in Berlin. He was deported from Berlin on October 27–29, 1941, to the Łódź ghetto. He was deported from Łódź to Chełmno on May 4, 1942. He perished in Chełmno on May 4, 1942.

VISSER, Pauline: Born on August 1, 1873, in Emden. She was deported from Berlin on October 24, 1941, to the Łódź ghetto. She was deported from Łódź to Chełmno on May 12, 1942. She perished in Chełmno on May 12, 1942.

VÖLKE, Dora: Born on May 2, 1902, in Berlin. She was deported from Berlin on October 24, 1941, to the Łódź ghetto. She was deported from Łódź to Chełmno on May 4, 1942, where she perished.

VOGEL, Georg: Born on October 6, 1882, in Wollstein. He was deported from Berlin on October 18, 1941, to the Łódź ghetto. He was deported from Łódź to Chełmno on May 7, 1942. He perished in Chełmno on May 7, 1942.

VOGELSANG, Helga: Born on March 19, 1916, in Neus. She was deported from Düsseldorf on October 27, 1941, to the Łódź ghetto. She was deported from Łódź to Chełmno during September 1942, where she perished.

VOLLRATH, Marie: Born on October 12, 1884, in Stolp. She was deported from Berlin on November 1, 1941, to the Łódź ghetto. She was deported from Łódź to Chełmno on May 9, 1942. She perished in Chełmno on May 9, 1942.

VOOS, Gerson: Born on November 1, 1940, in Cologne. He was deported from Cologne on October 22, 1941, to the Łódź ghetto. He was deported from Łódź to Chełmno where he perished on May 10, 1942.

VORENBERG, Fanny: Born on April 22, 1889, in Kępno, Poland. She was deported from Cologne on October 22, 1941, to the Łódź ghetto. She was deported from Łódź to Chełmno during May 1942, where she perished.

VORREUTER, Eva: Born on September 27, 1913, in Berlin. She was deported from Berlin on October 24, 1941, to the Łódź ghetto. She was deported from Łódź to Chełmno on May 4, 1942. She perished in Chełmno on May 4, 1942.

VOSS, Erna: Born on February 18, 1923, in Embken. She was deported from Cologne on October 30, 1941, to the Łódź ghetto. She was deported from Łódź to Chełmno during May 1942, where she perished.

WACHS, Kathe: Born on April 2, 1904, in Poznań, Poland. She was deported from Berlin on October 24, 1941, to the Łódź ghetto. She was deported from Łódź to Chełmno during September 1942, where she perished.

WACHSNER, Sophie: Born on May 17, 1875, in Mysłowice, Poland. She was deported from Berlin on November 1, 1941, to the Łódź ghetto. She was deported from Łódź to Chełmno on May 12, 1942. She perished in Chełmno on May 12, 1942.

WACHTEL, Margarete: Born on January 6, 1911, in Berlin. She was deported from Berlin on November 1, 1941, to the Łódź ghetto. She was deported from Łódź to Chełmno on May 9, 1942. She perished in Chełmno on May 9, 1942.

WAGENER, Alfiede: Born on May 3, 1880, in Hamburg. She was deported from Hamburg on October 25, 1941, to the Łódź ghetto. She was deported from Łódź to Chełmno on April 20, 1942, where she perished.

WAGNER, Gertrud: Born on January 21, 1892, in Berlin. She was deported from Berlin on October 27–29, 1941, to the Łódź ghetto. She was deported from Łódź to Chełmno on September 11, 1942. She perished in Chełmno on September 11, 1942.

WAHRHAFTIG, Sophie: Born on January 26, 1920, in Berlin. She was expelled from Berlin on June 18, 1939, to Zbąszyń, Poland. She was deported from Berlin on October 27–29, 1941, to the Łódź ghetto. She was deported from Łódź to Chełmno on May 15, 1942. She perished in Chełmno on May 15, 1942.

WAJCER, Frida: Born on March 15, 1905, in Lubaczów, Poland. She was deported from Berlin on October 27–29, 1941, to the Łódź ghetto. She was deported from Łódź to Chełmno on May 12, 1942. She perished in Chełmno on May 12, 1942.

WAJCMAN, Cila: Born on May 5, 1914, in Berlin. She was deported from Berlin on October 27–29, 1941, to the Łódź ghetto. She was deported from Łódź to Chełmno on July 10, 1944. She perished in Chełmno on July 10, 1944.

WAKSBERG, Moszek: Born on October 12, 1886, in Wolanów, Poland. He was deported from Berlin on October 18, 1941, to the Łódź ghetto. He was deported from Łódź to Chełmno during September 1942, where he perished.

WALD, Rudolf: Born on November 1, 1905, in Stettin. He was deported from Berlin on November 1, 1941, to the Łódź ghetto. He was deported from Łódź to Chełmno on May 9, 1942, where he perished.

WALDE, Aron A. van der: Born on March 18, 1869, in Emden. He was deported from Berlin on October 24, 1941, to the Łódź ghetto. He was deported from Łódź to Chełmno on May 12, 1942. He perished in Chełmno on May 12, 1942.

WALDMANN, Henny: Born on October 3, 1884, in Rawicz, Poland. She was deported from Berlin on October 24, 1941, to the Łódź ghetto. She was deported from Łódź to Chełmno on May 15, 1942. She perished in Chełmno on May 15, 1942.

WALLACH, Abraham: Born on August 1, 1871, in Zaborów, Poland. He was deported from Berlin on November 1, 1941, to the Łódź ghetto. He was deported from Łódź to Chełmno on May 13, 1942. He perished in Chełmno on May 13, 1942.

WALLER, Elfriede: Born on March 13, 1891, in Cologne. She was deported from Hamburg on October 25, 1941, to the Łódź ghetto. She was deported from Łódź to Chełmno on May 4, 1942, where she perished.

WALTER, Erna: Born on October 4, 1900, in Berlin. She was deported from Berlin on October 18, 1941, to the Łódź ghetto. She was deported from Łódź to Chełmno on May 8, 1942. She perished in Chełmno on May 8, 1942.

WALZER, Henny: Born on June 10, 1899, in Kassel. She was deported from Hamburg on October 25, 1941, to the Łódź ghetto. She was deported from Łódź to Chełmno on May 15, 1942, where she perished.

WANGENHEIM, Bertha: Born on October 14, 1910, in Norden. She was deported from Cologne on October 30, 1941, to the Łódź ghetto. She was deported from Łódź to Chełmno where she perished on June 26, 1944.

WARSZAWSKI, Judes: Born on June 20, 1885. She was expelled from Zwickau to Poland. She was deported from the Łódź ghetto to Chełmno on September 11, 1942, where she perished.

WARTENBERGER, Ernestine: Born on July 14, 1878, in Berlin. She was deported from Berlin on October 24, 1941, to the Łódź ghetto. She was deported from Łódź to Chełmno on May 4, 1942. She perished in Chełmno on May 4, 1942.

WEBER, Johanna: Born on July 1, 1881, in Berlin. She was deported from Berlin on October 18, 1941, to the Łódź ghetto. She was deported from Łódź to Chełmno on May 8, 1942, where she perished.

WECHSELMANN, Salomon: Born on August 1879, in Berlin. He was deported from Berlin on October 24, 1941, to the Łódź ghetto. He was deported from Łódź to Chełmno on May 14, 1942. He perished in Chełmno on May 14, 1942.

WEGLEIN, Gertrud: Born on October 25, 1896, in Berlin. She was deported from Berlin on November 1, 1941, to the Łódź ghetto. She was deported from Łódź to Chełmno on May 7, 1942. She perished in Chełmno on May 7, 1942.

WEIGERT, Clara: Born on January 20, 1872, in Berlin. She was deported from Berlin on November 1, 1941, to the Łódź ghetto. She was deported from Łódź to Chełmno on May 9, 1942. She perished in Chełmno on May 9, 1942.

WEIL, Arnold: Born on August 31, 1929, in Cologne. He was deported from Cologne on October 30, 1941, to the Łódź ghetto. He was deported from Łódź to Chełmno where he perished on July 7, 1944.

WEILE, Ida: Born on April 3, 1872, in Löwen. She was deported from Berlin on November 1, 1941, to the Łódź ghetto. She was deported from Łódź to Chełmno on May 9, 1942. She perished in Chełmno on May 9, 1942.

WEILER, Irmgard: Born on December 4, 1907, in Bonn. She was deported from Düsseldorf on October 27, 1941, to the Łódź ghetto. She was deported from Łódź to Chełmno during September 1942, where she perished.

WEIMANN, Helene: Born on September 1, 1875, in Aachen. She was deported from Cologne on October 22, 1941, to the Łódź ghetto. She was deported from Łódź to Chełmno during May 1942, where she perished.

WEINBACH, Alfred: Born on June 25, 1885, in Vienna, Austria. He emigrated from Leer to Austria. He was deported from Vienna, on November 2, 1942, to the Łódź ghetto. He was deported from Łódź to Chełmno on May 20, 1942, where he perished.

WEINBAUM, Arno: Born on July 5, 1885, in Gołdap, Poland. He was deported from Berlin on October 18, 1941, to the Łódź ghetto. He was deported from Łódź to Chełmno on September 11, 1942. He perished in Chełmno on September 11, 1942.

WEINBERG, Fritz: Born on December 30, 1880, in Essen. He was deported from Düsseldorf on October 27, 1941, to the Łódź ghetto. He was deported from Łódź to Chełmno on May 7, 1942. He perished in Chełmno on May 8, 1942.

WEINER, Berta: Born on August 20, 1900, in Tarnów, Poland. She was deported from Berlin on October 27–29, 1941, to the Łódź ghetto. She was deported from Łódź to Chełmno on May 4, 1942. She perished in Chełmno on May 4, 1942.

WEINLAUB, Margarete: Born on January 27, 1889, in Berlin. She was deported from Berlin on November 1, 1941, to the Łódź ghetto. She was deported from Łódź to Chełmno on May 8, 1942, where she perished.

WEINSCHENK, Ida: Born on January 24, 1882, in Neunkirchen. She was deported from Berlin on October 18, 1941, to the Łódź ghetto. She was deported from Łódź to Chełmno on May 8, 1942. She perished in Chełmno on May 8, 1942.

WEINTRAUB, Leja: Born on September 29, 1885, in Podlipie, Poland. She was deported from Berlin on October 27–29, 1941, to the Łódź ghetto. She was deported from Łódź to Chełmno on September 12, 1942. She perished in Chełmno on September 12, 1942.

WEISENBERG, Ida: Born on December 10, 1910, in Berlin. She was deported from Berlin on October 24, 1941, to the Łódź ghetto. She was deported from Łódź to Chełmno during September 1942, where she perished.

WEISNER, Luise: Born on April 29, 1893, in Königsfeld. She was deported from Düsseldorf on October 27, 1941, to the Łódź ghetto. She

was deported from Łódź to Chełmno on May 11, 1942. She perished in Chełmno on May 12, 1942.

WEISS, Gertrud: Born on November 27, 1898, in Schönsee. She was deported from Berlin on October 27–29, 1941, to the Łódź ghetto. She was deported from Łódź to Chełmno on July 10, 1944. She perished in Chełmno on July 10, 1944.

WEISSBROD, Margot: Born on May 9, 1922, in Berlin. She was deported from Berlin on October 27–29, 1941, to the Łódź ghetto. She was deported from Łódź to Chełmno on May 5, 1942. She perished in Chełmno on May 5, 1942.

WEISSFELDT, Paula: Born on December 3, 1884, in Emmereich. She was deported from Düsseldorf on October 27, 1941, to the Łódź ghetto. She was deported from Łódź to Chełmno on May 6, 1942. She perished in Chełmno on May 7, 1942.

WELTMANN, Anna: Born on January 28, 1902, in Czyżów Szlachecki, Poland. She was deported from Berlin on October 18, 1941, to the Łódź ghetto. She was deported from Łódź to Chełmno on May 8, 1942. She perished in Chełmno on May 8, 1942.

WELZER, Else: Born on June 15, 1900, in Tyrawa Wołoska, Poland. She was deported from Berlin on October 24, 1941, to the Łódź ghetto. She was deported from Łódź to Chełmno on July 3, 1944. She perished in Chełmno on July 3, 1944.

WENDRINER, Paula: Born on May 2, 1885, in Stettin. She was deported from Berlin on October 24, 1941, to the Łódź ghetto. She was deported from Łódź to Chełmno on September 12, 1942. She perished in Chełmno on September 12, 1942.

WERDESHEIM, Marjem: Born on August 28, 1904, in Kolbuszowa. She was deported from Berlin on November 1, 1941, to the Łódź ghetto. She was deported from Łódź to Chełmno on May 9, 1942. She perished in Chełmno on May 9, 1942.

WERNER, Laura: Born on August 18, 1887, in Haynau. She was deported from Berlin on October 18, 1941, to the Łódź ghetto. She was deported from Łódź to Chełmno on May 8, 1942. She perished in Chełmno on May 8, 1942.

WERTHEIM, Kurt: Born on October 24, 1886, in Berlin. He was deported from Berlin on October 24, 1941, to the Łódź ghetto. He was deported from Łódź to Chełmno on May 4, 1942, where he perished.

WERTHEIMER, Anna: Born on December 3, 1876, in Wolfhagen. She was deported from Cologne on October 22, 1941, to the Łódź ghetto. She was deported from Łódź to Chełmno during May 1942, where she perished.

WESCHE, Otto: Born on June 10, 1879, in Berlin. He was deported from Berlin on October 27 -29, 1941, to the Łódź ghetto. He was deported from Łódź to Chełmno on May 4, 1942. He perished in Chełmno on May 4, 1942.

WESTFELD, Elisabeth: Born on December 30, 1898, in Hamburg. She was deported from Hamburg on October 25, 1941, to the Łódź ghetto. She was deported from Łódź to Chełmno on September 10, 1942, where she perished.

WESTHEIMER, Karl: Born on February 8, 1880, in Ottweiler. He was deported from Cologne on October 22, 1941, to the Łódź ghetto. He was deported from Łódź to Chełmno during May 1942, where he perished.

WESTPHAL, Erna: Born on September 27, 1901, in Berlin. She was deported from Berlin on October 24, 1941, to the Łódź ghetto. She was deported from Łódź to Chełmno on September 12, 1942. She perished in Chełmno on September 12, 1942.

WEYL, Elise: Born on April 14, 1874, in Barmen-Elberfeld. She was deported from Düsseldorf on October 27, 1941, to the Łódź ghetto. She was deported from Łódź to Chełmno on May 7, 1942. She perished in Chełmno on May 8, 1942.

WIDMANN, Gabriele: Born on July 9, 1929, in Liegnitz. She was imprisoned in the *Sammelstelle Levetzowstrasse*, Berlin. She was deported from Berlin on October 18, 1941, to the Łódź ghetto. She was deported from Łódź to Chełmno on May 8, 1942. She perished in Chełmno on May 8, 1942.

WIENER, Cacilie: Born on June 13, 1881, in Rabka-Zdrój, Poland. She was deported from Berlin on October 27–29, 1941, to the Łódź ghetto.

She was deported from Łódź to Chełmno on May 6, 1942, where she perished.

WIESENFELD, Isaak: Born on December 22, 1903, in Tyczyn, Poland. He was expelled from Leipzig to Poland on October 28, 1938, to Poland. He was deported from the Łódź ghetto to Chełmno on April 13, 1942, where he perished.

WIESENTHAL, Margarete: Born on December 6, 1888, in Bolzenburg. She was deported from Berlin on October 27–29, 1941, to the Łódź ghetto. She was deported from Łódź to Chełmno on May 5, 1942. She perished in Chełmno on May 5, 1942.

WIESNER, Feige: Born on June 26, 1878, in Turka, Poland. She was deported from Berlin on October 24, 1941, to the Łódź ghetto. She was deported from Łódź to Chełmno during September 1942, where she perished.

WIESZANSKY, Lina: Born on December 14, 1887, in Kaukehmen. She was deported from Berlin on October 18, 1941, to the Łódź ghetto. She was deported from Łódź to Chełmno on May 8, 1942, where she perished.

WIHL, Friedrich: Born on July 20, 1899, in Krefeld. He was deported from Düsseldorf on October 27, 1941, to the Łódź ghetto. He was deported from Łódź to Chełmno on May 7, 1942. He perished in Chełmno on May 8, 1942.

WILK, Erich: Born on August 8, 1885, in Potsdam. He was deported from Berlin on November 1, 1941, to the Łódź ghetto. He was deported from Łódź to Chełmno on May 8, 1942. He perished in Chełmno on May 8, 1942.

WILL, Heinz: Born on December 21, 1934, in Berlin. He was deported from Berlin on October 27 -29, 1941, to the Łódź ghetto. He was deported from Łódź to Chełmno on September 4, 1942. He perished in Chełmno on September 4, 1942.

WILLDORF, Marie: Born on August 11, 1887, in Berlin. She was deported from Berlin on October 24, 1941, to the Łódź ghetto. She was deported from Łódź to Chełmno on May 4, 1942. She perished in Chełmno on May 4, 1942.

WILLNER, Hersch: Born on August 12, 1879, in Mława, Poland. He was deported from Cologne on October 30, 1941, to the Łódź ghetto. He was deported from Łódź to Chełmno during May 1942, where he perished.

WINDMÜLLER, Adolf: Born on May 5, 1880, in Emden. He was imprisoned in Sachsenhausen Concentration Camp from November 1938, to December 15, 1938. He was deported from Berlin on October 18, 1941, to the Łódź ghetto. He was deported from Łódź to Chełmno on May 8, 1942. He perished in Chełmno on May 8, 1942.

WINTER, Adele: Born on December 17, 1885, in Gelsenkirchen. She was deported from Düsseldorf on October 27, 1941, to the Łódź ghetto. She was deported from Łódź to Chełmno on May 7, 1942. She perished in Chełmno on May 8, 1942.

WISCH, Siegfried: Born on March 24, 1881, in Poznań, Poland. He was deported from Berlin on October 24, 1941, to the Łódź ghetto. He was deported from Łódź to Chełmno on May 4, 1942. He perished in Chełmno on May 4, 1942.

WITTENBERG, Adolf: Born on March 6, 1888, in Lubasz, Poland. He was deported from Berlin on October 29, 1941, to the Łódź ghetto. He was deported from Łódź to Chełmno on June 26, 1944. He perished in Chełmno on June 26, 1944.

WITTKOWSKI, Emma: Born on December 13, 1883, in Gostyń, Poland. She was deported from Berlin on November 1, 1941, to the Łódź ghetto. She was deported from Łódź to Chełmno on May 6, 1942. She perished in Chełmno on May 6, 1942.

WOHL, Ella: Born on September 21, 1890, in Wilhelmshaven. She was deported from Hamburg on October 25, 1941, to the Łódź ghetto. She was deported from Łódź to Chełmno on May 15, 1942, where she perished.

WOHLFELD, Max: Born on October 30, 1882, in Lubenia, Poland. He was deported from Berlin on October 18, 1941, to the Łódź ghetto. He was deported from Łódź to Chełmno on May 8, 1942. He perished in Chełmno on May 8, 1942.

WOLF, Arthur: Born on July 25, 1890, in Bad Sobernheim. He was deported from Berlin on November 1, 1941, to the Łódź ghetto. He was deported from Łódź to Chełmno on May 8, 1942. He perished in Chełmno on May 8, 1942.

WOLFF, Albert: Born on August 27, 1899, in Strasburg. He was deported from Berlin on October 24, 1941, to the Łódź ghetto. He was deported from Łódź to Chełmno on May 4, 1942. He perished in Chełmno on May 4, 1942.

WOLFFS, Betty: Born on November 19, 1877, in Aurich. She was deported from Berlin on October 24, 1941, to the Łódź ghetto. She was deported from Łódź to Chełmno on September 7, 1942. She perished in Chełmno on September 7, 1942.

WOLFFSKY, Martha: Born on February 3, 1874, in Laurahütte, Poland. She was deported from Berlin on October 24, 1941, to the Łódź ghetto. She was deported from Łódź to Chełmno on September 7, 1942. She perished in Chełmno on September 7, 1942.

WOLFRAM, Clara: Born on December 7, 1878, in Neustettin. She was deported from Berlin on October 18, 1941, to the Łódź ghetto. She was deported from Łódź to Chełmno on May 8, 1942, where she perished.

WOLFSOHN, Johanna: Born on July 11, 1878, in Piassutten. She was deported from Berlin on October 24, 1941, to the Łódź ghetto. She was deported from Łódź to Chełmno on May 4, 1942. She perished in Chełmno on May 4, 1942.

WOLKOMIRSKY, Scheina: Born on October 11, 1879, in Nowogrudok, Russia. She was deported from Berlin on November 1, 1941, to the Łódź ghetto. She was deported from Łódź to Chełmno on May 9, 1942. She perished in Chełmno on May 9, 1942.

WOLKOWITSCH, Isaak: Born on January 15, 1918, in Barmen-Elberfeld. He was expelled from Wuppertal on October 28, 1938, to Zbąszyń, Poland. He was deported from the Pabiance ghetto during May 1942, to the Łódź ghetto. He was deported from Łódź to Chełmno on July 12, 1944, where he perished.

WOLLENBERG, Else: Born on January 16, 1902, in Konstanz. She was deported from Berlin on October 18, 1941, to the Łódź ghetto. She was deported from Łódź to Chełmno on May 8, 1942. She perished in Chełmno on May 8, 1942.

WOLLHEIM, Eva: Born on July 10, 1882, in Mrocza, Poland. She was deported from Berlin on November 1, 1941, to the Łódź ghetto. She was deported from Łódź to Chełmno on May 8, 1942. She perished in Chełmno on May 8, 1942.

WOLLMANN, Meta: Born on May 20, 1899, in Borek, Poland. She was deported from Berlin on October 18, 1941, to the Łódź ghetto. She was deported from Łódź to Chełmno on May 8, 1942. She perished in Chełmno on May 8, 1942.

WOLLSTEIN, Bertha: Born on September 21, 1881, in Berlin. She was deported from Berlin on November 1, 1941, to the Łódź ghetto. She was deported from Łódź to Chełmno on May 8, 1942. She perished in Chełmno on May 8, 1942.

WOLLSTEINER, Berta: Born on January 7, 1881, in Czarnków, Poland. She was deported from Berlin on October 18, 1941, to the Łódź ghetto. She was deported from Łódź to Chełmno on May 8, 1942, where she perished.

WONGLESZEWSKI, Jakob: Born on December 20, 1933, in Cologne. He was deported from Cologne on October 30, 1941, to the Łódź ghetto. He was deported from Łódź to Chełmno during September 1942, where he perished.

WONGROWITZ, Adolfine: Born on July 10, 1888, in Wronki, Poland. She was deported from Berlin on November 1, 1941, to the Łódź ghetto. She was deported from Łódź to Chełmno on May 9, 1942. She perished in Chełmno on May 9, 1942.

WORECZEK, Ilse: Born on September 7, 1907, in Altenburg. She was deported from Berlin on October 27–29, 1941, to the Łódź ghetto. She was deported from Łódź to Chełmno on May 5, 1942, where she perished.

WORTMANN, Elise: Born on July 28, 1882, in Breslau. She was deported from Berlin on October 18, 1941, to the Łódź ghetto. She was deported from Łódź to Chełmno during September 1942, where she perished.

WRESCHNER, Rosalie: Born on May 11, 1873, in Rogoźno, Poland. She was deported from Berlin on October 18, 1941, to the Łódź ghetto. She was deported from Łódź to Chełmno on May 8, 1942. She perished in Chełmno on May 8, 1942.

WRONKER, Frieda: Born on May 21, 1901, in Essen. She was deported from Düsseldorf on October 27, 1941, to the Łódź ghetto. She was deported from Łódź to Chełmno on May 7, 1942. She perished in Chełmno on May 8, 1942.

WRZESINSKI, Kathe: Born on December 21, 1894, in Danzig. She was deported from Berlin on October 27–29, 1941, to the Łódź ghetto. She was deported from Łódź to Chełmno on May 4, 1942. She perished in Chełmno on May 4, 1942.

WÜRTENBERG, Ella: Born on December 19, 1910, in Heinrichswalde. She was deported from Berlin on October 18, 1941, to the Łódź ghetto. She was deported from Łódź to Chełmno on February 8, 1943, where she perished.

WÜRZBURGER, Berta: Born on January 26, 1896, in Binau. She was deported from Düsseldorf on October 27, 1941, to the Łódź ghetto. She was deported from Łódź to Chełmno on May 7, 1942. She perished in Chełmno on May 8, 1942.

WULF, Alfred: Born on July 17, 1897, in Cologne. He was deported from Cologne on October 30, 1941, to the Łódź ghetto. He was deported from Łódź to Chełmno during September 1942, where he perished.

WUNDERLICH, Margarethe: Born on October 8, 1894, in Neustettin. She was deported from Hamburg on October 25, 1941, to the Łódź ghetto. She was deported from Łódź to Chełmno on May 10, 1942, where she perished.

WUNDERMACHER, Lotte: Born on January 1, 1903, in Berlin. She was deported from Berlin on November 1, 1941, to the Łódź ghetto. She was deported from Łódź to Chełmno on September 12, 1942. She perished in Chełmno on September 12, 1942.

WUNDERMANN, Anna: Born on December 14, 1906, in Słomniki, Poland. She was deported from Düsseldorf on October 27, 1941, to the Łódź ghetto. She was deported from Łódź to Chełmno during September 1942, where she perished.

WUNSCH, Margarethe: Born on September 15, 1887, in Berlin. She was deported from Berlin on October 24, 1941, to the Łódź ghetto. She was deported from Łódź to Chełmno on May 14, 1942. She perished in Chełmno on May 14, 1942.

WURMANN, Margarete: Born on June 13, 1879, in Schivelbein. She was deported from Berlin on October 18, 1941, to the Łódź ghetto. She was deported from Łódź to Chełmno on May 8, 1942, where she perished.

WYK, Isaac: Born on March 22, 1868, in Emden. He was deported from Berlin on October 24, 1941, to the Łódź ghetto. He was deported from Łódź to Chełmno on May 12, 1942. He perished in Chełmno on May 12, 1942.

ZACHARIAS, Dina: Born on May 18, 1899, in Langenschwalbach. She was deported from Düsseldorf on October 27, 1941, to the Łódź ghetto. She was deported from Łódź to Chełmno on May 7, 1942. She perished in Chełmno on May 8, 1942.

ZACK, Amalie: Born on February 22, 1891, in Heddesheim. She was deported from Cologne on October 30, 1941, to the Łódź ghetto. She was deported from Łódź to Chełmno during May 1942, where she perished.

ZANDER, Martha: Born on May 4, 1880, in Berlin. She was deported from Berlin on October 27–29, 1941, to the Łódź ghetto. She was deported from Łódź to Chełmno on September 12, 1942. She perished in Chełmno on September 12, 1942.

ZANDERS, Albert: Born on July 5, 1881, in Dülken. He was deported from Cologne on October 30, 1941, to the Łódź ghetto. He was deported from Łódź to Chełmno during May 1942, where he perished.

ZANGENBERG, Herta: Born on March 7, 1895, in Berlin. She was deported from Berlin on October 24, 1941, to the Łódź ghetto. She was

deported from Łódź to Chełmno on May 4, 1942. She perished in Chełmno on May 4, 1942.

ZAUDERER, Brucha: Born on May 3, 1908, in Krechowice, Poland. She was deported from Düsseldorf on October 27, 1941, to the Łódź ghetto. She was deported from Łódź to Chełmno on May 7, 1942. She perished in Chełmno on May 8, 1942.

ZEIDLER, Frieda: Born on May 6, 1895, in Deutsch Lissa. She was deported from Düsseldorf on October 27, 1941, to the Łódź ghetto. She was deported from Łódź to Chełmno on May 7, 1942. She perished in Chełmno on May 8, 1942.

ZEIMANN, Benno: Born on May 7, 1902, in Gniezno, Poland. He was deported from Berlin on October 24, 1941, to the Łódź ghetto. He was deported from Łódź to Chełmno on May 5, 1942. He perished in Chełmno on May 5, 1942.

ZELKOWICZ, Maria: Born on July 3, 1920, in Forst. She was expelled from Forst on October 28, 1938, to Zbąszyń, Poland. She was deported from the Łódź ghetto to Chełmno on March 30, 1942, where she perished.

ZELLERMAYER, David: Born on February 5, 1884, in Alt Fratautz. He was deported from Berlin on October 27–29, 1941, to the Łódź ghetto. He was deported from Łódź to Chełmno on May 5, 1942. He perished in Chełmno on May 5, 1942.

ZIEGLER, Herta: Born on June 14, 1893, in Stargard. She was deported from Berlin on November 1, 1941, to the Łódź ghetto. She was deported from Łódź to Chełmno on May 8, 1942. She perished in Chełmno on May 8, 1942.

ZIEL, Selma: Born on December 22, 1877, in Potsdam. She was deported from Berlin on October 24, 1941, to the Łódź ghetto. She was deported from Łódź to Chełmno on May 4, 1942. She perished in Chełmno on May 4, 1942.

ZILBERMANN, Gitla: Born on September 13, 1885, in Konin. She emigrated from Danzig to Poland. She was deported from the Łódź ghetto to Chełmno, where she perished on September 10, 1942.

ZILVERSMIT, Hedwig: Born on April 25, 1895, in Schwerte. She was deported from Cologne on October 30, 1941, to the Łódź ghetto. She was deported from Łódź to Chełmno during May 1942, where she perished.

ZIMBLER, Gittel: Born on December 17, 1875, in Czernowitz, Rumania. She was deported from Berlin on November 1, 1941, to the Łódź ghetto. She was deported from Łódź to Chełmno on May 9, 1942. She perished in Chełmno on May 9, 1942.

ZIMBLER-FIEDLER, Malka: Born on October 11, 1877, in Czernowitz, Rumania. She was deported from Berlin on November 1, 1941, to the Łódź ghetto. She was deported from Łódź to Chełmno on May 9, 1942. She perished in Chełmno on May 9, 1942.

ZIMMERMANN, Elsa: Born on July 26, 1890, in Malstatt. She was deported from Berlin on October 24, 1941, to the Łódź ghetto. She was deported from Łódź to Chełmno on May 4, 1942. She perished in Chełmno on May 4, 1942.

ZINN, Erna: Born on January 28, 1889, in Elsdorf. She was deported from Cologne on October 30, 1941, to the Łódź ghetto. She was deported from Łódź to Chełmno during May 1942, where she perished.

ZITRIN, Charlotte: Born on March 21, 1879, in Bielsko-Biała, Poland. She was deported from Berlin on October 18, 1941, to the Łódź ghetto. She was deported from Łódź to Chełmno on May 4, 1942, where she perished.

ZLOTNICKI, Ida: Born on March 22, 1870, in Schlochau. She was deported from Berlin on October 27–29, 1941, to the Łódź ghetto. She was deported from Łódź to Chełmno on May 5, 1942. She perished in Chełmno on May 5, 1942.

ZLOTNIK, Joseph: Born on August 27, 1938, in Hamburg. He was deported from Hamburg on October 25, 1941, to the Łódź ghetto. He was deported from Łódź to Chełmno on March 30, 1942, where he perished.

ZUCKERMANN, Heinrich: Born on May 8, 1876, in Poznań, Poland. He was deported from Berlin on October 27–29, 1941, to the Łódź

ghetto. He was deported from Łódź to Chełmno on May 4, 1942. He perished in Chełmno on May 4, 1942.

ZURNDORFER, Elisabeth: Born on April 18, 1901, in Pirmasens. She was deported from Düsseldorf on October 27, 1941, to the Łódź ghetto. She was deported from Łódź to Chełmno on May 7, 1942. She perished in Chełmno on May 8, 1942.

ZWEIG, Wita: Born on June 23, 1872, in Peczenizyn. She was deported from Berlin on October 24, 1941, to the Łódź ghetto. She was deported from Łódź to Chełmno on May 4, 1942. She perished in Chełmno on May 4, 1942.

ZYDOWER, Siegfried: Born on June 30, 1930, in Berlin. He was deported from Berlin on October 18, 1941, to the Łódź ghetto. He was deported from Łódź to Chełmno on March 5, 1942. He perished in Chełmno on March 5, 1942.

ZYGELMAN, Abram: Born on June 1, 1889, in Częstochowa, Poland. He was expelled from Hamburg on October 28, 1938, to Zbąszyń, Poland. He was imprisoned from October 28, 1938, to the summer of 1939, in the Zbąszyń Internment Camp. He was deported from the Łódź ghetto to Chełmno, where he perished.

ZYSKIND, Sala: Born on November 11, 1924, in Berlin. She was deported from Berlin on November 1, 1941, to the Łódź ghetto. She was deported from Łódź to Chełmno on March 4, 1942, where she perished.

Chapter XII
The Perpetrators
Sonderkommando Kulmhof Garrison

This chapter contains the information mostly compiled from the work Artur Hojan started in 2011. The list of the *Kulmhof* garrison was incomplete and has been added to from my own research in writing this book. In addition to the work Artur undertook based on the findings of Judge Władysław Bednarz investigations, the statements of Walter Piller and Hermann Gielow, a number of publications have been consulted; these include *Chełmno Witnesses Speak*, Patrick Montague's book, *Chełmno and the Holocaust*, the book by French L. MacLean, *The Camp Men*, Claude Lanzmann's *The Shoah*, and *Those Were the Days*, by Klee, Dressen and Riess. Also consulted were various accounts in the National Archives in Kew, the archives of the Wiener Library in London, and NARA in Washington DC.

Whilst a complete listing of personnel may never be known, this is one of the most comprehensive lists provided to date. Further works by future authors may even include more names. We hope that our list of names and biographical details, where known, helps other researchers in their efforts. Of course it has to be stressed that there may be some errors with this listing, for example: similar sounding names, mistakes made by witnesses, and so on. Whilst a great deal of care has been taken, we apologize in advance for any errors made.

Background

The Chełmno death camp came under the direct command of *SS-Obergruppenführer* Wilhelm Koppe, who was born at Hildesheim on June 15, 1896. He served as the Higher SS and Police Leader for the *Warthe*, until November 9, 1943, when he took over from Friedrich-Wilhelm Krüger, as Higher SS and Police Leader "*Ost*," the highest-ranking SS and Police Officer in the *Generalgouvernement*.

Koppe worked closely with Arthur Greiser, the *Gauleiter* of the *Warthegau*, and Greiser continually meddled in the affairs of Chełmno death camp, particularly in relation to the Łódź Ghetto, which was managed by Hans Biebow.

The first small group that arrived in Chełmno to take charge of the establishment of the camp were *SS* members from the *Sicherheitspolizei*, some of whom had been involved in the T_4 extermination programme, aimed at the psychologically impaired and physically handicapped people in the *Warthegau* and East Prussia. In addition, around 100 men came from one of the *Schutzpolizei* battalion's stationed in Łódź.

All the commanding posts were held by *SS*-men from the *Sicherheitspolizei*. The members of the *Schutzpolizei* were divided into three sub-units called *Kommando's*. These were the "Transport *Kommando*", the "Palace *Kommando*" and the "Forest *Kommando*". The first of the sub-units was responsible for guarding the deported prisoners from the railway station in the village of Powiercie as well as those brought directly to Chełmno. The "Palace *Kommando*" guarded the victims in the grounds of the palace. The "Forest *Kommando*" was responsible for sentry duty around the Forest Camp grounds in the Rzuchów forest. They were also responsible for burying, and later burning the corpses. They additionally oversaw the covering up of all traces of the crimes committed there.

Walter Piller testified on June 15, 1945, whilst in Russian captivity about the conditions of the garrison at Chełmno:

> All the members of the *SS-Sonderkommando* received supplies in accordance with basic principles. Dinner was prepared in the camp kitchen and every member received two additional portions (for the day and night) from the canteen. These were the highest standards among all German military units. Although I cannot say exactly how many grams of bread, butter, sausage, honey, marmalade and other products they received, the amounts were certainly satisfactory.
>
> Apart from this, every member of the unit received a bottle of vodka every 10 days and 10 cigarettes a day. Apart from the regular salary, every 15 days everyone received an additional payment from the administrative officer, *Polizei-Sekretär* and *SS-Sturmscharführer* Görlich. *SS-Hauptsturmführer* Bothmann would get 18 *RM* (*Reichsmark*) a day. All

the other *SS* members along with *Polizei-Leutnant* Burmeister, and *Polizeimeister* Lenz received 15 *RM* a day, while the remaining officers of the reserves -12 *RM* a day.

In addition each of them received a packet of washing powder and a piece of soap. Everybody had to pay for cigarettes in the canteen managed by *SS-Hauptscharführer* Erwin Schmidt. The money for special additional payments came from the *Reich* Governor's Office in Poznań. Also general maintenance costs were covered by the district self-government offices (*Gauselbstverwaltung*).

In addition, *SS-Hauptsturmführer* Bothmann received an extra supply of vodka and cigarettes to be available to offer guests, such as officers sent by *Gauleiter* Greiser or for Greiser himself should he have chosen to come. When Chełmno was visited by the *Gestapo*, the commanding officer from the *Gestapo* headquarters in Łódź, Dr. Bradfisch, the *Oberregierungsrat* and *SS-Obersturmbannführer* or someone of his administration, then supplies were also taken from the allotments managed by *SS-Scharführer* Burmeister. As far as I know, no extra money was paid for shooting Jews.

However, *SS-Hauptscharführer* Runge received an extra bottle of vodka after he completed the two crematoriums. Also the drivers who transported ashes of the cremated Jews at night back and forth from the River Ner got an additional bottle of vodka. I cannot recall who these drivers were. The unit paid for the accommodations, the delivery and the laundering of bedclothes. The staff only had to pay the Polish staff for cleaning the quarters and washing undergarments. As far as I know, each member of the unit employed a Polish woman for this work. At first, five or more police officers were accommodated in one house; later all lived in one larger house in order to be able to react quickly whenever it was necessary.[167]

Rozalia Peham, who married *Schutzpolizei Rottwachtmeister* Josef Peham, who became a member of *Sonderkommando Kulmhof*, testified before Judge Władysław Bednarz in Koło, on June 26, 1945, and she recalled that:

> Among the members of the *Sonderkommando Kulmhof*, I knew Gustav Laabs (a chauffeur of the "black automobile"), Richter, Burmeister, Hans Rose and Gottlieb Gassman, who came from Stuttgart and escaped to Switzerland. He was Hans Messingschlager's chauffeur, also a chauffeur Hert, who came from Łódź.

---

[167] *Chełmno Witnesses Speak*, Konin – Łódź 2004, pp. 179–180.

When my husband worked in Chełmno he received a wage of 150 German Marks monthly and 10–13 German Marks a day as *Schweige-Geld*.[168] From my husband I received a gold watch, a gold bracelet and a gold ring with some stone. These things came from Chełmno. He did not pay anything to anybody for them.

On the following day, June 27, 1945, in Koło, Rozalia Peham provided another testimony before Judge Władysław Bednarz:

> I would like to point out that almost all members of the *Sonderkommando* operating in Chełmno in 1942 and at the beginning of 1943 were killed. Only seven of them returned to Chełmno, namely Bothmann, Richter, Görlich, Laabs, Schmidt, Burmeister and one more whose name I cannot remember. Several other members of the *SS-Sonderkommando* "Bothmann" also survived. There were those that got wounded and did not return to the front or were transferred to other units, not as vulnerable as the *SS-Sonderkommando* "Bothmann". Plate died together with my husband. Before being transferred to Chełmno, my husband did service in Łódź. Before the transfer, he and his colleagues were told they would go to Chełmno for *"Einsatz"* (Operation). After their arrival, Bothmann told them they would have the honour to eliminate the enemies.

Chełmno Death Camp—Commandants Listed in Chronological Order

LANGE, Herbert
November 1941–February 1942

Born on September 29, 1909, in Menzlin, Pomerania, Germany: He studied Law but failed to obtain a degree and joined the Nazi Party on May 1, 1932 (Party Number 1159583) and in August of the same year joined the *SA*. The following year on March 1, 1933, he joined the *SS* (*SS* Number 93501). He subsequently joined the police force, becoming a *Kriminalkommissar*. During 1939, Lange was promoted to the rank of *SS-Untersturmführer*, and in August of the same year he went to Frankfurt an der Oder, which was the assembly point for *Einsatzgruppe VI* commanded by *SS-Oberführer* Erich Naumann, prior to the invasion of Poland.

---

[168] Money for Silence – Rozalia Peham – Statement June 27, 1945.

On September 12, 1939, *Einsatzgruppe VI* arrived in Poznań (*Posen* under German occupation) in the *Warthegau*. A *Sonderkommando* (special unit) under the command of Lange was formed. He received orders from Arthur Greiser, the *Gauleiter* of the *Warthegau*, to establish a concentration camp in *Posen*. In addition to this, Lange was also involved in the *"Intelligenzaktion Posen"*, which was the Nazi murder *"Aktion"*, aimed at the Polish elite and potential resistance leaders in the Wielkopolska region, as part of the Nazis *"Generalplan Ost"*.

Herbert Lange served as the Commandant of Fort VII in *Posen* for only a very short time, literally 6 days from October 10, to October 16, 1939; his role being to select the site and recruit the camp staff and admit the first prisoners. Following this he was appointed head of the *Sonderkommando* Lange, which was responsible for carrying out a series of "Euthanasia *Aktionen*", in the Wielkopolska region, using a mobile gas van, and executions by shooting. Lange played a leading role in the development of the gas van along with experts from the *Kriminaltechnisches Institut (KTI)* in Berlin, which was constructed on the chassis of an *Opel Blitz* truck, in the garages of the *Posen Gestapo*. Alfred Trenker, deputy head of the *Gestapo* in *Posen*, testified that Lange had told him in the summer of 1940 that he (Lange) had to travel to Berlin and the *RSHA* several times because of conferences and meetings concerning the suitable types of gassing vans.

Lange and his *Sonderkommando* between October 1939 and June 1940, conducted a series of "Euthanasia *Aktionen*" using a gas van at asylums in Owińska, Dziekanka in Gniezno, Kościan, Warta, Kochanówka near Łódź, Gostynin and others. It is estimated that during these actions in the stationary gas chamber at Fort VII in *Posen* and in the gas van at least 10,000 patients were gassed using carbon monoxide and combustion gases.

Lange's accomplishments in the "Euthanasia *Aktionen*" in Poland were highly regarded, and as a result of this he was promoted to *SS-Obersturmführer*, during April 1940. Following the euthanasia campaign in the *Warthegau*, his unit was sent to the Soldau (Działdowo) Camp. Wilhelm Rediess, the Higher *SS* and Police Leader for Prussia, hired the *Sonderkommando Lange* to murder 1558 mental patients for 10 *RM* per head. After the murderous activities in Soldau, the *Sonderkommando Lange* went to the Netherlands on holiday.

Later Lange was responsible for mass killings in the Konin region, but his official position from the end of November 1940, until taking up the position of Commandant of the Chełmno death camp was as the Head of the Economic Crimes Department of the Criminal Police in *Posen*.

Whilst in *Posen*, the *Sonderkommando Lange* was requested in August 1941, by Erich von dem Bach Zelewski, the Higher SS and Police Leader *Mitte*, to attend his headquarters in Baranowicze, and give a demonstration of the killing-process he employed.

In October 1941, his services were sought again, to clear out three asylums in Novgorod. A Junkers JU52 aircraft was supplied to transport Lange, some of his *Kommando*, and equipment. This was probably carbon monoxide bottles and piping to convert the rooms to provisional gas chambers.

Herbert Lange, having been promoted to the role of *SS-Hauptsturmführer* on September 1, 1941, arrived in Chełmno village on November 15, 1941, along with a small number of SS Officers, and immediately set to work establishing the death camp. The first mass gassing took place on December 8, 1941. Lange ran Chełmno death camp with an iron fist, and became furious when things did not go to plan.

In February 1942, Herbert Lange was transferred from Chełmno, to the *Reich* Main Security Office, in Berlin, where he served under *SS-Brigadeführer* Arthur Nebe, as a *Kriminalrat,* and in July 1944, he was actively engaged in rounding up the conspirators who had planned and carried out the failed attempt on Adolf Hitler's life on July 20, 1944. His work on this was rewarded when he was promoted to the rank of *SS-Sturmbannführer*. Herbert Lange was killed in action at Niederbarim, near Berlin on April 20, 1945.

SCHULTE, Wilhelm
February – March 1942

Born on June 23, 1912, in Altena, in North Rhine-Westphalia, Germany, to Wilhelm and Wilhelmina Hast. He had five siblings. He did not finish his school education and found employment as an unskilled laborer working in different places and factories. On November 1, 1940, he joined the police. First he served in Vienna, Austria, and he was posted to Łódź, Poland, where he directed a police battalion that guarded the Jewish ghetto.

Between the early part of 1942 and the spring of 1943, he served at the Chełmno death camp. For the short period of time between Herbert Lange being transferred to Hans Bothmann taking his place, Schulte served intermittently as the Camp Commandant. When Chełmno was liquidated and the German personnel left on April 11, 1943, he was posted to serve in the *Prinz Eugen* Division in the Balkans. At the end of the War he was captured by the Yugoslavs. After being released he worked in various metallurgical plants. He was married twice, and had three children. During the Chełmno Trial in Bonn, West Germany during 1962, he was found guilty of War crimes and sentenced to 13 months and 2 weeks in prison, but the sentence was never imposed.

BOTHMANN, Hans Johann
March 1942–April 1943
March 1944–January 1945

Born on November 11, 1911, in Lohe-Rickelshof, Schleswig-Holstein, Germany. In 1932, Bothmann joined the *Hitlerjugend* (Hitler Youth) and on June 1933, he became a member of the *SS*. His *SS* Number was 117630 and his *NSDAP* Number was 3601334.

After the invasion of Poland, Bothmann arrived in *Posen* with other members of *Einsatzgruppe VI*. He was a member of the State Police based in *Posen*, with the rank of *SS-Hauptsturmführer* and *Kriminalkommissar*.

On March 9, 1942, Hans Johann Bothmann, arrived in Chełmno, to take over as Commandant of the death camp there. He performed this role in both the first phase of Chełmno's operation between

March 1942 and April 1943, and when the second phase occurred between the months of March 1944, until January 1945, when the camp was liquidated for the second and final time.

After this date all 85 members of the *SS-Sonderkommando Kulmhof*, with Bothmann as Commandand were posted to join the 7. *SS-Freiwilligen – Gebirgs-Division Prinz Eugen* (7th *SS* Volunteer Mountain Division *Prinz Eugen*. This unit was involved in the fight against partisans in Yugoslavia and they suffered very heavy casualties. A number of the former personnel who served in Chełmno were killed in active service.

In March 1944, Bothmann and his unit returned to Chełmno and re-established the death camp. On June 23, 1944, the first of ten transports left the *Litzmannstadt* ghetto bound for Chełmno. This resettlement *"Aktion"* lasted until July 14, 1944, and some 7,186 Jews perished in the death camp. These individuals were among the last remaining Jewish workers still left in the *Litzmannstadt* ghetto. The ghetto was finally liquidated with mass transports to the Auschwitz-Birkenau camp in Upper Silesia.

Walter Piller, another member of the *Sonderkommando* Bothmann, who served as Bothmann's deputy, testified after the War: that Bothmann stood 187 centimeters tall, had thin blond hair, a characteristic high-pitched voice and blue eyes.

Chełmno was liquidated on January 17, 1945. Bothmann reported to the *Gestapo* headquarters in *Posen*, and he was posted to Wałcz, where he served as a liaison officer of the Security Police to *Reichsführer-SS* Heinrich Himmler.

Hans Bothmann was a brutal figure, responsible for the death of countless thousands in the gas-vans. He also personally killed around 300–400 people. Hans Bothmann hanged himself in a British internment camp in Heide, on April 4, 1946.

Chełmno Death Camp—Garrison
A-Z
Listed in Alphabetical Order

ADLER, Alois: Born on April 20, 1914, in Fretteroda. He was a member of the *Schutzpolizei* and he served in the *SS-Sonderkommando Kulmhof* during the first stage. According to the findings of investigating Judge Władysław Bednarz, he was treated at the hospital in nearby Koło. No further details are known.

AHLSCHLAGER, Hans: Born on November 8, 1919, in Karow, Germany. He served in the *SS-Sonderkommando Kulmhof* during the first phase. According to the findings of investigating Judge Władysław Bednarz, he was treated at the hospital in nearby Koło. No further details are known.

ALBRECHT, Rudolf: Born on November 11, 1907, in Wola Karubowa, Poland. He served in the *SS-Sonderkommando Kulmhof* during the first phase. According to the findings of investigating Judge Władysław Bednarz, he was treated at the hospital in nearby Koło. No further details are known.

BAR, Helmut: *Wachtmeister.* No further details are known.

BARTEL: *Wachtmeister.* No further details are known.

BASLER: *SS-Oberscharführer.* He arrived in Chełmno during late December 1941, or early January 1942. He drove a gas-van but did not stay long in Chełmno.

BECK, Heinrich: A member of the *Schutzpolizei*, with the rank of *Oberwachtmeister*, he arrived in Chełmno from *Litzmannstadt*, along with other *Schutzpolizei* members, on March 3, 1942.

BEHM, Alfred. He was believed to have served with Herbert Lange during the euthanasia *Aktionen* in the *Warthegau*. He served in Chełmno during the first phase as Transport Commander. It is thought that Behm was taken prisoner by the Russians at the end of the War. His fate is unknown.

BIERNISCH: Mentioned in the statement of *SS-Hauptscharführer* Hermann Gielow. No further details are known.

BLEI: Recalled by Szymon Srebnik as a guard, who treated the Jews badly.

BLENCH: *Wachtmeister.* No further details are known.

BOCK, Walter: Born on June 16, 1912, in Clenze, Lower Saxony, Germany. He was the son of farmer Heinrich Bock and Wilhelmina Reisner. After attending primary school he worked on farms. During 1939, he tried to join the *Wehrmacht,* but the German Army rejected him.

On February 2, 1940, he joined the Police Battalion 310 in Berlin-Spandau, where he immediately received the rank of *Wachtmeister.* In October 1940, he was posted with his unit to Częstochowa, in Poland. He suffered from depression and spent several weeks in an infirmary in Berlin.

After he recovered, Bock completed an NCO course and he was posted to a police battalion in *Litzmannstadt.* From July to October 1941, he attended a training course at a police school in Pelplin, Tczew County in Poland. On January 30, 1942, he was promoted to the rank of *Oberwachtmeister* and then a month later he was sent as a volunteer to Chełmno death camp. He served mostly at the Palace, guarding the loading of the gas vans. He remained in Chełmno until April 1943, when the first phase ended.

Bock was posted to serve in the *Prinz Eugen* Division in the Balkans, where he took part in combat patrols. Due to syphilis he suffered from mental problems. At the end of the War he was captured in Croatia, but he escaped from there to Austria. There he was re-captured by British forces and imprisoned in a Prisoner of War (POW) camp in Lienz. In 1946, he was released from internment. He passed the de-nazification process established by the Allies after the War, because he did not mention his service in the Chełmno death camp. Initially unemployed, he later served in the police in Hannover, in Germany, but retired due to ill-health issues in 1957. He was married twice. He was acquitted in the Bonn Trial in 1962.

BOGE, Otto: *Wachtmeister.* Boge was in charge of the Polish *Arbeitskommando* during the first phase of the camp's operation. He was photographed with the *Kommando* in the Palace courtyard. No further details are known.

BOHM, Josef: *SS-Rottenführer.* Born on July 26, 1911. He was transferred from the *SS-Wachtkommando Posen*, to serve in Chełmno during the first phase of the camp's operation.

BOLLMANN: *Unterwachtmeister.* According to Szymon Srebnik, he was one of the more humane guards.

BURMEISTER, Ernst: Born on April 4, 1899, in Goldberg, Lower Silesia. He was the son of Robert Burmeister and Augusta Hornisch. Robert Burmeister was a Silesian coal-miner and later a farmer. In 1913, he graduated from elementary school. He wanted to be a hairdresser but his parents persuaded him to be a tinsmith. In 1917, he was drafted into the army and he fought on the Western Front, where he was decorated with the award of the Iron Cross (Second Class).

In July 1920, he joined the police, and between the years of 1921 and 1939, he served in the police garrison in Frankfurt am Main. In November 1939, he was sent to a police battalion in *Litzmannstadt*, where he was promoted to the rank of *Revierleutnant*. He was a member of the guard company that guarded the *Litzmannstadt* Jewish ghetto.

In the autumn of 1943, along with about 30 other policemen he joined the so-called *"Wetterkommando"* commanded by *SS-Hauptsturmführer* Hans Legath. This *Kommando* undertook the exhumation and the burning of the corpses from the mass graves in the *Warthegau*. These people were Poles murdered by the members of *Einsatzgruppe VI* at the beginning of the Second World War. After the *Wetterkommando* was disbanded in the spring of 1944, Burmeister returned to *Litzmannstadt* before being posted to Chełmno death camp. At Chełmno he was responsible for guarding the Jewish workers in the camp.

On August 8, 1944, Burmeister and other members of the police detachment were sent to Warsaw to fight in the Warsaw Uprising, instigated by the Polish Home Army. He was seriously wounded in the fighting and was treated in a military hospital in *Litzmannstadt*.

Shortly before the arrival of the Red Army he returned to Germany via Lower Silesia, where he was arrested by the British forces during May 1945. He was released from a Prisoner of War (POW) camp in the autumn of 1945. After the War he was dismissed from the police service. He worked occasionally at various locations in Germany until 1948. He was twice married and had one child. During the Chełmno Trial in Bonn, West Germany in 1962, he was sentenced to serve three and a half years in prison.

BURMEISTER, Walter: Born on May 2, 1906, in Ahlbeck, a municipality of Heringsdorf on the island of Usedom on the Baltic Coast. He was the son of Georg Burmeister and Klara Knüppel. After he completed his schooling in 1920, he joined his father's sheet metal workshop. In 1932, he graduated from a trade school and a year later in October 1933 he joined the *SS* and was promoted to the rank of *SS-Rottenführer*. He joined the Nazi Party in 1937 and from the autumn of 1938, he served in a police unit in Oranienburg, near the Sachsenhausen Concentration Camp.

Later Walter Burmeister joined the *Waffen-SS* and took part in the campaign against Poland in September 1939. After a few weeks he was transferred to the *SS-Totenkopf* Division in Dachau, where he performed the role of chef in the kitchen. In 1940, he took part in the French campaign where he was wounded.

In January 1940, he was transferred to the State Police headquarters in *Posen*. He worked in the economics crimes department, whose chief was Herbert Lange. In the summer of 1941, he was assigned to the motor unit and he became the personal driver of Herbert Lange. During the late summer and autumn of 1941, he travelled together with Lange, throughout the *Warthegau* looking for suitable sites to establish a death camp. They started to establish a death camp in Chełmno on November 15, 1941. He served in the Chełmno death camp until the camp was disbanded in April 1943.

He was then posted with other members of the *Sonderkommando Kulmhof* to serve in the *Prinz Eugen* Division in the Balkans, where he was head of the kitchen. He was then promoted to the rank of *SS-Unterscharführer*. From March 1944, to January 17, 1945, he served once again in the Chełmno death camp. Shortly before the arrival of the Red Army he travelled with Hans Bothmann to *Posen*.

He returned to Germany and was injured in a bombing raid on May 2, 1945, and was hospitalized. He was held in an internment camp in Neuengamme until October 1947. After his release from the internment camp he worked occasionally for farmers, and he worked as a tinsmith. He was married with one child, and then divorced. In the

Chełmno Trial in Bonn during 1962, he was sentenced to serve thirteen years in prison.

BÜRSTINGER, Erwin: Based on the testimony by Walter Piller in 1945, Erwin Bürstinger was born in Austria, and was aged about thirty-eight years of age. He was 170 centimeters tall, had thin dark hair and was married. He served in the first phase in Chełmno until the camp was liquidated in April 1943. He was responsible for all of the vehicles and often stood in for other drivers when they were sick, including driving the gas-vans.

When Chełmno was liquidated in April 1943, he was transferred to the secret field police in the Balkans. He returned to the Chełmno death camp in March 1944.

CHRISST, Johann: Born on October 23, 1905, in Kramwinkel. He served in the *SS-Sonderkommando Kulmhof* during the first phase. According to the findings of investigating Judge Władysław Bednarz, he was treated at the hospital in nearby Koło. No further details are known.

DANIEL: He was a member of the *Schutzpolizei*, with the rank of *Oberwachtmeister*, and he served in the *SS-Sonderkommando Kulmhof* during the second phase of its operation. Szymon Srebnik recalled that he was cruel towards the Jews.

FIEDLER, Gustav: He was a *Polizeihauptwachtmeister* in the *Litzmannstadt* ghetto and he was transferred to Chełmno in January 1942. At the Chełmno death camp he supervised the bone grinder in the *Waldlager*, during the first phase. He did not return to Chełmno in March 1944, but attended a training course and was subsequently posted to Greece, where he fought against partisans. He was wounded in 1945, and was transferred to Copenhagen, Denmark, where he fell into the hands of Danish resistance fighters. He survived this and was arrested after the War for his membership in the SS, but was released in 1948.

His involvement with Chełmno death camp did not come to light for many years, but he was eventually arrested and stood trial in Kiel, West Germany and on November 26, 1965, he was found guilty of War crimes and sentenced to 13 months and two weeks in prison.

FILER, Walther: He was an *SS-Unterscharführer* in rank. No other details are known.

GASSMANN, Gottlieb: As recalled by Rozalia Peham, the wife of sentry Josef Peham, he originated from Stuttgart.

GIELOW, Hermann: Based on the testimony by Walter Piller in 1945, Hermann Gielow was about 46 years old. He was born and lived in Berlin. He was 170 centimeters tall, with thin dark blond parted hair and he was married.

He was transferred as a driver from Legath's *Wetterkommando* to the *SS-Sonderkommando Kulmhof,* in 1944. He drove a truck between Chełmno and the *Waldlager,* transporting Jews to their death. He was taken prisoner by the Red Army during the battle for *Posen.* The Soviets interrogated him and then he was handed over to the Polish authorities. His trial commenced on April 25, 1949, in Kalisz. He was found guilty of War crimes and was sentenced to death. The appeals court in *Posen* (Poznań) upheld the verdict and the sentence was carried out on May 16, 1950.

GÖDE, Karl: An *SS-Hauptscharführer* in rank, he arrived in Chełmno in early January 1942, and he performed the role of assistant to Fritz Ismer, who was responsible for the safekeeping of the valuables confiscated from the victims. No further details are known.

GÖRLICH, Wilhelm: Based on the testimony by Walter Piller in 1945, Wilhelm Görlich was born in the Sudetenland, was 162 centimeters tall, was of a stocky build and married. He served in the *Gestapo* in Inowrocław and then worked for the *Gestapo* in *Posen.* He was posted to Chełmno death camp in April 1942, where he was responsible for the safekeeping of confiscated valuables, such as gold, precious stones, rings, banknotes, coins and other items. He transported them at regular intervals to the *Litzmannstadt* ghetto authorities. He also paid the soldiers their salaries, and gave them food stamps entitling them to receive certain food rations. Wilhelm Görlich was wounded in the fighting for *Posen.* He was taken prisoner by the Soviet Army during 1945. He was tried for War crimes and sentenced to 25 years in prison, but was in fact released in 1949.

GRAF, Hermann: Born on March 15, 1920. He served in the *SS-Sonderkommando Kulmhof* during the first phase. According to the findings of investigating Judge Władysław Bednarz, he was treated at the hospital in nearby Koło. No further details are known.

HAASE: A member of the *Schutzpolizei*. He served in the *SS-Sonderkommando Kulmhof* during the second phase. He was shot and killed by the Jewish workers on January 17, 1945, during the revolt in the granary, where *Polizeimeister* Lenz was also killed.

HÄFELE, Alois: Born on July 5, 1893, in Gündlingen, Baden Württemberg. He was the son of Armand Häfele and Emma Wolf. His mother died two years after his birth. His father had a small farm. He graduated from primary school in 1908, and he started to learn how to become a baker.
During the First World War he served in the Navy on a battleship, and he was awarded the Iron Cross (Second Class). After the First World War ended he worked as a baker in Karlsruhe. From 1920, he served in the police. In 1940, he was admitted to the Nazi Party and the SS (*SS* Number 354180). He served as a police constable in Częstochowa and *Litzmannstadt* in occupied Poland, and in Mannheim, Germany.
Häfele arrived in the Chełmno death camp on January 28, 1942, and there he was responsible for organizing the Jewish *Arbeitskommando* in the Palace. When the camp was liquidated in April 1943, he served in the *Prinz Eugen* Division in the Balkans. During August 1943, due to his age, he was sent to a *Waffen-SS* Gendarmerie unit in Buchenwald. In March 1944, he returned to Chełmno, where he stayed until the camp was liquidated for the last time on January 17, 1945. Shortly before the arrival of the Red Army, he went to Berlin in a truck with Gustav Laabs..Walter Piller testified that Häfele lived in Kassel, was 50 years old, with grey hair and gold front teeth. He avoided captivity and he retired in 1951. He was married with two daughters. In the Chełmno Trial during 1962, he was sentenced to fifteen years in prison, which was subsequently reduced to a thirteen year sentence.

HAGEN, Fritz: Born on December 10, 1908, in Munich. He served in the *SS-Sonderkommando Kulmhof* during the first phase. According to the findings of investigating Judge Władysław Bednarz, he was treated at the hospital in nearby Koło. No further details are known.

HAIDER, Simon: Born on December 16, 1894. He served in the *SS-Sonderkommando Kulmhof* during the first phase. According to the findings of investigating Judge Władysław Bednarz, he was treated at the hospital in nearby Koło. No further details are known.

HANNES: *Wachtmeister* in rank; he served at the crematoriums in the *Waldlager*, according to Jewish survivor Mieczysław Zurawski, during the second phase of Chełmno's operation.

HARDT, Herman: Born June 26, 1912, in Duisburg. He served in the *SS-Sonderkommando Kulmhof* during the first phase. According to the findings of investigating Judge Władysław Bednarz, he was treated at the hospital in nearby Koło. No further details are known.

HARTER, Erich: Born June 23, 1920, in Charlottenhof. He served in the *SS-Sonderkommando Kulmhof* during the first phase. According to the findings of investigating Judge Władysław Bednarz, he was treated at the hospital in nearby Koło. No further details are known.

HEILBRUNNER, Johann: Born November 13, 1919, in Strobnitz, Oberdonau, Czech Republic. He served in the *SS-Sonderkommando Kulmhof* during the first phase. According to the findings of investigating Judge Władysław Bednarz, he was treated at the hospital in nearby Koło. No further details are known.

HEINL, Karl: Born on April 11, 1912, in Hausham, in the municipality of Miesbach, Bavaria. He was the son of Karl Heinl and Anna Voit. His father who was a coal miner died during the First World War. In 1916 or 1917, he moved with his mother and step-father to Duisburg. He went to primary school and initially struggled, often missing lessons. But he eventually graduated from school with good results.

After school he learned the trade of a butcher, but from 1931, he worked as a messenger, and he received money from social assistance. He became a member of the Nazi Party on May 1, 1933. One year later, after completing military training, he was admitted to the police in Cologne. Then he served in various military and police regiments, and he took part in the Austrian "*Anschluss*" and the invasion of Czechoslovakia.

Later he served in the police in Gorzów Wielkopolski and *Posen*. Whilst some accounts state he arrived in Chełmno in January 1942, his own personal testimony places him in Chełmno at least a month earlier, when the garrison was first being established.

At Chełmno he was responsible for organizing the camp guard duty at the "Palace" and the Forest Camp, until the camp was liquidated in April 1943. He then saw service in the *Prinz Eugen* Division in the Balkans. He took part in heavy fighting and was wounded twice. He received the Iron Cross (First and Second Class) and other decorations.

After the War, Heinl was interned by the British forces until 1947. Later he worked as a policeman and a steelworker. He was married and divorced twice. He was sentenced to 7 years in prison at the Chełmno Trial in Bonn during 1962, for assisting in the murder of Jews at Chełmno.

HENSEN, Friedrich: Born on November 29, 1920, in Hagen, North Rhine-Westphalia. He was married to Charlotte, neé Mittlestadt and the couple had two children.

He provided a statement to the British forces on July 13, 1945. A lot of the dates he recalls are contradictory. As a member of the police, he served in the Police Training Battalion in Pohlitz between April 1940, and March 1941, where he served in the SS Police Division at Katscher and from March 25, 1941, he served in the police administration in Litzmannstadt.

In July 1942, he was posted to SS-Sonderkommando Kulmhof and he worked in the Forest Camp, where the Jews were killed in gas vans and buried. He witnessed the bodies being exhumed and burnt, whilst he kept guard. He mentioned by name a number of the Chełmno garrison.

In his statement he claims he left Chełmno in December 1944, but there is no mention of what he did when the camp was first liquidated in April 1943. He was captured by British forces on April 15, 1945, in Hagen.

HERING, Oskar: He arrived in Chełmno along with Gustav Laabs on May 3, 1942, from *Posen*. He drove the gas vans during the first phase of the camp's operation. He died fighting at Vratanica, Serbia, on October 4, 1944.

HERTE: As recalled by Rozalia Peham, the wife of sentry Josef Peham, he was sent to *Litzmannstadt* for trading in gold.

HEUKELBACH, Wilhelm: Born on February 28, 1911, in Kierspe, North Rhine-Westphalia, the only son of Theodor Heukelbach and Else Kurschuss. His father died during the First World War and his mother remarried. He completed primary and secondary schools and later worked on the farm of his step-father, who died in 1926.
To avoid service in the army, he joined the police force in 1939, and after completion of police training he was deployed on guard duties in Cologne and later on in *Litzmannstadt*. He arrived from *Litzmannstadt*, to the Chełmno death camp on April 10, 1942, where he was a guard.
When Chełmno death camp was liquidated in April 1943, he was posted to the *Prinz Eugen* Division in the Balkans, where he took part in heavy fighting, and was promoted to the rank of SS-*Hauptscharführer*. During 1944, he served in a police-gendarmerie unit in Weimar-Buchenwald, and then later in a *Panzer* Grenadiers unit near Prague. He was captured and interned by the American forces until 1947. He was married, with two daughters. During the Chełmno Trial in Bonn, during 1962, the sentence of 13 months, two weeks in prison was dismissed.

HOFFMANN, Kurt: Operated the bone grinder in the *Waldlager*, during the first phase of Chełmno death camp's existence.

HÜFING, Gustav: Gustav Hüfing, from Wesel, arrived in Chełmno on March 24, 1942, from *Litzmannstadt*, to perform the role of Head of the *Polizeiwachtkommando*. According to Rozalia Peham, the wife of sentry Josef Peham, Hüfing lived in *Adolf Hitler Strasse* in *Litzmannstadt*.

HULL, Hermann: He served for several weeks in the SS-*Sonderkommando Kulmhof*. He was posted to Holland. No further details are known.

HUT, Kurt: Born on June 5, 1920. He served in the *SS-Sonderkommando Kulmhof* during the first phase. According to the findings of investigating Judge Władysław Bednarz, he was treated at the hospital in nearby Koło. No further details are known.

HUTNER: Recalled by Szymon Srebnik and fellow sentry Bruno Israel. He treated the Jews kindly, and he served in both phases of the death camps existence.

ISLINGER, Josef: Born on September 7, 1919, in Einhausen, Hesse. He served in the *SS-Sonderkommando Kulmhof* during the first phase. According to the findings of investigating Judge Władysław Bednarz, he was treated at the hospital in nearby Koło. No further details are known.

ISMER, Fritz: Arrived in Chełmno in early January 1942. He was responsible for the valuables confiscated from the victims during the first phase of the camps existence. He was posted to the Balkans, and he remained there, whilst other members of the *Sonderkommando Kulmhof* returned to the *Warthegau* in March 1944.
He fell ill in April 1944, and spent some time in hospital, then served in the *SS Panzer* Division *Frundsberg*. After the War ended, he was later questioned during 1960, regarding his service in Chełmno. No charges were ever brought against him.

ISRAEL, Bruno: Born on August 19, 1906, in Łódź. He was born to Lukiusz and Linda König. Before the Second World War he worked as a dyer for the company Leber and Lewandowski. He signed the *Volksliste* in 1940, and started working for the *Hilfspolizei* in 1941.
In 1943 he was drafted into the *Gendarmerie* with the rank of *Wachtmeister* and in July or August 1944 he was posted to the *Sonderkommando Kulmhof*, where he took part in transporting deportees to the *Waldlager*. He left Chełmno in January 1945, and went to *Posen* with other members of the *Sonderkommando*. He was tried in Poland and sentenced to death, but his sentence was commuted to life in prison. He was released from prison on December 12, 1958.

JACOB, Hans: Mentioned in J. Przybylski's testimony. No further details are known.

JAKUBOWSKI, Feliks: Born on November 20, 1911, in Hamber am Rhein. He was a member of the *Schutzpolizei* with the rank of *Oberwachtmeister*. He served in the *SS-Sonderkommando Kulmhof* during the first phase. According to the findings of investigating Judge

Władysław Bednarz, he was treated at the hospital in nearby Koło. No further details are known.

JUNK, Ludwig: Born on February 28, 1920. He served in the *SS-Sonderkommando Kulmhof* during the first phase. According to the findings of investigating Judge Władysław Bednarz, he was treated at the hospital in nearby Koło. No further details are known.

KARZER, Mois: He was a member of the *Schutzpolizei*, with the rank of *Oberwachtmeister*. He served in the *Sonderkommando Kulmhof* during the second phase. No further details are known.

KLOSE: He was a member of the *Schutzpolizei*, with the rank of *Oberwachtmeister*. He served in the *Sonderkommando Kulmhof* during the second phase. He was described by witnesses as middle-aged, tall and fat. He was recalled by Szymon Srebnik.

KRAUS, Oskar: He was a member of the *Schutzpolizei*, with the rank of *Oberwachtmeister*. He served in the *Sonderkommando Kulmhof* during the second phase. No further details are known.

KRETSCHMER, Erich: Based on the testimony by Walter Piller in 1945, Erich Kretschmer was about 40 years old and was born in Saxony. He was 172 centimeters tall, with a gold tooth. He served in both phases of the Chełmno death camp's existence, from the time of Herbert Lange and Hans Bothmann.

He was responsible for transporting Jews; he used to escort the Jews to the narrow-gauge railway in Chełmno. He also transported the Jews in trucks from the church in Chełmno to the forest camp. When Chełmno was liquidated he was loaded onto a truck along with the baggage of the commanders and the SS troops, and they travelled to *Posen,* and then on, to Frankfurt an der Oder. No further details are known.

LAABS, Gustav: Born on December 20, 1902, in Eleonorenhof, Kreis Greifenberg, Pomerania. He was the son of Hermann Laabs and Anna Mauck. His father was a milker who died in 1919. Two years after Gustav's birth the Laabs family moved further afield. He was a good pupil in primary school and when his schooling was completed, he became a milker like his father.

In 1920, Laabs joined the *Reichswehr* as a cavalryman, and after leaving the army in 1921, he moved to Szczecin, where he worked until 1927 in various factories. During 1922, he married for the first time; he had seven children, two of whom died. Between 1927 and 1930, he was a taxi driver, but later he was unemployed.

On November 1, 1932, he became a member of the Nazi Party and the *SS*, his *SS* Number was 48181; soon he was promoted to the rank of *SS-Unterscharführer*. As a soldier in the *Wehrmacht* he took part in the occupation of the Sudetenland. On November 1, 1938, he became a driver for a branch of the *SD* in Szczecin and was promoted to the rank of *SS-Oberscharführer*. He became the personal driver of *SS-Brigadeführer* Erich Naumann.

In 1939, he was again drafted into the *Wehrmacht* and took part in the campaigns against Poland in 1939, and a year later against the French. After this campaign ended, he returned to Szczecin and was once again promoted, this time to the rank of *SS-Hauptscharführer*. During the autumn of 1941, he was transferred to the *Reich* Main Security Office (*RSHA*) in Berlin, where he was responsible for repairing cars.

In May 1942, Gustav Laabs was ordered to report to the *SS* and Police Headquarters in *Posen*, where he was vaccinated against typhoid, pledged to silence and posted to the *Sonderkommando Kulmhof*. He arrived in Chełmno on May 3, 1942, and immediately started to drive the gas-vans. He stayed in Chełmno until the camp was liquidated during April 1943.

Along with other members of the *Sonderkommando* he was sent to the *Prinz Eugen* Division in the Balkans. During his stay in Yugoslavia he did not participate in any combat actions. In March 1944, he returned to Chełmno, along with other members of the *SS-Sonderkommando* Bothmann and he stayed there until January 1945. After the dissolution of the death camp along with Häfele he went by truck to Berlin and later reported to an *SS* Military Police unit in Weimar-Buchenwald. In March 1945, he became unwell and was taken to a military hospital in Altenburg. In April 1945, he was captured by American forces and sent to a Prisoner of War (POW) camp in Bad Kreuznach. This camp was taken over by the French forces and Laabs and other prisoners were taken to a camp near Paris.

He was released from French captivity in October 1946, and he found employment as a driver in a number of locations within Germany. In February 1958, he divorced his first wife and married Maria Wecker, with whom he had a son. Gustav Laabs was tried at the Chełmno Trial in 1962, and he was sentenced to serve 15 years in prison that was reduced to 13 years after an appeal.

LANG, Harold: He was the first head of the Police guard at Chełmno for a brief time during the first phase, and was replaced by *Polizeioberleutnant* Harri Maas, within the first month of the establishment of the death camp.

LENZ, Wilhelm: Based on the testimony by Walter Piller in 1945, Wilhelm Lenz was a married man of around 50 years of age, from Silesia. Lenz was a member of the *Schutzpolizei* with the rank of *Polizeimeister*. Lenz served under Herbert Lange and Hans Bothmann, as chief of the *Waldlager*. He was an extremely brutal killer, known as "Big Whip" to the Jewish prisoners. When Chełmno was disbanded, Lenz served in the *Wetterkommando* commanded by *SS-Hauptsturmführer* Hans Legath.

Wilhelm Lenz was killed on the night of January 17, 1945, as he entered the Granary on the "Palace" grounds to remove the Jewish workers in groups of five for execution. Lenz was overpowered and dragged into the Granary. The Jews inside called out that Lenz had hung himself, but probably they killed him and *Schutzpolizei* member Haase, as well. The Granary was set on fire, and Lenz and Haase's charred bodies were buried along with the Jewish workers and craftsmen who perished, in the grounds of the "Palace."

LOSCHAK, Friedrich: A member of the *Schutzpolizei*, with the rank of *Polizeiwachtmeister*, as recalled by Friedrich Hensen. No further details are known.

MAAS, Harri: *Polizeioberleutnant* Harri Maas replaced Harold Lang, but the day after his arrival at Chełmno, he was accidentally sprayed in the face with disinfectant and replaced three days later.

MADERHOLZ, Friedrich: Born on November 7, 1919, in Weissenburg, Bavaria, the son of Johann Friedrich Maderholz and Babette Katheder. He graduated from primary school but he was a poor pupil. He wanted to be a carpenter and locksmith, but he could not perform calculations on machines. He became an unskilled farmer.

At the end of 1939, under the influence of propaganda posters he joined the police and he served in Vienna, Bolesławiec in Silesia, and in Stuttgart. In May 1941, he was posted to *Litzmannstadt*. On March 13, 1942, he was posted to the Chełmno death camp, where he performed guard duty. When the camp was dismantled in April 1943, he was posted to serve in the *Prinz Eugen* Division in the Balkans.

During this period of service he was promoted to the rank of *SS-Unterscharführer*, but in November 1943 he was severely wounded by shrapnel from an exploding grenade, and as a result his leg was amputated up to the thigh. He spent the rest of the War in hospitals under treatment. He was interned until 1946, and then he found employment in factories that employed war-invalids. He was married to Margareta Spatz, whom he met in Chełmno and they had three children. During the Chełmno Trial in Bonn during 1962, he was sentenced to 13 months, two weeks in prison, but on appeal the sentence was dismissed.

MALZMÜLLER, Theodor: He was a member of the *Schutzpolizei*, with the rank of *Polizeiwachtmeister*, and he served in Police Guard Battalion XXI in *Litzmannstadt*, before being posted to the *Sonderkommando Kulmhof*. He arrived at Chełmno death camp on November 27, 1941, and he worked as a guard on sentry duty in the *Waldlager*. When the Chełmno death camp was dismantled in April 1943, he was posted to serve in the *Prinz Eugen* Division that fought against the partisans in Yugoslavia.

MEHRING, Anton: Born on March 25, 1920, in Offenbach Am Main, Hesse, the son of Ludwig Mehring and Elise Simon. His father was a stone-mason. He completed elementary school and became a tanner. In May 1940, he was admitted to the police and assigned to the *SS* Police Division in Upper Silesia, and from there was posted to *Litzmannstadt*.

He was then posted to the *SS-Sonderkommando Kulmhof* and he arrived in Chełmno on March 27, 1942, where he served as a guard in both the "Palace" and the *Waldlager*. He returned to *Litzmannstadt*, and was posted to an *SS* Battalion in the Netherlands. In November 1943, he was assigned to a *Wachtkommando* in Obersalzburg. He remained there until the end of the War until he was captured by American force. When he was released from American internment, he found employment as a scrap merchant, a forest worker and a laborer in a chemical factory. From 1955, Mehring was the owner of a tavern. He was married with two sons. During the Chełmno Trial in Bonn in 1962, he was acquitted.

MEIER, Kurt: He was recalled by Friedrich Hensen to be a member of the *Schutzpolizei* with the rank of *Polizeiwachtmeister*, who served at the Chełmno death camp.

MICHALSKI, Paul: He was recalled by Friedrich Hensen to be a member of the *Schutzpolizei* with the rank of *Polizeiwachtmeister*, who served at the Chełmno death camp.

MÖBIUS, Kurt: Born on May 3, 1895, in Magdeburg, the son of August Möbius and Franziska Roder. He was educated in both primary and secondary schools, but achieved poor results. He found employment as a blacksmith. During the First World War he fought on the Western Front and also on the Eastern Front, where he was wounded. He was awarded the Iron Cross (Second Class).
After the War ended he worked as a locksmith in Dessau, and in 1924 he joined the police force. In the spring of 1941, at his own request, he was transferred to a Police Battalion in *Litzmannstadt*. On December 19, 1941, he arrived in the Chełmno death camp, where he was responsible for all of the work carried out in the "Palace." Following some conflict with the Head of the *Polizeiwachtkommando*, Gustav Hüfing, in September 1942, he was moved to a Police Battalion in *Litzmannstadt*.
He fled before the Red Army arrived and returned to Dessau, where he was wounded. He was captured by Soviet forces and interned in a Soviet camp. Later he worked in a Buna plant in Dessau. In the summer of 1949, he escaped to the Federal Republic of West Germany, because he feared that with the Buna plant decommissioning he would be sent as a specialist to the Soviet Union. He found work in various locations. He collected a police pension, but concealed the fact that he had served at Chełmno. After retirement, he worked at a petrol station as a night watchman. He was married, with four

children. At the Chełmno Trial in Bonn, he was sentenced to serve 8 years in prison.

MÜLLER: Remembered by Szymon Srebnik as a sentry who allegedly died in Warsaw.

NETZL, Ernst: He was mentioned as having served at Chełmno death camp, in the testimony provided by Margareta Maderholz, formerly Spatz. No further details are known.

NEUMANN, Friedrich: An *SS-Hauptscharführer* in rank, he was replaced as head of the administration office in Chełmno by Wilhelm Görlich in April 1942. His ultimate fate is unknown.

OSTERMEIER, Josef: He was recalled by Friedrich Hensen to be a member of the *Schutzpolizei* with the rank of *Polizeiwachtmeister*, who served at the Chełmno death camp.

OTTO, Herbert: Born on October 9, 1901, in Dresden. He joined the Nazi Party (Number 97592) and the *SS* (*SS* Number 11544). Herbert Otto was among the first group of *SS* men assigned to the Chełmno death camp. As an *SS-Obersturmführer* in rank, he was the deputy commandant under both Herbert Lange and Hans Bothmann. After the Chełmno death camp was dismantled in April 1943, he was posted to the 7th *SS* Division *Prinz Eugen*. He was killed in action on May 6, 1945, near Prague.

OTTO, Rudolf: A member of the *Schutzpolizei*, he served as a guard in Chełmno. No further details are known.

PEHAM, Josef: He was a member of the *Schutzpolizei* with the rank of *Rottwachtmeister* who was posted to Chełmno after serving in Litzmannstadt. He married Rozalia Peham on April 1, 1943. She was a German who had settled in Skobielice, Chełmno Community, where she ran a farm with her mother, and thanks to her testimony before Judge Władysław Bednarz we know so many details of her husband's life and other members of the *Sonderkommando*. At Chełmno Josef Peham guarded the Jews being unloaded at Koło station, he also carried out guard duty in the *Waldlager* and sentry duty at the Zawadki Mill. When the *Sonderkommando* was liquidated in April 1943, Josef

Peham was posted to the 7th SS Division *Prinz Eugen*. He was killed in action.

PETERS, Willi: As recalled by Rozalia Peham, the wife of sentry Josef Peham, he was married to a German woman from Rzuchów.

PILLER, Walter: Born on December 14, 1902, in Berlin-Spandau, Falkensee, the son of Albert Piller and his wife Minna, neé Meier. His father, who was a foreman, died in 1942. From the age of 6–14 he attended a primary school in Spandau, from which he was expelled in his final year, but during the three years that followed he mastered the trade of a turner in an artillery workshop in Spandau.

After losing his job, he applied for employment in the Berlin police department. He was supported in his application by *Hauptmann* Balke, whom he had met on a swimming training course. Upon passing the entrance examination, Piller was accepted as a police officer candidate on August 20, 1924, and he graduated from the police academy in Brandenburg-an-der-Harvel. A year later, he became an *Unterwachtmeister* and was transferred to Berlin, where he served in various Berlin Emergency Police Departments in Charlottenburg, Wilmersdorf, as well as in the West police group headquarters. He was also appointed as a sports instructor in the emergency departments. He also served as a *Revier-Oberwachtmeister*. On August 20, 1936, he left the Berlin Security Police, but was still a member of the police reserve forces.

Walter Piller was then employed as a temporary worker in the Teltow County Savings Bank with its headquarters in Berlin, and he applied for a post in the Criminal Police (*Kripo*) but due to long waiting lists, he decided to join the *Gestapo* as a Criminal Officer. He was now married to Marta Buchholz since April 1935, and in his own words,"was in a difficult financial situation." At the end of 1937, he was appointed to work in the *Gestapo* headquarters, where after a three-month trial period and passing an examination in criminology, he was promoted to the rank of *Kriminal-Oberassistent*. His work consisted of checking people's suitability to work in arms production plants, and protecting dignitaries at political rallies.

On August 20, 1939, Walter Piller was assigned to *Einsatzkommando II* of the Security Police during the Polish campaign. His role in Poland was to travel by car searching every police building in large cities and towns, in order to go through police files, and to secure police registers of Polish political organizations. His unit reached the Fortress of Modlin, near the end of the campaign, and from there he was posted to *Posen*. From *Posen*, he was transferred to Inowrocław, where he worked in the *Gestapo* post there, and he moved his family from Berlin to Inowrocław.

When the *Gestapo* post in Inowrocław was closed on November 1, 1943, he was posted to the *Wetterkommando Legath*, where all corpses of Polish citizens executed by firing squads that had been buried in the forests in the territory of the *Gestapo* headquarters in the *Posen* area, had to be dug up and cremated on site.

When the *Wetterkommando* Legath's unit was disbanded in early 1944, Walter Piller was transferred to the *Gestapo* in Łódź, but in March 1944, he was posted to the *SS-Sonderkommando* Bothmann at *Kulmhof*. At *Kulmhof*, Bothmann appointed Piller to serve as his deputy, whilst being responsible for overseeing the Jewish *Arbeitskommando* in the "Palace", and the barracks in the *Waldlager*.

When the *Sonderkommando* was disbanded on January 17, 1945, Piller made his way to *Posen* where he was wounded on February 21, 1945, by a shell from a heavy howitzer at a command post near the *Posen* Citadel. Two days later on February 23, 1945, he was captured by the Russians and held captive in the *NKWD* Prisoner of War Camp No. 173, in *Posen*. Walter Piller was put on trial by the Polish authorities. He was found guilty of War crimes and was executed on January 19, 1949, in Łódź.

PLATE, Albert: Born on December 31, 1903, in Rüstringen, Lower Saxony. He was an *SS Hauptscharführer* and *Kriminalsekretär* in rank and he was Bothmann's deputy during the first phase. When the camp was liquidated in April 1943, Plate was posted to the 7th SS Division *Prinz Eugen*. He was severely wounded and committed suicide on October 4, 1944, in Yugoslavia.

RAUDZUS, Friedrich: He was recalled by Friedrich Hensen to be a member of the *Schutzpolizei* with the rank of *Polizeiwachtmeister*, who served at the Chełmno death camp.

REIBLINGER, Anton: He was recalled by Friedrich Hensen to be a member of the *Schutzpolizei* with the rank of *Polizeiwachtmeister*, who served at the Chełmno death camp.

REISSNER, Sepp: He was recalled by Friedrich Hensen to be a member of the *Schutzpolizei* with the rank of *Polizeiwachtmeister*, who served at the Chełmno death camp.

RICHTER, Albert: An *SS-Sturmscharführer* in rank. No further details are known.

RICHTER, Herbert: Based on the testimony by Walter Piller in 1945, Richter was aged about 37, with dark, slightly grey hair, 172 centimeters tall and had a long face. He had his own house in *Posen* and was married. Richter was an *SS-Hauptscharführer* in rank.
Richter was in Chełmno during both the first and second phases of the camp's existence. In Chełmno he was responsible for sorting the clothes and valuables as well as standing in for the drivers of the gas-vans. When the camp was finally liquidated on January 17, 1945, he made his way to *Posen*. Walter Piller recalled that Richter was probably wounded in the fighting with the Red Army in the Citadel in *Posen*.

ROMBACH, Erich: He was recalled by Friedrich Hensen to be a member of the *Schutzpolizei* with the rank of *Polizeiwachtmeister*, who served at the Chełmno death camp.

ROSE, Hans: He was recalled by Rozalia Peham, the wife of sentry, Josef Peham.

ROSS: A member of the *Schutzpolizei* with the rank of *Wachtmeister*. No further details are known.

RUNGE, Johannes: Based on the testimony by Walter Piller in 1945, Runge was aged about 40, 176 centimeters tall, with dark blond hair and a low forehead. He was married and lived in *Posen*. He was an *SS-Hauptscharführer* in rank. Runge was at Chełmno from the very beginning and he was responsible for building the crematoria in the *Waldlager* and was in charge of one of the crematoria. After Chełmno had been dismantled, Walter Piller testified that Runge had last been seen with Hermann Gielow in a combat unit under the command of *Hauptmann* Kohler after fighting in the Hugger Brewery in *Posen*. He probably died of his wounds after being captured by the Soviet Army in February 1945.

RUWENACH: Recalled by Bruno Israel as a member of the *Schutzpolizei* with the rank of a *Wachtmeister* who had a camera in Chełmno, and who took numerous photographs of the camp that survived the War. Szymon Srebnik recalled that he treated the Jews well and assisted the Jewish prisoner Finkelstein in his ultimately unsuccessful escape bid.

SCHALLING, Franz: He was a member of the police who served in *Litzmannstadt* before being posted to Chełmno, on November 25, 1941. He performed guard duty in a sentry box in front of the "Castle." He was interviewed by Claude Lanzmann for the film "Shoah."

SCHEFLER, Wilhelm: A member of the *Schutzpolizei* with the rank of *Wachtmeister*. No further details are known.

SCHMERSE, Wilhelm: He was recalled by Walter Piller from his days with the *Wetterkommando* Legath and at Chełmno. He was a *Kriminal-Sekretär* and *SS-Sturmscharführer* in rank. He was aged 42, born in Mark Brandenburg, 178 centimeters tall, with blond parted hair. He was divorced. He served in the *Gestapo* post in Inowrocław, and when that was closed down he served in a *Gestapo* post in Włocławek. He then served with Walter Piller and others in the *Wetterkommando* Legath, whose mission was to exhume and cremate the corpses of Polish citizens executed by firing squads and buried in the forests in the territory of the *Gestapo* headquarters in the *Posen* area. When the *Wetterkommmando* was being disbanded, Wilhelm Schmerse and Walter Piller attended a training course for *SS* Leaders in Rabka, near Kraków, in the *Generalgouvernement*. Both Wilhelm Schmerse and Walter Piller were assigned to *SS-Sonderkommando* Bothmann in Chełmno, once they had returned the equipment and vehicles to the Security Police in *Posen*. Wilhelm Schmerse was to be assigned to the post of deputy commandant to Bothmann. However, after only two days he fell ill, and was taken to the hospital in Inowrocław, where he underwent stomach surgery. Walter Piller then took his place at Chełmno, as deputy commandant.

SCHMIDT, Erwin: Based on the testimony by Walter Piller in 1945, Schmidt was aged about 35, born in the Sudetenland. Schmidt was 180 centimeters tall, with thick dark blond hair, and he had a gold front tooth. He was married and lived in Łódź. He served in Chełmno under Hans Bothmann, where he managed the canteen and supplied the unit with provisions. He was an *SS-Hauptscharführer* and when Chełmno death camp was liquidated in April 1943, he was posted to to the 7th *SS* Division *Prinz Eugen*, where he fought against partisans in the Balkans.

He returned to Chełmno in March 1944, and he was a member of *SS-Sonderkommando* Bothmann until the camp was dissolved on January 17, 1945. He made his way to *Posen*, where he was wounded in the fighting for Grollman's Fort and was apparently killed during the fighting for the Citadel in *Posen*, according to Walter Piller.

SCHNEIDER: A member of the *Schutzpolizei* with the rank of *Oberwachtmeister*. According to Szymon Srebnik, a Jew jumped out the church window and threw himself at Schneider, who shot him dead.

SCHOFFNER: A member of the *Schutzpolizei,* with the rank of *Wachtmeister* who arrived in Chełmno from *Litzmannstadt*. According to Szymon Srebnik he was short, of slim build, with blond hair, and no facial hair.

SCHONBECK, Heinz: He was recalled by Friedrich Hensen to be a member of the *Schutzpolizei* with the rank of *Polizeiwachtmeister,* who served at the Chełmno death camp.

SEIDENGLANZ, Stefan: Based on the testimony by Walter Piller in 1945, Seidenglanz was born near Vienna, 170 centimeters tall, and married. Seidenglanz was a driver and a member of the *NSKK (Nationalsozialistisches Kraftfahrer-Kommando)* in the resettlement headquarters in Łódź. He served in both phases of Chełmno's existence, and he was an *SS-Hauptscharführer* in rank and he performed the role of a driver.

SIMON, Bruno: A member of the *Schutzpolizei* with the rank of *Oberwachtmeister*. He was a guard in the *Waldlager*. He drowned in the River Ner on July 24, 1944.

SLIWKE, Arthur: He was a member of the *Schutzpolizei* with the rank of *Wachtmeister*. He was recalled by fellow guard, Bruno Israel, as being atrocious towards the Jews. Sliwke shot the Jewish man Finkelstein, whilst he was escaping.

SOMMER, Max: Born on February 9, 1902. He was an *SS-Unterscharführer* in rank and he served in Chełmno from the beginning of the death camp's existence. He was responsible for the segregation of the victims' valuables. In January 1945, when Chełmno death camp was liquidated, Max Sommer went to Berlin. Walter Piller stated during his trial, that Max Sommer had died before the end of the War.

SORGE, Herbert: Born on January 22, 1920. He served in the *SS-Sonderkommando Kulmhof* during the first phase. According to the findings of investigating Judge Władysław Bednarz, he was treated at the hospital in nearby Koło. No further details are known.

STEINBAUER, Josef: Born on March 23, 1920. He served in the *SS-Sonderkommando Kulmhof* during the first phase. According to the findings of investigating Judge Władysław Bednarz, he was treated at the hospital in nearby Koło. No further details are known.

STEINKE, Alexander: Born on March 16, 1912, in Bytsch, in Poland. He was a member of the *Schutzpolizei* with the rank of *Polizeioberwachtmeister*. At the end of May 1942, one of the Sauer gas vans exploded and Alexander Steinke suffered burns and had to be taken to the hospital in *Warthbrücken*, where he was treated. Once he recovered from his injuries he returned to his duty at the death camp. He was acquitted of War crimes at the Chełmno death camp during the Chełmno Trial in Bonn, 1962–1963.

STROHMEIER, Johann: Born on August 16, 1920, in Gros Sankt Florian, Styria, in Austria. He served in the *SS-Sonderkommando Kulmhof* during the first phase. According to the findings of investigating Judge Władysław Bednarz, he was treated at the hospital in nearby Koło. No further details are known.

THIELE, Ernst: Based on the testimony by Walter Piller in 1945, Thiele was an *SS-Hauptscharführer* in rank. He was aged about 48, and was born in Berlin. He was 178 centimeters tall, with thin dark blond parted hair. He was married and lived in Inowrocław. He served in the *Wetterkommando* Legath as a driver for Hans Legath. When the *Wetterkommando* was disbanded, he was posted to SS-*Sonderkommando* Bothmann in *Kulmhof* in the second phase. Thiele perfomed the same driving duties as Gielow, and later he transported chopped wood to the cremation sites, as well as food to the *Waldlager*. He also drove the trucks that took away ashes to be disposed of in the Warta River, according to Walter Piller.

QUAAS, Gerhard: Born on April 26, 1920. He served in the *SS-Sonderkommando Kulmhof* during the first phase, as a member of the *Schutzpolizei* with the rank of *Unterwachtmeister*. According to the findings of investigating Judge Władysław Bednarz, he was treated at the hospital in nearby Koło. No further details are known.

VINKEN, Arthur: Born on November 29, 1909, in Łódź, Poland. He served in the *SS-Sonderkommando Kulmhof* during the first phase. According to the findings of investigating Judge Władysław Bednarz, he was treated at the hospital in nearby Koło. No further details are known.

VOGT, Hans: Born on May 23, 1920, in Westerenger, North Rhine-Westphalia. He served in the *SS-Sonderkommando Kulmhof* during the first phase. According to the findings of investigating Judge Władysław Bednarz, he was treated at the hospital in nearby Koło. No further details are known.

WALLSCHIETZ, Hermann: Born on April 2, 1920. He served in the *SS-Sonderkommando Kulmhof* during the first phase. According to the findings of investigating Judge Władysław Bednarz, he was treated at the hospital in nearby Koło. No further details are known.

WALTHER, Franz: A gas van driver, who arrived in Chełmno in December 1941, or January 1942. No further details are known.

WILDERMUTH, Jakob: He served in the *SS-Sonderkommando Kulmhof* during the first phase. According to the findings of investigating Judge Władysław Bednarz, he was treated at the hospital in nearby Koło. He was a witness during the Chełmno Trial in Bonn during 1962–1963.

WORNSHOFER, Toni: He was a driver at Chełmno. No further details are known.

ZAJDLER, Karol: He served in the *SS-Sonderkommando Kulmhof* during the first phase. He was responsible for camp supplies and the kitchen. No further details are known.

ZESSIN, Hans: Born on February 16, 1911, in Steinwald, Northern Bavaria. He served in the *SS-Sonderkommando Kulmhof* during the first phase. According to the findings of investigating Judge Władysław Bednarz, he was treated at the hospital in nearby Koło. No further details are known.

ZIMMERMAN: He was a member of the *Schutzpolizei* with the rank of *Wachtmeister*. He served in the *SS-Sonderkommando Kulmhof* during the second phase. No further details are known.

Chapter XIII
The Polish *Arbeitskommando*

JASKOLSKI, Lech: He was one of the members of the group of prisoners incarcerated in cell 62, in the Fort VII prison in *Posen*. He took part in the euthanasia *"Aktionen"* in the *Warthegau*, under Lange's supervision. When the death camp at Chełmno was established, he was sent there with his colleagues to form the Polish *Arbeitskommando* until the death camp was liquidated during April 1943.
He returned to the Fort VII prison in *Posen* after Chełmno was liquidated. Later that year, he was employed by Legath's *Wetterkommando* until that unit was disbanded in 1944. Jaskolski, together with three other Poles who served in the *Wetterkommando*, was transferred to the Zabikowo transit camp that was under the control of the *Posen Gestapo*.
On June 23, 1944, Jaskolski was sent to the Auschwitz Concentration Camp, but after only two weeks he was transferred to the Mauthausen Concentration Camp in Austria. His stay there was brief and he was sent to the recently opened Linz III sub-camp. He was liberated by the American forces and he settled in southern France. His further fate is unknown.

LIBELT, Marian: He was sent from a prison in Rakoniewice along with Wacław Świtała to a cell in Fort VII, in *Posen*, which bore the designation "SK." He took part in the euthanasia *"ens"* in the Warthegau, under Lange's supervision. When the death camp at Chełmno was established he was sent there with his colleagues to form the Polish *Arbeitskommando*.
In Chełmno, he was accidentally trapped inside a gas-van during the loading procedure and gassed on January 14, 1942. His body was taken back to the grounds of the mansion and buried there by his fellow members of the Polish *Arbeitskommando*. It is believed that his body was exhumed later and turned over to his family.

MALICZAK, Henryk: Born circa 1903, he was a gardener by profession. He was arrested in November 1939, and imprisoned by the *Gestapo* in the town of Kościan. After three weeks he was transferred to a cell in Fort VII, in *Posen*. The cell was designated with the letters "*SK.*" He took part in the euthanasia "*Aktionen*" in the *Warthegau*, under Lange's supervision. When the death camp at Chełmno was established he was sent there with his colleagues to form the Polish *Arbeitskommando*. He served there until the camp was closed down in April 1943, and then he returned to Fort VII, in *Posen*.

He then served with Jaskolski, Skrzypczynski and Mania in the *Wetterkommando* and was later an inmate in the Żabikowo transit camp near *Posen*. From there, Maliczak was transferred to Auschwitz Concentration Camp with his colleagues on June 23, 1944.

On July 4, 1944, this group of four were transferred to the Mauthausen Concentration Camp in Austria. His stay there was brief and he was sent to the recently opened Linz III sub-camp. He was liberated by the American forces in May 1945.

Maliczak returned to Poland after the War ended and settled in Piotrkowice. This key eyewitness and participant in the history of *Sonderkommando* Lange and the Chełmno death camp was interviewed in 1962, by a correspondent for Czechoslovakia's Rudeho Prava and was questioned twice by the Polish authorities during 1964 and 1967. No charges were ever brought against him, and he died on May 4, 1982.

MANIA, Henryk: He was a teenager studying metalwork in September 1939, when the Germans invaded Poland. He was arrested for allegedly trying to poison a German. After working for a few weeks repairing roads and railway tracks he was transferred from a prison in his home town of Wolsztyn, to Fort VII in *Posen*, where he eventually found himself in a cell with the designation "*SK.*" He took part in the euthanasia "*Aktionen*" in the *Warthegau*, under Lange's supervision. When the death camp at Chełmno was established he was sent there with his colleagues to form the Polish *Arbeitskommando*. He served there until the camp was closed down in April 1943, and then he returned to Fort VII, in *Posen*.

He then served with Jaskolski, Skrzypczynski and Maliczak in the *Wetterkommando* and was later an inmate in the Żabikowo transit camp near *Posen*. From there, Mania was transferred to Auschwitz Concentration Camp, with his colleagues on June 23, 1944. On July 4, 1944, this group of four were transferred to the Mauthausen

Concentration Camp in Austria. His stay there was brief and he was sent to the recently opened Linz III sub-camp. He was liberated by the American forces in May 1945.

After the War ended, Mania returned to Poland and his hometown of Wolsztyn, but he was soon forced to leave. Local residents whose relatives died in Fort VII claimed Mania survived because he collaborated with the Germans. Mania settled in Szczecin, via Poznań.

Mania's legal problems began in 1949, following a case of mistaken identity. The Polish authorities initiated a series of investigations over the following three decades looking into his wartime activities, but no charges were ever brought against him. With the collapse of Communism in Poland, the Institute of National Remembrance re-examined the case and conducted its own investigations. Mania was arrested in November 2000, found guilty of complicity in genocide and was sentenced to eight years in prison. Despite the conviction, the elderly Henryk Mania was released, and he simply vanished into obscurity.

PIEKARSKI, Franciszek: He was a forester by profession, and he was the eldest member of the group of prisoners incarcerated in cell 62, in the Fort VII prison in *Posen*. He took part in the euthanasia *"Aktionen"* in the *Warthegau*, under Lange's supervision. When the death camp at Chełmno was established, he was sent there with his colleagues to form the Polish *Arbeitskommando*, until the death camp was liquidated during April 1943, and this group returned to Fort VII in *Posen*. He died in Fort VII, on July 29, 1943, allegedly from heart failure. According to Maliczak, Franciszek Piekarski died in Fort VII, as a result of a blood clot.

POLUBINSKI, Stanisław: He was one of the members of the group of prisoners incarcerated in cell 62, in the Fort VII prison in *Posen*. He took part in the euthanasia *"Aktionen"* in the *Warthegau*, under Lange's supervision. When the death camp at Chełmno was established he was sent there with his colleagues to form the Polish *Arbeitskommando* until the death camp was liquidated during April 1943, and this group returned to Fort VII in *Posen*. According to Henryk Mania, Polubinski was murdered in Fort VII after being caught smuggling a letter within the prison.

SKRZYPCZYNSKI, Kajetan: He was one of the members of the group of prisoners incarcerated in cell 62, in the Fort VII prison in *Posen*. He took part in the euthanasia *"Aktionen"* in the *Warthegau*, under Lange's supervision. When the death camp at Chełmno was established he was sent there with his colleagues to form the Polish *Arbeitskommando*, until the death camp was liquidated during April 1943, and this group returned to Fort VII in *Posen*.

He then served with Jaskolski, Mania and Maliczak in the *Wetterkommando* and was later an inmate in the Żabikowo transit camp near *Posen*. From there, he was transferred to Auschwitz Concentration Camp, with his colleagues on June 23, 1944. On July 4, 1944, this group of four were transferred to the Mauthausen Concentration Camp in Austria. His stay there was brief and he was sent to the recently opened Linz III sub-camp. He was liberated by the American forces in May 1945. Skrzypczynski emigrated to Sydney, Australia in 1950, and he died of a heart attack on December 19, 1992, in Australia.

SZYMANSKI, Stanisław. He was one of the members of the group of prisoners incarcerated in cell 62, in the Fort VII prison in *Posen*. He took part in the euthanasia *"Aktionen"* in the *Warthegau*, under Lange's supervision. When the death camp at Chełmno was established, he was sent there with his colleagues to form the Polish *Arbeitskommando*.

He died in Chełmno at four o'clock in the afternoon on September 19, 1942, according to a notice received by his family. Szymanski was killed due to his alleged involvement in selling jewellery from the victims murdered in the Chełmno death camp.

Chapter XIV
Testimonies and Trials

The following testimony was made by the former Chełmno guard, Friedrich Hensen, shortly after the end of the Second World War, to the British Army in Germany. Allowances need to be made as English is not the native tongue of the person being interrogated.

Statement By:

Friedrich Hensen

Report of My Activity by the SS Special Detachment in Kulmhof (Chełmno)

Rheinberg – July 13, 1945

Nationality: German

Date of Birth: November 29, 1920

Profession: Police File Sergeant

From 25.04.1940 to 02.07.1940 Police Training in Pohrlitz

From 02.07.1940 to March 1941 SS Police Division at Katscher Oberschlesien

25.03. 1941 to January 1945 Police administration in *Litzmannstadt*

From the Police administration I was assigned in July 1942 to December 1943 to the *Gestapo* and came to the SS Special Detachment in *Kulmhof,* District *Warthbrücken* in Poland.

15.04. 1945 I came into captivity to Hagen at the Police Quarters

Exact Statement of your activity and occupation

Police file sergeant at Pohrlitz Niederdonau.

Were you a member of the *NSDAP*?

No.

Last Service Rank

Police file sergeant.

Report of my activity by the *SS* Special Detachment in *Kulmhof*

Appears the police file Sergeant Friedrich Hensen belonging to the *SS* Special Detachment in *Kulmhof*, District *Warthbrücken* in Poland and says after being made familiar with the subject of the interrogation and exhorted to deposit the real truth, what follows:

Personality: My name is Friedrich Hensen, born the 29 November 1920, in Hagen, Nordrhein-Westfalen. Living in Hagener Strasse, Hagen. I am married with Charlotte Hensen, by birth Mittelstadt, and have two children aged 2 years and 10 months.

In July 1942[169], I was assigned as Police member to the *SS* Special Detachment to *Kulmhof*, District *Warthbrücken*, in Poland, by the *Gestapo*. This detachment composed of about 120 *SD* and Policemen. The leader of the Detachment was Criminal Commissioner Bodman[170]

This camp was indirectly under command of *SS* Himmler—our mission consisted of the extermination of the Jews. I myself was incorporated as a guard. The extermination of the Jews went on as follows:

The Jews were brought by lorry and train to *Kulmhof*. There, all valuables were taken away from them by the detachment and then follows the undressing. After the undressing they came in closed boxlike lorries, which contained about 80–100 persons. In the lorry a pipe went from the motor to the box, in which the Jews were sitting. By starting the motor the gas went inside of the car and within 10 minutes the whole crew was dead. Correspondent they were buried in the wood. Mass graves with evaluation of 20 to 30, 000 were turned out. The Jews were comprised of men, women, children and aged. Also transports with syphilis and typhus diseased came in. They were not gassed but killed by neck-shot.

---

[169] Incorrectly listed as July 1941.
[170] Should read Bothmann.

In the beginning of the year 1941,[171] the Jews were not buried but burned. The buried were exhumed again and burned in the wood-ground built box-formed furnaces. My mission was to keep free the ways running by. I received 11 *Marks* pay daily. The valuables, money, jewels and textile articles were sent to the Ghetto administration of *Posen*.[172] Only young people came to this confinement detachment. The following *SD* men and Policemen of the Special Detachment are known to me, as those chiefly responsible:

Rank	Name	Other Information
Chief *SS* Company Leader	BODMAN	Should be BOTHMANN
SS Lieutenant	PLATE	From Bochum
Police Sergeant	RAUDZUS	
Ditto	REISSNER	
Ditto	LOSCHAK	
Ditto	OSTERMEIER	
Ditto	MICHALSKI	
Ditto	MALZMÜLLER	
Police Master	LENZ	
Ditto	HEIDER	
Police Sergeant	REIBLINGER	
	SCHONBECK	
	ROMBACH	

Where the above-mentioned men are staying now, I cannot state with the best knowledge. I became separated from these people afterwards. I still heard then that the detachment until December, one month before it was disbanded in January 1945.[173] I myself was one and a half years with this detachment until December, one month before it was disbanded.

---

[171] Should read 1942.
[172] Should read Łódź.
[173] Incorrectly stated as January 1944.

The Jews were brought daily with 120 to 150 men in the cellars from a house we called the "Castle." They had to execute heavy work with a very small bread and soup portion. They had to sleep on the stone floor, as the sleeping accommodation, the objects they had on their bodies in the daytime were used. Day and night the Jews were so vexed, thrashed and tortured that they committed suicide.

The photo news of Katyn in the newspapers are to our conviction pictures taken by the Germans of the Jews, who have been murdered by this *SS* Special Detachment. It was only a propaganda purpose for the foreign countries. To take photos from the entire surroundings of *Kulmhof* was most severely forbidden. I cannot say further about this, while this notice contains everything what I have seen and experienced.

I have made these statements to the best of my knowledge and conscience, and I warrant with my own person for the justness of the same.[174]

Testimony by Bronisław Falborski on June 11, 1945.

During the Nazi occupation I worked in the "*Kraft*" garage in Koło (Asnyka Street) as a mechanic. I worked in the firm from April 1942, to 1943. I cannot remember the exact dates. Our firm repaired cars belonging to *SS-Sonderkommando Kulmhof*. Once they told us to repair a vehicle designed for gassing. I cannot tell exactly when this event took place. I think it might have been in the summer of 1942.

The car might have been about 2.50 meters high. Its length was 6 meters. It was a black box-shaped vehicle. The roof was almost flat, and formed a right angle with the walls. It seemed to be covered with sheet metal, though I am not sure. I have not seen the engine. I did not notice the make of the car. The door was locked with a bolt and key. The van was guarded by a few gendarmes and I could not examine its construction closer. I did not notice if there were any gas

---

[174] WO 309/374, National Archives Kew.

masks hanging in the cabin. I do not remember if the car had the registration plates.

I was told to repair the car. I had to change the packing (gasket) between the elastic part of the exhaust pipe and the part leading to the interior of the load-carrying body. The exhaust pipe was not made of uniform material, as in a regular car, but was composed of three parts. The middle part was elastic, just like a hose. It could be linked with the pipe leading to the load-carrying body, directing the exhaust fumes inside, or with the tail pipe extension and then the exhaust fumes were directed outside.

When they brought the vehicle, the pipe was directed to the interior. The packing between the two pipe-fittings had worn out and I was told to change it. I put in asbestos packing and fixed the fittings with four bolts. I enclose a self-made sketch of the exhaust pipe, including the linking element between the exhaust pipe and the pipe directing the gas to the interior. Being urged all the time, I finished the job after half an hour.

At that time people working in the garage were: Zygmunt Roszak, Zbigniew Dudzinski (both in the army), Szablewski Marian (works in the town of Kutno at the railroad station), Jankowski, Junkiert, Lewandowski (I do not know their names or addresses), Zenon Rosa (presently working at the post office).

Apart from this case, I had never witnessed a repair of any *SS-Sonderkommando Kulmhof* car designed for gassing. Right before starting working in the "*Kraft*" garage, I had been working as a chauffeur for May, a forest manager. Because of my job I often appeared in the Chełmno wood. Many times I saw cars going to the wood and back. The vehicles looked just like the one I later repaired in the "*Kraft*" garage. It seemed to me there were only two trucks, the same size. They would pass each other on the way. I cannot tell how long each ride took—it might have lasted half an hour, maybe an hour.

Three times I saw a specially adjusted furniture van, which now remains in the grounds of the former Ostrowski's firm. The first time I saw the car, was in the wood, the second time on the road, and the third time when it was leaving the Chełmno palace courtyard. I saw the vehicle every few days. It was in the spring of 1943. The last time I saw the van was in the grounds of the Ostrowski's firm and I am absolutely sure it was the same car (the same size, shape, color).[175]

Testimony by Władysław Dabrowski on June 13, 1945.

During the German occupation I worked as a railroader. I could observe the arriving transports of Jews. The railroad transports were already coming in the winter of 1942. The Jews were led to the synagogue on foot. There was a rule that the Jews had to stand in rows of threes, but the rule was often neglected.

In the summer of 1942, throughout a period of a few months, the same train brought transports from Łódź to Koło. The train consisted of over twenty covered rail cars, mostly 15-ton cars. Usually there was one railroad car for the escort. The cars were extremely crowded. At the beginning I counted how many times the transports came to Koło bringing Jews. I stopped counting after reaching 101. I knew there was no end to it. The train usually came between midday and 2p.m.

Then the people were loaded into narrow-gauge railroad boxcars. There they had to crowd even more. There was no permanent set of narrow-gauge railroad cars used every day, though sometimes it seemed that some of the cars were used several times. The trains bringing Jews were serviced exclusively by German conductors. In order to load the Jews on the narrow-gauge railroad, the train coming from Łódź was directed to the track number 4 and later to the reloading track. The reloading was extremely brutal. I saw twice Jews killed on the railroad platform.

Before the train from Łódź started arriving at regular basis, there had been some irregular arrivals. During the initial period the Jews were driven off from the railroad station directly to the synagogue. It was

---

[175] Chełmno Witnesses Speak, Konin – Łódź 2004, pp. 149–150.

hard to estimate the number of the transported Jews. According to my estimate the first transports carried 1,200–1,500 people. Later there were about 1,000 each time. Initially the Jews carried their luggage themselves; later the belongings were left at the station and loaded onto trucks. When the Jews were transported by the narrow-gauge railroad, one car was used as a storage place for the luggage.

In some cases, Jews were brought to Chełmno exclusively by trucks. I do not know where they were from. The road leading to Chełmno stretched along the railroad track, so I could observe the events taking place in the road. When the first transports arrived, we—the railroaders could talk to the Jews. They told us that there would be a large ghetto in Chełmno and there were large estates where they would work. We learned that they were brought from Łódź. Later the contact with the Jews was broken, as it was forbidden to approach them.

In 1943, there was an interval in transports. It lasted several months. I cannot determine how long. In the spring of 1942, there was also an interval, but soon after many Jews were transported, also from abroad. The German conductors told me these were Jews from Vienna and Czechoslovakia. They were treated well and were not beaten. They were well dressed and did not speak Polish. The train in which they arrived consisted mainly of passenger cars (but there were no Pullman cars). I saw two such transports at a close distance. In each transport there were over 1,000 people. The transports were escorted. There were not many of them from abroad.

In the summer of 1944, we received an order to clear the reloading track because there would be many transports arriving in Chełmno which would have to be reloaded into the narrow-gauge railroad cars. But the transports did not come—the Chełmno camp was liquidated at the end of 1944.

During the liquidation process, *Sonderkommando -SS* men came to the railroad station and took some things to Chełmno. Those were wooden chests, iron and wooden barrels. Earlier they took away some machines. The machines were transported with the use of a tractor. It was hard to realize what the *SS*-men's intentions were as some of the things were sent somewhere, while others (the new ones—barrels, chests, and even a fold-away barrack) were transported to Chełmno.

I do not know the names of the *SS*-men. I have never talked to them. I did not see Poles brought to Chełmno and I have never heard about it. The last transports were two large trains from Poznań and one from Konin. Once—in 1943, on a warm day, but I cannot remember the exact date—a train brought many Jewish children from Łódź. Among them were a few older people. The children were aged 6–15. They were treated just as bad as the adult Jews. I know nothing about the alleged inspection of the *Gestapo* commission from Berlin.[176]

Statement of Theodor Malzmüller on June 27, 1960.

When we arrived we had to report to the camp commandant, *SS-Hauptsturmführer* Bothmann. The *SS-Hauptsturmführer* addressed us in his living quarters, in the presence of *SS-Untersturmführer* Albert Plate (Bothmann's deputy). He explained that we had been detailed to the *Kulmhof* (Chełmno) extermination camp as guards and added that in this camp the plague boils of humanity, the Jews, were exterminated. We were to keep quiet about everything we saw or heard; otherwise we would have to reckon with our families' imprisonment and the death penalty.

We were then allocated our places in the guard unit (*Wachtkommando*), which consisted of about fifty to sixty police officers from the 1st Company *Litzmannstadt* Police Battalion. As I recall, there were also some officers from the 2nd Company in it. The officer in charge of the guard unit was *Oberleutnant* Gustav Hüfing. He was from Wesel.

The guardroom was situated in the village of *Kulmhof*. The unit members were accommodated in houses in the village. The duties of the guard unit consisted of (1) maintaining the security of the

---

[176] Chełmno Witnesses Speak, Konin – Łódź 2004, pp. 147–148.

guardroom. (2) Guarding the so-called "castle" yard and (3) guarding the so-called "camp in the wood."

The extermination camp was made up of the so-called "castle," and the camp in the wood. The castle was a fairly large stone building at the edge of the village of *Kulmhof*. It was here that the Jews who had been transported by lorry or railway were first brought. The Jews were addressed by a member of the *Sonderkommando* in the castle courtyard. I myself once heard one of these speeches when I was on guard duty in the castle courtyard for a day in December 1942.

When a lorry had arrived, the following members of the *SS-Sonderkommando* addressed the Jews: (1) Camp Commandant Bothmann, (2) *SS-Untersturmführer* Albert Plate, from North Germany, (3) *Polizei-Meister* Willi Lenz, from Silesia, (4) *Polizei-Meister* Alois Häfele,[177] from Württemberg. They explained to the Jews they would first of all be given a bath and deloused in *Kulmhof* and then sent to Germany to work. The Jews then went inside the castle. There they had to get undressed. After this they were sent through a passageway on to a ramp to the castle yard where the so-called "gas van" was parked.

The back door of the van would be open. The Jews were made to get inside the van. This job was done by three Poles, who I believe were sentenced to death. The Poles hit the Jews with whips if they did not get into the gas-van fast enough. When all the Jews were inside the door was bolted. The driver then switched on the engine, crawled under the van and connected a pipe from the exhaust to the inside of the van. The exhaust fumes now poured into the inside of the truck so that the people inside were suffocated. After about ten minutes, when there were no further signs of life from the Jews, the van set off towards the camp in the wood, where the bodies were then burnt.

During the period that I was in the guard unit, most of the time I did sentry duty in the interior of the camp in the wood. The camp was in a clearing in the woods between *Kulmhof* and *Warthbrücken*. As

---

[177] Incorrectly listed as Haberle, in his statement.

a guard just within the camp perimeter, I frequently saw mass graves filled with the bodies of Jews who had been exterminated, being dug up by the Jewish *Arbeitskommando*. The bodies were then burnt in two incinerators.[178]

Statement by Walter Burmeister on January 24, 1961.

As soon as the ramp had been erected in the castle, people started arriving in *Kulmhof* from *Litzmannstadt* in lorries.... The people were told that they had to take a bath, that their clothes had to be disinfected, and that they could hand in any valuable items beforehand to be registered.

On the instructions of *Kommandoführer* Lange, I also had to give a similar talk in the castle to the people waiting there—how often exactly I can no longer say today. The purpose of the talk was to keep the people in the dark about what lay before them. When they had undressed they were sent to the cellar of the castle and then along a passage-way on to the ramp and from there into the gas van. In the castle there were signs marked "To the Baths."

The gas vans were large vans about 4–5 meters long, 2.20 meters wide and 2 meters high. The interior walls were lined with sheet metal. On the floor there was a wooden grille. The floor of the van had an opening which could be connected to the exhaust by means of a removable metal pipe. When the lorries were full of people the double doors at the back were closed and the exhaust connected to the interior of the van.

The *Kommando* member detailed as the driver would start the engine straight away so that the people inside the lorry were suffocated by the exhaust gases. Once this had taken place, the union between the exhaust and the inside of the lorry was disconnected and the van

---

[178] Klee, Dressen, Riess, *Those Were The Days*, Hamish Hamilton, London 1991, pp. 217–218.

was driven to the camp in the woods where the bodies were unloaded.

In the early days they were initially buried in mass graves, later incinerated. I then drove the van back to the castle and parked it there. Here it would be cleaned of the excretions of the people that had died in it. Afterwards it would once again be used for gassings. I can no longer say today what I thought at the time or whether I thought of anything at all. I can also no longer say today whether I was too influenced by the propaganda of the time to have refused to have carried out the orders I had been given.[179]

Statement by Kurt Möbius on November 8, 1961.

In addition, *SS-Hauptsturmführer* Lange said to us that the orders to exterminate the Jews had been issued by Hitler and Himmler. We had been drilled in such a way that we viewed all orders issued by the head of state as lawful and correct. We police went by the phrase, "Whatever serves the state is right, and whatever harms the state is wrong." I would also like to say that it never even entered my head that these orders could be wrong.

Although I am aware that it is the duty of the police to protect the innocent; I was however, at that time convinced that the Jewish people were not innocent but guilty. I believed all the propaganda that the Jews were criminals and sub-humans, and that they were the cause of Germany's decline after the First World War. The thought that one should oppose or evade the order to take part in the extermination of the Jews never entered my head either. I followed these orders because they came from the highest leaders of the state and not because I was in any way afraid.[180]

---

[179] Ibid., pp. 219–220.
[180] Ibid., pp. 220–221.

Investigations and Trials.

In 1946, Judge Władysław Bednarz published his findings about the Chełmno death camp in a 74-page book titled, *Oboz Stracen w Chełmnie nad Nerem* (The Death Camp in Chełmno –on-Ner). On March 29, 1947, despite having sufficient material to go to trial, the District Court in Łódź decided to suspend criminal proceedings against Alois Häfele and others, until they had been arrested and handed over to the Polish authorities.[181]

During 1959, with the establishment of the Central Office of the State Justice Administration for the Investigation of National Socialist Crimes, the German authorities began collecting information about the Chełmno death camp. Formal charges of complicity in mass murder were brought against 12 former members of the *Sonderkommando Kulmhof* on July 5, 1962. The trial commenced on November 26, 1962, in Bonn, West Germany, with 12 former members of the Chełmno garrison facing justice.

The verdicts were as followed:

Name	Verdict	Appeals
Walter Bock	Acquitted	
Anton Mehring	Acquitted	
Alexander Steinke	Acquitted	
Wilhelm Heukelbach	13 months, 2 weeks in prison	Sentence Dropped
Friedrich Maderholz	13 months, 2 weeks in prison	Sentence Dropped
Wilhelm Schulte	13 months, 2 weeks in prison	Sentence Dropped
Gustav Laabs	15 years in prison, loss of civil rights for 10 years	Reduced to 13 years in prison

---

[181] P. Montague, *Chełmno and the Holocaust*, I.B. Tauris and Co. Ltd, London 2012, pp. 178–179.

Walter Burmeister	13 years in prison, loss of civil rights for 10 years	
Alois Häfele	15 years in prison, loss of civil rights for 10 years	Reduced to 13 years in prison
Kurt Möbius	8 years in prison, loss of civil rights for 6 years	
Karl Heinl	7 years in prison, loss of civil rights for 5 years	
Ernst Burmeister	3 and a half years in prison	

International Military Tribunal—Nuremberg.

During the International Military Tribunal (IMT) held at Nuremberg, which began on November 20, 1945, and concluded on October 1, 1946, the Chełmno death camp was not investigated in any great detail. Only two documents cover Chełmno. The most comprehensive is a document covering the report on Chełmno by Judge Władysław Bednarz, which described the camp and the method of extermination in some detail.[182]

The second document is a statement by Rudolf Höss, the Commandant of Auschwitz, describing his visit to Chełmno in September 1942, to witness the exhumation and cremation methods being tested by *SS-Standartenführer* Paul Blobel. On his return to Auschwitz, Höss immediately employed the methods gleaned from Chełmno, in Birkenau to dispose of the corpses of those murdered in Bunker II.[183]

---

[182] IMT Nuremberg Document – USSR 340 – Wiener Library WL 1655/1553.
[183] IMT Nuremberg Document – NO 4498B – Wiener Library WL 1655/3375.

Adolf Eichmann Trial—Jerusalem 1961.

During the Adolf Eichmann Trial in Jerusalem in June 1961, three former Chełmno death camp inmates testified, they were: Michał Podchlebnik, Shimon Srebnik and Mieczysław Zurawski.

Michał Podchlebnik testified in Session 65, on June 5, 1961. He described how he was taken by the police to Chełmno in late 1941. He worked in the forest camp digging pits and unloading the dead bodies from the gas vans. He recalled finding Chazkel Jakubowicz, who came from his home-town of Koło, still alive in the gas van.[184]

Shimon Srebnik also testified on the same day that his father was shot in the street whilst walking with him in the Łódź ghetto. He was deported from the Łódź ghetto at the age of thirteen, to the Chełmno death camp. During the trial, he described how Bothmann, the camp commandant terrorized the Jews through undertaking brutal physical exercises:

> On Sabbath days, he would come whenever he was in the mood for a little fun. He would come, call out four men—I was always the fifth—and say to us: "You see this finger?" We answered: "Yes." He would ask: "What is this?" A finger he would say to us: "No that is not a finger! If I do this," he pointed his thumb downwards. "You lie down, if I do this," he pointed his thumb upwards. "You stand!"
> And he moved it this way and that, in either direction, and we lay down and we got up. If I saw that he was watching I began to get up. The others were getting up and lying down all the time. Once he told them to get up and they were no longer able to do so, they had no breath left. He said to them, "You cannot get up?" They were not even able to speak.
> He asked me "*Spinnefix*" (this is what he called me)... "You too cannot stand up?" I answered: "Yes I can," and I got up, for I had not done all these exercises. He pulled out his revolver, went up to them and killed them.[185]

Mieczysław Zurawski also took the stand on June 5, 1961 and he described how he was deported from Łódź to Chełmno during July

---

[184] www.Nizkor.org (Complete Eichmann Transcripts) Session 65, June 5, 1961.
[185] Ibid.,

1944. He recalled how the *SS* began to liquidate the camp in the forest during September to October 1944:

> We took them (the barracks) down. There were about a hundred men who remained for this work and to remove all the traces. We took apart the crematoria and took apart the places where it said, "Bath-house," and "To the Doctor." These were taken apart and all this was carted off to Koło, and when we were taken away, they dressed us so that one could not tell we were Jews. The gas vans were also taken in the direction of Koło.
> On Sunday, there was no work. So they lined us up with bottles on our heads and had their game of target practice. Those whose bottle was hit stayed alive, and those they hit in the head, fell, and the others had to bury them.[186]

---

[186] Ibid.,

Chapter XV
Epilogue

The first attempt to uncover what had happened at Chełmno was started by a Jewish survivor who had lost his family in the death camp. Jakub Waldman began collecting testimonies from local villagers and from three survivors still in the area. He also participated in the initial visit to the camp by a delegation from the Main Commission for the Investigation of German Crimes in Poland and the Central Jewish Historical Commission during May 1945. The documents he put together are now located in the Jewish Historical Institute (ZHI) in Warsaw. Jakub Waldman passed away in Turek on September 1, 1945.[187]

On May 24, 1945, the above-mentioned commission travelled from Łódź to Chełmno, where they examined the former mansion and the forest camp. They travelled to Koło, where they visited the synagogue and the Ostrowski works, where a vehicle thought to be a gas-van, was parked.

On June 6, 1945, the Polish Ministry of Justice appointed Judge Władysław Bednarz to conduct an official investigation into what happened at the Chełmno death camp. He started work immediately, collecting evidence and recording testimonies from people in the area who had witnessed the atrocities committed by the *Sonderkommando Kulmhof*. He also recorded testimonies of survivors from Podchlebnik, Srebnik and Zurawski.

On the grounds of the former mansion, the pit where worthless items had been burned was excavated and they recovered partially burnt papers, including a 31-page journal, apparently written by a member of the *Waldkommando*. Only 11 of the pages contained entries, written in pencil. Also found in the pit were about 24,200 spoons, 4,500 knives, 2,500 forks and large quantities of pots and pans, eye-glasses and many other items. In addition, various types of

---

[187] P. Montague, *Chełmno and the Holocaust*, I.B. Tauris and Co. Ltd, London 2012, pp. 176.

jewellery, watches, and paper money were found, US dollars, Soviet rubles and German *Reichmarks*.

The money, jewellery and other objects of value that had been recovered from this pit, were placed in boxes, catalogued and deposited in a bank in Łódź, until they were transferred two months later to the Polish National Treasury.

In the former Forest Camp area, Judge Bednarz attempted to secure the area, as locals were stripping the site bare, the external fence had been removed and some of the railroad rails used as grating for the crematoria had been carted off. As with other former death camp sites like Treblinka, this area saw a number of "treasure hunters" descend on the former camp site.

In the nearby town of Koło, Judge Bednarz secured the site of the old synagogue and the Jewish Council building which was located next to the synagogue. The walls inside were covered with handwritten notes left by the people who had passed through it during the first period of the death camp's existence. Among the hundreds of inscriptions only one was found which indicated that the writer knew the fate that awaited them. It read, "Jews don't wait—you will be here one day, then you will be taken to the ovens—transport 13."

The floor of the synagogue was littered with more than 5,000 pairs of shoes. They had arrived, like other shipments before them, via Poznań for repairs. The items were sent by the *Nationalsozialistische Volkswohlfahrt*, a Nazi welfare organization that received goods originating from the death camp. The origin of the shoes was common knowledge among the welfare workers. The shoes were probably thrown away. The smaller synagogue in Koło was demolished in 1989, the larger synagogue in Koło was destroyed by the Nazis in September 1939. Today, the site of the former synagogues is an empty lot, with a small memorial showing the synagogue.

Also in Koło at the former Ostrowski Works, Judge Bednarz examined a van that had been left there by the *Sonderkommando Kulmhof*. There is some doubt as to whether this gas-van was used to gas people or disinfect clothes. Szymon Srebnik thought it was, but Zurawski and guard Bruno Israel thought it was used to disinfect clothes, at least during the second phase. Certainly this may be so in the second phase, when the transports were much reduced, but in the murderous first phase all three gas vans were in use, and therefore a view could be formed that this indeed was a gas-van from the first phase of Chełmno's existence.

On July 30, 1945, during the Judge Bednarz investigation, three mass graves containing the remains of 55 Poles were exhumed in the area of the former forest camp. These Poles had been taken from the prison in Koło and murdered in the forest by shooting, before the camp was established in November 1941. On Sunday, August 5, 1945, the corpses were placed in caskets and given an on-site Christian burial during a nation-wide solemn ceremony, attended by representatives of various political parties, social organizations and members of the investigating commission. A large wooden cross was erected over the grave in memory of those Poles, murdered by the Nazis.

In 1946, Judge Władysław Bednarz published his findings in a 74-page book that we have already covered in the previous chapter.[188]

During 1957, a small monument was erected over the common grave of the last members of the Jewish workers who died in the early morning hours of January 18, 1945. The Jewish communities from Łódź and Włocławek erected the memorial. The memorial bears the inscription written in Polish and Hebrew: "A place sanctified by the blood of thousands of victims of the genocidal Nazi murderers. Honour their memory."

The bodies of the Jewish *Hauskommando* members were never given a proper burial. What is not commonly known, is that the remains of 2 policemen—Haase and the sadistic killer, Willi Lenz, were also buried with the murdered Jewish workers.

In the early 1960's, the Polish government decided to build a monument on the grounds of the former forest camp. The monument was dedicated on September 27, 1964. The memorial consists of a concrete structure, six to seven meters thick, some 35 meters by 36 meters, supported on five pyramid-shaped legs. The front—the

---

[188] P. Montague, *Chełmno and the Holocaust*, I.B. Tauris and Co. Ltd, London 2012, pp. 176–178.

side facing the road, features a bas-relief representing the victims. To the right is inscribed the Polish word *"Pamietamy"*—"We remember." Extracts of the note written by the Jewish craftsmen in the granary, penned by Izaak Siegelman, are inscribed on the back of the monument.[189]

In 1975, the area of the former forest camp underwent landscaping improvements, an asphalt road, paths and squares were laid out and decorative shrubs were planted. Further work along these lines was carried out in the early 1980's. During the summers of 1986 and 1987, the District Museum in Konin commenced archaeological work in the former forest camp area, with a view to establishing a museum there. Three years later, on June 17, 1990, a small museum was opened on the grounds of the former forest camp. Where the crematoria stood during 1941–1943, fragments of one of the crematoria's foundations were discovered during the evacuations and were put on display.

Near the crematorium a "Wall of Remembrance," which measured thirty-seven-and a half meters long and just over two meters high with the inscription "To the memory of the Jews murdered in Chełmno 1941–1945," was erected. The concrete wall also features a gate over which is inscribed in Hebrew: "The gate through which the just will pass." In addition to this "Wall of Remembrance," additional memorials have been erected over time, representing the Jewish communities murdered on these grounds, from locations such as Bełchatów, Brzeziny, Gabin and Łódź.

On August 7, 1991, an updated tablet was unveiled at the gravesite of the Poles who were shot in the forest during 1939. On the same day, a new monument was unveiled, an obelisk in memory of Stanisław Kaszynski, who was murdered on the mansion grounds on February 3, 1942, after being arrested for writing letters to the Swiss Consulate in Łódź, describing what was occurring in Chełmno.

A memorial cemetery was unveiled on August 22, 1994, on the grounds of the former forest camp to mark the 50th anniversary of

---

[189] P. Montague, *Chełmno and the Holocaust*, I.B. Tauris and Co. Ltd, London 2012, p. 179.

the liquidation of the Łódź ghetto. The initiative was headed by the Turek Compatriots' Association from Israel, and features Jewish headstones salvaged from nearby Turek.

The District Museum in Konin, through analyzing aerial photographs taken in 1958 and 1979, shows two important structures in the former forest camp; a field furnace from the first phase of the camp's operation and a crematorium used in the second phase. In 1998, the Museum in Konin purchased the land that included the grounds of the former mansion.

Between the years 1997 and 2001, the museum discovered waste pits within the grounds of the former mansion used to burn worthless items; they also excavated the former mansion itself, down to the foundations. They found numerous items, such as tools used by the tailors and shoemakers who worked in the basement. The excavation also revealed the floor plan of the basement area. Visitors to the site today can see the stairs leading down to the basement and the corridor through which thousands made their last journey on this earth, into the waiting gas-van.

During 2003 and 2004, further archaeological work was conducted in the former forest camp area and the location of the two main crematoria from the first phase and the two crematoria from the second period were established. Mass graves and individual objects were also found.[190]

On Monday, September 12, 2005, Cameron Munro, Artur Hojan, Lukasz Postaremczak and Chris Webb set off from our overnight hotel in Turek, for our trip to Chełmno and the surrounding important places connected with the camp. An extract from my daily journal, parts of which were published in the book *Postcards from the Past* published in 2009, records what we saw that day:

After breakfast we drove to Dąbie, to meet our guide for the day, Zdzisław Lorek, better known as Lorek, for obvious reasons. Lorek, without wasting any time, took us to the former Jewish Quarter, and the first site we visited was the church in the town which the Nazis

---

[190] P. Montague, *Chełmno and the Holocaust*, I.B. Tauris and Co. Ltd, London 2012, pp. 180–181.

used as a storage place for goods confiscated from the deportees sent to Chełmno. The next place we visited was the former Jewish synagogue, which had now been converted into flats. Lorek managed to speak to one of the owners and he allowed us into the roof space, where there was a beautiful Hebrew inscription in yellow writing on a blue background. This inscription was a real treasure from a vanished world.

The next thing we saw in the former ghetto area was the Rabbi's house, and then we made our way to the edge of the village to the former house of *SS* Doctor, Rolf König, who was on good terms with Chełmno Commandant, Hans Bothmann, and where drinking parties took place, involving members of the death camps' staff. At the rear of the house are garages and according to Lorek, Dr. König's driver had started the engine and was almost gassed as he had used a fuel mixture used in the gas-vans.

The 975 Jews who lived in Dąbie were taken to Chełmno on December 14, 1941, where they were murdered.

Lorek then suggested we visit Grabow, which was where Szlamek Bajler, who had escaped from Chełmno on January 19, 1942, made contact with Rabbi Jakub Szulman, to warn him of what was happening at Chełmno. The synagogue and the Rabbi's house are still standing. The synagogue and former Rabbi's house are now a storage place and the Rabbi's house is now an office. We return to the car after taking photographs, to the small main square, which contains the former Jewish houses where Poles were interviewed in the Claude Lanzmann's film "Shoah."

The 1240 Jews who lived in Grabow were gassed on April 10, 1942, in Chełmno.

Next stop on our schedule was the Koło station, which was virtually unchanged in sixty years, apart from a modern looking footbridge. Koło station is approximately 12 kilometers from the village of Chełmno. It was at this station that deportees arriving from Łódź and other places in the *Warthegau* in trains were transferred to the narrow-gauge railway for the one way journey to Powercie. Whilst the station is virtually unchanged, the main track and the narrow-guage railway tracks have been moved and relaid during the electrification of the line.

Leaving the station we make our way to the former ghetto area, where we see the space that used to hold the large and small Jewish synagogues. The Jews of Koło, some 3,500, were ordered to congregate in front of the *Judenrat* next to the synagogue on December 8–10, 1941, and they became the first victims of Chełmno death camp.

We take photographs of the houses that once were homes to the Jews of Koło, and at the rear of the former ghetto area, we arrived at the former Ostrowski factory, which was where Judge J. Bronowski from the Regional Court in Łódź inspected the gas van from Chełmno in October 1945. Artur Hojan entered into a discussion with an elderly factory security guard who explained that the hanger shown in the famous photograph of the 1945 inspection had been knocked down after the War, and that the gas van had stayed on site until the 1960's, when it was sold to a local car dealer.

We then drove from Koło station to Powercie, which is where the deportees to Chełmno were unloaded and went by foot to the mill at Zawadka. The Jewish deportees were kept in the mill overnight before being taken in lorries to the "Castle" in Chełmno, where they were gassed. The mill was destroyed during the 1980's and all you can see now is the remains of the foundations. There was also a bridge at the mill, where the ashes from the crematorium in the *Waldlager* were thrown into the River Warta, but only some wooden posts remain.

Now we drove in Lukasz Postaremczak's car to the site of the former death camp in Chełmno village, and we parked up on the former "Palace" grounds. We visit the small office / museum and purchase some books on Chełmno, such as *Chełmno Witnesses Speak* and *The Extermination Center for Jews in Chełmno-on-Ner*.

We move towards the ruins of the former "Palace." Looking towards the church, we see the remains of the underground basement that the Jews passed through after undressing, to go up the ramp to the waiting gas van. It started to rain so we rushed into the former Granary building; this had now been converted into an excellent museum, and this gave us the opportunity to take some photos of the exhibits recovered from various archeological research, such as beer bottles and so on....

With the rain finally abating, we once again gathered around the "Palace" ruins, where Lorek and Artur provided a detailed description of the extermination process and the destruction of the "Palace" in the spring of 1943.

We returned to the car and turned left onto the main road heading towards Koło, following exactly the same route the gas vans took to the *Waldlager* site in the Rzuchów Forest. The journey is short and the sun is now shining after the heavy rain. After a brief stop in the museum, which is small but excellent, Lorek takes us on a tour of the mass graves area, and the cremation sites.

Recent archeological research sites were visited. Lorek explained that the Nazis carried out experimental cremations in 1942, and he was of the opinion that there were at least nine cremation sites; some were much larger than others. We stopped by some freshly dug long ditches at the rear of the crematoria ruins. These archeological digs had been carried out to see if they contained any bodies, but they didnot.

A large party of Jewish students arrived at the cremation site, as we were looking at the remains of the dismantled crematoria, which we photographed from all angles. The Jewish students posed by the nearby memorial, with their unsmiling armed security guards looking on; this is a wall with an arch towards the right hand side, with the inscription "Pamieci Zydow Pomordowanych w Chełmnie 1941–1945."

We leave the former *Waldlager* site and head back into Chełmno village, where we dropped Artur Hojan and Cameron Munro off, and Lukasz's agreed to take Lorek to his home, when it started to rain again heavily. The rain poured down, accompanied by thunder and lightning, as we crossed the new motorway construction site. We found Lorek's home and drove across a field to his place, whilst the lightning forked towards the earth.

We now had to return to Chełmno village and pick up Artur and Cameron; we crossed the River Ner with the church looming in the distance. We found ourselves again on the motorway construction site, which had now, with the rain, turned into a sea of mud. Understandably, with no road markings, we got hopelessly lost, but luckily we came across a group of construction workers, and we followed their van back to Chełmno village, where we met up with Artur and Cameron.

Our visit to Chełmno had come to an end, and as it got dark we set off on the road to Łódź to continue the next part of our research trip, accompanied by more violent thunder and lightning storms.[191]

We visited Chełmno again in 2009, this time accompanied by my friend Professor Matthew Feldman from Northampton University. We visited more or less the same places, but we went to Krośniewice and Sompolno for the first time. The 1,000 Jews from Sompolno went to Chełmno on February 2, 1942, and the 900 Jews from Krośniewice went to Chełmno on March 2, 1942. All the Jews perished at the Chełmno death camp.

In the village of Chełmno itself, we saw the house where Erhard and Marthe Michelsohn lived, virtually opposite the church, and the former *Deutsches Haus*, which once was the village fire station. We then drove to the former *Waldlager* to see the ruined crematoria and the other cremation sites.

---

[191] Chris Webb – Daily Journal – Research Trip September 2005 – extracts contained in the self-published book *Postcards From the Past*, Cranleigh, 2009.

Appendix I
Letter from Rabbi Szulman—Grabow

Rabbi Jakub Szulman
Postcard to Łódź Ghetto
January 19, 1942

My Dearest Ones!

I have not replied to your letters, since I did not know exactly what was being rumoured. Now, to our great misfortune, we know everything. An eyewitness, who by chance, was able to escape from hell, has been to see me. I learned everything from him. The place where everyone is being put to death is called Chełmno, not far from Dąbie; people are burned in the nearby forest of Łochów.

People are killed in one or two ways: either by shooting or by gassing. This is what happened in the towns of Dąbie, Izbica Kujawska, Kłodawa and others.

Recently, thousands of Gypsies have been brought there from the so-called Gypsy Camp in Łódź and for several days thousands of Jews from Łódź are being brought and the same is done to them.

Do not think that a madman is writing; unfortunately it is the cruel and tragic truth (Good God). O Man, throw off your rags, sprinkle your head with ashes, or run through the streets and dance in madness.

I am so worried by the sufferings of Israel, my pen can write no more. I feel my heart is breaking. But perhaps the Almighty will take pity and save the "last remnants of our people!"

Help us, O Creator of the World!

Grabow, January 19, 1942
Jakub Szulman

Appendix II
List of Transports to Chełmno

Date	Origin of Transport	Number of People Deported
1941		
December 7–11	Koło	3,500
December 14	Dąbie	975
December	Dobra	1,100
1942		
January 2–9	Łódź (Roma)	4,300
January 10–12	Kłodawa	1,000
January 13	Bugaj	600
January 14–15	Izbica Kujawska	1,000
January 16–29	Łódź	10,003
February 2	Sompolno	1,000
February 22–28	Łódź	7,025
March 1–31	Łódź	24,699
March 2	Krośniewice	900
March 3	Żychlin	3,200
March	Ozorków	500
March 26	Kutno	6,000
April 1–2	Łódź	2,349
April 10	Grabow	1,240
April 10–11	Łęczyca	1,750
April 16–17	Gostynin	2,000
April 16–17	Gąbin	2,150
April 17	Sanniki	250
April 22	Osięciny	300
April	Brześć Kujawski	200
April	Piotrków Kujawski	550

April 30-May 2	Włoclawek	3,500
May 14–15	Łódź	10, 914
May 17–18	Pabiance	4,000
May 19–20	Brzeziny	3,000
May 22	Ozorków	300
June 10–11	Radziejów Kujawski	630
July 20	Stary Czachulec	10,000
July	Lutomiersk	750
August 11–13	Bełchatów	4953
August 14	Szadek	450
August 22	Sieradz	1,400
August 22–24	Warta	1,353
August 24–28	Łask	2,600
August	Wieluń	10,000
August 25–26	Zduńska Wola	10,900
September 1–2 September 7–12	Łódź	15, 685
September 14	Zelów	6,000
1944		
June 23	Łódź	562
June 26	Łódź	912
June 28	Łódź	803
June 30	Łódź	700
July 3	Łódź	700
July 5	Łódź	709
July 7	Łódź	700
July 10	Łódź	700
July 12	Łódź	700
July 14	Łódź	700
Grand Total		172, 230

Appendix III
Inspection Protocol—
Ostrowski Factory Koło

Koło, 13 October 1945.

Persons present: Judge J. Bronowski from the Regional Court in Łódź for the purpose of inspecting the vehicle found in Koło on the area of the former "Ostrowski" factory at present owned by the County Vehicle Office in Koło. The inspection determined the following:

Details of driver's cab and engine:

Inscription on the radiator grill: "Magrius"

Length of the vehicle: 8.3 meters

Average width: 2.1 meters

Width of the rear: 2.32 meters

Length of engine: 1.65 meters

Width of radiator: 67 centimeters

Height of radiator: 80 centimeters

Rear Compartment

Length: 5.25 meters

Height: 2.43 meters

Width: 2.32 meters

The rear compartment is in the form of a sealed plank box, painted a grey-green colour. The roof is concave and covered with tar paper. In each side wall there is a rectangular opening measuring 46 cms x 15 cms lined with tar paper, at a height of 2 meters above the edge of the lowest plank. At the rear of this compartment there is a double-door, which occupies the whole width of the compartment and suspended on three pairs of hinges. Beaten into the paint of the doors there is the inscription "Otto Kohn Spedition, Ruf 516 Zeulen... da i. TH."

On the front mud-guard there is the inscription "Atü 5.8" and on the door of the driver's cab "40 km" in black paint on a white disc. The two driver's doors are 1.55 meters in height; 1.4 meters long; and 2.3 meters wide. The seats and steering wheel are missing, as is the tachometer on the dashboard. Under the bonnet, the engine is a 6-cylinder "Deutz" run on Diesel. Also missing are the dynamo, starter, ventilator, air filter and fuel pump. On a plaque on the engine there is the inscription:

"Humboldt-Deutz A.G. "Magrius Werke" Ulm (Donau) Baujahr 1939. Lieferdat739 Abn- Stempel. Fahrgestell Nr. 9282/38. Nutzlast kg 2700. Fahrgestell-Baumuster 023. Eingewicht 4980kg. Motor Baumuster FoM 513 zul. Gesamt gew. 7900 Leistung P.S. 105 cm3 7412. Zulässige Achsendrücke vorn kg 2400 hinten 5500."

The front wheels are missing, as well as the differential and headlights. The doors are 7 cm thick, and the walls of the rear compartment 8 cm thick. The inside walls, the doors, floor and trapdoors of the rear compartment are lined with 2 mm thick galvanized iron. The interior edges are packed with triangular wooden cleats 6 cm wide and 4 cm thick.

In the forward part of the rear compartment, on the side cleats, there are ladders 2.04 meters wide. The interior galvanized iron is badly corroded. The doors are secured shut by round iron rods that run lengthwise across the doors to two hooks at the ends, and fastened shut by a padlock. The doors are lined with tar paper. At the rear there are insertions for hooks.

With this the inspection was concluded.[192]

---

[192] Holocaust Historical Society Archives.

Appendix IV
The Extermination Center

From a Document Received by the Polish Jewish Labor Party "Bund"

In October 1941, the entire Jewish population of Konin County—some 3,000 persons—was driven together in Zagórów. Every Jew was compelled to pay 4 *Reichsmarks* and to subject himself to a medical examination. This examination, imposed on all men, ages 14 to 60, and all women, ages 14 to 50, had as its purpose, ostensibly, to determine each individual's ability to work. Following this examination the Jews were herded into trucks and sent off 60 at a time. Each could take with him a kit of personal necessities weighing no more than one pound. Their journey was to the Kazimierz woods, in the area of Zagórów, where the Jews were led into the woods. From that moment on, no more was heard of the Jews, and every trace of them was lost. Searches, letters of inquiry, or specially—dispatched messengers—in the *Reich* itself or in the Districts controlled by the Government-General—proved fruitless.

In mid-December, similar expulsions of Jews took place in Koło County. In that county, the entire Jewish population of Koło (2,000 persons), and of Dombie-on-Narew (1,000 persons), were taken to the same woods. Some time afterwards, in early January 1942, the same fate befell the Jews of the following towns: Kłodawa (46 persons on January 2 and 4); Izbica, Kujawy County (45 persons on January 9). From January 15 onwards, groups of Jews that had been driven out of the Łódź ghetto, began to arrive in Chełmno. The first group was composed of 750 families – some 3,000 persons. In that manner, thousands upon thousands passed through Chełmno. They were not told where they were being taken—or why. Unofficially, however, the Germans spread various rumors among their victims: that in Chełmno, a Jewish community would be created for the entire county; that this was but a part of the plan to settle all Jews in the vicinity of Pinsk, or in Galicia, and so on, and so on.

All Jews who had been taken, disappeared. Despite the fact that the Germans planned the entire procedure to the minutest detail, carefully co-ordinating all of their activities, and maintaining the strictest secrecy, all particulars are nevertheless now known.

The arriving groups would first be taken into the Chełmno church. There the Jews would lay down their belongings and be brought into the castle. The church and its vicinity would be lined with uniformed *Gestapo* agents and civilians. Then, too, there would be stationed, in the area surrounding the church, a large number of gendarmes. At no time did victims of two separate transports have the opportunity of meeting. The arrivals were, at the start, treated very courteously and kindly. They were helped in getting down from the truck, and so on.

An elderly German in his 60's attired in civilian clothes was especially amiable. The Jews would be taken into a large well-heated chamber, lined with ladders as one finds in a public bath. From this chamber, stairs led down to a ramp-like structure. On the sides were a number of cellars. In one of these cellars, the elderly German, to whom we have referred, addressed the new arrivals, telling them that the entire transport was due to be sent to the ghetto in Łódź, that the men would be employed in factories, at trades and in commerce; that the women would be given jobs in house-keeping and the children sent to school. However, before going to the Łódź ghetto, they must bathe in the castle bath, submit to disinfection, and permit also their clothing to be disinfected. Following this talk, they would be told to disrobe—the women to their underwear, the men to their shirts and garters. Whatever personal documents, valuable articles and money the Jews had in their possession, they were told to turn in.

Finally, the entire group would be led, through the previously mentioned steps, into the "bath." In reality however, they were taken through a bitterly-cold hallway to the ramp. There, the Germans' treatment of the Jews would suddenly change. With whips and gun butts the Jews would be driven into an automobile. The automobile was a large, grey truck, whose rear door was locked hermetically, permitting no air to get in. The walls of the truck were lined with tin, the floor—with ladders, under which were pipe openings, approximately 15 centimeters in diameter, covered with sieve wire. These pipes were part of the gas mechanism found at the front of the car and regulated by the chauffeurs. After the victims were thrown into the truck it was sealed.

The car would drive into the woods, some 7 kilometers away, and travel about 15 minutes. On the left of the road, some 200 steps from the path, one came upon the execution place, encircled with gendarmes, who were armed with machine guns. In one corner was a big dig-out, 5 meters deep and one by one-and-a-half meters wide—below, and five meters wide – above. At this spot, around 30 Germans were gathered (gendarmes, SS-men, and civilians), and from 20-50 Jewish grave-diggers, naked, but for the shirts they wore.

The truck would halt about 100 meters from the grave. The chauffeur, who served both as chauffeur and as executioner, would turn on the gas apparatus and leave the truck. From the truck would come stifled cries, howls, and poundings on the walls. After a quarter-hour, all would be quiet. Then the chauffeur would go into the truck driver's compartment, and turning on an electric switchlight, peer through the window into the truck's gas chamber. Having made certain that the victims were dead, he would drive the truck nearer towards the grave. After a five-minute wait, the SS officer would order the truck to be opened.

No sooner was the truck chamber opened than a stinging odor of gas filled the air. A little while thereafter, eight Jewish grave-diggers would proceed with their job. Four would toss down the dead bodies, two of their colleagues would haul the corpses into the graves, while two others would place them in position. The men and women who perished in the chamber looked as though they were simply asleep, but were smeared with excrement—probably because of the effect of the gas and the horrible fear.

Two German civilians[193] would again examine every corpse, so as to rob the dead of their last belongings. They would fling off rings from the fingers and lockets too. With pliers, they would extract gold

---

[193] These were in fact members of the Polish *Arbeitskommando*.

teeth from the mouths of the victims, and make certain there were no hidden articles of value on the backs of the men, or in the sex organs of the women. The desecrated and robbed bodies would then be placed in rows in the grave, under the direction of the SS man who, twig in hand, supervised all operations. The head of one victim would be laid at the feet of another, and in the spare room that remained, children were placed. One such sector totalled 200 victims.

After mid-January 1942, the layers were covered with chloride powder, so as to remove the nauseating odor. Daily, victims from 6 to 9 transports would be buried in this manner described above. After a thorough cleansing, the truck would depart. The Lubrodzer Woods were at all times guarded by gendarmes, so that the only witnesses of the executions were the unfortunate grave-diggers, who were confined in the cellars of the castle.

At seven-o'clock in the morning they would receive bitter, lukewarm coffee and dry bread—taken from the kits that the Jews had brought with them. After breakfast, the cellar doors –clamped down with a triple lock—were opened, and an SS officer would command, "Juden heraus." The officer would himself never go into the cellar, fearing acts of violence on the part of the victims. After having ascertained their number again and again, the Germans would throw them into the truck and take them to the place of execution. There, the "job" would take the entire morning.

For lunch they would again receive bitter, cold coffee and frozen bread. Of the group of grave-diggers, eight, who were busy at their "job" in the dug-out, were not permitted to leave their posts at all. At noon-time, they would receive, in the real dug-out, one portion of coffee. In the evening, these eight would be commanded to lie down in the grave—facing the corpses, whereupon one of the SS men would riddle their brains with machine gun bullets. The grave-diggers who survived, would fill in the graves of the new victims, and at about 5 o'clock return to the cellar.

There were times, however, when the diggers worked until late in the night, in the glare of floodlights (when they buried transports of victims from Łódź for example). Without being granted the slightest respite, the grave-diggers were under surveillance—from the moment they left the cellar in the morning, until they returned at night. Any sign of fatigue, on the part of the diggers, would result, right there and then, in death, or in lashes on the back.

The surviving grave-diggers were all certain that eventually they would all be murdered. The guards—adding to the misery of the men—compelled them to join in choral chants, such as, "Wir danken Adolf Hitler für das Essen." On numerous occasions, the diggers tried to escape, smash windows, and inform the outside world of what was happening in Chełmno. They threw letters out of the stove chimney, and out of autos. Finally, three grave-diggers succeeded in escaping, and it is from them that we have the present chronicle.[194]

---

[194] The Massacre of a People – What Democracies Can Do, Jewish Frontier Association, New York 1943, WL OSP 2176.

Appendix V
My Tribute to Artur Hojan

Fig. 40   Artur Hojan (Ada Hojan)

Artur Hojan

1973–2013

Artur Hojan was born on August 7, 1973, in Głogów, Lower Silesia, in Poland. He lived in Kościan and he graduated from the Technical Secondary School there and went on to earn a degree in Geology at the Adam Mickiewicz University in Poznań. After his graduation, he sought a career as a journalist and reporter and he was awarded a prize for journalism in a national competition, named in honor of Stefan Batory. Artur loved climbing in the mountains, and was a member of the "Club Alpine" in Poznań, during breaks from his studies. He also loved the sea, and was particularly fond of the Baltic coast and Riga. His favorite city in Poland was Wrocław.

He loved reading books and watching films, such as "Knife in the Water." His favourite actor was Jack Nicholson and his favorite directors were Roman Polanski and Andrzej Żuławski. He also loved some British television programmes such as "Fawlty Towers" and "You rang M'Lord." He was also very keen on listening to music, by such bands as Kraftwerk and Tangerine Dream. He also liked the jazz great Chick Corea.

However, one of his great loves was history and whilst researching his first book, he came into contact with the Nazi Euthanasia murder programme; his book *Terra Incognita* was published in 2002. One of his relatives, his uncle Leszek Woliński was incarcerated in Gross Rosen Concentration Camp, and his stories inspired Artur to research this subject more extensively.

Following the publication of *Terra Incognita*, a fitting memorial was erected in Jarogniewice Forest where the gas vans travelled, from the Kościan psychiatric hospital and the victims were buried by the Nazis. The unveiling of this memorial was marked by the attendance of Szewach Weiss, the former Israeli Ambassador to Poland, and this took place on September 25, 2002.

I first met Artur in Kraków, on the ARC trip to Poland in July 2004. Artur acted as a guide and translator, although his English was a bit rusty as one of the banks in Kraków will testify, when I tried to cash some Traveller's cheques. Luckily we became firm friends and a year later in September 2005, Cameron Munro and I returned to Poland and experienced a very interesting trip that visited a number of places, including Poznań, Kościan, Chełmno, Warsaw and Treblinka. Artur organized and planned the whole trip, and it was without doubt the most impressive Holocaust related research trip that I have ever been on.

Artur was a well-respected expert on Herbert Lange and the *SS-Sonderkommando* at Chełmno, as well as the general history of the Chełmno death camp and the Euthanasia actions carried out in the *Warthegau* area of Poland, similar to the mass murder programme carried out by the Nazis in the *Reich*, under the *T4* codename. As a result of our trip and Artur's knowledge, I published a book titled *Postcards from the Past*. Artur designed the cover and helped me with drawings and text, which gave a day-to-day account of our trip.

Artur and Cameron who had co-founded the Tiergartenstrasse 4 Association based in Berlin, put on a memorable presentation in

Kościan during our trip, called "The Chronicles from Dead Places." The presentation was held in the theatre on Bernardynska Street and was extremely well attended. One of those who attended was Mr. Marian Koszewski, a survivor from Auschwitz Concentration Camp, who spoke briefly and warmly about the presentation.

We repeated part of our 2005 trip four years later in 2009, this time we were accompanied by Professor Matthew Feldman and Cameron Munro. Artur once again took care of all of the planning and bookings. We visited a host of places such as Koło, Dąbie, Krośniewice, Kutno, Sompolno, Chełmno and Łódź. We spent the final day in Warsaw, where Artur took us to see a remaining part of the Warsaw ghetto wall, and the building which used to be the *Gestapo* Headquarters in Al. Szucha. Artur brilliantly rescued my bag, containing my passport, flight tickets and camera, which I had stupidly left in the taxi that took us to the ZIH building.

In the afternoon we parted at the Main Station in Warsaw, on June 5, 2009, and this was sadly the last time we saw each other in the flesh. Over the years that followed we spoke via Skype and communicated regularly by e-mails. I watched with pride as Cameron, Artur and others developed the Tiergartenstrasse 4 Association into a well-respected Holocaust research organization. They have produced many publications and given lectures on a wide range of Holocaust related topics. Artur went out at night in December 2013, and tragically never returned.

Artur will be greatly missed by his wife Adrianna and their young daughter Zuzia, and by his other family members and friends.

I will always remember him with great affection and he will always remain in my heart. I hope that in some small way, I have through this book provided a legacy for his research and unfinished work caused by his untimely death in December 2013.

Artur Hojan

Rest In Peace our dear friend.

Gone but never forgotten.

Chris Webb, with considerable help from Ada Hojan and the Hojan Family.

Illustrations

Fig. 1   Pre-War Chełmno and Kalisch Postcard (Chris Webb Private Archive)

Fig. 2   Posen Gestapo Headquarters (Chris Webb Private Archive)

Fig. 3 Chełmno Schloss Pre-War – Chełmno Museum (Cameron Munro)

Fig. 4   Kulmhof 1941 – Chełmno Museum (Cameron Munro)

Fig. 5   Transport of Jews at Koło – Chełmno Museum (Professor Matthew Feldman)

Fig. 6 Transport of Jews Arrive – Chełmno Museum (Professor Matthew Feldman)

Fig. 7 Polish Arbeitskommando and Guards in Kulmhof – Chełmno Museum (Cameron Munro)

Fig. 8   Gas Van in Koło after the War and Gustav Laabs – Chełmno Museum (Cameron Munro)

Fig. 9   Group Photo of Polish Arbeitskommando in Chełmno (Holocaust Historical Society)

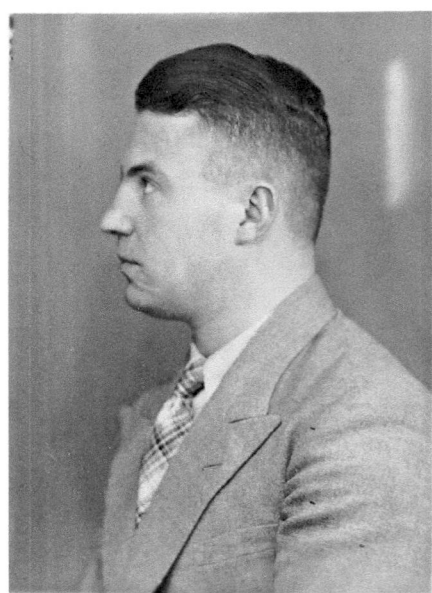

Fig. 10 Herbert Lange (Bundesarchiv, BE2-2011/A-2119. Reprint with kind permission.)

Fig. 11 Hans Bothmann (Holocaust Historical Society)

Fig. 12   Kosten (Kościan) Sanatorium 1941 Postcard (Chris Webb Private Archive)

Fig. 13   Warthbrücken Vogelschau Showing the Old and New Synagogue (Chris Webb Private Archive)

Fig. 14   Warthbrücken Wartime Postcard (Chris Webb Private Archive)

Fig. 15   Warthbrücken Riga Gasthaus Postcard (Chris Webb Private Archive)

Fig. 16 Inside of a Gas Van (Courtesy of The Wiener Library)

Fig. 17 Hans Bothmann's Quarters in Kulmhof (Courtesy of The Wiener Library)

Fig. 18 Chełmno Granary (Courtesy of The Wiener Library)

Fig. 19 Interior of a Gas Van (Courtesy of The Wiener Library)

Fig. 20–22 Waldlager 1945 (Courtesy of The Wiener Library)

Fig. 23   Radegast Litzmannstadt (Chris Webb Private Archive)

Fig. 24   Chełmno Church 2005 (Chris Webb Private Archive)

Fig. 25   Chełmno Kommandantur 2005 (Chris Webb Private Archive)

Fig. 26   Chełmno Schloss Ruins and Church 2005 (Chris Webb Private Archive)

Fig. 27   Chełmno Granary 2005 (Chris Webb Private Archive)

Fig. 28   Chełmno Schloss Ruins 2005 (Chris Webb Private Archive)

Fig. 29   Chełmno Waldlager Mass Graves 2005 (Chris Webb Private Archive)

Fig. 30   Chełmno Waldlager 2005 (Chris Webb Private Archive)

Fig. 31   Chełmno Schloss Ruins 2009 (Chris Webb Private Archive)

Fig. 32   Chełmno Former Deutsches Haus 2009 (Chris Webb Private Archive)

Fig. 33   Chełmno Waldlager Crematorium ruins 2009 (Professor Matthew Feldman)

Fig. 34   Koło Railway Station 2005 (Cameron Munro)

Fig. 35   Koło – Factory where gas-van was found 2005 (Chris Webb Private Archive)

Fig. 36   Grabow Synagogue and Rabbi's House 2005 (Cameron Munro)

Fig. 37   Dąbie Church 2005 – Used by the SS Sonderkommando Kulmhof as a storehouse (Chris Webb Private Archive)

Fig. 38   Dąbie – Dr. Königs House 2005 (Cameron Munro)

Fig. 39   Zawadka Mill Owners House (Cameron Munro)

Fig. 40   Chełmno Sign 2005 (Cameron Munro)

Fig. 41   Artur Hojan (Ada Hojan)

Documents, Drawings, Maps

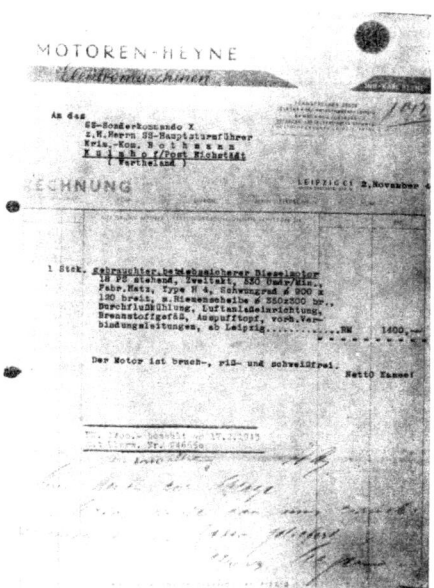

Doc. 1   Kulmhof Motoren-Heyne Invoice (Artur Hojan)

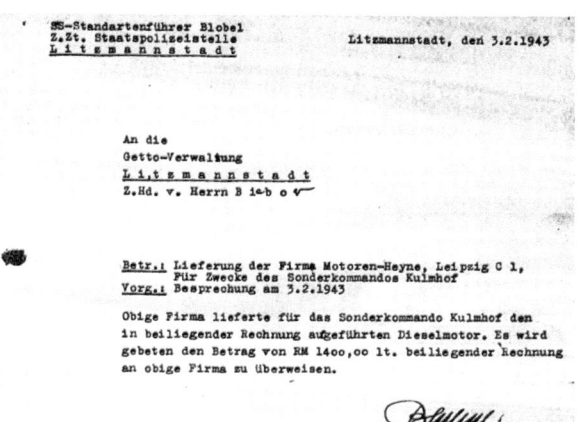

Doc. 2   Paul Blobel Motoren-Heyne Invoice (Artur Hojan)

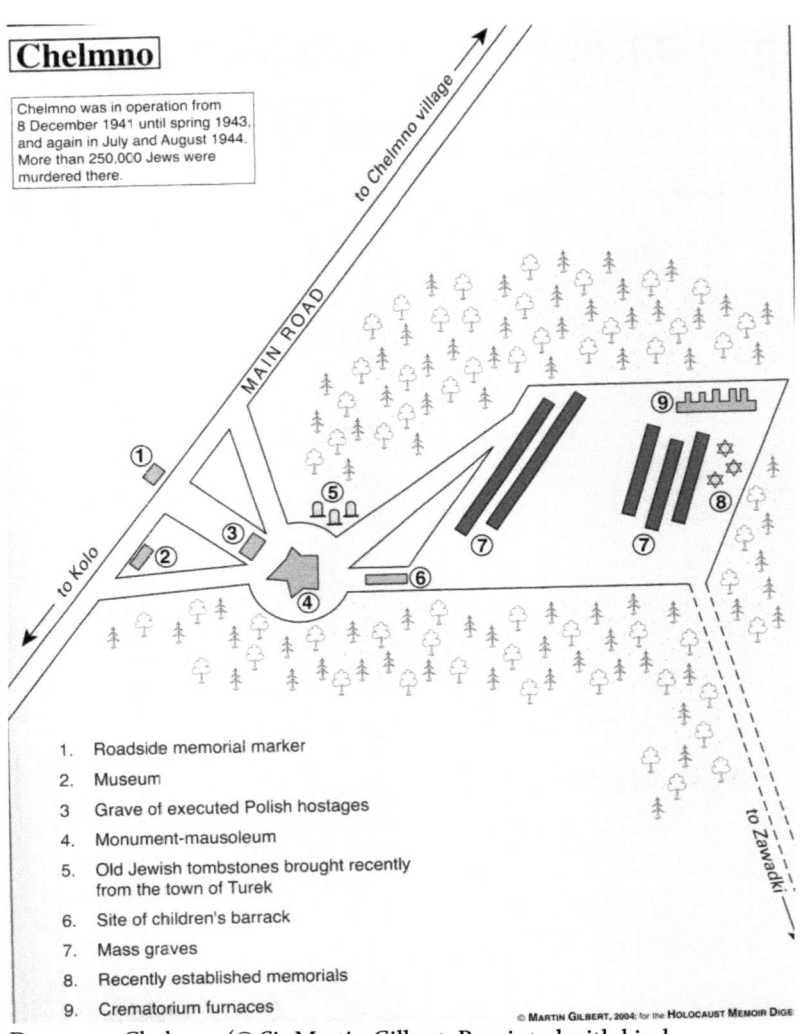

Doc. 3 Chełmno (© Sir Martin Gilbert, Reprinted with kind permission).

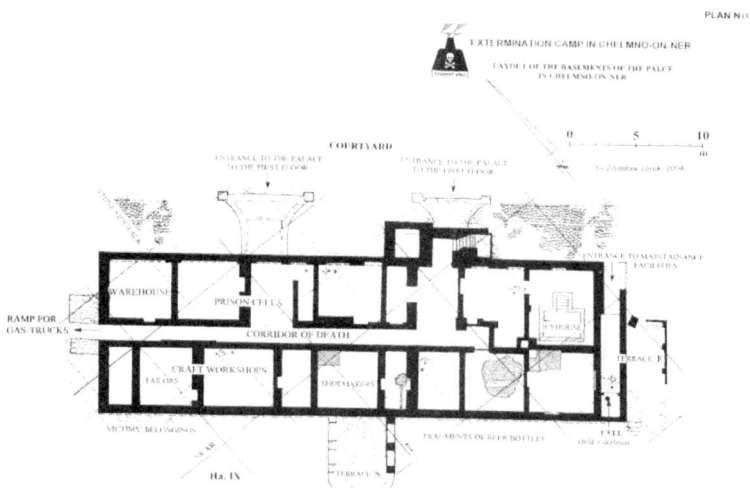

Doc. 4 Chełmno Palace Basement Drawing (© Muzeum Martyrologiczne w Żabikowie. Reprinted with kind permission)

hohensalza nr. 51   9/1   1500-

den herrn reichstatthalter
abteilung roem. 2 -

p o s e n =
================

trifft: zwei fleckfiebererkrankungsfaelle im kreise warthbruecken,
zug   : ohne.

richterestatter: medizinalrat dr. habil. mayer.

die polen stanislaus p o u b i n s k i und lech j a s k u l s -
i erkrankten als hilfsarbeiter eines H -sonderkommandos im
nsatz am judendurchgangslager k u l m h o f kreis warthbruecken
de dezember bzw. anfang januar grippeaehnlich und wurden am 4. und
januar in das kreiskrankenhaus warthbruecken mit eindeutigen zei-
en einer fleckfiebererkrankung eingeliefert. weil- felix-reaktionen
hen noch aus. die erforderlichen maszmahmen sind nach dem amts-
rztlichen bericht vom 7. januar getroffem.=

r reg.praes.
hensalza.+

703   nr.   51   9.1.42   rsth/ posen /-abel==

Doc. 5   Kulmhof Correspondence – Two Poles with Typhus (Artur Hojan)

Landrat
Gesundheitsamt —
Dr.K./Br.

Wartbrücken (Kolo)
Reg.-Bez. Hohensalza
24.1.42

Vertraulich!

An den
Herrn Regierungspräsidenten
Hohensalza

Betrifft: Fleckfieberfälle Kajetan Skryposzynski und Piekarski Franz aus Kulmhof.

Hiermit berichte ich, daß im Laufe des 23.1.42 die beiden Angehörigen des polnischen Arbeitskommandos in Sonderkommando Kulmhof Kajetan Skryposzynski geb. am 14.7.1917 und Franz Piekarski beg. am 3.6.1884 wegen Fleckfieberverdacht ins Kreiskrankenhaus Wartbrücken gebracht worden sind. Die beiden polnischen erkrankten unter denselben stürmischen Erscheinungen wie die derzeit wegen Fleckfieberverdacht ins Krankenhaus eingewiesenen Polen des Sonderkommandos in Kulmhof. Bei beiden liegt die Temperatur um 40°. Beide haben an objektiven Krankheitserscheinungen eine schwere Kreislaufschwäche und ein makulöses Exanthem, welches besonders dicht auf der Brust und den vorderen Seiten der oberen Extremitäten besteht. Bei beiden besteht ein Milztumor. Subjektiv klagen die Kranken über heftige Kopf- und Halsschmerzen und über ein starkes Krankheitsgefühl. Blut zur Untersuchung auf die Reaktion von Weil-Felix wurde auf meine Veranlassung heute entnommen und per Eilboten andas Staatl. Medizinaluntersuchungsamt gesandt. Über das Ergebnis geht Ihnen sofortiger Bericht zu. Der Skryposzynski Kajetan ist einer von den beiden polnischen Gefangenenarbeitern, bei denen das Auftreten des Fleckfiebers in Anbetracht dessen, daß er besonders exponiert arbeitete, erwartet wurde. Der 2. Arbeiter über den ich in dem vorigen Bericht andeutete, daß man den Ausbruch des Fleckfiebers bei ihm erwartete, ist inzwischen aus anderen Gründen verstorben. Bei Piekarski Franz kam die Erkrankung insofern überraschend, als daß er lediglich am Material arbeitete, welches durch die das Material absendenden Behörden als nicht Fleckfieberverdächtig und läusefrei bezeichnet wurde.

Es wurdenscher von mir am gestrigen Tage folgende Maßnahmen angeordnet und zum großen Teil durchgeführt:

1. Entlausung der Unterkünfte des polnischen Arbeitskommandos mit deren gesammten Zubehör, einschließlich ihrer Insassen.
2. Entlausung der Unterkünfte und ihres Zubehörs der Mitglieder des Sonderkommandos.
3. Um eine erneute Verlausung der Einrichtungen des Sonderkommandos wirksam zu verhüten, wurde das in Kulmhof beschäftigte jüdische Arbeitskommando strengstens abgesondert. Da es Nachts im Kulmhofer Schloss untergebracht ist, muß ein besonderer Eingang, der von sonst niemand benutzt wird, geschaffen werden, unter Benutzung mit Desinfektionsmitteln ausgespritzt wird.
4. Darüber hinaus wurde angeordnet, daß das jüdische Arbeitskommando täglich nach beendetem Dienst völlig entlaust in seine Unterkünfte geht. Die Kleidungsstücke werden über Nacht entlaust. Die gleichen Maßnahmen wurden für das polnische Arbeitskommando angeordnet, gleich ob es mit Fleckfieberverdächtigen oder mit Läusenbehafteten in irgend eine Berührung kommt.
Für diejenigen des Sonderkommandos und derjenigen Angehörigen der polnischen Arbeitskommandos, die mit Juden schlechthin im Rahmen des Arbeitsprozesses in Berührung kommen, wurden Schutzanzüge angeordnet und bestellt; die Lieferung wird in 4 - 5 Tagen erfolgen können.
Um für die sachgemäße Durchführung Gewähr zu haben, wurde von mir für diese vordringlichen Arbeiten der Gesundheitsaufseher Otto Schmarz dem Sonderkommando bis auf Weiteres täglich für eine gewisse Zeit zur Verfügung gestellt. Die Arbeiten werden mit Instrumenten und Mitteln die das Sonderkommando stellt, bewältigt, sodaß dem Gesundheitsamt selbst keine Kosten entstehen können.
Ich selbst werde mich alltäglich an Ort und Stelle von dem Stand der Arbeit überzeugen. Da entgegen der Auffassung des Sonderkommandos die polnischen Arbeiterunterkünfte und zum Teil die Sonderkommandounterkünfte verlaust waren, mithin grundsätzlich als Fleckfieberverdächtig zu gelten haben, bitte ich wenn möglich um Überlassung weiterer Portionen Impfstoff, um diesen gegebenenfalls verimpfen zu können.

i.V.

Medizinalrat.

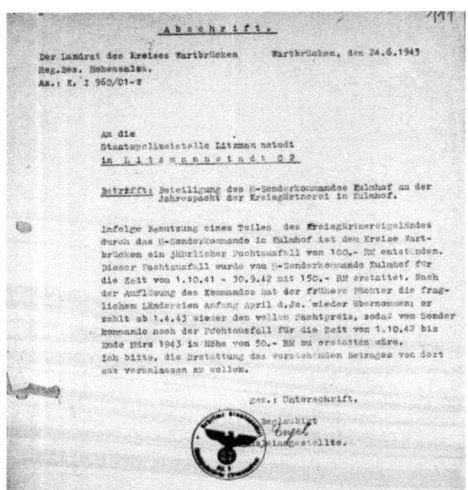

Doc. 8   SS Sonderkommando Kulmhof – Correspondence re Kreisgartnerei (Blue Stars Archive)

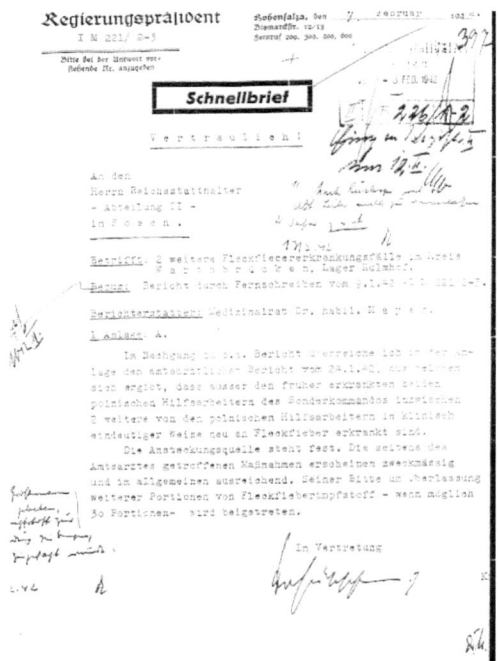

Doc. 9   Kulmhof – Correspondence 2 further cases of Typhus (Blue Stars Archive)

112

Geheime Staatspolizei Litzmannstadt, den 28. Juni 1943
Staatspolizeistelle Litzmannstadt **Getto-Verwaltung**
- L I - Litzmannstadt
Eing 3 0. AUG 1943
An
Abschriftlich Abteilung durch
gegen Rückgabe an Herrn KOS. P l a t e
SS-Feldpost-Nr. 47 188 C

mit der Bitte um Aussprache bzw. Bescheinigung der sachlichen Richtigkeit.

Im Auftrage:
Lenk

/En.

SS-Dienststelle Feldpost.Nr. 43059 O.U., den 13.8.1943.

Geheime St...
Staats... Litzmannstadt
2 2 AUG. 1943

Urschriftl.

der Geheimen Staatspolizei
Staatspolizeistelle Litzmannstadt
z. Hd. v. Pol.Oberinsp. L e n k

in L i t z m a n n s t a d t

zurückgesandt.
Der Pachtausfall des vom SS - Sonderkommando
benutzten Kreisgärtnereigeländes in Kulmhof für die
Zeit vom 1.10.1942 bis Ende März 1943 in Höhe von 50 RM.
(fünfzig) muß noch beglichen werden.
Die sachliche Richtigkeit wird hiermit bescheinigt.

Im Auftrage:
Plate,
SS - Untersturmführer.

Doc. 10 Letter from Albert Plate in Kulmhof to Lenk in Litzmannstadt
(Blue Stars Archive)

Doc. 11   Kulmhof Fuel Report (Blue Stars Archive)

Doc. 12   Kulmhof Fuel Report for Individual Vehicles (Blue Stars Archive)

Aufstellung über die in der Zeit vom 1. - 5.3.1942
von Bf Widzew Radegast nach Warthbrücken beförderten
Pj- Züge.

Tag	Bef. Juden	Begleiter	Zusammen	Transport- kosten RM Rpf		Begleiter Rückfahrt	Fahrtkosten RM Rpf	
1.3.	501	13	514	1439	20	13	72	80
2."	510	13	523	1464	40	13	72	80
3.	502	13	515	1442	--	13	84	--
4.	660	13	673	1884	40	13	72	80
5.	801	13	814	2279	20	13	72	80
6.	812	13	825	2310	--	13	72	80
7.	801	13	814	2279	20	13	72	80
8.	851	13	864	2419	20	13	72	80
9.	785	13	798	2234	40	13	72	80
10.	790	13	803	2248	40	13	72	80
11.	780	13	793	2339	40	13	72	80
12.	701	13	714	2106	30	13	72	80
13.	651	13	664	1958	80	13	72	80
14.	602	13	615	1814	30	13	72	80
15.	601	13	614	1811	30	13	72	80

Doc. 13   Transport Details from Radegast Station in Litzmannstadt to Warthbrücken March 1942 (Blue Stars Archive)

Litzmannstadt, den 2. September 1944.

Treibstoff-Meldung:

Lfd. No:	Art des Wagens:	Pol. No:	Benzin:	Rohöl:	Motoröl:	Besitzer.	Kraftfahrer.
1.	L.K.Wg.	19 240.	20 ltr.	==	==	Gettovwltg.	Bielenkow.
2.	L.K.Wg.	19 347.	10 "	==	==	"	Kwiatkowski.
3.	Schlepper.	19847.	==	15 ltr.	==	Städt. Fuhrp.	Woitzniak.
4.	L.K.Wg.	19 240.	70 "	==	2 ltr.	Gettovwltg.	Bielenkow.
5.	Tempo.	47 552.	10 "	==	0,4 "	"	Domainski.
6.	L.K.Wg.	45 639.	==	==	1 - "	"	Marczinkows
7.	L.K.Wg.	19 240.	20 "	==	==	"	Bielenkow.
8.	L.K.Wg.	19 459.	==	510 "	21 "	"	Rother.
9.	L.K.Wg.	19 347.	20 "	==	==	"	Kwiatkowski
10.	L.K.Wg.	19 459.	==	220 "	10 "	"	Sirakowski
11.	L.K.Wg.	19 240.	10 "	==	==	"	Bielenkow.
12.	L.K.Wg.	19 240.	20 "	==	==	"	Bielenkow.
13.	L.K.Wg.	45 639.	==	==	1 "	"	Marczinkowsi
14.	L.K.Wg.	19 240.	20 "	==	==	"	Bielenkow.
15.	L.K.Wg.	71 449.	49 "	==	==	S.S.Polizei.	Laabs.
16.	L.K.Wg.	71 449.	45 "	==	==	S.S.Polizei.	Laabs.

Bestand am 1. September abends:

Benzin: 1 632 ltr. (Eingang 1 182 lr.)
Rohöl: 2 330 " (1 698 ")
Motoröl: 104,1 "

Lagerverwaltung
Gettoverwaltung
Balater Ring

Doc. 14   Fuel Obtained Record in Litzmannstadt by Gustav Laabs (Blue Stars Archive)

Abschrift

Der Höhere SS- und Polizeiführer
beim Reichsstatthalter in Posen
im Wehrkreis XXI
Tgb. Nr.: 332/42 g

Posen, den ... Aug. 1942

Geheim!
Stempel:
Persönlicher Stab
Reichsführer
Schriftgutverw......
Nr. AR/31/23

An den
Reichsführer-SS Persönlicher Stab
z. Hd. SS-Obersturmbannführer Dr. Brandt
B e r l i n S W 11
Prinz-Albrecht Str. 8

Betr.: Pelzsachen aus Kulmhof für die Waffen-SS

Lieber Kamerad Brandt!

Der Reichsführer-SS hatte seinerzeit angeordnet, daß die bei der Aktion in Kulmhof anfallenden Pelzsachen der Waffen-SS zur Verfügung gestellt werden sollten. Als bisheriges Ergebnis melde ich dazu, daß am 27. Juni 1942 ein Waggon voll ungezählter Pelzsachen an das Bekleidungsamt der Waffen-SS in Ravensbrück zur Absendung gekommen ist.

Es ist damit zu rechnen, daß im Herbst noch weitere Pelzsachen anfallen.
Ich bitte Sie, den Reichsführer-SS entsprechend zu unterrichten.
Mit kameradschaftlichen Grüßen und

H e i l H i t l e r

Ihr W. Koppe

Doc. 15 Kulmhof Fur Collection (Yad Vashem)

SS-Sonderkommando

Einschreiben!

An den
    Inspekteur der Sicherheitspolizei
              und des SD
    z.Hd.v.SS-O'stuf, B a u m

Kulmhof, den 1.

in P o s e n.

Betrifft: Kameradschaftabend anläßlich des Gauleiterbesuches.
Bezug: Mündl. Anordnung des Gauleiters.
Anlagen: 1

In der Anlage überreiche ich eine Rechnung über einen Kameradschaftsabend, zu welchem das SS-Sonderkommando durch den Gauleiter G r e i s e r eingeladen wurde. Der Gauleiter hat gebeten, ihm die Rechnung zur Begleichung vorzulegen. Ich bitte deshalb, diese dem Gauinspekteur G e i s l e r zuzuleiten.

SS-Hauptsturmf. d.
Kriminalkommissar

Doc. 16   Invoice for Kameradschaftabend in Warthbrücken (Yad Vashem)

Der Inspekteur der Sicherheitspolizei
und des SD in Posen
II C b. Tgb.Nr. 102/43 Ba./D.

Posen, den 2. April 1943

Urschriftlich
an die
NSDAP Gauleitung Wartheland
z.Hd.v.Gauinspekteur Pg. Helmut Geisler
P o s e n
Schloßfreiheit 11

Der Reichsstatthalter
5. APR 1943

In der Anlage wird ein Schreiben des SS-Sonderkommandos Kulmhof nebst einer beigefügten Rechnung in Höhe von RM 237.69 mit der Bitte um Kenntnisnahme überreicht.

Im Auftrage:

SS-Obersturmführer.

Doc. 17   Ibid.,

Gaststätte "Riga"
Gustav Richter
Wartbrücken, Poststr. 9
Telefon Nr. 29

Wartbrücken, den 8.3. 1943.

RM. 237.89 bez. am 18.6.1943
mit Verrechnungsscheck Nr.394090

R e c h n u n g

an das Sonderkommando der SS -Kulmhof, vom Kameradschaftsabend
am 5.3.43.- in der Gaststätte "R i g a"-Wartbrücken.

92 Mann Abendessen, Lokalmiete, wegen Ausfall	RM.192.75.-
10 Fl. Sodawasser	2.20.-
83 ½ Liter u. 25/ 0,3/Liter Bier	42.94.-
	R M .237.89.-

Zweihundertsiebenunddreissig & 89 Pfg.

Festgestellt:
Görlich
Polizeisekretär
4.5.43

Wartbrücken, 8.3. 43,-

Gaststätte "Riga"
Gustav Richter
Wartbrücken, Poststr. 9

Geheim!

An die Reichsstatthalterbehörde   h i e r ,
mit der Bitte um Bezahlung aus dem für die
Judenaktion bestimmten Fonds.
Posen, den 20.4.43.

Doc. 18   Gaststätte Riga, Warthbrücken Party Bill (Yad Vashem)

Doc. 19 Maderholz, Friedrich, Kulmhof Garrison – Extract from Personal File (Yad Vashem)

B. B. Nr. = 20363

Fragebogen
zur Erlangung der Verlobungsgenehmigung
(von Frauen sinngemäß ausfüllen)

Name (leserlich schreiben): Burmeister Walter Heinrich Wilhelm
in SS seit Oktober 1933 Dienstgrad: Rottenführer   SS-Einheit: 2/74
in SA von ____ bis ____, in HJ von ____ bis ____
Mitgliedsnummer in Partei: ____   in SS: 135 871
geb. am 2. Mai 1906 zu Ahlbeck-Seebad   Kreis: Usedom-Wollin
Land: Preußen   jetzt Alter: 29 Jahre   Glaubensbek.: ev.
Jetziger Wohnsitz: Ahlbeck-Seebad   Wohnung: Lindstraße 2
Beruf und Berufsstellung: Zimmer- u. Fußballplatz-Meister (beim Vater)
Liegt Berufswechsel vor? nein
Außerberufliche Fertigkeiten und Berechtigungsscheine, z. B.:
   Führerschein, Sportabzeichen: Führerschein 3 b
   Sportauszeichnungen: ____
Ehrenamtl. Tätigkeit: ____
Dienst im alten Heer: Truppe ____ von ____ bis ____
   Reichswehr ____ von ____ bis ____
   Schutzpolizei ____ von ____ bis ____
Letzter Dienstgrad ____
Frontkämpfer: ____ bis ____ verwundet ____
Orden und Ehrenabzeichen einschl. Rettungsmedaille: ____
Welcher Konfession ist der Antragsteller? ev.   die zukünftige Braut? ev.
(Als Konfession wird auch außer dem herkömmlichen jedes andere gottgläubige Bekenntnis angesehen.)
Ist neben der standesamtlichen Trauung eine kirchliche Trauung vorgesehen? Ja — Nein.
Gegebenenfalls nach welcher konfessionellen Form? ev.

Lebenslauf:
Als Sohn des Klempnermeisters Georg Burmeister und dessen Ehefrau Klara geb. Knüppel bin ich Walter Heinrich Wilhelm Burmeister am 2. Mai 1906 in Ahlbeck-Seebad geboren.

Doc. 20 Burmeister, Walther, Kulmhof Garrison – Extract from Personal File (Yad Vashem)

B.U.Nr. 19990

Fragebogen
zur Erlangung der Heiratsgenehmigung
(von Frauen sinngemäß auszufüllen)

Name (leserlich schreiben): Herbert Lange
in SS seit: März 1933   Dienstgrad: Rottenführer   SS-Verband: Stapo Aachen
Mitgliedsnummer in Partei: 1.159.583   in SS: 93501
geb. am 29.9.1909 zu Manglin   Kreis: Anklam
Land: Pr.   jetzt Alter: 25   Glaubensbek.: evangel.
Jetziger Wohnsitz: Aachen,   Wohnung: Mozartstraße 17/19
Beruf und Berufsstellung: Kriminal-Kommissar u. R.
Liegt Berufswechsel vor? nein
Außerberufliche Fertigkeiten und Berechtigungsscheine, z. B.:
  Führerschein, Sportabzeichen: Führerschein 3 b
  Sportauszeichnungen: nein
Ehrenamtl. Tätigkeit: nein
Dienst im alten Heer: Truppe: nein   von   bis
  Reichswehr: nein   von   bis
  Schutzpolizei: nein   von   bis
Letzter Dienstgrad: —
Frontkämpfer: nein   bis   verwundet
Orden und Ehrenabzeichen einschl. Rettungsmedaille: nein

Lebenslauf:

Am 29. September 1909 wurde ich als Sohn des Schmiedemeisters Max Lange und seiner Ehefrau Anna, geb. Hoffmann, in Menglin b/Anklam geboren. Meine Jugend verlebte ich in Kratzwied, wo mein Vater eine Stellung beim Eisenwerk einnahm. Mein Vater starb aber schon im Jahre 1920. In Kratzwied besuchte ich zunächst die Knaben-Volksschule, später

Doc. 21   Herbert Lange, Kulmhof Commandant Fragebogen – Extract from Personal File (Wiener Library)

Doc. 22 Hans Bothmann Kulmhof Commandant Fragebogen – Extract from Personal File (Wiener Library)

Namentliche Aufstellung
der leitenden Personen bei der

a) Ghettoverwaltung:

1. Biebow, Amtsleiter
2. Ribbe, 1.stellv.Amtsleiter
3. Hämmerle, 2.stellv.Amtsleiter u.Einkauf
4. Mayer, Warenverwertung
5. Luchterhand, Korrespodent
6. Seifert, Warenverwertung
7. Straube, Textilverarbeitung
8. Gennewein, Finanzverwaltung
9. Eisner, Lagerverwalter in der Herm.-Göring-
10. Czarnulla, Personalabteilung
11. Degner, Transportabteilung
12. Fiedler, Taxator für Wertsachen

Baluter-Ring

13. Schwind, Lagerverwalter am Baluter-Ring
14. Andrä, Vertreter
15. Petershagen, Transportwesen am Baluter-Ring
16. Schaumburg, Lederverwertung
17. Schuster,

b) beim Ältesten der Juden:

1. Rumkowski, Ältester
2. Rosenblatt, 1.Vertreter u.Chef des Ordnungsdien
3. Jakubowicz, 2.Vertreter u.Fabrikationswesen
4. Fuchs, Dora, Sekretarin des Ältesten.
5. Herzberg, Zentralgefängnisleiter
6. Warszawski, Textilverteilung

Doc. 23 List of German Officials and Judenrat Members in the Litzmannstadt Ghetto (Yad Vashem)

Doc. 24 Hans Bothmann visits Litzmannstadt to meet with Biebow and Dr. Bradfisch (Yad Vashem)

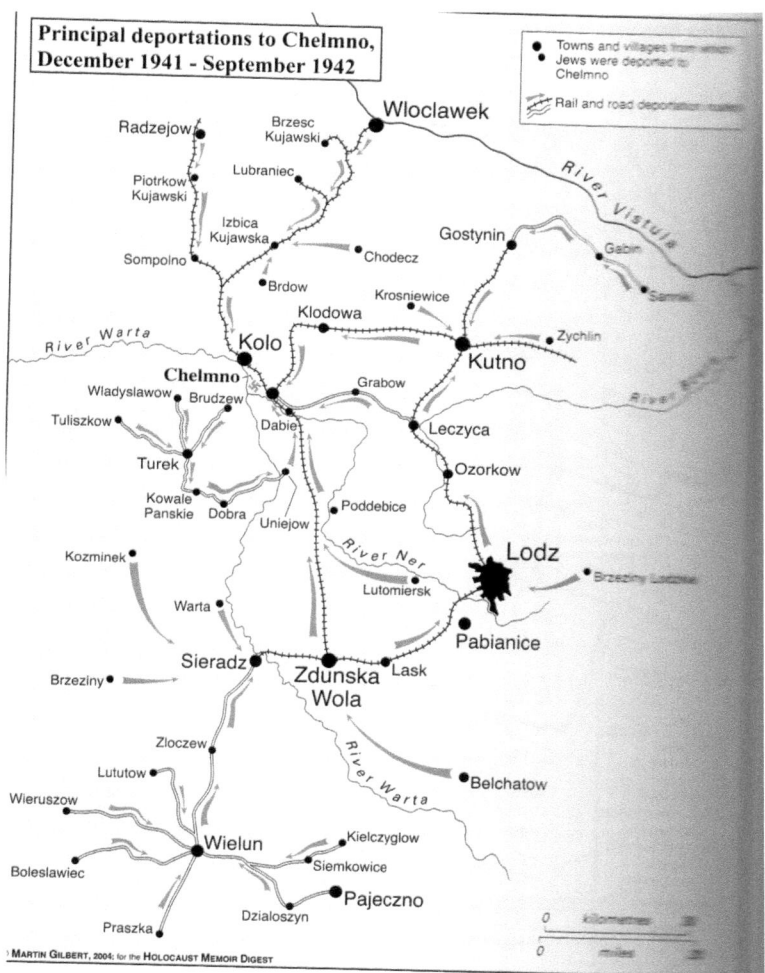

Doc. 25   Principal Deportations to Chełmno, December 1941–September 1942 (© Sir Martin Gilbert, Reprinted with kind permission)

Lfd.Nr.	Trsp.	Trsp.Nr.	Name	Vorname	Strasse	Alter
151.	II	502	Bloch	Käthe	Hohenstein.70	1892
152.	II	511	Brauer	Herta	Fisch 15	1911
153.	II	512	Brauer	Walter	"	1906
154.	II	520	Bohrmann	Paulina	" 21	1874
155.	II	521	Bohrmann	Dina	"	1875
156.	II	522	Bohrmann	Amanda	"	1882
157.	II	543	Braun	Mina	Hohenstein,70	1890
158.	II	544	Bachenheimer	Salomon	"	1879
159.	II	545	Bachenheimer	Waldemar	"	1926
160.	II	546	Bachenheimer	Mathilde	"	1885
161.	II	555	Beutler	Marian	Reiter 11	1905
162.	II	561	Basch	Helene	"	1901
163.		855	Baumann	Hans	Rembrandt 10	1877
164.	II	892	Basch	Therese	"	1892
165.	II	865	Beck	Marie	"	1877
166.	II¹	29	Bergenthal	Nanette	Gnesener 26	1868
167.	III	30	Bergenthal	Ernst	Stofchen 22	1891
168.	III	31	Bergenthal	Else	"	1896
169.	III	99	Bunzl	Irma	Rembrandt 10	1888
170.	III	246	Brumlik	Karl	"	1876
171.	III	254	Brodsky	Mayer	"	1887
172.	III	262	Baer	Leopold	"	1896
173.	III	278	Brunner	Richard	"	1892
174.	III	279	Brumlik	Anna	"	1884
175.	III	305	Berkendorf	Emanuel	Ranch 18	1894
176.	III	306	Benkendorf	Marta	"	1906
177.	III	307	Benkendorf	Susi	"	1933
178.	III	311	Bustina	Moritz	Rembrandt 10	1903
179.	III	312	Bustina	Marie	"	1903
180.	III	313	Bustina	Helene		1934

Doc. 26   Transport List Litzmannstadt – Kulmhof – May 5, 1942 (State Archives Łódź)

Table of Equivalent Ranks

Reichsführer-SS	Reichs Leader
SS-Oberstgruppenführer	General
SS-Obergruppenführer	Lieutenant General
SS-Gruppenführer	Major General
SS-Brigadeführer	Brigadier General
SS-Oberführer	Senior Colonel
SS-Standartenführer	Colonel
SS-Obersturmbannführer	Lieutenant Colonel
SS-Sturmbannführer	Major
SS-Hauptsturmführer	Captain
SS-Obersturmführer	First Lieutenant
SS-Untersturmführer	Second Lieutenant
SS-Sturmscharführer	Sergeant Major
SS-Hauptscharführer	Master-Sergeant
SS-Oberscharführer	Sergeant First Class
SS-Scharführer	Staff Sergeant
SS-Unterscharführer	Sergeant
SS-Rottenführer	Corporal
SS-Sturmmann	Acting Corporal
SS-Oberschütze	Private First Class
SS-Schütze	Private

Glossary of Nazi Terms

Abteilung: A branch, section or sub-section of a main department or office. Also a military or paramilitary unit of up to battalion strength, i.e. approximately 700 men

Aktion Reinhardt: The code name used in honor of Reinhard Heydrich for the mass murder of Polish Jewry

Allgemeine-SS: General body of the SS consisting of full-time, part-time, and inactive or honorary members, as distinct from the *Waffen-SS* (see entry for *Waffen-SS*)

Amt: A directorate or an office of a ministry

Amtsgruppe: A branch of a *Hauptamt*

Anschluss: The Annexation of Austria to the German *Reich* in March 1938

Arbeitsamt: Labor Office

Arbeitslager: Labor / Work Camp

Außenstelle / Außendienststelle: Out-station of an office, agency or ministry

Befehlshaber der Sicherheitspolizei und des SD: Commander in Chief of the Security Police and Security Services

Einsatzkommando: Special Unit

Gau: One of the 42 main territorial divisions of the Nazi Party

Gauleiter: The highest-ranking party official in a *Gau*, responsible for all political and economic activity, mobilization of labor and civil defence

Geheime Staatspolizei (Gestapo): Secret State Police that became *AMT IV* of the *RSHA* in September 1939. Headed by *SS-Gruppenführer* Heinrich Müller

Generalgouvernement: German occupied Poland, administered by Hans Frank from his headquarters in Kraków

Hauptamt: A main or central office.

Höhere SS und Polizeiführer: Higher *SS* and Police Leader. Himmler's personal representative in each military region. Also established in the occupied territories. Nominally the commander of all *SS* and Police units in his area, as well as acting as the liaison officer with the military and senior regional authorities

Judenrat: Jewish Councils established by the Nazis for Jewish self-administration, in all its various facets: food, housing, labor allocation, welfare, police, economic and social

Kanzlei des Führers: Hitler's Chancellery

KdS: Commander of the Security Police and Security Services

Kommando: A brigade, squad, or detail

Kommissariat: A Regional Headquarters of the Police; also a political administration in the occupied eastern territories (for example *Reichskommissariat Ukraine*)

Kreishauptmann: The principal district official in the *Generalgouvernement* and occupied territories

Kreisleiter: District Party Leader

Kriminalkommissar: Lowest rank in the upper officer class of the Criminal Police

Kriminalsekretär: Next rank up from Kriminalassistent

Landesforstamt: State Forestry Office

Landrat: Head of District Administration

Leitstelle: A Regional Headquarters of the *Gestapo* or *Kripo* established at the Headquarters of a Military District or capital of a county

Luftwaffe: German Air Force headed by Hermann Göring.

Nationalsozialistisches Kraftfahrkorps (NSKK): National Socialist Motor Corps

Nationalsozialistische Volkswohlfahrt: National Socialist Social Welfare

Ordnungspolizei (ORPO): Order Police. The regular uniformed police, comprising the *Schutzpolizei, Gendarmerie* (rural constabulary), and *Feuerschutzpolizei* (fire-fighting police), together with certain technical and auxiliary services

Organisation Todt: A paramilitary government organization used mainly for the construction of strategic highways and military installations. *Organisation Todt* Head was Fritz Todt until his death in 1942.

Radegast: Radogoszcz Station in Łódź where the Jewish transports left for Chełmno and Auschwitz

Reichsgau: One of 11 regions formed from territories annexed by the *Reich*

Referat: A sub-section within a *Gruppe*

Referent: The official in charge of a *Referat*

Reichsführer-SS: *Reich* Leader of the *SS*. Heinrich Himmler's *SS* title from June 1936.

Reichskriminalpolizeiamt: Berlin Headquarters of the *Kriminalpolizei (Kripo)* which in September 1939 became *Amt IV* of the *RSHA*

Reichssicherheitshauptamt (RSHA): *Reich* Security Main Office formed in September 1939, and combined the *Sicherheitspolizei* and the *Sicherheitsdienst*. It was both an *SS-Hauptamt* and a branch of the *Reich* Ministry of the Interior

Reichstag: German National Parliament

Schlosskommando: Castle Unit

Schutzpolizei (Schupo): Protection Police. The regular uniformed municipal constabulary, forming the bulk of the *Ordnungspolizei*

Sicherheitsdienst (SD): Security Service. The intelligence branch of the *SS*, headed by Reinhard Heydrich

Sicherheitspolizei (Sipo): Security Police, comprising of the *Kripo* and *Gestapo*, headed by Reinhard Heydrich

Sonderkommando: A special unit of the *SS* employed for police and political tasks in occupied territories. Also used to denote the special brigades of prisoners in Auschwitz-Birkenau Concentration Camp who worked in the crematoria in the mass murder process

Spezialwagen: Special van

SS-Leibstandarte "Adolf Hitler": Adolf Hitler's bodyguard regiment. The oldest of the *SS* militarized formations, established in 1933. Commanded by Joseph "Sepp" Dietrich

SS- und Polizeiführer: *SS* and Police Leader. In command of a district in the occupied territories, subordinate to the *Höhere SS und Polizeiführer*

Standarte: *SS* or *SA* formation equivalent to a regiment, i.e. approximately 3,000 men

Sturmabteilung (SA): Storm Detachment, also called the "Brown Shirts" in accordance with their uniform. The original Nazi paramilitary organization founded in 1921

Sturmbann: An *SA* or *SS* unit, equivalent to a battalion, i.e. 750–1,000 men

SS-Totenkopfverbände: *SS* Death's Head units that guarded the concentration camps. In 1939, they formed the nucleus of the *SS-Totenkopf* division, one of the first field formations of the *Waffen-SS*

SS-Verfügungstruppen: The pre-War militarized formations of the *SS*, renamed the *Waffen-SS* in 1939

Volksdeutsche: Ethnic Germans

Volksliste: German People's List. Nazi Party Racial Registration

Waffen-SS: Fully militarized *SS* formations. Initially composed of the *SS-Verfügungstruppen* and the *SS-Totenkopf* units. During the Second World War it comprised of 40 divisions, both German and non-German units

Waldkommando: Forest Unit

Wehrkreis: Military region, usually indicated on maps by a Roman numeral

Wehrmacht: The German Armed Forces

Wetterkommando: "Weather Commando" unit used to exhume and destroy traces of genocide in the *Warthegau.*

Wirtschafts- und Verwaltungshauptamt (WVHA): Administration and Economic Main Office of the *SS.* Formed from the *SS-Hauptamt Haushalt und Bauen* during 1940. Headed by Oswald Pohl, the *WVHA* supervised the *SS* economic enterprises and administered the concentration camps.

Selected Bibliography

ADELSON, Alan and LAPIDES, Łódź Ghetto (Viking Penguin, New York, 1989)

ARAD, Yitzhak, Bełżec, Sobibór, Treblinka (Bloomington, Indiana University Press, 1987)

Chełmno Witnesses Speak (Konin, Łódź, 2004)

DOBROSZYCKI, Lucjan, The Chronicle of the Łódź Ghetto 1941–1944 (Yale University Press, New Haven and London, 1984)

GILBERT, Martin, The Holocaust—The Jewish Tragedy (Collins, London, 1986)

HILBERG, Raul, The Destruction of the European Jews (Holmes and Meier, New York, 1985)

KL Auschwitz, Seen By The SS (Auschwitz Museum, 1978)

KLEE, DRESSEN, REISS, Those Were The Days (Hamish Hamilton, London, 1991)

KOGON, LANGBEIN, RUCKERL, Nazi Mass Murder (Yale University Press, 1993)

KRAKOWSKI, Shmuel, Chełmno: A Small Village in Europe (Yad Vashem, Jerusalem, 2009)

LANZMANN, Claude, Shoah (Pantheon Books, New York, 1985)

MACLEAN, French L, The Camp Men (Schiffer Military History, Atglen PA, 1999)

MONTAGUE, Patrick, Chełmno and the Holocaust (I.B. Tauris and Co Ltd, London, 2012)

REES, Lawrence, Auschwitz, The Nazis and the Final Solution (BBC Books, London, 2005)

REITLINGER, Gerald, The Final Solution (Vallentine, Mitchell, London, 1968)

WEBB, Chris, The Bełżec Death Camp (Ibidem-Verlag, Stuttgart, 2016)

Unpublished Works

GORCZYCA, Krzysztof, and LOREK, Zdzisław, *Day after day in the extermination camp Kulmhof. An attempt of event calendar 1941–1945*, March 2005

HOJAN, Artur, *Chełmno SS*

WEBB, Chris, *Daily Journal—Research Trip to Poland*, September 2005

Sources and Acknowledgements

Websites

www.bundesarchiv.de/gedenkbuch

www.deathcamps.org

www.holocausthistoricalsociety.org.uk

www.holocaustresearchproject.org

www.Nizkor.org (The Complete Eichmann Trial Transcripts)

http://thefifthfield.com

ynng.Yadvashem.org/names

Archives

Blue Stars Archives, UK

Bundesarchiv, Berlin, Germany

Ghetto Fighters House, Israel

Holocaust Historical Society, UK

National Archives Kew, London, UK

National Archives (NARA), Washington DC, USA

Tall Trees Archive, UK

United States Holocaust Memorial Museum (USHMM), Washington DC, USA

Wiener Library, London, UK

Yad Vashem, Jerusalem, Israel

Acknowledgements

Bordon Library, Forest Centre, Whitehill, UK

BÖLTER, Florian, ibidem-Verlag, Hannover, Germany

DEMPSEY, Patrick, Holocaust Author, USA

FALKSOHN, Howard, Wiener Library, London, UK

FELDMAN, Professor Matthew

GILBERT, Sir Martin

HOJAN, Adrianna

JAROS, Marek, Wiener Library, London, UK

KATZ, Lilli – Mai

KUCHERENKO, Alla, Yad Vashem, Israel

KUWALEK, Robert

LANGE, Valerie, ibidem-Verlag, Hannover, Germany

LOREK, Zdzisław, Poland

LÖWENTHAL, Mark

MÜHLBERGER, Tania Helene, Warwick/Würzburg BA Hons. Graduate in modern languages and literature

MOESER, Lutz, Bundesarchiv, Berlin, Germany

MUNRO, Cameron, T4 Association, Berlin, Germany

NIXON, Tom, Graphic Design

OREN, Zvi, Director of Archives, Ghetto Fighters House, Israel

PARZER, Robert, T4 Association, Berlin, Germany

PURMANN, Reinald, T4 Association, Berlin, Germany

SPYRAKIS, Heather

SPYRAKIS, Mark

SZUKALAK, Marek

TREGENZA, Michael, English Historian and Author, Lublin, Poland

WEBB, John

WEBB, Shirley

ZIOLKOWSKA, Dr. Anna, Director of the Zabikowie Museum

Index of Names

A

Aaron, Selma 151
Abendroth, Margarete 151
Abraham, Anna 152
Abramsom, Meir 99
Abramczyk, Flora 152
Adam, Hertha 152
Adelheim, Johanna 152
Adler, Alois 370
Adler, Anschel 152
Ahlschlager, Hans 370
Albersheim, Whilhemine 152
Albert, Clara 152
Albert, Karl -Wilhem 36
Albrecht, Rudolf 370
Alembik, Chaya 152
Alexander, Bertha 152
Allmeier, Adelheid 153
Alpert, Jakob 153
Alsberg, Martha 153
Altmann, Adolf 153
Altschul, Karoline 153
Amster, Dora 153
Anders, Lizzie 153
Andres, Ferdinand 153
Anschel, Berta 153
Anschlawski, Selma 154
Antmann, Sofie 154
Apfel, Henny 154
Apfelbaum, Ettel 154
Apisdorf, Regina 154
Apt, Gertrud 154
Archenhold, Julius 154
Arends, Karl 154
Arendstein, Gertrud 155
Arendt, Klara 155
Arensberg, Erich 155
Armer, Rudolf, 155
Arndt, Arthur 155

Arnstein, Doris 155
Aron, Abraham 155
Aronade, Rosa 155
Aronsohn, Elisabeth 155
Aronson, Edith 156
Arronge, Emilie 156
Artmann, Fidel 156
Asch, Berta 156
Ascher, Franz 156
Atlas, Cirla 156
Auerbach, Emma 156
Aumann, Selma 156
Ausaderer, Ruth 157
Aussenberg, Lina 157
Awerbuch, Frieda 157

B

Bab, Arthur 157
Babiacki, Schlomo 52
Bach, Albert 157
Bach-Zelewski, Erich von dem 32, 367
Bachenheimer, Johanna 157
Bächer, Margarete 158
Bachmann, Wally 157
Bachschütz, Flora 157
Back, Berta 157
Bagainski, Julius 158
Bahr, Alfred 158
Bähr, Hedwig 158
Bajler, Fela 147
Bajler, Szlamek 46-47, 61, 68-69, 75, 82, 147, 421
Balai, Emma 158
Ball, Hedwig 158
Balke 387
Balsam, Zita 159
Bamberger, Joseph 159
Bandmann, Alama 159

Bar, Albert 158
Bar, Helmut 370
Baran, Margarete 159
Barme, Bertha 159
Barnas, Minna 159
Baron, Henriette 159
Bartel 370
Bartels, Clara 159
Baruch, Berta 159
Bärwald, Emma 158
Basch, Helene 160
Baschwitz, Cacilie 160
Basler 45, 370
Bassfreund, Adele 160
Batory, Stefan 437
Bauer, Felix 160
Baum, Amalie 160
Baumann, Gertrud 160
Baumblatt, Anna 160
Bäumel, Wilhelm 158
Baumer, Abraham 160
Baumgarten, Bertha 161
Bauser, Erna 161
Becht, Dr. Walther 32, 107
Beck, Heinrich 76, 370
Becker, Else 161
Beder, Ibka 104
Beder, Mala 104
Beder, Paul 103
Beder, Regina 104
Beder, Sala 104
Beder, Schimson 104
Bednarz, Władysław 61, 127, 131,
 140-141, 148, 150, 362, 364-365,
 370, 374, 376-377, 379-381,
 386, 392 -394, 411-412, 416-418
Beer, Anna 161
Beermann, Carola 161
Behm, Alfred 38, 370
Behr, Abraham 161
Behrens, Alina 161
Beier 115
Bein, Betty 161
Beith, Gunther 162

Belau, Emma 162
Belitzer, Regina 162
Benda, Emmy 162
Bendik, Jenny 162
Bendit, Bernhard, 162
Benger, Hermann 162
Benjamin, Adele 162
Benzian, Margarete 163
Benzion, Herta 163
Berek 127
Berend, Franz 163
Berg, Alfred 163
Bergel, Marianne 163
Berger, Alexander 163
Bergmann, Betti 163
Berkheim, Alfred 163
Berkowicz, David 163
Berl, Gertrud 164
Berlowski, Waclaw 31
Berlin, Emmy 164
Berlowitz, Anna 164
Bermann, Jenny 164
Berndt, Rosa 164
Bernhard, Irene 164
Bernhardt, Adelheid 164
Bernhaut, Jakob 164
Bernsohn, Hermann 165
Bernstein, Antonie 165
Bernthal, Edith 165
Besen, Josefine 165
Besteher, Hedwig 165
Besthof, Alma 165
Bettelheiser, Hermann 165
Bettenhausen, Alice 165
Bettmann, Leo 165
Beutler, Marion 166
Bezen, Bilba 166
Bibedgal, Schmuel 52-53
Biberfeld, Dorothea 166
Bibo, Elsa 166
Bick, Anna 166
Biebow, Hans 69, 77, 96 -97, 105,
 125, 139, 363
Bier, Albertine 166

Biermann, Margarete 166
Biernisch 370
Biesunski, Adele 166
Bilski, Charlotte 166
Bing, Manfred 167
Birkenfeld, Leopold 88
Birmann, Josef 167
Birn, Samuel 167
Bistram, Baron von 34
Blach, Betti 167
Blancke, Otto 167
Blankenstein, Martha 167
Blass, Auguste 167
Blatt, Isaak 167
Blattberg, Osias 168
Blaukopf, Berko 168
Blaustein, Berthold 168
Blei 371
Bleich, Markus 168
Blench, 371
Blimbaum, Sofie 168
Blitstein, Gertrud 168
Blitzblum, Friedrich 168
Blobel, Paul 91-92, 94-95, 105, 109, 113, 412
Bloch, Helga 169
Block, Ida 169
Bluhm, Hedwig 169
Blum, David 169
Blumenau, Clara 169
Blumenfeld, Ilse 169
Blumenkron, Mathilde 169
Blumenrath, Berta 169
Blumenthal, Albert 169
Blumgardt, Erich 170
Boas, Clara 170
Bock, Heinrich 371
Bock, Renate 170
Bock, Walther 371, 411
Boge, Otto 83, 371
Bohm, Elsa 170
Bohm, Josef 372
Bohrmann, Amanda 170
Bondy, Johanna 170

Bonem, Alice 170
Bonheim, Margarete 170
Bonifacius, Lotte 170
Borchardt, Hanna 171
Bochert, Anna 171
Bollmann 372
Borck, Emil 171
Borkowski, Samuel 171
Bornheim, Margot 171
Bornstein, Jakob 171
Borodkin, Rosa 171
Boroschek, Karl 171
Borowski, Mendel 172
Bothmann, Hans 76, 78-79, 81, 83, 85-86, 91-93, 106 -107, 110-111, 115-117, 119, 121-122, 124-126, 128, 134-135, 138, 140, 142-144, 363- 365, 368-369, 373, 381, 383,386, 388, 390-391, 393, 401-402, 407-408, 413, 421
Botshaim, Hindla 172
Bouscher, Eduard 172
Boygen, Sonja 172
Brach, Milli 172
Brack, Ilse 172
Brack, Viktor 29
Bradfisch, Dr. Otto 110, 125, 144, 364
Bragenheim, Erna 172
Bram, Erwin 172
Bramm, Hertha 172
Brandt, Alfred 173
Brasch, Arno 173
Brau, Adolf 173
Brauer, Herta 173
Braun, Frieda 173
Braunschweiger, Ella 173
Breitenstein, Johanna 173
Bremer, Regina 173
Breslauer, Adele 174
Bressler, Moritz 174
Breumann, Ella 174
Breiger, Klara 174
Brill, Neuma 174

Brilles, Hedwig 174
Bringer, Ida 174
Brinitzer, Erna 174
Brink, Joseph 174
Brinn, Julius 175
Brodek, Frieda 175
Broder, Nelly 175
Brodt, Charlotte 175
Bromberger, Anni 175
Bronowski, Judge J. 422, 429
Bronstein, David 175
Bruch, Ludwig 175
Bruchfeld, Lotte 175
Brück, Gisela 176
Bruck, Julia 175
Bruckmann, Max 176
Brückmann, Henny 176
Brüggermann, Else 176
Brünell, Hannelore 176
Brumel, Gertrud 176
Buchmeier, Rosalie 176
Bucholz, Gertrud 176
Bucholz, Martha 387
Bud, Elise 177
Büchenbacher, Sophie 177
Bukofzer, Erich 177
Bula, Antoni 31
Bullemer, Johanna 177
Buonaventura, Fritz 177
Burchard, Sara 177
Burchardi, Regina 177
Burg, Martin 177
Burger, Johanna 177
Burgmann, Betty 178
Burmeister, Ernst 119, 121, 125-126, 137, 372, 412
Burmeister, Georg 373
Burmeister, Robert 372
Burmeister, Walter 32-33, 37-38, 94, 112, 117, 122-123, 128, 144, 363-365, 409, 412
Bürstinger, Erwin 37-38, 86, 112, 117, 122, 124, 129, 144, 374
Burzinska, Cyria 178

Buschhoff, Hilde 178
Butow, Anna 178
Buttner, Lucie 178
Buxbaum, Emma 178
Bythiner, Kurt 178
Bytinski, Ursula 178

C

Cahen, Ruth 99
Cahn, Hedwig 179
Callmann, Johanna 179
Calm, Else 179
Calmer, Richard 179
Cammitzer, Hertha 179
Capauner, Johanna 179
Cappel, Fanny 179
Caro, Gunda 179
Carsch, Adele 180
Caspari, Salomon 180
Casparius, Franziska 180
Caspary, Hedwig 180
Casper, Marie 180
Cassel, Artur 180
Cassirer, Hilde 180
Cendrowicz, Ruchla 180
Chaim, Johanna 181
Chaskel, Martin 181
Checinski 99
Chmielnieka, Ester 181
Chojnacki, Lena 181
Chraplewski, Bianka 181
Chraplowsky, Arnold 181
Chrisst, Johann 374
Cibulski, Edith 181
Claessen, Hans 181
Cleffmann, Josefine 182
Cohen, Anna 182
Cohn, Anneliese 182
Cohnen, Hugo 182
Conrad, Ella 182
Conrak, Conrah 182
Coper, Calman 182
Coppel, Erna 182

Corea, Chick 438
Cornel, Margit 183
Cossmann, Ida 183
Courant, Nuscha 183
Cremer, Pauline 183
Croner, Frieda 183
Cudkowicz, Rolf 183
Custodis, Elise 183
Cwern, Jan 183
Cytryn, Henni 184
Czapski, Else 184
Czarnulla, Erich 96

D

Dabrowski, Wladyslaw 405
Dagowitsch, Feige 184
Dahl, David 184
Dahlheimer, Flora 184
Dannann, Friederike 184
Damzog, Ernst 120, 144
Daniel 374
Daniel, Else 184
Danielsohn, Frida 184
Dankowski 63
Dannenbaum, Charlotte 184
Danziger, Paula 185
David, Gertrud 185
Davidmann, Max 185
Davidsohn, Ella 185
Davidson, Martha 185
Dawidowicz, Bronislawa 185
Dejaco, Walter 105
Delik, Else 185
Dember, Julia 185
Dessler, Erna 186
Dettmann, Anni 186
Deutsch, Fritz 186
Dienstfertig, Ella 186
Dietrich, Marta 186
Dimenstein, Eva 186
Dingfelder, Kathe 186
Djuk, Maria 186
Dobrin, Else 186

Dobriner, Flora 187
Dobrowolski, Else 187
Dokschitzki, Miron 187
Domb, Max 187
Dombrower, Edith 187
Dominsky, Rebekka 187
Dongus, Dr. Walter 95
Dorn, Meta 187
Draheim 70-71
Dratwa, Sara 187
Dreifus, Hedwig 188
Dresdner, Herta 188
Dressen, Wiili 362
Dressler, Ruchla 188
Dreyfus, Albert 188
Dreyfuss, Bernard 188
Drobinski, Liba 188
Drucker, Ester 188
Drutowski, Elli 188
Dubinska, Lea 189
Dudzinski, Zbigniew 404
Dunje, Hermann 189
Dymentmann, Chaim 189

E

Eckstein, Elly 189
Edel, Hermann 189
Edelstein, Fanny 189
Eger, Margarete 189
Eggener, Alfred 189
Ehrenbaum, Marta 190
Ehrenfeld, Ladislaus 190
Ehrlich, Edith 190
Ehrmann, Simson 190
Eichel, Frieda 190
Eichelbaum, Alice 190
Eichengrun, Betty 190
Eichenwald, Herta 190
Eichmann, Adolf 60-61, 148-150, 413
Eichold, Mathilde 191
Eigenfeld, Isaak 191
Eiger, Ruth 191

Eisenberg, Alfred 191
Eisenblatt, Albert 191
Eisenfeld, Sara 191
Eisenstab, 52
Eisenstadt, Gertrud 191
Eiserfey, Ilse 191
Eisig, Frieda 191
Eisner, Sophie 192
Elbert, Lieselotte 192
Elias, Auguste 192
Elkan, Ida 192
Elsbach, Ella 192
Emanuel, Bertha 192
Emmering 99
Engel, Bella 192
Engelhard, Betti 192
Ephraim, Emillie 192
Eppenheim, Hilda 193
Epstein, Helene 193
Erlich, Wolek 130
Erlich, Henoch 130
Ermann, Rosa 193
Ermolnikoff, Frieda 193
Erszter, Betty 193
Eschen, Blanka 193
Esser, Erna 193
Esserholz, Veronika 193
Ettinger, Abraham 194
Ewerth, Wilhelm 194

F

Fabian, Erna 194
Fabisch, Hedwig 194
Färber, Siegfried 194
Faibusch, Esther 194
Falborski, Bronislaw 403
Falk, Auguste 194
Falkenhausen, Betty 194
Falkson, Helene 195
Familier, Gerda 195
Feber, Regina 195
Feder, Fanny 195
Federmann, Paula 195

Feibusch, Jenny 195
Feiertag, Johanna 195
Feige, Selma 195
Feiler, Esther 195
Feld, Klara 196
Feldhahn, Alfred 196
Feldmann, Elly 196
Feldman, Professor Matthew 424, 439
Feldmar, Walli 196
Fells, Anne 196
Felsenthal, Bruno 196
Fenichel, Zerline 196
Fenster, Eva 196
Ferber, Berta 197
Fernich, Helene 197
Fertig, Sareli 197
Feuer, Jenny 197
Feuerstein, Heinz 197
Feybusch, Julius 197
Fichtelberg, Sandor 197
Fickelburg, Dr. 45
Fidelmann, Erna 197
Fiedler, Gustav 77-78, 94, 374
Filer, Walther 375
Finger, Anna 197
Fink, Adele 198
Finkel, Jenny 198
Finkels, Tana 198
Finkelstein 132, 134, 138, 141, 390, 392
Finkelstein, Flora 198
Fischel, Rita 198
Fischer, Heinz 198
Fischlerman, Hinda 198
Flanzreich, Marion 198
Flatau, Frieda 199
Flatauer, Rudolf 199
Flatow, Alice 199
Fleischer, Ida 199
Fleischmann, Johanna 199
Fliess, Hella 199
Flonder, Itta 199
Förster, Lilli 199

Fogel, Elias 199
Fontheim, Harry 200
Fränkel, Alma 200
Frajermann, Chaja 200
Frank, Berta 200
Franke, Taube 200
Franken, Erna 200
Frankenstein, Ella 200
Frankenthal, Edith 200
Frankfurt, Carl 201
Fraystmann, Chawa 201
Freimark, Therese 201
Freimuth, Emil 201
Freireich, Hinda 201
Freitag, Rosa 201
Frenkel, Selma 201
Frensdorf, Erich 201
Freudenberg, Gertrud 202
Freudenreich 106
Freund, Walter 202
Freundlich, Johanna 202
Frey, Clara 202
Freyberg 32
Friedberg, Kurt 202
Friedberger, Gerd 202
Friede, Elisabeth 202
Friedeberg, Henriette 202
Friedemann, Erna 202
Friedensohn, Meta 203
Friedheim, Rosa 203
Friedlander, Albertine 203
Friedlich, Laja 203
Friedman 104
Friedmann, Albert 203
Fröhlich, Anne 203
Fröling, Flora 203
Frohnhausen, Frieda 203
Frohwein, Ella 204
Fromm, Dorothea 204
Frost, Georg 204
Früchter, Berta 204
Fruchtzweig, Emillie 204
Fruh, Else 204
Frühling, Else 204

Fuhrmann, Maria Regina 88
Frydland 130, 133
Fuchs, 119
Fuchs, Albert 204
Fuchs, Gunther 96
Funk, Hermann 96
Fürst, Julie 204
Fürstenberg, Elfriede 205
Fultheim, Bianka 205
Furmanski, Elly 205

G

Gabriel, Adolf 205
Gärtner, Helene 205
Gandzior, Frieda 205
Gans, Berta 205
Gappe, Paula 205
Garai, Moritz 206
Gassman, Gottlieb 364, 375
Geckel 112
Gedalje, Amalie 206
Geisel, Helene 206
Geisenheimer, Frieda 206
Geissler, Charlotte 206
Geizmann, Aron 206
Geldern, Elli 206
Geller, Henry 206
Gembicki, Renate 206
Gembitz, Auguste 207
Gendler, Werner 207
Geppert, Rachela 207
Gerber, Max 207
Gerechter, Anna 207
Gerothwohl, Ignatz 207
Gerolis 71
Gersmann, Flora 207
Gerson, Alfred 207
Gerstel, Dorothea 208
Gersztenzang, Szlama 208
Gessler, Ernst 208
Gewerz, Egon 208
Gidion, Jenny 208

Gielow, Hermann 117, 121, 129, 144, 150, 362, 370, 375, 389, 393
Gimpel, Frieda 208
Giter 51
Gladtke, Elsa 208
Glajtman, Estera 208
Glassenapp, Kathe 208
Glasser, Else 209
Glass, Benno 209
Gleitmann, Laja 209
Glicenstein, Chaja 209
Glogowski, Max 209
Glück, Olga 209
Glucks, Richard 105
Gluskin, Abraham 209
Gnieslaw, Laja 209
Göde, Karl 45, 375
Göritz, Rosa 209
Götz, Margarete 210
Götzer, Paula 210
Götzhoff, Rosa 210
Goldbarth, Sara 210
Goldberg 62
Goldberg, Ferdinand 210
Goldberg- Weltmann, Artur 210
Goldeman, Charlotte 210
Goldenring, Charlotte 210
Goldfinger, Gertrud 211
Goldfreund, Margarete 211
Goldman, Mahmens 53-54
Goldmann, Elisabeth 211
Goldring 100
Goldschild, Valeria 211
Goldschmidt, Bernhard 211
Goldstaub, Rosa 211
Goldstein, Else 211
Goldstrom, Ilse 211
Goldstücker, Max 211
Goldwasser, Maria 212
Golyscheff, Jakob 212
Gompertz, Jenny 212
Gondorf, Erna 212
Gonsenheimer, Henny 212
Gordon, Alfred 212

Gorlich, Wilhelm 117, 122, 143, 363, 365, 375, 386
Gossele, Oswald 122
Gossels, Elise 212
Gotheiner, Horst 212
Gotthelft, Berta 213
Gottlieb, Selly 213
Gottreich, Lilian 213
Gottreich- Jacobsohn 213
Gottschalk, Frieda 213
Gowa, Paula 213
Grabischewski, Schmul 213
Grabiszewski, Sofie 213
Grabowski 59
Gräfner, Rosa 213
Grätzer, Ella 214
Graf, Hermann 36, 376
Graff, Gertrud 214
Graumann, Max 214
Grebermann, Ellen 214
Greiser, Arthur 29, 83-84, 110-111, 115-116, 150, 363-364, 366
Grell, Kathe 214
Gries, Kurt 214
Griess, Martha 214
Grödel, Albert 214
Grojnowski (see Bajler, Szlamek)
Gronowski, Erika 214
Gros, Elsbeth 215
Gross, Manasche 215
Grosman, Manfred 215
Growald, Edith 215
Grün, Pinkus 112
Grüneberg, Charlotte 215
Grunfeld, Meir 150
Grünberg, David 215
Grünewald, Margarete 215
Grünfeld, Minna 216
Grünspahn, Fritz 216
Grünthal, Hugo 216
Grünwald, Kate 216
Grumach, Fritzi 216
Grünau, Janette 216
Grundmann, Ella 216

Grünsfeld, Bertha 216
Gülzer, Bertha 216
Günther, Adolf 217
Guggenheim, Mathilde 217
Gulko, Hirsch 217
Gumpertz, Margarete 217
Gunzenhauser, Julie 217
Gütermann, Selma 217
Gutfeld, Berta 217
Guth, Julius 217
Gutkind, Dora 217
Gutman, Anna 218
Guttmann, Elly 218
Gutwilen, Abraham 218
Gutwillig, Jenta 218

H

Hass, Lilli 218
Haase 140, 376, 383, 418
Haber, Albert 218
Hachenberg, Adele 218
Hackelberg, Hilde 218
Häfele, Alois 68, 72, 77, 81, 85, 87, 110, 117, 127, 132, 134, 142-143,376, 382, 408, 411-412
Häfele, Armand 376
Hagelberg, Jenny 219
Hagen, Fritz 376
Hahn, Heinz 219
Haider, Simon 37-38, 83, 377
Haimann, Hannelore 219
Hain, Karoline 219
Hakesberg, Kurt 219
Halber, Friederike 219
Halbersberg, Sara 219
Halle, Margarethe 219
Halter, Moniek 51, 55-56, 58
Hamburger, Hulda 219
Hammel, Fritz 220
Hannes 377
Hanno, Else 220
Hardt, Hermann 377
Harf, Moritz 220

Harlam, Peter 220
Harter, Erich 377
Harth, Erna 220
Hartog, Adolf 220
Hartogsohn, Lea 220
Hasfeld, Eva 220
Hauer, Helmut 221
Hauptmann, Benno 221
Hauser, Berta 221
Hausmann, Eva 221
Hayum, Ilse 221
Hecht, Hermann 221
Heffner, Ruth 221
Heidemann, Frieda 221
Heider 402
Heidt, Martin 221
Heilberg, Rosi 222
Heilborn, Herbert 222
Heilbronn, Helene 222
Heilbrunn, Ruth 222
Heilbrunner, Johann 377
Heilner, Irma 222
Heim, Irene 222
Heimann, Adelheid 222
Heimbach, Anna 222
Heimberg, Edgar 223
Hein, Rosa 223
Heine, Fritz 223
Heineberg, Else 223
Heinemann, Emma 223
Heinl, Karl 36, 38, 377-378, 412
Heinrich, Leonard 223
Heiser, Paula 223
Held, Marie 223
Heldberg, Laura 224
Hellenstein, Hedwig 224
Heller, Charlotte 224
Hellmann, Max 224
Hellwitz, Wilhelmine 224
Helmann, Klara 224
Henle, Gert 224
Henlein, Anna 224
Hensen, Charlotte 378, 401

Hensen, Friedrich 378, 383, 385, 388-389, 391, 400-401
Hentschel, Margarete 224
Hepner, Kathe 225
Hercberg, Salomon 77
Hermann, Erich 225
Hering, Oskar 85-87, 112, 122, 378
Herkner, Fritz 113
Herrscher, Rosel 225
Herrschander, Helene 225
Herschberg, Charlotte 225
Herstatt, Hubert 225
Herszkowicz, Josef 94, 112
Hert, 364, 379
Hertz, Maximillian 225
Herz, Adelheid 225
Herzberg, Else 225
Herzberger, Leon 226
Herzenberg, Irene 226
Herzfeld, Hannelore 226
Herzog, Paula 226
Hess, Benno 226
Hesse, Max 226
Hessenberger, Martha 226
Heuckelbach, Theodor 379
Heuckelbach, Wilhelm 82, 93, 379, 411
Heumann, Selma 226
Heydemann, Hugo 227
Heydrich, Reinhard 85, 95
Heymann, Berta 227
Hiller, Frieda 227
Himmelrick, Kathe 227
Himmelweit, Irma 227
Himmler, Heinrich 32, 83-84, 110, 115, 119, 144, 369, 401, 410
Himmler, Siegmund 227
Hinrichs, Emma 227
Hinz, Gertrud 227
Hirsch, Adolf 227
Hirschberg, Gertrud 228
Hirschel, Rosa 228
Hirschfeld, Johanna 228

Hirschfeldt, Fritz 228
Hirschhahn, Rosa 228
Hirtz, Eugen 228
Hitler, Adolf 29, 40, 367, 410, 435
Hoberg, Karola 228
Hoch, Regina 228
Hochberger, Zilli 229
Hochdorf, Arnold 229
Höflich, Henriette 229
Hoffmann, Elenore 229
Hoffman, Kurt 94, 379
Hoffstadt, Margot 229
Hofmann, Jenny 229
Hohenstein, Adel
Hojan, Adrianna 439
Hojan, Artur 362, 420, 422-424, 437-439
Hojan, Zuzia 439
Holdstein, Alfred 229
Holländer, Adelheid 229
Holstein, Betty 230
Holz, Bernd, 230
Holzknecht, Berta 230
Holzmann, Dora 230
Hope, Rolf 230
Hopp, Clara 230
Hopstein, Estera 230
Horn, Albert 230
Hornich, Augusta 372
Hornik, Regina 231
Horwiitz, Susanne 231
Horwitz, Elfriede 231
Höss, Rudolf 105-106, 412
Hössler, Franz 105-106
Hufing, Gustav 77-78, 379, 385, 407
Hull, Hermann 379
Hüneberg, Margarete 231
Huskiel 127
Hut, Kurt 379
Hutner 380
Hüttner, Cacilie 231
Huffmann, Erna 231

Humberg, Erich 231

I

Icek, Abram 231
Ickovicz, Fiszel 231
Igla, Rivka 232
Iglick, Edgar 232
Ihring, Gertrud 232
Illfelder, Paula 232
Imhof, Amalie 232
Inow, Beatrice 232
Ires, val Spira 232
Isaac, Bella 232
Isaak, Alfred 232
Isay, Adolf 233
Isenthal, Katharina 233
Islinger, Josef 83, 380
Ismer, Fritz 45-46, 375, 380
Israel, Bruno 140, 380, 390, 392, 417
Israel, Hugo 233
Israelsohn, Zipora 233
Italiener, Gesine 233
Iwanter, Moritz 233

J

Jablonower, Josef 233
Jablonsky, Erna 233
Jachmann, Gertha 234
Jacht, Alice 234
Jacks, Else 234
Jacob, Amanda 234
Jacob, Hans 380
Jacobi, Rosa 234
Jacobius, Ruth 234
Jacobowitz, Martha 234
Jacobsohn, Alfred 234
Jacobus, Rosa 234
Jacoby, Anita 235
Jacubowitz, Gertrud 235
Jaffe, Paul 235
Jahisch, Perla 235
Jakob, Betty 235
Jakobi, Margot 235
Jakobs, Renate 235
Jakobstahl, Else 235
Jakubowski, Feliks 380
Jakubowitz, Anna 235
Jakubowicz, Chazkel 413
Jalowitz, Karl 236
Jankowski 404
Jankowski, Manja 236
Jansen, Eugen 46
Jarecki, Alphons 236
Jaskolski, Lech 39, 396-397, 399
Jaskulski, Edith 236
Jastrow, Amalie 236
Jastrzebski, Beniek 94, 112
Jean, Johanna 236
Jeidels, Frieda 236
Jerochim, Jenny 236
Jerozolmski, Szlama 236
Joachimstahl, Edgar 237
Joelsohn, Jacob 237
John, Ernestine 237
Jonas, Abraham 237
Jonassohn, Hans 237
Jonasson, Frida 237
Jong, Gerda 237
Jonscher, Liebe 237
Jordan, Johanna 238
Josel, Gertrud 238
Joseph, Else 238
Josephsohn, Alfred 238
Juda, Else 238
Judkiewicz, Noech Wolf 94, 112
Jülich, Hermann 238
Jüttner, Dorothea 238
Junk, Ludwig 381
Junkiert 404
Jurke, Ellen 238
Just, Alice 238
Just, Willi 91
Justmann, Yitzhak 99 -101, 147-150

K

Kaczynski, Kurt 239
Kämpfer, Ellen 239
Kaffe, Meta 239
Kahl, Grete 239
Kahn, Alfred 239
Kahn, Alfred 239
Kahnweiler, Lilli 239
Kain, Siegbert 239
Kainer, Henriette 239
Kaiser, Emmy 239
Kalb, Erna 240
Kalenscher, Regina 240
Kalischer, Meta 240
Kaliski 63
Kallmann, Marie 240
Kalmuszewicz 127
Kaltenbrunner, Dr. Ernst 111
Katheder, Babette 383
Kaminski, Bunim 99
Kaminski, Hannah 240
Kaminsky, Gertrud 240
Kamp, Edith 240
Kann, Klara 240
Kanter, Kurt 241
Kantorowicz, Leo 241
Kaplan, Georg 241
Karfiol, Klara 241
Kargauer, Norbert 241
Kariel, Veronika 241
Karpe, Thomas 241
Karzer, Mois 381
Kaschmann, Isaac 241
Kassel, Rosalie 241
Kastellian, Adele 242
Kaszynski, Stanisław 72-74, 419
Kaszynski, Karolina 74
Katz, Max 242
Katzenberg, Jenny 242
Katzenellenbogen, Eva -Lucie 242
Katzenstein, Anneliese 242
Kauffmann, Paula 242
Kedziorek, Rosa 242
Keller, Arnold 242
Kelman, Betty 243
Kempinski, Meta 243
Kempler, Edith 243
Kerbs, Frieda 243
Kern, Alice 243
Kerp, Frieda 243
Kick, Henriette 243
Kiefer, Ida 243
Kiewe, Frieda 243
Kiksmann, Jacob 244
Kimel, Abraham 244
Kinsky, Henriette 244
Kiriasefer, Sigmund 244
Kirschbaum, Hedwig 244
Kirschberg, Eva 244
Kirschenbaum, Jenny 244
Kirschner, Paula 244
Kirstein, Henriette 245
Kisch, Erna 245
Kiwi, Hermann 245
Kiwit, Emmy 245
Klaber, Klementine 245
Klandt, Clara 245
Klarer, Jacob 245
Klarmann, Regina 245
Klebe, Margot 245
Kleczewski, Werner 246
Klee, Ernst 362
Klee, Kurt 246
Klefisch, Sibylia 246
Kleimann, Malka 246
Klein, Herbert 246
Klestadt, Friedrich 246
Klinger, Johanna 246
Klopstock, Paula 246
Klose 381
Kloss, Grete 246
Klüger, Sara 247
Kluge, Rosalie 247
Knapp, Henri 247
Knecht, Regina 247
Kniebel, Josef 247

Knopf, Jenny 247
Knüppel, Klara 373
Koburger, Melanie 247
Koch, Joachim 247
Kochmann, Berthold 247
Köln, Erich 248
Kohler 144, 390
Kohn, Otto 430
Koltan, Icek 130
Koltan, Mojsze 130
König, Klara 248
König, Linda 380
König, Dr Rolf 421
Königsberger, Alice 248
Königsfeld, Dorothea 248
Kösten, Ida 248
Königheim, Paula 248
Kogon, Hersch 248
Kohlagen, Therese 248
Kohls, Berta 249
Kohn, Alfred 249
Kolatzki, Berta 249
Konegen, Frida 249
Kongrecki, Auguste 249
Koninsky, Henriette 249
Koppe, 29, 83, 362-363
Koppel, Pauline 249
Korant, Anna 249
Kornblum, Johanna 249
Korngold, Rifka 250
Korte, Lilly 250
Koslowski, Henriette 250
Kossmann, Johanna 250
Kostezki, Rachila 250
Koszewski, Marian 439
Kotek, Elias 250
Kowalski, Hinda 250
Kraft 403
Krakauer, Else 251
Krakowski, Hirsch -Leib 99
Kramarski, Max 251
Kramarzinsky, Frieda 251
Kramer, Joef 251
Krämer, Selma 250

Kramp, Rudolf 122, 125, 130
Kranold 79
Kratz, Jacob 251
Krebs, Johanna 251
Kreissberg, Mincia 251
Krekler, Hedwig 251
Kresse, Henriette 251
Kreiger, Abraham 252
Kretschmer, Erich 37-38, 81-82, 117, 127-128, 130, 381
Krisch, Hermann 252
Krohn, Gertrud 252
Kron, Selma 252
Kronenberger, Augusta 252
Kronheim, Ulrike 252
Krüger, Friedrich-Wilhem 362
Krüger, Hedwig 252
Krypka, Clara 252
Krzewacki, 54-55, 66
Kuba, Adolf 252
Kuczina, Henriette 253
Kühns, Irma 253
Kufert, Icek 253
Kugelmann, Robert 253
Kulp, Anna 253
Kuntz, Frieda 253
Kunz, Max 253
Kuperberg, Helena 253
Kupfermann, Josef 254
Kupferschmied, Sara 254
Kuppermann, Henriette 254
Kuropatwa, Therese 254
Kurschuss, Else 379
Kurz, Ellen 254
Kurzberg, Hulda 254
Kurzondkowski, Meta 254
Kurzweg, Doris 254
Kussel, Hugo 254
Kutner, Sophie 255
Kuttner, Olga 255
Kuznicki, Frayda 255
Kuznitzky, Martha 255

L

Laabs, Gustav 85-86, 112, 117, 121-122, 129, 138, 364-365, 376, 378, 381-383, 411
Laabs, Hermann 381
Lachmann, Betty 255
Landau, Anna 255
Landeck, Clara 255
Landecker, Frieda 255
Landesmann, Ruth 256
Landsberg, Veronika 256
Lang, Harold 40, 383
Lang, Martha 256
Lang- Puchof, Josefine 256
Lange, Herbert 29- 33, 36-38, 41, 46, 68, 72-73, 76, 110, 119, 365-368, 370, 373, 381, 383, 386, 396-399, 409-410, 438
Lange, Julius 256
Lange, Dr. Rudolf 144
Langstadt, Else 256
Lanoch, Hanna 256
Lanzmann, Claude 40, 89, 148-149, 362, 390, 421
Lapidas, Erna 256
Lasch, Leonore 257
Laser, Lilli 257
Lasker, Hermann 257
Laski, Caesar 257
Laszlo, Angela 257
Lau, Rabbi Moshe 99
Lau-Levi, Naphtali 150
Laufer, Netty 257
Lautmann, Sara 257
Lazarus, Leopold 257
Leber, Sabine 257
Lebram, Max 258
Ledermann, Regina 258
Lefebre, Horst 258
Leffmann, Emil 258
Legath, Hans 117-118, 120-121, 125, 372, 375, 383, 388, 390, 393, 396

Lehmann, Anna 258
Leibenhaut, Golda 258
Leibholz, Georg 258
Leipziger, Meta 258
Leiser, Hermann 258
Leistner, Adele 259
Lejbusiewicz, Chawa 259
Lemberg, Dr 96
Lemle, Johanna 259
Lenneberg, Hermine 259
Lenhoff, Sarah 259
Lenz, Amalie 259
Lenz, Wilhelm 36-38, 84, 93, 111, 117-118, 120- 122, 127-128, 130 - 131, 133, 140-143, 364, 376, 383, 402, 408, 418
Leopold, Else 259
Lermer, Rose 259
Leschziner, Wilhem 259
Les, Emma 260
Lesek, Mosche 53-54
Less, Avner 60
Lesser, Leonie 260
Lessner, Meta 260
Letocha, Liesbet 260
Leufer, Henny 260
Levano, Paula 260
Leven, Hermann 260
Levenbach, Margarethe 260
Levi, Cilly 260
Levin, Berthold 260
Levisohn, Manfred 261
Levison, Fanny 261
Leviton, Hedwig 261
Levy, Edgar 261
Lew, Jonas 112
Lewandowski 404
Lewandowski, Manfred 261
Lewi, Hedwig 261
Lewien, Julius 261
Lewin, Charlotte 261
Lewinowska, Minka 262
Lewineck, Margarete 262
Lewinski, Erna 262

Lewinsohn, Betty 262
Lewith, Karoline 262
Lewkowicz, Alfred 262
Lewy, Max 262
Leyser, Leopold 262
Libelt, Marian 39, 396
Libowski, Grete 262
Librach, Gitla 263
Lichtenstein, Alice 263
Lichtheim, Margarete 263
Lichtigfeld, Sala 263
Lichtmann, Oskar 263
Liebenthal, Edith 263
Liebermann, Bianca 263
Lieblein, Jenni 263
Liebrecht, Walter 264
Lievendag, Meta 264
Liffmann, Moritz 264
Lillenfeld, Hilde 264
Lillenheim, Chana 264
Lillenthal, Albert 264
Lindemann, Armin 264
Lindenstrauss, Arthur 264
Lindmann, Anita 264
Link, Editha 265
Linker, Jetty 265
Linz, Karoline 265
Lion, Helene 265
Lipmann, Margot 265
Lippmann, Melanie 265
Lipschitz, Georg 265
Lisek, Pessa 265
Lissack, Ida 265
Lissauer, Gerda 266
Lissner, Rieke 266
Liszewsky, Anneliese 266
Lithauer, Ernst 266
Littmann, Lydia 266
Littwack, Liesbeth 266
Liwschitz, Gregor 266
Loeb, Emmy 266
Löbenstein. Ella 267
Löffler, Else 267
Lövinski, Frieda 267

Löwe, Angelika 267
Löwenbach, Else 267
Löwenberg, Arthur 267
Löwenheim, Johanna 267
Löwenkopf, Chana 267
Löwensberg, Ernst 267
Löwenstein, Anna 268
Löwenthal, Arthur 268
Löwi, Emmy 268
Löwy, Betty 268
Lohn, Rael 268
Lomnitz, Elfriede 268
Lorber, Hannchen 268
Lorch, Johanna 268
Lorek, Zdzisław 420- 421, 423
Lorenz, Meyer 268
Loriig, Siegfried 269
Loschak, Friedrich 383, 402
Loser, Manfred 269
Loszynski, Gustav 269
Louis, Irma 269
Lubasch, Frieda 269
Lubascher, Kurt 269
Lubelsky, Ruth 269
Lubiner, Fiszel 99
Lubinski, Richard 269
Lubranzcyk, Erna 269
Luca, Lucian 270
Lucas, Betty 270
Luchtenstein, Hedwig 270
Ludnowsky, Wilheline 270
Ludwicki, Antoni 141 -142
Ludwicki, Hela 142
Ludwig, Paula 270
Lübeck, Edmund 270
Lypold, Berthold 270

M

Maas, Dina 270
Maas, Harri 383
Machtynger, Roza 271
Maclean, French L 362
Maderholz, Friedrich 76, 383, 411

Maderholz, Johann 383
Maderholz, Margareta 386
Mängen, Klara 271
Märker, Carl 271
Magasiner, Bertha 271
Magier, Abraham 271
Magnus, Elisabeth 271
Mahnke, Sara 271
Maier, Frieda 271
Mainzer, Walter 271
Majer, Geszyp 112
Major, Marja 272
Malbin, Ruth 272
Maliczak, Henryk 30, 39, 112, 396-399
Malinowski, Clara 272
Malkus, Lydia 272
Malsch, Amalie 272
Malzmüller, Theodor 40, 110-111, 384, 402, 407
Mamber, Rosa 272
Mamelok, Grete 272
Manasse, Frieda 272
Mandel, Hedwig 273
Mandels, Dr Sima 139
Mandelbaum, Wanda 273
Mandelsohn 130
Mandus, Luise 273
Manes, Margarete 273
Mangold, Ella 273
Mania, Henryk 39, 397-399
Mann, Paula 273
Mannes, Julius 273
Mannheimer, Albert 273
Mansbach, Johanna 273
Mantel, Jacob 274
Manteuffel, Elfriede 274
Marchand, Emma 274
Marcus, Charlotte 274
Marcuse, Hedwig 274
Marczak, Dorothea 274
Margoniner, Georg 274
Margoninski, Martha 274
Margulius, Abraham 274

Markert, Clara 275
Markiel, Rose 275
Markiewicz, Julius 275
Markowitz, Else 275
Markschiess, Markscies, 275
Markus, David 275
Markuse, Bertha 275
Marschner, Karlheinz 275
Marwilski, Arthur 276
Marx, Andreas 276
Maschkowski, Hugo 276
Masum, Anna 276
Mathes, Johanna 276
Mathews, Julius 276
Mattissohn, Jeanette 276
Matzdorf, Felix 276
Mauck, Anna 381
Mautner, Alice 277
May, Heinrich 44, 70, 75, 78-79, 91-93, 404
May, Lilli 277
Mayer, Alfred 277
Meerfisch, Sara 277
Meersand, Frieda 277
Mehler, Alfred 277
Mehring, Anton 384 -385, 411
Mehring, Ludwig 384
Meier, Eva 277
Meier, Kurt 385
Meigners, August 277
Meilich, Hugo 277
Meinhardt, Jenny 278
Meitlis, Elsa 278
Melhorn, Dr 78-79
Meller, Debora 278
Menahini, Michan 278
Mendel, Arno 278
Mendels, Alwine 278
Mendelsohn, Casper 278
Mendheim, David 278
Menkis, Ryfka 279
Mentsch, Josef 279
Menz, Ilse 279
Merzbach, Gertrud 279

Meschoulam, Albert 279
Messerschmidt, Hertha 279
Messingschlager, Hans 364
Messow, Elfriede 279
Metzenberg, Charlotte 279
Metzger, Raicha 279
Meyer, Alice 280
Meyerfeld, Emma 280
Meyerhof, Fritz 280
Meyerhoff, Henriette 280
Meyers, Emillie 280
Meyerowitz, Bogdan 280
Michaelis, Erich 118, 120-121
Michaelis, Gertrud 280
Michalski, Paul 385, 402
Michel, Auguste 280
Michels, Betty 280
Michelsohn, Erhard 33, 107, 424
Michelsohn, Martha 89, 424
Michelson, Mordechai 99
Mielzynski, Flora 281
Milchner, Flora 281
Mickiewicz, Adam 437
Mildenberg, Julius 281
Milgram, Ilda 281
Miller, Dr 130
Miloslawski, Arnold 281
Mindus, Franziska 281
Minner, Agnes 281
Miodownik 127
Misch, Berta 281
Mischkowsky, Margarete 282
Miszczak 142, 149
Mitschker, Meta 282
Mitz, Sylvia 282
Mode, Hertha 282
Möbius, August 385
Möbius, Kurt 43, 71, 81, 85, 385, 410, 412
Möhring, Frieda 282
Möllerich, Selma 282
Mönch, Bertha 282
Mohl, Johanna 282
Monderer, Margot 282

Monetta, Sara 283
Montague, Patrick 362
Morawicki, Martha 283
Morawiecki, Lea 283
Mordkiewicz, Abram 130
Mordkiewicz, Mordka 130, 139
Moritz, Karola 283
Morozewicz, Father Karol 37
Moschkowitz, Elfriede 283
Moser, Marie 283
Moses, Albert 283
Moszkowitz, Margem 283
Mottek, Sylvia 283
Motulski, Lilly 284
Mucha, Emma 284
Müller, 386
Müller, Dorothea 284
Muller, Heinrich 60-61
Munro, Cameron 420, 423-424, 438-439
Münzer, Fanny 284
Mularski, Siegfried 284
Muszkat, Milva 284
Myrants, Ruth 284

N

Nachschön, Loiuse 284
Nachtigall, Minna 285
Nadel, Markus 285
Nadler, Fryda 285
Nagel, Maximillian 285
Nager, Elsbeth 285
Natannsen, Hugo 285
Nathan, Hedwig 285
Naumann, Erich 29, 365, 382
Nebe, Arthur 367
Nehab, Sella 285
Nelken, Schmul 286
Nellhaus, Wilhelm 286
Netter, Flora 286
Netzl, Ernst 386
Neubauer, Joachim 286
Neubieser, Flora 286

Neuburg, Julius 286
Neuberger, Chloe 286
Neuding, Henriette 286
Neugarten, Johanna 286
Neuhaus, Ruth 287
Neuhof, Mathilde 287
Neumann, Friedrich 38, 386
Neumann, Hans 287
Neumark, Manfred 287
Neumüller 65
Neustadt, Johanna 287
Neustadter, Lina 287
Neuwahl, Ines 287
Nicholson, Jack 437
Niclas, Julia 287
Niendorf, Elfriede 287
Nielsen, Kate 288
Nomberg, Charlotte 288
Nordman, Mosze 99
Nosseck, Betty 288
Nossek, Hildegard 288
Nüssbaum, Charlotte 288
Nüssbaum, Julie 288
Nüssholz, Moses 288
Nussbaum, Aron 95, 112

O

Oberländer, Friedel, 288
Oberschutzky, Hedwig 289
Oberfest, Henryk 130, 139
Obst, Paula 289
Obstler, Rosalie 289
Östreich, Henny 289
Öttinger, Arno 289
Ohnhaus, Moses 289
Oling, Jenny 289
Oliskiewicz, Jan 73-74
Oliven, Else 289
Opfer, Paula 290
Oppel, Alice 290
Oppenheim, Clara 290
Oppenheimer, Adolf 290
Orbach, Elly 290

Orchudescm, Kate 290
Orenstein, Marion 290
Ortheiler, Rachel 290
Oscher, Luise 290
Osser, Hans 291
Ostberg, Hedwig 291
Oster, Benny 291
Ostermeier, Friedrich 386, 402
Ostromogliski, Lessa 291
Ostrowski (firm) 130, 404-495,
  416-417, 422, 429
Ostowski, Willy 291
Ostwald, Johanna 291
Oswald, Georg 291
Otto, Herbert 36, 38, 386
Otto, Rudolf 386

P

Packsher, Franziska 291
Paderstein, Daisy 291
Pagener, Sofie 291
Pakin, Taube 148-149
Pander, Kaethe 292
Panitsch, Nathan 292
Panke, Helene 292
Pappenheimer, Carl 292
Pariser, Johanna 292
Paschwalski, Szmul 130
Paskusz, Roschen 292
Paul, Kathe 292
Peglau, Rolf 292
Peham, Josef 95, 364, 379, 386-387
Peham, Rozalia 95, 364-365, 375, 379, 386-387, 389
Peiser, Arthur 293
Pels, Juda 293
Pelzer, Margot 293
Pelziger, Justine 293
Peretz, Alice 293
Pergament, Erich 293
Pergamenter, Berta 293
Peritz, Hilda 293

Perl, Liebe 293
Perlinski, Hugo 294
Perlmutter, Chana 294
Perlstein, Alice 294
Peters, Willi 387
Pfeil, Moritz 294
Phiebig, Hans 294
Philip, Sophie 294
Philipp, Paula 294
Philippi, Marie 294
Phillipps, Emilie 295
Philippsohn, Frieda 295
Philippstein, Jenni 295
Philipson, Hans 295
Philpstahl, Gertrud 295
Pianka, Minna 295
Pich, Betty 295
Pick, Else 295
Piekarski, Franciszek 39, 398
Piella, August 70
Pilcer, Martin 295
Piller, Albert 387
Piller, Minna 387
Piller, Walter 117, 119, 121-123, 130, 142-143, 362-363, 369, 374-376, 381, 383, 387, 389-393
Pincus, Anna 296
Pinkowitz, Jenny 296
Pinkus, Jakob 296
Pinoff, Harry 296
Pinthus, Frieda 296
Piorkowsky, Alice 296
Pippersberg, Gerd 296
Pitrowski, Meir 51
Plaat, Recha 297
Plass, Franziska 297
Platau, Hedwig 297
Plate, Albert 68, 71-72, 76, 78, 83-85, 91, 111-112, 388, 402, 407-408
Platz, Ruth 297
Plaut, Anna 297
Plessner, Bertha 297
Plocker, Fajwel, 94

Plocker, Felek 112
Plocker, Moniek 112
Plocker, Mojzesz 94
Poch, Dora 297
Podbielski, Eva 297
Podchlebnik, Michal 42, 57, 60-61, 68-69, 148, 413, 416
Podchlebnik, Mordka 63
Pöderl, Selma 298
Pohl, Oswald 115
Pohlmann, Jontof 298
Polak, Ernst 298
Polanski, Roman 437
Politzer, Max 298
Polke, Wally 298
Pollack, Camilla 298
Pollaczek, Rosa 298
Polley, Elsa 298
Polnsker, Erna 297
Polubinski, Stanislaw 39, 45, 398
Popper, Rudolf 299
Porn, Anna 299
Posner, Elise 299
Postaremczak, Lukasz 420, 422
Prager, Leo 299
Prava, Rudeho 397
Praszker, Gerszon 51
Preller, Hedwig 299
Preuss, Max 299
Prinz, Selma 299
Proskauer, Dr. 130
Proskauer, Gerda 299
Przyblska, Mrs 141
Przybylski, J. 380
Pulka, Gerda 299
Punitzer, Herbert 300
Putziger, Arthur 300

Q

Quass, Gerhard 393

R

Rabbinowitz, Martha 300
Radomsky, Else 300
Radwantzer, Erna 300
Rak, Levi 300
Rand, Anna 300
Randerath, Adele 300
Raphaelson, Frieda 301
Rappaport, Malwine 301
Raps, Roschen 301
Rasba, Chaye 301
Rathaus, Chaskel 301
Ratkowski, Gertrud 301
Ratz, Szosza 301
Rau, Cacillie 301
Raudzus, Friedrich 388, 402
Rauff, Walter 91
Rauch, Estera 301
Rawack, Klara 302
Rebensaft, Feige 302
Rechtschaffen, Minna 302
Reder, Rosalie 302
Redner, Berta 302
Rediess, Wilhelm 31, 366
Reiblinger, Anton 389, 402
Reich, Moniek 128, 133-134
Regensburger, Amalie 302
Rehfeld, Lisbeth 302
Reich, Julius 302
Reich, Moniek 128, 133, -134
Reichenberg, Gerta 303
Reichenstein, Laura 303
Reichhardt, Lotte 303
Reichmann, Martha 303
Reider, Sonja 303
Reif, Maria 303
Reilinger, Flora 303
Reinemann, Irma 303
Reinhard, Johanna 303
Reins, Selma 304
Reismann, Bruno 304
Reissmann, Arthur 304
Reissner, Alice 304

Reissner, Sepp 389, 402
Reisner, Wilhelmine 371
Reiwald, Anna 304
Reversz, Hedwig 304
Rewald, Oskar 304
Reyersbach, Margarete 304
Ribbe, Friedrich 94, 97
Richter, Albert 96, 389
Richter, Herbert 81, 117, 122-123, 364-365, 389
Riehs, Helene 305
Riesenfeld, Ella 305
Riess 362
Riess, Edith 305
Ring, Jenny 305
Ringelblum, Emanuel 46, 147
Ringer, Dora 305
Risch, Paula 305
Robert, Flora 305
Rochocz, Zerline 305
Rockmann, Margarete 305
Rödelheimer, Julius 305
Roder, Franziska 385
Röhmann, Edith 306
Roer, Josef 306
Röttgen, Emilie 306
Rogoff, Gregor 306
Roj, Abram 148-149
Roj, Icek 148
Roj, Sura 148
Rolle, Pauline 306
Rombach, Erich 389, 402
Romm, Recha 306
Rose, Hans 364, 389
Rose, Max 306
Rosemann, Anna 306
Rosen, Rudolf 307
Rosenbaum, Arnold 307
Rosenberg, Albert 307
Rosenblatt, Erna 307
Rosenbluth, Debora 307
Rosendahl, Wilhelm 307
Rosendorf, Heinz 307
Rosenfeld, Ida 307

Rosenkranz, Louise 308
Rosenow, Gertrude 308
Rosenrauch, Manfred 308
Rosenstein, Erna 308
Rosenstern, Richard 308
Rosenstiel, Adele 308
Rosenstock, Henriette 308
Rosenthal, Aharon 52-53
Rosenthal, Alice 308
Rosentretter, Fanny 309
Rosmarin, Benjamin 309
Rosner, Else 309
Ross 389
Roszak, Zygmunt 404
Rotenberg, Fanny 309
Roth, Ernestine 309
Rothenberg, Hanna 309
Rother, Adolf 309
Rothfels, Roni 309
Rotholz, Auguste 309
Rothschild, Johanna 310
Rothstein, Selma 310
Rottenstein, Rosalie 310
Rubach, Stanislaw 116
Ruben, Albert 310
Rubens, Anna 310
Rubensohn, Hertha 310
Rubenstein, Jakob 310
Rubenstein, Paula 311
Rubin, Efraim 310
Rubinfeld, Ida 310
Rublach, Luba 311
Rudeitzki, Frida 311
Rudermann, Cacilie 311
Rübsteck, Amalia 311
Rückersberg, Berta 311
Rüdenberg, Else 311
Ruhr, Albert 311
Rumkowski, Mordechai Chaim 57, 69, 94, 102, 137
Rumper, Leja 312
Runge, Hannes 37, 38, 84, 106, 117, 122, 124, 127-128, 130, 133, 138-139, 142, 144, 364, 389

Russ, Frieda 312
Russeck, Passel 312
Ruwenach 141, 390
Rynarzewski, Dora 312

S

Saalfeld, Gertrud 312
Saban, Ida 312
Sabatzky, Willy 312
Sabel, Amanda 312
Sabor, Eva 312
Sachs, Ilse 313
Sack, Josefine 313
Salazin, Frieda 313
Salinger, Eva 313
Salm, Berta 313
Salmon, Mathilde 313
Salomon, Alfred 313
Salomonis, Johanna 313
Salzmann, Arthur 313
Samaskewitz, Marga 314
Samosch, Rosa 314
Samter, Gertrud 314
Samuel, Hertha 314
Sanders, Johanna 314
Sandheim, Else 314
Sandmann, Rosa 314
Sarner, Gertrud 314
Sass, Fanny 314
Saul, Georg 315
Sax, Betty 315
Schachmann, Jette 315
Schalling, Franz 40-42, 390
Schäfer, Rosalie 315
Schallenberg, Hildegard 315
Schalscha, Else 315
Schanzer, Betty 315
Schapira, Lucie 315
Schapiro, Louise 315
Scharlinski, Charlotte 316
Schattschneider, Else 316
Schauer, Helene 316
Schaul, Marta 316

Scheff, Gabriele 316
Scheffler, Rosa 316
Schefler, Wilhelm 390
Scheiberg, Klara 316
Scheidemann, Ella 316
Scheier, Leopold 317
Schein, Fanny 317
Scheiner, Hedwig 317
Scheinwechsler, Ernestine 317
Schemel, Bruno 317
Schendel, Jenny 317
Scherbel, Arthur 317
Schermann, Elise 317
Scherz, Aron 318
Scheuer, Rosa 318
Scheye, Ruth 318
Scheyer, Alice 318
Schiefer, Mathilde 318
Schiffer, Else 318
Schild, Marta 318
Schiltzer, Rosa 318
Schilzer, Grete 318
Schimmelmann, Frieda 319
Schindel, Karla 319
Schindler, Gitta 319
Schleimer, Meta 319
Schlesinger, Fritz 319
Schlewinsky, Johanna 319
Schliz, Amalie 319
Schloss, Chana 319
Schloss, Valeska 319
Schmelzer, Loiuse 320
Schmerse , Wilhelm 118, 120-121, 390
Schmidt, Betty 320
Schmidt, Erwin 117, 122, 144, 364-365, 391
Schmiedmayer, Gerda 320
Schmitz, Selma 320
Schmoll, Agnes 320
Schmul, Rosi 320
Schmulowitz, Gideon 320
Schnapp, Feleg 320
Schneider 391

Schneider, Hulda 321
Schnitzer, Sara 321
Schnock, Heinz 321
Schnog, Seligmann 321
Schnook, Henny 321
Schoffner 391
Schömann, Frieda 321
Schön, Isfried 321
Schönbach, Henriette 321
Schonbeck, Heinz 391, 402
Schönfeld, Hildegard 321
Schönfeldt, Amalie 322
Schönhorn, Gertrude 322
Schönthal, Recha 322
Schops, Clara 322
Schor, Dora 322
Schorsch, Roschen 322
Schott, Hanna 322
Schramm, Benjamin 323
Schrank, Helene 323
Schreiber, Karl 323
Schriever 94
Schröder, Helene 323
Schrubski, Byanka 323
Schubach, Max 323
Schüftan, Else 323
Schüler, Jacques 323
Schüller, Pauline 323
Schulde, Gertrud 324
Schulte, Wilhelm 76-77, 81, 85, 367, 411
Schulz 33, 39
Schulz, Sara 324
Schulze, Martha 324
Schuster, Olga 324
Schwab, Ruth 324
Schwalb, Golda 324
Schwarz, Albert 324
Schwarzmann, Rachel 325
Schweizer, Josefine 325
Schwenk, Erich 325
Schwerin, Else 325
Schwind 122
Secklels, Selma 325

Seckl, Friedrich 325
Seefeld, Bernd 325
Seelig, Rosa 325
Seginer, Isaak 325
Seide, Elfriede 326
Seidemann, Moritz 326
Seidenglanz, Stefan 117, 391
Seiferheld, Milian 326
Seifert, Franz 97, 104
Selbiger, Rosa 326
Selig, Rita 326
Seligmann, Amalie 326
Semmler, Jakob 39
Senft, Amalie 326
Sereeth, Gisela 326
Servos, Julius 327
Sichel, Werner 327
Siegelman, Izaak 419
Siemontowski, Ilse 327
Sierakowiak, Dawid 101-102
Silberbach, Adolf 327
Silberberg, Emma 327
Silberblatt, Rosel 327
Silbermann, Bertha 327
Silberstein, Rosa 327
Silbiger, Moritz 327
Simenauer, Lucie 328
Simke, Elfriede 328
Simon, Alice 328
Simon, Bruno 137, 391
Simon, Elise 384
Simon - Wolfskehl, Erna 328
Simons, Berta 328
Simonstein, Martha 328
Simson, Selma 328
Singer, Elsa 328
Sinski, Jakub 329
Sippel, Mathilde 329
Sistic, Erna 329
Sitzmann, Karl 329
Siuda 62
Sklarz, Clara 329
Skrzypczynski, Kajetan 39, 397, 399

Slatopolski, Horst 329
Sliwke, Arthur 138, 141, 392
Slotowski, Paul 329
Smolarski, Faivel 329
Sobersky, Herbert 329
Sobotki, Johanna 330
Sollinger, Hanna 330
Solms, Else 330
Sommer, Hedwig 330
Sommer, Max 37-38, 117, 122, 392
Sommerberg, Julie 330
Sommerfeld, Johanna 330
Sommerfeldt, Margot 330
Sommerhauser, August 330
Sonn, Levi 331
Sonnenberg, Emma 331
Sonnenblick, Blima 331
Sonnenfeld, Arthur 331
Sonnenmark, Elise 331
Sorge, Herbert 392
Sorin, Rosa 331
Sorsky, Marie 331
Sostheim, Alfred 331
Spandau, Valeska 331
Spanier, Bella 332
Spatz, Margareta 384
Speier- Holstein, Samuel 332
Sperling, Karolina 332
Spet, Emma 332
Speyer, Else 332
Spicker, Heinz 332
Spiegel, Johanna 332
Spiegler, Leopold 332
Spieldoch, Paula 333
Spielmann, Joachim 333
Spira, Arthur 333
Spiro, Erna 333
Spitz, Gisela 333
Spitzer, Berta 333
Sporn, Adelheid 333
Springer, Gisela 333
Squar, Elvira 333
Srebnik, Hava 149

Srebnik, Szymon 127, 131, 138, 140, 149, 371-372, 374, 380-381, 390-391, 413, 416-417
Stadthagen, Lucie 334
Stahl, Leon 334
Stajer, Gecel 95
Stark, 143
Steckel, Margarete 334
Steier, Jakob 334
Stein, Dora 334
Steinbauer, Josef 392
Steinberg, Selma 334
Steiner, Sophie 334
Steinfeld, Bernhard 335
Steinhagen, Max 335
Steinhart, Moritz 335
Steinke, Alexander 88, 392, 411
Steinweg, Sophia 335
Steinischewski, Benno 335
Stephan, Henriette 335
Stern, Adolf 335
Sternberg, Ellen 335
Sternefeld, Karl 335
Sternfeld, Max 336
Sternheim, Selma 336
Sternlicht, Regina 336
Sternschuss, Rosa 336
Stich, Hedwig 336
Stiebel, Jakob 336
Stiefel, Hannelore 336
Stitzky, Elsa 336
Stock, Eva 337
Stockmann, Rosa 337
Stoppelmann, Minna 337
Stosberg 120
Strasburg, Iser 95, 112
Strauss, Agnes 337
Streisand, Margarete 337
Strohmeier, Johann 392
Strumpfner, Alma 227
Struzik, Elli 337
Studinski, Hedwig 337
Sturmlaufer, Estera 338
Stupp, Abraham 108

Stutzinski, Jenny 338
Sultan, Hedwig 338
Surth, Jakob 338
Susskind, Hedwig 338
Sussmann, Carla 338
Swarsensky, Margarete 338
Swiatlowski, Fedora 338
Swietoplawski, Gershon 55
Switala, Waclaw 396
Szablewski, Marian 404
Szajnfeld, Martha 338
Szama, Ika 112
Szamatulski, David 339
Szigelzky, Werner 339
Szlamowicz, Szyja 94, 112
Szmulewicz, Luser 339
Szplit 63
Sztajn, Dr 99
Szulman, Rabbi Jakob 60, 147, 421, 425
Szumiraj, Zemed 112
Szumiraj, Zemad 112
Szycman, Adolf 339
Szydlowski, Martin 339
Szykman, Rosa 339
Szkudlarek, Waclaw 101
Szymanski, Stanislaw 39, 106, 399
Szymkie, Motel 94
Szyndelmacher, Gitla 339

T

Talan, Rika 339
Tann, Meta 340
Tannenwald, Leonore 340
Tasselkraut, Dorothea 340
Taubenschlag, Gerhard 340
Tauber, Malke 150
Tausk, Bertha 340
Teich-Birken, Isaak 340
Teicher, Helene 340
Teitelbaum, Helene 340
Teller, Sara 340

Temkin, Rabbi Mosze 99
Tetteles, Cilli 341
Teutsch, Paula 341
Thalmann, Arthur 341
Thiele, Ernst 117, 121, 392-393
Thiele, Johanna 341
Thon, Feigel 341
Tichauer, Cacilie 341
Tobias, Thekla 341
Todtmann, Fritze 341
Toporski 95
Törlitz, Franziska 342
Toller, Louis 342
Trachtenbrodt, Kate 342
Träger, Jakob 342
Traub, Elsa 342
Treitelfeld, Hermann 342
Trenker, Alfred 366
Treuherz, Dora 342
Trompeter, Feigel 342
Troplowitz, Rosa 342
Tucholski, Dorothea 343
Tuerk, Hulda 343
Tugendhat, Marta 343
Tusst 122
Tworoger, Markus 343

U

Ucko, Else 343
Uffenheimer, Ludwig 343
Ullmann, Julia 343
Ulrich, Henriette 343
Unger, Emma 344
Uram, Fanny 344
Utitz, Jeanette 344

V

Valk, Sara 344
Vasen, Adelheid 344
Veit, Paula 344
Verstandig, Gerhard 344
Vinken, Arthur 393

Visser, Pauline 344
Vogt, Hans 393
Voit, Anna 377
Völke, Dora 345
Volk, Dr 115
Vollrath, Marie 345
Voos, Gerson 345
Vorenberg, Fanny 345
Vorreuter, Eva 345
Voss, Erna 345

W

Wachs, Kathe 345
Wachsner, Sophie 346
Wachtel, Chaskiel 94
Wachtel, Margarete 346
Wachtel, Smlek 112
Wachtel, Symcha 112
Wagener, Alfriede 346
Wagner, Gertrud 346
Wahrhaftig, Sophie 346
Wajcer, Frida 346
Wajcman, Cila 346
Wajs, Dr 130
Wajsberg 99
Waksberg, Moszek 346
Wald, Rudolf 347
Walde, Aron 347
Waldmann, Henny 347
Waldman, Jakub 416
Wallach, Abraham 347
Waller, Elfriede 347
Wallshietz, Hermann 393
Walter, Erna 347
Walter, Franz 45, 393
Walzer, Henny 347
Wangenheim, Bertha 347
Warszawski, Dawid 102
Warszawski, Judes 347
Wartenberger, Ernestine 348
Webb, Chris 420
Weber, Johanna 348
Wechselmann, Salomon 348

Wecker, Maria 383
Weglein, Gertrud 348
Weigert, Clara 348
Weil, Arnold 348
Weile, Ida 348
Weiler, Irmgard 348
Weimann, Helene 348
Weinbach, Alfred 349
Weinbaum, Arno 349
Weinberg, Fritz 349
Weiner, Berta 349
Weiner (Szlamek Bajler) 67-68
Weinlaub, Margarete 349
Weinschenk, Ida 349
Weintraub, Leja 349
Weisenberg, Ida 349
Weisner, Luise 349
Weiss, Gertrud 350
Weiss, Szewach 438
Weissbrod, Margot 350
Weissfeldt, Paula 350
Weltmann, Anna 350
Welzer, Else 350
Wendriner, Paula 350
Werdesheim, Margem 350
Werner, Laura 350
Wertheim, Kurt 351
Wertheheimer, Anna 351
Wesche, Otto 351
Westfeld, Elisabeth 351
Westheimer, Karl 351
Westphal, Erna 351
Weyl, Elise 351
Widawski, Chaim 99 -100, 147-150
Widawski, Chaya 149
Widawski, Joshua 149
Widmann, Gabriele 351
Wieczorek 140
Wiener, Cacilie 351
Wiesenfeld, Isaak 352
Wiesenthal, Margarete 352
Wiesner, Feige 352
Wieszansky, Lina 352

Wihl, Friedrich 352
Wildermuth, Jakob 43, 393
Wilk, Erich 352
Will, Heinz 352
Willdorf, Marie 352
Willner, Hersch 353
Windmüller, Adolf 353
Winter, Adele 353
Wisch, Siegfried 353
Wittenberg, Adolf 353
Witjowski (Szlamek Bajler) 59
Wittkowski, Emma 353
Wohl, Ella 353
Wohlfeld, Max 353
Wolf, Arthur 354
Wolf, Emma 376
Wolff, Albert 354
Wolffs, Betty 354
Wolffsky, Hertha 354
Wolfram, Clara 354
Wolfsohn, Johanna 354
Wolinski, Lesek 438
Wolkomirsky, Scheina 354
Wolkowitsch, Isaak 354
Wollenberg, Else 355
Wollheim, Eva 355
Wollmann, Meta 355
Wollstein, Bertha 355
Wongleszewski, Jakob 355
Wongrowitz, Adolfine 355
Woreczek, Ilse 355
Wornshofer, Toni 394
Wortmann, Elise 355
Wreschner, Rosalie 356
Wronker, Frieda 356
Wrzesinski, Kathe 356
Würtenberg, Ella 356
Würzburger, Berta 356
Wulff, Alfred 356
Wunderlich, Margarethe 356
Wundermacher, Lotte 356
Wundermann, Anna 357
Wunsch, Margarethe 357
Wurmann, Margarete 357

Wyk, Isaac 357

Z

Zacharias, Dina 357
Zack, Amalie 357
Zajdler, Karol 394
Zander, Martha 357
Zanders, Albert 357
Zangenberg, Herta 357
Zauderer, Brucha 358
Zarak, Chaskel 94, 112
Zeidler, Frieda 358
Zeimann, Benno 358
Zelkowicz, Maria 358
Zellermayer, David 358
Zenon, Rosa 404
Zessin, Hans 394Ziegler, Herta 358
Ziel, Selma 358
Zilbermann, Gitla 358
Zilversmit, Hedwig 359
Zimbler, Gittel 359
Zimbler- Fiedler, Malka 359
Zimmermann 66
Zimmermann 394
Zimmermann, Elsa 359
Zinn, Erna 359
Zitrin, Charlotte 359
Zlotnicki, Joseph 359
Zuckermann, Heinrich 359
Zulawski, Andrzej 437
Zurawski, Mordka 127, 131, 138, 141-142, 150, 377, 413, 416-417
Zurndorfer, Elisabeth 360
Zweig, Wita 360
Zydenfeld 127
Zydower, Siegfried 360
Zygelman, Abram 360
Zylberszac, Baruch 99
Zyskind, Sala 360

ibidem*.eu*